THE DEVELOPMENT OF

ACADEMIC

FREEDOM

IN THE UNITED STATES

By RICHARD HOFSTADTER

and WALTER P. METZGER

IN LITTERIS
LIBERTAS
1754·1893

NEW YORK

COLUMBIA UNIVERSITY PRESS

COPYRIGHT © 1955 COLUMBIA UNIVERSITY PRESS, NEW YORK

First printing 1955
Second printing 1956

PUBLISHED IN GREAT BRITAIN, CANADA, INDIA, AND PAKISTAN
BY GEOFFREY CUMBERLEGE: OXFORD UNIVERSITY PRESS
LONDON, TORONTO, BOMBAY, AND KARACHI

Library of Congress Catalog Card Number: 55-9435

MANUFACTURED IN THE UNITED STATES OF AMERICA

THE DEVELOPMENT OF ACADEMIC FREEDOM IN THE UNITED STATES

A STUDY PREPARED FOR THE
AMERICAN ACADEMIC FREEDOM PROJECT
AT COLUMBIA UNIVERSITY
Robert M. MacIver, Director

AMERICAN ACADEMIC FREEDOM PROJECT

26574

Louis Finkelstein, Chancellor, The Jewish Theological Seminary of America

Frank P. Graham, Ex-President, University of North Carolina

Theodore M. Greene, Professor of Philosophy, Yale University

Rufus C. Harris, President, Tulane University

Edward C. Kirkland, Professor of History, Bowdoin College

Mrs. Eugene Meyer, Trustee, Barnard College

The Rev. J. Courtney Murray, S.J., Woodstock College and Seminary

J. Robert Oppenheimer, Director, The Institute for Advanced Study

Charles Seymour, Ex-President, Yale University

Mrs. Arthur Hays Sulzberger, Trustee, Barnard College

Ralph A. Ulveling, Director, The Detroit Public Library

Sir Llewellyn Woodward, The Institute for Advanced Study

In addition the following gentlemen served on the Panel for part of the time but owing to other demands on their time found it necessary to resign from this activity.

John S. Dickey, President, Dartmouth College

A. Whitney Griswold, President, Yale University

Erwin N. Griswold, Dean of the Law School, Harvard University

Lewis Webster Jones, President, Rutgers University

This project, the first to undertake its particular task of investigation in this country or elsewhere, is an outcome of the initiative and the generosity of Louis M. Rabinowitz. His offer to finance it, made to Columbia University in the spring of 1951, was readily welcomed by the University authorities, and under the leadership of Dr. Grayson Kirk a committee, headed by Dean Louis M. Hacker, was appointed to make the necessary arrangements. Professor R. M. MacIver was made its Director. The study was planned to consist of two parts, one a historical survey of the rise, development, and vicissitudes of academic freedom in this country, the other an analysis of the contemporary situation and a study of the problems it presents, against a background designed to bring out the significance of academic freedom and its relation to the society in which we live. The first part, *The Development of Academic Freedom in the United States,* was entrusted to Professors Richard Hofstadter and Walter P. Metzger, both of the History Department of Columbia University. The second part was undertaken by the Director. The

work is now published in two companion volumes. The general theme of
these books is the same as that of Columbia University's Bicentennial activities in 1954—"Man's right to knowledge and the free use thereof."

In the furtherance of the work a Panel of Advisers was enlisted, which
held several two- or three-day sessions besides giving to the working staff
the benefit of their comments and criticisms on the various sections of
the study as they were initially drafted. The Executive Committee joined
with the Panel in these activities and was also brought together for special discussions. It owes a great debt to this distinguished group of associates; their suggestions have been throughout most helpful. However,
it should be clearly understood that neither the Panel of Advisers nor the
Executive Committee is in any way to be held responsible for the conclusions expressed by the authors. The same, it need scarcely be said, is
true of Columbia University. Thanks are due for the University's very
generous hospitality to the Project and for its willingness to manage the
grant made by the Louis M. Rabinowitz Foundation.

PREFACE

A CADEMIC FREEDOM has become one of the central issues of our time. It has been our aim in this volume to write an account of the problem of academic freedom in American colleges and universities from the founding of the first college to the recent past. While we have tried to provide historical perspective on the current struggle over intellectual freedom in higher education, we have tried also to avoid the pitfall of interpreting the past solely from the standpoint of present issues and current anxieties. Ours is an analytical history, not a full-throated polemic for academic freedom. We have no desire to conceal an ineluctable prejudice on behalf of freedom of thought, and we hope and expect that this inquiry will be a history, not an autopsy. Our commitment to freedom has no doubt affected in many ways our treatment of the problem, but our foremost intention has been to shed new light on the history of the academic man and the complex circumstances under which he has done his work, in the faith that an enlargement of understanding will in the end be an enlargement of freedom.

One of our earliest decisions in planning this work was to make it more than a running account of "cases." To write only about the outstanding violations of freedom would be to treat the story of academic freedom as though it were nothing but the story of academic suppression. The cases are, in a sense, the pathology of the problem. The distortions that would arise from dealing with them alone are comparable to those that would be found in a history of the labor movement telling only of strikes, a history of science telling only of the encroachments of theology, or a history of political democracy devoted only to its defeats. It is, of course, an important part of our concern to learn what forces in society have ranged themselves against the freedom of teaching and research and what successes they have scored; but we have also been interested to know what freedom has meant to successive generations of academic men, to what extent they have achieved it, and what factors in academic life itself, as well as in American culture at large, have created and sustained it.

We consider it as much a part of our task to explain why freedom exists as to explain why it has been limited.

Cases, moreover, serve only as guides to the nature of the problem; they do not exhaust its meaning. To ask what it was that men wanted to be free about, why the freedoms they claimed were considered by other men to be improper or dangerous, what arguments were employed on both sides, and where the power lay to settle the issues is to pass from the academic institutions to the community that supported them, set their goals, and (in America at least) governed them. Such questions have led us to try to tell our story against the background of the religious, intellectual, and political issues that gave to academic controversies their special urgency and broad social significance. They have taken us not only into the discussion of such matters as the development of the American form of academic government and the professional organization of academic men, but also into the educational policies of religious denominations, the history of theological controversies, the rise of Darwinism in American thought, and the relations between men of business and men of learning.

Broad as our scope has been, we have not dealt with every aspect of the theme. We have discussed primarily the freedom of faculty members and have dealt with the issue of freedom for students only at those points where the two have converged. In our minds the history of student freedoms and student discipline is a matter of comparable importance, but it is a large and in many respects a separate question that deserves a treatise of its own. We have also confined ourselves to college and university education. Those who are interested in the history of freedom of teaching in schools below college grade will be enlightened by Howard K. Beale's two earlier volumes, *A History of Freedom of Teaching in American Schools* (1941) and *Are American Teachers Free?* (1936). Finally, we have brought our story to a close without treating, except by occasional reference, the current crisis in academic freedom; but this is analyzed in the companion volume sponsored by the American Academic Freedom Project, Professor Robert M. MacIver's *Academic Freedom in Our Time*.

There is a sharp difference between the main concern of Part One, which deals with the American college down to the period just after the Civil War, and that of Part Two, which deals with the modern American university. Part One deals with an age overshadowed by religious and theological questions, Part Two with an age preoccupied with science and social problems. Part One begins with an introductory chapter touching upon some phases of the history of intellectual freedom in the universities of Western Europe up to the time of the Reformation. No reader should imagine that this chapter presumes to be even an abbreviated history of intellectual freedom in the universities of Europe—several volumes would be necessary to accomplish that task—but it seemed desirable to touch upon this background in order to bring the long history of this issue, and the various forms it has taken, to the attention of readers who might be excessively preoccupied with recent events and American conditions. Moreover, while it was clear that whatever we might write on the subject of academic freedom before the Reformation would be more than ordinarily incomplete and inadequate, we did not want to indulge ourselves in the provincialism of beginning our story as though the problem originated with the founding of Harvard College in 1636.

The rest of Part One deals with what might be called the prehistory of academic freedom in our own country. It treats of a period when colleges were under denominational control and there were hardly any universities worthy of the name. In the denominational colleges the problem of academic freedom as we now understand it was hardly posed, for the sponsors of such colleges, on the whole, did not intend that they should be to any significant degree intellectually free, and the men who taught in them had for the most part only the slenderest aspirations toward intellectual freedom. Our inquiry into the severe limitations upon freedom in the old colleges should not be taken as a total indictment of their services to their students and the community or as a denial of their right to exist. But in the pre-Civil War era the denominational colleges not only accorded an inadequate measure of freedom to those who taught and studied in them, but their friends and sponsors were disposed to choke, sabotage, and destroy such attempts as were made to establish larger and more capacious institutions supporting advanced scholarship and providing the conditions of university freedom. Despite these limitations, collegiate education before the Civil War had its own merits and on occasion its significant controversies and gestures toward academic freedom; the period was also one of educational agitation when most advanced thinkers presaged the coming era of university development.

Since religious commitments and sectarian aspirations did so much to create the restrictive atmosphere of the old college and to cramp the early work of the rising university, religious leaders figure in an exceptionally prominent way among the opponents of intellectual freedom in the first half of our story. We hope that no reader will infer from this a commitment to aggressive secularism on the part of the authors. While there are still circumstances under which religious interests can restrict the free expression to which the secular mind is entitled, we are also aware that there is now some likelihood that here or there the unconsciously secularist bias of our formally "religious" but too often spiritually hollow society will impinge upon the full development of the genuinely religious student or scholar. Nor have we forgotten that some of the same religious denominations that a hundred years ago were culpable for their indifference or opposition to intellectual freedom have in recent years produced some of its most impassioned and powerful spokesmen.

With the coming of the modern university, the theme of Part Two, the entire situation was transformed within the life span of a single generation. The university, not the college, became the model institution. While in the ante-bellum period the very existence of the entrenched denominational colleges limited or checked the emergent universities, in the later period the development of universities reshaped in some measure all but the most backward colleges. The emergence of the university was nothing less than an educational revolution in the United States. Research took a place along with teaching as a major function. The methods and concepts of science displaced the authority of religion. The academic profession took on, for the first time in a full measure, the character, aspirations, and standards of a learned profession. Within the university, the growth of resources, the proliferation of activities, the assemblage of large faculties gave impetus to bureaucratization—to tenure rules, formal procedures of promotion and dismissal, the delegation of authority. A self-conscious and well-formulated rationale for academic freedom appeared, framed in terms to fit the new realities of academic life. Aspirations for intellectual freedom that had been expressed in the denominational era only by pioneers or rebels in the colleges were now understood and endorsed by powerful figures of the educational world. While freedom in the modern university was, as it always has been, only imperfectly realized in practice, those who would oppose and limit freedom were now for the first time in our history put upon the moral and intellectual defensive. It may put some of our current difficulties into perspective to realize that the academic freedom which is now under fire is not an ancient prerogative but an acquisition of relatively recent date.

It is impossible to acknowledge by name all the scholars—almost three
score of them—who have given freely of their time by reading drafts,
offering criticism, catching errors, and providing us with access to materials, but our sincere gratitude goes out to them. Without their help this
study would have been far less adequate. We are indebted above all to
Louis M. Rabinowitz, who conceived the American Academic Freedom
Project and brought to it not only ample resources but the close interest
of a generous heart and mind. We are grateful for our association with
Robert M. MacIver, the director of the American Academic Freedom
Project, whose advice and criticism have been of value on many occasions,
and who has consistently shown a quality that must be recommended to
administrators of academic research projects—a wise and cordial regard
for individuality and independence. Finally, without the help of our research assistants, Francis Wilson Smith, Joseph Katz, and Juan Linz,
this work would have taken far longer and would have rested on a much
less sufficient base of information.

A word on the nature of our collaboration. Although each author has
assumed full and final responsibility for a part of the text—Hofstadter
for Part One, Metzger for Part Two—the interpretive structure of this
volume and all the major problems that have arisen have been objects of
frequent discussion, as the text has been of mutual criticism. Thus, except
for the fact that it contains no collaborative prose, this has been in every
sense a collaborative enterprise. On most of the broad issues the authors
have found themselves—not always at the beginning but usually at the
end of discussion—in substantial agreement on the meaning of the facts.
If there are still marginal inconsistencies in interpretation or in tone, they
remain in the text not through an oversight but as a consequence of our
resolve not to try to submerge individual differences for the sake of an
unnecessary uniformity.

RICHARD HOFSTADTER
WALTER P. METZGER

Columbia University
in the City of New York
April, 1955

CONTENTS

CONTENTS

PART TWO: THE AGE OF THE UNIVERSITY
by *Walter P. Metzger*

Part One

THE AGE OF THE COLLEGE

by RICHARD HOFSTADTER

I: THE EUROPEAN HERITAGE

CORPORATE POWER IN THE MIDDLE AGES

Aᴄᴀᴅᴇᴍɪᴄ ғʀᴇᴇᴅᴏᴍ is a modern term for an ancient idea. Although the struggle for freedom in teaching can be traced at least as far back as Socrates' eloquent defense of himself against the charge of corrupting the youth of Athens, its continuous history is concurrent with the history of universities since the twelfth century. The university is in its origin a medieval institution. The first universities of the Middle Ages emerged gradually, often at centers of clerical learning like the cathedral schools, when the numbers of students and masters grew large enough to require some formal organization. Five universities—Salerno, Bologna, Montpellier, Paris, and Oxford—may be said to have come into existence and reached varying degrees of distinctness and complexity by the end of the twelfth century; and by the end of the thirteenth, the first great century of university development, seventeen others had been founded in Italy, France, Spain, Portugal, and England. Rashdall, in his classic study *The Universities of Europe in the Middle Ages,* enumerated seventy-eight that had been founded in Europe to the end of 1500; most of them were still in existence in that year.[1]

In constitutional form we may distinguish two great traditions stemming from two archetypal universities, Paris and Bologna. Bologna, which began as a center for the study of civil law and soon became noted for canon law as well, was patronized very largely by wealthy or noble families, whose sons were both laymen and clergymen. The teachers themselves were frequently laymen, comparatively free of ecclesiastical supervision or jurisdiction. As foreigners and strangers in Bologna, the

---

[1] Hastings Rashdall, *The Universities of Europe in the Middle Ages* (3 vols.; 1895, ed. by F. M. Powicke and A. B. Emden, Oxford, 1936). Salerno was always chiefly a medical school, while Montpellier in the twelfth century had faculties of medicine and law; in 1289 Montpellier was formally constituted as a general university, or *studium generale,* although it had long functioned in that capacity. Among the later universities discussed by Rashdall, 23 were founded in the fourteenth century and 33 in the fifteenth.

students needed organization; as mature and usually wealthy scholars, they were capable of managing their own affairs and setting terms to the teachers. At Bologna, therefore, the gilds, which *were* the university, were organizations of the students, and the masters were hardly more than the hired men of the students, by whom they were subjected to a rigid and detailed academic discipline.[2]

Paris, a center of theological studies and arts, was by contrast a gild of the masters. There the masters and students were either clerics or were so regarded, and the masters' organizations were the units of the university structure. The Italian, Spanish, and Portuguese universities were modeled after Bologna, while most of the German universities and the two in England were modeled after the University of Paris. Some French universities were universities of masters, but others, notably in the South, were of a mixed nature, fusions of the Parisian and Bolognese types.

In intellectual concerns and ecclesiastical relations the two traditions also diverged. The universities of Italy and some in France were notable individually for their work in civil law or medicine, some of them later for natural philosophy. Founded at centers of commerce where ancient Roman traditions had not been altogether lost, the Italian universities were somewhat secular in their preoccupations. A separate faculty of theology had no place in the early organization of the Italian universities, for instance, and in later stages of the universities' development the study of theology was given but secondary or slight importance. Ecclesiastical interference was comparatively moderate, and, when exercised, was the instrument of political rather than doctrinal objectives.[3]

In the North, notably at Paris and Oxford, theology and philosophy reigned, although many northern universities also taught law and medicine. In those northern centers that specialized in theology and where the study of law was also carried on, the legal studies tended to emphasize canon law. At Paris canon law was of much significance, but civil law was not encouraged. Some northern *studia,* however, among them Orléans and Bourges, were distinguished in civil law. Thus while the southern institutions were at first greatest as centers for the pragmatic studies

---

[2] *Ibid.,* I, 149–51, 195–97. The doctors at Bologna much later formed their own faculty gilds that controlled the eligibility and some activities of their members.

[3] *Ibid.,* II, 62. In the thirteenth century theology was taught only at Paris, Toulouse, Oxford, and Salamanca. The papacy did not encourage the multiplication of faculties of theology, and young institutions often avoided it until long after their founding. Stephen d'Irsay, *Histoire des universités,* I (Paris, 1933), 161, 177.

of law and medicine and were intimately linked through their personnel with local aristocracies, many northern institutions took their cue chiefly from the University of Paris, which was the center of a pan-European intellectual influence resting above all upon its faculties of theology and arts. The northern institutions were more acutely torn than the southern ones by the doctrinal controversies of the Middle Ages and ultimately by the bitter struggles of the Reformation.

A study concerned with the general intellectual history of Europe might well give equal attention to both these university traditions; but for our purpose, which is to shed some light on the background of American higher education, a somewhat stronger emphasis on the northern tradition is desirable. During the Middle Ages the intellectual relations between Paris and Oxford were always close. Cambridge was modeled in a broad sense on Oxford; and Cambridge, together with the English dissenting academies, was the primary formative influence on Harvard and most of the American colonial colleges.[4] To examine a few of the theological and philosophical quarrels that ruffled the northern universities is also to deal with some of the central issues in the history of intellectual liberty.

The modern lay reader, under the influence of an old rationalist stereotype, often thinks of the Middle Ages only as an age of dogma and suppression. Unless, however, the diversity of the social background of the medieval university is envisaged, unless the full vigor of the clash of interests and doctrines in its intellectual milieu, notably in the thirteenth and fourteenth centuries, is seen, neither the remarkable corporate power of the university nor the independence and boldness of some of its outstanding masters will be appreciated fully.

In the social structure of the Middle Ages the universities were centers of power and prestige, protected and courted, even deferred to, by emperors and popes. They held this position chiefly because great importance was attached to learning, not only as a necessary part of the whole spiritual enterprise, but also for its own sake. Great nobles, powerful clerics, men of wealth and influence, could go into a career of learning with the feeling that it was a fit thing to do with their lives. Such a theo-

---

[4] Only much later, in the post-Civil War era, was the English influence on American higher education superseded to an important degree by the example of the German universities. For the impact of the German universities see below, Chap. VIII. Among the colonial institutions of America, only one, William and Mary, was more profoundly influenced by Oxford than by Cambridge.

logical center as the University of Paris stood at the heart of the spiritual life of the age; at Paris for a time sat most of the great masters of philosophy and the great refiners of doctrine from all Europe.[5] If the universities were spiritual centers, they were scarcely less important as agencies of practical life, whose work was as relevant to the ecclesiastical and political life of the thirteenth and fourteenth centuries as the modern university is to the scientific and industrial life of our time.[6] They provided vocational training for the clerical functionaries of church and state—for notaries, secretaries, legates, and lawyers. Much of the strength of the universities rested upon the personal loyalty of former students or masters who were in places of power, who had an intimate and respectful knowledge of the services of the universities, and who were formally bound to them by oaths of loyalty, informally (and perhaps more effectively) by ties of sentiment.[7]

In internal matters the universities had the prerogative of self-government. They were autonomous corporations, conceived in the spirit of the gilds; their members elected their own officials and set the rules for the teaching craft.[8] Although the most prized teaching license, the *ius ubique docendi,* which gave the scholar the theoretical right to teach at any university,[9] could be granted only by *studia* so authorized by emperors, popes, or kings, internal matters of institutional government were in the hands of those immediately connected with learning. Each faculty made its own rules. Each faculty elected its own head and held its own assemblies—and it is significant of the internal vitality of the corporate body that assemblies were held very often and in secret—while the university as a whole had its general assembly, the congregation.[10]

[5] For an estimate of "The Medieval University in Church and Society," see F. M. Powicke, *Ways of Medieval Life and Thought* (Boston, 1951), pp. 198–212.

[6] Rashdall conjectured that at the close of the Middle Ages a larger portion of the population received a university education than is the case in modern countries. *Cambridge Medieval History,* VI (Cambridge, 1929), 601. Presumably this comparison would not apply to the United States, which in the twentieth century has come to offer a university education, or a facsimile thereof, to an unprecedented portion of the total population.

[7] For the text of such an oath see Lynn Thorndike, ed., *University Records and Life in the Middle Ages* (New York, 1944), pp. 103–5.

[8] The terms *universitas* and *collegium* meant a collectivity, corporation, or any organic group or gild.

[9] For the limitations on this right see Rashdall, *Universities of Europe,* I, 13–15. Of less general application was another teaching license, the *licentia docendi,* which gave the right to teach in the diocese in which it was granted.

[10] For a discussion of the organization of the University of Paris in relation to

While great feuds could and did develop within the universities—examples are those at Paris between the faculties of arts and theology and between the secular clergy and the members of the mendicant orders—the universities were aware that their prestige and power depended upon their capacity for cohesion.[11] As Sir Maurice Powicke says, they were "intensely self-conscious and self-important."[12] The universities were encouraged in this self-importance by the fact that the faculties of the great institutions—Bologna, Paris, Oxford—were consulted again and again on vital questions of doctrine and law, and were expected to state their findings and intervene in ecclesiastical and social affairs. In the early fourteenth century, for instance, the theologians of the University of Paris, with the support of the French king, humbled the Avignon Pope, John XXII, who in his capacity as a private theologian had espoused a doctrine concerning the beatific vision against which they had pronounced almost a century before. In this case they reaffirmed their earlier judgment and appealed to the king to enforce it, a strategy which wrung from the pope a reply "as humble and apologetic as if he were a young student in Paris in danger of losing the bachelor's degree for heresy."[13] Ultimately the pope rather equivocally retracted. At crucial junctures in the affairs of the Church, like the Council of Constance, the universities played an important part. When Henry VIII turned to the English universities for a judgment on his divorce—one of the most famous instances of university consultation—he was acting in a well-established tradition; but that in this instance the judgment was extracted rather than freely given was a sign that the autonomy of the universities had been considerably diminished.

At the time of their greatest independence the universities lived in the interstices of medieval society, taking advantage of its decentralization and the balance of its conflicting powers to further their own corporate interests. The absence of a monolithic structure of power, the existence of a real plurality and diversity of interests within the frameworks of both

---

its corporate power and intellectual freedom see Mary Martin McLaughlin, "Intellectual Freedom and Its Limitations in the University of Paris in the Thirteenth and Fourteenth Centuries," unpublished Ph.D. dissertation (Columbia University, 1952), pp. 31–32. We are heavily indebted to this study.

[11] "Do not divide, always cohere," preached one of the chancellors of Paris, "as individuals we are nothing." D'Irsay, *Histoire*, I, 148.

[12] Powicke, *Medieval Life and Thought*, p. 183.

[13] Rashdall, *Universities of Europe*, I, 553; cf. McLaughlin, "Intellectual Freedom," pp. 362–69.

the ecclesiastical and secular powers, put the universities in a position in which they were not easily overwhelmed. They appealed to king or council against pope, to pope against king or bishop, and to kings and popes alike against truculent town governments.

Moreover, they had weapons of their own that put them above the level of mere appellants and gave them independent bargaining power. Among these weapons was the cessation or suspension of lectures, the academic equivalents of the modern strike. A still more powerful device arose, oddly enough, from their very poverty. Unhampered in the beginning by physical apparatus, great libraries, worldly goods, and substantial college foundations, they could and on occasion did migrate, taking with them their large numbers of students and profitable trade. Such migrations were one of the means of the early spread of universities, since at times migrations resulted in new foundations.[14]

In quarrels with local authorities the universities defended themselves with such vigor—and success—that Rashdall speaks of them as living off their misfortunes. Students were commonly young and riotous, and they regularly made enemies among the townspeople, who resented their privileges and their licentiousness. A major conflict at the University of Paris occurred in 1228–29 when successive forays by students and townsmen, arising out of a tavern brawl, caused the regent, Blanche of Castile, to send a company of soldiers against the students. When several students were killed, the masters suspended lectures in protest. Dissatisfied with the immediate results, they went further: they resolved that if justice were not done to the university within a month, they would disband it for six years, and even then would not return unless satisfactory redress had meantime been given. Nor was this an idle threat: most of the masters and scholars actually left. Many went to Oxford and Cambridge, which were much strengthened by their arrival, others to the smaller *studia generalia* or the cathedral schools of France. The dispersion lasted almost two years. It resulted in the recall of the papal legate who had advised the fatal attack and the issuance of an order from Gregory IX to the King and the Queen Mother that they punish the offenders. It is unclear what other redress was granted to the masters, but the episode was followed by a series of papal bulls enlarging the privileges of the university, among them the bull *Parens scientiarum* (1231), which gave the university

[14] Eleven institutions are known to have originated in this fashion down to 1456; see the table in Rashdall, *Universities of Europe*, I, xxiv.

apostolic sanction for the right to suspend lectures and ratified its authority to make its own statutes and punish violators by expulsion. Serious limitations were imposed upon the power to punish scholars possessed by the bishop and the university's chancellors. Several years later the university was given another important exemption, the *ius non trahi extra,* that made it impossible for students to be cited to ecclesiastical courts at a distance from Paris.[15]

Somewhat comparable was the aftermath of the riot of St. Scholastica's Day at Oxford in 1355. The townsmen made a frightful organized assault on the university in which scholars were beaten, tortured, and killed. After lectures had been suspended by the masters for several months, the Bishop of Lincoln put the town under interdict and the king ordered a commission of inquiry. Scores of townsmen were arrested and the mayor of Oxford was imprisoned. Under a new charter the greater part of the government of the town and the regulation of its trade was now turned over to the university. A large company of specified municipal officers was put under obligation to attend an annual mass on St. Scholastica's Day for the souls of the murdered clerks and to make a token offering of a penny apiece in their memories—a quaint practice that was not abolished until 1825.[16]

The very solidarity of the masters in such instances suggests more than *esprit de corps*—it suggests discipline. If masters were to undertake a cessation of lectures or migration in a body, if an entire university, or at least a faculty of theology or canon law, was to render corporate judgments on vital issues, some internal regime that would encourage if not compel agreement was necessary.[17] The idea of corporate action, corpor-

---

[15] Rashdall, *Universities of Europe,* I, 334–43.

[16] Charles E. Mallet, *A History of the University of Oxford* (Oxford, 1924), pp. 160–63; Rashdall, *Universities of Europe,* III, 96–103. Rashdall observes, concerning the frequency and bitterness of Oxford's town and gown riots: "There is probably not a single yard of ground in any part of the classic high Street that lies between S. Martin's and S. Mary's which has not, at one time or another, been stained with blood. There are historic battlefields on which less has been spilt." *Ibid.,* III, 96.

[17] In this respect the modern university can be contrasted with its medieval forerunner. The modern university emphasizes that it has no corporate judgment on disputed public questions. It expects, at least in the United States, that its professors in the course of such public activities as they choose to engage in will dissociate their own opinions from the university's reputation, and it hopes, often in vain, that the public will understand that the professor speaks only for himself. The recent tendency among some academic men in the United States to propose more rigorous academic self-discipline or self-censorship in return for an anticipated broader respect for university independence from the community shows a disposition, how-

ate judgment, and corporate power implies some sacrifice of individual independence. Thus, far from being an unqualified guarantee of individual freedom, the corporate power of the university was in some important respects at odds with it. Every corporate unit of the University of Paris, for instance—the nations, the colleges, and the separate faculties—adopted statutes and ordinances affecting almost every conceivable facet of academic life, from trivial details of dress to the subjects and methods of lectures and disputations. (In addition the Dominicans and Franciscans within the academic community were subject, under penalty of the loss of their academic privileges, to the regulations of their own orders.) To insure an understanding of and obedience to the regulations, upon their admission to the faculties masters were expected to take oaths in which they promised to obey the statutes, keep university secrets, and observe cessations. Such oaths give evidence of the premium placed by the university upon its code of internal discipline.[18] A recent student of the history of the University of Paris concludes:

More important in the history of freedom in the university than the sporadic intervention of ecclesiastical authorities were the efforts of the masters themselves to regulate and sometimes to restrict the teaching of their colleagues. For the liberties which enabled them to exercise their intellectual functions made possible also the corporate imposition and enforcement of restrictions. Now it was the institution and its parts which not only claimed freedom but exercised control.[19]

From this it should not be inferred either that the solidarity of the universities was complete (for internal feuds were in fact a vital part of university history), or that the corporate power of the universities involved a net loss to the personal freedom of their members. Far more than the modern university the medieval university was a self-contained intellectual community; not only did the daring and the novelties it produced come from within, but the pressure for intellectual conformity also came chiefly from within. But some faculty, some order, some corporate interest was likely to fly to the aid of most unorthodox thinkers, and it

---

ever unwitting, to move somewhat closer to the medieval equipoise between corporate autonomy and academic freedom. The difference—and the difficulty—is that the modern American university neither shows the militancy nor enjoys the respect of the medieval university.

[18] On oaths see Rashdall, *Universities of Europe,* I, 378–80; the university seems at length to have called for so many oaths that their sanctity and value were seriously deflated.

[19] McLaughlin, "Intellectual Freedom," pp. 28–29.

was rare indeed that anyone stood alone. In return for their loyalty, teachers were surrounded by an institutional framework that supported their pride and security as men of learning and offered them a vigorous defense against interference. Indeed, in great crises the positions even of such notable heretics as Wyclif and Huss were for a time strengthened by powerful support given them within their universities. As in so many of the relations of medieval life, the interplay between corporate power and individual freedom was complex and many-sided.

PERSONAL FREEDOM IN THE MIDDLE AGES

Freedom, if it is to be meaningful, must ultimately be exercised by individuals. When we turn from the corporate position of the medieval universities and their faculties to the role of the individual thinker, we find him working under conditions that cannot simply be described as free or unfree. He existed, if he had something important to say, in a state of tension between submission to authority and self-assertion.

The term authority, of course, is ambiguous. We must distinguish between positive authority and the authority of tradition. Positive authority —that is, external pressure in the form of positive acts brought to bear by academic or ecclesiastical or civil power—leaves its open record in the form of regulations and prohibitions, censures and censorship, and overt acts of persecution. While the intimidating effects of positive authority are not measurable, its rise and decline can at least be traced by the historian with some degree of specificity. But the authority of traditional belief and the power of deferential habits of thought are intangible; they are woven into the whole texture of intellectual life, and their influence can be assessed only in a highly impressionistic way. When Henry Osborn Taylor speaks of deference to authority as "a first general quality of mediaeval thought," [20] what he means is authority in the second of these two senses. The inherited pattern of deference to philosophic authority, as well as the traditional desire for salvation itself—a goal superior to inquiry—were doubtless far more imposing and consistently operating inhibitions on free speculation than were the formal acts of the Church.[21]

[20] Henry Osborn Taylor, *The Mediaeval Mind*, II (Cambridge, 1949), 327–28.
[21] Cf. Taylor, *Mediaeval Mind*, II, 326: "even in the great twelfth and thirteenth centuries, intellectual inquiry was never unlimbered from bands of deference, nor ever quite dispassionately rational or unaffected by the mortal need to attain a salvation which was bestowed or withheld by God according to His plan authorita-

In all ages the weight of tradition presses in varying degrees upon the capacity of the individual to pose new hypotheses and find new truths. In the Middle Ages tradition was, if Taylor is right, particularly formidable; but to say that it suppressed originality and destroyed the power of the scholastics to produce novelty would be to fly in the face of the intellectual resourcefulness of academic men during the twelfth, thirteenth, and fourteenth centuries. As C. R. S. Harris argues:

It is undeniable that the dogmas of the Church exercised an influence which was paramount. But this influence was psychological rather than authoritative in the sense of external compulsion. . . . At the height of its maturity medieval thought displayed a latitude which is truly surprising; the speculations of the twelfth and thirteenth centuries contain a diversity which quite belies the notion of any orthodoxy rigorously imposed from without.[22]

The intellectual freedom of the medieval scholar existed within the framework of an authoritative system of faith upheld by vigilant positive authority. The fact that a certain kind of freedom existed within that framework is undeniable; the value that is assigned to it will vary in accordance with the religious and philosophic convictions of the observer. If it were one's sole aim to compare the medieval with the modern world one might with justice emphasize the gravity of the restrictions on inquiry in the medieval university as they appear to the modern intelligence. But since it is our purpose to enter sympathetically into the spirit of the medieval academic experience and to understand the function of the medieval university from the point of view of its period, it is necessary to take for the moment a relativistic view, accepting as given the medieval framework of ideas.

---

tively declared." One can only refer the reader to Taylor's brilliant discussion of this theme (II, 323–28), and the critical comments by Maurice De Wulf, *Philosophy and Civilization in the Middle Ages* (Princeton, 1922), pp. 170–72.

[22] C. R. S. Harris, *Duns Scotus,* I (Oxford, 1927), 40; the order of the sentences has been transposed here. The inherent complexities of the problem of freedom in the medieval framework are illustrated by the same writer when he observes a few pages later, apropos the recantation of Roscellinus: "No dialectic, however persuasive, could be tolerated which imperilled the doctrine of the Church. . . . Whenever a conflict arose between faith and reason, the result was a foregone conclusion; the freedom of thought was limited not so much by an external authority . . . as by the psychological convictions of the unanimous consensus of Christendom, which was impervious to argument, however cogent, and totally unaware of any inconsistency in its attitude." *Ibid.,* p. 47. The illustration, however, does not quite fit the point, for Roscellinus' recantation seems to have been impelled more by external authority in the form of the Council of Soissons than by psychological conviction.

While the tension between faith and inquiry, between the individual and traditional authority, involves hardly less than the history of medieval thought, it is possible at least to convey some idea of the extent to which positive authority was brought to bear and the means used to confront or evade it. Here we may take the fields of philosophy and theology as a touchstone—but it should be emphasized that this procedure is somewhat prejudicial to the Middle Ages, for these two were the most difficult and controversial areas, not the freest. In such fields as law and medicine, grammar and logic, mathematics, statics, optics, and meteorology,[23] prescribed limits were far less restricting than they were for philosophers and theologians, and, as the late C. H. Haskins pointed out, "experiment and research were much freer than has been supposed." [24] The scientific subjects were pursued about as freely if not as effectively as they were in antiquity or in early modern times, and in some of them the groundwork was laid for the development of early modern science. The striking antagonism between religion and science that we find in early modern times was not so characteristic of the Middle Ages, when men of science, so often clerics themselves, maintained a deferential view of theology but went on quietly with their work. Lynn Thorndike once dropped the challenging remark that

there seems no adequate proof for a single specific instance of persecution of men of science by the church for purely scientific views in the twelfth and thirteenth centuries. The occasions when such men got into trouble and when we know the reason why, are just those occasions when they left science to dabble in theological or ecclesiastical concerns.[25]

[23] These subjects are designated here in accordance with modern, not medieval, terminology. In the Middle Ages the lines were not so sharply drawn, and these subjects (except for law and medicine) were pursued as secular studies in the faculty of arts.

[24] C. H. Haskins, *The Renaissance of the Twelfth Century* (Cambridge, Mass., 1939), pp. 360–61; see his discussion of freedom of thought, pp. 360–65, and in *The Rise of the Universities* (New York, 1923), pp. 68–78. Other brief discussions of freedom in the medieval university are those of A. J. Carlyle in F. S. Marvin, ed., *Progress and History* (Oxford, 1916), pp. 89–90, De Wulf, *Philosophy and Civilization in the Middle Ages,* pp. 71–72, and Edgar N. Johnson, "The Background of the University Tradition," in *Freedom and the University* (Ithaca, 1950). G. G. Coulton takes a much dimmer view than most writers of medieval freedom in his *Medieval Panorama* (Cambridge, Mass., 1938), Chap. XXII and *passim,* as he does in his other writings.

[25] Lynn Thorndike, "Natural Science in the Middle Ages," *Popular Science Monthly,* LXXXVII (September, 1915), 279. For a single case in the fourteenth century that may possibly be an exception to this generalization, see Thorndike's *A History of Magic and Experimental Science,* Vol. II (New York, 1929), Chap.

Even in theology and philosophy there was a significant margin for
the movement of the mind. Confronted as they were by the task of putting
together the traditions of classical philosophy with the teachings of Scripture and the symbology of the faith, the Christian thinkers found themselves working in a realm of inquiry that left large, and to them significant, areas of inquiry open to argument and susceptible to the innovative
force of great minds. A hierarchy of authorities might be accepted and
defined, but the authorities themselves did not agree, and thus their pronouncements had to be construed, reconciled, even on occasion contradicted, by reason. "Authority," said Alain de Lille in the twelfth century,
"has a nose of wax that can be turned in any direction." [26] When in his
Sic et non, which appeared before the opening of the university era,
Abelard ranged together the conflicting opinions of authority on point
after point, he was quickening a major method of scholastic criticism.
The supreme art of the scholastics was dialectic; and while dialectic had
limitations of its own it fed the need of the masters for the clash of mind
against mind.[27] It was from the Middle Ages that early modern education
inherited the disputation as an academic form, whose value as a medium
for the cultivation of ordered thought and cogent expression should not
be minimized.[28]

LXXI. Not always, of course, was the line between scientific and theological
concerns a clear one.

In such a field as medicine the weight of traditional authority seems far more
important in impeding progress than the positive intervention of the Church. The
Church attempted to keep clerics from practicing medicine, but for reasons of
church discipline, not out of hostility to medical knowledge. Possibly this tendency
to make medicine more of a laic profession was an aid to its development. Dissection
was not, as often asserted, forbidden by the Church, and dissections became fairly
common after 1300. Progress in anatomy was chiefly obstructed by a traditional
deference to Galen and Avicenna so intense that teachers of anatomy could ob-
stinately see in a corpse what Galen said would be there, even when it was not, or
would attribute discrepancies to changes in the text made by translators or copiers.

[26] Maurice De Wulf, *The History of Mediaeval Philosophy* (New York, 1952),
I, 222–23.

[27] Late medieval developments in formal logic also helped to lay some of the
foundations for early modern science.

[28] See the brief appreciation of the disputation in Meyrick H. Carré, *Phases of
Thought in England* (Oxford, 1949), pp. 94–99. The author remarks (p. 99):
"The persistent effort to meet objections against a philosophical position was an
education in agile and searching thought. . . . An Oxford or Cambridge scholar
of the thirteenth century was obliged to penetrate deeply into the principles in which
he believed. . . . The universities afforded a more thorough training in strenuous
abstract thinking than was afforded in any later period in England." James J. Walsh
has pointed to the enduring pedagogical value of the disputation in colonial American colleges in his *Education of the Founding Fathers of the Republic* (New York,
1935), Chap. X and *passim.*

If some social and professional factors made for timidity on the part of the medieval scholars, others encouraged daring and forcefulness. If there were timid masters of the sort Godfrey of Fontaines rebuked when he wrote: "Masters should be diligently aware lest, frightened where there is nothing to be feared, they think they have good reason for being silent when there is none; few are to be found who can be blamed for excess in speaking truth, but many indeed for silence," [29] the very existence of such an exhortation bespeaks the presence of men of a different turn of mind. One is struck by the appearance among the outstanding scholars of figures of enormous independence and self-confidence, even of arrogance—men of the temper of Abelard, Roger Bacon, and William of Ockham. Some scholars, coming from noble families, added the pride of learning to the pride of place.[30] But whether the scholar's origin was high or low, he was given to feeling that the man of knowledge should have an exalted role in the world. Moreover, he might well be ambitious, like men in other high places, and there was no great distinction to be won by those who could only parrot what had been handed down to them. The greatest numbers of students flocked to hear arresting and stimulating minds like Abelard's; the highest honors were won by ambitious constructions like that of Aquinas—among whose propositions, it should be remembered, were several once cited as unorthodox. Mediocrity might be docile, but high aspiration pressed nervously at the outer limits of the received doctrines. The roll of those whose ideas received some measure of unfavorable attention from some ecclesiastical authority from the twelfth to the fourteenth century is impressive—Roscellinus, Abelard, Gilbert de la Porée, Roger Bacon, Siger de Brabant, Peter John Olivi, Arnald of Villanova, Meister Eckhart, William of Ockham, Nicholas of Autrecourt, Pietro d'Abano, Marsilius of Padua—even Peter Lombard and Aquinas.[31]

One must conclude that the medieval period was neither the nightmare of dogmatism, cruelty, and suppression that it was held to be by the rationalist scholars of the nineteenth century nor the magnificently open ground for free expression that some modern medievalists at times seem

[29] McLaughlin, "Intellectual Freedom," p. 2.
[30] Cf. De Wulf's suggestion that the formulation of the conceptualist doctrine may have been related to the proud individualism of the sons of chevaliers (*Philosophy and Civilization in the Middle Ages*, p. 59).
[31] This list leaves out not only many lesser figures but also such men as Joachim of Floris and Ramon Lull, who were not university teachers but had much influence in the universities.

to be portraying. Intellectual freedom has, of course, both its objective and subjective aspects. A man is objectively free insofar as his society will allow him to express novel or critical ideas without the threat of formal or informal punishment of any serious kind. He is subjectively free insofar as he *feels* free to say what he wishes. Subjective freedom may exist without objective freedom wherever men are so completely confined by the common assumptions of their place, time, or class that they are incapable of engendering any novel or critical ideas that they care to express, and where in fact the expression of such ideas would be dangerous. Such men would be conscious of no restraints, but they would not be free. A high degree of intellectual freedom may be said to exist where both subjective and objective freedom prevail in a considerable measure, and where the latter is present in reasonable proportion to the former. Modern scholars agree that there was considerable liberty in the medieval universities. The range of that liberty was much narrower than that which exists in universities reared under the modern democracies and in the spirit of modern scientific inquiry. But to set up the full range of ideas that can be safely professed in the universities of a modern democracy as an absolute standard for other ages would be perhaps marginally illuminating but unhistoric. Grant the limits of the faith, more elastic than we sometimes incline to believe, within which the medieval scholar himself was usually content to work, and one finds that the range of problems that he dealt with, the variety of solutions, the area of choice that confronted him, were still considerable. Subjectively and objectively he enjoyed a measure of freedom—large enough to make possible creative work of great value but limited enough to bring creative thinkers again and again into conflict with authority—most commonly the authority of their own university colleagues. When such conflicts arose it was not always authority that, in the long run, triumphed.

To define clearly either the difference or the similarities between medieval and modern freedom of inquiry is a task for a far larger study than ours. But one difference that will at once strike the inquirer is that between the two conceptual models of intellectual inquiry and between the amount of emotional tension connected with unorthodox ideas in the Middle Ages and the present day. The modern academic community in a democratic state, although often unable fully to realize it, assumes the right of free inquiry. The medieval academic community, although frequently and intentionally breaching it, assumed the right of some author-

ity to exercise censorship and proscription in theology and on such conclusions of philosophy as were deemed to encroach upon theology. While
the Middle Ages sought for unity and completeness in these fields,[32]
the modern mind generally accepts as not only inevitable but desirable
the existence of a plurality of philosophical perspectives. In many fields
there is available to modern inquiry an elaborate apparatus of verification
for which there was no adequate medieval counterpart; and the process
of verification lowers the level of intellectual animus, takes the center of
authority out of the realm of the personal and political, and refers it to
criteria that are impersonal and detached. The medieval model of inquiry was limited by the presence of a hard core of accepted doctrine,
authoritatively established, which was defined and enforced, made obligatory on all thinkers at the risk not only of their worldly position but of
their spiritual privileges and possibly even their eternal souls. Each new
accretion of knowledge was expected to be consistent with sound doctrine. Assumed was the desirability, indeed the inevitability, of a single
system of truth, anchored in God, and elaborated by man in accordance
with a rigorous system of inference.[33] (Of course, the unsettled questions relating to that system were admitted by all but the most anti-
intellectualist thinkers to be numerous and important.) Medieval scholars
seem for the most part not to have desired to challenge this model of
truth when considered abstractly; most of them accepted the notion of a
system stemming from a central body of authority, and the concept that
somewhere the power must be located to define with finality the limits of
truth and of inquiry. In the concrete, however, they were never able
to agree on the substantive questions of what could be inferred from or
what interfered with the central core of the faith, or on the jurisdictional
question of who should have the authority to condemn which propositions
and under what circumstances. In short, while they submitted themselves
to the Church and the broader principles of the faith, both inwardly, it
would seem, and outwardly, some of them did not feel obliged to accept
the idea that the hierarchy represented the true Church. It was of the

[32] On this theme in medieval culture see De Wulf, *Philosophy and Civilization in
the Middle Ages,* Chap. V. Perhaps it should be added that this quest for ideal
unity was itself in part a product of the actual diversity of the Middle Ages.

[33] In theory philosophy was to enjoy independence of theology, but the major
philosophical issues had a way of being bound up with theological ones. Thus
twelfth-century logical and ontological discussions were associated with heresies
concerning the Trinity, while the thirteenth-century reception of Aristotle led some
thinkers toward allegedly anti-Christian views.

utmost importance that the outline of the Church's authority was never precisely drawn, even though everyone might think it desirable that the matter should somehow be capable of settlement.

From the standpoint of the Church itself, freedom existed not by design but by default. The exercise of daring and initiative in touchy areas of thought went on not because the Church recognized or openly encouraged the individual's right of free inquiry, but because the Church, at various times and in varying degrees, found it unnecessary, undesirable, inexpedient, or impossible to suppress the work of scholars who were often well protected, tenacious, and powerfully motivated. Very often the Church intervened in intellectual life only because the disputes in the university led to insistent charges of heresy by some group of scholars that could not be ignored.

The various condemnations and censures of the thirteenth and fourteenth centuries, it is true, add up to an enormous imposition on inquiry in philosophy and theology. That it was not a fatal imposition is much to the credit of the scholars whose beliefs were questioned; in many cases they showed a hardihood and stubbornness in the pursuit of truth that outlasted and even reversed condemnations. Modern scholarship tends to emphasize the variety, boldness, and ultimate fruitfulness of the academic work of the thirteenth and fourteenth centuries. These qualities were achieved under difficult circumstances; the considerable measure of freedom enjoyed by many distinguished masters in the great days of the medieval university was not handed to them as a generous offering of Church or society, but was laboriously and patiently wrested from meddlesome colleagues, bishops, or papal legates at much sacrifice. One cannot escape the feeling that intellectual life in the medieval university, as compared with that of our own age, was lived at an exceptionally high voltage, that the morale and tenacity of the medieval masters at their best marks a high point in the history of the human spirit.

In justice to the Church it should be said that if its theory did not allow for freedom of thought, its practice was far from consistently repressive. Before the emergence of the university system, indeed, the Church had been rather inefficiently organized for the repression of speculation.[34] For centuries it had of necessity been much more concerned with the defense of its temporal interest than with the detailed definition

---

[34] Cf. the discussion of the subject by A. J. Macdonald, *Authority and Reason in the Early Middle Ages* (Oxford, 1933).

of points of dogma or with interference with the work of scholars.[35] The cathedral schools had been relatively free from interference by positive authority in their substantive intellectual tasks, although in the matter of their external administration a considerable amount of ecclesiastical exhortation and some regulations were forthcoming.[36] The Church seems to have had, at the beginning of the university era, no regular mechanism for the censorship of scholarly work.[37] However, in the twelfth century, when some individual thinkers seemed to be veering into dangerous ground, the Church began to raise a heavy hand, in the form of the condemnation of books or doctrines deemed heretical; such condemnation usually proceeded from the councils of bishops. Notable in this respect were the condemnations of some of the ideas of Roscellinus, Abelard, and Gilbert de la Porée. These were serious and harmful incursions upon freedom of speculation. They inhibited, but could not altogether quiet, their victims; they checked the growth of, but did not stifle, new ideas. Repeatedly it happened that ideas that were subject to condemnations long afterward continued to receive respectful attention from scholars. The notions of some nominalist writers, for instance, might be condemned and yet survive for generations to excite agitated controversy in the schools. Aristotle was proscribed at one point and yet became the established object of study and source of authority for the next generation.

During the very period in which the university system was taking form, the attitude of the Church was growing much harsher. At the same time it found itself more capable, when it was considered necessary, of carrying out organized repression. In the thirteenth century, an age of increasingly defined doctrine and also of well-organized heresy, the Church reached the zenith of its power, spiritual and temporal. The Waldensian and Albigensian movements had made the Church's officials alert to the danger of its destruction, and about 1230 the existing, relatively informal,

[35] Even J. B. Bury, in his rationalist polemic, *A History of Freedom of Thought* (New York, 1913), concedes that before the end of the twelfth century the Church was far from systematic in its pursuit of heresy, that it was "mainly guided by considerations of its temporal interest, and was roused to severe action only when the spread of false doctrines threatened to reduce its revenues or seemed a menace to society" (pp. 55–56).

[36] See the brief survey by E. P. Pride, "Ecclesiastical Legislation on Education, A.D. 300–1200," *Church History*, XII (December, 1943), 235–54. D'Irsay concludes that this tradition was substantially continued in the early university period. *Histoire*, I, 149–50.

[37] G. B. Flahiff, "The Ecclesiastical Censorship of Books in the Twelfth Century," *Mediaeval Studies*, IV (1942), 1–22.

means for the location and trial of heretics were replaced by the systematic machinery of the Inquisition. But intellectual life had already been enormously quickened by the recovery of the greater part of the works of Aristotle. The philosophical and doctrinal ferment was further complicated by the rise of the mendicant orders and the problems they created by their entrance into the universities, where conflicts arose between regulars and seculars and between Dominicans and Franciscans. Thus the universities arose in a period of ecclesiastical and doctrinal turmoil and considerable repression, and at least one of them (Toulouse, in 1229) was founded for the specific purpose of providing a doctrinal antidote to the heresies of Languedoc.[38]

The Church had always been far more concerned about doctrinal deviations that had a practical bearing upon its safety and power than upon those that were primarily of academic significance and offered it no fundamental challenge. Gregory of Heimburg in the fifteenth century sardonically declared that it was safer to discuss the power of God than the power of the popes.[39] Thus the existence of heretical movements or tendencies among the population at large made certain positions more dangerous for teachers to espouse. A suggestion playfully discussed in the dialectical process was one thing; an idea that corresponded with a popular heresy, a schismatic tendency, an attack on the friars, or the antipapal objectives of some powerful prince was quite another. Heretical scholars who risked their necks over matters of such fundamental importance might survive, but only by the grace of powerful protectors far

[38] Cf. Rashdall, *Universities of Europe*, II, 162: "It was . . . recognized that even among the clerks of Paris the spirit of inquiry and bold speculation had made great advances: at Toulouse the danger was to be avoided by a careful choice of teachers." However, when the masters of Toulouse issued a circular letter in 1229 to invite other teachers to join them, they promised: "Those who wish to scrutinize the bosom of nature to the inmost can hear here the books of Aristotle which were forbidden at Paris. What then will you lack? Scholastic liberty? By no means, since tied to no one's apron strings you will enjoy your own liberty." Thorndike, *University Records and Life in the Middle Ages*, p. 34.

[39] H. C. Lea, *A History of the Inquisition of the Middle Ages* (New York, 1887), III, 569. This principle was more applicable during the days of the secularized Renaissance popes than it had been earlier. Cf. Mandell Creighton, *Persecution and Tolerance* (London, 1895), p. 109: "Leo X was tolerant of the philosophic doubts of Pomponazzi concerning the immortality of the soul, because such speculations were not likely to affect the position of the Papacy; but could not allow Luther to discuss the dubious and complicated question of indulgences, because it might have disastrous effects upon the system of papal finance."

For evidence, however, on the extent to which issues of ecclesiastical politics were discussed at Paris, see McLaughlin, "Intellectual Freedom," Chaps. IV, V.

stronger than the universities themselves. Thus in the early fourteenth century, Marsilius of Padua, at one time a rector of the University of Paris, an opponent of papal power, and one of the most significant political thinkers of the Middle Ages, fled from Paris in the company of John of Jandun, who shared his opposition to papal power, to the court of Louis of Bavaria, where both men placed themselves under the German emperor's protection. William of Ockham, after preaching somewhat similar views, took the same course. Toward the end of the century John Wyclif, an influential theologian at Oxford, was protected by John of Gaunt, the Duke of Lancaster, one of the most powerful men in England. For his political opposition to the Church Wyclif found widespread backing, not only from John but within Oxford; but when he went on to espouse a sweeping range of heresies touching upon the Eucharist, he lost many friends and was expelled from the university along with some of his followers. Further prosecution was probably prevented only by his death, which occurred when the controversy inspired by his teaching was still raging.[40] Not long afterward, John Huss, the rector of the University of Prague, was condemned by the Council of Constance and, despite strong support both in his university and among the Bohemian populace, was brought to the stake.[41] A century later Martin Luther, who was teaching at the University of Wittenberg at the time he posted his ninety-five theses, survived and triumphed only with the protection of powerful lay lords.

But these are all spectacular cases in which men who were playing an important role in political and religious life happened to be doing so as occupants of academic posts. That Wyclif, Huss, and Luther were all academic men, like many other prominent reformers of the age, is testimony to the significance of academic life even after the great age of the medieval universities was over, but the fate of these men belongs more intimately to the broader story of religious liberty than to that of intellectual freedom in the universities. Their histories would be a poor point from which to estimate the situation of the characteristic academic man, or to test the common processes of academic life. What of the more typical university masters whose teaching led them a little off the beaten path?

Presumably Paris, with its great influence and its conspicuous place in

---

[40] For Wyclif and Lollardry at Oxford see Mallet, *History of Oxford*, I, 221–40, and the more recent study by Joseph H. Dahmus, *The Prosecution of John Wyclyf* (New Haven, 1952), esp. Chap. III.

[41] Rashdall, *Universities of Europe*, II, 225–34.

the Church, supplies a somewhat untypical example of university affairs. It serves, however, to confront us with the most intense realization of the medieval struggle between freedom and authority. It was the center of European intellectual life, destined not only to find some of its masters' works under censure or condemnation but to be in the end a center of settled authority in its own right. During the thirteenth century Paris was rocked by a series of crises in whose course the masters waged an intermittent struggle against the watchdogs of authority, papal, episcopal, and academic.

The first and most severe of these crises, which grew out of the increasing worries of ecclesiastical authorities over heresies outside and bold speculative thinking inside the university, was a manifestation of the generally heightened concern for doctrinal orthodoxy shown in the Fourth Lateran Council in 1215. From the standpoint of the masters, particularly those of the arts faculty, this struggle was an attempt to preserve under mounting pressure the freedom they already enjoyed.

In 1210 a council of bishops, for the first and only time, treated a speculative movement among the Paris masters very much as it would have treated a popular heresy. Amalric de Bène, a master of arts who had turned to the study of theology, had developed a system of thought, influenced by Neoplatonism and particularly by the work of John Scotus Erigena, which has been described as pantheistic. Some of his own colleagues had censured him and he had appealed to the pope, but their judgment was upheld and he was compelled to retract his errors. A number of his followers, however, carried on with the implications of his work and developed it into an heretical movement that had already spread outside the university itself. A synod at Paris not only condemned a list of relevant errors but acted with a severity that was "unique in the history of the medieval university of Paris." [42] The same synod (in which, it should be noted, some of the masters of the university took part) condemned and burned the writings of David of Dinant, a teacher whose works showed the influence of the rediscovered writings of Aristotle. While the characteristic penalty for masters who were recusant under accusation was the loss of ecclesiastical and teaching offices, and perhaps excommunication, the dissenters of 1210 were shown little mercy. Ten of the heretics who followed Amalric, all either masters or former stu-

[42] McLaughlin, "Intellectual Freedom," p. 26; cf. pp. 25–26, 57–60 for this movement. See also Rashdall, *Universities of Europe,* I, 354–56.

dents at Paris, were degraded from their clerical rank and released to the secular authority; four others were degraded and imprisoned for life. Nine or ten were burned in November, 1210. Thus they were treated not as academic men customarily were, but as the Inquisition was later to treat popular heretics, and probably because their belief was regarded in the same light as a popular heresy. One might have expected a repressive action of such savagery to quiet for an indefinite period any experimentation with further novelties or heresies. In fact it was followed by a period of remarkable speculative activity,[43] and by a notable expansion in the work and interests of the arts faculty.

The outbreak of bold philosophizing that conservative theologians were complaining of at Paris from the late twelfth through the early years of the thirteenth century was now climaxed by an intellectual revolution centering around the rediscovery of the greater part of the works of Aristotle, which had been unknown to Latin Christianity. Now the older and more traditional teachers in the theological faculty were challenged by younger men who liked to mix their theology with philosophy; and the theological faculty found itself disturbed by the tendency of the philosophers in the arts faculty to address themselves to questions previously the concern of theologians.[44]

The story of the reception of the new Aristotle is a good example of how the institutional inconsistencies of the Church and the tenacity of some of the masters helped intellectual innovation. In what seems to have

[43] Thirty years after the executions of 1210 Albertus Magnus still found it worth while to refute in detail the ideas of David of Dinant. This seems to have been part of a general effort to prevent Aristotle from being compromised by such heterodox followers. See G. Théry, *Autour de décret de 1210* (Paris, 1925).

[44] Two significant mid-century cases seem to have arisen in good part as a consequence of internal rivalries. In 1247 John of Brescain was cited before the papal legate, the chancellor, masters of theology, and others on the ground that he had repeatedly espoused several errors in teaching logical exercises. With him was involved a Master Raymond who had already been imprisoned. It was decided that John of Brescain, for introducing theological questions and heretical opinions into logical exercises, should be deprived of the right to teach and expelled from the city and diocese of Paris. McLaughlin, "Intellectual Freedom," pp. 81–83. Another very bitter constitutional struggle, that between the secular clergy and the mendicant friars over the place of the latter in the university, resulted in an important case in 1256. William of St. Amour, a leader among the secular masters, had written an apocalyptic tract against the mendicant orders, pointing to the rise of these orders as a sign of the coming of the Antichrist and the end of the world. Despite remarkably bold support among the secular masters, his book was condemned. He refused, unlike some of his fellows, to retract, was banished from France and suspended forever from preaching or teaching. Rashdall, *Universities of Europe*, I, 385–89.

been an original effort to choke off at its source the impending revolution, the synod of 1210 had forbidden the reading or teaching at Paris of some unspecified works of Aristotle on natural philosophy, an act which was ratified in 1215 by the papal legate, who confirmed a body of statutes drawn up by the masters. But the intellectual riches of the new Aristotle were a powerful temptation. Presumably there was at first no public violation of the prohibition, but one of the chancellors complained that the forbidden works were being read secretly, another that the students liked nothing but to read forbidden books. By 1228 Pope Gregory IX was warning the faculty of theology against trying to confirm theological doctrines by resorting to philosophy. In 1231 he opened the door to a retreat by the Church when he authorized the prior of the Dominicans to absolve all masters and students who had violated the prohibition against lecturing on or reading the forbidden books, and the masters of arts were told that they were not to use these books until they were purged of objectionable matter. Such a purgation seems never to have taken place—at any rate it would have been difficult to solve the problem by such a procedure, for Aristotle had to be taken in hand and interpreted more or less whole in order to be Christianized. In the 1240s, for instance, Roger Bacon openly flouted the fading prohibition by lecturing on the proscribed books, and at this time Aristotle seems to have been rapidly gaining in popularity among both the faculties of arts and theology.[45] Gradually the internal opposition to the new Aristotle collapsed. In 1243 the new pope, Innocent IV, repeated Gregory's promise of an expurgation and for the first time extended the prohibition to the University of Toulouse, where the new Aristotle had been freely taught for fourteen years. But by 1255 Aristotle was not only studied but was prescribed reading in the faculty of arts at Paris, even though no expurgation had been made. Thus within a period of thirty years, thanks to the stubbornness of the masters and the laxity of the authorities, his natural philosophy had run the entire range from unqualified proscription to general use.[46]

[45] The literature on the gradual dissolution of the prohibition is briefly reviewed by Stewart Easton, *Roger Bacon and His Search for a Universal Science* (New York, 1952), pp. 35–45; cf. McLaughlin, "Intellectual Freedom," pp. 60 ff.

[46] Oddly enough, the now obsolete and unenforceable prohibition was actually renewed as late as 1263. Mandonnet suggests that the Church saw real value in the study of Aristotle but was inhibited by fear of the heresies he might unleash. It could not without serious inconvenience either lift or enforce its ban, and therefore found an advantage in allowing the situation to remain ambiguous. Pierre Mandonnet, *Siger de Brabant et l'Averroisme latin au XIIIme siècle* (Louvain, 1911), pp. 22–26.

A second major crisis, involving both the implications of the Aristotelian revolution and the struggle of the masters of arts for autonomy, came in the 1270s. Moslem scholars had long been familiar with the natural philosophy of Aristotle, and when this part of his work dawned on the Christian thinkers it was with the guidance of Arab and Greek commentators. Among the great commentators on the Aristotelian texts was Averroës of Córdoba, a doctor by profession, who died in 1198. The commentaries of Averroës became so widely read in the Latin world that he was known as "the commentator" in the same sense that Aristotle was "the philosopher." As a learned commentator on the Peripatetic, Averroës was useful and acceptable, but his own philosophical views were heretical both in the Moslem and the Christian worlds, for he believed that the individual soul expires with the body, that matter is eternal rather than created, and that all possible intellect in the human species is ultimately one.[47] His philosophy was widely professed in Spain and his commentaries caused more than a ripple in the arts faculty at Paris.

The leader of the Parisian "Averroists" was a master of arts, Siger de Brabant. When Bishop Tempier of Paris condemned the doctrines of Averroës in 1270, declaring that all who knowingly taught or asserted them were excommunicated, Siger went on calmly and only a bit more prudently with his teaching. Seven years later, when Pope John XXI complained to Bishop Tempier about the dangerous errors circulating at Paris, the bishop, urged on by a group of zealous masters of theology, responded by condemning indiscriminately 219 propositions of various sorts, including some upheld by Aquinas. The issue was joined as to how far the thought of Aristotle might be carried and how real was the philosophical autonomy of the arts faculty.[48] Siger and one of his associates,

[47] The principal contentions of Averroism that aroused concern in the Christian world were: that God knows nothing outside Himself, and that He does not have knowledge of particulars, and that human actions are not ruled by divine providence; that the world is eternal, and there was no first man; that there is only one intelligence for all men, that the individual soul dies with the body, and that the soul after death could not suffer from a corporeal fire; that the world is governed by necessity and is under the influence of the celestial bodies, and that the human will acts only within the realm of necessity.

[48] On Siger and heterodox Aristotelianism see Fernand van Steenberghen, *Siger de Brabant d'après ses oeuvres inédites,* Vol. II: *Siger dans l'histoire de l'aristotélisme* (Louvain, 1952). The terms "Averroism" and "Averroists" have often been used rather loosely to designate some of the heterodox Aristotelians, who cannot in fact always be assumed to have been followers of Averroës or even to have been profoundly influenced by him. The use of the conventional terms in the text should not be taken as necessarily implying a close affiliation between Latin writers and Averroës.

Bernier of Nivelles, seem to have been summoned before the Inquisitor-General of France, although it is uncertain that they ever obeyed. Siger appealed to the protection of the Roman court and was imprisoned in a mild custodial fashion with another of his followers (Bernier was restored to favor), and then apparently spent his remaining years at the papal court at Orvieto, where he was murdered by a demented clerk. To many of his contemporaries Siger appeared not as a heretic but as a great martyr to philosophical independence and freedom of thought. Dante in the *Paradiso* put him in heaven, at the left hand of Thomas Aquinas.[49] The Averroistic strain of rationalism survived not only at Paris, where it can be seen in the work of John of Jandun and others in the fourteenth century, but above all at Padua and Bologna. It seems to have contributed significantly to the primary skeptical currents of the late Middle Ages.[50]

At Paris, despite Siger's incarceration, the continued struggle of the arts faculty for its independence from the theologians was won by the close of the thirteenth century. After 1277 "there was no further effective intervention on the part of the theologians in either the organization or the studies of the arts faculty," [51] and the pride and self-confidence of the masters of arts henceforth increased. Another philosophic crisis, however, took place in the first half of the fourteenth century, partly in connection with the work and influence of William of Ockham. Ockham was cited to the papal curia in 1324 by a commission of Paris and Oxford theologians which, after carefully examining his work for all of three years, censured fifty-one articles, not only in theology but in metaphysics, natural philosophy, psychology, and logic. Yet no official condemnation ever seems to have resulted from this examination, and a quarter-century after the event the Paris masters seem to have been unaware of it.[52] Ockham's doctrines caused so much tumult, particularly among the younger scholars, that the public and private reading of his works was prohibited by the arts faculty at Paris in 1339. Again in the following year the prohibition was renewed, but under circumstances that suggest that the object

[49] Canto X, 136–38. To Averroës himself Dante assigned an easy place in Hell, the limbo of the unbaptized, along with some very distinguished company. *Inferno,* Canto IV, 144.

[50] Cf. Anneliese Maier, *Die Vorläufer Galileis im 14. Jahrhundert* (Rome, 1949), Chaps. IX, X.

[51] McLaughlin, "Intellectual Freedom," p. 133; for the exercise of this autonomy see Chap. III.

[52] *Ibid.,* pp. 354–56. On the examination of Ockham see A. Vacant and E. Mangenot, *Dictionnaire de théologie catholique,* Vol. XI, col. 889 ff.

was now rather to quiet some of the more obstreperous anti-Ockhamists.[53] One of the scholars affected by the action of 1340 was Nicholas of Autrecourt, a leading philosophical skeptic of the fourteenth century. Six years later Nicholas was gravely censured by a papal commission for teachings repudiating the entire framework of the now altogether orthodox Aristotelian thought and for propounding doctrines that were held to be a menace to the faith. But the censure neither erased his influence nor ended his career, for he seems to have been, not long after, still dean of the cathedral at Metz and still in possession of the degrees and benefices of which he was supposed to have been deprived.[54] The outcome of these two cases, like the earlier reception of Aristotle, illustrates the futility of such intervention against important ideas.

FAITH, REASON, AND COMMUNICATION

Something must be said concerning the degree of awareness of the issue of freedom among the medieval masters and the devices they used to challenge or circumvent authority. It would be less true to say that they had an elaborate rationale for freedom of thought than to say simply that they were driven to claim and exercise a measure of freedom by the nature of their task.[55] They were aware of themselves as members of a great fellowship, extending across the ages, as men whose lives were dedicated to the search for truth and whose work was subject to harassment by the ignorant or uncharitable. From Latin sources they knew of Plato's *Apology* and on occasion found some personal meaning for themselves in the persecution of Socrates and his great self-defense.[56] The conditions of their profession as teachers made it urgent for the more original masters to maintain an area in which their minds could move about.

[53] See Ernest A. Moody, "Ockham, Buridan, and Nicholas of Autrecourt: The Parisian Statutes of 1339 and 1340," *Franciscan Studies,* VII (June, 1947), 113–46.

[54] McLaughlin, "Intellectual Freedom," pp. 190–220; cf. J. R. Weinberg, *Nicolaus of Autrecourt* (Princeton, 1948), p. 3.

[55] Cf. McLaughlin's conclusion that the typical response of the thirteenth- and fourteenth-century masters to restriction was not to analyze the issue as a problem in freedom and to expound a theory but "simply to claim freedom as a practical necessity in the fulfillment of those intellectual functions which they were ever concerned to define and extend." "Intellectual Freedom," p. 388. Sir Maurice Powicke is content to sidestep the problem with the remark that "they were not so perplexed as we are by the problem of freedom, for they believed that truth is one, and would be seen later. They had quite enough freedom to be contentious, and they liked controversy." *Medieval Life and Thought,* p. 212.

[56] Thorndike, *History of Magic and Experimental Science,* II, 639–40.

Without some philosophical differentiation that stamped them as men with something singular to say, how could they attract students or teach with vigor? [57]

Before the beginning of the university epoch the conflict between authority and individual scholars of distinction had led to a series of actions against speculative freedom. Abelard, despite his own earnest intention to put dialectic in the service of faith,[58] was among those who fell under criticism. It was not uncommon, either in the theological and philosophical revival of the twelfth century or afterwards, for philosophers to hurl at each other the accusation of heresy—Abelard himself was not above using this device as a kind of dialectical *coup de grâce*—and the question was inevitably raised by his critics whether his use of dialectic had not become dangerous to sound doctrine. His enemies, he complained, had argued that it was unlawful for a Christian to treat of things that do not pertain to the faith. He replied with a burst of self-assertion that reveals the extent to which his kind of intellectualism would carry him in his claims to freedom:

It is wonderful if I must not discuss what is permitted them [i.e. his critics] to read. . . . Truth is not opposed to truth . . . as falsehood may be opposed to falsity, or evil to evil . . . but rather all good things are in accord. All knowledge is good, even that which relates to evil, because a righteous man must have it. Since he may guard against evil, it is necessary that he should know it beforehand; otherwise he could not shun it. Though an act be evil, knowledge regarding it is good; though it be evil to sin, it is good to know the sin, which otherwise we could not shun. . . . If therefore it is not wrong to know, but to do, the evil is to be referred to the act and not to the knowledge. Hence we are convinced that all knowledge, which indeed comes from God alone and from his bounty, is good. Wherefore the study of every science should be conceded to be good, because that which is good comes from it; and especially one must insist upon the study of that *doctrina* by which the greater truth is known. This is dialectic, whose function is to distinguish between every truth and falsity: as leader in all knowledge, it holds the primacy and rule of all philosophy. The same also is shown to be needful to the Catholic Faith, which cannot without its aid resist the sophistries of schismatics.[59]

[57] That novel ideas were being advanced in the twelfth century with a considerable awareness of risk is indicated by Adelard of Bath's remark that his generation was so unreceptive to novel ideas that authors commonly published new views by attributing them to others. Thorndike, *History of Magic and Experimental Science*, II, 24–25.

[58] On faith and reason in Abelard see J. G. Sikes, *Peter Abailard* (Cambridge, 1932).

[59] Taylor, *The Mediaeval Mind*, II, 379.

What Abelard had to say was naturally written from the standpoint of a devout man who, even though some of his own theological notions were condemned, considered it the primary business of intellect to defend the faith. This belief in the value of intellect was the outstanding quality in his heritage. It was by the power of reason, not by force or mere preachments, that he hoped to impel heretics to return to the faith.[60] Similarly, in pedagogy he placed a high value upon the cultivation of dialectical skill as opposed to the mere imparting of information. In his *Sic et non,* which was written for the benefit of young students, he counterposed the contradictory statements of great authorities on important theological questions. By encouraging such a method for the teaching of the young, he quickened the tradition of dialectical rigor.[61] It was his objective, he said, by raising issues from the "apparent repugnancy" in the writings of the holy Fathers to excite the students "to search out the truth of the matter, and render them the sharper for the investigation. For the first key to wisdom is called interrogation, diligent and unceasing. . . . By doubting we are led to inquiry; and from inquiry we perceive the truth." [62]

As we have seen, the accepted Christian ideal of the intellectual enterprise was that of a system of knowledge partly stemming from and entirely consistent with the faith. While no one challenged the concept in principle, it had to be qualified repeatedly in practice if there was to be any considerable measure of freedom of thought. Freedom implies choice, and choice implies the existence of diversity of ideas and beliefs. The struggle of the dissident scholars against positive authority therefore consisted chiefly of taking advantage of intellectual or political methods by which a real plurality of intellectual opportunities and perspectives could be maintained within the ideal structure of unified doctrine.

The boldest, probably the most effective, and yet the quietest of all these methods was the simple one of ignoring condemnations and censures without openly challenging them—for masters again and again continued to discuss and even to assert ideas that positive authority had condemned as erroneous. It was by just this kind of stubbornness, as we have seen, that the new books of Aristotle, once under proscription

[60] *Ibid.,* II, 380.
[61] Sikes, *Peter Abailard,* Chap. IV.
[62] Taylor, *The Mediaeval Mind,* p. 335. Cf. Adelard of Bath's perspicuous argument for following reason rather than authority. Thorndike, *History of Magic and Experimental Science,* II, 28–29.

at Paris, were opened to general study there. A second method, suited
to the pluralistic structure of medieval society and the lacunae in the
organization of the Church, was to act upon a geographical plurality of
truths—that is, to ignore in one diocese a prohibition that had had its
origin in another. Thus one finds a mid-fourteenth-century master like
Jean Buridan expressing some doubts as to the validity of the indiscriminate condemnations of 1277, remarking that he had heard a famous
doctor of theology say that it would not be improper for someone to
uphold outside of the diocese of Paris an opinion that was contrary to the
decisions of the Bishop of Paris.[63] Nor was this a mere flippancy. Before
the beginning of the Inquisition the Church had left the defense of the
faith against heresy in the hands of the bishops. With the development
of the Inquisition, the popes and the inquisitors became the guardians of
orthodoxy so far as popular heresies were concerned, but in academic
matters the officials of the universities and the bishops continued to
bear the primary responsibility. This tradition of decentralization worked
to the advantage of the academic community. Tempier's condemnations
of 1277 had, in fact, no binding force outside the university and diocese
of Paris. To put them into effect at Oxford required another separate
and somewhat different censure by Archbishop Robert Kilwardby—
presumably the result of an understanding between the two men—in
which the doctrines of Thomas Aquinas were singled out.[64] This action
was, of course, even more freely ignored at Paris than the little-observed
condemnation of its own bishop, and at Oxford it was far from effective.

Still another factor that gave protection to the masters was that their
primary function was to teach, and in teaching the process of communication was informal.[65] Often the only evidence of the heterodoxy of the
teacher would be in the notes of the students. It was also possible for
scholars who wished either to communicate ideas of questionable orthodoxy for the consideration of others, or to cross the line that was
supposed to separate philosophical from theological inquiry, to express
in advance their willingness to submit to the judgment of the theologians

[63] McLaughlin, "Intellectual Freedom," p. 179.
[64] A brief account of the condemnations in relation to intellectual changes is
given by Maurice De Wulf, *The History of Mediaeval Philosophy* (London, 1939),
II, 224–232. The Parisian condemnation of Aquinas' propositions was retracted by
the Bishop of Paris in 1325, two years after St. Thomas' canonization.
[65] Étienne Gilson, *La Philosophie au moyen âge* (Paris, 1947), p. 413.

or the Church.[66] Since it was common to assume that heresy existed only where there was pertinacity in error, this was sometimes helpful.

Attacks on inquiry did not go without frequent direct and open challenge. While some masters might choose simply to circumvent such attacks, open criticism was often made. The lengths to which some masters were prepared to go in making direct challenges on behalf of freedom may be illustrated from the writings of Godfrey of Fontaines, a late-thirteenth-century secular master of the Paris faculty of theology, a regent master for thirteen years, who was elected to the bishopric of Tournai in 1300. A highly respected figure, frequently known after his death as *doctor venerabilis,* Godfrey indulged in discussions both of doctrine and church policy. He was one of a number of masters, regular and secular, who refused to acknowledge the validity of the condemnations of 1277. Not only did he continue to discuss some of the doctrines condemned, like the idea of the eternity of the world, but he scathingly criticized the indiscriminate condemnations themselves. He denied the right of a prelate to condemn doctrines as heretical, asserting that this concerned the whole community of the faithful and could be done only by a council or by the pope. To bind men, he asserted, to an opinion on questions on which there may be a diversity of views without danger to faith would impede the pursuit of truth. Since the conflict of opinion among learned men would stimulate discussion, the truth would be discovered more readily if men were left free to seek through discussion not what is more pleasing but what agrees with right reason.[67]

Godfrey denounced as ignorant and naive the condemnations of 1277 and called upon Bishop Tempier's second successor, Simon de Bucy, to revoke his act:

[66] Cf. Buridan, when he discusses the problem of whether there is an infinite immobile space beyond the visible heavens: "I leave the determination of all that I say in this question to the theologians and I wish to acquiesce in their determination." McLaughlin, "Intellectual Freedom," p. 178. Sometimes the retractions came only after the event. Meister Eckhart, when he got into difficulties just before his death, avowed his willingness to retract anything he had ever written or said that might be deemed erroneous and heretical, just as though it had never been uttered. "Although I may err," he argued, "I cannot be a heretic; for the first pertains to the intellect, the second to the will." *Ibid.,* p. 361.

[67] See the discussion of Godfrey of Fontaines' rationale for freedom in McLaughlin, "Intellectual Freedom," pp. 271–80, 310–11, 314–15 and Maurice De Wulf, "Étude sur la vie, les oeuvres et l'influence de Godefroid de Fontaines," *Mémoires de l'Académie Royale de Belgique,* Ser. 2, Vol. I, Classe des Lettres et des Sciences (Brussels, 1906), Chap. III.

If right reason or an authority demonstrates that that which a prelate con-
demns as false and erroneous is true; or even, without being absolutely certain, that the condemned thesis is probable . . . ; or again if it is susceptible
of being made the basis of contrary opinions, it appears that both excommunication and condemnation are equally erroneous, since they hinder inquiry
into and knowledge of the truth. Certainly it is not proper that any individual
should take it upon himself alone to resist that measure . . . but one should
ask that the prelate himself revoke the condemnation and excommunication.
For even if it is true that to maintain them does not entail a danger to salvation, it does involve a blow to perfect understanding, for it would deprive
men of freedom of research into truths through which their understanding
would be in no small measure improved. And then, what a scandal in the
eyes of both many believers and unbelievers that prelates should be so
ignorant and naive as to hold as erroneous and contrary to faith that which
is irreconcilable neither with faith nor with good morals! [68]

It was by no means unusual that this master should have invoked the
criterion of *intellectual competence* in theology as a thing far more
relevant than the bishop's formal place in the hierarchy as a warrant for
repudiating his authority.[69]

The impact of Aristotelianism itself brought substantive changes in
the pursuit of knowledge that proved to be profoundly liberating. By
opening up whole unfamiliar realms to inquiry it created a necessity for
some workable equipoise between the traditional and universally accepted claims of belief and the desire of scholars to pursue secular studies.
Institutionally such an equipoise was found at Paris in the growing autonomy of the faculty of arts. Intellectually it was manifested in the
separation of reason from faith, of philosophy from theology, and of
logical and epistemological inquiry from ontological considerations.

Broadly speaking, three views prevailed as to the significance of the
vast new world of knowledge and speculative activity that was opened

[68] De Wulf, "Étude sur la vie," pp. 40–41.

[69] Godfrey goes on to say of the current bishop that while he is eminent in the
literature of canon and civil law, his knowledge of theology is not sufficient to
warrant his trying to correct the condemned articles without the advice of masters
competent in the subject. *Ibid.,* p. 46. Godfrey could hardly bring himself to excuse
the bishop for this. He was aware, however, that the masters would not have been
found in complete agreement on some of the articles, a consideration which he felt
would have justified the bishop in simply abstaining from action.

For a brief but extraordinarily strong statement in behalf of freedom of thought
in physics, logic, and grammar when these do not pertain to theology, see William
of Ockham as quoted by Friedrich Ueberweg, *Grundriss der Geschichte der Philosophie,* II, ed. Bernhard Geyer (Berlin, 1928), 582. Ockham's position goes beyond
Godfrey's in its forthrightness.

up by the new Aristotle. One school, that of the traditionalists, preferred to eschew it. A second, in which St. Thomas Aquinas was pre-
eminent, set about with great ingenuity to Christianize Aristotle and
construct a philosophical synthesis out of Peripateticism and the Christian faith. Still another school, which has been commonly called that of
the Latin Averroists but which might more accurately be designated as
that of the heterodox Aristotelians, was confronted with a knotty problem arising from its desire to explore as fully as possible the views of
Aristotle in the arena of natural reason without being confined by a
primary concern with the consequences for Christian faith. This school,
whose most notable figure was Siger de Brabant, was confronted with
the problem of the relations of faith and reason in an acute form.

A gap had appeared between those ideas that it was safe and proper
to profess as true and some ideas about which the philosophy of Aristotle
tempted one to speculate—the eternity of the world, the unity of intellect,
the immortality of the individual soul, the providential character of God.
Some of the conclusions of Aristotle, faithfully pursued, seemed to challenge Christian faith. Siger tried to solve this problem by emphasizing
the distinction between the natural order (the object of philosophical
attention) and the supernatural order (the sphere of theology and faith).
He held that while the operations of man's natural reason might necessarily lead to one conclusion, it was possible by faith to maintain the
opposite as true. Like Averroës himself, the Latin Averroists were
accused by their opponents of maintaining the theory of the "double
truth"—that is, of asserting that what is true in theology can be false
in philosophy, and vice versa.[70] Such a self-contradictory position was

[70] Averroës, who himself once suffered exile for opinions not altogether congenial
to the Moslem world, made a famous attempt to reconcile the claims of philosophy
and theology in a work that did not become known in the Latin world until the
fourteenth century. In his little treatise *The Agreement of Religion and Philosophy*
Averroës delineated three levels of discourse that exist for three different types of
men: the first is operative among the great mass of men, who are moved only
by rhetoric; the second is for those (the theologians) who like to have their religious
views somewhat rationalized by dialectical interpretation; the third is for the
philosophers who, like Aristotle, seek for certain demonstration. Averroës believed
that social strife over matters of faith might be avoided if these three types of
discourse were kept separate—if the populace were never confronted with matters
of theology, if theologians never tried to be philosophers, and if philosophers stayed
clear of theology. Of course it was the philosophers who strove for the profound, the
ultimate, the certain truth, which the theologians apprehended less clearly, and the
masses crudely through the means of symbology and simple legend. Averroës
believed, moreover, that it was a mistake for the learned to try to communicate
their findings to the masses. Although his appeal was rather seriously flawed by the

in fact espoused by no one.[71] Averroës himself had maintained that the real truth was to be found in the full exercise of natural reason; while Siger, although claiming that philosophical truth expressed the utmost capacities of man's natural reason, conceded nonetheless that where it conflicted with revealed faith the claims of faith must be taken as superior. The Latin Averroists in their most radical formulations declared only that philosophical conclusions are "necessary"—that is, inevitable within the framework of natural rationality—even though they might be contrary to the findings of the faith, which are really *true*.[72] It was the business of the philosopher, Siger maintained, to explain the natural order, which is accessible to experience and reason. But by divine intervention a supernatural order may be instituted, concerning which the philosophical conclusions that are true on the hypothesis of a purely natural order will not hold.[73] Through revelation one may have access to truths beyond the reach of natural reason.

Some students have suggested that Siger's abstract willingness to submit to the doctrines of the faith, while toying speculatively with the most heterodox suggestions of natural philosophy, was merely a protective device that was to enable him to teach as a freethinker. One of the earlier students of his work concluded that the religious faith of the Latin Averroists was "at least rather feeble if not altogether fictitious," and considered their work "a disguised form of free thought." [74] The preponderant opinion, however, including the most recent and thorough

---

tones of condescension with which Averroës referred to theologians, there seems little doubt that he was trying to arrive at a strategy for social peace and intellectual tolerance. He was also trying, however roughly, to make a point in what we would now call the sociology of knowledge. Having inherited the tradition of a lofty and tolerant culture, and having been sustained by two Caliphs and the upper classes and banished by pressure from intolerant theologians and an ignorant populace, it was natural for him to approach the problem from the standpoint of a broadminded elitist. See Ibn Rochd (Averroës), *Traité décisif sur l'accord de la religion et de la philosophie,* trans. and ed. by Léon Gauthier (Algiers, 1942), esp. pp. 25 ff., and the discussion in Étienne Gilson, *Reason and Revelation in the Middle Ages,* pp. 39–66.

[71] Etienne Gilson, "La Doctrine de la double vérité," in *Études de philosophie médiévale* (Strasbourg, 1921), p. 68.

[72] Van Steenberghen, *Siger de Brabant,* p. 688.

[73] *Ibid.,* p. 694; cf. the discussion of this subject, pp. 677–88. This makes it easier to understand why some of the boldest thinkers of the fourteenth century liked to place the greatest emphasis on divine omnipotence.

[74] Mandonnet, *Siger de Brabant et l'Averroisme latin au XIIIme siècle,* pp. 190–95; cf. pp. 149–52.

inquiry,[75] leans to the view that Siger was entirely sincere in his professions of faith. This elusive question of sincerity, which is unlikely ever to be settled with finality, is an issue of some importance to the history of intellectual freedom. But if motives and subjective states cannot be assessed with certainty, results sometimes can; it is at least clear that the duality between faith and reason that found its inception in the problems of the heterodox Aristotelians tended to free the speculative mind from doctrinal limitations by making it possible to follow the play of natural reason while paying full respect to the demands of faith.

A somewhat more challenging problem of historical interpretation is raised by the writings of John of Jandun in the fourteenth century, whose sincerity as a Christian is doubted by some scholars, like Gilson, who readily credit the sincerity of Siger. By John of Jandun's time Aristotelianism had become so securely established and the rights of the arts faculty so generally respected that he can hardly be considered an innovator in the manner of Siger. But he was a notable figure, and his writings show a certain insouciance of tone that has made his meaning suspect. He is disquieting, as Gilson says, not so much for his matter as his manner.[76] In his case it has seemed much more likely than in Siger's that he was using the now conventional obeisance to orthodoxy as a mask behind which to express a fundamental irreverence.[77] "I do believe that that is true," he writes concerning an article of faith, "but I cannot prove it. Good luck to those who can!" He concludes a long

[75] Van Steenberghen, *Siger de Brabant,* pp. 689–700. Gilson also resolves this question in Siger's favor (*Reason and Revelation in the Middle Ages,* pp. 59–60), while De Wulf seems to have it both ways, arguing on one page that Siger "in order to shelter himself . . . adopted a prudential attitude" (*History of Mediaeval Philosophy,* II, 161) and on the next that he was sincere (*ibid.,* pp. 162–63).
Whatever the true intentions of the Latin Averroists, the consequences of their approach were feared by some church authorities. Tempier's condemnations of 1277 include those who say that what they are writing is true according to philosophy but not according to the Catholic faith, as if there were two contradictory truths.
[76] Gilson, "La Doctrine de la double vérité," p. 65.
[77] Stuart MacClintock in a recent review of the literature, however, argues forcefully in favor of the ultimate sincerity of the Latin Averroists, and concludes that they can best be understood as trying simply to establish an autonomous area for the play of the mind in accordance with the principles of natural reason without, in their religious profession, really deviating from the tenets of the faith. In effect, nonetheless, their attitude did involve a radical circumscription of the realm of faith. Stuart MacClintock, "John of Jandun and the Problem of Latin Averroism," unpublished doctoral dissertation (Columbia University, 1951), esp. pp. 91 ff. and 103 ff. Cf. the discussion of this school by A. J. Rahilly, *Studies,* II (September, 1913), 301–24; III (March, 1914), 686–713.

argument in which he demonstrates the philosophical impossibility of the idea of creation by asserting that we ought to believe it anyway. "Let it be added," he ends, "that creation very seldom happens; there has never been but one, and that was a very long time ago." [78] When we find the same writer telling us that belief is simply a habit induced by listening to certain teachings from childhood,[79] we may well wonder if we are not, as Gilson suggests, listening to some daring precursor of the Enlightenment who is carrying on with criticism of the faith without unduly endangering himself.[80] John did in the end find it necessary to leave Paris, but it was not his rationalism but his antipapal politics that drove him off to the court of Louis of Bavaria.

Unlike John of Jandun, many of the fourteenth-century masters were trying to free themselves from the trammels of an Aristotelianism that had hardened into an orthodoxy. In many respects the position of these men vis-à-vis possible charges of heresy was much simpler than that of their predecessors of the 1270s. While the Averroists had found themselves ranged against dogmatic religion, the new critical writers were interested chiefly in attacking dogmatic philosophy and liberating themselves from philosophic authority. It was thei goal to question Aristotle or to raise problems in natural philosophy that he had not considered. Having more than one authoritative tradition to appeal to, they could subtly turn upon itself the whole apparatus of authoritative definition.[81]

The method of probable argument, which became a commonplace among the fourteenth-century masters and was employed to notable effect by Nicholas of Autrecourt, made possible the development of philosophical criticism and the exploration of new ideas without presuming to offer a direct challenge to the faith. In employing the method of hypothetical statement and dealing in probabilities rather than assertions of necessary truths, those who followed the method of probable argument also found themselves in the possession of an intellectually liberating technique.[82] They unambiguously denied upholding what had

---

[78] Gilson, *Reason and Revelation in the Middle Ages,* pp. 61–63.

[79] McLaughlin, "Intellectual Freedom," p. 182.

[80] See MacClintock's reasons, however, for suspecting this judgment, in "John of Jandun," pp. 112–21 and *passim.*

[81] McLaughlin, "Intellectual Freedom," pp. 188–89.

[82] We have drawn on the explication of "probabilism" in Weinberg, *Nicolaus of Autrecourt,* Chap. VI. The nub of the difference between Siger's approach to truth and that of later probable argument, insofar as it bears on the problem of heresy, is that while Siger maintained that certain philosophical propositions con-

been so unfairly attributed to the earlier Averroists—the idea that truths can be opposed. But they insisted that there is a legitimate arena of speculative and probable argument in which certain undenied truths of the faith can actually be less probable in the light of pure reason than their contradictories.[83] Human information, mental powers, and types of argument, they held, are at any time quite limited. Errors and limited comprehension are inevitable. While some things are absolutely certain from experience or logic and others must be believed certain as articles of faith, there is still a third ground for the proper operation of the mind—the area of probability, which is where man must work when all those factors making for uncertainty are in play. Men arrive through reason at propositions which are probable to them, and which may be in themselves true or false but cannot, at the moment, be *known* as true or false. Thus one can disputatively, and in a sense experimentally, advance a wide range of propositions as the best yield of current information and reason, without being prepared to profess them as true.[84] It is

---

trary to faith are *necessary* in reason, the "probabilists" held that such propositions are merely the most probable that can be achieved by the best human reason at a given time and with a given set of data.

For convenience we have followed Weinberg in using here the term "probabilism," although it did not come into general use until near the end of the sixteenth century, when it denoted a particular theory in moral theology.

[83] Thus one Pierre de Ceffons wrote: "I do not fall into that error that I say that this is true according to Aristotle but not according to faith, because I know that truths are never opposed. . . . Although it is erroneous to say that God is not three and one and that the world had no beginning, it is nevertheless not erroneous to assert that, faith aside, it is more *probable* that God is not three and one or that the world never began than to assert their opposites. For nothing prevents some false propositions from being more probable than some true ones." *Ibid.*, pp. 116–17.

[84] Nicholas avowed at his trial at Avignon that he had done precisely this, and that he was prepared to retract those of his propositions that his judges found heretical and blasphemous. He had, he said, stated them only disputatively, not definitively and did not mean to adhere to them pertinaciously. His defense was dismissed as a "foxy excuse," but it is difficult to say whether or not this was a fair judgment. *Ibid.*, pp. 6, 114–15; McLaughlin, "Intellectual Freedom," pp. 213–15. As an alternative to the theory that Aristotelians of Siger's caliber and the later "probabilists" were really rationalists who tried to protect themselves through "foxy" and insincere professions of faith, and the opposite theory that they were unable to see any gaps between their philosophical rationalism and their fideism in theology, one can envisage still a third possibility that somewhat reconciles the two—namely, that their minds were sundered by the duality of their social roles and that they had developed completely functional and humanly satisfactory dual mentalities. On one hand they were believing Catholics who accepted revealed truth and had no desire to spread heresies or subvert the faith; on the other they were passionate intellectuals, scholars, teachers, profoundly moved by the quest for knowledge and the desire for achievement.

easy to see that under such criteria of knowledge the rich and significant ground of inquiry for some thinkers might be entirely in the area of probable and hypothetical statement, and that here some very fresh and remarkable things might be said. The work of such a master as Jean Buridan, a great fourteenth-century precursor of modern science, shows how the method of probable argument and hypothetical statement could be identified with honestly tentative ways of thinking, the capacity for suspension of belief, modesty of assertion, tolerance of differences and ambiguities, and the spirit of intellectual play.[85]

Thus scholastic thought from the early fourteenth century onwards was characterized by a radical separation between the sphere of the senses, reason, and natural knowledge on one side and the sphere of faith and revelation on the other. There was a growing tendency to give up the effort to demonstrate the truths of faith by reason and to rely solely on revelation or intuition for their foundation. Central in the philosophy of William of Ockham, this separation of faith and reason became completely familiar in the schools.[86] In the minds of many thinkers one of its chief functions was to protect the faith from new currents of philosophical skepticism and natural inquiry (Ockham, for instance, was a passionately devout Christian), but in time it also had the contrary effect of protecting philosophical skepticism from inquisitive guardians of the faith.[87] And perhaps in the long run of propagating skepticism; for it was not, as De Wulf remarks, a far cry from saying that the ideas of faith are inaccessible to reason to saying that they are

[85] See McLaughlin's discussion of Buridan in relation to the problem of freedom, "Intellectual Freedom," pp. 156–90.

[86] Gilson, *La Philosophie au moyen âge,* pp. 638 ff., 655.

[87] This stratagem had a long subsequent history. Thus even as late as the seventeenth century Francis Bacon is to be found arguing for a twofold theory of truth and asserting that "the more absurd and incredible any divine mystery is, the greater honour we do to God in believing it; and so much the more noble the victory of faith." In commenting on the passage in which this quotation appears, Basil Willey finds his confidence in Bacon's sincerity shaken by "the ceremonial and formal obeisance about many of his salutes to religion." He concludes, however, that "Bacon's desire to separate religious truth and scientific truth was in the interests of science, not of religion. He wished to *keep science pure from religion;* the opposite part of the process—keeping religion pure from science—did not interest him nearly so much. . . . Religious truth, then, must be 'skied', elevated far out of reach, not in order that it may be more devoutly approached, but in order to keep it out of mischief. But having secured his main object, namely, to clear the universe for science, Bacon can afford to be quite orthodox (just as, in another context, he can concede poetry to human weakness)." Basil Willey, *The Seventeenth Century Background* (New York, 1934), pp. 28–29.

contrary to reason. This radical dissociation of faith and reason seems, in any case, to have had a valuable function in the development of late medieval philosophy and science. It can hardly be coincidental that the two schools that are now considered to have mediated the fruitful continuity between medieval and early modern science, the Ockhamists at Paris and the Paduan Averroists,[88] both resorted to philosophical techniques that in some measure freed speculation and inquiry by divorcing their consequences from the tenets of the faith. For a time, as we shall see, such a formula even became within limits acceptable to authority itself. While it grew out of the substantive problems of the thought of the thirteenth century and afterward, this separation of natural reason from faith seems to have become a protective convention among some of the later writers.

What was most commonly referred to in the earlier days as the differentiation between revealed truth and natural reason also became transmuted later into a differentiation between revealed truth and scientific hypothesis as well. Thus in the fourteenth century Nicole Oresme, after summarizing with striking cogency the case for the diurnal rotation of the earth, added a passage deferring on grounds of faith to the movement of the heavens and remarking that this additional instance of the conflict between articles of faith and natural reason could really be useful in the defense of the faith; [89] while Jean Buridan, after suggesting that the celestial orbs were moved by an inherent impetus rather than by intelligences, added that he asserted this only tentatively and sought further

---

[88] For a brief account see John Herman Randall, Jr., "The Development of Scientific Method in the School of Padua," *Journal of the History of Ideas,* I (April, 1940), 177–206.

[89] "It appears thus that it cannot be shown by any experience that the heavens are moved by a daily movement. . . . It cannot be concluded by reasons that the heavens may be moved. And third, reasons have been offered to the contrary, that it is not so moved. Nevertheless all hold and I believe that it is so moved and that the earth is not: 'God has established the sphere of the earth, which shall not be moved'—the arguments to the contrary notwithstanding, for these are persuasions which do not lead to evident conclusions. But considering all that has been said, it is possible to believe that the earth is so moved and that the heavens are not, and it is not evident to the contrary. And, in any case, it seems on the face of it, as much or more against natural reason, as are either all or some of the articles of our faith. And thus what I have said for fun in this manner could be of value in confuting or reproving those who would attack our faith by rational arguments." From *Le Livre du ciel et du monde* (1377) translated in James Bruce Ross and Mary Martin McLaughlin, *The Renaissance Reader* (New York, 1953), p. 583. Did Oresme, in the face of his own reasoning, really believe that the earth does not move? On this as in other matters we merely seek enlightenment from historians of medieval thought, and humbly submit to their judgments.

judgment on the matter from the theologians.[90] And in 1543, when Copernicus' friends and editors published the dying man's *De revolutionibus orbium coelestium,* one of them, the Lutheran Andreas Osiander, inserted a protective anonymous preface in which it was declared that the work provided only another hypothesis for the use of astronomers, not a new description of the universe: "For it is not necessary that these hypotheses be true, nor even probable, but this alone is sufficient, if they show reasoning fitting the observations." [91]

THE NEW LEARNING AND THE NEW SCIENCE

In the late fourteenth century and in the fifteenth, there was some shift in the center of intellectual gravity as some of the North Italian universities became infused with the scientific teachings that had flourished at Oxford and Paris, and other universities to the east, notably Prague and Heidelberg, rose in eminence. New interests and new areas of inquiry—humanistic scholarship and scientific investigation—were now beginning more and more to be fostered outside the universities as well as within them, and outside Italy the relative importance of universities in the sum total of intellectual life tended to be smaller. In some institutions, moreover, professors and students became negligent, and academic requirements degenerated into empty forms. As late scholasticism became more preoccupied with the details and refinements of intellectual systems that had passed beyond their first great days of formulation and advancement, the intellectual life of the universities lost some of its appeal. One important function, however, the universities did not lose— that of supplying the fundamental education of great men of achievement in all lines of creative work. Even those leading humanist scholars and writers, for instance, whose fate it was to do their work outside university walls, were for the most part educated within them. The great political critics of the papacy were men whose dialectic had been sharpened in the schools. The precursors and early leaders of the Reformation—Wyclif, Huss, and Luther—were university men; and when, in the

[90] The passage from Buridan is quoted in Anneliese Maier, *Die Impetustheorie der Scholastik* (Vienna, 1940), p. 85.

[91] Dorothy Stimson, *The Gradual Acceptance of the Copernican Theory of the Universe* (Hanover, N.H., 1917), pp. 28–30. The text of this preface is in Edward Rosen, *Three Copernican Treatises* (New York, 1939), pp. 24–25, along with a discussion of the philosophical strategy behind it and Copernicus' own rejection of the idea, pp. 22–33.

early days of the Reformation, Luther found himself in combat with Pope Adrian VI, the struggle was led on one side by a theologian of Wittenberg and on the other by a theologian from Louvain.

While the intellectual vitality of the universities varied greatly from place to place, their power and corporate autonomy were quite generally declining, for these depended upon characteristics of medieval organization that were waning—the supremacy of the popes, the universality and integrity of the Church, the extranational and primarily ecclesiastical character of intellectual life. Some of the weapons of the universities had lost their force. Migrations, which had done so much at the beginning to diffuse the university system and strengthen university power, proved in the long run to be self-limiting. Both migrations and cessations had depended for their effect upon the scarcity as well as the effectuality of the services rendered by the university. The result of the migrations, together with the great numbers of new university foundations of the fourteenth and fifteenth centuries, was to overbuild the university system to a point at which the University of Paris begged the pope not to authorize any more foundations. In the last quarter of the fifteenth century new foundations did in fact finally dwindle to nothing. Migrations were now an empty threat, and talk of cessation was more likely under the new conditions to bring university faculties under the retaliatory hand of secular power than it was to win new privileges or safeguard the old. As universities became more heavily endowed with college foundations and other properties, and as their intellectual life became increasingly committed to permanent libraries, they became timid and immobile, and their financial dependence provided princes and municipalities with a pretext for unprecedented intervention in their affairs. But it had been, above all, the pluralism of medieval life that provided these powerful corporations with the source of their autonomy; as national states arose, sovereigns, princes, and parliaments took upon themselves the right to meddle in the internal affairs of universities, appointing and discharging professors at will and mocking at the former pride and autonomy of the masters.[92]

Paris itself remained a center of corporate power long after the creative intellectual life centering upon its famous masters had passed. But this power, once associated with the creativity of its teachers, now seemed to rest primarily upon its role as a center of orthodoxy, its ability to

[92] D'Irsay, *Histoire,* I, 191–222, sketches the decline of the medieval university.

limit the freedom of others. The Paris theological faculty began to intervene regularly in spheres ordinarily belonging to the Inquisition, and by the late fourteenth century had virtually supplanted the Inquisition as the judge of heresy for Paris and northern France.[93] It was this body that drew up the articles convicting Joan of Arc of heresy. The latter-day role of Paris in church affairs reached a peak with its place in the Council of Constance, 1414–18, but its function as a political sounding board seems to have long continued.[94] Like lesser universities, it was ultimately victimized by the growing power of the monarchs and other secular agencies of government. In 1446 the Parlement of Paris became the supreme tribunal of the university by order of a royal edict which was intended to stop the intervention of the university in attempts of the Crown to tax the wealthy academic clergy. The university remained contentious, however, until the reign of Louis XI, when its attempt to check the monarch's demand to control its rector was utterly defeated and its autonomy was completely broken. The university's final act of self-assertion came in 1499, when it called a cessation to protest against new infringements on its privileges. This protest was hastily withdrawn in response to dire threats from Louis XII, who revoked the right of cessation itself.[95] Such independence as the university continued to have now existed only on the sufferance of the kings.

Oxford, which had enjoyed an independence, if not an authority, comparable to that of Paris, remained throughout most of the fourteenth century the arena of vigorous philosophical thought, concerning which Wyclif once complained that a new logical system sprang up every twenty years.[96] The suppression of Wyclif's own school, however, marked the turning point in the history of his university. Since he taught a doctrine of the Eucharist that struck at the heart of Catholic theology and a doctrine of clerical poverty that struck at the prevailing practices of

[93] McLaughlin, "Intellectual Freedom," pp. 381–85.

[94] D'Irsay, *Histoire,* I, 191–95.

[95] Rashdall, *Universities of Europe,* I, 425–32. Louis XI had also interfered with the curricular freedom of the university in 1474, when he promulgated an edict proscribing the nominalist writers in the faculties of arts and theology. Fifteenth-century scholastics divided broadly into the ancients and the moderns, the former of which were the standard realist writers in the tradition of Aquinas and Albertus Magnus and the latter the nominalistic followers of Ockham. In proscribing the moderns Louis XI was binding Paris to a course of action less liberal than that of some institutions that offered alternate courses in both philosophical persuasions. Within less than a decade, however, nominalism was again permitted at Paris.

[96] Carré, *Phases of Thought in England,* p. 144.

the Church itself, it is not surprising that the bishops should have sought to quiet him or that they should have had the authorization of the Crown. What was remarkable was the loyalty Wyclif commanded within the university and the stubbornness with which it, in common with a very large section of public opinion, defended him. Even for some years after the chancellor of the university received a papal bull demanding that Wyclif be turned over to the Primate and Bishop of London, he was supported at Oxford. His followers in the university and the town, who were prepared to resist Wyclif's suppression by force of arms, were at length put down only by the united power of the Crown and the Church; but even after Wyclif's death there was so much Lollardy left at Oxford that new repressive intervention was undertaken in 1408, more than two decades afterward. Wyclif's Bible was then prohibited, university teachers were forbidden to teach heretical doctrines or allow discussion of the sacraments or essential articles of faith, a monthly inquisition into heresy was ordered in all colleges and halls, and a rigid censorship was imposed. When Archbishop Arundel went beyond these measures to demand that the university itself appoint a commission to draw up a formal list of Wyclif's errors, he met with sabotage and rioting before he had his way. In 1411, when he proposed to make a visitation of the university, which was a violation of its traditional papal privileges, the scholars defied him, fortified the church against him, celebrated Mass in the face of the interdict, and poured into the streets with arms to rout his followers. Only the forceful intervention of the Crown established the archbishop's authority in the end, and compelled the scholars to acknowledge his power of visitation. With this the independent spirit of the Oxford scholars was broken at last.[97] The comparable suppression of the Hussites a few years later added to the chill that settled over the northern universities.[98]

In the development of humanistic learning the Italian universities took the leadership, as they had earlier done with medicine and law and were later to do with physical science. Toward the end of the fourteenth century the infiltration of Greek influences and the collection of Greek manuscripts was already well under way, and by the middle of the fifteenth century, when humanistic learning was rapidly spreading in

[97] Mallet, *History of Oxford*, I, 221–40.
[98] Cf. James B. Mullinger, *A History of the University of Cambridge* (London, 1888), p. 60; Mallet, *History of Oxford*, I, 338. See also Clara P. McMahon, *Education in Fifteenth-Century England* (Baltimore, 1947), Chap. II.

the North, the first great generation of Italian Hellenists had already passed from the scene.[99] While it brought new interest and energy to university life throughout Europe, the development of humanist learning took place under new conditions in which the relative position of the universities in the whole of intellectual life was considerably lowered. The universities of the Middle Ages had been well knit into the ecclesiastical system, and university men could be credited with a large proportion of the sum of intellectual work. Humanism grew up within the framework of a well-developed system of patronage in which learning was fostered not so much by the universities as by princes and nobles, the *haute bourgeoisie,* and the Roman court itself. Significantly, the indispensable libraries of the great age of humanist scholarship were gathered almost entirely by princes and private persons, while the universities played a very small part.[100] A secular intellectual life was emerging on a scale hitherto unknown; and for this reason the presence or absence of intellectual freedom in the universities represents a considerably less significant part of the whole story of intellectual liberty in the humanist period than it did at the peak of the Middle Ages.

There existed, nonetheless, a problem of intellectual freedom for the academic humanists, particularly in the northern universities, a problem which posed itself in a far different form from that which had been characteristic of the medieval university. In Italy, to which the northern humanists almost universally turned for their first draughts of classical learning, skepticism was rife, and the measure of latitude permissible to free thought was very broad. The papacy itself became for a time hardly more than a secular institution, served by men like Guicciardini, who disdained it, and Valla, who had struck a scholarly blow at its historical pretensions to temporal power. It was Italian learning primarily, and not that of the North, that Ariosto characterized when he asked, "Why is it that learning and infidelity go hand in hand?" [101] During the age of the Renaissance popes a remarkable degree of latitude was given, albeit inconsistently, to Italian thinkers. The machinery of the Inquisition existed, and might at any time be called into action; and yet widespread freedom of thought must always have acted as a temptation to boldness.

[99] D'Irsay, *Histoire,* Vol. I, Chaps. X, XI.
[100] Myron P. Gilmore, *The World of Humanism* (New York, 1952), pp. 184–86.
[101] Preserved Smith, *The Age of the Reformation* (New York, 1920), p. 628.

The case of Pietro Pomponazzi, the foremost academic philosopher of Italy in the early sixteenth century, suggests how far one might go, if he had the proper connections, under the system of licensed hypocrisy that for a time prevailed in Italy. In 1516 Pomponazzi, who had been for over two decades a professor, first at Padua, then Ferrara, and finally at Bologna, published his famous treatise on the immortality of the soul, a problem which had for the Italians of the period an especially lively speculative interest. For his skepticism Pomponazzi might be considered among the first of the modern philosophers. But for his interest in certain problems inherited from the Aristotelian scholastics, and notably in those raised by Averroës for thinkers of what was loosely called the "school of Padua," he might well be placed among the more tenacious of the latter-day scholastics.[102] It may be enough to say here of Pomponazzi's work that it denied that one could by rational Aristotelian methods prove the immortality of the soul as maintained by the Christian Church, that its conception of ethics was far more naturalistic than Christian, and that it bowed to orthodoxy in the traditional manner of the "double-truth" school by concluding that faith shows that the soul is immortal.[103]

Pomponazzi's book was published in the face of a decree, issued only three years before by a Lateran Council, against philosophical skepticism concerning the immortality of the soul.[104] The thinness of Pom-

[102] On Pomponazzi see the discussion by John Herman Randall, Jr., in Ernst Cassirer, et al., The Renaissance Philosophy of Man (Chicago, 1948), pp. 257–79, and the text, pp. 280 ff.

[103] The Averroists denied that the individual soul was immortal because it did not possess the attribute of intelligence, but granted it a kind of collective immortality insofar as it participated in the unity of intellect. Pomponazzi denied the possibility of rationally demonstrating the existence of intelligence independent of corporeal embodiment.

Pomponazzi's formula, which proved acceptable to the papacy, was this: "I do not firmly adhere to anything which I have said in my book, save in so far as the Apostolic See determines. Whatever, therefore, I may have said, whether it be true or false, whether it be in accordance with the faith or contrary to it, I ought not in any way to be held heretical." In reply to one of his critics he declared: "He will not find that in any part of my little treatise I have affirmed that the soul is mortal. I have only said that Aristotle thought so, and that immortality cannot be proved by natural reason, but is to be held by sincere faith." Mandell Creighton, A History of the Papacy from the Great Schism to the Sack of Rome, V (London, 1901), 272, 274. Cf. Pomponazzi's careful phrasing in his original treatise, Cassirer, et al., Renaissance Philosophy of Man, pp. 302–3, 379, 381.

[104] Creighton, however, points to the apologetic, hortatory, and toothless character of this decree not as evidence of suppression but as "significant testimony to the decay of dogmatic theology." Ibid., p. 222.

ponazzi's use of the "double truth" stratagem did not escape the clergy, who appealed to the Doge of Venice to suppress him. The Doge ordered the book burned, and Pomponazzi seems to have felt it discreet to stay away from Venice; but when Pope Leo X was petitioned to suppress Pomponazzi, he neglected to prosecute the philosopher, partly because of the intercession of Cardinal Gonzaga (to whom Pomponazzi dedicated one of his books) and the humanist Cardinal Bembo. Far from intimidated by the possibility of prosecution, Pomponazzi followed his critique of immortality with an attack on the clergy. Nor did his independence harm his professional career. Other Italian universities clamored for him, and the Bolognese magistrates were eager enough to keep him in their university to confirm his professorship for eight years and raise his salary. At his death Cardinal Gonzaga erected a monument to him in his native town of Mantua. The incident perhaps represents the zenith of the Italian skepticism of the period, which before many years went into eclipse under the combined impact of the Reformation struggle and the decline of Italian political and cultural life.

Despite the immense authority of Italian learning among the humanists of the northern universities, neither the skepticism nor the frequently cynical character of Italian thought was disseminated as readily as the model of Italian scholarship itself. Academic humanism in the North was predominantly pious, moderate, and compromising. Conservative churchmen foresaw that the intellectual concerns of the humanists, as well as their interest in church reform, might have subversive implications, but subversion was far from the intent of the humanists themselves. They were not schismatics, they wanted to lead no movement of revolt against the Church; indeed, they wanted to see no popular movement of any kind. If they wanted to be free to criticize the corruptions that had become so common in the Church or the superstitions that prevailed so widely among the populace, their purpose was not to undermine the Church's moral authority but to purge and strengthen it. The touchstone was the Reformation itself: while some of the humanists had initial sympathies with Luther, the leaders turned overwhelmingly against the Reformation when the break finally came, and most of them died within the bonds of the faith.[105]

[105] But concerning the complexities of this relationship and the tie between some humanists and Protestantism, see Paul Kalkoff, "Die Stellung der Deutschen Humanisten zur Reformation," *Zeitschrift für Kirchengeschichte,* XLVI (Gotha, 1928), 161–231.

Indeed, the ideal of such men as Erasmus, Colet, and Lefèvre d'Étaples was to put letters into the service of Christ, for among them the strain of literary and esthetic concern was subordinate to the textual and philological. Unlike the scholastics, the humanists were not so much concerned with dialectics or the subtleties of dogma as they were with getting at the true spirit of Christianity through a proper reading of the sources. Erasmus was revolted at the thought that people read Holy Scripture in the Vulgate when the Greek text was available for a more accurate reading. "I should wish," he once wrote, "that this simple and pure Christ might be deeply impressed upon the mind of men, and that I deem best attainable in this way, that we, supported by our knowledge of the original languages, should philosophize *at the sources* themselves." [106] Similarly Sir Thomas More, when the study of Greek at Oxford was made the object of a demonstration on the part of the traditionalist or "Trojan" faction there, wrote a letter to the authorities in which he defended humanistic education on the primary ground not of its professional usefulness— although for this also high claims could be made—but because it could "train the soul in virtue" and "build a path to Theology through Philosophy and the Liberal Arts." [107]

One sometimes gets the no doubt exaggerated impression that to the northern humanists religion was a combination of sound morals and sound philology that should be taken altogether out of the hands of the vulgar masses who had no Greek. Huizinga comments on Erasmus' failure to see that

[106] J. Huizinga, *Erasmus of Rotterdam* (London, 1952), p. 109; cf. Chaps. XII, XIII, *passim*.

[107] "This fellow declares that only theology should be studied; but if he admits even that, I don't see how he can accomplish his aim without some knowledge of languages, whether Hebrew or Greek or Latin; unless, of course, the elegant gentleman has convinced himself that there is enough theology written in English or that all theology can be squeezed into the limits of those [late scholastic] 'questions' which he likes to pose and answer, for which a modicum of Latin would, I admit, suffice. But really, I cannot admit that Theology, that august Queen of Heaven, can be thus confined. Does she not dwell and abide in Holy Scripture? Does she not pursue her pilgrim way through the cells of the holy Fathers: Augustine and Jerome; Ambrose and Cyprian; Chrysostom, Gregory, Basil and their like? The study of theology has been solidly based on these now despised expositors of fundamental truth during all the Christian centuries until the invention of these petty and meretricious 'questions' which alone are today glibly tossed back and forth. Anyone who boasts that he can understand the works of the Fathers without an uncommon acquaintance with the languages of each and all of them will in his ignorance boast for a long time before the learned trust his judgment." Gilmore, *The World of Humanism*, p. 214.

his conceptions of the Church, the sacraments and the dogmas were no longer purely Catholic because they had become subordinated to his philological insight. He could not be aware of it because, in spite of all his natural piety and his fervent ethical sentiments, he lacked the mystic insight which is the foundation of every creed.[108]

Their aristocratic outlook, their disdain for the grosser forms of popular religious practice and belief, their scholarly niceties, and their lack of interest in doctrine or dialectics kept the humanists of the North free from heresy and prevented them from having broad popular influence, while their insistence on the value of letters to the religion of the civilized man put them in the position of having something positive to bring to the Church. In them the desire for freedom took the form of a desire for complete latitude for scholarship within a limited but significant area of inquiry.

For all their moderation, the humanists found enemies among the conservatives in the Church and the traditional scholastics within the universities. Humanism was a threat to academic vested interests. Good churchmen, moreover, recognizing in the moralistic and rationalistic criticisms of the humanist scholars the first rumblings of what became the Reformation, saw that their concern with philological accuracy might in the end lead to questions about some church practices that hung upon philologically precise interpretations of scriptural texts. With the scholastics the humanists had to wage an open and bitter warfare, in the course of which the humanists expressed unreservedly their disdain for the sterility of scholastic exercises, for the traditional concern with forms and refinement of doctrine, and for the bad Latin and negligible Greek of their opponents. Paradoxically, in their repudiation of scholastic modes of thought they reacted toward a kind of intellectual indifferentism that can almost be called anti-intellectualistic, yet is intimately linked with the development of a spirit of tolerance. "We have defined so much," Erasmus lamented,

that without danger to our salvation might have remained unknown or undecided. . . . The essentials of our religion are peace and unanimity. These can hardly exist unless we make definitions about as few points as possible and leave many questions to individual judgment. Numerous problems are now postponed till the oecumenical Council. It would be much better to put off such questions till the time when the glass shall be removed and the darkness cleared away, and we shall see God face to face.[109]

[108] Huizinga, *Erasmus of Rotterdam*, p. 136.   [109] *Ibid.*, p. 116.

In this frame of mind a man was prepared neither to persecute others nor to espouse ideas with such passion as to risk persecution for them, as scholars had done in the great days of scholasticism.[110]

If the humanists committed many injustices in their estimation of scholasticism, these were matched by the discriminations practiced against them in the universities by a combination of schoolmen and churchmen. Although the humanists, like the early thirteenth-century Aristotelians, had the advantage of being associated with a fresh and powerful impetus to new learning, they made their way in many northern universities slowly and under disadvantages. Through most of Erasmus' life the firmly entrenched upholders of the old systems and ideals succeeded in maintaining their supremacy in the schools.[111] Many humanist careers that might well have graced the universities were sustained by private patronage or within separate academies, and the resistance of the university conservatives to humanism helped to keep much of the most significant intellectual work outside of university walls.

Humanism made its way in the universities with varying degrees of success. At Paris a Catholic humanist like Lefèvre d'Étaples and for a time even an heretical one like Louis Berquin was protected from the reactionary theologians of the Sorbonne by King Francis I, who discriminated sharply between learned men whom he wished to indulge and popular heretics whom he suppressed without hesitation.[112] Although an effort at Louvain to combine the doctrinal orthodoxy of Paris with humanist scholarship met with a measure of success during the years from 1490 to 1520, the place was the despair of Erasmus, who left it because its atmosphere was oppressive.[113] In England the humanists at both uni-

---

[110] Erasmus had much sympathy with some of the practices of an heretical sect, the Bohemian Brethren, but to them he wrote: "You must not think that any words of mine will bring you support; indeed my own influence, such as it is, requires the backing of others. If it is true that my writings are of any value to divine and useful learning, it seems to me unwise to jeopardize their influence by proclaiming publicly the agreement between us: such actions might lead to their being torn from the hands of the public. Forgive me this caution, you will perhaps call it fear. . . ." P. S. Allen, *The Age of Erasmus* (Oxford, 1914), pp. 295–96.

[111] *Ibid.*, p. 257; cf. Henry Osborn Taylor, *Thought and Expression in the Sixteenth Century* (New York, 1930), I, 151–52. Gerhard Ritter, however, has emphasized the superficial character of the conflicts between humanism and scholasticism, "Die geschichtliche Bedeutung des deutschen Humanismus," *Historische Zeitschrift*, CXXVII (1923), 393–453.

[112] See Georg Florian Münzer, *Franz I und die Anfänge der Französischen Reformation* (Freiburg, 1935).

[113] D'Irsay, *Histoire*, I, 255–57; Huizinga, *Erasmus of Rotterdam*, pp. 149–50.

versities, while at first faced with bitter opposition from within, made their way under powerful protectors like Cardinal Wolsey, Archbishop Warham, Bishop Fisher, Sir Thomas More, and Henry VIII himself.[114] In Germany Cologne played a reactionary role like that of the Sorbonne, while Erfurt was most hospitable to humanism.

It was Germany that provided the *cause célèbre* of northern humanism in the case of Pfefferkorn and Reuchlin. The incident began when Johann Pfefferkorn, a converted Jew, proposed that several new disabilities should be imposed upon the Jews, among them that all their books, with the exception of the Old Testament, should be delivered up to be burned. With the support of the Dominicans and the emperor's sister, he succeeded in persuading Emperor Maximilian to authorize the destruction of such books. When Pfefferkorn's procedure was found objectionable by the Archbishop of Mainz, the controversy over the propriety of burning the books was referred in 1510 to the faculties of four universities and to a few private scholars, among whom was Johann Reuchlin. Reuchlin, then in his middle fifties, was probably the outstanding scholar in Germany.[115] Educated at the universities of Freiburg, Basel, Orleans, and Poitiers, he was not only a Greek scholar but a great Hebraist. Having always earned his living under patronage and as a private teacher, he was not, strictly speaking, an academic man, but he was a hero to the entire learned world in Germany, academic and otherwise. One of his enthusiasms, which perhaps dates from his acquaintance with Pico della Mirandola during his Italian travels, was his interest in the cabala, in which he thought might be found the answers to some of the perplexing questions of Neoplatonic and Christian philosophy.

To a man with Reuchlin's Hebraic interests nothing could be more shocking than the proposed destruction of the very means of his intellectual existence. His connections with and indebtedness to some of the more learned Jews of his time had not placed him above the measure of prejudice that was common for his times.[116] He did not object, he said in reply to the inquiry, to the destruction of those few Jewish books which were solely and expressly aimed at Christianity; but the rest of the Jewish

[114] Mallet, *History of Oxford,* Vol. I, Chap. X; James Bass Mullinger, *The University of Cambridge from the Earliest Times to the Royal Injunctions of 1535* (Cambridge, 1873), Chap. V.

[115] Francis Griffin Stokes, in the introduction to his translation of the *Epistolae obscurorum virorum* (London, 1909), p. xxvi; this introduction gives a brief account of the controversy.

[116] Ludwig Geiger, *Johann Reuchlin* (Leipzig, 1871), pp. 162–64, 249–51.

literature, including the Talmud, the cabala, commentaries, sermons, and other writings were of use to the Christian religion and to knowledge, and he saw no reason why this ancient literature, long tolerated in Christian law, should be destroyed. The conversion of the Jews themselves—the supposed purpose of Pfefferkorn—could best be served by a careful study of their literature and thought. This opinion inspired an attack on Reuchlin by Pfefferkorn, and a reply by Reuchlin which was alleged by the theologians to be heretical. The Inquisitor-General, Jacob Hochstraten, collected a parcel of condemnations from the faculties of the German universities and the University of Paris and summoned Reuchlin to a trial at Mainz. When Reuchlin appealed to the Holy See, the case went to the bishops of Speyer and Worms; and when the Bishop of Speyer found Reuchlin free of heresy, Hochstraten carried the embarrassing issue once more to Rome.

The Reuchlin case came before Pope Leo X at almost the same time as did that of Pietro Pomponazzi, and one might expect, judging from the sheer merits of the issues, that the pontiff who had dealt so liberally with the controversial speculations of the Italian would have thrown out of court the far less imposing case against the German. But before the issue had ground altogether to its conclusion, new rumblings of discontent had been heard from Wittenberg; and even though a commission of experts advised the papal curia in Reuchlin's favor, Leo decided, in 1520, that the book in question was offensive, ordered it to be suppressed, and enjoined silence on Reuchlin. The pope was not prepared to add to his German troubles an affront to the Dominicans and the universities of both Germany and France.[117] Reuchlin himself, although impoverished by the expenses of the proceeding, carried on with his work, spending the few years remaining to him as professor of Greek and Hebrew at Ingolstadt and then Tübingen. He died in 1522, while the bitter controversy aroused by Luther was raging, firm in the bosom of the faith.

While the Reuchlin case was still under consideration there appeared a scathing document that Herder has called the *Don Quixote* of German theology—*The Letters of Obscure Men,* a product of the humanist circle at Erfurt.[118] This work is something of a landmark in the history of the intellectual class in the sense that for the first time it rallied the public

[117] Creighton, *A History of the Papacy,* VI, 60.
[118] On authorship see Stokes, introduction to *Epistolae obscurorum virorum,* pp. lvi–lxviii.

opinion of the learned world around an issue of interest to scholars. It is, of course, an exercise in pure *ad hominem,* for its sole effect is to pour ridicule on the ignorance and hoggishness of the traditional party. In this it was, according to common report, enormously effective. At a time when the attention of the world of western learning was focused upon the case of the Jewish books it crystallized the sentiments of the liberals and gave expression to the utter disdain with which the humanists regarded their opponents. But this intensely personal attack upon the Colognists (as the Pfefferkorn-Hochstraten party was called) has only a marginal significance for the history of the notions of tolerance and intellectual freedom. It was not a sober defense of free learning. It was a ribald assault on the limitations and foibles of the conservatives. Erasmus, with his characteristic urbanity, saw at once that neither the Colognist accusations of heresy nor the personal ridicule of the Erfurt group dealt with the fundamental issue of how religion and learning could best be served. In a magisterial letter of 1519 he rebuked Hochstraten for his part in the proceedings, especially his effort to obscure the question by pressing the factitious charge of infidelity and heresy. "Separate the person from the issue," he insisted. "A man can err, and then his error is to be condemned, but his honor ought to be saved, the scientific effort esteemed, with which he enlightens and serves theology rather than obscuring or fighting it." [119] To Erasmus the form taken by the controversy seemed to endanger rather than advance learning. And while many modern writers find in its outcome a moral victory for the cause of humanist scholarship, the evidence for such a view is extremely vague; what is perhaps clear is that the conflict showed how unready were both conservatives and reformers in the world of learning to discuss a problem of free inquiry from the standpoint of some criterion of the welfare of either religion or learning. The temper of the controversy presaged not the advancement of learning but the maelstrom of the Reformation.

[119] Geiger, *Johann Reuchlin,* p. 430; for Erasmus' role see pp. 427–35. An interesting opinion that reflects the thoroughgoing elitist position of the humanist scholar was expressed by Mutianus Rufus, the leader of the Erfurt circle and one of the most enlightened of the humanists. Although wholeheartedly on Reuchlin's side, he expressed during the early stages of the dispute his disapproval of anything that would agitate the masses, who must be left with their simple views of religion, lest they be stirred up against the Empire, the Church, and the men of learning. One sees here an anxious anticipation of the Reformation and an accurate reflection of the humanist feeling that church reform must not become a popular affair. See Karl Völker, *Toleranz und Intoleranz im Zeitalter der Reformation* (Leipzig, 1912), pp. 19–20.

Whatever their problems, the early humanists had been fortunate to work in an age when the ecclesiastical unity of Christendom had not yet been profoundly riven by the reformers. The great achievements of early modern science, however, took place within an atmosphere of bitterness, dogmatism, and intimidation. Since the universities after the beginning of the Reformation were under still closer church-state control and surveillance, and more favorable circumstances for innovation were provided under private auspices, early modern science tended more and more to flourish outside the universities. Thus, while the Italian universities carried on the most significant intellectual activity in Christendom, the share of the universities elsewhere in the sum of intellectual work was again substantially reduced.

The history of the Copernican system suggests that the Church had grown somewhat less hospitable to astronomical speculation than it had been during the fourteenth and fifteenth centuries. Nicole Oresme and Albert of Saxony had spoken with impunity of a moving earth. Nicholas of Cusa had toyed with several daring ideas about the universe which were rather similar to those that were to cost Bruno his life;[120] for all this he remained Bishop of Brixen and later became a cardinal. By the time of Copernicus the atmosphere was not so free. Copernicus himself might have brought his ideas forward several years before he did had he not been at odds with his bishop (partly for personal reasons, partly over his friendship for the Protestant scholar Rheticus). When he finally arranged for the publication of his *De revolutionibus orbium coelestium* (1543) after many years of delay, it was done only after carefully discussing the matter with his friends, Cardinal von Schönberg and Bishop Tiedemann Giese, and under the protective cover of a carefully written preface in which the work was dedicated to Pope Paul III, a scholarly man whose intellectual interests and character were such as to promise that there would be no persecution.[121] Even after these precautions, Osiander, as we have seen, felt it discreet to add another safeguard by inserting without Copernicus' consent the anonymous preface in which the device of hypothetical statement was employed.

Launched with all this caution, the Copernican system did not at first

[120] On the influence of Nicholas of Cusa on Bruno see Dorothea Waley Singer, *Giordano Bruno* (New York, 1950), pp. 54–59; Nicholas' actual scientific accomplishments are discussed by Lynn Thorndike, *Science and Thought in the Fifteenth Century* (New York, 1929), Chap. VII.

[121] Rosen, *Three Copernican Treatises*, pp. 26–27.

arouse anything like the furor that might have been anticipated. Part of its quiet reception may perhaps be credited to the last-minute precaution of Copernicus' editors. But more surely its failure to draw the fire of officialdom can be attributed to the fact that it was not widely accepted by scientists themselves.[122] This was not entirely due to fear (although there were men like Kepler's teacher, Professor Maestlin of Tübingen, who believed in and who was widely known as a teacher of the Copernican system, but who espoused the Ptolemaic system in his published textbook),[123] but can be traced in substantial measure to the fact that there were many intrinsic unresolved difficulties about the Copernican system that troubled even men of open mind.[124] Tycho Brahe, the leading astronomer of Europe, did not adopt it. The Roman Church was largely indifferent to it, the Protestants with their greater bibliolatry were contemptuously opposed,[125] and civilized minds like Montaigne, Bodin, and Bacon did not accept it. At the close of the sixteenth century the doctrine still had few supporters. It was Giordano Bruno who by elaborating the new theory into a vision of the universe first alerted the Church to its dangers.

In his survey *Science since 1500,* H. T. Pledge makes the suggestive remark that "it is philosophies rather than scientific discoveries which are persecuted." [126] While there are undoubtedly some exceptions to this generalization—Galileo represents not the least of them—it seems that the severe findings of science, under their simple armor of matter-of-fact, frequently stood a better chance of escaping the inquisitor's eye than the speculations of grand theorists. So it was in the case of Bruno, who combined with his great imagination and remarkable courage a tremendous capacity for provocation. The story of Bruno's career as a wandering scholar in the university world would in itself provide a lengthy footnote

[122] Stimson, *The Gradual Acceptance of the Copernican Theory of the Universe,* p. 32 and *passim.*

[123] *Ibid.,* p. 48; even Galileo continued out of a spirit of compliance to teach the Ptolemaic cosmology at Padua in the 1590s after being persuaded of the Copernican system. J. J. Fahie, *Galileo* (London, 1903), pp. 39–40.

[124] These are assessed lucidly by Herbert Butterfield, *The Origins of Modern Science, 1300–1800* (London, 1950), Chaps. II and IV. Cf. Francis R. Johnson, *Astronomical Thought in Renaissance England* (Baltimore, 1937), Chap. IV.

[125] During Copernicus' lifetime Luther said of him: "The fool wants to overthrow the whole art of astronomy. But as Holy Scripture declares, Joshua bade the sun stand still, and not the earth." Stimson, *The Gradual Acceptance of the Copernican Theory of the Universe,* p. 39n. On Melanchthon, Calvin, Montaigne, and Bodin, *ibid.,* pp. 39–48.

[126] H. T. Pledge, *Science since 1500* (London, 1947), p. 54.

to the history of intellectual liberty. The fact that this heretical and im-
mensely difficult man was able to live for many years in the university
world offers a morsel of evidence that intellectual liberties were not totally
absent from the northern *studia* of the late sixteenth century,[127] but his
wanderings and discomforts likewise make it clear that genius and originality were far from sufficient to provide a scholar with a secure career.
Bruno was a profoundly unorthodox thinker, seemingly without any real
attachment to any of the standard theological positions of his day. His
end is perhaps too familiar to require much comment; it forms one of
the ugliest passages in the history of the Inquisition. There can be little
doubt today that he was persecuted chiefly for his theological ideas, and
that his views pertaining to or deriving from science were of only incidental significance. But what is most pertinent here is that by reopening
the horrible but by no means novel prospect of an infinity of worlds he
caused authority to give full attention to the dangerous implications of
Copernicanism, and that his burning in 1600 marks the turning point from
official indifference or liberality to persecution.[128] The day was not far
distant when a campaign would be inaugurated to prevent Galileo from
proclaiming the results of his observations.

Galileo had no sooner published his *Sidereus nuncius* (1610), which
reported his telescopic observations, than he was listed as a suspect in the
secret books of the Inquisition. Within a few years the jealousy of scientific rivals, the religious scruples of the Dowager Grand Duchess of Tus-
cany, and the suspicions of the Dominicans and Jesuits had combined to
arouse vigilance against him. A professor at Pisa was soon forbidden to
discuss the double motion of the earth even within the customary formula
of probability. In 1616 Copernicus' *De revolutionibus,* after almost three

[127] See his touching words of gratitude to Wittenberg, quoted in Wilhelm Dilthey,
*Weltanschauung und Analyse des Menschen seit Renaissance und Reformation,
Gesammelte Schriften* (Leipzig, 1914), II, 509.
[128] One could probably argue that Bruno all but sought persecution by his manner
and methods, and that his devotion to his ideas only resulted in a setback to the
advance of scientific knowledge. Cf. the remarks by Mark Graubard, "Persecution
as the Pathology of Freedom and Authority," in Lyman Bryson, *et al.,* eds., *Freedom
and Authority in Our Time* (New York, 1953), especially pp. 399–401. In fact,
the ethic of tact, moderation, compromise, and concentration upon the essentials is
an altogether defensible one in relation to the problem of freedom. The sole danger
is that the entire onus of manifesting these qualities may be thrown upon those
standing for innovation, while they ought to be with equal reason demanded of the
authorities. Noteworthy in Bruno's case is his somewhat belated appeal to the
double truth tradition, which was of course quite fruitless. See Harald Höffding,
A History of Modern Philosophy (New York, 1950), I, 120–21.

quarters of a century, was put on the Index as subject to correction; [129] and, while the record here is obscure and controversial, Galileo was apparently given some inkling at this time that further discussion of the condemned opinion would have its dangers. Galileo abjured,[130] and went on with his work, much troubled, until his admirer Cardinal Maffeo Barberini became Pope Urban VIII. Imagining that the time was again opportune to assert the truth, Galileo appeared in 1630 before the Grand Master of the Sacred Palace with a new manuscript in dialogue form in which the two great cosmologies were discussed. After much study the pope's representatives gave permission for the publication of the work upon condition that the hypothetical form of statement be used and that some of the pope's own reasoning concerning the question of the tides be incorporated. Accordingly Galileo's *Dialogue on the Two Chief Systems of the World* was published in 1632 under the cover of an introduction in which Galileo asserted that he was "taking up . . . the Copernican side of the question, treating it as a pure mathematical hypothesis . . ." [131] Despite his compliance with the forms, it was obvious that the work was a powerful plea for the truth of the Copernican system, not as a mathematical convenience but as a description of the universe. Also, Galileo's enemies prevailed upon the pope to believe that his own point of view had been subtly ridiculed. Galileo was charged with violating the decree of 1616 and maintaining the heliocentric system contrary to Scripture. An old and ailing man, he was summoned to Rome in 1633, tried, threatened with torture, and subjected to the humiliation of recanting and disavowing what he knew to be true, and sentenced to custodial imprisonment that lasted until his death in 1642.[132]

[129] Copies of the book were allowed to circulate provided all passages dealing with the motion of the earth were altered so as to assert that this idea, although false, was introduced merely as a mathematical hypothesis for simplifying calculations. The works of Copernicus, Galileo, and Kepler were removed from the Index in 1835.

[130] He did, however, send a copy of one of his works to the Archduke Leopold of Austria, under the protective cover of a very touching letter in which he offers his ideas not as true—for to do so has been condemned by the authorities—but as "a poetical conceit or a dream." "But," he adds pathetically, "even poets sometimes attach a value to one or another of their fantasies, and I likewise attach some value to this fancy of mine." Fahie, *Galileo,* p. 180.

The case of Galileo, notably the question of exactly what happened in 1616, is fraught with many complexities that we have had to pass over. See Karl von Gebler, *Galileo Galilei and the Roman Curia* (London, 1879), and Léon Garzend, *L'Inquisition et l'heresie . . . à propos de l'affaire Galilée* (Paris, 1912).

[131] *Ibid.,* p. 247.

[132] The legend that Galileo muttered his defiance of the Inquisitors is not credited

The most important literary document occasioned by Galileo's persecution was Tommaso Campanella's *The Defense of Galileo,* which appeared in 1622 at a time when its author, a Calabrian, was serving his twenty-seven years of imprisonment at the hands of the Spanish government. As a consequence of the discontents in Calabria this remarkable monk had been accused of heresy and of plotting against the state, and had resumed his philosophic and literary labors as soon as the physical circumstances of his imprisonment had been sufficiently lightened to make it possible. An intensely loyal Catholic, for all the novelty of his philosophical and social ideas, Campanella later secured the aid and protection of the pope, which made it possible for him to spend his last years at liberty in France. Although his most famous work is his utopia, *The City of the Sun* (1623), his *Defense of Galileo* has been called "the first reasoned argument to be published in support of the freedom of scientific investigation." [133] The tract was written after Campanella had learned of Galileo's initial encounters with the Church, but before the latter's final trial and sentence, which Campanella, as a loyal Catholic, accepted. The Calabrian was a complex and often seemingly inconsistent thinker, and it is difficult in a brief passage to do justice to the character of his defense. Despite its anticipation of modernity, its argument would probably not have seemed strange to Adelard of Bath, Abelard, St. Thomas Aquinas, or Godfrey of Fontaines. In broad outline the book attempts to establish two things: that there is nothing canonical, so to speak, about the ideas of Aristotle, least of all his cosmology; and that with proper exegesis it is possible to make a consistent harmony between new scientific discoveries and Scripture. The strategy of the book is quite compelling. Campanella seems to be trying to urge the Church out of its growing rigidity and into an intellectual statecraft that he feels is closer to the flexibility and liberality of its earlier policies. Its tone, as well as its argument, is such as to give comfort to those modern scholars who like to emphasize the continuity between the thought of the Middle Ages and early modern times. In true medieval fashion the book shows great deference to authority—

---

by modern scholarship. He did something more sensible: he continued, despite failing health and eyesight, to carry on his scientific work to the end, doing tremendously important work in dynamics in the face of obstacles to publication imposed by the Church. Fahie, *Galileo,* Chap. XV. The most recent study, Giorgio de Santillana's *The Crime of Galileo* (Chicago, 1955), appeared too late to be drawn upon for these pages.

[133] Robert B. Sutton, "The Phrase *Libertas Philosophandi," Journal of the History of Ideas,* XIV (April, 1953), 311.

the authority of Scripture, of the Church Fathers, of St. Thomas, of the Lateran Councils—but always with the purpose of deposing the authority of Aristotle, and of providing authoritative precedents for the findings of Galileo.[134]

Although his particular application of his views to the case of Galileo was such as could have been made only by a man of considerable learning and ingenuity, Campanella's line of argument was composed upon familiar premises that had long been used to confute obscurantists. Indeed, perhaps the most striking thing about this early modern defense of scientific freedom is its thoroughly medieval tone. God had given man his reason and his senses in order that he make use of them, and to fail to do so is to "transgress the natural law of God." Moreover, truth does not contradict truth. Therefore there can be no contradiction between nature, "the created book of God's wisdom" and Scripture, "the revealed book of His divine wisdom." Wisdom is to be sought in "the whole book of God." What we learn of nature through reason and our senses must therefore be legitimate and consistent with the rest of God's truth, properly understood. But, as to the proper understanding of Scripture, there is a difference between its "mystical meaning for the wise" and its "obvious meaning for the vulgar." (How consistently this distinction runs through the early justifications of free thought!) The learned know that Scripture needs sound interpretation and that this does not always come easily. Since natural knowledge cannot be inconsistent with the true meaning of Scripture, advances in natural knowledge may give us clues to interpretation. The miracle of Joshua, then, is no less a miracle when we know that the sun is at rest—it is merely a miracle the mechanics of which is better understood.[135]

Campanella not only strikes this blow at Biblical literalism, but he keeps the problem of freedom of inquiry uppermost in mind. He quotes St. Thomas Aquinas as having said that "new theories always may be in-

134 "Saint Thomas," Campanella writes characteristically, "teaches that Aristotelianism is not a doctrine of faith. . . . The Fathers and the two masters of the scholastics, Saint Thomas and Peter Lombard, support more than they oppose Galileo, and Scripture favors more than it censures him." Grant McColley, tr. and ed., The Defense of Galileo ("Smith College Studies in History," Vol. XXII [April–July, 1937]), pp. 35–49. Campanella stressed the heretical potentialities of Aristotelianism. Ibid., pp. 40–42.

135 Ibid., pp. 18, 27, 28, 30, 54. The passage on Joshua is obscure, but Campanella seems to be suggesting that a miracle did take place, the mechanical form of which can be interpreted as well by the Copernican as the Ptolemaic system; cf. the reasoning of Oresme in 1377, Ross and McLaughlin, Renaissance Reader, p. 582.

troduced under the name of philosophy, and such theories should not be opposed on the grounds that they are contrary to faith . . ." and St. Gregory as having said that "if scandal develops because of truth, it is desirable that we permit scandal to be born, for by it truth will be left standing." [136] "Effective discussion," he declares, "is made sterile by bondage." [137] He expresses the modern confidence that error cannot survive: "If Galileo's theory be unsound it will not endure"; therefore, it is unnecessary to forbid it.[138] Significant too is the appearance in his text, possibly for the first time, of the phrase *libertas philosophandi,* freedom of philosophizing, which was the fruit of the medieval autonomy of philosophy and was the forerunner of more modern terms like *Lehrfreiheit* and "academic freedom." This phrase became fairly common usage in the seventeenth century.[139]

Of course Campanella's argument was ignored by the Church. After Galileo's abjuration and final sentence, copies of both were sent to all inquisitors and papal nuncios that they might notify their clergy and all the professors of mathematics and philosophy at the universities. Special care was taken to see that those at Florence, Padua, and Pisa were notified.[140] It is impossible to measure the extent of the blight that fell on such science as there was in the universities, or upon men of learning in general. Presumably many were like Descartes (of whom it has been said that he had no vocation for martyrdom), who had prepared a physical treatise which he was about to release when he learned of Galileo's trial, and who promptly suppressed his own work.

We think of the seventeenth century as a century of genius, of great

---

[136] McColley, *Defense of Galileo,* pp. 34, 67. St. Thomas is quoted from the preface to his *Tract against the Errors of the Greeks,* where he is arguing for a certain autonomy of philosophy from the faith. St. Gregory is quoted from a commentary on Ezekiel.

[137] *Ibid.,* p. 33.   [138] *Ibid.,* p. 37.

[139] *Ibid.,* p. 33: "I have shown that liberty of thought [or liberty of philosophizing] is more vigorous in Christian than in other nations." Cf. Sutton, "The Phrase *Libertas Philosophandi,*" p. 311 and *passim.* Actually the phrase had been used in a slightly different form by Bruno in 1588, Kepler in 1610, and Galileo in 1612, as Sutton shows. Among those who used it later in the seventeenth century were Descartes and Spinoza. The subtitle of the latter's *Theologico-Political Treatise* (1670) reads: *Containing Certain Discussions Wherein is Set Forth That the Freedom of Philosophizing Not Only May, without Prejudice to Piety and the Public Peace, be Granted; But Also May Not, without Danger to Piety and the Public Peace be Withheld.* The phrase itself was perhaps new, but the idea, as many a medieval master could have testified, was old.

[140] Stimson, *The Gradual Acceptance of the Copernican Theory of the Universe,* pp. 67–68.

advances in all branches of science, of brilliant philosophy and liberal theology. Although work of much importance to science was carried on at Leiden and Cambridge, there was a tendency for such investigation to be fostered more effectively in scientific societies. Most of university life was still substantially bounded by the medieval curriculum, the Latin language, and Greek thought. Its science was the science of Ptolemy, Euclid, Aristotle, Galen, and Hippocrates. Ecclesiasticism and confessional requirements were all but universal, and freedom of thought was neither practiced nor professed. "The teacher," ran one statement of the predominant ideal,

is not to permit any novel opinions or discussions to be mooted; nor to cite or allow others to cite the opinions of an author not of known repute; nor to teach or suffer to be taught anything contrary to prevalent opinions of acknowledged doctors current in the schools. Obsolete and false opinions are not to be mentioned at all even for refutation nor are objections to received teaching to be dwelt on at any length. . . . In philosophy Aristotle is always to be followed and St. Thomas Aquinas generally.[141]

The exceptions to this generally bleak picture existed where universities were sponsored by municipalities and where the hand of ecclesiasticism rested less heavily—at the northern Italian universities, in Holland, where Leiden was notably hospitable to science and where Cartesianism had its warmest reception, and at Halle, Heidelberg, and Altdorf.[142] But even at Padua Vesalius found that he had to conform to Galen and met so much opposition to novel discovery that he lost his temper and left for the court of Spain.

At the University of Paris tradition was everything. The university was still the censor of books, and in 1626 the death penalty was prescribed by civil authority for anyone who published without university authorization, while another rule forbade any teacher to hold or teach anything against the ancient authors. Although Descartes had dedicated his *Discourse on Method* to the Sorbonne, the Paris theologians in 1663 had his works, except as corrected, put on the Index. In 1671, when the Archbishop of Paris warned all four faculties against allowing any opin-

141 Quoted from Acquaviva, the Jesuit general, by Martha Ornstein, *The Role of Scientific Societies in the Seventeenth Century* (Chicago, 1938), p. 215; the factual material in this paragraph is drawn from that work, Chap. VIII. See also D'Irsay, *Histoire*, Vol. II, Chap. XV, and Friedrich Paulsen, *The German Universities* (New York, 1906), pp. 42–44.

142 Some aspects of the situation in German universities are dealt with in A. Tholuck, *Das Akademische Leben des Siebzehnten Jahrhunderts* (Halle, 1853).

ions that might breed doctrinal confusion, his warnings were accepted without a dissenting voice. Only with modest exceptions was the picture different in England, where the Laudian statutes of 1636 enjoined Aristotle upon the faculties. Oxford, to be sure, had a striking upsurge of scientific interest around the middle of the century, but most of this was attributable to Oxford residents without formal connection with the university, and it petered out when most of these men went to London.[143] At Cambridge something of a turning point occurred in 1663 with the endowment of the Lucasian professorship of mathematics and astronomy, which was to be filled by Newton from 1669 to 1702; but it was the Royal Society, not the university, that showed the more alert interest in Newton's work. Only at the dawning of the eighteenth century, when some universities expressly adopted the principle of *libertas philosophandi* and even Paris (in 1720) set Descartes beside Aristotle, did the more traditionalist institutions show some signs of yielding to the times.

THE IDEA OF TOLERATION

The modern idea of academic freedom has been developed by men who have absorbed analogous ideas from the larger life of society. From modern science they have taken the notion of a continuing search for new truths, fostered by freedom of inquiry, verified by objective processes, and judged by those who are competent. From commerce they have taken the concept of a free competition among ideas—hence the suggestive metaphor of a free market in thought. From the politics of the liberal state they have taken the ideas of free speech and a free press and an appreciation of the multitude of perspectives in a pluralistic society. From religious liberalism and from the long historical development which led to the taming of sectarian animus have come the ideas of toleration and religious liberty [144] by which they have benefited.

While it would be idle to attempt to establish priorities of importance

[143] Ornstein, *Role of Scientific Societies in the Seventeenth Century,* pp. 92 ff., 241–47; on university science at mid-century see James B. Conant, "The Advancement of Learning during the Puritan Commonwealth," *Proceedings of the Massachusetts Historical Society,* LXVI (Boston, 1942), 3–31.

[144] By religious toleration we mean a state policy under which religious groups other than the established church are permitted to carry on worship; by religious liberty a policy under which worship is freely allowed to all groups and no civil disabilities are attached to membership in any church. By tolerance we mean simply an attitude of forbearance and a disposition to extend toleration or religious liberty.

among these forces, it is clear that modern intellectual liberty on any considerable scale was an impossibility until the ferocious dogmatism and intolerance that flourished with the Reformation and Counter Reformation were in some measure quieted. Thus religious tolerance and religious liberty were the historical matrix of intellectual freedom within such traditionally religious institutions as the universities. As modern science and modern liberal politics may be said to have provided the conceptual models for the positive content of academic freedom, tolerance and religious liberty may be said to have cleared the ground for it by eliminating or moderating its most formidable obstacles, notably the union between church and state. Academic freedom and religious freedom have one root in common: both are based upon the freedom of conscience, hence neither can flourish in a community that has no respect for human individuality.

Traditionally Protestantism is quite rightly credited with having led to immense gains in personal freedom by forcing a breach in religious authority, by creating religious diversity, and by asserting the rights of the individual conscience. This, however, was no part of the intention of the major Protestant reformers; it was an outcome of two centuries of laborious historical evolution. The immediate consequences of the Reformation were disastrous to tranquillity and to intellectual freedom. With the Reformation the genial secularization that had been under way within the Roman Church was abruptly ended, and with it disappeared most of that inconsistent but highly valuable indulgence for critical thought that the Church had allowed. Toward science and learning, toward the rights of conscience, the major Protestant groups were no more indulgent than the Roman Church, which now became far more severe than before in its attempts to meet these new challenges to its power.

Toleration and religious liberty made headway not because men were wise enough to anticipate and avoid the consequences of persecution but because they had witnessed and endured those consequences for more than two centuries after Luther's manifesto of 1517. Toleration and religious liberty slowly won acceptance where men of power and authority learned to consider them necessary to civil order and flourishing commerce; [145] where religious minorities and small sects protested with some

[145] A notable case was that of the *politiques* in France, who although chiefly Catholics were driven by the disorder of their country to advocate toleration as

effect against persecution; where secularized thinkers and ethical Christians spoke out in behalf of freedom of thought and conscience or of the softer principles of Christian morality. And yet progress along these lines was so slow in making itself felt in academic life that even in America, where the multitude of religious denominations made mutual accommodation imperative, the application of toleration to academic life had only limited results for many generations. For about two hundred and fifty years after the founding of Harvard in 1636, the very form in which the problem of freedom was posed in American colleges—insofar as there was a formulation of the problem of freedom—was set by the conditions of religious sectarianism; and the ebb and flow of both liberty and achievement in collegiate education could be measured by the rise and fall of tolerance and religious liberalism. Part I of this volume traces that story, but before we can focus upon the American scene itself a final word must be said about the forms in which the rationale for tolerance was inherited.

From the standpoint of one who believed in the doctrine of exclusive salvation—that is, one who felt that heresy damns souls and that there was no salvation outside the bounds of his own confession—there had always been a rigorous logic behind persecution. To do anything less than try to force the heretic to conform seemed an abandonment of his soul; to permit him to infect others with damning ideas would be to compound this sin. There were, moreover, Scriptural admonitions to which appeal could be made, especially the fatal text of Luke: "Compel them to come in." In fact, however, a dual tradition existed within Christianity, and it was possible to find authoritative Scriptural or patristic justification either for persecuting or tolerating—often, as in the case of Augustine, within the writings of a single authority.[146]

In order to persecute, three things, at least, were necessary: the persecutor must be sure that he was right on the point of dogma at issue; he

---

an expedient in the interests of national concord and unity. Close to them was Jean Bodin, who significantly looked to the educational process under the guidance of the state as the means by which that unity of sentiment, once provided by religion, could be instilled in the children. See especially his *Oeuvres philosophiques,* ed. Pierre Mesnard (Paris, 1951), pp. 57 ff.

[146] This discussion of persecution owes much to Roland Bainton's article, "The Struggle for Religious Liberty," *Church History,* X (June, 1941), 96–124, which says a great deal in small compass, and to the same author's introductory essay in his translation of Castellio's *Concerning Heretics* (New York, 1935). An extremely suggestive analysis is that of Johannes Kühn, *Toleranz und Offenbarung* (Leipzig, 1923).

must be sure that the issue was important (i.e., vital to salvation) and not inessential; and he must be convinced that coercion is actually effective. The advance of arguments for toleration or religious liberty is the story of the progressive weakening of one or another of these assumptions in different times and places. While for the firm Catholic it was unthinkable to doubt either of the first two of these assumptions, the development within Catholicism, prior to the Reformation, of mysticism, humanism, and sectarianism had already set in motion currents of thought and feeling that weakened the determination to persecute. Mystics turned attention away from dogma and toward personal and inward religious experience, and introduced an element of subjectivism that made for mutual forbearance. Humanists also disparaged dogma, partly because they wanted freedom of investigation in those areas that to them were of most concern, but partly too because of the emphasis upon Christian ethics in their thinking.[147] Sectarianism, as expressed within the Church by the Spiritual Franciscans, set obedience to God above obedience to the pope (later this principle of mundane resistance was extended by others to other religious authority). The Reformation, by releasing innumerable substreams of religious thought and setting the example of successful resistance to authority, shattered the possibility of common agreement upon enforceable principles and ultimately allowed these three seeds of liberalism to take root and grow. By establishing an open competition of sects, it made inevitable an ultimate appeal to individual conscience and individual choice. Under the impact of generations of increasingly rationalistic criticism men came to doubt their own certainty in matters of faith and to understand more and more widely the import of Montaigne's remark that it is setting a very high value on one's ideas to burn men for them. As the importance of doctrinal differences receded, the importance of conduct as a criterion of true religion rose. The exercise of Christian charity came to be considered far more important than what John Locke called "nice and intricate matters that exceed the capacity of ordinary understandings." [148] There was a tendency to try to cut down on the number of points considered essential to religion, and by the same token

[147] Cf. Erasmus: "You will not be damned if you do not know whether the Spirit proceeding from the Father and the Son has one or two beginnings, but you will not escape damnation if you do not cultivate the fruits of the Spirit which are love, joy, peace, patience, kindness, goodness, long-suffering, mercy, faith, modesty, continence, and chastity." Bainton, introduction to Castellio's *Concerning Heretics*, p. 33.

[148] *A Letter concerning Toleration*, 1689 (New York, 1950), p. 15.

to minimize the number of differences deemed worth persecuting men for.[149]

Finally, while there were, as we have said, powerful reasons for toleration which stemmed from considerations of secular expediency, there were distinctively religious reasons for toleration which stemmed from psychological impulses that had long had their formulation in Christian ethics.[150] As George Lincoln Burr once wrote,

It was not science, not reason, that put an end to inhumanity in so many fields: the pedants were as cruel as the bigots. Reason came in only to sanction here reforms which had been wrought in spite of her. The real antagonist of theology and of rationalism alike was the unreasoning impulse of human kindliness.[151]

Pious men saw that forced acceptance of a faith would not be sincere, that instead of saving souls, it created hypocrites; [152] and many of them found in the acts of persecution a breach of Christian charity far more objectionable than any notions of the alleged heretic.[153]

Some writers came to see the very search for religious truth and the willingness to endure persecution for it as a religious merit, a token of spiritual sincerity that contrasted nobly with the readiness of some men to submit to coercion. It was argued that religious conversion should be sought by humility, devotion, and persuasion, rather than by force, and many liberals expressed their confidence that truth would in the long run

[149] This attempt to strip off inessentials often had a practical urgency when it seemed that by so doing some Protestant groups otherwise close together might be able to unite. This distinction between fundamentals and inessentials, however, could cut both ways, for authority might argue that if some matters were really inessential to the main body of faith the nonconformists were being obstinate and petty for stickling over them. Thus Laud, who was strong on discipline and matters of form but broadminded about doctrine, still grated upon the Puritans. In the end it was realized that what is fundamental to one sect is not to another, and the whole distinction tended to break down. Bainton, "The Struggle for Religious Liberty," pp. 103–5.

[150] Thus even W. E. H. Lecky in his History of the Rise and Influence of the Spirit of Rationalism in Europe (1865; London, 1946), part II, p. 30, concedes concerning the rise of toleration in England that "the most illustrious of the advocates of toleration were earnestly attached to positive religion."

[151] Roland H. Bainton and Lois Oliphand Gibbons, George Lincoln Burr, His Life: Selections from His Writings (Ithaca, N. Y., 1943), p. 56.

[152] Cf. Erasmus: "That which is forced cannot be sincere, and that which is not voluntary cannot please Christ." Bainton, introduction to Castellio's Concerning Heretics, p. 34.

[153] For a beautiful example of the precedents for tolerance in mystical and devotional literature of the waning Middle Ages see Chap. XVI of Thomas à Kempis' Imitation of Christ.

command assent. Thus out of centuries of argument for religious tolerance certain perspectives emerged that, in a more secular context, were
readily translated into arguments for intellectual freedom. Fallibilism—
the recognition that man is prone to error and that to this no one can
presume himself an exception—became a leading theme in the rationalist
tradition.[154] With it came the recognition that the truth is not static, but
is progressively unfolded, and that the quest for truth is itself a human
activity deserving of respect as an ultimate value. Some religious writers
understood, before it became a commonplace in the history of science,
the principle that error may have its value, or its indispensable place, in
the search for truth.[155] And finally the humanist idea that personal piety
and morals are more important than doctrinal tenets could easily be translated into the secular principle that it is only misconduct, not opinions,
that should make one liable to prosecution or to disabilities.

The impulse to persecute had, among other things, its psychological
sources, and these were projected into theology in the form of a harsh
conception of the nature of both God and man and of the relation between them. Men who were pre-eminently concerned with justice on
earth were more likely to believe that the decrees of God were also limited by considerations of justice and were not the products of an arbitrary
and inscrutable will. Those theologies that emphasized the charity, mercy,
and justness of God in terms amenable to human reason, that asserted the
ability of man to better his nature and help himself toward salvation, were
most disposed to tolerate; while those theologies that held to a wrathful
and arbitrary God whose decrees were beyond human scrutiny and
preached predestination and the helplessness and wretchedness of man
were more consonant with persecution.

The argument for tolerance entered into modern thought through many
channels, of which we can choose but one illustration. If a single work
must be chosen from early modern history as a repository of the argument
for tolerance to set beside Campanella's later defense of Galileo, it would
probably be Sébastien Castellio's *Concerning Heretics,* which appeared in

[154] Actually the roots of this idea can be found in the fourteenth and fifteenth
centuries.

[155] In 1531 the mystical apostate Lutheran, Sebastian Franck, put it in these
terms: "Truth, when set over against error, shines forth only the more clearly and
steadily. That is why God permitted heresies to arise, and it is expedient that there
should be lies for the proving and establishing of the truth, for every proposition
carries with it and demands its contrary." Quoted in Bainton's translation of
Castellio's *Concerning Heretics,* p. 188.

1554 as a protest against the burning of Servetus in Geneva the previous year at the behest of Calvin.[156] Castellio, a Frenchman by birth, who had been called by Calvin to be rector of the college at Geneva but had broken with Calvin over theological questions, was at the time professor of Greek at the University of Basel. A few years earlier he had published a Latin translation of the Bible in whose footnotes and dedicatory preface (to Edward VI of England) he had already made a plea for tolerance. Castellio's *Concerning Heretics* was answered on Calvin's behalf by Theodore Beza. The views it expressed led to Castellio's being hounded almost to the point of leaving Basel and seeking refuge elsewhere, but he hung on until his death in 1563.

The greater part of Castellio's book consisted of excerpts from authoritative writers from patristic times down to such immediate predecessors as Erasmus and Sebastian Franck, who had argued either for liberty or for very mild penalties for heretics. Its dedication to Duke Christoph summarized Castellio's own views, which were profoundly affected by the humanistic emphasis on conduct as opposed to beliefs. Christ had commanded men to "live together in a Christian manner, amicably, without controversy and contention, loving one another." Nothing then could be more repugnant to the nature and will of Christ than to strangle and burn others who differ on matters of faith. Others may be sincere, they may cling to their different ways not out of contumacy or obstinacy but out of a sincere fear of offending Christ (for his servant Paul had enjoined men not to do anything about which they were in doubt).[157] Castellio professed to hate heretics himself, but he was troubled by the thought that men might be held for heresy who were not heretics, and that punishment might be carried far beyond what was demanded by Christian discipline. He saw that there had already come to be so many sects that if each one persisted in regarding the others as heretical, persecution might go on endlessly. He denied that there was an inevitable linkage between doctrine and morals, insisting that good lives could be lived by men of many different opinions.[158]

Castellio's book was widely read on the Continent, but nowhere was it so influential as in Holland. There the liberal-minded Erasmian scholar

[156] On Castellio and Servetus see Earl Morse Wilbur, *A History of Unitarianism: Socinianism and Its Antecedents* (Cambridge, 1947), Chaps. XIII and XIV.

[157] Romans 14:23.

[158] Bainton's translation of Castellio's *Concerning Heretics,* pp. 121–40; cf. Castellio's other remarks on this theme, *ibid.,* pp. 257 ff.

and writer, Dirk Volkertszoon Coornhert, made himself thoroughly familiar with Castellio, translated two of Castellio's pamphlets and tried to popularize his arguments. A layman and a former secretary of state, Coornhert belonged to the liberal and cultivated minority in Holland that found itself out of sympathy with the rigorous orthodox Calvinism of the Reformed Church. His denial of the doctrine of predestination and his advocacy of toleration for all the major religious groups brought him the disapproval of the orthodox ministers, who forbade him to publish his views. They also arranged for a formal answer to his heresies; and at this juncture occurred one of the most interesting episodes in modern intellectual history. Among those summoned to reply to Coornhert was one Jacobus Arminius, a minister of Amsterdam who had studied under Beza at Geneva, and who was thus thought to be eminently equipped to defend predestination and capital punishment for heretics. "The acute and distinct Arminius," as Milton was to call him, set about to restudy the question with care, and in consequence almost completely reversed his position, adopting tenets very close to those of Coornhert himself.[159] Arminius became the founder of a theological movement of wide influence among the Dutch clergy and laity.

The full terms of the theological argument between the Arminians and the Calvinists are endlessly complicated. Suffice it to say that the Calvinists had one of the most impregnable arguments for the validity of persecution, for according to them its purpose was not to persuade or to save —the efficacy of which could always be readily doubted—but simply and purely to punish for the greater glory of God. Its implicit premise was that such punishment was gratifying to God, an assumption that could be doubted but hardly disproved.[160] Arminianism was essentially a criticism of Calvinist theology from an ethical standpoint. The Arminians held that God was limited by his own regard for justice.[161] They objected to

[159] On Arminianism and the split in Dutch Calvinism see A. W. Harrison, *The Beginnings of Arminianism* (London, 1926) and the same author's *Arminianism* (London, 1937); see also Petrus J. Blok, *History of the People of the Netherlands* (New York, 1900), Vol. III, Chaps. XIV, XV.

[160] Some critics pointed out that if the eternal fate of the heretic's soul was predestined, punishments and means of coercion could not in any case save him. Thorough Calvinists were not very much affected by this, for in their view heresy was above all an offense to God, and hence more serious than any offense to man, such as murder or treason, that ordinarily called for capital punishment.

[161] Cf. Arminius: "God can indeed do what He wills with His own; but He cannot will to do with His own what He cannot rightfully do, for His will is circumscribed within the bounds of justice." Harrison, *Arminianism*, p. 21.

the idea that God had found it necessary to decree damnation in order then to effect salvation. This, they asserted, made God Himself the author of sin. Moreover, they objected that the Calvinists' doctrines left the great multitude of men without hope of salvation, while providing a few with an arrogant sense of election contingent upon no ethical qualities. They insisted that Christ had died not only for the elect, as the Calvinists would have it, but for "the world"—that is, for all men. They held that the grace of God is indispensable to man, but not irresistible, and that it would be possible to fall from grace—a notion that was meant to induce a necessary moral discipline into the behavior of the elect. All this tended to soften the image of God's arbitrary judgment, to make ethics more important at the expense of dogmatics, and to suggest doubts to the persecuting mind. Thus while the Arminians preached toleration for the compelling reason that they were a minority subject to persecution, they also developed a theology that was in consonance with toleration.

Arminius himself was made professor of theology at Leiden and remained in that post until his death in 1609, despite the objections of the senior professor of theology, Gomarus, to his unorthodoxy. Because of the hospitality of Leiden to Arminians, the orthodox faction opened their own university at Groningen in 1614. At the Synod of Dort, 1618–19, the Arminian faction, the Remonstrants, were with finality judged to be heretics, after which the persecution of their leaders was greatly intensified. One, Oldenbarnevelt, was put to death. Another, Hugo Grotius, the great theorist of international law, made a dramatic escape from imprisonment. Arminius' follower and successor at Leiden, Vorstius, was harassed and humiliated there, excluded from teaching, charged with Socinianism, and finally, after the decision of the Synod, expelled from his professorship.[162] In England the struggle in the churches of the Netherlands was followed with great interest. Ironically, while the preachers of Arminian persuasion were being hunted down in Holland, English Puritans, regarding that country as a sanctuary, were fleeing there from the hostility of James I.

In one respect the Arminians taught doctrines that were quite congenial to English authority: as a religious minority with more influence among powerful lay politicians than they had among the clergy, they naturally turned to doctrines of church-state relationships that favored civil

[162] *Ibid.*, pp. 52–59; cf. Harrison, *The Beginnings of Arminianism,* Chap. VI.

authority over religious affairs and denied any independent ecclesiastical jurisdiction. In their view the state was entitled to inspect and maintain the purity of the church—a doctrine most repugnant to Calvinists—but was not to act in any controversial matter to enforce the will of the majority or to interfere with individual conscience.[163] James I, for all his hostility to the Puritans, had been a Calvinist, and had thrown the weight of English influence on the side of the orthodox faction at the Synod of Dort. Under Charles I and Laud, however, the Arminian combination of liberal theology, secular autocracy, and stern church discipline became extremely congenial to the reigning trend, and the high-church party became deeply affected by Arminian ideas. Laud favored the Arminians for places in the church to the degree that when a divine asked what it was that the Arminians held, the answer was: all the best benefices and livings in England. From the standpoint of our present interest, what is important is that Arminian thought worked as a powerful leaven among the leading English clergy for religious rationalism and toleration. This is not to say that the first English Arminians were primarily interested in the philosophy or practice of toleration. But such ideas, latent in the theology they had adopted, began to be asserted. Nor is it to say that the English theologians were incapable of thinking up their own objections to Calvinism and that every deviation from orthodoxy can be attributed directly to Arminian sources. Arminianism became, in fact, a rather loosely used word for latitudinarian thinking, and in the American colonies, as we shall see, was an indiscriminate epithet for any variety of latitudinarian heresy. But Arminianism was an important opening wedge for the later development of English rationalism and English toleration. The latitudinarian theologians of the seventeenth and early eighteenth centuries found in it an important starting point. One finds traces of its influence in the Cambridge Platonists, in liberal Puritans like Milton, in later rationalists like Locke, and in the Unitarians and Universalists. From this latitudinarian tradition, which was the tradition of greatest influence for liberalism in the American colonies, stems the development of much of the liberalism of Harvard and of the later American Episcopal colleges.

Slow as the principles of toleration were to win adherence in the field of civil policy, they were still slower to make headway in the universities, with their traditional religious commitments. For university studies the

---

[163] Arminian political theory is discussed by Douglas Nobbs, *Theocracy and Toleration* (Cambridge, 1938), esp. Chap. II.

first consequences of the Reformation were disastrous.[164] Under the territorial confessional states the last remnants of corporate autonomy disappeared, and the long process by which the secular state had been encroaching upon the university reached its climax. The same formula that had been used to bring peace at Augsburg was the effective formula governing intellectual life: *cuius regio, eius universitas*. The king or the prince determined what faith was to be professed by his subjects and by those who taught or studied in his university; such freedom as was to be had could be found only by migrating. The university was now a completely confessional institution; and while the same might indeed have been said of the medieval universities as well, it meant something far more rigid and inflexible now that confessional allegiances and dogmatic differences were everything. A certain pluralism in philosophical tradition, as we have seen, enlarged and liberated the intellectual life of the medieval universities, despite their theoretical doctrinal unity. But in the full flush of the Reformation confessional considerations were dominant and everything could be a confessional consideration. When the Duke of Prussia, for instance, was disposed to take with full seriousness the Lutheran hostility to Aristotle, the study of the Peripatetic, and with him practically all study of philosophy at Königsberg, was suppressed.[165]

Exceptions there were, of course, to the dominant practices of the hidebound universities with their confessional oaths, but these came only toward the close of the sixteenth century. Leiden, founded in 1575 by William the Silent to honor the city for its resistance to the Spanish, reflected the liberalism and cosmopolitanism of the Netherland towns, and became "the earliest university of Europe to follow an intentional and consistent policy of academic freedom." [166] Professors were not required to make any doctrinal commitments in their simple oath of loyalty to the university and the city; Jews were admitted as students and private teachers; a Catholic professor, driven to resign by Protestants in the town because he defended religious persecution, was invited by the burgomasters and curators to return; and the university began to have the reputation as a refuge of learned men that it continued to keep during the seventeenth

---

[164] D'Irsay, *Histoire,* Vol. I, Chap. XIII, emphasizes the unfortunate consequences of the Reformation; see also Paulsen, *The German Universities,* pp. 36–37.

[165] D'Irsay, *Histoire,* I, 324–26.

[166] Robert B. Sutton, "European and American Backgrounds of the American Concept of Academic Freedom, 1500–1914," unpublished doctoral dissertation (University of Missouri, 1950), pp. 41–42.

century. The liberalism of Leiden was severely impaired after the Synod of Dort, when the Arminians were driven out, and it went into eclipse after 1676, when a professor was expelled for espousing Cartesianism.[167] Helmstedt, founded at about the same time as Leiden in the domains of the dukes of Brunswick-Wolfenbüttel, primarily to propagate Lutheran orthodoxy, nonetheless enjoyed at the end of the century a modest reputation for freedom, and retained the services of the liberal theologian Calixtus. That it was, however, far advanced on the path to liberalism later taken by the German universities is dubious.[168]

In England the Reformation was an act of state that began with the humbling of the universities. Henry VIII extracted favorable judgments on his divorce by employing threats against the universities, and followed his initial victory with the sweeping Royal Injunctions of 1535. These injunctions, which involved political interference beyond anything the universities had experienced, called for an oath of loyalty, set some of the conditions of lecturing, threw out the *Sentences* of Peter Lombard and required that all divinity lectures be given directly on the Scriptures, proscribed the "frivolous questions and obscure glosses" of Duns Scotus and his followers, and banned the study of the canon law.[169] It has been said that when the king's commissioners at Oxford found the torn leaves of Scotus' works driven by the wind through the quadrant of New College they were witnessing the final downfall of scholasticism in England. Like most attempts to draw sharp lines in intellectual history, this is an exaggeration; but what is true is that the divorce question and the Royal Injunctions put an end to whatever was left of the insulation and repose of the university scholars. From the time of the Lutheran controversy, when the early Protestant sympathizers at Cambridge had held secret meetings,[170] to beyond the middle of the seventeenth century, controversial theology was the most vital interest of university men and the story of university life was so intimately interwoven with the development of the English Reformation that the history of academic controversy is al-

[167] On Leiden see *ibid.*, pp. 42 ff., and Harrison, *Arminianism*, and *The Beginnings of Arminianism*.

[168] Sutton, "European and American Backgrounds," pp. 50 ff.

[169] See the account of the Reformation in Mullinger, *The University of Cambridge . . . to the Royal Injunctions of 1535*, Chap. VI, and for the injunctions see pp. 629–32.

[170] The Cambridge scholars who were infected with Lutheranism, many through smuggled books, met outside the colleges in the White Horse Inn, where it was felt they would be safer. On this episode see Mullinger, *ibid.*

most identical with that of the Reformation itself. During the religious upheavals of the Tudor era the men of the universities who did not conform to the reigning orthodoxy enjoyed no more immunity or peace than other dissenters or other clerics. They found themselves in a world of harassments, visitations, enforced confessional oaths, and burnings. Under Edward VI a vigorous and oppressive visitation took place that led to the exodus of many Romanist divines, while under the Marian reaction the leading Protestants left in large numbers and the universities became theaters and even agencies of the latest persecutions. Still another wave of exiles, now Catholics, left with the coming of Elizabeth, and at the beginning of the Elizabethan era the universities reached one of their low points.

With the growing moderation of the Elizabethan age and the return to the universities of many of the Marian exiles who had been in Holland or Switzerland, Calvinism took firm root among the theologians of the church, and in its wake came the Puritan breed. While Oxford, although not without its Puritans, became the stronghold of episcopacy, Cambridge was significantly infiltrated by the theologians of the Puritan party. Thomas Cartwright, the intellectual leader of the growing Puritan party, held forth at Cambridge for a few years, but for his doctrine of church government was removed from his professorship in 1571 over the opposition of the majority of the younger masters of arts. This action was supplemented by the imposition upon the university of a number of statutes that effected a constitutional reorganization, weakening the university organization in favor of the colleges and replacing the liberal and broadly representative mode of government by an oligarchy.[171] Many Puritans, among them Walter Travers and William Ames (whose theology was to be so influential in New England), sought safety in exile. Ames went from Christ's College to the University of Franeker, where as professor of theology he had a broad influence upon European Protestantism.[172] Still Puritanism was not rooted out of Cambridge. In 1584 Sir Walter Mildmay, Chancellor of the Exchequer and Elizabeth's trusted adviser, established Emmanuel College as a training ground for the ministry. His sympathy for the Puritans was quite properly suspected;[173] the college

[171] On Cartwright and the Elizabethan statutes see James B. Mullinger, *The University of Cambridge from the Royal Injunctions of 1535 to the Accession of Charles I* (Cambridge, 1884), pp. 207–41.

[172] *Ibid.*, pp. 510–12.

[173] "I hear, Sir Walter, you have been erecting a Puritan foundation," said

became a center of Puritan thought, and incidentally the primary nursery of the learned minds of New England.[174] By 1596, when a controversy raged between Calvinists and Arminians, the Calvinists at Cambridge were strong enough to oust from his post as Lady Margaret Professor of Theology an Arminian opponent, Peter Baro, who had offended them in one of his sermons.[175] As yet no quarter was given by either side in academic controversies, and no broadly accepted sanctions existed to prevent opposing sides from using naked power as a means of settling disputes. The theological disputants of the late sixteenth and early seventeenth centuries felt that the points at issue were far too grave to leave much room for the pale decencies of intellectual freedom. But some freedom did survive,[176] not because men believed as yet that the universities ought to be committed to it, but because so many and so complex and rapid changes had taken place in the religious life of England that there was persistent doctrinal uncertainty. Moreover it was the good fortune of the English that their bitterest conflicts arose not so much over broad theological issues as over questions of church government and liturgy, and men who were ready to conform on the latter could often find some intellectual elbow room for the former.

The end of the Catholic threat, however, only freed the Puritan and episcopal factions in the English church for a fuller expression of their mutual animosity, and as the breach widened the position of the Puritans became increasingly difficult. Under James I an oath of loyalty to the episcopal form of church government and the liturgical practices of the Church of England was imposed on all candidates for university degrees, confirming a requirement of the Act of Supremacy (1559) and fixing upon the conscience of the universities a blight that was not satisfactorily removed until 1871.[177] Now earnest Puritans could no longer complete a course of university studies. In 1628 all disputations on the Thirty-nine

---

Elizabeth. "No, Madam," was the answer, "far be it from me to countenance any thing contrary to your established laws, but I have set an acorn, which when it becomes an oak, God alone knows what will be the fruit thereof." *Ibid.*, p. 312; cf. pp. 310–14.

[174] On Emmanuel College and Harvard see Samuel Eliot Morison, *The Founding of Harvard College* (Cambridge, 1935), Chap. VI.

[175] Mullinger, *The University of Cambridge . . . to the Accession of Charles I*, pp. 347–50.

[176] See Mallet, *History of Oxford*, II, 89, on the views of contemporaries.

[177] The governing ideal was succinctly stated in the royal letter to the Chancellors: "The universities are the nurseries of learning and should be free from all factions." Mullinger, *The University of Cambridge . . . to the Accession of Charles I*, p. 457.

Articles of the Church of England were forbidden at either university, thus curtailing discussion of many of the matters that were most central in university intellectual life. Archbishop Laud's intensified campaign against the Puritans brought him to look closely into the orthodoxy of his own Oxford and stamp out the remnants of Puritanism there. As chancellor of the university after 1629, Laud patronized it liberally with one hand while doing his best to suppress its remaining freedoms with the other. He enriched it with benefactions, adorned it with buildings, and at the same time assured that it would be "the headquarters of the Arminian faith in England, an institution of orthodoxy, decorous, disciplined, and correct." [178] From its vice-chancellor he required a detailed weekly report of its discipline and doctrine, for there was hardly a matter so small as to be beneath his notice. In the Laudian Statutes, confirmed in 1636, the life of the university was codified and its government and conduct minutely prescribed; a measure of oligarchy was introduced such as the Elizabethan statutes had brought to Cambridge.

Such, in barest outline, was the state of the English universities in relation to the problem of religious freedom at the time of the founding of Harvard and the beginnings of collegiate education in America. The impact on America of later English developments may be seen from the colonial point of view in Chapter II, but one further development in English education may be anticipated here—the emergence of the dissenting academies. With the Restoration and the Act of Uniformity (1662) about a fifth of the divines of England who would not conform were ejected from their pastoral or academic positions (among them, it may now be noted, twelve who had been educated at Harvard and had returned to England during the Commonwealth or Protectorate). The university men among them set about to build new lives for themselves tutoring the sons of the dissenting nobility and gentry and educating the nonconformist ministers of the future. Out of these activities emerged a series of remarkable educational institutions whose value to subsequent English education, especially during the palsied days of the universities, was profound, and whose influence on American collegiate education was far from negligible.[179]

[178] H. R. Trevor-Roper, *Archbishop Laud* (London, 1940), p. 116; for Laud's chancellorship see also Chap. VIII and Mallet, *History of Oxford,* Vol. II, Chap. XVII.

[179] Irene Parker, *Dissenting Academies in England* (Cambridge, 1914), and H. McLachlan, *English Education under the Test Acts* (Manchester, 1931), are in-

From the Restoration to the beginning of the nineteenth century the academies employed the best educational energies in England. At first staffed each by a single tutor, and only afterwards by larger faculties, they grew and prospered and multiplied, and passed from an early phase of suppression by the authorities into one of recognized public existence. Their student bodies, at first composed of the sons of clerics and others primarily interested in religious issues, expanded to include a large middle-class public and even many children of conforming Anglicans. Their moral regimen and academic standards were higher, their fees lower, than the universities, and they offered work of university grade. Soon they were competitors sufficiently formidable to provoke agitation by the universities for their complete suppression. As for their course of studies, their original founders were too well versed in the classical studies to abandon them, but as one might expect of dissenters, were somewhat more hospitable than the universities to scientific and practical learning, so that the curricula of the academies combined classicism with a not excessive dash of utilitarian flavor.[180] Studies suited to budding clerics were in time somewhat subordinated to those suited to the budding middle class of England. In these institutions were educated such men as Daniel Defoe, Bishop Joseph Butler, the dissenting educator Philip Doddridge, Joseph Priestley, the Reverend Thomas R. Malthus, William Hazlitt, and James Martineau, among a distinguished list of leaders in politics, learning, and business. Students in some of the academies during their heyday were treated to a measure of liberality in thought and pedagogical practice that would have been altogether unfamiliar in the universities.[181] Locke was widely read among them at a time when the *Essay*

formative on these institutions, and their American impact is discussed by T. J. Wertenbaker, *Princeton: 1746–1896* (Princeton, 1946), pp. 81–89. See also Eugene D. Owen, "Where Did Benjamin Franklin Get the Idea for His Academy?" *Pennsylvania Magazine of History and Biography,* LVIII (1934), 86–94.

[180] Students of the history of the curriculum will be interested in comparing the early eighteenth-century course of studies at Yale or Harvard with that taught, say, at Sheriffhales Academy. See Parker, *Dissenting Academies in England,* p. 70, McLachlan, *English Education under the Test Acts,* p. 46.

[181] Priestley, who went to Northampton Academy, recalled: "In my time the Academy was in a state peculiarly favourable to the serious pursuit of truth, as the students were about equally divided upon every question of much importance, such as liberty and necessity, the sleep of the soul, and all the articles of theological orthodoxy and heresy; in consequence of which, all these topics were the subject of continual discussion. Our tutors also were of different opinions; Dr. Ashworth taking the orthodox side of every question and Mr. Clark, the sub-tutor, that of heresy, although always with the greatest modesty. Our lectures had often the air

concerning Human Understanding was forbidden at Oxford, and much of their work was carried on in a spirit of modified rationalism and modified Puritanism.[182] From them and their graduates, as from that solid middle-class England that they so capably served, there came to America during the early eighteenth century an unmeasured stream of influence and example which could hardly have been other than liberalizing and which must in some degree have been responsible for the notable gains of American education during the earliest years of the American Enlightenment.

By the early eighteenth century, when collegiate education in America was just beginning to proliferate outside the limits of Cambridge, Massachusetts, the European universities were still largely bound by confessional requirements. At the peak, judged by standards of freedom, was such an interdenominational institution as Leiden, which in its hour of glory stood almost alone. On the Continent, where the Reformation had made its mark, the scholar could free himself from the limits of the confessional university only by migrating to the region where the religion of his choice was enforced (by 1648 the formula *cuius regio* had been extended to include Calvinists as well as Lutherans and Catholics). In England the nonconformists could leave or ignore the universities and teach in the dissenting academies. By and large, one could not exchange views and freely discuss fundamental confessional matters within the walls of a single institution, although there were a number of extrafundamental matters that one might safely exercise one's mind upon. On the margins of theology there was a greater and growing freedom for philosophical speculation, insofar as the principle of *libertas philosophandi* was winning recognition.

---

of friendly conversations on the subjects to which they related. We were permitted to ask whatever questions and to make whatever remarks we pleased, and we did it with the greatest, but without any offensive, freedom. The general plan of our studies which may be seen in Dr. Doddridge's published lectures was exceedingly favourable to free inquiry, as we were referred to authors on both sides of every question, and even required to give an account of them." Parker, *Dissenting Academies in England,* p. 103.

[182] At the close of the eighteenth century these academies turned toward the work of propagating the principles of particular nonconformist bodies and away from the task of offering the best possible liberal education with the result that they lost much of their special distinction. Parker, *Dissenting Academies in England,* pp. 123, 136.

II: HARVARD COLLEGE FROM DUNSTER TO LEVERETT

THE COLONY AND THE COLLEGE

The early New England Puritans were a determined people whose religion was a stern school for the discipline of character. They had been able to take up their abode in a wilderness because they had the strength to risk all the uncertainties of the New World in order to realize religious principles. In this they were sustained by the belief that it was not their own wills but the will of God that had sent them to the American strand. They were picked, as Cotton Mather later asserted, "by no human contrivance, but by a strange work of God upon the spirits of men" that inspired them "to secede into a wilderness, they knew not where, and suffer in that wilderness they knew not what." [1]

If they were a chosen people—if God had sifted a whole nation to send choice grain into the wilds of North America—it must be for some high and significant purpose, they thought, and the Puritans believed that they well understood what that purpose was. They were here to demonstrate to all England, indeed to all Europe, that their ideals of religion and church policy were sound. They were here to found, under the auspicious conditions provided by a virgin continent, a Holy Commonwealth in which Puritan ideals could be sustained and realized as it was obviously impossible to do in England during the time of Archbishop Laud. They were to establish a community that would make them the vanguard of international Protestantism.

The Puritans saw themselves in a special relation to God which involved special privileges and obligations. Since they were doing God's work, it was only to be expected that particularly powerful efforts would be made by satanic forces to undermine them. They were prepared to make the strenuous efforts necessary to guarantee that the Holy Com-

[1] Cotton Mather, *Magnalia Christi Americana* (1702; Hartford, Conn., 1820), II, 219.

monwealth would not be subverted either from without, whether it be by pagan Indians or mad Quakers, or from within by the defection of some of their own breed. Under the stress of their holy task and their singular problems, it was hardly to be expected that they would be a tolerant people. True, they had been persecuted themselves,[2] and they did not embrace the idea of persecution without qualifications. They had simply withdrawn, they felt, to form their own society in the wilderness, and they had not invited or compelled men of other faiths who did not share their vision of the Holy Commonwealth to come with them to Massachusetts Bay. Baptists, Quakers, Antinomians, and other heretics could find places for themselves elsewhere in the wilderness—there was room enough. The characteristic Puritan punishment for heresy was banishment, and when they resorted to the more drastic expedient of hangings, as they did in the case of some Quakers in 1659 and 1660, it was after the victims, warned and banished, had returned to provoke them with their agitations.

Not surprisingly the Puritans held to the classic views concerning toleration and heresy. As Nathaniel Ward put it in his *Simple Cobbler of Aggawam,* anyone who was willing to tolerate the active propagation of a religion other than his own was simply not sincere in it. A state that would give liberty of conscience in matters of religion might just as well give liberty of conscience in its moral laws. Experience would teach Christians that it was far better to live in a united, if somewhat corrupt, state than in a state "whereof some Part is Incorrupt, and all the rest divided." One might (as the Puritans did) close one's eyes for convenience to the deviations of some citizens who did not openly challenge the established way, but one could not in any case concede their right openly to divide the conscience of the community.[3] Most of the Puritans seem to have accepted the distinction between fundamental points of doctrine, meaning those without which man cannot be saved, and others which were merely circumstantial points, on which men might differ in judgment

---

[2] The frequency of this experience among the first generation is attested by the biographies and family stories of the early presidents of Harvard. Henry Dunster seems to have left England because of his nonconformist principles. Charles Chauncy had been twice imprisoned for his opposition to Laud's regulations. Leonard Hoar had been silenced by the Act of Uniformity and had given up his ministry in Hants. Increase Mather, the first American-born president, was the son of Richard Mather, who had been suspended from his ministry in Lancashire.

[3] Perry Miller and Thomas H. Johnson, *The Puritans* (New York, 1938), pp. 227–32.

without prejudice to the salvation of either side.[4] In his famous argument with Roger Williams, John Cotton shrank from the accusation of persecution for conscience. It was not lawful, he said, to persecute anyone "for Conscience sake Rightly informed." But "for an Erronious and blind Conscience," once the apostolically enjoined double admonition (Titus 3:10) had been given, it was legitimate to proceed against the heretic; for, after all, in fundamental points the word of God was so clear that the heretic could not help but be convinced of the error of his ways after one or two admonitions, and hence any further persistence on his part was not really out of conscience but actually *against* his own conscience. Thus it was never for true conscience but only for sinning against his conscience that a man was persecuted.[5]

Those among the Puritan tribe who persisted in heresy—in the willful choice, that is, of false doctrine—must be prepared after due warning and argument to accept banishment if they would not stop uttering their beliefs. Those from outside, who like the Quakers tried to impose themselves upon the community, faced something worse than banishment. As a relatively homogeneous group that had not yet to reckon with the problem of a diversity of active faiths, the American Puritans were much firmer in their resistance to the idea of toleration than were their English counterparts. The English Independents had among them so many sects of various kinds that mutual toleration was a practical necessity if they were to hold together as a political party. The American Puritans saw this tolerance as a lamentable softness in their English friends. They felt as though they had been cut off from their roots and that they stood alone in their singleminded pursuit of God's way, for they had hoped that English Independency, which looked up to the writings of such New England intellectuals as Cotton, Hooker, and Shepard, would be the instrument through which their own success in God's work would be broadcast first to England and then to Europe. Thus while a liberal Independent like Milton was writing the *Areopagitica* his brethren in the New

---

[4] See John Cotton, "The Answer of Mr. John Cotton . . ." *ibid.,* pp. 217–18. An election sermon delivered by Urian Oakes in 1673 indicates the extent to which the more liberal New England Puritans might go. Compassion should be shown for the infirmities of men's minds, he said, and it was the duty of the magistrate to tolerate some errors, notably those that were "extrafundamental," small, or inconsiderable, and maintained in a "modest and peaceable" manner. Much depended also upon "the Condition of the State. . . . Hence that may be tolerable in one State, that is not in another." John L. Sibley, *Biographical Sketches of Graduates of Harvard University* (8 vols.; Cambridge, Mass., 1873–1951), I, 175–77.

[5] Miller and Johnson, *The Puritans*, p. 218.

World were determining to continue in their ways. The English Independents, on their side, were in fact embarrassed by having the New Englanders thrown in their faces when they advocated toleration. As George Downing, the former Harvard tutor, wrote in 1645 from England to his cousin, John Winthrop, Jr., "the law of banishing for conscience . . . makes us stinke every wheare." [6]

It may seem at first blush a startling paradox that Harvard College, founded in a community so dedicated to the enforcement of religious unity, should have become the university that for three centuries held the leading position for liberality of thought in American higher education. The historical developments that produced this paradox give the early history of Harvard a special significance for our story; for the seeds of Harvard liberalism were actually planted with Puritanism itself, and they sprouted not long after the first generation of American Puritans had passed on to their rewards.

Unquestionably Harvard was meant to be the orthodox instrument of the community and its faith. At the time of Harvard's founding there was a common anxious concern for the preservation of sound teaching. Boston had just been rocked by the antinomian controversy precipitated by Anne Hutchinson and her followers, a controversy perhaps most significant, so far as the difficulties of maintaining orthodoxy were concerned, for the fact that in its turbulent course Master John Cotton, one of the most authoritative expositors of the New England Way, narrowly escaped being disastrously involved. While many modern students will find in the Hutchinson movement a healthy note of religious individualism, it must be understood that to the Puritans Anne Hutchinson's teachings not only implied religious and social anarchy but were identified with a kind of popular anti-intellectualism.[7] At least three Puritan historians recorded that one of the reasons for the choice of Cambridge (first known as Newtown) for the site of the college was the fact that its pastor, Thomas Shepard, a preacher of great authority, influence, and appeal to the young, had succeeded in keeping Newtown "spotless from the contagion of the opinions" that had disturbed the people of Boston.[8]

But if Harvard was to be a center of orthodoxy, it was also to be the

[6] Quoted by Samuel Eliot Morison, *Builders of the Bay Colony* (Boston, 1930), p. 249.

[7] Samuel Eliot Morison, *The Founding of Harvard College* (Cambridge, Mass., 1935), Chap. XIII, esp. pp. 175–76.

[8] *Ibid.*, pp. 182–83.

home of a learned and rational ministry. Probably in greater measure than any other Protestant group the Puritans inherited the scholastic impulse to rationalize faith and the belief that learning has a high and vital place in religion. Puritan services emphasized neither ranting exercises in emotionalism nor the repetition of an esthetically appealing ritual, but rational discourses blending thought, piety, and scholarship. From an early date a strong effort was made to provide a common-school training good enough to produce a literate population that could follow the discourses of the clergymen and read Scripture for itself. There was an extraordinary number of university-educated men among the first generation of Puritans. Before 1646 about a hundred Cambridge men and about one third that number from Oxford emigrated to New England, so that the community in which they settled had one university-trained scholar for every forty or fifty families. From these men, says Professor Morison, were recruited the founders and first governors of Harvard College; from their loins sprang most of the first generation of Harvard students. These university-trained emigrants were the people who founded the intellectual traditions and scholastic standards of New England. They created a public opinion which insisted on sound schooling at whatever cost; and through their own characters and lives they inculcated among a pioneer people a respect for learning.[9] They expected their clergy to realize high standards of scholarship. All but 5 percent of the colonial clergymen of the New England Congregational churches were degree holders.[10] The

[9] Morison, *The Founding of Harvard College,* pp. 40–41; cf. pp. 358–410 for brief personal sketches of this body of educated immigrants. Among them were 100 from Cambridge, 32 from Oxford, 3 from Dublin, 2 each from Leiden and Franeker, and 1 from Padua; 87 held B.A.'s, 63 M.A.'s, 3 B.D.'s, and 1 M.D. In New England these men contributed (counting more than once any who had more than one occupation) 98 ministers, 27 magistrates, deputies, and lawmakers, 15 schoolmasters, 5 businessmen, and 3 physicians. Among the Cambridge colleges, Emmanuel was by far the most conspicuous, contributing 35 men, including John Harvard, John Cotton, and Thomas Hooker. Harvard's first president, Henry Dunster, came from Magdalene, its second, Charles Chauncy, from Trinity. *Ibid.,* pp. 360–62.
[10] Frederick Lewis Weis in *The Colonial Clergy and the Colonial Churches of New England* (Lancaster, Mass., 1936), finds that there were in New England 2,064 colonial clergymen of all denominations, from 1620 to 1776, of which 1,586 were Congregationalists. Figures for all denominations are not provided; but while Baptists and Separatists had clergies of which respectively 89 percent and 81 percent did not hold degrees, 95 percent of the Congregational ministers held degrees. Among the degree-holding clergy of all denominations up to 1776, 57 percent came from Harvard; 26 percent from Yale; 6 percent from Cambridge; 3 percent from Princeton; 2.5 percent from Oxford, and a scattering from other institutions, including not only American colonial colleges but Edinburgh, Glasgow, Dublin, Aberdeen, and Geneva. See the tables, *ibid.,* pp. 15–16.

B.A. degree by itself was not considered a sufficient attainment for a truly learned Congregational minister; the usual candidate for the clergy went on to take his M.A., for which he had to wait three years (not all of which, however, was required to be spent in study). During the seventeenth century Puritan clergymen were commonly addressed as "Master" in England and New England because they had commonly taken the Master's degree.

As early as 1636, when the population of Massachusetts Bay could hardly have been more than 10,000, the Puritans, "dreading to leave an illiterate Ministry to the Churches, when our present Ministers shall lie in the Dust," legally established a college which began instruction two years later. The fact that this fear of an illiterate clergy was the immediate and urgent motive for the founding of the college has led to some disagreement among historians over whether it was intended to be a theological seminary or a divinity school. The question is almost without meaning, for the theological seminary belongs to an age of specialized education of the sort the Puritans did not know. The tradition of liberal learning, as it had come down from the Middle Ages and had been broadened by the Renaissance, was the sole collegiate education they knew— and this was the fare of all students, whether their ultimate vocation was to be clerical or secular. That students planning for secular lives, notably for public leadership, would go to the college was undoubtedly expected, but no one thought that their interests required a different curriculum from those of future clerics. In 1650, when the General Court provided a charter for the college, the training of ministers was not mentioned among the specified purposes: "the advancement of all good literature, artes and Sciences" and "the education of the English and Indian youth of this Country in knowledge: and godliness." [11] Urian Oakes, the fourth president of the college, spoke common sentiments in his election sermon of 1673 when he called for "able instruments to manage church and state affairs" and to maintain "our civil and ecclesiastical state . . . in good plight and condition." [12] It is not surprising, then, to learn that during the seventeenth century only a little over 40 percent of all Harvard's students and about 52 percent of her graduates became ministers.

[11] See Morison, *The Founding of Harvard College,* pp. 247–51, on the early statements of the objects of the college. For an interesting defense of liberal education for ministers, see President Charles Chauncy's commencement sermon of 1655, as extracted in Miller and Johnson, *The Puritans,* pp. 705–7.

[12] Quoted in T. J. Wertenbaker, *The Puritan Oligarchy* (New York, 1947), p. 140.

Harvard may actually be considered less ecclesiastical than Oxford or Cambridge, in the sense that a smaller proportion of her students became clergymen.[13] It may be a just summation to say that while Harvard's purposes were not conceived to be secular—since nothing was entirely secular in a Holy Commonwealth—they were not entirely ecclesiastical. It was also implicitly understood that the teaching in the college would be committed to the doctrinal orthodoxy of the New England Congregational Way; and if no formal tests or oaths of conformity were imposed, it was not because conformity was not expected but because the community was at the beginning so homogeneous in religious conviction that such requirements were felt to be superfluous.

One of the primary problems in founding and maintaining the college was to secure a satisfactory president. From the beginning the presidency of Harvard College was intended to be a post of no mean status in New England, equal at least to the outstanding ministerial offices of the province. The president must be a learned clergyman, with a capacity for leadership. What made it difficult to meet these requirements was that the outstanding pastors were unable to get releases from their congregations; and when one considers the uncertainty of the college's finances it seems doubtful that many were willing to try. It became necessary to look to newly arrived young Masters, who came without congregational assignments, as was the case with the college's first "Master," the scapegrace Nathaniel Eaton, and its first president, Henry Dunster; or to find an eminent pastor who happened to be ready to move, like Charles Chauncy, the second president. The salaries paid by the poorly financed college were never alluring. The complaints of the presidents about their personal poverty and that of the college are a *leitmotif* of its early history. On the whole it must be said that after their original mistake with Master Eaton the Overseers did well. Six presidents were appointed during the seventeenth century, and four of these—Henry Dunster, Charles Chauncy, Urian Oakes, and Increase Mather—were notable men. The three admin-

---

[13] Morison, *The Founding of Harvard College,* pp. 247, 247–48n. Not only did students pass from the college into a wide variety of occupations, but their social recruitment itself was fairly wide. The sons of ministers and magistrates loom very large at first, but shortly after the middle of the century there is a notable increase in the proportion of sons of artisans, tradesmen, and modest farmers. The college from an early date in its history was an agency of social mobility in a society that seems on the whole rather stratified. See Morison, *Harvard College in the Seventeenth Century* (Cambridge, Mass., 1936), I, 74–75 and II, 450–51 for figures on the student body.

istrations of Dunster, Chauncy, and Mather covered forty-eight years, the greater part of Harvard's history before 1700.

The early Harvard presidents, like other American college presidents for more than two centuries afterwards, were not only administrative but teaching officers. For more than a hundred years, however, the primary teaching personnel at Harvard consisted of two or three young men designated as tutors. It was not until 1722 that the college had a professor, not until after 1720 that it had as many as four tutors in service at one time. Unmarried men in their early twenties, residents of the college hall who supervised the lives as well as the studies of undergraduates, the tutors were usually future clergymen waiting and studying for the required three post-baccalaureate years for their M.A. degrees. Normally they resigned their tutorships as soon as a ministerial call came to them, since their teaching careers were in their own minds no more than a way of marking time. Until near the end of the seventeenth century a tutor's pay was not sufficient to constitute an inducement to remain in the post. Tenures were brief. Henry Dunster complained in 1653 that tutors came and went at such a rate that "ever and anon all the work committed to them falleth agen on my shoulders." [14] Under his successor the average length of service was only two and a half years, and until the long absentee presidency of Increase Mather when the outstanding tutors, John Leverett and William Brattle, stayed for twelve years, a three-year tutorship was most typical. Thereafter the span of a tutor's teaching life began to lengthen. The average tenure of eighteen tutors hired from 1697 to 1742 comes to almost nine and a half years.[15]

[14] Morison, The Founding of Harvard College, p. 449.

[15] These calculations omit the unusually long and devoted career of the famous "Father" Flynt, which would distort the average. Henry Flynt, whose tutorship stretched from 1699 to 1742, was the son of a Dorchester minister. After receiving his Harvard M.A. he was invited to preach at Norwich, Connecticut, in 1695, but having discovered that he did not like preaching, he returned to Harvard a few years later to begin the career that won him the affections of generations of students. In 1718 he declined the rectorship of Yale. It is from his teaching that Shipton dates the end of the rapid succession of transient tutors that had been customary. Clifford K. Shipton, Sibley's Harvard Graduates (Vols. IV–VIII of John L. Sibley, Biographical Sketches of Graduates of Harvard University, 8 vols.; Cambridge, Mass., 1873–1951), IV, 163. But it was not until the term of another famous tutor, Thomas Robie (1714–23), that tenures regularly became extended to eight or nine years or more. Robie, like Flynt, tried preaching after graduation, but was accused of unorthodoxy because of his liking for the works of Tillotson. He turned to science, became skilled in meteorology and astronomy, and was admitted to the Royal Society. Ibid., V, 452. Toward the close of the seventeenth and the beginning of the eighteenth century one finds a larger proportion of ex-tutors going into secular occupations,

The fugitive teaching careers of these early tutors is a matter of much moment for the history of American education. Since there were greater inducements in the ministry for learned young men, it was impossible to staff the college with anything but transient teachers, whose interest in the college and in teaching was secondary. Such teachers could hardly play a role of importance in the government of the college, nor were they likely to raise issues of intellectual or religious freedom. (If they had any deviations they were attached to, they were well advised to postpone airing them until they had established themselves in the affections and confidence of some congregation.) The early history of Harvard is silent as to matters bearing on the freedom of these young instructors,[16] and it is not until the period of the Great Awakening that a clear case arises among them. The only figure of importance among the instructional officers was the president himself. Here the record has something to tell, for controversies over intellectual freedom in American collegiate education begin with the first president of the first college, Henry Dunster.

THE DUNSTER CASE

In June, 1654, eighteen years after the enactment that created Harvard, its president, Henry Dunster, was obliged to present his resignation to the Overseers. Although the event naturally bears only the remotest resemblance to a modern academic freedom case, it was the first instance in American history in which a college official's tenure in his post was broken by a conflict between his personal beliefs and the established opinion of the community.

---

chiefly into public service. One also finds a significant number of men who, like Flynt and Robie, studied for and momentarily entered the ministry but gave it up out of incapacity or lack of enthusiasm. By contemporaries this might well have been taken as a sign of the times.

[16] The only stir in the college before the days of Increase Mather in which tutors were involved seems to have had little to do with religious or intellectual differences. President Hoar was forced to resign in 1675 under circumstances the precise causes of which were a mystery to contemporaries and remain one to historians. They seem to have involved personal issues. Hoar, it appears, alienated both students and tutors (who may have been whipped up against him by his successor, Urian Oakes, pastor of the church in Cambridge and evidently an aspirant to the presidency). Hoar was supported by the Overseers, magistrates, and ministers, but when the entire student body deserted the college after the commencement exercises of 1674, his resignation became necessary. The case suggests, at least, that a president could not hold the college together, much less carry on with constructive

It is by a technicality, or perhaps by default, that Dunster can be called Harvard's first president. His regime was preceded by that of Nathaniel Eaton, designated "Master" rather than "President," whose brief steward-ship had been cut short by his own mismanagement and brutality and by the slovenliness of his wife, who boarded the students. Eaton was dis-missed by the magistrates of the province at the end of his first year. Harvard had been closed for the academic year 1639–40, its existence little more than a legal fiction after this abortive beginning, when the newly arrived young minister Henry Dunster, a graduate of Magdalene College, Cambridge, took charge of its fortunes. During the fourteen years of his administration, Dunster did well for the young institution. Working with meager funds, he established the curriculum and the insti-tutional forms of the college, obtained its charter in 1650, and brought it to such repute that its students, who numbered upwards of fifty, included boys sent from Bermuda, Virginia, New Amsterdam, and even from Eng-land, where Oxford and Cambridge accepted its degrees, *ad eundem gradem.* "No American college president," writes Samuel Eliot Morison, ". . . has succeeded in doing so much with so little money." [17]

In 1653, when income reached a low point, Dunster appealed to the General Court for more ample funds for the coming academic year. The Court replied with an irritating financial investigation which seemed to cast his probity or competence into question; whereupon he sent the com-mittee of inquiry a long memorandum rehearsing the various grievances that he had developed during his presidency. The investigation caused the Court to grant the Overseers some new financial prerogatives, which Dunster found "questionable and offensive." It may be that his difficulties with the Overseers weakened Dunster's attachment to his post and subtly prepared his mind for the espousal of a heresy that would be as irritating to the authorities as their intrusions had been to him. This is conjec-ture; what is undeniable is that Dunster, who had hitherto shown no signs of heresy and whose first three children had been baptized in the Cam-bridge Church, refused to present for baptism his fourth child, born in

---

plans of the sort Hoar had, if he did not enjoy some respect and confidence among tutors and students. For an account of the incident see Morison, *Harvard College in the Seventeenth Century,* II, 401–8.

[17] Morison, *Harvard College in the Seventeenth Century,* I, 38; for the most satisfactory account of the financial investigation of 1653–54 and the Dunster case, see pp. 302–19; see also Jeremiah Chaplin, *Life of Henry Dunster* (Boston, 1872), Chaps. IX–XIII.

the fall of 1653 just at the time when the General Court's unfavorable reaction to his petition was beginning to rankle. The community was soon excited by the sensational news that the president of Harvard College had become entangled, as Cotton Mather later wrote, in "the snares of Anabaptism." [18]

In denying the scriptural validity of infant baptism, Dunster was touching upon a sore issue. For some years the colony had been agitated over serious questions concerning who should be eligible for baptism and who could be members of the church. These questions, which as we shall see were not resolved until the Half-Way Covenant of 1662, went straight to the heart of the New England Church polity. The prevailing view was that while Scriptural evidence for the baptism of infants left something to be desired, the practice seemed to be a logical deduction from Scripture and from the necessities of Puritan institutions. Moreover, opposition to infant baptism was associated in the Puritans' minds with the Anabaptists, with "enthusiasm," with currents of religious feeling that they heartily detested.[19] In arriving at the conviction that no infants could properly be baptized, Dunster came to a conclusion that was considered dangerous and altogether unacceptable, but he came to it not as an Anabaptist or enthusiast but as a misguided member of the Congregational community who stumbled into an error in the course of contemplating the community's own problems. This fact alone makes intelligible some of the gentler aspects of the controversy in which he became involved.

When one compares it with the rancorous and cruel banishment of Anne Hutchinson and the banishment of Roger Williams, and the imprisonment and whippings that had already been administered to Baptists and the brutal treatment and final execution of Quakers that was to come a few years later, the treatment accorded Dunster seems considerate. The magistrates arranged in Boston a private debate, or "conference," after the fashion of the formal disputation, between Dunster and several champions of orthodoxy; this only had the effect of hardening the president in his heretical ways. A few months later the General Court, observing that "it greatly concernes the welfare of this country that the youth thereof be educated, not only in good literature, but sound doctrine," rec-

---

[18] Cotton Mather, *Magnalia Christi Americana*, II, 10.
[19] See the account of the situation in Perry Miller, *From Colony to Province* (Cambridge, Mass., 1953), Chap. VI.

ommended to the Overseers and the selectmen of the towns of the province that they refuse to keep as teachers or officers of schools or colleges any persons "that have manifested themselves unsound in the fayth, or scandelous in theire lives, and not giving due satisfaction according to the rules of Christ."

Dunster had not been dismissed, and he could have kept his job if he had promised to be silent about his unacceptable convictions, for everything in the case indicates that the magistrates and ministers never lost personal confidence in him.[20] Dunster, however, submitted a curious letter of resignation which made no clear reference to religious issues but dwelled at some length on the recent investigation of the college and the expansion of the powers of the Overseers at the expense of the Corporation. The General Court gave Dunster the opportunity to take a month to reconsider. Evidently they still hoped that he could be persuaded to swallow his heresy, and it may be inferred that the internal affairs of the college were, in the minds of all concerned, more vital than doctrinal issues. But a month later Dunster closed his presidency with the utmost finality when he interrupted a baptismal service at Cambridge with a startling speech against infant baptism and the "corupcions stealing into the Church."

His subsequent notice to the Overseers that he had not reconsidered was a formality. Accepting his resignation, the Overseers tendered the presidency of the college to Charles Chauncy, a learned pastor at Plymouth. Chauncy was sound on the baptism of infants but he held to a nettlesome deviation in the conduct of the ceremony itself: he believed in baptism by total immersion rather than sprinkling. This was a pardonable practice in doctrine, but, as Governor Bradford said, it was "not so conveniente in this could countrie"; and it threatened to have more bearing on infant mortality than infant immortality. Chauncy accepted the presidency with the condition attached that he remain severely silent on the alleged necessity of immersion, and on another of his peculiarities, his belief that the Lord's Supper could properly be celebrated only at evening.

[20] The extent to which Dunster had been esteemed is suggested in an earlier letter to John Winthrop from the Rev. Thomas Shepard, the trusted pastor of the church at Cambridge, in which he observed: "Your apprehensions agaynst reading and learning heathen authors, I perswade myselfe were suddenly suggested, and will easily be answered by H. Dunstar, if you should impart them to him." Chaplin, *Life of Henry Dunster,* p. 48.

As for Dunster, he continued to enjoy consideration at the hands of the Overseers; he was permitted to remain in the president's house for several months after his resignation took effect. But the county court at Cambridge found him guilty of having interrupted the baptismal service, for which he was publicly admonished. A few years later a debt of £40 that he owed to the Colony was forgiven by the General Court "as a gratuity for his good service" to the college. Dunster removed to the town of Scituate in Plymouth Colony which was hospitable to dissenters and where he seems to have found opportunities to preach. He often visited Massachusetts Bay, remained a member of the Cambridge Church, and in 1659 died, as Cotton Mather put it, "in such harmony of affection with the good men, who had been the authors of his removal from Cambridge, that he, by his will, ordered his body to be carried unto Cambridge for its burial, and bequeathed legacies to those very persons." [21]

Plainly the case of Henry Dunster was a gentlemen's disagreement. The offender was treated not as a subversive outsider but as a member of the inner elite who happened to fall out of line on one item of doctrine but whose discretion could still be trusted, even after all attempts at persuasion had failed.[22] His own mild acquiescence to the code that compelled his resignation is also illuminating, especially since it contrasts so sharply with his strong assertion of his views and rights both in matters of college policy and theological doctrine. Plainly he felt himself to be doctrinally on solid ground; but even to him, the victim of expulsion, there seems to have existed no sanction in the form of a code of educational or intellectual decorum to which he could appeal to justify his remaining in the presidency while publicly proclaiming an unpopular tenet. He did not say that he had, as the college's president, a right to his opinion; he could only stoutly maintain that his opinion was right. As a trusted and familiar figure in the community he was given a chance to argue for this opinion with other learned clergymen, although it must have been a foregone conclusion that he would not convince them.[23] The concept

[21] See Mather's account of Dunster in *Magnalia Christi Americana,* I, 367; the will is in Chaplin, *Life of Henry Dunster,* pp. 303–8.

[22] The Puritans made a distinction between the Baptists themselves, who were totally objectionable, and members of their own group who happened to oppose only their baptismal practices. Cf. Kenneth Murdock, *Increase Mather* (Cambridge, Mass., 1926), pp. 138–39, 142.

[23] The text of Dunster's debate with the orthodox ministers, transcribed evidently with several minor errors, may be found in Chaplin, *Life of Henry Dunster,* pp. 289–301. Of course the purpose of the debate was not to give Dunster a chance to

upon which his tenure at Harvard was based was presumably the same as that upon which the New England clergy held their offices. These men considered themselves engaged in a solemn covenant with their congregations which could be broken on either side only for the gravest reasons. It might well have been felt that accepting the presidency of Harvard College involved an implicit covenant under which the president was to remain loyal to the essential doctrines of the New England Way. Having departed at a significant point from these doctrines, and having failed to persuade New England's doctrinal leaders that his views were correct, it is understandable that Dunster may have thought his resignation obligatory under the terms of his covenant. He never argued that a college is a place in which the search for truth is to be carried on through free inquiry and the exchange of views. He apparently agreed with his opponents that it is a place in which the received truth is to be passed on, and so thinking, he quietly and gracefully accepted his defeat.

THE DECLINE OF THE HOLY COMMONWEALTH

In order to realize the purposes of the Holy Commonwealth the early Puritan leaders had striven to maintain complete unity in Massachusetts Bay, and they had done so with a firmness that ruled out all possibility of articulate dissent. By the 1660s it was clear that against those who would invade their community with an alien vision, whether they were complete outsiders like the Quakers and Baptists or would-be members of their own group like the followers of Anne Hutchinson or Roger Williams, the Puritans had maintained themselves with great success. What they could not do was to remain what they were, to preserve among themselves that unity and conformity which they had expected to retain. The pristine Congregational ideals were so demanding and the Puritan spirit was so dynamic that it proved impossible to freeze the spiritual and doctrinal life of Massachusetts Bay in the eternal pose that the sculptors of the Holy Commonwealth demanded. Plagued by internal differences over church polity and secular politics, and confronted by the besetting problem of relations with an uncongenial government in England, the guardians of the Puritan ideal conducted after 1660 a long strategic retreat. As they

---

persuade the others, but chiefly to give them a chance to persuade him. One of his former students, Jonathan Mitchel, had been swayed for a time by Dunster's views, but finally cast them off as coming from the Devil. Shipton, *Sibley's Harvard Graduates,* I, 148–49.

gradually backed into a policy of growing freedom and toleration, their college passed into the hands of those elements in the community whose liberal tendencies laid the foundations of the Harvard tradition of freedom.

As a chosen people, living under a special covenant with God, the Puritans did not believe that any of their fortunes were attributable to environmental circumstances or accidents. Since they were under the special charge and care of God, everything that befell them, they thought, had a divine meaning, a cosmological significance. If they were subject to an invasion of witches, it was because the Devil had special reason for trying to storm God's own bastion on earth. A pestilence, a famine, an Indian attack, a storm—these were signs of God's disfavor to the group, just as an accident, an illness, a business loss were signs of His disfavor to the individual.[24] It was characteristic, then, for the Puritan conscience to entertain a particularly lively sense of sin under conditions of adversity; for adversity itself was the surest proof to a covenanting people that sin was still within it. The hunger and insecurity of life in a raw wilderness made many occasions for the middle- and lower-middle-class Englishmen who led the Puritan settlements to give thought to the state of their souls. It was the hardness of life that was felt to be consistent with the Puritan temper at its most rigorous.[25]

But it was precisely at this point that the Puritan spirit, as it worked out its destiny in seventeenth-century America, contained the materials of its own destruction. If misfortune went hand in hand with sin, it followed that prosperity was a token of virtue. As the colony grew, as trade flourished and an urban aristocracy arose, the means of sin and luxury were provided. At the same time the very presence of these means seemed to betoken a state of grace that would permit some spiritual relaxation. Even had it been of any use, the Puritan preachers were not free under

[24] In the Puritan conscience the sense of guilt was heightened by adversity, which was interpreted as divine punishment. For vivid personal illustrations, see Murdock, *Increase Mather*, p. 51; Barrett Wendell, *Cotton Mather* (New York, 1891), p. 50.

[25] A view accepted by the author of an early (1630) promotional pamphlet urging settlers to go to New England on the ground, among others, that life was hard there. "If men desire people to degenerate speedily, and to corrupt their minds and bodies too, and besides to tole in theeves and spoilers from abroad, let them seek a rich soil, which brings in much with little labor: but if they desire that Piety and godliness shall prosper accompanied with sobriety, justice, and love, let them choose a Country such as this is—which may yield sufficiency with hard labor and industry." Quoted in Sanford H. Cobb, *The Rise of Religious Liberty in America* (New York, 1902), p. 154.

their own doctrine to rail against the coming of prosperity. God had provided well-being, as He had provided everything else. "Their gain is their godliness," as a current aphorism had it. But it was the surest evidence of human depravity that godliness was not well sustained after gain had been assured. The clergy who clung to the old dispensation found themselves in a merciless dilemma: "[They] could not demand that people stay poor, for their economic opportunities were specifically opened by the providence of God; on the other hand, they could not quietly acquiesce in letting New England go the way of all flesh." [26] As a consequence, the sermons of the New England clergy sounded a constant note of lamentation, heard even as early as the 1640s, which "swelled to an incessant chant within forty years. By 1680 there seems to have been hardly any other theme for discourse, and the pulpits rang from week to week with lengthening jeremiads." [27]

A further difficulty—not unrelated to the first—was that the Puritans had founded the Holy Commonwealth as a sect, and they were now in the process of becoming a church. They had started out with the hopelessly demanding notion that no one could become a member of their churches (and with that a full-fledged citizen, for suffrage ran with church membership) who was not, so far as any human agency could determine, a regenerate soul, a pure saint. Access to the sacraments—which they regarded not as instruments by which a man might be saved but only as instruments by which his Covenant with God could be sealed—was in strictest theory to be reserved for those who were spiritually prepared for them. Adults were considered to be prepared to partake of the Holy Communion only after they had undergone a religious conversion and had given a public account of their experience of regeneration. As for infants, while the Puritan fathers had some difficulties about the validity of baptizing them—it was on this question that Dunster fell—they thought they had Scriptural reason for believing that children could be fairly assumed to inherit, in a sense, the grace of their fathers. Hence, children of church members were eligible for baptism.

A problem arose with the passing of the first generation. Young people were growing to adulthood who had not experienced the persecutions of

---

[26] Perry Miller, *The New England Mind: The Seventeenth Century* (New York, 1939), p. 475.

[27] *Ibid.*, p. 472; for a full treatment of this theme see Chap. XVI, and the same author's *From Colony to Province*, Chaps. I–III. Cf. Herbert Schneider, *The Puritan Mind* (New York, 1930), Chap. III.

the Old World, the passage to the New, the trials of deracination, the hardships of the wilderness—who did not, in brief, share to the full the vision of the Holy Commonwealth or the stern temper that was required to realize it. For such persons, significantly, the rigors of the personal accounting demanded for access to Communion became embarrassing. They might well be willing to accept exclusion from Communion as a consequence, but what of their children? Would they be eligible for baptism? To deny baptism, and hence church membership, to such persons would have meant to have by far the greater part of the community outside the congregations. It would have torn up the fabric of the Holy Commonwealth. To permit baptism would be to make an inconsistent compromise with the original dream of a church of pure saints by filling the churches with presumably unregenerate persons.

After years of debate a compromise was reached at the Synod of 1662 in the Half-Way Covenant: the unregenerate could be half-way members of the churches; their children could be baptized, but neither they nor their children would be eligible for Communion. This was a workable compromise in practice, but it seemed to sacrifice theological consistency to considerations of church polity, and it was roundly opposed by a minority of the parsons and a majority of the laymen.[28] The adoption of the Half-Way Covenant marked the first serious formal departure from the old ways. Not only did it constitute in itself a relaxation from the pristine ideals and practices, but it left issues over which the community continued to be divided. Before very many years had gone by the Reverend Solomon Stoddard, one of the most influential men in the province, established an ecclesiastical empire of his own in the Connecticut Valley in which the practice was adopted of allowing professing Christians to take Communion even when they could not claim that they were in a state of grace. In some respects, notably in his emphasis on the irrational sovereignty of God, Stoddard's theology was more "conservative" than that professed by the clerics of Boston, but he opened the Lord's Supper to the unregenerate on the ground that it could be an instrument of conversion. Over this he waged with Increase Mather a bitter theological

---

[28] In view of the criticisms usually made of the Puritan clergy, it is worth noting that at this point the clergy espoused the "liberal" side of the issue while the laity opposed this extension of baptism. Perry Miller characterizes the opposition to the Half-Way Covenant as "an uprising of the crowd against the majesty of scholastic learning." *From Colony to Province*, p. 105.

battle which was of particular importance because it involved institutional practices as well as abstract issues. The controversy left a rent in the Holy Commonwealth that could not easily be mended.

The controversy over "Stoddardeanism" disturbed a community that was already in difficulties over its relations with the Crown. The Restoration in England had posed serious new problems for the Puritans by making it necessary for them to pretend—as they had not had to pretend under the Commonwealth or the Protectorate—to be something other than what they were. Oddly enough, while English policy after the Restoration was probably if anything less tolerant than that of the Puritans, its pressure on New England worked for toleration there. The Puritans had to walk carefully lest they offend the Crown and put their charter in jeopardy. In 1662 they had a letter from the king confirming the Massachusetts charter but demanding that Anglicans be free to worship, that persons of honest lives not be denied the Lord's Supper, and that religious restrictions on the suffrage be abandoned. These demands they were able to avoid or craftily evade, but only because of easy-going English administration. Again, however, the rent in the Holy Commonwealth was widened by the appearance of a party, chiefly mercantile, that was out of sympathy with efforts to realize the old ideals at the cost of angering the king. "By 1670 the holy society had become like any other society outside the national covenant, sundered into two opinions, not over a basic theological or even ecclesiastical question, but over one of political expediency." [29] Under the threat of external interference and internal disunity the defenders of the old New England Way found themselves unable to maintain the purity and unity of their society. Baptists and Quakers persisted in settling among them, and could not, as in the old days, be driven out. In 1665 a group of Baptists formed a church in Boston and carried on with it in spite of prison sentences.[30] Three years later the General Court sentenced the sect to banishment, but the law was never enforced. Quakers, who had begun in the early 1660s to have meetings in private homes, began to worship more openly in 1674. As early as 1665 a law was passed permitting them to go about their secular business, although it was not until 1697 that they were able to demonstrate

[29] Miller, *From Colony to Province,* p. 128; our account of the various factors in the decline of the Holy Commonwealth draws heavily upon Books I and II of this work.
[30] Cobb, *Rise of Religious Liberty in America,* pp. 228–29.

their acceptance by the construction of a solid brick meetinghouse on Brattle Street.[31]

As the trade of the Northern colonies became more important, and as the Crown became preoccupied with tighter organization for the sharpening imperial struggle with France, maintenance of the long-standing freedom and independence of New England became impossible. In 1684 the charter of the Massachusetts Bay colony was revoked. In 1686 the Dominion of New England was created under the autocratic governorship of Sir Edmund Andros, and the traditional agencies of colony government in Massachusetts were abolished. In the same year the Puritans, to their horror, saw the Old South Church occupied forcibly for the holding of an Anglican service, after which the first Anglican Church, King's Chapel (1688), was built in Boston.[32]

The establishment of the Dominion, catastrophic as it was, was at first accepted by most of the Puritans as a punishment for sin. Before long, however, the combined threat of the Dominion to trade, land titles, the liberties of Englishmen, and the promise of the New England Congregational Way turned almost the entire province bitterly against the Dominion and its governor. Even the pro-English faction fell apart. When the

[31] See Rufus Jones, *The Quakers in the American Colonies* (London, 1911), Chaps. V, VI; R. P. Hallowell, *The Quaker Invasion of Massachusetts* (Boston, 1887); Cobb, *Rise of Religious Liberty in America,* pp. 217 ff.

A high point in the progress of the free conscience in America had been reached in 1657, when a band of English Quaker missionaries was hospitably received at Newport and the commissioners of the other colonies requested their banishment, threatening reprisals if it were not forthcoming. To which the Rhode Islanders replied that they had no law among them by which the Quakers could be punished for exercising freedom of conscience. "And we, moreover, finde, that in those places where these people aforesaid, in this colony, are most of all suffered to declare themselves freely, and are only opposed by arguments in discourse, there they least of all desire to come, and we are informed that they begin to loath this place for that they are not opposed by the civill authority, but with all patience and meekness are suffered to say over their pretended revelations and admonitions, nor are they like or able to gain many here to their way; surely we find that they delight to be persecuted by civill powers, and when they are soe, they are like to gain more adherents by the conseyte of their patient sufferings, than by consent to their pernicious sayings: And yet we conceive, that theire doctrines tend to very absolute cuttinge downe and overturninge relations and civill government among men, if generally received." *Rhode Island Records*, I, 376 ff. In 1702, when Cotton Mather published his *Magnalia Christi Americana,* he accepted the Rhode Island approach to the Quakers. He would not, he said, defend the past persecutions of them. "I am verily perswaded these miserable Quakers would in a little while (as we have come *now* seen) have come to nothing, if the civil magistrate had not inflicted any civil penalty upon them." *Magnalia,* II, 453.

[32] For the early growth of Episcopacy in Boston see Henry W. Foote, *Annals of King's Chapel* (Boston, 1882), Vol. I, Chaps. II–V.

news of the Glorious Revolution reached Massachusetts in 1689 it precipitated a local uprising that effectually dissolved the Dominion government. The newly established rapport with England, however, brought
fresh issues. The Act of Toleration of 1689 seemed to indicate that the
Puritans could be left alone, like other dissenters, with their church system, but they were reluctant to assume the position of an ordinary dissenting sect. The original ideal of the founders had been to purify the
Church of England itself, and they had always professed—although the
profession had grown increasingly hollow—to be still inside that body.
It would be difficult to carry on this pretense and continue with the
exclusion of Anglicans, difficult to live as the beneficiaries of a tolerating
regime without extending to dissenters among themselves a little at least
of the toleration now enjoyed by all Englishmen except papists. Such
toleration was indeed demanded by their own new charter of 1691. Dissenters could no longer be treated as Anne Hutchinson and Roger Williams and the Baptists and Quakers had been treated by the first generation of New Englanders. Thus the proponents of the main line of tradition, for example Increase and Cotton Mather, began during the 1690s
to sing the praises of a measure of toleration that their venerated ancestors would have scorned. Unfortunately, admitted Increase Mather, the
people of New England had been "in some matters relating to Conscience
and difference of opinion . . . more rigid and severe than the primitive
Christians or the Gospel doth allow of." But "tell them," said his son
Cotton, "That New England has Renounced whatever laws are against a
Just Liberty of Conscience." [33] This swing toward a mood of tolerance
may have been, at least in the beginning, an act of expediency more than
a heartfelt change. But, for whatever reason, toleration was being
preached by men who had good right to consider themselves the lineal
inheritors of the ideals of the founding fathers. That the Mathers could
find a good word for toleration was a measure of the distance that the
New Englanders had come. They had paid, perhaps, no more than a reasonable price for the restoration of self-government and the liberties of
Englishmen. But it must be observed that these were *secular* considerations. The Puritans had found themselves in a world too complex for the
simplicities of the Holy Commonwealth, and they had yielded. The
changes were too sweeping to leave their college untouched.

[33] Miller, *From Colony to Province,* pp. 166, 167.

THE EMERGENCE OF HARVARD LIBERALISM

The years from 1684 to 1707 saw the rise within Congregationalism of a "liberal" faction led by William and Thomas Brattle, the Reverend Benjamin Colman, and John Leverett. The struggle between this group and the "conservatives" led by Increase and Cotton Mather culminated, so far as Harvard was concerned, in 1707 when John Leverett was made president of the college. Any historian who wishes to portray this conflict in its full significance for the college runs the risk of exaggerating its significance for the community as a whole or misrepresenting the issues involved. What was at stake was not a matter of theology, for the liberals still considered themselves reasonably good Calvinists and could probably have subscribed to a common confession of faith with the conservatives without any sense of misrepresenting themselves. Moreover, the conservatives were exactly what that word in its better sense implies—they were not totally unenlightened or inflexible reactionaries.[34] The victory of the liberals was neither a revolution nor a *coup d'état;* it can best be compared to what happens in modern American politics when one of our two major parties—both adhering loyally to the same political system and a common set of presuppositions and each containing within itself elements of liberalism and conservatism—ousts the other.

The feud between the liberals and the conservatives thus had rather the quality of a family quarrel than a battle to the death. One cannot overlook the fact that the Mathers, with whatever misgivings, consented to preach when the liberals opened the Brattle Street Church, that Benjamin Colman remained an intimate friend of Cotton Mather and was charged by the aging Increase with the defense of the churches, that he delivered eulogies at the funerals of both the Mathers, and called Increase "a Father to us all." Nor is it desirable to forget the latter-day conversion of the Mathers to toleration, or that "liberal" tendencies in natural philosophy could be found in Increase Mather, and that many students have seen overtones of deism in his son's work *The Christian Philosopher*.[35]

[34] A serious attempt to do justice to the Mathers and to the New England clergy as a whole during the period from 1680 to 1725 that should be read by all students who have been raised, say, on V. L. Parrington's version of the Puritans, is Clifford K. Shipton's "The New England Clergy of the 'Glacial Age,'" *Publications of the Colonial Society of Massachusetts*, XXXII (Boston, 1937), 24–54.

[35] Cf. Shipton: "Both the Mathers were among the theological progressives of their generations, but they lived long enough to be passed by their swiftly moving times, and to have their seventeenth-century religious theatricals become ridiculous

The lines of controversy were vague and shifting, the issues usually more personal and factional than doctrinal. And if intellectual change was as inexorable as it was gradual, it may well be because Puritanism contained within itself some of the materials of the Enlightenment, as is believed by many modern students. Such considerations, at any rate, go far to explain why the very considerable intellectual changes that took place at Harvard between 1680 and 1720 were not symbolized by a single spectacular issue or *cause célèbre,* but by a series of relatively minor incidents and sly maneuvers.

What gave the liberals their significance for the fate of the Holy Commonwealth was not quite so much that they were radically liberal or that they won control of the college, but that they existed at all; for the original dream of the Commonwealth had not contemplated the emergence of parties but the maintenance of unity. It was the signal achievement of the liberals that they brought directly into the heart of Boston and the citadel of ministerial learning the great blessings of diversity and conflict. For Harvard College itself and for New England intellectual life their victory was truly momentous, for it set the institution on a path which it has never deserted and paved the way for a series of cumulative minor victories that established Harvard's place in the vanguard of intellectual liberalism.[36] Harvard began its existence at a time when one theology and one religious group held sway in the colony. By the beginning of the eighteenth century that sect split into two factions and students from both wings attended the college. Even the orthodox faction was taking a broader view of things than it had in earlier days. The college was well advanced in the transition from the Puritan age to the age of the Enlightenment. At Harvard the eighteenth century began, in a sense, with the inauguration of Leverett in 1707. Yet in all this there was no sudden abandonment of the covenant theology, no sudden onslaught against Calvinism. The real departure that was visible at the time of Leverett's succession was not in dogma, but rather in temper and in church prac-

---

in the eyes of younger persons who read the *Spectator* . . .'" "The New England Clergy of the 'Glacial Age,' " p. 30. The character and significance of the difference between the liberals and conservatives in this era is discussed by Miller, *From Colony to Province,* Chap. XXVII.

[36] This is not to deny that Harvard had always been more liberal than the mean average of the Puritan community itself. For some eloquent remarks on the place of Harvard in Puritan liberalism see Clifford K. Shipton, "Puritanism and Modern Democracy," *New England Historical and Genealogical Register,* CI (July, 1947), 87–88.

tice. The new group did not at once drop the old tenets of the Congregational Way, but they did neglect conspicuously to show the full rigor of the pristine Puritans. Emotionally they relaxed. The liberals flourished among the wealthy, leisured, and aristocratic elements in the province, while the appeal of the conservatives was somewhat stronger in the villages where the old conditions were still more in evidence and folkish piety held its own. The liberals associated on terms of ease with the Anglicans in the province and began to intermarry with them. Some of them perhaps dipped more frequently into Tillotson than they did into Calvin. If they did not see any reason for espousing wholeheartedly the tenets of the latitudinarian writers, they saw no reason for not reading them or putting them under proscription.

During the last crucial phase in the fortunes of the Holy Commonwealth, Increase Mather, the most eminent defender of the faith, both in politics and religion, was also president of Harvard College. It was one of the pivotal facts of his regime that Mather was a nonresident president. Ironically, the college, which was languishing when he took over in 1685 and flourishing when he resigned in 1701, became the beneficiary of his salutary neglect.[37] The "teacher" of the Second Church in Boston, the theological and ideological leader of the old order, and long a fellow of the Harvard Corporation, Mather was the outstanding figure in New England. He found himself too busy ever to assume in full the responsibilities of his Harvard office. During the sixteen years of his presidency he was settled in Cambridge for only a few months. He gave up his pastorate in Boston only for a short period toward the end, and that at the urgent demand of the General Court; for four whole years he was absent on the colony's business in England. He had spent some of the pleasantest days of his life in England as a young man, and his appetite for English society was whetted anew by his four-year sojourn. He seems to have longed for any occasion that might present itself for his permanent removal to England, whether as agent for the colony or pastor of a congregation. After England the society of provincial Boston, not to speak of the mudholes of Cambridge, failed to satisfy his ambitions. He was a supremely able man, a fact appreciated by no one so well as himself and his son Cotton; but so far as Harvard College was concerned his pride was precisely the kind that goeth before a fall. The status quo at Harvard

[37] Morison, *Harvard College in the Seventeenth Century,* Vol. II, Chaps. XXII and XXIII, is severe in his interpretation of Mather's role at Harvard; Murdock, *Increase Mather,* defends Mather at all possible points.

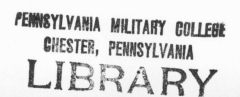

was never so much in need of a watchdog as during his regime, when he was busy elsewhere trying frantically to repair the innumerable weak spots in the defenses of the Holy Commonwealth.

It had been the intention of the founders that Harvard College reproduce the English collegiate way of living, which required the common residence of both students and tutors and demanded, at its best, the constant supervision of a resident presiding officer. Mather, if we are to judge by the advice he gave at the founding of Yale, as well as by his own presidential conduct, had little respect for this conception of the college.[38] He bitterly resisted the many suggestions of the General Court that he take up residence in Cambridge, invoking his unwillingness to desert his pastorate (which he would readily have sacrificed, however, if a call had come from an English congregation), and several times offering to resign instead.[39] And although he understood its importance in the life of the colony, he had a certain unconscious disdain for the college itself, which he once revealed to the representatives of the General Court, when he asked: "Should I leave off preaching to 1500 souls . . . only to Expound to 40 or 50 Children, few of them capable of Edification by such Exercises?"[40]

This attitude was one of the causes of Mather's undoing so far as his aspirations for the intellectual role of the college were concerned. During his commuting presidency the sole tutors of the college, and during his absence its sole resident governors, were John Leverett and William Brattle, who became tutors and fellows of the Corporation in 1685 and 1686 respectively and remained together until 1697. Both were able men and good teachers, many of whose students were devoted to them. To them is attributable the progress made by the college during the last fifteen years of the century. Both were members of mercantile and magisterial families that were in short order to be aligned against Mather. They were relatively liberal in their attitudes, and for twelve years the future intellectual elite of the Bay Colony passed under their tutelage and theirs alone.

[38] Morison, *Harvard College in the Seventeenth Century,* II, 499–500.

[39] That these resignations were regularly refused is explained by Morison with the conjecture that it would have been difficult to prevent the election of Cotton Mather as Increase's successor, something that even Increase's partisans feared. "For Cotton Mather was a typical infant prodigy grown up, pedantic and conceited, meddlesome and tactless, unsympathetic to the aspirations of youth and intolerant of their failings. Cotton as President would have emptied Harvard College. . . ." *Ibid.,* pp. 502–3.

[40] Samuel Sewall, *Diary* (Boston, 1878), I, 493.

When Increase Mather returned from his four-year mission in England bearing the reluctantly accepted Massachusetts Charter of 1691, he confronted an intolerably complex set of tasks. On one side he was trying to fend off the formidable threat of Stoddardeanism to the old Covenant ways. On the other he had the emergent liberals of Boston and Cambridge to cope with—and this was most important for the college. But he also had to reconcile the province to the imperfect charter and with its royal governor—the best charter he had been able to secure. In this he was confronted with the opposition of a "popular" faction consisting chiefly of people who were dissatisfied with the concessions he had made in London.[41] This group, more out of concern with crippling his political power and preventing his return to England than love for the college, continuously made a point of invoking the residency requirements for the college president and ultimately succeeded in confronting Increase with the choice of giving up his office or residing in Cambridge.

Still another task that plagued Mather was that of securing a new charter for the college itself, which was considered to be legally dead inasmuch as it had been chartered under a now obsolete regime. However, this last was a delicate task and one that proved in the end to be too much for him, for it would be difficult to get a royal charter without Anglican visitation, and what he needed to fulfill his aims was an extremely sectarian instrument strong enough to fend off both the Anglicans from without and the liberals from within. Already, he knew, the college under the tutorship of Leverett and Brattle had suffered from too latitudinarian a management to suit his taste. Thus for ten years Mather tried, with draft after draft, to replace the legislative charter of 1650 with a royal charter that would satisfy his sectarian requirements.

The story of Mather's charter maneuvers is unbearably tedious. It may be enough to say here that they reached their climax in 1699 when he inserted into a proposed charter a provision that no one could be president or vice-president of the college or a fellow of the Corporation who would not declare himself to be and continue in adherence to the New England Congregational Way. No such sectarian requirement had been set forth in the 1650 charter, nor even in the various charter bills and

41 For factional and ecclesiastical politics in this period, see Everett Kimball, *The Public Life of Joseph Dudley* (New York, 1911) and Clayton Harding Chapman, "Life and Influence of Rev. Benjamin Colman," unpublished Doctor of Theology dissertation (Boston University, School of Divinity, 1947), Chap. IV.

disallowed charters of the past seven years.[42] Not surprisingly the royal governor, Lord Bellomont, offended at the open exclusion of Anglicans (although the exclusion was actually aimed at the liberals), vetoed the charter.[43] In his desperation Mather indicated that since he could not obtain such a religious test he preferred to have no charter at all—which would have reduced Harvard to the level of an unincorporated divinity school without the power to award degrees.[44] His efforts were futile, and in 1707, after a legal interregnum of many years, the college reverted to the 1650 charter, which has been ever since its fundamental instrument of government.

In the meantime Mather had become embroiled in a new controversy involving not only his political opponents in the Governor's Council but also the tutors at the college. During his earliest years at Harvard he had maintained harmonious relations with his tutors. He had himself at first commended "the liberal mode of philosophizing" in the study of logic at Harvard, in accordance with which students were "pledged to the words of no particular master," but could consult Aristotle, Petrus Ramus, Descartes, or Bacon; and it may be no more than a coincidence that tutor William Brattle had made his slight innovations in the logical theses in 1689 shortly after Mather left for England.[45] It was not logic, however, but religion that was crucial, and here tutors Leverett and Brattle seem to have strayed out of the strait and narrow. One of their students, many years later, recalled that

they recommended to their Pupils the reading of Episcopal authors as the best books to form our minds in religious matters and preserve us from those narrow Principles that kept us at a Distance from the Church of England as apostates from the Primitive Faith . . . the Number of friends to the Church of England in that Country is at least ten times I may say twenty times more since these Gentlemen govern'd the college than they were before.[46]

[42] Morison, *Harvard College in the Seventeenth Century,* II, 524; see Murdock, *Increase Mather,* pp. 353–55.

[43] Many years afterward, in 1725–27, the rectors of the two Episcopal churches of Boston petitioned the Overseers for seats on that board on the ground that they qualified by virtue of being "teaching elders" of Boston churches, who, under a law of 1642, were automatically Overseers. Without incurring any difficulties with the representatives of the Crown the Overseers dismissed this application for what it was worth. See Josiah Quincy, *The History of Harvard University* (Cambridge, Mass., 1840), Vol. I, Chap. XVII and pp. 560–74.

[44] *Ibid.,* II, 526–27.

[45] See Miller, *The New England Mind,* pp. 118, 121; what Brattle had done was chiefly to translate the standard Ramist terms into Cartesian ones.

[46] Morison, *Harvard College in the Seventeenth Century,* II, 505–6.

Presumably Mather sniffed out the odors of latitudinarianism; at any rate, upon his return in 1692 we find him tightening up the teaching of theology and narrowing the studies: "I caused the masters of Art to begin disputations in Theological Questions, with a design to put down Arminianisme." [47]

Mather now saw more clearly than before the vital role of the college in staving off "Degeneracy & Apostasy," and the importance of "care that the Tutors there be such as shall make Conscience to Establish the Young Scholars in these Holy Principles of Truth." [48] In 1697 he wrote an Epistle to the Church and the scholars at Cambridge in which he reminded Leverett and Brattle that the well-being of the Church depended upon the college, and added:

Nor are the Churches like to continue pure Golden Candlesticks, if the Colledge, which should supply them, prove Apostate . . . You that are Tutors there, have a Great Advantage put into your Hands (and I pray God give you Wisdom to know it!) to prevent it. The Lord hath made you Fathers to many Pupils. You will not deny but that He has made me a Father to you. It was my Recommendation that brought you into that Station. And therefore, as my Joy will be Greater to see you Acquit your selves Worthily, so my earnest Sollicitudes for it must needs be the more, on that Account.[49]

Which was a slightly elliptical way of saying to the tutors that since they held offices upon his nomination, it was their duty to teach as he pleased. A few weeks later an association of ministers met in the college hall and expressed their awareness of "the tendencies which there are amongst us towards Deviations from the good Order wherein our Churches have . . . been happily established and continued." [50]

It was too late. Leverett and Brattle were already about to leave their tutorships for other posts, Brattle for the ministry and Leverett for politics. Their work had been done, had indeed already made a notable contribution to liberality of thought in Massachusetts. Moreover, they were already well involved with a group of well-to-do young men who were about to make the greatest breach in the church policy of New England since the Half-Way Covenant. They joined with William Brattle's brother Thomas, who was treasurer of the college, and other influential men in the group which in 1698 formed the new Brattle Street Church and called the Reverend Benjamin Colman, a student of Leverett's, as its pastor. The new church promptly abandoned the half-way

[47] *Ibid.*, II, 503; cf. I, 280 and 280n.   [48] Murdock, *Increase Mather*, p. 330.
[49] Morison, *Harvard College in the Seventeenth Century*, II, 542.
[50] *Ibid.*, p. 543.

membership of the sort that had been institutionalized in 1662. Its members issued a challenging manifesto in which, despite their pledged loyalty to the Westminster Confession, they asserted that baptism would be given to the children of any professing Christians who wished to educate their children in the Christian religion; and that while Communion would be available only to those whose sanctity was ascertainable by the minister, the congregation would not "impose upon any a public relation of their experiences." Thus some of the worst aspects of Stoddardeanism had been brought right to Boston. The conservatives were now confronted with an organized liberal wing, fortified by a wealthy membership and close rapport with the governor and his circle.

A few years later Mather himself, after an enforced trial at residence in Cambridge which he found quite intolerable, indicated to the General Court that they would do well to think of another president. He was succeeded by Samuel Willard, one of his chosen colleagues on the Harvard Corporation, who followed his example in not surrendering his pastorate of the Old South Church. It seemed ironically inconsistent to have unseated Mather only to get another nonresident, and indeed the statutes called for a man who lived in Cambridge; but the members of the Court evaded the issue by the ingenious if transparent device of calling Willard the vice-president, which was the title he held until his death.

Willard, a graduate of the Harvard class of 1659, was quite as orthodox as Increase Mather but far less militant and powerful.[51] His six-year tenure proved to be an interregnum, which was abruptly ended one day in 1707 when he "cut his finger while eating oysters," fell into a convulsion, and died. The fellows of the Corporation (then a temporary body which had been gradually infiltrated by the liberals) nominated John Leverett for the presidency. The Mathers were horrified. "To make a lawyer, and one who never affected the study of Divinity, a praesident for a College of Divines, will be a very preposterous thing, a thing without precedent," wrote Cotton Mather who had hoped for the presidency himself. But "the Churches might yett be saved" if the General Court would reject Leverett.[52] Unfortunately for the position of the Mathers, the notion that Leverett represented a threat to the churches was not too widely shared. The General Court had before it an address from thirty-nine ministers (of whom nineteen or twenty had been Leverett's pupils

[51] Miller suggests, however, that the young men educated under Willard provided the last-ditch resistance to the catholic spirit of Colman. *From Colony to Province*, pp. 450–51.

[52] Morison, *Harvard College in the Seventeenth Century*, II, 552–53.

in Harvard College) endorsing him in affectionate terms and commending his ratification as a service to the religion and learning of the province. That the tutorship of Leverett and Brattle had proved to be a significant source of political power is manifest in the prominence of Leverett's pupils among the signers, as it is in the ministers' observation that "under the Wise and faithful Government of him and the Reverend Mr. Brattle of Cambridge the greatest part of the now rising Ministry in New England were happiely Educated." [53]

A deadlock seemed nonetheless to be impending in the General Court when the acceptance of Leverett's nomination by the Governor's Council was not concurred in by the House, which represented more closely the rural piety of the province. Governor Dudley then suggested an ingenious compromise; in return for the House's acceptance of Leverett, the governor and council would discard the temporary settlement under which Harvard had been governed since 1700 and restore the charter of 1650, a gratifying admission of the hitherto uncertain right of the General Court to charter a college without sanction from the Crown. Only after this bargain was consummated did the House realize that the restoration of the 1650 charter would automatically reduce the Corporation from seventeen members to seven, and put into the hands of the governor the power to select from the large temporary Corporation a small group acceptable to him and Leverett.[54]

John Leverett, born in the year of the Half-Way Synod, was forty-five. The grandson of Governor John Leverett and the son of a lawyer who "maintained but an indifferent character," he inherited wealth and readily took a place among the prominent men of affairs in Massachusetts. Before leaving his tutorship he had been elected representative for Cambridge in the General Court; he had subsequently studied law and served as justice of the peace and judge of the Supreme Court, speaker of the House, and member of the provincial council. An old friend of Governor Dudley, he had also served the province on important missions. A political conservative securely anchored in the dominant faction of the colony, befriended by a large part of the ministry, and favored by an amenable Corporation, he entered the presidency in a strong position.[55]

For the first time in its history, the college Corporation found itself

[53] *Ibid.*, pp. 551–52.　　　　　[54] *Ibid.*, p. 555.
[55] On Leverett see the sketch in the *Dictionary of American Biography* and Shipton, *Sibley's Harvard Graduates*, III, 180–98; for Leverett's conservative views, see Morison, *Harvard College in the Seventeenth Century*, II, 554.

consistently at odds with a significant portion of the community; and the very qualities that made it possible for Leverett to found "the liberal tradition of Harvard University" [56] kept Leverett's regime under the glare of criticism. The Reverend Benjamin Colman, who had resided at Oxford and Cambridge, thought that "no Place of Education can well boast a more free Air than our little College may." [57]

Much of Leverett's sixteen-year reign at Harvard coincided with the era of peace and prosperity that followed the Treaty of Utrecht in 1713. Harvard expanded with the colony, and a large part of the increase in its undergraduate body came from the well-to-do gentry of the seaport towns who were fattening on land speculation and the triangular trade. This inundation from the very element that had done the most to dilute the pristine spirit of Puritanism took the college a long way further in the direction in which it had been moving. Harvard men, who had traditionally been designated in a Biblical way as "Sons of the Prophets" and were now referred to simply by Leverett as "Sons of Harvard," were increasingly being educated simply as young gentlemen, and began to conduct themselves—with cards, horse races, and "profane swearing"— as young gentlemen of means usually did. In self-defense the more devout students organized societies for worship and discussion. But even the theological side of the college was relaxing. At a meeting of the Overseers in 1718 Leverett was attacked by Judge Samuel Sewall on the ground that there had been some "intermission of the Exposition of the Scriptures." [58] Leverett was also subject to occasional sniping by the Mathers, and although his position was too strong to make subversion of his regime possible, his financial support was somewhat constricted during a period of rising prices and he died heavily in debt.[59]

Leverett's regime was also disturbed by the battle over self-government by the Corporation, which will be discussed in the next chapter, and by one investigation by the Overseers, the first of a long series of heresy-

[56] Samuel Eliot Morison, *Three Centuries of Harvard* (Cambridge, Mass., 1936), p. 75.
[57] Ebenezer Turell, *The Life and Character of the Reverend Benjamin Colman* (Boston, 1749), p. 123; among the novelties was the award to Colman's young friend, an Italian Jew, Judah Monis, of the Master's degree in 1720; even before his conversion to Christianity, Monis became Instructor of the Hebrew Language, 1722–60. This was at a time when in most of the universities of the Western world, including Oxford and Cambridge, Jews along with dissenting Christians were barred from degrees by religious tests and oaths. Cf. Chapman, "Life and Influence of Rev. Benjamin Colman," pp. 142–43.
[58] Shipton, *Sibley's Harvard Graduates*, III, 188.   [59] *Ibid.*, pp. 189, 191–92.

hunts in the history of American higher education. The investigation (1723) seems to have been precipitated by charges made by Cotton Mather to the effect that students were privately reading "plays, novels, empty and vicious pieces of poetry, and even Ovid's Epistles, which have a vile tendency to corrupt good manners," that tutors were assigning books on theology "that have rank poison in them," and that a Harvard College education had become an impediment rather than an asset to a good ministerial career. The Overseers' Committee of Visitation was headed by the honorable Samuel Sewall—the same who in days past had humbly stood before his congregation in solemn repentance for his part in the witchcraft trials—and its report was a temperate affair which mentioned lapses both in orthodox instruction and in student morals but made no strong recommendation for change in the conduct of the college.[60]

One of Harvard's signal academic gains during Leverett's presidency was also intimately linked with the advance of tolerance when an endowment for a professorship of divinity was accepted from a Baptist layman. In 1719 and 1720 a London merchant, Thomas Hollis, gave generous gifts to Harvard for poor scholars and divinity students, gifts which were followed by a request from John Leverett and Benjamin Colman for funds to create a divinity professorship. Hollis, who seems to have been attracted by the growing liberalism of the college in a colony where his coreligionists had been persecuted in the past,[61] readily

[60] On the investigation see Quincy, *History of Harvard,* I, 316–21. The essential finding of the committee, so far as intellectual freedom is concerned, was: "That there does not appear to have been any greater recommendation of books in Divinity to the students, but that they have read promiscuously, according to their inclinations, authors of different denominations in religion; and by some information given, the works of Tillotson, Sherlock, Scott and Lucas, are generally most used." The strongest stricture on student morals was this: "That, although there is a considerable number of virtuous and studious youth in the College, yet there has been a practice of several immoralities; particularly stealing, lying, swearing, idleness, picking of locks, and too frequent use of strong drink; which immoralities, it is feared, still continue in the College, notwithstanding the faithful endeavors of the rulers of the House to suppress them."

Miller has concluded that the conservatives were chiefly agitated by the fact that the liberals, while still holding to Calvinism in its broad outlines, were quietly forsaking the particular offshoot of it, the Covenant theology, that had so long been the marrow of New England divinity. See *From Colony to Province,* Chap. XXVII.

[61] Such is Professor Morison's conclusion (*Three Centuries of Harvard,* p. 66). Murdock, however, points triumphantly to the fact that Hollis' interest in Harvard

complied. The sole qualification attached was that no candidate for the professorship "should be refused on account of his belief and practice of adult baptism"—a stipulation not intended to exclude anyone but to assure the donor that men of his own denomination would not be objects of discrimination. He also required that during his lifetime the names of those nominated for the professorship be submitted for his approbation. The Corporation greeted this endowment, the first chair in Harvard's history, with enthusiasm, but the Overseers balked at accepting it without redefining Hollis' language in such a way as to make possible the exclusion of candidates other than those who adhered to the strict New England Way. Hollis' specifications had called for a Master of Arts and a communicant of the Congregational, Presbyterian, or Baptist church, and a man of "sound and orthodox principles." It could be said that the donation was not received in the best of faith. The Overseers, while they swallowed for policy's sake the eligibility of a Baptist, chose to construe the words "sound and orthodox" in their own way and not in Hollis'. Leverett's son-in-law Edward Wigglesworth, the first choice of the Corporation, was accepted for the Hollis Chair, but only after an examination into his orthodoxy commanded by the Overseers, in which he was specifically questioned (*pace* Mr. Hollis!) on "the divine right of infant baptism," as well as other dogmas. Although Hollis was not fully apprised of the Overseers' miscarriage of faith, he did grow alarmed as to the use to which his funds might be put; especially was he alarmed at "the late uncharitable reflections of some upon the Baptists as not orthodox." [62] Having been asked for his portrait for the college hall, he wrote:

---

dated from Increase Mather's four-year sojourn in England, and adds: "If Harvard's liberality was what appealed, it must, then, have been its liberality prior to 1690, or, its liberality under Mather!" (*Increase Mather,* pp. 276–78 and 278n.) Possibly, but it should not be forgotten that the liberality of Harvard under Mather was ascribable in large part precisely to Mather's absence and neglect, and to the presence of Leverett and Brattle. Over thirty years passed between Hollis' first expression of interest in Harvard and the creation of the Hollis Professorship of Divinity, and at the time of the donation Hollis was in correspondence with the liberal Colman. For a full account of the donation see Quincy, *History of Harvard University,* Vol. I, Chap. XII. This is not to say that the Mather dynasty did not still have its hand in the business. Cotton Mather, although he had sent his son Samuel to Harvard, seems to have been busy trying to divert Hollis' interest to Yale College! *Ibid.,* I, 226–29, 524–28. Chapman, "Life and Influence of Rev. Benjamin Colman," pp. 132 ff.

[62] Quincy, *History of Harvard University,* I, 258.

I doubt not but that they are pleased with my moneys, but I have some reason to think, that some among you will not be well pleased to see the shade of a Baptist hung there, unless you get a previous order to admit it, and forbidding any indecency to it . . . I pray to God [he charitably added], to allay the un-Christian heats, that have been among you of one sort and another. Be at peace, and continue not to divide and bite one another.[63]

Leverett and his Corporation had been forced to connive at the actions of the Overseers, but by not forcing the issue they won both the professorship itself and the occupant they chose to designate. Edward Wigglesworth proved to be a liberal and inquiring scholar and an effective teacher, and he lived to see most of the pulpits of Massachusetts and northern New England filled by ministers who had learned their divinity from him.[64] He was succeeded by his son Edward, the two in succession occupying the Hollis Professorship from 1722 to 1792. "It was the Wigglesworths," says Professor Morison, "who trained the pioneers of liberal Christianity in New England—the ministers who led the way out of the lush but fearsome jungles of Calvinism into the thin, clear light of Unitarianism." [65]

To make theology the touchstone of intellectual freedom is perhaps one-sided, for this was of course the exposed nerve of Puritanism. If receptivity to new ideas can be taken as an index of freedom, the receptivity of Harvard men in the areas of science and philosophy speaks well for the early college. The development of science will be discussed elsewhere, but it may be pertinent to point out here that the old ideal of *libertas philosophandi* was familiar and acceptable to both liberals and conservatives in the age of Increase Mather and John Leverett. "In philosophical matters," wrote Leverett in 1711,

Harvardians philosophize in a sane and liberal manner, according to the manner of the century; in logic as in Physics they are neither sceptics nor dogmatics. . . . For what is Natural Philosophy, unless a system in which natural things are explained; and in which that hypothesis is certainly the best by which the greater part of natural phenomena are most fully and clearly explained; these things are to be sought and required. Without any manner of doubt whatever, all humane matters must be tested by Philosophy. But the same license is not permissible to Theologians.[66]

[63] *Ibid.*, pp. 258–59.   [64] Shipton, *Sibley's Harvard Graduates,* V, 552.
[65] Morison, *Three Centuries of Harvard,* p. 68; the Hollis scholarships were also liberally administered by the Corporation. One of the first was given to John Callender, who became the Baptist minister of Newport.
[66] Morison, *Harvard College in the Seventeenth Century,* I, 168; cf. the sentiments of Increase Mather, p. 167.

Clearly the ancient distinction between philosophy and theology in respect to freedom of inquiry was still operative at Harvard at the beginning of the eighteenth century. That this philosophical freedom was actually exercised is clear from the readiness with which both the logical systems of Petrus Ramus, the intellectual guide of the Puritans, and Aristotle, his foe, were accepted and studied, and also by the ease with which the categories of Cartesian logic were introduced toward the end of the seventeenth century.[67]

To this philosophical latitude must be added a growing practical toleration. By the beginning of the eighteenth century the dominant sect had split into two factions, and students from both wings were present in the college; they were occasionally exposed to the work of Anglican theologians; they were joined by Baptist students (who were present on scholarships); the professorship of divinity, no less, bore the name of a Baptist merchant; a cleavage was beginning to appear between theology and ethics; and even the orthodox wing of Congregationalism was taking a broader view of religion than in the earlier days.

With all this change, the evidence that is available shows no sign that anything quite like modern notions of intellectual freedom had yet been formulated. Still less is there a specific justification for academic freedom. Men often spoke of liberty of conscience but never applied it to the teaching function. College teaching was not a recognized career, and tutors lacked even the faintest trace of a professional consciousness, for the very good reason that college teaching was as yet far from being a profession. It was not customary to say either that intellectual freedom was an asset to the community or that the individual had a right to free conditions for the growth and development of his mind. The Dunster case showed that in his day the only appeal was to the correctness of the individual's deviant opinion, not to his right to have one.

There is hardly more evidence for a clearly delineated rationale for freedom of inquiry at the opening of the eighteenth century than there was at the beginning of Harvard. But by that time two general sanctions had emerged: gentlemanliness and tolerance. When Judge Sewall accosted Leverett before the Overseers over the neglect of religious exercises at the college, Leverett responded, in the words of Sewall's diary,

[67] Morison, *Harvard College in the Seventeenth Century,* I, 187 ff. The logical compendium prepared in 1687 by William Brattle on the basis of Descartes was used as a textbook until 1765. *Ibid.,* p. 193.

by seeming "to be surprised at my treating him in this manner. I did not use to do so. Neither did he use to treat me so. This complaint was made twice at least. Many spoke earnestly, that what was said [i.e. by Sewall] was out of season." [68] The short account we have of this interchange says much about the social situation in which college practices under Leverett were challenged. The spokesman of orthodoxy was fended off by an appeal to the standards of good manners: he was treating another gentleman in less than courtly fashion and was "out of season"—a stratagem sufficient in this case to put Sewall on the defensive, but one that would have been swept aside by one zealot in the company of other zealots. A certain regard for gentlemanliness had always been one of the Puritan virtues, but it had not always been so powerful an inhibition on sectarian bigotry or brutality. [69] With the rise of a wealthy class of gentry this regard increased in strength to the point where decorum was beginning to be of roughly comparable importance with principle.

The advance in tolerance was another index of the decline of the religious scruples of the pristine Puritan age; for tolerance is, unfortunately, too often the virtue only of those who do not care excessively. It becomes a necessity of peace, trade, security, and culture not to care overmuch when a religious monopoly is replaced by religious duopoly or by diversity. The split within Congregationalism, the presence of Anglicans and Baptists, the pressure from England—all of these introduced such endless possibilities for bitter struggle that peace and quiet would have been totally impossible if religious differences had been pushed to the limit. Nor should it be imagined that the more orthodox were unaware of this. In 1718, when a pastor was ordained in the Baptist Church of Boston, three Congregational pastors took part. Among them was Cotton Mather, who preached a sermon in which he spoke of bygone religious persecutions in these terms:

Good men, alas! have done such things as these. New England also has in former times done something of this aspect, which would not now be so well approved: in which, if the brethren, in whose house we are now convened, met with anything too unbrotherly, they now with satisfaction hear us ex-

---

[68] Sewall, *Diary*, III, 202–3.

[69] Per contra, see F. A. Christie, "The Beginnings of Arminianism in New England," *Papers of The American Society of Church History*, Second Series, III (New York, 1912), 157: "To be orthodox one did not need to be fanatic or disrespectful, and certainly politeness is no sure proof of theological laxity." But when politeness is invoked as of comparable importance with good dogma and sound practice, something has happened to the Puritan spirit.

pressing our dislike of everything which looked like persecution in the days that have passed over us.[70]

And even old Increase, who died in 1728, liked to boast in his last days that Harvard College "forever indifferently Instructs and Rewards all Scholars of whatever different Perswasions in Christianity among us." [71]

[70] Cobb, *Rise of Religious Liberty in America,* p. 223.
[71] Miller, *From Colony to Province,* p. 481.

III: THE COLONIAL COLLEGES

THE AMERICAN PATTERN:
DENOMINATIONAL SPONSORSHIP

Bʏ ᴛʜᴇ ᴍɪᴅᴅʟᴇ of the eighteenth century there had emerged an American system of collegiate education different not only from the English models with which Americans were most familiar but from all others as well. In three features the early American system was unique. First, while American collegiate education, like that of Europe, was the ward of religion, its pattern of essentially private denominational sponsorship, with a modest admixture of state supervision, was new. Second, unlike the European universities, American colleges had no connection with professional and advanced faculties—that is to say, they were colleges but not, strictly speaking, universities. American colleges did not, like those of Oxford and Cambridge, multiply and cluster at great centers of learning; they were small and scattered, and after the Revolutionary era they were to become numerous as well, so that the educational effort of the American people was increasingly diffused. In the nineteenth century, as we shall see, this tendency got completely out of hand. The third unique characteristic was that the early American colleges developed a system of lay government—that is, a system in which the major decisions were made by boards of nonresident governors who were not teachers [1]—that remains characteristic of American higher education to this day. In order to understand later developments in the colleges insofar as they affected the status, the freedom, and the initiative of teachers, we must first understand the origins of lay government and the emergence of America's distinctive pattern of denominational sponsorship, a pattern which was not modified or replaced on any considerable scale until after the Civil

[1] The term *lay government* threatens to be confusing when applied to this early period when ministers were so prominent on governing boards. What we mean by lay government of academic institutions is simply government by persons other than the faculties—i.e., nonautonomous government. Applied to churches, the same term, of course, means government by those who are not clergymen.

War. Later, in analyzing the nineteenth-century colleges, we will trace the consequences of the diffusion of effort in American education.

The first three colleges, Harvard (1636), William and Mary (1693), and Yale (1701), were founded by the established churches of their respective colonies.[2] Then, after the settled churches had become too austere, too doctrinal, and too remote from the religious needs of the people, the religious scene was revitalized by the Great Awakening, inspired by the preaching of such men as Theodore J. Frelinghuysen, William Tennent and his sons, Jonathan Edwards, and by the five rousing evangelistic trips of the great English revivalist, George Whitefield. This series of revivals led to splits in the Congregational, Presbyterian, and Baptist groups that had important consequences for education. Princeton (1746) was founded by New-Side Presbyterians who hoped to show that they too, for all their revivalist fervor, could continue the New England tradition of an educated ministry. Both Brown (1764) and Queen's College (1766, later Rutgers) were founded by revivalistic groups, the first among the Baptists of Rhode Island, the second among Frelinghuysen's followers in the Dutch Reformed Church. Dartmouth (1769), the last of the colonial establishments, grew out of an Indian missionary school organized with Whitefield's help by Eleazar Wheelock, a Congregational pastor who had caught the current "enthusiasm." The two most secular of the colonial schools, King's College (1754, later Columbia) and the College of Philadelphia (1755, later the University of Pennsylvania) were still not untouched by religious rivalries, since both were shared and fought over by Anglicans and Presbyterians.

While the early colleges developed under religious sponsorship and a large measure of religious control, it does not follow that their religious purposes wholly account for their character. The common statement that they were in effect theological seminaries is altogether untrue. We have seen that Harvard was never a mere religious seminary with the sole purpose of training ministers. The stated purposes of other early institutions, as expressed in their charters, also included references to liberal education and the service of the public.[3] What is true is that the

---

[2] Dates, in all cases, are those of the first charters. In naming colleges whose titles later underwent a change, we have followed convenience rather than consistency.

[3] William and Mary's charter, unlike Harvard's, did say that it was to be a "seminary of Ministers of the Gospel," but added the more general goal "that the youth may be piously educated in good letters and manners." Yale's spoke of fitting youth "for publick employment, both in church & civil state," Princeton's simply of in-

desire to educate a suitable, orthodox body of native clergymen could be plausibly asserted to be the most urgent and immediate reason for founding the majority of the colonial colleges, perhaps seven out of nine. But it is equally true and equally important that their curricula were not those of divinity schools but of liberal arts schools, and that among those denominations that tried to maintain high standards for their clergy, additional postgraduate study in divinity was expected. It must also be remembered that early in the eighteenth century the clergymen graduates became a minority among all graduates. The proportion declined sharply throughout the eighteenth century, at the close of which about four fifths of all graduates were going into other vocations.[4] Not one of the colonial colleges required students to subscribe to a particular religious creed as a condition of admission. The founders of Brown, the most liberal college among them, not only ruled out sectarian differences as an object of classroom instruction but barred religious tests for members of the faculty.[5]

The sectarian allegiance of a college was usually expressed by the religious adherence of its president. The charters of King's College, Brown, and Queen's College specified that their presidents must be, respectively, an Anglican, a Baptist, and a member of the Dutch Reformed Church. And although their charters did not demand it, Yale and Harvard could hardly think of anyone but a Congregationalist, Princeton anyone but a Presbyterian.

structing them "in the learned Languages, and in the Liberal Arts and Sciences." If there was any trend among the later colleges in their statements of purpose, it was toward a more secular tone. See Edgar W. Knight, *A Documentary History of Education in the South before 1860* (Chapel Hill, N.C., 1949), I, 401; Franklin B. Dexter, *Documentary History of Yale University* (New Haven, 1916), p. 21; Thomas J. Wertenbaker, *Princeton, 1746–1896* (Princeton, 1946), pp. 396–97; Herbert and Carol Schneider, eds., *Samuel Johnson . . . His Career and Writings* (New York, 1929), IV, 222–24; Elsie Clews, *Educational Legislation and Administration of the Colonial Governments* (New York, 1899), pp. 303–8.

[4] Bailey B. Burritt, *Professional Distribution of College and University Graduates* (Washington, 1912), pp. 14, 22, 75, gives figures that should be good approximations. For figures on Princeton graduates to 1794 see Varnum L. Collins, *President Witherspoon: A Biography* (Princeton, 1925), II, 222. The importance of education for the ministry has been a source of some controversy. See, for example, Winthrop S. Hudson's angry polemic, "The Morison Myth concerning the Founding of Harvard College," *Church History,* VIII (June, 1939), 148–59.

[5] Walter C. Bronson, *The History of Brown University, 1764–1914* (Providence, R.I., 1914), pp. 3–4, 506; this liberality was practiced as well as professed, so far as choice of faculty was concerned. *Ibid.,* p. 101. In 1774 the Corporation at Brown added specifically that the children of Jews were free to enter the institution and enjoy the freedom of their religion. Reuben A. Guild, *Early History of Brown University* (Providence, R.I., 1897), p. 150.

The most noteworthy departure from the practice of the first three colleges to be made by those institutions that were founded around the middle of the century and afterwards is the introduction of interdenominational representation on boards of control. While the last six colonial colleges were all identified in varying degrees with a single dominant church, five had interdenominational representation. With the exception of Dartmouth they did not enjoy, as had the earlier colleges, the privilege of being founded by an established church.[6] The founders of the later colleges, in order to establish their institutions, had been forced to allay the hostility of other denominations by allotting them some place on governing boards, while their subsequent need to broaden the base of their financial support and enlarge their student bodies also contributed to softening their sectarian features. King's College, despite its Anglican affiliation, had among its charter members the pastors of four churches of other denominations in New York City. The College of Philadelphia, which grew out of a nonsectarian academy chartered in 1749, was reorganized and broadened in 1779 as the University of Pennsylvania (although it had already been infiltrated by the Presbyterians), an arrangement under which six of the twenty-four trustees were to be the senior members of each of the principal religious denominations of the city, including the Roman Catholic. The pretensions of the two most prominent denominations were recognized by making the first provost an Anglican divine and the first vice-provost a Presbyterian. At Brown, where the Baptists had a clear preponderance in both units of the dual governing board, the Congregationalists, Anglicans, and Quakers together held fourteen out of thirty-six seats among the trustees, while among the fellows only eight of twelve could be Baptists.[7] The spirit of interdenominational concession was least in evidence at Queen's College, yet even Queen's included four state officials among its forty-one trustees, and still others of the twenty-eight laymen named to its original board were not members of the Dutch Reformed Church.[8] Only a little less sectarian was Dartmouth, where three mem-

[6] This must be qualified for King's College insofar as the English and Dutch Churches shared a form of joint establishment dating from the promise of the English upon the surrender of New Amsterdam not to subvert the religion of the Dutch settlers. The first charter of King's College required that the president be a member of the English Church "as by law established."

[7] Clews, *Educational Legislation and Administration* . . . , pp. 259, 300–308; Edward P. Cheyney, *History of the University of Pennsylvania* (Philadelphia, 1940), pp. 122–25; Edward C. Elliott and M. M. Chambers, *Charters and Basic Laws of Selected American Universities and Colleges* (New York, 1934), pp. 415–16.

[8] William H. S. Demarest, *A History of Rutgers College, 1766–1924* (New Bruns-

bers of the first board were Anglican laymen and New Hampshire officials.[9]

The tendency toward interdenominational representation, although a sign of growing tolerance, did not mean that the denominations had composed their differences and forgotten their hostilities. On the contrary, interdenominational representation came about precisely because sectarian bickering was so acute that hostile factions had to be quieted in some diplomatic way if the new institutions were to have a chance of success. The founding of King's College seemed for a time to be seriously jeopardized by animosities between Anglicans and Presbyterians, while differences between the same groups affected the early development of the College of Philadelphia. Brown was founded only after an angry tussle between Baptists and Congregationalists. Sectarian pride kept the governing board of Queen's College from accepting union with Princeton at a time when Queen's was staggering toward total collapse. As for Dartmouth, the mere suspicion that the Bishop of London might be made an ex-officio trustee caused Eleazar Wheelock to consider removing his projected college from New Hampshire to another province. As late as 1779 the suspicion inspired in the dissenting sects of Virginia by the Anglican background of William and Mary destroyed Jefferson's plans to revamp the institution, even though these plans involved a diminution of its denominational character.[10]

In sum, the desire to dominate and the fear of being dominated had by no means died out in sectarian breasts, but the capacity to do mischief to each other had been greatly diminished, and the necessity of reckoning with outsiders brought about a greater flexibility in educational planning.

The later eighteenth-century colleges were opened at a time of ex-

---

wick, N.J., 1924), pp. 62, 74–76; Clews, *Educational Legislation and Administration* . . . , pp. 338–39. The early spirit of Queen's College was expressed by Theodore Frelinghuysen when he said of the other denominations, "We have no business with their colleges; they may erect as many as they please, and must expect to maintain them too, themselves. Let everyone provide for his own house." Demarest, *History of Rutgers,* p. 39. Perhaps it was this attitude that made it so difficult to keep Queen's College alive.

[9] Frederick Chase, *A History of Dartmouth College and the Town of Hanover* (Cambridge, 1891), pp. 121n, 642.

[10] On these developments see *A History of Columbia University* (New York, 1904), Chap. I; Dorothy Rita Dillon, *The New York Triumvirate* (New York, 1949), Chap. II; Cheyney, *History of the University of Pennsylvania,* pp. 122–23; Bronson, *History of Brown University,* pp. 122–23; Chase, *History of Dartmouth,* pp. 114–20, 125–26; Sadie Bell, *The Church, the State, and Education in Virginia* (Philadelphia, 1930).

panding religious liberty. To be sure, this expansion was for the most part neither planned nor welcomed. The articulate Protestant leaders of colonial settlement had been—with few notable exceptions like Roger Williams and William Penn—firmly opposed to toleration. But while they rejected it as a principle they yielded increasingly to it out of necessity or expediency. A large number of sects poured into or emerged within the colonies during the eighteenth century, and none was strong enough to attain dominance. In the absence of a majority strong enough to exercise coercion, some mutual forbearance became a simple necessity. Indeed the situation of the various sects provided an example for free political organization that was not lost upon American observers. "In a free government," wrote Madison in Number 51 of *The Federalist,*

the security for civil rights must be the same as that for religious rights. It consists in the one case in the multiplicity of interests, and in the other of the multiplicity of sects. The degree of security in both cases will depend on the number of interests and sects.[11]

Also working for tolerance were the example of English opinion and English law under Cromwell and after the Act of Toleration of 1689, as well as the influence of English governors who reflected the preference of the mother country (and of some of the Catholic and Quaker proprietors) for economic prosperity rather than sectarian bickering. The developments of the eighteenth century accentuated the trend toward tolerance, as the sects moved somewhat closer together in the face of common problems—the threat of an Anglican episcopate and the rise of rationalism and Deism. Even the development of revivalistic factions among the Presbyterians, Baptists, and later the Methodists contributed surprisingly to the atmosphere of religious latitude. The New-Side apostles, despite their intolerant impulses, realized that their type of emotional religion would only benefit by the destruction of the formal institutions and establishments that had been created by their predecessors and opponents; such destruction would clear the way for movements that exalted the force of spirit over external discipline and traditional arrangements. Finally, the growth of rationalism itself created a liberal-minded elite, the flower of which were such men as Franklin, Adams, Jefferson, and Madison, and which was fundamentally indifferent to doctrinal issues and impartially tolerant of all the sects.[12]

[11] *The Federalist,* ed. by Edward Mead Earle (Washington, 1937), pp. 339–40.
[12] The forces working for religious liberty are discussed by W. W. Sweet, "The American Colonial Environment and Religious Liberty," *Church History,* V (March,

THE AMERICAN PATTERN: LAY GOVERNMENT

Of great significance for later struggles over intellectual freedom was the American system of academic government which had taken on its essential features by the middle of the eighteenth century. Nowhere outside the United States and Canada are modern universities governed by boards of laymen. The system of lay government has created special problems for free teaching and scholarship in America. The essence of lay government is that the trustees, not the faculties, *are,* in law, the college or university, and that legally they can hire and fire faculty members and make almost all the decisions governing the institution. This has hampered the development of organization, initiative, and self-confidence among American college professors, and it has contributed, along with many other forces in American life, to lowering their status in the community. Other professional groups have far greater power to determine the standards and conduct of their own professions.[13]

To contrast without qualification the European system of academic self-government with the American system of lay government would, however, be misleading. While European universities, particularly those of the Continent, are formally self-governing, they are still not entirely free from the influence of church and state. American universities and colleges, particularly the best private institutions, have developed a system under which the balance of governmental power is actually distributed among trustees, administration, and faculty. Formally empowered with almost all the prerogatives of government, trustees in such institutions have in fact delegated most of them to the administrations or the faculties, retaining chiefly the prerogative of budgetary decisions and the right of intervention in broad policy. Faculties have a very large voice, often in effect the controlling voice, in matters of appointment, promotion, and curriculum. Legally still powerless, they are nonetheless potent agencies of academic government in the most reputable colleges and universities.

1935), 43–56, and Perry Miller, "The Contribution of the Protestant Churches to Religious Liberty in Colonial America," *ibid.,* pp. 57–66. Cf. Evarts B. Greene, *Religion and the State* (New York, 1941), Chap. III.

[13] American academic government is discussed in relation to the problems of academic freedom by Robert M. MacIver in *Academic Freedom in Our Time* (New York, 1955), Part II. See also the discussion of the freedom and status of American professors by Richard Shryock, "The Academic Profession in the United States," *Bulletin of the American Association of University Professors,* XXXVIII (Spring, 1952), 32–70.

How this measure of informal self-government has grown up within the framework of the plenary legal powers of the trustees is an important part of our story.[14]

When all necessary qualifications have been made, however, the fact remains that lay government has been one of the most decisive factors in the problem of academic freedom in America, and its origin and development are central to our concern. The American system of lay government was not planned by the founders of the colonial colleges, who were themselves familiar chiefly with the altogether different system of the English universities. Rather it grew out of the conditions of religious and social life in the New World.[15]

In at least three important respects the American situation was unique. The first was that while the European universities had been nurtured for centuries on the medieval gild traditions of faculty self-government, the American colleges were not only Protestant institutions but had been founded in a totally Protestant milieu, sharply cut off from many medieval traditions. The medieval universities were ecclesiastical agencies founded at a time when the Church was still effectually guarding its institutions from the incursions of lay power. Both the church principle of ecclesiastical independence and the gild principle of corporate self-government provided the universities and society at large with dominant models of autonomy. This autonomy the Protestant Reformation had

[14] See below, Chap. V, pp. 232–38; Chap. VI, pp. 308–9.

Lest the American system be excessively depreciated, one may add that it is naive to suppose, whatever the formal and traditional sanctions underlying freedom of teaching and scholarship, that any universities anywhere can be altogether free from the pressures that the community brings to bear. One need only look at the interplay between the "autonomous" medieval universities and the Church, at the impact of the Reformation upon universities, or even to probe a little at the genial facade of German *Lehrfreiheit,* to see that European practices of academic government have hardly eliminated inhibitions from academic life. In justice to the role of laymen in education, it should also be said that their intervention has on occasion been salutary. After academic self-government had led to stagnation and decay at Oxford and Cambridge, Parliamentary intervention in the middle of the nineteenth century led to admirable reforms. See A. I. Tillyard, *A History of University Reform* (Cambridge, 1913). In the United States many colleges were being rescued at the same time by the intervention of their alumni. See below, Chap. VI.

[15] It is suggestive, in this respect, that the Protestant universities of Canada have undergone a parallel constitutional evolution, embracing an original scheme of lay government later qualified by the growth of a considerable degree of informal faculty government. In the early Canadian institutions the roles of ex-officio trustees drawn from political positions seems even more important than in the American colleges, and political events—elections, the changes of governors—had decisive influence on the fortunes of Canadian colleges.

sharply circumscribed. As we have seen, the proud self-sufficiency, and with it much of the intellectual freedom, that had been characteristic of the medieval universities at their zenith went into decline. Moreover, the principle of the freedom of the church hierarchy from intervention by laymen was sharply challenged—not least by the Puritans, of whom it has been remarked that they gave the layman a larger part in the control of the local church than he had enjoyed since the Roman emperors became Christian.[16] Now it was not a very drastic step from admitting men who were not clerics into the government of churches to admitting those who were not teachers into the government of colleges. Just as gild self-government and church autonomy were models for the organization of the medieval universities, so nonconformist Protestant church government provided new and different models for the American colleges. In England itself, while the method of founding colleges at Oxford and Cambridge was not changed by the Reformation, educational foundations of lower than university grade had begun to be placed under the control of incorporated bodies of lay trustees in the sixteenth century.[17]

American Protestants did not consider that they were destroying intellectual freedom by extending the policy of lay government from churches to colleges. Indeed they considered it one of their contributions to civilization that they had broken up the priestly autonomy of advanced education and had brought it under the control of the community.[18] Of course the early founders of American colleges did not depart very far from

[16] Samuel Eliot Morison, *Three Centuries of Harvard* (Cambridge, Mass., 1936), p. 71.

[17] See Edward H. Reisner, "The Origin of Lay University Boards of Control in the United States," *Columbia University Quarterly*, XXIII (March, 1931), 68–69.

[18] "Since the Reformation from Popery, the Notion of the Sanctity of Colleges and other Popish Religious Houses has been exploded. . . . The Intention herein was not to destroy the Colleges or the Universities, and rob the Muses, but to rescue them from Popish Abuses, and reduce them to a Constitution more agreeable to the Original Design of Universities [i.e., in antiquity], and more dependent upon the Civil Power. From this time they have been considered as Lay-Communities. . . . And in forming new Universities, and Colleges, the British Nation has perhaps made them a little more pompous, in Compliance with Customs introduced into the ancient Universities in *Popish* Times; which Customs being of long Standing they chose to suffer to continue in them. But the Protestant Princes, and Republicks, and States, in whose Territories there was no University before, had no Regard to any Popish Usages or Customs in erecting Colleges, and Universities, and only endowed them with such Privileges and Powers, and Officers, as were properly School Privileges, Powers and Officers." [Benjamin Gale] *A Reply to a Pamphlet Entitled the Answer of the Friend in the West* (n.p., 1755), pp. 47–48. Significantly, the author of these remarks was a partisan of the somewhat more liberal faction that sought to wrest the control of Yale from Thomas Clap.

the traditional assumption that institutions of higher learning should be run largely by clerics, but if clerics were expected to share the government of churches they might also be expected to share the government of colleges. Such early efforts as were made to increase the corporate autonomy of teaching bodies were not identified with any movements toward greater liberality in thought, but rather with narrow clerical interests, conservatism, and orthodoxy. As we shall see, Mather at Harvard in the seventeenth century and tutors Sever and Welsteed in the early eighteenth century sought to augment corporate autonomy for reasons that had little to do with freedom, while the clerics at William and Mary seem to have been interested only in their own salaries and privileges. Likewise, Thomas Clap at Yale, defending the independence of that institution against the intervention of the Connecticut legislature, was fighting for conservative theology and sectarian purity. Paradoxical as it may seem to those who read the situation with twentieth-century values in mind, the growing religious and intellectual liberalism of eighteenth-century America was identified in the colleges not with corporate autonomy but with lay government. Not until the nineteenth century, when lay government had been long established, was this situation reversed.

The second reason for lay government was that while the European universities evolved out of long-established communities of scholarship and teaching, the first American colleges were created, in a sense, as artifacts by communities that had to strain very limited resources to support them. This meant that infant institutions in the American colonies had to be carefully nursed for many years before they developed into stable colleges capable of standing on their own feet. During this period of infancy the lay boards of control exercised sweeping powers that they were later reluctant to give up, being, like other parents, unwilling to accept the fact of their own obsolescence. Moreover, the prominent role of private benefactions guaranteed that this obsolescence would never be complete; institutions dependent upon renewed surges of good will in the lay community were more sensitive to lay opinion than were those that relied upon stable clerical livings or regular parliamentary appropriations.

Finally, while in Europe a body of men belonging to what could be called a teaching profession existed before the emergence of the universities, the colleges in America were created first, and only afterwards did a considerable body of professional teachers emerge. The idea of the self-governing university had been based upon the assumption that teachers were mature professionals; the first American teachers were preponderantly youthful amateurs. In a raw community like early colonial America the opportunities for a man of learning outside the realm of teaching were too great to leave many first-rate men available for the ill-compensated, low-status positions that were the lot of those whose whole lives would be given to the instruction of boys. As we have seen in Chapter II, the first teaching staffs at Harvard were composed of future ministers for whom teaching was only a temporary occupation, a preamble to a clerical career. In the later colleges this was also the case, with the exception, as we shall see, of William and Mary. So long as the bulk of college teaching was in the hands of groups of youngsters for whom teaching was only a by-path to more desired careers, faculty self-government was bound to seem less acceptable, indeed less meaningful, than it did in European universities numbering among their masters many great and influential men of learning. For over a century and a half American collegiate education relied chiefly on young tutors, having in all its faculties only a handful of professors of some maturity and length of tenure.[19] Harvard had been established for more than eighty-five years, Yale for more than fifty, and Princeton for more than twenty before each had its first professor, and it was to be many years more before regular professors outnumbered transient tutors. The only secure and sustained professional office in American collegiate education was that of the college president himself. He alone among the working teachers of the early colleges had, in the community and before the governing boards, the full stature of an independent man of learning. To this situation can be traced the singular role and importance of the American college or university president.

Lay government created more problems than it solved, and to these problems the college president provided an answer—at least the best answer that could be found. Lay boards of trustees were absentee proprietors, and in the bustling America of colonial days they usually had very little leisure to devote to their colleges. Small as they were, these colleges had promotional problems, staff problems, disciplinary problems,

[19] From the standpoint of ecclesiastical organization one might say that while in Europe the clerics who were responsible for education were the teachers themselves, in America the clerics responsible for education were trustees and the teachers were only *future* clerics.

servant problems, curricular problems—and to none of these could the busy trustees consistently give enough attention. Thus between the trustees, who had the legal capacity but not the time or energy to govern, and the teachers, who were considered too young and too transient to govern, there was created a power vacuum. This vacuum the presidents quickly began to fill.

The early college president played a multiple role. As a cleric and learned man he taught. As a member of the governing board he participated in major decisions. As a leading citizen of his community he promoted his institution. As a faculty member he led the teaching staff. As a preacher he prayed and sermonized for the students. Since he was subject in most cases to dismissal by governing boards, he was the subordinate of the trustees, and yet as the man most familiar with college affairs he was also the leader of the governing board. In relation to his tiny teaching staff he was a leader or a boss, depending upon his situation and temperament. Unlike the European rector, he was not elected by the teachers nor in any formal way accountable to them. Teachers came and went as a matter of course. The president remained until he died or resigned or, in rare cases, was ousted by his board. The tutors, being temporary servants, had little reason to resist or hamper his authority.[20] The trustees, although they appointed and could replace him, could not displace him. In legal theory they were the college, but in the eyes of the community, and often in his own eyes, the president was the college. Upon his reputation and his promotional energies its place in the community chiefly depended. He became at once its dynamic center of authority, its symbol, and its spokesman. He occupied and in a sense created an office which has no equivalent in academic systems outside the United States. The prestige and pride that elsewhere were vested in the faculties came to center in him—and there, with some modification, they have remained to this day.

For a long time, in most colleges, the president was the only teacher who possessed enough status, power, and confidence to wage a battle with the trustees or repressive forces in the community on behalf of religious or intellectual freedom. Thus, from the time of Henry Dunster down to the Civil War period, the outstanding college controversies of this sort involved presidents more often than professors, and tutors

[20] The president might make a practice of consulting tutors, however, and his absence or illness might leave them with large powers of discretion.

hardly at all. In some of these cases it is hard to determine to what extent the controversy was a purely administrative affair and to what extent it involved intellectual issues. But the fact remains that in the transition of both freedom and power from lay trustees to faculty members, insofar as that transition has taken place, the president played an important and constructive part. In the early days of the colleges it was quite difficult for trustees to find a man endowed with all the qualities needed for vigorous college leadership. Those institutions that could not find a strong president or would not give him sufficient powers frequently languished. The man who had the necessary qualifications thus found himself in a good bargaining position, and if he was astute, he often saw to it that he came into his office with a strong hand.[21] Strong presidents, to be sure, could make great difficulties, as the opponents of Mather and Clap could testify; but strong presidents, like Ezra Stiles and John Witherspoon, made strong colleges, and ultimately—though this was much later indeed—they made strong faculties. In the transit of powers of decision to the faculties, as in the struggle for freedom of thought, many of the outstanding college presidents contributed their full share.

THE BEGINNINGS OF LAY GOVERNMENT

The development of the first two colonial colleges, Harvard and William and Mary, suggests that their founders intended to emulate the governmental conditions of the English colleges with which they were familiar, but that circumstances impelled them in the direction of lay government. Oxford and Cambridge were governed by their own faculties. The scholars made their own rules and appointed their own officers, and neither the Crown nor the donors of college properties normally made claims to participate in academic government. The colleges, which had grown out of student residence halls, were managed by the elected col-

---

[21] A good illustration in the Revolutionary period is that of Ezra Stiles, who made an extremely canny reconnaissance of the terrain before he accepted the presidency of Yale. Almost a hundred years later James Burrill Angell made the trustees of the University of Michigan all but stand on their heads before he went from Vermont to Michigan. One of his predecessors at Michigan, Henry L. Tappan, had been treated harshly by the trustees and in a manner very unfavorable to the freedom of the institution. This was one factor in Angell's caution. See the fascinating letters in Wilfred B. Shaw, ed., *From Vermont to Michigan: Correspondence of James B. Angell* (Ann Arbor, 1936).

lege heads and the "fellows"—and in English usage no one who was not a college fellow taught in a college. College and university authorities ran their own affairs and administered their own finances. There seems to be no evidence that the founders of Harvard College at first intended to depart from these familiar and respected practices of academic government. But when Harvard was created by legislative enactment in 1636, it seemed impossible to commit to a group of men as yet unknown and unchosen the full powers of management of the resources that were to be put at the disposal of the college by the General Court. (The wisdom of the founding fathers, from their own point of view, in keeping control in their own hands was shown by the early history of the institution, for its first head, Master Nathaniel Eaton, was a scapegrace and its first president, Henry Dunster, turned heretical.) Hence the college was placed under the control of a board of Overseers consisting of six magistrates and six ministers. Until a charter was granted in 1650, the Overseers were the sole governing body of the college. In 1642 the legislature reorganized them, appointing as members of the board all the magistrates of the province, its governor and deputy governor, the president of the college and the "teaching elders" of the churches of the six adjoining towns.[22] The first board under this statute numbered, in addition to the president, eleven public officers and nine ministers.

The disadvantages of trying to manage a college through such an external agency, with scattered members of whom only one, the college president, was in close and continuous contact with college business, soon became clear; and it seems to have been at President Dunster's insistence that a corporate charter was secured. The disparity between the position of the college teachers, who were no more than transient employees of the Overseers, with much responsibility but no power, and the autonomous position of the English universities was painfully obvious. The charter of 1650 seems to have been meant in part to eliminate this anomaly by creating the Corporation of the college as a separate governing body, to be composed of the president, the treasurer, and

[22] Magistrates meant the Assistants of the province who were annually elected by the freemen. Teaching elders meant both the "pastors" and the "teachers" of the churches involved. A fully staffed church was expected to have two ordained ministers. On the reorganization of 1642 see Samuel Eliot Morison, *The Founding of Harvard College* (Cambridge, Mass., 1935), pp. 325–28. Subsequent measures changing the composition of the Overseers are printed in Edward C. Elliott and M. M. Chambers, *Charters and Basic Laws of Selected American Universities and Colleges* (New York, 1934), pp. 216–24.

five fellows. The power to elect their own successors, to manage the college's property and act for it in law, to hire college servants, and to make rules and by-laws was vested in the Corporation—but that body was to secure the consent of the Overseers on all important decisions and to submit to its arbitration in cases of disagreement. The charter thus seems to have embodied a compromise between the familiar English conditions of faculty self-government and the practice that had prevailed at Harvard since 1636. The Corporation was to take the initiative in all matters, but the Overseers were endowed with a veto.

Thus the disparity between the inherited English ideal of self-government and the conditions of provincial life led to a system of dual control; and, as we shall see in the case of William and Mary, dual control was to result there also from the action of the same forces. In one respect this dual system formally emulated English practice, for it was customary for English colleges to have an external agent of government called the Visitor. But usually the function of the Visitor was only to act as an umpire when disputes arose, and many English colleges actually had no Visitor in 1600. Plainly the role of Harvard's Overseers would have been far greater than the traditional visitorial function, even if the provisions of the charter of 1650 had been observed.

In fact, those provisions were not observed, and Harvard was not governed in accordance with the charter. In spite of its mandates, the Overseers, not the Corporation, elected the two presidents who followed Dunster, hired and paid the fellows, and issued orders governing the college servants. The Overseers, after fourteen years of ascendancy, were evidently not prepared in 1650 to yield their prerogatives to a very small group of very young men.[23] Nor, evidently, were the young men, who were destined in any case to be teachers for only a few years, especially interested in challenging this usurpation by the Overseers of the Corporation's charter prerogatives. Faculty self-government was thus forestalled at the beginning by the simple fact that there was as yet no teaching profession. Nothing could be more misleading than to describe early Harvard College, as one student of academic government

[23] Professor Morison points out that in 1650 President Dunster himself had just turned forty, the treasurer was twenty-six, and the average age of the five fellows was about twenty-four. *Harvard College in the Seventeenth Century* (Cambridge, Mass., 1936), I, 11. On early Harvard government see *The Founding of Harvard College,* Chaps. XV, XXII, and *Harvard College in the Seventeenth Century,* Chaps. I, XXIII, XXIV.

has done, as a "tutor's college." [24] Not only did the early Corporation neglect to exercise most of the fundamental powers of academic government, but even within the Corporation the place and power of the tutors was severely limited at the outset. As Morison puts it, "the Harvard Corporation never functioned like an English collegiate body, and began to evolve into something else before the ink was scarce dry on the Charter." [25] It had evidently been Dunster's intention to follow the English pattern: every teacher of undergraduates was to be a fellow, and no nonresidents were to be fellows. (Some residents might be fellows, without teaching, if they were present at the college in some scholarly role.) As it turned out, some of the teaching fellows began to resign shortly after the granting of the charter, and the revenues of the college proved far too meager to provide stipends for the five fellowships mentioned in the charter. During the rest of the seventeenth century there were apparently never more than three tutors at the college (often only two), and hence never more than three resident fellows.[26] The rapid turnover of the tutors made the Corporation an unstable body, despite the longer ex-officio tenures of the presidents and the treasurers. Even in Dunster's time neighboring ministers who had been tutors began to get seats on the Corporation; beginning in the 1670s it became customary to give seats to ministers who had never been tutors. Morison concludes that until the Corporation was reorganized under President Leverett in 1707 "the President governed the College with the aid of such Overseers as were interested, and treated the tutors as senior students assisting him in discipline and instruction, rather than his fellows." [27]

After 1707 it became a regular practice to appoint tutors without granting them the status of fellows of the Corporation. Finally, in 1780, the Corporation became a totally nonresident body, except, of course, for the president himself. Businessmen and lawyers began to be elected to the Corporation, and with this development the functions of the Over-

[24] John E. Kirkpatrick, *The American College and Its Rulers* (New York, 1926), Chap. I.

[25] Morison, *Harvard College in the Seventeenth Century*, I, 14.

[26] For the tutors, fellows, and other officers, with their terms of office as nearly as they can be determined, see Albert Mathews in *Publications of the Colonial Society of Massachusetts*, XV (1925), lxvi, lxvii, and clii, ff. On the meaning of the word "fellow" see pp. cxxxii–cxxxv. Before 1690 there were only three fellows appointed who were not tutors, but there were additional fellows whose tenures as fellows was far longer than their resident careers as tutors. From 1690 to 1728 there were seventeen fellows who never served at any time as tutors.

[27] *Harvard College in the Seventeenth Century*, I, 15.

seers became more and more vestigial.[28] With only minor qualifications
it can thus be said of the Harvard Corporation that while it was in any
serious measure a resident body of teachers it did not govern, and that
when it finally took on the functions of government it was a group of
nonresident men who were not teachers.[29]

William and Mary, the second colonial college to be chartered, resorted, like Harvard, to a dual system of government that included one
unit that was expected to take charge in the absence of a body of teachers
and another unit that was expected at length to embody the will of the
faculty. But while at Harvard the supposed "faculty" unit, the Corporation, contained non-teaching members from very early times and became the real agency of government only after it had become almost
entirely a body of laymen, at William and Mary the faculty unit, the
President and Masters (or Professors), was always a body of resident
masters in the English tradition. Its right to control the college, how-

---

[28] The primary reason for the initial steps taken to replace ministers by businessmen in 1779 and 1784 seems to have been the financial difficulties faced by Harvard
in the Revolutionary period and immediately after. Josiah Quincy, *The History of
Harvard University* (Boston, 1860), Vol. II, Chap. XXXI; Morison, *Three Centuries
of Harvard*, pp. 153–60.

[29] In 1721 a constitutional issue arose out of the antagonism between Leverett and
the conservatives. Two tutors, Nicholas Sever and William Welsteed, claimed that
by virtue of being resident teachers and stipendiaries of the college they were
entitled to seats on the Corporation. In presenting their case to the Overseers, they
relied upon the alleged meaning of the charter of 1650 and the intention of its
framers to follow the English practice of including all "fellows" in the management
of colleges. While their conception of the intent of the founders was probably
correct, it ran counter, of course, to long-standing Harvard usage. At the time the
conservative faction had great strength in the Overseers and the General Court,
and the entire move represented an effort through Sever and Welsteed to remove
from the Corporation two recently appointed ministers of the liberal faction,
Benjamin Colman and Nathan Appleton, who would have to leave if the others
were seated. Fortunately for Leverett, the Royal Governor, Samuel Shute, was
feuding with the legislature. He took the side of the liberals and made it clear that
he would invoke Royal authority if necessary to prevent any further attempt to alter
the traditional practice to the disadvantage of Leverett's Corporation. The fullest
account of the controversy is in Quincy, *History of Harvard*, Vol. I, Chaps. XIII
and XIV, with documents, pp. 546–56. A briefer and more detached account is that
of Morison in *Three Centuries of Harvard*, pp. 69–73. See also the comments by
Shipton in *Sibley's Harvard Graduates*, V, 92–93, and VI, 154–55, and the text of
Sever's argument before the legislature in *Proceedings of the Massachusetts Historical Society*, XVI, 54–67.

For a later effort to minimize the power of the Overseers and strengthen the
Corporation, see Shipton's sketch of Nathan Prince in *Sibley's Harvard Graduates*,
VI, 272–73, and Nathan Prince, *An Account of the Constitution and Government of
Harvard College* (n.p., n.d. [1742]).

ever, was always under dispute by the lay unit, the Visitors—and in the end the Visitors won a complete victory.

From the early seventeenth century there had been talk of a college for Virginia, but it was not until 1693 that the Reverend James Blair, commissary for the Bishop of London and head of the Anglican church in Virginia, returned to England and secured the royal charter that authorized the creation of the college.[30] Financed by aid from the Crown and the provincial government, as well as by subsequent private gifts, William and Mary was an agency both of the church and the state. The charter created four schools: a common school for Indian children; a grammar school at which Greek and Latin were to be taught to post-elementary students; a "philosophy school," or college; and a divinity school. In addition to the president, who was not expected to teach, there were to be six "professors," two each in the divinity school and college and one to head each of the lower schools. A board of Visitors was estab-lished, consisting of fourteen laymen and four clergymen, with the power to appoint the president and the masters and to make the rules and statutes of the college. They were to co-opt their successors. The Reverend Blair was made both a Visitor and the president of the college for life, while Governor Francis Nicholson was among the Visitors. In the English tradition a chancellor—i.e., a protector, adviser, and agent at the court —was included, an office filled by the Bishop of London. It was further provided that when the college was founded and established its properties and revenues should be transferred from the Visitors to the President and Masters, and that the latter body was to be a body politic with per-petual succession, empowered to conduct the college's business affairs.[31]

[30] Basing his argument partly on Commissary Blair's familiarity with the uni-versities of Aberdeen and Edinburgh, A. Bailey Cutts has made a case for the importance of a Scottish influence on the American pattern of lay government. "The Educational Influence of Aberdeen in Seventeenth Century Virginia," *William and Mary Quarterly*, Second Series, Vol. XV (July, 1935), pp. 229–49. How-ever, his parallel between the academic senate at Aberdeen and the William and Mary system is not very convincing. The real clash at William and Mary seems to have been between Oxford ideals and American realities. See Courtlandt Canby, "A Note on the Influence of Oxford upon William and Mary College in the Eight-eenth Century," *William and Mary Quarterly*, Second Series, Vol. XXI (July, 1941), pp. 243–47.

[31] So large a part of the records of William and Mary have been lost, especially for its earliest years, that its history cannot be written with the thoroughness that is possible in the case of the other colonial colleges. However, from the beginning of the *William and Mary College Quarterly*, First Series, Vol. I, and in the pages

Teachers and members of the governing board were required to take an oath subscribing to the Thirty-nine Articles of the English church.

The text of the charter suggests that the college government was intended to follow the English pattern so far as possible—it even provided for a representative of the college in the House of Burgesses to be named by the President and Masters (not, it should be noted, by the Visitors)—which leads one to suspect that its founders assumed that the ultimate transfer of the college properties into the hands of the President and Masters would carry with it the fundamental power of control, leaving the Visitors in some such incidental position as that occupied by Visitors in England. However, if this was the intention, the charter failed to anticipate the effects of American conditions upon the power structure of the college. So long as the right to make the statutes and choose personnel was in the hands of the Visitors, they were in a position to govern if they chose to do so.

Revenues were inadequate, and the institution was long in getting under way. Indeed, while its charter was the second to be granted in the colonies, William and Mary became the third college in actual operation, for Yale was graduating students long before William and Mary was able to offer a college curriculum. There is no evidence that anything resembling the regular college curriculum of the time was offered before 1729, when the full complement of teachers as provided by the charter was at last engaged, a body of statutes drawn up, and the transfer of college properties and revenues from the Visitors to the President and Masters was finally made.[32]

By this time, however, the Visitors had been engaged in the active and

---

of its successor, the *William and Mary Quarterly,* documents shedding much light upon its history have appeared. It is inexpedient to cite all these items in detail. The text of the charter, together with many of the most important surviving documents, is printed in Edgar W. Knight, *A Documentary History of Education in the South before 1860,* I, 368–552. See also *Virginia Magazine of History and Biography,* IV (October, 1896), 161–75. A good brief historical sketch may be found in Lyon G. Tyler's *Williamsburg* (Richmond, 1907), pp. 110–204. See also the anonymous sketch, *The History of the College of William and Mary from its Foundation, 1660, to 1874* (Richmond, 1874), and Herbert Baxter Adams, *The College of William and Mary* (Washington, 1887).

[32] The grammar school was open by 1694, the Indian school by 1711. The sole faculty member who had served any length of time at "college" teaching, the Rev. Hugh Jones, asserted in 1724 that William and Mary "at present . . . scarcely merits the name of a college." See Knight, *Documentary History of Education in the South,* pp. 493, 498, and *The Official Letters of Alexander Spotswood* (Richmond, 1865), pp. 166–67. Cf. Samuel Eliot Morison, "American Colonial Colleges," in *Rice Institute Pamphlet,* XXIII (October, 1936), 261n.

detailed supervision of the embryonic college and its associated schools for almost thirty-five years, and a precedent for their continuous interference had been firmly established. Even after the transfer was made, the right to make the laws and statutes of the college was still theirs, and later they seem to have construed from this a right to intervene in academic affairs when they chose.[33] As a consequence the legal structure of the college was utterly anomalous: the faculty found itself formally empowered to exercise control of its business transactions, while the Visitors were legally left (through their control of the statutes) with broad and intrusive rights of intervention in academic matters. That such a condition had been the intent of the charter seems very doubtful. However, there seem to have been few difficulties of much academic importance for some years after the transfer. From 1729 to about 1755 the President and Masters probably enjoyed more self-government than did the faculty of any other early American college.[34] Having surmounted its early period of poverty and neglect, the college flourished between the middle of the century and the time of the Revolution, a period in which Thomas Jefferson and many other distinguished students graduated.

During the 1750s William and Mary became the center of a series of contentions between the faculty and the Visitors that was a part of a larger struggle over clerical salaries between the clergy and laymen of the province. The right of individual members of the faculty to marry and reside outside the college and to combine professorships with church functions became the subject of occasional disputes, while the right of the faculty body as a whole to appoint college officers and servants, bestow scholarships, manage revenues, and control college discipline without interference precipitated a running argument over the constitution of the college. The peculiar ambiguities of the charter and the sweeping powers exercised in the past by the Visitors gave ample cause for confusion.[35] The faculty, consisting almost entirely of Oxford men

[33] This in spite of the injunction made by the two survivors of the original board of Visitors when they drew up the Statutes of 1728 to the effect that the Visitors should "not suffer themselves to be troubled, except in Matters of great Moment, where there is some Difficulty to be got over, or some Corruption or ill Practice to be reformed, or a new Statute to be made, or some other weighty business to be transacted." Knight, *Documentary History of Education in the South*, p. 507.

[34] See Lyon G. Tyler, "Early Courses and Professors at William and Mary College," *William and Mary College Quarterly*, First Series, Vol. XIV (October, 1905), pp. 71–83.

[35] The clearest account of the controversies is that of Tyler, *Williamsburg*, pp. 144 ff. See also H. J. Eckenrode, *Separation of Church and State in Virginia* (Rich-

accustomed to far greater academic autonomy, put up a spirited resistance to lay control, insisting that beyond the making of the statutes the Visitors had enjoyed no rightful powers over the college since 1729 except in cases in which violation of the statutes was alleged. Since the faculty could appeal to the Bishop of London against the decisions of the Visitors they were not without recourse, and they won a number of concessions. But in the end it was inevitable that the powerful gentry of Virginia would win out over a handful of stubborn clerics. Whatever vestiges of faculty autonomy remained after the 1760s were swept away by the Revolution, during which Jefferson, as governor of Virginia and a member of the Visitors, attempted to transform his alma mater into a state university. In this he failed because of the hostility of the dissenting sects of Virginia to an institution with Anglican traditions.[36] But he did manage to reorganize and in a considerable measure to secularize it. In 1790 a legal action taken by a dismissed master resulted in a decision of sweeping importance by the Virginia Court of Appeals which in effect reaffirmed the extensive powers that had long been exercised by the Visitors and confirmed their right to remove professors.[37] Thus ended at William and Mary the only sustained attempt by college teachers to reproduce in the colonies the English pattern of academic autonomy. The independence and militancy of its faculty had been remarkable, but they had rested on forces outside the American milieu—the Privy Council, the Church of England, the Bishop of London—and no comparable situation was possible after the Revolution.

THE ARCHETYPES OF LAY GOVERNMENT

Harvard and William and Mary had one significant experience in common: the early emergence of a dual system of control, followed by the

mond, 1910), Chap. II; John E. Kirkpatrick, "The Constitutional Development of the College of William and Mary," *William and Mary Quarterly,* Second Series, Vol. IV (April, 1926), pp. 95–108; William S. Perry, *Historical Collections Relating to the American Colonial Church* (Hartford, 1870), I, 456–57, 468–69, 473, 517–18, 523–24 and *passim;* "Journal of the President and Masters of William and Mary College," *William and Mary College Quarterly,* First Series, Vol. V (October, 1896), pp. 85–89; Vol. V (April, 1897), pp. 224–29. Some light is shed on the relation of the faculty of William and Mary to the Visitors by H. L. Ganter, ed., "Documents Relating to the Early History of the College of William and Mary," *William and Mary Quarterly,* Second Series, Vol. XX (1940), *passim.*

[36] For an account of the impact of the Revolution on William and Mary see Bell, *The Church, the State, and Education in Virginia,* pp. 171–88.

[37] Bracken *v.* the Visitors of William and Mary, 1 *Call* 495–514 (1790).

ultimate concentration of power in the hands of the lay board and the subordination of the faculties. At William and Mary, unlike Harvard, the faculty body had after 1729 the character if not the strength of a group of resident masters in the English tradition, a unique situation explained in part by the ample resources that made possible six teachers of professorial stature and in part by their strong outside support. At Harvard the primary teaching officers, the tutors, played a much smaller role; and there the president became the only effective spokesman for the faculty. William and Mary illustrates more clearly the transition from the medieval university ruled by a clerisy to the modern American college ruled by laymen; while Harvard, more distinctively Protestant and distinctly American from the outset, had neither the hierarchical-gild model of control nor the resources and faculty to emulate the English colleges. Despite their support in England, however, the scholars at William and Mary, like the Virginia clerics generally, failed to command enough respect and assent in the local community to maintain their control of the college. Therefore, neither Harvard nor William and Mary, with their transitional forms and their dual boards of control, provided the characteristic models for American college government. For the most part, early American colleges, like modern American universities, were governed by unitary lay boards of control formally endowed with absolute and unqualified powers of decision. In the establishment of this pattern the most powerful models and centers of influence were the third and fourth colleges to be chartered, Yale and Princeton, and it is the government of these schools in the eighteenth century that we must now examine to see how the American mold was formed.

Yale was a creation of Harvard men. Its ten original trustees were clergymen, nine of whom had the benefits of a college education at Harvard. Its first five presiding officers were Harvard graduates. But while Harvard was enmeshed in administrative entanglements and ambiguities for more than seventy years after its founding, the legal distribution of authority in early Yale was simple: its first charter, granted by the legislature in October, 1701, gave to its trustees the authority to "erect, form, direct, order, establish, improve, and at all times in all suitable ways for the future to encourage" [38] the "collegiate school" which later was named for Elihu Yale. Their powers embraced

---

[38] For the text of the first charter of 1701, as enacted by the General Court of Connecticut, see Dexter, *Documentary History*, pp. 20–23.

the choice of their successors (who were to be Connecticut ministers over the age of forty), the choice of the rectors and teachers of the school, the payment of these and other employees, and the management of all properties and finances. In law, and for a long time to come in fact, their powers of government were absolute.

The chief problem confronting the Connecticut clerics who founded Yale was to safeguard the legal future of their college. It was on this account that they were troubled by the events at Harvard during the previous fifteen years. When the charter of the Massachusetts colony itself was vacated in 1684, the charter that had been granted to Harvard College by the Massachusetts legislature automatically became a legal nullity. Thus despite the several attempts that had been made in the meantime to secure a charter for Harvard, the older institution was still, at the time of Yale's founding, in law (although not, of course, in fact) a dead institution. While Connecticut, unlike Massachusetts, had not had its charter annulled when it was brought into the Dominion of New England, it had before it the ominous example of the Bay Colony. At that very moment there was a bill before Parliament to annul the charters of the New England colonies. Thus the Connecticut clerics faced a dilemma: to get a charter from the legislature was to risk the total dissolution of the college, as the charter might readily be voided by the Crown if the college received unfavorable attention; but to seek a royal charter was to run the risk, as the Massachusetts men had learned, of inviting royal and episcopal interference. Yale's founders decided to solve this problem as best they could by getting a charter from the colonial legislature and by masquerading their college under the most trivial guise, hoping that English indifference to or ignorance of colonial affairs would leave it unmolested.[39] Hence they called it not a "college" but by the more modest title "collegiate school"; hence they called its head not the president, as at Harvard, but the "rector"; hence they ambiguously authorized its trustees to issue "degrees or licenses," whatever that might mean. They had every intention of founding a college of the same grade and merit as Harvard, but for the time at least had no desire to proclaim it as such.

It has often been said that Yale was started because its founders

[39] The clearest statement of this problem is that of William L. Kingsley in William L. Kingsley, ed., *Yale College: A Sketch of its History* (New York, 1879), I, 21–24.

were primarily concerned with having a center of orthodoxy that would serve Congregationalism more faithfully than did the backsliding college in Cambridge.[40] While there can hardly be any doubt that Yale's founders meant to establish a sound orthodox institution, it is unlikely that the emergent latitudinarianism of Harvard frightened them excessively or that it provided the primary impulse for a Connecticut college. The desire for a college less expensive, nearer to home, and more satisfying to local pride had been expressed in Connecticut more than fifty years earlier and seems never to have disappeared.[41] Perhaps the most significant departure from Harvard's practice that was made at the beginning was the dropping of the dual form of government urged upon the Connecticut men by their Massachusetts correspondents and advisers. One can only hazard the guess that the planners of Yale found no merit in the periodic tug-of-war that they knew had gone on at Harvard between the Overseers and the Corporation, and that they intended to keep as tight-reined a control as possible over their own school. Whatever their reason, their decision marks a momentous break in the origins of American academic government, the dividing line between the dual system of the first two charters and the single board that was to be the almost universal pattern ever afterwards. That they did not admit non-clerics to the Yale Corporation (in this they spurned another recommendation from Massachusetts) may have been the consequence of their interest in upholding the legal proposition that they had already founded an institution when they applied to the General Court of Con-

[40] An interpretation expressed by Quincy, *History of Harvard University,* I, 197–200, and elaborately refuted by Prof. James L. Kingsley of Yale in *American Biblical Repository,* Series 2, Vol. VI (July, 1841), pp. 177–95; Vol. VI (October, 1841), pp. 384–404; and Vol. VII (January, 1842), pp. 175–207.

[41] The traditional conservatism of Yale may have originally made the older view plausible, and it is true that Moses Noyes, a brother of one of the first trustees and himself a trustee for many years, observed in 1723 that the initiators of Yale had given as their reason that Harvard was "under the Tutorage of Latitudinarians." Dexter, *Documentary History,* p. 242; cf. Simeon E. Baldwin, "The Ecclesiastical Constitution of Yale College," *Papers of the New Haven Historical Society,* III (New Haven, 1882), 406–8. But Connecticut was at the time far less troubled than Massachusetts by latitudinarian tendencies. Also it seems significant that the recommendation of some of the Massachusetts conservatives that the diligent study of the Westminster Confession and Ames' *Medulla* should be prescribed for all scholars was quietly ignored at Yale. Dexter, *Documentary History,* pp. 8–9, 15–19. See also Dexter, "The Founding of Yale College," *Papers of the New Haven Colony Historical Society,* III (New Haven, 1882), 1–3, and "Yale College in Saybrook," *ibid.,* VII (New Haven, 1908), 129–30.

necticut for a charter. To admit new members to the board of trustees might be to reopen the question.[42] It has also been suggested that laymen were excluded "because there were really so few active educated men then in Connecticut outside of the clergy, so few laymen who would endure labor and sacrifice for the ideal of higher education." [43]

So far as the powers of the president were concerned, Yale's experience was quite similar to Harvard's, and this is the more striking when we realize that the original group of trustees, who well knew what difficulties had been created for Harvard by the dominating person of Increase Mather, intended to keep the rector a subordinate figure. Their first set of rules allowed tenure on good behavior to the rector and other officers. During the early days of the fledgling collegiate school, when a permanent site had not yet been agreed upon, its first two rectors were trustees who combined ministerial duties with supervising the tutors and teaching. In 1718 the school was at last settled at New Haven and given the name of Yale College. It was not very long after the secure establishment of the school that its rector loomed very large in its affairs. The first rector not chosen from the original group of trustees was the Reverend Timothy Cutler, who as we shall see had to leave because of his conversion to episcopacy. The second, the Reverend Elisha Williams, whose rectorship began in 1726, was admitted to the board of trustees, and after some years began to preside at meetings of the Corporation.

The larger, the more complex, the more prosperous the college grew, the more did the prestige and power of its presiding officer grow. The emergence of the rector as the dynamic force in the college merely had to wait upon the appearance of a tactful or forceful man who enjoyed the confidence of the trustees.[44] Williams was succeeded in 1739 by the Reverend Thomas Clap, an able and domineering man, who quickly enlarged the position of the rector by assuming as a right the leadership of the Corporation that had been delegated as a privilege to Williams. Clap's influence led to the new charter of 1745, which transformed the Corporation, now styled the President and Fellows, into a body in which the president became in law what Clap had made him in fact, the dy-

[42] Dexter, "The Founding of Yale College," p. 23; see also the considerations urged by J. L. Kingsley in *American Biblical Repository,* VI, 186.

[43] Dexter, "The Founding of Yale College," p. 16.

[44] An extremely illuminating study of the growth of the rector's and then the president's powers is Dexter's "An Historical Study of the Powers and Duties of the Presidency in Yale College," *Proceedings of the American Antiquarian Society,* New Series, Vol. XII (October, 1896), pp. 27–42.

namic center and the head of the governing body.[45] Clap's arbitrary conduct later became unpopular and led to a movement among some of the
gentry of Connecticut to subject the college to a committee of visitation
from the legislature. Clap was able to forestall this by an ingenious defense of the autonomy of the college,[46] but finally in 1792, long after his
day, an arrangement was concluded under President Ezra Stiles that
settled the antagonism and for a time ended the separation of the college
and the state. The governor, the lieutenant-governor, and six senior assistants in the council were admitted into the Corporation in return for
material benefits to the college, including funds for a new dormitory and
future professorships. For eighty years Yale was governed by a Corporation of such a mixed composition of private and public fellows; state officers were at last replaced by six Yale alumni, elected by their peers.[47]

Princeton, Yale's offspring, reproduced Yale's basic pattern by vesting all powers of government in its trustees, but its organization was in
several respects a new departure in American academic history. It was
the first college chartered after the impact of the Great Awakening and
the enlarged toleration of eighteenth-century life had been felt. It was the
first non-Anglican college to get a royal charter, the first case in which the
Crown unambiguously recognized the existence of a distinctive American system of lay government for colleges; it was the first to be chartered
in a province that had no established church, and the first to have a
strong intercolonial influence that raised it from the beginning above the
level of a local agency.

In one respect Princeton was an outgrowth of the expansion of New

[45] For the text of the charter of 1745, under which, with its amendments, Yale is
still governed, see Elliott and Chambers, *Charters and Basic Laws,* pp. 588–93. The
laws drawn up by Clap for the college in 1745 anticipated the later emergence of
faculty participation in Yale's government insofar as they required the president
to consult with the tutors "in all cases of difficulty and importance." However,
"the participation of the Tutors in Faculty deliberations was far more a matter
of form than of reality" in Clap's time. Dexter, "An Historical Study," pp. 36–37.
For later faculty participation see George W. Pierson, *Yale College: An Educational
History, 1871–1921* (New Haven, 1952), Chaps. VII and VIII, esp. pp. 133–35.

[46] Thomas Clap, *The Annals or History of Yale-College* (New Haven, 1766)
esp. pp. 69–76. See Dexter, "The Founding of Yale College," pp. 10 ff. and 22–23,
and "Thomas Clap and His Writings," *Papers of the New Haven Colony Historical
Society,* V (New Haven, 1894), 247–74. For a contemporary critique of Clap's
position from a legal standpoint see [Samuel Whittlesey Dana] *Yale-College Subject
to the General Assembly* (New Haven, 1784).

[47] The negotiations of 1792 are accounted for in F. B. Dexter, ed., *The Literary
Diary of Ezra Stiles,* III (New York, 1901), 452–58, 460–69; for later changes see
Elliott and Chambers, *Charters and Basic Laws,* p. 589n.

England. For years before its founding the Puritans had begun to leave Massachusetts and Connecticut, spreading out across Long Island, down into New York, and on into New Jersey. In the middle colonies the Yankees rubbed elbows with the older stocks and the new immigrants, with the Dutch, Scots, Germans, and Scotch-Irish of these provinces; and Congregationalists found themselves confronted for the first time with a complex religious environment in which they encountered Presbyterians, Quakers, Baptists, Lutherans, Mennonites, and members of the Dutch Reformed Church.[48] In this new environment Congregationalism itself tended to change, chiefly toward acceptance of the Presbyterian form of church organization; for the loose form of organization that prevailed in New England had been fostered by the religious homogeneity of the early days, by the system of town organization, and by the advantageous position of the established church. While even Connecticut Congregationalists had shown some tendencies toward closer organization, those who went farther south found it all but an imperative necessity. The township system and the privileged position in the state legislatures that gave Congregationalists the cohesion they had had in New England were lacking in New York, New Jersey, and Pennsylvania, while the presence there of several other religious bodies seemed to make cohesion more necessary than ever. Thus New England Calvinism, with the expansion of New England, tended to become Presbyterian in government, and it was more in the Presbyterian than the Congregational form that it propagated itself throughout the country. In adopting Presbyterianism, the New Englanders found themselves in the same synods and presbyteries with the Scots and Scotch-Irish, to whom this form of organization was long familiar. Princeton was in a measure the joint product of the traditional New England educational enthusiasm and the political and organizational strength of Presbyterianism.

It was the product, too, of a religious schism brought by the Great Awakening. The Presbyterians were divided into two factions by a difference in attitude toward the new religious "enthusiasm," the integrity of the minister's domain, and the education of the ministry. The Old-Side faction disapproved of the religious excitements of the Awakening. Their staid traditional clergy were troubled by the revivalist practices of itinerant ministers who frequently confronted them with competing agents of

[48] Thomas J. Wertenbaker, *The Founding of American Civilization: The Middle Colonies* (New York, 1938), Chaps. IV and V.

salvation who not only invaded their territories but often attacked the settled clerics themselves as cold and unregenerate. There was, moreover, the issue of education: the Old Side, insisting upon regular training at colleges and universities, were opposed to licensing ministers who fell short of the traditional standards.[49] Those New-Side men who had Congregational backgrounds were particularly sensitive to the charge that their faction was rearing a substandard ministry. It was a group of such men in New York and New Jersey, determined to set adequate educational standards and discouraged by the hostility of Yale under President Clap to the Awakening, who made the first movement to found Princeton. (Six of the seven trustees named in the original Princeton charter were Yale men, while one was from Harvard.)

In 1746, despite the opposition of the Anglican clergymen of the middle colonies, Governor John Hamilton granted a charter to a small group of New York and New Jersey ministers and laymen to found the College of New Jersey (the name was not legally changed until 1896). In this first charter three prominent New York laymen of unimpeachable New-Side Presbyterian affiliations and four New Jersey clergymen were named trustees with power to co-opt other trustees to the number of twelve. The trustees were given the full powers of management, including the hiring and firing of the president and all faculty members. Two years later, after the institution had already been feebly launched, the new royal governor, Jonathan Belcher, persuaded the trustees to accept a second charter. Belcher was a good Calvinist, but he feared that the college might be attacked by the other religious denominations if it did not have a closer affiliation with the province. With some difficulty, he was able to persuade the trustees to accept an enlargement of the board from twelve to twenty-three; this step added the governor and four members of his council, together with three prominent Pennsylvania laymen, and preserved the clerical majority by adding eight ministers. It was also required that the trustees (not the faculty or the students) take an oath of loyalty to the Hanoverian succession, which could be adopted by anyone but recusant Catholics.

In other vital respects the text of the charter was the same as that of two years before. Retained but slightly reworded was the provision of the 1746 charter that the trustees could not exclude

[49] John Maclean, *History of the College of New Jersey* (Philadelphia, 1877), I, 24–60.

any Person of any religious Denomination whatsoever from free and Equal Liberty and Advantage of Education, or from any of the Liberties, Priviledges or immunities of the Said College on account of his or their speculative Sentiments in Religion and of his or their being of a Religious profession Different from the said Trustees of the College.[50]

This clause, the first such statement of tolerant principles in an American college charter, reflected at once the necessity of placating the Anglicans and Quakers and the difficulties of a dissenting church that was securing a charter from an Anglican monarch. But the fact of primary significance is that with Princeton we have the first instance of a college founded under the characteristic conditions of the America of the eighteenth, rather than the seventeenth, century: religious and ethnic heterogeneity, schismatic differences brought by the Awakening, and growing mutual accommodation and tolerance. Harvard, William and Mary, and Yale, being colleges chartered for established churches, had had an intimate relation in each case with the state, receiving substantial amounts of financial assistance and becoming subject, especially in the case of the two New England schools, to a great deal of intervention by the state legislatures.[51] Of necessity Princeton carried on without state aid and was substantially free of state control.[52]

The appearance in Princeton's charter of a clause opening the college to students who were not of the trustees' religious persuasion should not, however, be taken as mitigating the sectarian commitment of the institution. Even after the breach within the Presbyterian church had been outwardly healed, the New-Side faction kept its hands upon the reins. The Old-Side leaders proposed in 1766 that in return for the election of a president chosen by them and the appointment of a genuine faculty of professors they would guarantee substantial donations.[53] This proposal

[50] The text of both charters can be found in Wertenbaker, *Princeton*, pp. 396–404. The text of the first charter, which was lost for over a century and a half and hence unknown to Princeton historians before Wertenbaker, is not conveniently available elsewhere. For later constitutional changes see Elliott and Chambers, *Charters and Basic Laws*, pp. 431–33. The non-denominational clause was thought to be required to conform to the 1664 charter of the province. See Charles W. Shields, "The Origin of Princeton University," *Memorial Book of the Sesquicentennial Celebration of the Founding of the College of New Jersey* (New York, 1898), pp. 455–60, on the role of Governor Belcher in working for the liberality of the college.

[51] William Wallace Smith, "The Relations of College and State in Colonial America," unpublished doctoral dissertation (Teachers College, Columbia University, 1949), Chaps. II–IV.

[52] Maclean, *History of the College of New Jersey*, I, 67–68.

[53] Varnum L. Collins, *Princeton* (New York, 1914), pp. 67–68.

the trustees rejected, fearing synodical control; instead they chose as their new president the distinguished Scottish theologian, Dr. John Witherspoon. This proved a strategic choice, for the new president was a man of such caliber as to enable the college to put its stamp upon the church instead of being merely controlled by it.[54] Witherspoon, who promptly Americanized himself, became a figure of much ecclesiastical and political influence (he was a delegate to the Continental Congress from New Jersey for most of the period from 1776 to 1782), and proved to be acceptable to both Presbyterian factions.[55]

With the development of Princeton we have the characteristic pattern for American private college government: control through a unitary board of nonresident, nonacademic persons; [56] the presence on the board of clergymen either in equal numbers to laymen or in predominant strength; a denominational affiliation of some kind, but hospitality to matriculants of other sects; the centrality, in the institution's governance and development, of the strong president; the essential independence, despite the occasional presence of state officials on boards of control, from either control or support by the state. The later colonial colleges might vary this formula to a greater or lesser degree. But after the Revolution, and during the first decades of the nineteenth century, as the American college system emerged from the eastern states and spread through the South and West in the wake of settlement, it was the pattern begun by Yale and set by Princeton which was most emulated. In the early national period the work of founding and managing colleges remained primarily in the hands of the churches, and two main

[54] See *ibid.*, pp. 62–93 for the best discussion of factors bearing on college control in this period.

[55] Varnum L. Collins, *President Witherspoon: A Biography* (Princeton, 1925), is an important study. Such was the confidence of the trustees in Witherspoon that in 1770 they resolved to turn over to him "the sole direction as to the Methods of Education to be pursued in this Seminary" (*ibid.*, I, 134–35).

[56] Among the colonial charters one, that of Brown, reverted to the dual board of control. It seems uncertain whether the model in this case was the bicameral legislature of the state or the Harvard system, which Brown's closely resembled. Brown's board consisted of a group of trustees, who resembled Harvard's Overseers, and a body of fellows, resembling the Harvard Corporation. The president was an ex-officio member of the Fellows. Basic policy decisions were made by the joint concurrence of the two boards, as in a bicameral legislature, although the awarding of degrees and the "Instruction and immediate Government of the College" were vested in the president and fellows; so also was the drafting of college statutes, subject to the approval of the trustees. Aside from the president, no faculty members were fellows. Walter C. Bronson, *A History of Brown University, 1764–1914* (Providence, R.I., 1914), pp. 500–507. Bowdoin, among the later New England colleges, also adopted a dual board, in this case a clear imitation of Harvard's.

streams of influence can be discerned, one emanating from Yale and
spreading into the Northwest and the other emanating from Princeton
and spreading into the South and the Southwest.[57] The diffusion of the
influence of Yale and Princeton might be illustrated in several ways.
Perhaps none is more dramatic than the prominence of their graduates
among college presidents. Among 110 presidents of 75 colleges in operation before 1840, 36 were graduates of Yale and 22 of Princeton—the
two institutions together providing more than half the total.[58]

SUPPORT AND CONTROL

The earliest colleges had been founded at a time when private resources
were much too feeble to maintain them, and support by the state was a
necessity. The close of the colonial period saw the ideal of the private
college well established. The intimate relations between the first colonial
colleges and the states have caused one student of the subject to declare
that the first three colleges were in effect under state control, and to imply a vague analogy with the state universities of a later age.[59] But since
all three institutions were founded under the aegis of established churches,
this statement can easily be misleading. It is hardly more valid than the
assertion that the colleges were controlled by the churches. It is perhaps
less startling but more correct to say that the colleges were governed
by the church-state complex. In Massachusetts the magistrates usually
consulted and often deferred to the ministers. Anne Hutchinson, for instance, was condemned and excommunicated by a church synod, but she
was tried and banished by civil authorities. Similarly, the clergy took the
initiative in the prosecution of the Quakers, but the legislation controlling

[57] George P. Schmidt, *The Old Time College President* (New York, 1930),
pp. 25–28; Wertenbaker, *Princeton*, pp. 113–17. Donald R. Come has written an
illuminating account of the diffusion of Princeton's example, "The Influence of
Princeton on Higher Education in the South before 1825," *William and Mary
Quarterly*, Third Series, Vol. II (October, 1945), pp. 359–96.

[58] Schmidt, *The Old Time College President*, p. 96. The others were recruited
as follows: Union 13, Brown 12, Dickinson 10, Dartmouth 9, Harvard 8, and a
scattering accounting for the remainder. Dickinson itself, however, was profoundly
influenced by Princeton, as Dartmouth was by Yale.

[59] Smith, "Relations of College and State in Colonial America," pp. 1–4, and
passim. The author confounds his own thesis with respect to Massachusetts when
he points out that the suffrage act of 1631 guaranteed "that the affairs of the civil
government would remain largely under the control of the Church" (*ibid.*, p. 9).
It is confusing when a college is "controlled" by a state that in turn is "controlled"
by the church.

them was enacted by the General Court and enforced by the magistrates.[60] In similar fashion the General Court often interfered in the affairs of Harvard—and not merely through the Overseers, on which board it was represented, but also directly through legislative action. It was the General Court, not the Overseers, that took action against President Dunster and received his resignation, and that called upon Increase Mather either to reside in Cambridge or vacate the presidency. In Connecticut the Assembly, although not represented on the governing board of Yale, showed its interest by ordering the trustees to finish a building at New Haven, intervening in the choice of a rector and the permanent location of the school, examining finances on many occasions, and looking into the religious condition of the college. Dependent as they were upon state aid, the two New England colleges were in no position to resist such interference even if they so chose. William and Mary, in a stronger position because of its larger fixed income, was subjected to less detailed intervention; but the personnel of the board of Visitors there was closely interlocked with the membership of the Governor's Council and the House of Burgesses. The college's situation at Williamsburg, the capital of the province, was a token of its intimate relation with the state, as well as a great academic advantage.[61]

In the last thirty years before the outbreak of the Revolution both state aid and state interference diminished as the burden of support shifted from government to private individuals. The first three colleges had relied chiefly upon governmental support in the form of annual grants or assigned revenues from a particular source. But the later schools, largely because of sectarian hostilities and inhibitions, could not safely call upon the state governments, and thus benefited from state aid only in a marginal and incidental way. King's College got some public help, the College of Philadelphia less, and Dartmouth only two very small grants, while Princeton, Brown, and Queen's College received nothing.[62]

The founding and continuation of the later colleges were made possible by the development of a widespread interest in higher education among

[60] Greene, *Religion and the State,* pp. 42–46.

[61] For state action bearing on the colleges see Smith, "Relations of College and State in Colonial America," Chaps. I–III.

[62] Smith summarizes state aid to the colonial colleges, *ibid.,* pp. 33–38, 58–64, 77–80, 89–114, 142–43; cf. the table compiled by Clews, *Educational Legislation and Administration* . . . , p. 501, which represents schematically and approximately the grants and appropriations of the colonial governments to colleges and schools.

the well-to-do, an interest intense enough to bring contributions from thousands of individuals in the colonies, the British Isles, and even other parts of the Empire. Important bequests were still quite rare; most of the funds were raised through subscriptions, some through the riskier and less popular means of private lotteries.[63] The pressing need for private funds gave prestige to trustees like Gilbert Tennent of New Jersey and Morgan Edwards of Brown and administrators like William Smith of the College of Philadelphia and John Witherspoon of New Jersey, all of whom were outstandingly successful as fund raisers. It also underlined, however, the importance of the churches, through which a great deal of the solicitation was carried on, especially in the British Isles. British contributors were often impatient of American sectarian disputes, and the necessity of raising funds from them added some leverage to the movement toward tolerance in the colleges.[64] Colonial assemblies seem not to have been disposed to intervene officiously in the management of educational institutions that they were not supporting, and the later colonial colleges manifest a decided shift toward private control along with private support. Harvard and Yale, with their traditional involvements with the states, became disentangled more slowly, receiving their last grants in 1823 and 1831 respectively.[65] They were legally relieved of their liability to substantial state intervention after 1819 by the implications of the Dartmouth College case.

Direct legislation was not, of course, the only measure of state interest in the colleges. With the exception of Yale, Brown, and the College of Philadelphia, the colonial colleges had ex-officio representatives of the state officialdom, including the governors, on their boards of control, a relationship which arose out of the necessity either of securing a state charter or a royal or proprietary charter with some governor's benevolent intervention. Where political matters, factional feuds, church differences, or the interests of the state or Crown were involved, trustees representing

[63] For the sources of college support in the period 1745–75 see Beverly McAnear's valuable account, "The Raising of Funds by the Colonial Colleges," *Mississippi Valley Historical Review,* XXXVIII (March, 1952), 591–612. McAnear estimates that over £20,000 was raised in the colonies by private subscriptions and about £12,000 through lotteries. Bequests accounted for £7,402, public grants for £2,776. More than £21,000 was netted from British sources, whose aid was widely considered indispensable to the success of a colonial college. Suggestive but frequently inaccurate on the support of the colleges is Jesse B. Sears, *Philanthropy in the History of American Higher Education* (Washington, 1922).
[64] See, for example, Maclean, *History of the College of New Jersey,* I, 234.
[65] Smith, "Relations of College and State in Colonial America," pp. 137–38.

the political order were thus on hand to express themselves. On the Harvard Overseers and the governing board of Dartmouth the state officials comprised about half the membership.[66] At Philadelphia after 1779 and Yale after 1792 state officials were added, leaving only Brown, an inheritor of Rhode Island's church-state separatism, without such a relationship.[67]

The respective places of laymen and clerics on boards of control also deserve notice. By the terms of the charters (and these arrangements tended to perpetuate themselves for long periods), four of the colonial colleges—Harvard, Princeton, Brown, and Dartmouth—had governing boards on which clerical and lay trustees were quite evenly balanced. Three—William and Mary, King's College, and Queen's College—were mixed but clearly dominated by the laymen, while one, the College of Philadelphia, consisted entirely of laymen.[68] Yale's board, until its reconstitution in 1792, was the only one composed entirely of clergymen.[69]

A mere enumeration of the number of clerical and nonclerical trustees, however, perhaps underestimates the religious character of the colleges.

[66] At William and Mary only the Governor was an ex-officio representative of the state on the Visitors, but the overlapping of the province's governing groups provided others informally. At Princeton the governor was the sole state member. Twelve political officials were ex-officio members of the King's College board, including the first Lord Commissioner for Trade and Plantations, ten state officers, and the Mayor of New York City. Four out of forty-one trustees at Queen's College were in this category. Six of Dartmouth's twelve trustees were state officials (five from New Hampshire, one from Connecticut), but were not designated as ex-officio members.

[67] The revision of the College of Philadelphia's constitution in 1779 made six state officers ex-officio members of a board of nineteen, but the other members named were almost all state officers also. Another revision in 1791 maintained similar state representation. Yale, of course, added eight state officials to its board of eleven members in 1792.

[68] The statement concerning the College of Philadelphia needs some qualification. One of the original trustees, Richard Peters, had taken orders in the Church of England and had come to America as a clergyman. Differences between himself and his rector caused the suspension of his license by the Bishop of London. Although he remained a figure of some influence in the church in Pennsylvania, he had been living the life of a layman for twelve years before becoming a trustee of the academy out of which the college grew. Thomas H. Montgomery, *A History of the University of Pennsylvania from Its Foundation to* A.D. *1770* (Philadelphia, 1900), pp. 92–95.

[69] William and Mary had four clerics out of eighteen trustees; Queen's, thirteen out of twenty-eight (and a charter provision specified that ministers must not be over one third of the Board); King's College, seven clerics (including the Archbishop of Canterbury and the president of the college) out of forty-four. Brown may be said to have had a balanced board by virtue of the fact that ministers had a clear preponderance among the fellows, laymen among the trustees.

Ministers tended to be more assiduous in their attendance at meetings. The presidents who, as we have seen, provided so much of the dynamic leadership, were clergymen. And laymen themselves were very commonly chosen with their denominational affiliations clearly in mind, and often with reference to their position as pillars of their church communities. Perhaps most important of all, the college itself seems to have been thought of very largely in the light of its religious relationships, and the role of a college trustee had more of the pastoral character than it came to have in later times. Trustees, while governing the business affairs of the colleges, thought of themselves also as the moral and spiritual guardians of the students, and indeed often of the faculties; and pious laymen, leaving their businesses to attend board meetings, seem to have shorn themselves, to a degree, of their usual roles to assume the moral and intellectual garb of pastors-for-the-moment, inquiring closely into the regularity and character of religious services at the college and examining the spiritual nature and moral discipline of the undergraduates.

Thus even though the colleges were committed to the governance of laymen, these laymen found in the role and demeanor of the clerics a subtly influential archetype for their own behavior; the religious inheritance of the colleges created a kind of priesthood of the trustees. This was a process that could also work in the opposite direction, for the responsibilities of fund raising and administration tended to make men of affairs and business managers out of the clerics who became college presidents.[70] The management of colleges was indeed one of the many areas of life in which the unspecialized society of the eighteenth-century colonies created its versatile men.

One may find difficulties in disentangling the roles of church and state in college sponsorship, but one thing seems clear: aristocratic control and aristocratic values were universal. Colonial America may have been a more democratic society and may have offered more opportunities for class mobility than the contemporary societies of Europe. But as compared with the open and fluid society of the first half of the nineteenth century, or with the image of "frontier democracy" that is all too often freely pictured in general books on American history, the society of the American colonies was one dominated by an aristocracy of land and commerce, an aristocracy difficult of access to rising members of the middle class and all but closed to those who started very poor. To be

[70] This was notably true at Princeton and Brown.

sure, opportunities to earn an independent livelihood, to be free from poverty and gross insecurity, were exceptionally good for those who started in life with little but a willingness to work; but this was a far cry from opportunity to enter the ranks of the rich and powerful. A privileged class, strengthened by ties of intermarriage, existed in each province and at length spread across colonial boundaries; it seems to have grown stronger and become more sharply defined in the eighteenth century than in the seventeenth. "There was, in fact," writes a distinguished student of the colonial period, "in almost every colony a definite ruling class [which] dominated the local political machinery, filled all or nearly all the important local offices, . . . spoke on public matters in behalf of all . . . [and] used its power very largely for the benefit of its own members. . . ." [71] Attached to this ruling class were the outstanding professional men of the colonies, and on its periphery were the most acceptable leaders of a class of solid citizens of the sort represented by Benjamin Franklin.[72] It was to serve the traditional and aristocratic needs of this upper crust that the colonial colleges, with their conservative adherence to the classical curriculum, were designed, while the middle classes beneath them, whose base was small shopkeeping and special crafts, were generally satisfied to send their children to good private academies with curricula based less upon the classics and more upon a program of practical studies.[73]

It was the aristocracy that was primarily concerned with the colonial colleges, the well-to-do class that gave the bulk of private support, and the ruling group that provided the trustees.[74] When a governing board sat down to consider the affairs of the colonial college, there was usually assembled at the same table a group of men who were accustomed to seeing each other frequently at the counting houses, in each others' homes, and in the vestries of the churches, and whose family relationships could

[71] Leonard W. Labaree, *Conservatism in Early American History* (New York, 1948), p. 2. Chap. I of this volume has a brilliant account of the ruling families of what Labaree calls the conciliar aristocracies of the colonies. See also James Truslow Adams, *Provincial Society, 1690–1763* (New York, 1927), Chap. III, and Henry Graff's forthcoming study of the backgrounds of the signers of the Declaration of Independence.

[72] Carl and Jessica Bridenbaugh, *Rebels and Gentlemen* (New York, 1942), Chap. I.

[73] *Ibid.*, Chap. II; cf. Clifford K. Shipton, "Secondary Education in the Puritan Colonies," *New England Quarterly*, VII (December, 1934), 658–61.

[74] Cf. the comments of Cheyney, *History of the University of Pennsylvania*, pp. 30, 104, 111, 123, 131, 148; Demarest, *History of Rutgers College*, pp. 61–64; Guild, *Early History of Brown*, pp. 54–58.

be represented only by a complicated network of crisscrossing lines.[75] Even in Connecticut, which a man like Samuel Johnson considered hardly better than a mobocracy,[76] and which was in fact less clearly aristocratic than many other colonies, the bonds of kinship were conspicuous, and the clerical founders of Yale were quite elaborately interrelated.[77]

[75] A study of the members of the first Board of Trustees of the College of Philadelphia provides us with a microcosm of the economic and social world of the colonial elite. There were twenty-four trustees, of whom three quarters were Anglicans. At least fourteen were wealthy from investments in trade or land or a combination of the two, and many had inherited such wealth. Four were lawyers, four physicians, one an ex-clergyman turned to public service and the Indian trade, and one, Benjamin Franklin, was a scientist, inventor, author, and diplomat, as well as a man of business. No fewer than twenty-one held public offices at one time or another; most of them held multiple offices during their lives, including many of the highest positions in the provincial government and the municipal government of Philadelphia. Fourteen of the trustees were closely related to other trustees, either directly or through their siblings or children. Their interwoven connections become doubly complicated when family relationships are carried down a few generations and when they are compounded with business partnerships. One trustee, for instance, Thomas Lawrence, was associated in the shipping business first with another trustee, James Logan, and then with the elder brother of a second fellow-trustee. One of Lawrence's sons married the daughter of a trustee, while his daughter married a trustee's son. Samuel McCall, Jr., was a brother-in-law of two trustees, while two of his daughters married trustees (one of whom was the son of a trustee). The zenith of this kind of interrelationship is represented in the life of Charles Willing, the son of a Bristol merchant who came to Philadelphia in 1728 after his elder brother had already established a mercantile business there. In 1731 Willing married the sister of Dr. William Shippen, Sr., another of the original trustees. Of their four daughters, two married trustees, one married the son of a trustee, and the fourth married Col. William Byrd of Westover. They also had a son, Thomas, who became Chief Justice of the Supreme Court and joined the Board of Trustees in 1760. Thomas married the daughter of a trustee, and had a son who became a trustee in 1800 and a daughter who married a trustee. It is interesting that while many of the original trustees had good educations, only one held a college degree and that exposure to any portion of the undergraduate curriculum of the time was rare among them. No doubt this heightened their sense of the community's need for a college. In later years the kinship network left its mark upon the college staff. The daughter of trustee William Allen married into the famous DeLancey family of New York, and her grandson was William Heathcote DeLancey, Provost of the University of Pennsylvania, 1828–33. Dr. William Shippen's son, William Shippen, Jr., took his M.D. at Edinburgh and became the first professor of anatomy and surgery at the new medical school of the college. Trustee Philip Syng's grandson was Professor of Surgery, then Anatomy, at the University, 1805–31. Trustee Thomas Hopkinson's daughter married Dr. John Morgan, who was the first medical professor at the college. Data on the trustees was compiled by Mr. F. W. Smith, chiefly from sketches given in Montgomery, *History of the University of Pennsylvania,* pp. 53–108.

[76] Labaree, *Conservatism in Early American History,* p. 66.

[77] "The youngest trustee was Joseph Webb," remarks Dexter. "The fact he and Mr. Chauncy married sisters reminds us that the bonds of family connection between these early trustees were remarkably numerous. The same relationship existed

In sum, each of the early colleges was under the governance of men representing a fairly homogeneous social class and sharing a common conception of education. Although colonial politics was often the field of sharp partisan dispute, the social homogeneity of the immediate sponsors of the colleges, together with the absence from the curricula of topical economic or political subjects, kept the colleges relatively free from urgent controversy of this sort. The chief problems to appear within them— and they were by no means negligible—were those arising out of religious and intellectual differences within the governing group. On the whole the colonial elite need not have been ashamed of its educational achievement, for the colonial colleges, with all their weaknesses, made remarkable gains during the eighteenth century, not only in the direction of higher standards but of greater liberality. The sponsorship of an enlightened aristocracy has often been identified with such gains in American higher education.

---

between Mather and Andrew; Pierpont was the nephew of Pierson by one marriage, and the stepson of Buckingham by another; Noyes and Woodbridge were cousins; the children of Pierson and Woodbridge intermarried. . . ." "The Founding of Yale College," p. 31.

IV: RELIGION, REASON, AND
REVOLUTION

SECTARIANISM AND RESTRAINT

IN THE DEVELOPMENT of the American colleges, freedom of thought as a consciously formulated goal appeared first as religious freedom for students. Long before anyone spoke of freedom for teachers, the existence of religious freedom or toleration for undergraduates was commonly boasted as an outstanding asset of the eighteenth-century colleges. Princeton, summing up its own virtues for the public in 1764, was only repeating claims that had grown common among the other colleges when it asserted that its students were encouraged to exercise the right of private judgment and that the faculty did not dictate to them with "an air of infallibility." [1] Such a claim was a general point of pride among the colleges throughout the latter part of the century; and a college that openly violated this governing principle, as Yale did under President Clap, was bound to suffer for the breach.[2]

The tendency of the colleges to take pride in the toleration they accorded undergraduates, although observable at Harvard even in the late seventeenth century, was quickened after 1746 by competition among the colleges for students. In the financing of the colleges student fees were of crucial importance, and around the middle of the century an active competition for students emerged among the colleges from Phila-

---

[1] *An Account of the College of New Jersey* (Woodbridge, N.J., 1764), p. 28. Again in 1802, in the course of an appeal for funds, Princeton's sponsors looked back with pride to the fact that in the more than fifty years of its existence "we never, indeed, have been so attached to the dogmas of any religious sect as to impose them on our pupils. . . . No pupil with us has ever been questioned on the subject of his political creed, nor withheld from a full and free avowal of his sentiments, nor received any censure or disapprobation for making known his opinions either in speech or writing." John Maclean, *History of the College of New Jersey* (Philadelphia, 1877), II, 37–38.

[2] Even Thomas Clap paid lip service to it. See his claims in *The Annals or History of Yale-College* (New Haven, 1766), pp. 83–84.

delphia to Cambridge. While sectarian considerations did play some role in the choice of colleges by students and parents, low fees and sheer proximity seem to have been more decisive factors. Most college administrations, feeling that a single sect was unlikely to furnish enough students for the prosperity of their institution, chose in their public statements to advertise their nonsectarian character and to supplement this quietly by a more sectarian form of recruitment carried on by denominational pastors among the bright boys of their congregations.[3] The plea of sectarian loyalty, which might offend potential donors as well as potential students, was a risky one to use as a public argument. Once committed by their public announcements to nonsectarian conduct, however, the schools were mortgaged to it as an ideal.[4]

Educational theorists were much concerned that young men should have an education conducive to piety and good morals, to personal development, and to the wellbeing of society as a whole. But the needs and rights of faculty members were not commonly discussed in similar terms; teachers were assumed to be instruments rather than ends in themselves. It was expected of them that they be persons suitable for the development of the undergraduates in their tutelage and care—that is, they had to have some minimum of competence as teachers and they had to display piety and good morals because they were the exemplars of the young.[5] Beyond this, little was said of them. Even a man so sensitive to the necessary conditions of work for craftsmen in all spheres and so liberal in his ideas as Benjamin Franklin could write a little tract on the type of academy education best suited to the youth of Pennsylvania which included no more than a single perfunctory sentence on the men

[3] An excellent analysis of the problem is Beverly McAnear's "The Selection of an Alma Mater by Pre-Revolutionary Students," *Pennsylvania Magazine of History and Biography*, LXXIII (October, 1949), 429–40, esp. p. 435.

[4] Avoiding discrimination against students of sects other than the one that chiefly sponsored a college was not, however, quite identical with failure to proselytize among them. For instance, the Anglican atmosphere of the College of Philadelphia and the alluring inducements of Anglican orders seem to have swayed some of the Presbyterian youth, even though the faculty itself was largely Presbyterian. See Leonard J. Trinterud, *The Forming of an American Tradition* (Philadelphia, 1949), pp. 215–16.

[5] William Smith, in his *A General Idea of the College of Mirania* (New York, 1753), remarked (pp. 28–39) that all the masters must be of irreproachable character because the youth will emulate them. "The Masters . . . are truly affable, indefatigable and patient. . . . *Learning* in them, tho' universal, is but a secondary Qualification. Their amiable temper, mild Behavior, Forebearance and Placability, have long since struck Envy and Calumny dumb" (pp. 65–66). Good men and true, but rather subdued!

who were to teach them: "That the Rector be a man of good Under-standing, good Morals, diligent and patient; learn'd in the Languages and Sciences, and a correct pure Speaker and Writer of the *English* Tongue: to have such Tutors under him as shall be necessary." [6]

One of the earliest signs of recognition of the liberties of faculty members dates from 1772, when President John Witherspoon of Princeton, appealing to Englishmen in the West Indies for support, made a point of what he claimed was the atmosphere of liberty at that college. He made the conventional observations about the absence of religious discrimination, remarking that many students had completed the entire course without his ever becoming aware of their denominational preference.[7] But something of a landmark in educational discussion was his additional reference to the independence of the teachers:

There is no fear of being obliged to choose Teachers upon Ministerial [i.e., governmental] recommendation, or in compliance with the over-bearing weight of family interest. On the contrary the Trustees are naturally led, and in a manner forced to found their choice upon the characters of the persons and the hope of public approbation.

Thus, he assured his potential benefactors, those concerned in the government and instruction of the college were free from temptation "to a fawning cringing spirit and mean servility in the hope of Court favor or promotion." [8] Although a seminary of learning should not enter deeply into political contention, it should have an internal spirit of liberty, which is "infinitely preferable to the dead and vapid state of one whose very existence depends upon the nod of those in power."

The fact that Princeton did not derive its support all from one source, but was compelled to appeal to many interests, Witherspoon considered a distinct asset, since it conduced to freedom and tolerance: "Having no particular prop to lean to on one side, we are obliged to stand upright and firm by leaning equally on all." [9] The teachers in the college, too, being of varying religious principles, had had to adjust to each other.[10] Possibly this statement did not mean as much as it might have seemed on the surface—"court favor" had not been much of a problem in American education, and Witherspoon did not care to specify how widely the teach-

[6] Benjamin Franklin, *Proposals Relating to the Education of Youth in Pensilvania* (Philadelphia, 1749), p. 9.

[7] John Witherspoon, *Address to the Inhabitants of Jamaica and Other West-Indian Islands* (Philadelphia, 1772), pp. 25–26.

[8] *Ibid.*, p. 20.   [9] *Ibid.*, pp. 20–21.   [10] *Ibid.*, p. 25.

ers in the college actually differed in religion—but so far as it went, it represented a distinct advance over past expressions of college policy; at least a measure of freedom for college teachers was posited as an educational advantage of some importance.

During the greater part of the century, however, close religious conformity by teachers was commonly demanded as the norm. Such conformity was secured by what has always been the primary instrument of control, *restraint by recruitment:* that is to say, in the making of appointments an effort was commonly made to be sure at the beginning that the incoming president, professor, or tutor was one who accepted the requisite theological doctrines. That this method was quite self-consciously adopted at a very early stage can be seen in the case of President Chauncy, who was required to agree to keep quiet about his little doctrinal deviations before he was installed at Harvard in 1654. Again, when Edward Wigglesworth was appointed to the first professorship of divinity at Harvard, the Overseers forced the Corporation to test his orthodoxy.[11] Similarly, in 1756 the installation of Yale's first divinity professor, Naphtali Daggett, was attended by such an examination.[12] Yale not only indulged in such a practice but had also formalized its requirements in the laws drawn up by President Thomas Clap in 1745 by exacting of all incoming officers a public statement of assent to the Westminster Confession and the ecclesiastical discipline of the Connecticut Congregational churches as laid down in the Saybrook Platform of 1708.[13] Professors and tutors were subjected to some detailed examina-

[11] Shipton, *Sibley's Harvard Graduates,* V, 549; Josiah Quincy, *The History of Harvard University* (Cambridge, Mass., 1840), I, 253–56.

[12] The Corporation seems to have spent the better part of a day at this task. F. B. Dexter, *Biographical Sketches of the Graduates of Yale College,* 6 vols. (New York, 1885–1912), II, 154, 400. Daggett was examined "as to his principles of religion, his knowledge and skill in divinity, cases of conscience . . . and various other qualifications. . . . On the next day he preached in the College Hall, and then gave his assent to the Westminster Catechism and Confession of Faith, and to the Saybrook Platform; declared his belief that the Apostle's Creed, the Nicene Creed, and the Athanasian Creed agree with the Word of God; assented to the ninth of the Thirty-nine Articles of the Church of England, being that which relates to original sin; and ended by presenting an extended confession of his faith from his own pen, in which he renounced all the errors and heresies which commonly go under the name of Arianism, Socinianism, Arminianism, Pelagianism, Antinomianism, and Enthusiasm." William L. Kingsley, ed., *Yale College: A Sketch of Its History* (New York, 1879), I, 83–84.

[13] *Ibid.,* II, 16. While Clap put this test into the college laws, he did not introduce the practice, which was instituted by the Corporation after the startling apostasy of Rector Cutler in 1722. His own installation as rector in 1739 included giving proof of his orthodoxy, although he was himself probably much closer to orthodox

tion of the state of their faith even as late as the presidency of Ezra Stiles, which began during the Revolution.[14] The practice of careful recruitment and prior examination did not stop at Harvard with the elder Wigglesworth, as is shown by the discussions concerning the orthodoxy of President Holyoke before his installation in 1737 and the fact that the younger Wigglesworth, seated in the Hollis Chair of Divinity in 1765, went through an examination somewhat similar to that suffered by his father forty-three years earlier.[15] John Winthrop, the second occupant of the Hollis Professorship of Mathematics and Natural Philosophy, was treated more indulgently: the Board of Overseers twice voted down a proposal to examine him on his religious principles before ratifying his nomination. They examined him only on his competence in mathematics.[16] Princeton, like Harvard and Yale, made appointments with religious persuasion in mind. Its New-Side trustees firmly refused in 1766–67 to appoint the distinguished Francis Alison as president, even at the cost of much-needed financial support from the Philadelphia Old Side.[17] It is hard to say, however, whether or not this rejection was more attributable to dogmatic considerations than to factional stubbornness; for instead of Alison the trustees took John Witherspoon, who did not share their preference for the "New Divinity" of the Edwards-Bellamy-Hopkins school.[18]

The candid examinations of prospective appointees suggest that the consideration of doctrinal acceptability was all but universal; and where a president, professor, or tutor was installed without prior examination, the omission is more plausibly explained by the presumption that his principles were already well known than by the assumption that the boards of governors were liberal or indifferent to such matters. In interdenominational colleges more latitude existed for variety of belief, but no one seems to have contested the principle that a college officer's beliefs could properly be scanned before his appointment.

It might be inferred from the prevalence of restraint by recruitment that where clashes did take place between governing boards and college

---

Calvinism than the members of the Corporation that elected him. Shipton, *Sibley's Harvard Graduates*, VII, 31.

[14] Ezra Stiles, *Literary Diary* (New York, 1901), III, 18.

[15] Quincy, *History of Harvard*, II, 5–11, 131–32.   [16] *Ibid.*, II, 26–27.

[17] Thomas J. Wertenbaker, *Princeton, 1746–1896* (Princeton, 1946), pp. 48–51; Trinterud, *Forming of an American Tradition*, Chap. XII.

[18] Trinterud, *Forming of an American Tradition*, pp. 223–25.

officers over matters of belief, it would be because the officers underwent a change of mind during their tenures and announced for new principles that could not have been predicted at the time of their appointment. Such was in fact the case. It will be remembered that Henry Dunster's espousal of Antipedobaptism came suddenly and as a surprise to the Overseers after he had served Harvard for many years. A second such case occurred at Harvard in 1735, when Louis Langloiserie, who had been granted permission by the president and tutors to teach French to such students as desired it, was excluded from instruction at the college. A French Canadian immigrant who had embraced Protestantism, Langloiserie had been offering French instruction for almost two years when word got about that he held unsound doctrines. The Overseers authorized an investigation which showed that the instructor had recently been affected by some of the same tendencies toward "enthusiasm" that were associated with the Awakening, and that he had been proselytizing among some of the resident graduates. The Overseers resolved that the faculty had no authority to permit students to take French lessons from Langloiserie and that they must break off the relation immediately. They further resolved that they, the Overseers, had a right

to Examine into the principles of all those that are Employed in the instruction of the Students of the College upon any Just Suspicion of their holding dangerous tenents altho no Express Charge be Layed in against them. . . . and that no person chosen into such an office shal be accepted or Continued who refuseth when desired to give Satisfaction to this board as to their principles in religion.[19]

This resolution the faculty did not contest.

But undoubtedly the most celebrated case of an unexpected conversion was that of Rector Timothy Cutler at Yale in 1722, which shook the entire colony of Connecticut. Three years earlier Cutler, at thirty-five, had been called from his ministry at Stratford to become rector of the college, which at last had seemed to leave behind its infant struggles and had begun to experience a period of growth and prosperity. However, Yale had recently acquired the famous collection of books secured for it by Jeremiah Dummer, including those of the leading Anglican writers. Whatever

[19] The best account of the case is that of Albert B. Mathews, "Teaching of French at Harvard College before 1750," *Publications of the Colonial Society of Massachusetts*, XVII (1914), 216–32. Cf. the brief account in Edward Wigglesworth, *A Letter to the Reverend Mr. George Whitefield* (Boston, 1745), pp. 6–8, and Quincy, *History of Harvard*, I, 394–95, 574–76.

the real cause of the interest in episcopacy at Yale, these books seem to have quickened it, and it was not long before rumors were circulating that, as Cotton Mather put it, "Arminian books are cried up in Yale College for eloquence and learning, and Calvinists despised for the contrary." At the Yale commencement of 1722, when these suspicions had already been spread abroad, Cutler confirmed them in the most dramatic way by ending his prayer with the Episcopal form: "And let all the people say, Amen." The next day, Cutler, two of the tutors, and four ministers, including Samuel Johnson of West Haven, who was to become the first president of King's College, appeared in the college library to discuss with the Corporation their doubts of the validity of Presbyterian ordination. Once again, as in the Dunster case, what was at issue was not the right of the rector and tutors to hold simultaneously their offices and their unacceptable tenets, but simply who was right about the substantive theological issues.[20] Eventually Cutler, Johnson, and two others decided to leave Congregationalism and took Episcopal orders. The Corporation accepted the resignation of tutor Browne and "excused" Cutler from further service. They also provided that henceforth formal confessions of faith and examinations were to be demanded of future rectors and tutors. A tradition of candid watchfulness was begun at Yale.[21]

At Harvard the supervision of the religious and theological life of the college by the Overseers continued to be fairly severe through President Holyoke's regime, and for a time in 1747 there was even some talk in Massachusetts of an oath bill to impose Calvinism on Harvard.[22] Holyoke had not been president two years when the Overseers, who still represented far more accurately than the Corporation the conservative religious sentiments of the colony, intervened at a commencement by altering

[20] Also comparable with the Dunster case was the absence of abiding rancor. Cutler was by nature a difficult man; but Johnson, far from holding a grievance against his alma mater, maintained a friendly interest in it; and Episcopal ministers continued to attend there. W. L. Kingsley, *Yale College*, p. 54.

[21] F. B. Dexter, *Documentary History of Yale University*, pp. 231–34; *Yale Biographies and Annals*, I, 260, 270–73. For Samuel Johnson's account of the affair, Herbert and Carol Schneider, *Samuel Johnson . . . His Career and Writings*, (New York, 1929), I, 6–16. Shipton in his sketch of Cutler points to indisputable evidence that the rector had been guilty of duplicity in his dealings with the Yale Corporation, inasmuch as he had been planning to announce his conversion to episcopacy under circumstances which would cause the greatest consternation in Congregational ranks. "I now declare publicly," Cutler wrote to Thomas Hollis, "what I before believed privately." Shipton, *Sibley's Harvard Graduates*, V, 51–52.

[22] Samuel Eliot Morison, *Three Centuries of Harvard* (Cambridge, Mass., 1936), p. 87.

the form of the *quaestiones,* the Masters' disputations, forcing the Masters to put into an affirmative form of statement three theses raising questions concerning the trinity and other Christian doctrines.[23] Almost twenty years later a New-Light minister, who had been excluded from a place among the Overseers, stalked out of a commencement because he was outraged to hear the Masters arguing: Whether knowledge of even contingent singulars is appropriate to God. Unable to restrain his indignation, he wrote two anonymous letters to President Holyoke protesting against allowing the Masters to sport with the idea of God's omnipotence. Being at length forced to reveal his identity, he was answered gently by Holyoke, who pointed out that very challenging *quaestiones* (for instance, Intermediate knowledge is not premised of God) had been debated even in the days of Chauncy, Oakes, and Mather.[24]

While the greater part of the history of the colleges in the eighteenth century is one of progressive liberalization, at least in academic theory and curricular content if not in formal academic practices, there was one period in which this advance was checked in New England by the first developments connected with the Great Awakening: the decade falling approximately between 1740 and 1750. Ultimately the cause of toleration, and with it opportunities for liberalism in the colleges, was advanced by the schismatic tendencies of the Awakening in New England, but only after a period in which the first impact of the New-Light enthusiasms had brought a wave of sectarian and factional antagonisms and some efforts at repression. In all this the colleges were intimately involved. Not only were Harvard and Yale under the control of the Old-Light factions in their respective colonies, and thus knit into the fabric of the established order, but they were the centers for the supply of orthodox ministers; and one of the crucial issues of the Awakening—perhaps the most important practi-

---

[23] Quincy, *History of Harvard,* II, 23–25. The objectionable theses were: Whether the trinity of persons in the deity is revealed in the Old Testament, Whether creation from eternity involves a contradiction, and Whether to explain mysteries serves the cause of religion.

[24] Although the cleric insisted that he had no intention of harming the college or striking a blow at learning (the critics of freedom in the colleges never *meant* to harm them), this did not stop him from publishing his criticisms in a pamphlet, along with Holyoke's tactful, but to him unsatisfactory, answer. It is noteworthy that Holyoke took personal responsibility for the particular *quaestiones* introduced, and pointed out that they were in line with those debated in foreign Protestant universities. See A[ndrew] Croswell, *Testimony against the Prophaneness of Some of the Publick Disputes on the Last Commencement-Day* (Boston, 1760), esp. pp. 4–9. On Croswell's extremely contumacious career, see Shipton, *Sibley's Harvard Graduates,* VIII, 386–407.

cal issue—was the question of criteria for the ministry. In a colony like New Jersey, where there was neither an established church nor an established college, it was relatively simple for those attracted by the revivals to found their own schools and rear satisfactory ministers; but in Massachusetts and Connecticut, where the governance of the church order by the legislatures made possible the official repression or harassment of the New Lights, factional disputes took on an especial bitterness. So long as the Old Lights dominated it was difficult to found new churches of New-Light persuasion and impossible to found competing colleges. As pillars of the established order, the colleges naturally fell under criticism.

Since the New Lights represented a stern breed of Calvinism and the Old Lights were affected, if not by liberalism, at least by the decadence of the ancient principles, the modern student may be tempted to see in the battle between them some signs of a struggle between liberalism and reaction. It seems unlikely, however, that tolerance was in the beginning very thoroughly understood by either side; and if attempts to criticize or bully the colleges came chiefly from the ranks of the New Lights, one suspects that this was, while perhaps in part a product of their anti-intellectualism, still more attributable to the fact that, so far as control of the colleges was concerned, the New Lights were the Outs while the Old Lights were the Ins. Had the shoe been on the other foot, similar criticism of the colleges would probably have come from the opposite direction. But the more enlightened college authorities could hardly help but learn one lesson: there were grave disadvantages for serious educational work in too intimate a sectarian connection.

The first effect on the colleges of the factional antagonisms in the churches was to bring them under a wave of criticism for religious laxity and unorthodoxy. And this criticism came not merely from the more ignorant and ranting itinerant preachers of the revivals. No less a man than Jonathan Edwards in his *Some Thoughts concerning the Present Revival of Religion in New England* (1742) attacked the colleges in narrow terms as divinity schools gone sour. "The original and main design" of the colleges, he felt, was

to train up persons and fit them for the work of the ministry. And I would say in general, that it appears to me care should be taken, some way or other, that these societies should be so regulated, that they should, in fact, be nurseries of piety. Otherwise they are fundamentally ruined and undone as to their main design and most essential end. They ought to be so constituted that vice and idleness have no living there. . . . It seems to me a reproach to the land, that ever it should be so with our colleges, that, instead of being places of the greatest advantages for true piety, one cannot send a child thither without great danger of his being infected as to his morals. It is perfectly intolerable; and any thing should be done, rather than it should be so. . . . They should be . . . fountains of piety and holiness. There is a great deal of pains taken to teach the scholars human learning; there ought to be as much and more care thoroughly to educate them in religion, and lead them to true and eminent holiness. . . . And I cannot see why it is not on all accounts fit and convenient for the governors and instructors of the colleges particularly, singly, and frequently, to converse with the students about the state of their souls. . . .[25]

Such were the respects paid to the colleges by one of the most distinguished minds of the age. Presumably these strictures would have been less severe if the New Lights themselves had not been struggling to advance their persuasions under considerable pressure. We may wonder what Edwards' later tenure of the presidency of Princeton would have been like had it not been cut short after two months by his death.

More offensive than Edwards' criticisms were those made by George Whitefield a few years later. In 1744–45 Whitefield spent more than a year in New England during which he was drawn into furious controversy with the local orthodox ministers and the faculties of the colleges. His belief that the light of the New England colleges had now become "darkness that may be felt" and his charge that their spirit was ungodly received such wide currency that the faculties of both Harvard and Yale felt obliged to answer. The Harvard faculty issued a "testimony" in which they met Whitefield's charges with countercharges: he was an enthusiast, and hence an unreliable spiritual guide; he was "uncharitable, censorious, and slanderous"; he had accused the college of irreligion without giving evidence; he had cited the opinions of certain "godly ministers," but the ministers he was best acquainted with were those of Boston—who were themselves, as Overseers, a part of the government of the college. The faculty implied that Whitefield had drummed up his charges, and that in this as in many other respects he was a deluder of the people.[26] Whitefield replied with a hypocritical pamphlet full of half-disavowals and half-

---

[25] Jonathan Edwards, *Works* (New York, 1830), IV, 264–65.
[26] *The Testimony of the President, Professors and Hebrew Instructor of Harvard College . . . against the Reverend Mr. George Whitefield* (Boston, 1744), pp. 4, 8, 9–11.

regrets, ending with the statement that he still believed his assertions to be essentially true. Bad books were being read at Harvard College, and the failure of the tutors to pray with and examine the hearts of their students was, if nothing more, a sign of the general religious laxity of the times.[27]

This brought from Edward Wigglesworth a lengthy and formidable reply in which the entire state of the college was reviewed and Whitefield's charges laboriously and effectually refuted. Wigglesworth cited the Langloiserie case as evidence of the harmfulness of revivalist enthusiasm within a college. Pointing to Langloiserie's dismissal and the firing for his drunken habits of Isaac Greenwood, first Hollis Professor of Mathematics and Natural Philosophy, as illustrations of doctrinal and moral purity, Wigglesworth suggested that a college which was so unsparing with its own officers would hardly be indifferent to the morals of the children under its care. As to the latitudinarian theologians whose works were allegedly read there, the library records showed that Tillotson had not been borrowed once during the nine years from 1732 to 1741, nor Clarke for the past two years. The graduate divinity students read the orthodox Puritan divines far more than they did either Tillotson or Clarke. Finally, if it had been Whitefield's intention, as he said, merely to contribute to the religious reformation of Harvard, why had he not communicated his thoughts privately to its president or officers? Did he give a public airing to his views because he wished to discourage students from coming or potential donors from giving? [28]

The Yale faculty, then consisting of President Clap and three tutors, followed with a little counterblast of its own which in essence duplicated the Harvard countercharges and denials. This document was colored, in addition, by one of Clap's obsessional notions, namely that Whitefield had come to New England intending in the end to turn all its ministers out of their pulpits and "to introduce a Sett of Ministers into our Churches, by other Ways and Means of Education." Naturally one of the most effective ways of destroying the existing ministry of New England was "to vilify and subvert" its colleges, which would be a prelude to bringing in clergymen educated elsewhere. Certainly anyone who believed that the

[27] George Whitefield, *A Letter to the Reverend the President, and Professors . . . in Answer to a Testimony Published by Them* (Boston, 1745).

[28] Wigglesworth, *A Letter to the Reverend Mr. George Whitefield,* esp. pp. 6–8, 26–34. Whitefield seems indeed to have harbored no permanent grudge against Harvard. Almost thirty years afterward, when the Harvard Library was burned, he helped obtain books for a new library.

colleges were as bad as Whitefield charged would hardly believe them capable of supplying adequate ministers.[29]

These exchanges offer the novel spectacle of college faculties acting in a body to defend the reputation of their schools. It can hardly be said, however, that they were defending the existence of heterodoxy in the colleges; they were simply denying the truth of the charges and countering with charges of their own. Wigglesworth's satisfaction at Langloiserie's dismissal as evidence of Harvard's caution shows how far from the Harvard faculty's thoughts was the suggestion that a deviating teacher ought to be defended. The only matter of academic conduct on which there was a difference of opinion was whether tutors should indeed privately pray with and examine into the hearts of their students. Wigglesworth asserted that the tutors prayed with the students in church and that that was enough; it was the duty of every man to examine his own heart. Finally, it must be understood that the faculties were in this case simply acting in concert with a large part of the orthodox ministry in New England that had been outraged by some of Whitefield's preachings and accusations.[30] There was no flavor of independence in their acts of self-defense, merely a zeal to join the war of the factions that had been excited by the Great Awakening in New England.

SECTARIANISM AT YALE

The severest repressions growing out of the Great Awakening occurred in Connecticut. Yale under the regime of Thomas Clap as rector and president (1740–66) provides us with a case study in illiberalism, for there all the animus of sectarian passion was unleashed and there the restrictive measures that were being taken informally, partially, and sometimes rather apologetically at other colleges were made a formal part of the college laws and were openly defended. There an attempt was made to reduce one of the major colonial colleges to the status of a severely sectarian agency, foreshadowing many of the small church-dominated colleges that were to spring up in such profusion throughout the country in the early nineteenth century. The ultimate defeat of Clap's

[29] *The Declaration of the Rector and Tutors of Yale-College in New-Haven against the Reverend Mr. George Whitefield* (Boston, 1745), esp. pp. 8–12.

[30] For an account of the larger pamphlet war of which these college pamphlets were but a part, see Luke Tyerman, *The Life of the Rev. George Whitefield* (London, 1877), II, 123–42.

effort sheds light on the conditions that tended to broaden the horizons of higher education in the eighteenth century; for while Clap was certainly not the last tyrannical college president nor the last bigot, he was the last man in an eighteenth-century college to be powerful enough to go to such lengths.

Why did it happen at Yale, and why at that time? If the explanation which immediately comes to mind is correct—that Yale more or less accidentally came under the leadership of an exceptionally powerful and exceptionally bigoted sectary—then the incidents of Clap's regime have no more explanatory value than any other historical accident. It is undeniable that some of the acerbities of the situation are traceable to Clap's personal peculiarities, for he was more than ordinarily despotic and stubborn, and he had a streak of meanness.[31] It may also be allowed that the choice of this particular minister for Yale's rectorship in 1739 was an historical accident, in the sense that Clap's religious views were not a direct reflection of those of the Corporation that chose him: the Corporation consisted of vaguely liberal Old-Light men, while he was a vigilant and orthodox Calvinist.[32] It must be allowed, too, that the choice of such a man was perhaps a slight anachronism, because Yale had prospered for thirteen years under Elisha Williams, his predecessor, a man of more liberal and compromising spirit than Clap would have thought desirable. A member of a prominent Connecticut Valley family and a graduate of Leverett's Harvard, Williams was akin to Leverett in his versatility; he had studied law before turning to the ministry, and was actively interested in business and public affairs. His resignation from the college rectorship was widely attributed to his aspirations for the governorship. In 1744, while his successor was zealously harassing the young "enthusiasts" in Yale College and attempting to withhold a degree from a senior who had taken up a subscription to reprint one of Locke's letters on toleration,[33] Williams, as a sympathizer of the New Lights, wrote an extremely able pamphlet on religious liberty in which he argued from a Lockean

[31] See the sketch by Shipton in *Sibley's Harvard Graduates,* VII, esp. 48–49.

[32] That the Yale Corporation was dominated by moderates as early as 1723 is suggested by the fact that in that year they offered the rectorship to Edward Wigglesworth, who declined, evidently because of growing deafness. Dexter, *Yale Biographies and Annals,* I, 290, 312; Shipton, *Sibley's Harvard Graduates,* V, 550.

[33] The senior, however, forced Clap and the Corporation to award the degree by threatening to carry the matter to the king in council. Nothing was more frightening to college authorities. Benjamin Trumbull, *A Complete History of Connecticut* (New Haven, 1818), II, 183n.

standpoint the case for separation of church and state and denied the right of the civil magistrate to "make any penal Laws in Matters of Religion." [34]

But if Clap's point of view—or perhaps more accurately, his consecutive points of view—had not been rooted in the soil of Connecticut religion, it is doubtful that he would have held on as long as he did. Moreover, it seems a fact of striking significance that Yale under Clap was going through a process very similar to what Harvard had experienced under Mather, and the two situations have more in common than the presence of two forceful and rather doctrinaire old men. Harvard and Yale were both founded as colleges of sectaries and both had the problems incident to evolving into colleges of gentlemen. Both were Congregational, and both were founded under established churches. Both were founded under conditions of sectarian monopoly and each went through a period of strife when its religious environment became more pluralistic. One might be tempted to say that the troubles of Yale were due to consecutive attempts to make a college a partisan agency of a single religious faction. But Princeton was as much dominated by a single faction of Presbyterians as Yale was by a single faction of Congregationalists; and yet Princeton, founded as it was in the midst of greater religious diversity and without the benefits or disadvantages of an established church, was never plagued by the problems that beset Yale under Clap. (Indeed, competition from Princeton, where, as we have seen, quite a promotional asset was made of liberality toward the religion of students, was probably one reason for the later relaxation at Yale, since that liberality appealed to some of the same religious constituency in the same region.)

The essential reason for the acuteness of the situation at Yale was the existence of a religious establishment challenged by the sudden development of religious diversity in the Awakening. The presence of an establishment created the legal conditions of suppression, and the college became one of the agencies through which the two larger factions sought to make life difficult for each other and for the smaller dissenting groups. Yale was, in short, experiencing some of the same growing pains that Harvard had undergone earlier, but Connecticut, being more rural and less

[34] [Elisha Williams] *The Essential Rights and Liberties of Protestants: A Seasonable Plea for the Liberty of Conscience* (Boston, 1744), p. 1. On the authorship of this work see Shipton, *Sibley's Harvard Graduates*, V, 593; on Williams, see Shipton's sketch, *ibid.*, pp. 588–98, and Francis Parsons, "Elisha Williams," *New Haven Historical Society Papers*, VII (1908), 188–217.

commercial than Massachusetts, was slower to develop a critical aristocracy. Hence the change took place there at a later date and was attended
by sharper conflict.

In 1708 a representative group of Connecticut ministers had met at
Saybrook and adopted a confession of faith and a system of ecclesiastical
discipline under which the colony had enjoyed religious peace until the
period of the Awakening. There were in the province only small handfuls
of dissenters from the regime established in the Saybrook Platform, and
these dissenters—a few Baptists, Quakers, Episcopalians, and Rogerenes
—were granted liberty to worship in their own way while contributing to
the support of the established church; but the peace of the province
may be laid more to its fundamental homogeneity than to the breadth of
its tolerance.[35] The most formidable of these dissenting groups at the time
of the Awakening was the Episcopal, which, although practically nonexistent at the time of Rector Cutler's horrendous apostasy, had been
gaining in numbers and organizing new congregations for the past fifteen
years.

The Awakening alarmed the supporters of the standing order far more
deeply than had the rise of any of the pre-existing dissenting denominations, because it cut into the Congregational churches themselves. Although less infected with liberalism than the churches of Massachusetts,
many Connecticut congregations had shown signs of the same relaxation
that had been complained of so loudly in the sister colony since 1680.
Accordingly, when the Awakening came, even many of the essentially
conservative churchmen of Old-Light persuasion, despite their distaste
for extreme manifestations of "enthusiasm," could not resist seeing some
good in the great outpourings of the spirit of God that seemed to be
accompanying the revivals. Nor were the "liberal Calvinists" particularly alarmed at the tendencies toward stricter Calvinism that marked the
theological emphasis of the revivals. Two things, however, at length set
the greater part of the Old-Light men firmly against the revivals: one was
the tendency toward an extravagant amount of uninvited itinerant preaching by the revivalists (who were often far more exciting to local parish-
ioners than the sometimes dull clerics whose domains they were invading); the other was the tendency of the revivalists openly to discredit the
standing ministry, to insist that many of its members, being unregenerate,

[35] See M. Louise Greene, *The Development of Religious Liberty in Connecticut,*
Chaps. VI and VII. The Rogerenes were a tiny sect that had split off from the
Sabbatarians or Seventh-Day Baptists of Rhode Island.

were unworthy of their offices, and to charge them with various heresies, chiefly Arminianism. Thus while Whitefield had at first been greeted with cordiality by a large portion of the established ministry, his own censoriousness and the even less restrained preaching of men like Gilbert Tennent and James Davenport, soon created a multitude of enemies. It was one thing to welcome a visitor who might bring a new infusion of religious zeal to a complacent congregation; it was another to countenance itinerants who declared, in the words of Gilbert Tennent, that the regular ministers were "hirelings, caterpillars, letter-learned Pharisees, Hypocrites, Varlets, Seed of the Serpent, foolish Builders whom the Devil drives into the ministry, dead dogs that cannot bark, blind men, dead men, men possessed of the devil, rebels, and enemies of God." [36]

The ministers, who felt that they must fight back, were supported by many eminent Old-Light laymen who might have taken tolerant views of broad differences in theology had it not been for their belief that civil order could not be maintained without a large measure of religious conformity. Such men were alarmed not only because the established church was split into two factions, but because a body of Separatist Congregationalists had emerged. The church seemed to be threatened by disintegration; and this probably explains why the Consociated Congregationalists were for a time spurred to greater intolerance for deviant members of their own religious tradition than they were for Quakers or Episcopalians. In May, 1742, the Connecticut Assembly passed a series of restrictive laws: even regularly ordained ministers were not to preach in parishes other than their own except on invitation of the settled minister, at the risk of forfeiting the support of all the colony laws made for the benefit of the ministry; no church association was to license any minister to preach outside its precincts; bonds of a hundred pounds were levied to guarantee against a second offense of unauthorized itinerancy; and strangers from outside the colony found guilty of this offense were liable to expulsion as vagrants. [37] The toleration enjoyed by some dissenters since 1708 was repealed by the Assembly in 1743.

A time of troubles came to the religious life of the colony: there were excommunications and arrests; church members were imprisoned for

---

[36] *Ibid.*, pp. 237–38.

[37] Benjamin Trumbull, *Complete History of Connecticut*, II, 162–65. Under this law Samuel Finley, later to become president of Princeton, was arrested on his way to preach to a Separatist congregation in New Haven without legal standing, and expelled as a vagrant.

attending Separatist meetings or refusing to be taxed for the support of the establishment; officials who held New-Light beliefs were removed from public offices; ministers were rebuked and expelled from their churches; others had their salaries withheld. Baptist and Anglican churches gained recruits from the ranks of those who were disgusted by the factionalism and bitterness of the Congregationalists. Connecticut won a reputation for persecutions.[38]

At best this was a sorry milieu for a college, and it was Yale's misfortune to be under the leadership of an able but contentious man hardly capable of picking his way through the tangled briars of sectarianism. In formal theology Clap was actually closer to the troublesome New Lights than to the dominant Old Lights who controlled the Assembly and the college; but in his position on ecclesiastical politics and discipline he was for some years after his induction a pillar of the standing order. Unfortunately for Yale he conceived of the college primarily as a theological agency; and once this assumption was granted, the full involvement of the institution in factional struggles became inevitable, for the college was thus committed to enforcing the point of view of one or another of the participants instead of standing open as a school available to all. Clap's first move was an attempt to clamp down on New-Light tendencies in the college.

In this enterprise Clap had the support of the trustees, who, alarmed by the signs of interest in the revival within the college, resolved at the commencement of 1741 that any student who called a college officer or trustee "carnal" or "unconverted" should be required to make a public confession, and for a second such offense should be expelled. Later that year, young David Brainerd, who was destined to become one of the saints of New England Protestantism and to be immortalized in a modest way by Jonathan Edwards, made the mistake of saying of one of the tutors who had just been praying with the students, "He has no more grace than the chair I am leaning upon." It was characteristic of the atmosphere that had already been created by these controversies that a freshman who overheard Brainerd took the story to one of the women of the town, who reported it in turn to Rector Clap. And it was charac-

[38] Mary Hewitt Mitchell, *The Great Awakening and Other Revivals in the Religious Life of Connecticut* (New Haven, 1934), pp. 12–19. The fullest account is that of Benjamin Trumbull, *Complete History of Connecticut,* Vol. II, Chap. VIII. Cf. Maurice W. Armstrong, "Religious Enthusiasm and Separatism in Colonial New England," *Harvard Theological Review,* XXXVIII (April, 1945), 111–40.

teristic of Clap to call those who were reported to have been with Brainerd at the time and compel them to inform on their friend. When Brainerd refused to make a humiliating public confession in the college hall for a remark made in private conversation, he was expelled; and not even the intercession of such godly ministers as Aaron Burr, Jonathan Dickinson, and Jonathan Edwards, coupled with an apology from Brainerd, would cause Clap to relent and readmit him.[39]

In 1744 a new measure was taken against the New Lights: the trustees ruled that no one over twenty-one could be admitted as a freshman without special permission, an ordinance that was intended to bar some of the New Lights, many of whose most assertive adherents were over twenty-one at their entrance.[40] In the same year two students, John and Ebenezer Cleaveland, were reproached for attending Separatist church services with their parents while at home on vacation. Upon refusing to make the required confession in the college hall, they too were expelled.[41] The case aroused so much criticism that Clap and the tutors issued a pamphlet stating their side of the case. They pointed out that the Cleavelands had absorbed corrupt principles and dangerous errors, including that of antinomianism, from the "lay exhorters" whose services they had attended, and asserted "it would be a Contradiction in the Civil Government to Support a College to Educate Students to trample upon their own laws." [42] The logic of this was hardly answerable, given the repressive laws and the assumption that the college was to be as vigilant as possible an agent of the Old-Light faction. During the same year a member of the Corporation, being asked to account for his New-Light leanings, resigned rather than undergo an examination by his fellow trustees.[43]

It was at this point that Clap, taking advantage of the good favor he had with the Old Lights, secured the permanent charter of 1745; and the newly styled President now drew up a set of severe college laws which "smelled more of the Test Act and the English Cambridge than the laxity and theological vagueness of the new Cambridge in which he had stud-

[39] Jonathan Edwards, "Memoirs of the Rev. David Brainerd," in *Works* (New York, 1829), X, 50–51.

[40] Dexter, *Yale Biographies and Annals,* I, 754.

[41] *Ibid.,* p. 771; cf. Dexter, *Documentary History of Yale University,* pp. 368–72.

[42] *The Judgment of the Rector and Tutors of Yale-College concerning Two of the Students who were Expelled* (New London, 1745), esp. pp. 1–3, 10. Many years later, when the power of the New Lights had grown considerably, both Cleavelands were awarded their degrees. Dexter, *Yale Biographies and Annals,* II, 29 ff., 149 ff.

[43] Leonard Bacon, "The Corporation," in W. L. Kingsley, ed., *Yale College,* I, 177–78.

ied." [44] For some years there was quiet in the college. But by the middle 1750s, the continued growth of the New Lights put them in a position of approximate parity with the Old Lights in the Assembly; Clap, in the meantime, having fallen out with Joseph Noyes, the stubborn Old-Light pastor of the New Haven First Church, shifted his position until he was classified in the parlance of the time as a "political New Light." Thus the second half of his administration was spent in a feud with the Old Lights. Clap's first moves were to withdraw the students of the college from Noyes' church and to ask for the establishment of a professorship of divinity so that the college would have its own preacher. First, however, the Corporation resolved that every future officer of the college, including members of the Corporation itself, must declare for the Westminster Confession, and went on to prescribe quite elaborately just what it was proper to believe at Yale in matters theological. It was clearly stated that these principles were to govern Yale in perpetuity, and it was explicitly provided that a member of the Corporation could be examined if any other fellow suspected him of deviation from the prescribed articles. Of the professor of divinity a particularly elaborate confession of faith was demanded, in which he was to "renounce all such errors as shall in any considerable measure prevail at the time of his introduction." [45]

Clap's divinity professor, Naphtali Daggett, was examined and installed in March, 1756, and the college church was organized the following year. The next step in the campaign, an attempt on Clap's part to use against Joseph Noyes the new resolve of the Corporation concerning examination of its own fellows, miscarried badly. The Corporation tamely resolved in favor of the examination, but Noyes refused either to be examined or to resign from his position, and the proposal was too unpopular to be pushed any further in the face of such a determined stand. [46] By holding his ground, and thus setting bounds to heresy-hunting within the Corporation, Noyes undoubtedly did the college a great service,

---

[44] Shipton in *Sibley's Harvard Graduates,* VII, 33; the laws are reprinted in Dexter, *Yale Biographies and Annals,* II, 2 ff.

[45] The text of these resolutions, adopted in 1753, is given by Trumbull, *Complete History of Connecticut,* II, 316–19. Significant of the dogmatic confidence of the fellows was their promise to use Yale to maintain these tenets forever: "That we will always take all proper and reasonable measures, such as christian prudence shall direct, to continue and propagate the doctrines contained in these summaries of religion, in this college, *and transmit them to all future successions and generations;* and to use the like measures to prevent the contrary doctrines from prevailing in this society." *Ibid.,* p. 317; italics added.

[46] Dexter, *Yale Biographies and Annals,* II, 442–43.

although one of the historians of the Corporation has pointed out that he might have served it still more effectively and more consistently if he had objected twelve years earlier, when one of his New-Light opponents, Samuel Cook, had been forced to resign from the Corporation under the threat of just such an inquisition.[47]

The events of the 1750s aroused a storm of opposition in Connecticut. The movement to establish a professorship of divinity and a separate college church started a pamphlet war which had hardly died out when the attempted examination of Noyes began another. Many of the details of these controversies are beyond our concern; but some of the arguments shed light upon the conceptions of the college entertained by both sides, for the controversy raised many broad questions about the place of higher education in society and the relations of education to religion.

The clearest statements of the conservative position were in the writings of Clap himself. It is plain from an examination of his pamphlets that if he had had his way he would have forever frozen the development of the colleges in their original sectarian phase, for to him colleges were simply sectarian agencies, whose fundamental aim was not to teach the arts and sciences but to train orthodox and pious ministers.[48] They were religious societies, but of a special character because they reared the religious elite, the clergy. Thus the most vital thing in a college education was the internal religious life and the doctrinal soundness of the institution.

Should students, then, be permitted to worship variously and separately in accordance with their own choice, or that of their parents? To Clap this was inconceivable; no monitor could supervise the worship of students outside the college; their parents could not do so, so long as they committed them to the care of the college; but, above all, the uniformity, the conformity, which Clap's vision of a college unqualifiedly demanded,

[47] Bacon, "The Corporation," pp. 176–78. Dexter suggests that the move against Noyes was a bid on the part of the Corporation for support from the New Lights in the Legislature, where they were now a majority. Because of its Old-Light past, the college was not popular among the New Lights; but a show of concern for orthodoxy, and a personal blow at one of the leading members of the opposition, might win them over. *Yale Biographies and Annals,* II, 443.

[48] "Colleges are *Religious Societies* of a Superior Nature to all others. For whereas Parishes are Societies, for training up the *common People;* Colleges are *Societies of Ministers,* for training up Persons for the Work of the Ministry. . . . The great Design of Founding this School, was to Educate Ministers in our own Way." Thomas Clap, *The Religious Constitution of Colleges* (New London, Conn., 1754), pp. 4, 15.

could not be reconciled with diversity of religious practice. This led him to challenge commonly accepted parental prerogatives, as he had indeed done earlier in the Cleaveland case. For, as he said, if the parents were to say how their children should worship and thus take this decision out of the authority of the college, then there would be as many kinds of worship at college as there were different opinions of parents.[49] Such a state of affairs, which might seem quite acceptable to many who were steeped in the idea of tolerance, was to Clap simply shocking. He was aware that he might be reproached for violating liberty of conscience, but this he denied. "Under the Limitations of the Law," after all, any man could found such a college as his conscience might think fit. (This may have been formally true, but Clap must have known that at that time the liberty was more formal than real; one is reminded of Anatole France's famous remark about the majestic equality of the law.) In such a college, it would be fit and proper, once again, that uniformity should prevail in accordance with the will of the founder, which should always be followed. Any outsider who contributed funds to such a college should be aware— and this applied, said Clap, to the Anglicans who had given to Yale—that their money would be used to realize the purposes of the original founders, whose views differed from their own.[50]

In the realm of doctrine, Clap went on in another work to justify the system of tests that had been adopted at Yale for faculty members and Corporation fellows alike. He pointed out that a new scheme of divinity had been winning acceptance; this amounted in effect to a system of natural theology in which the doctrines of Calvinism were totally subverted.[51] After reflecting upon this system he insisted that minor deviations from orthodoxy could not safely be trifled with, because it could not be left up to heretics to define the significance of their own deviations. This was why the orthodoxy of teachers could not be satisfactorily established by anything short of a full and specific confession of faith.

[49] *Ibid.*, p. 14.

[50] *Ibid.*, pp. 14–20. These remarks were no doubt occasioned by some discontent with Clap's refusal in 1753 to allow the Episcopalian students in the college to attend regularly the Sunday services in the new Episcopal church. F. B. Dexter, "Thomas Clap and His Writings," *Papers of the New Haven Colony Historical Society*, V (New Haven, 1894), 256–57. Cf. the protest of Samuel Johnson against this policy. Schneider and Schneider, *Samuel Johnson*, I, 176–77. Episcopalian students, of course, never ceased to be welcome at Yale. Even Clap's primary concern was with the internal discipline of Connecticut Congregationalism.

[51] *A Brief History and Vindication of the Doctrines Received and Established in the Churches of New-England* (New Haven, 1755), pp. 19–23.

For a man may suppose or pretend, that the Ten Commandments are the most substantial Part of the Catechism, and that the Doctrines of the Divinity and Satisfaction of Christ, Original Sin, &c are but meer speculative *circumstantial* Points, upon which no great Weight ought to be laid. Such persons ought at least to declare what particular Articles they do *except,* that so others may judge, whether they are meer Circumstantials or not.[52]

It was dangerous, after all, to give up any one of a series of articles of faith, since they were a logical tissue and stood or fell together. Clap believed that the received doctrines of the Congregational churches were "of the utmost Consequence to the Salvation of the Souls of Men." He felt himself therefore duty bound "to do all that lies in my power, to continue and propagate those Doctrines; especially in the COLLEGE committed to my Care, since that is the Fountain from whence our Churches must be supplied." [53]

Uncompromising as they were, Clap's apologetics were of the sort to convince those already convinced and to alienate still more those who were opposed to him. Even before Clap's assault upon Noyes' position in the Corporation, the legislature had begun to falter in its annual financial support to Yale, and the college had fallen under attack because of its demand for a divinity professor.[54] After the movement against Noyes there was a fresh outburst of criticism in the course of which the entire concept of a narrow sectarian school was very closely examined. A broadminded Old-Light spokesman argued that the Corporation ordinance was unjust because a member could be called up on the suspicion of a single accuser; because the very election of Corporation members should have been taken as presumptive evidence of their worthiness to serve until some act gave evidence to the contrary; and because the mere fact of an examination would damage a man's character, even if he were acquitted. If "a Set of Narrow-Spirited Bigots" got on the Corporation, the writer warned, they would be in a position to harass other members and college officers who were "moderate, catholick, charitable Calvinists." [55] This was a clear warning to fellow Old Lights that to yield on this issue might be to sacrifice the entire control of the college to the most inquisitorial members of the opposing faction.

The author went on to attack Clap's concept of a college as a religious

[52] *Ibid.,* p. 37. Presumably Clap was referring to the Arminian distinctions between fundamental and non-fundamental doctrines of religion.
[53] *Ibid.,* p. 40.
[54] Dexter, *Yale Biographies and Annals,* II, 320–22, 366–68, 399.
[55] [Shubael Conant], *A Letter to a Friend* (New Haven, 1757), p. 10.

society. The president of Yale, he conceded, was a minister, but he presided as legal head and governor of the school, not as a clergyman. The fellows of the Corporation were, to be sure, ministers; but many trustees elsewhere were laymen and there was nothing intrinsically clerical in that office; moreover, they acted not in their capacity as ministers but under a civil appointment coming from a governmental charter. The tutors were not ministers, nor were the undergraduates; and of the latter it could safely be said on the basis of recent graduating classes that less than one quarter of them ever would become ministers. The sole member of the college who acted at the institution in his capacity as minister was the divinity professor. How then was Yale a society of ministers? In the curriculum? About three fourths of that was given to languages and arts, the rest to the study of divinity. No, a college was not simply a religious society, because it had other purposes than worship—some purely civil, others mixed. And while a church could conceivably be set up *within* a college, the right to do so did not lie, according to Congregational practice, in the president and fellows acting in their *political* capacity as governors of the college.[56]

What is displayed in such documents is an increasing critical awareness of the problems involved in the church-college relationship, and an emergent recognition of the fact that this relationship must be somewhat loosened if two or three religious factions were to use the college without continuous internecine strife. It is amusing to find some of the Old-Light worthies, now that they were themselves under pressure, dragging out arguments for tolerance and restraint that they had neglected to think of a few years before when they had driven a New-Light fellow off the Corporation and had been applauding Clap's reprisals against New-Light students. (It is similarly amusing to find Anglicans protesting bitterly against restrictions that were much less severe than those applied against dissenters at Oxford and Cambridge.) And yet the mere groping for these broader and more catholic principles had an independent value of its own; for after resorting to them instrumentally for a while, men began really to feel and believe them, and the road was opened for mutual peace.

The rest of the story of Clap's regime may be told briefly. He was besieged by rising restlessness in the colony at large, and by renewed petitions from formidable citizens for regular legislative visitation of Yale. Within the college itself his illiberalism continued, but it was met by stu-

[56] *Ibid.,* pp. 23–32.

dent rebellions (possibly stimulated in good part by parents or other persons outside the college interested in getting rid of the president), and in the end by desertions among the unhappy tutors.[57] Among Clap's final gestures of authority was the refusal of a gift of books because they included the works of an English divine of doubtful orthodoxy,[58] and the dismissal of two tutors for having espoused the grave heresy of Sandemanianism.[59]

After 1760 Clap's regime was under almost continuous pressure from two sides: on one there was the legal movement in the legislature to change the Yale charter by introducing legislative visitation into its government; on the other there was the more informal harassment of the college government by resident students, by parents, and in the end by the withdrawal of tutors. As we noted in Chapter III, the able old president successfully resisted the movement toward legislative changes in 1763 when he presented his effective but now discredited legal-historical account of the founding of Yale. But the growing unpopularity of the college in the community, a reaction not only to Clap's highhandedness, expulsions and discipline, and student fines,[60] but also to increased tuition

[57] See Dexter, *Yale Biographies and Annals,* II, 636–37, 723–24, 777; III, 167–68.
[58] *Ibid.,* II, 565–66; the potential donor was a Newport Baptist, the objectionable author the Reverend James Foster. Ezra Stiles felt that this act justified the charges of bigotry against Clap, and wrote him a powerful letter appealing for freedom of inquiry. "It is true," he conceded, "with this Liberty Error may be introduced; but turn the Tables the propogation [sic] of Truth may be extinguished. Deism has got such Head in this Age of Licentious Liberty, that it would be in vain to try to stop it by hiding the Deistical Writings: and the only Way left to conquer and demolish it, is to come forth in the open Field & Dispute this matter on even Footing. . . . Truth and this alone being *our* Aim in fact, open, frank and Generous we shall avoid the very appearance of Evil." Woodbridge Riley, *American Philosophy: The Early Schools* (New York, 1907), p. 217.
[59] Dexter, *Yale Biographies and Annals,* III, 93; the resignation was demanded of the two tutors in accordance with the test laws of 1753. The third tutor resigned with them in 1765, and the new tutors hired to replace them found themselves so uncomfortable that they, too, resigned. Kingsley, *Yale College,* p. 92. The Sandemanians were a tiny sect whose doctrine of salvation deviated drastically from that of Calvinism and allied theologies.
[60] John Trumbull, who was an undergraduate during Clap's last years, concluded that the fines were an anticipated part of the college's income (in "The Progress of Dulness," *Poetical Works* [Hartford, Conn., 1820] II, 38):

> Where kind instructors fix their price,
> In just degrees, on every vice,
> And fierce in zeal 'gainst wicked courses,
> Demand repentance of their purses;
> Till sin, thus tax'd, produces clear
> A copious income every year
> And the fair schools, thus free from scruples
> Thrive by the knavery of their pupils.

and poor fare in the college commons, was more than he could forever fend off. On the eve of commencement in 1765 a mob of students and townspeople assailed the home of the president, broke most of his windows, and slightly injured Clap himself.[61] During the following year students became so disorderly that life became impossible for the tutors; both tutors and students withdrew, and college functions were temporarily suspended.[62] Having brought the college to the brink of ruin, Clap resigned in 1766.

Clap's defeat ended the last attempt to impose upon one of the major colonial colleges the most restricting implications of a narrow sectarian commitment. It is noteworthy that the effective instrument of this defeat was the student body, which acted, one suspects, with parental backing. Clap had forestalled the movement in the assembly toward legal intervention; but there was no substitute for students, and when it appeared that the college was in danger of being all but emptied, it was clear that surrender must follow. By aligning the college vigorously first with one religious faction and then another, instead of holding it open to all in a catholic spirit, Clap had succeeded only in making for it too numerous and too determined a body of enemies. Had he merely tyrannized over tutors, he might have come to no difficulties; but to infringe conspicuously upon the religious liberties of students was to violate a sanction widely accepted in the community and necessary to the health of the college. The whole experience was an object lesson in the limitations of despotism and bigotry in a college whose role was as important as that of Yale in the mid-eighteenth century.

Clap was succeeded by Daggett, who was made president *pro tempore* for an interregnum that stretched out to eleven years. Although some signs of the same kind of student discontent that had plagued Clap were in evidence during Daggett's time, the man himself seems to have governed the college very loosely, being busy much of the time with the duties incident to his divinity professorship. Finally the Corporation, feeling the necessity of repairing some of the damage that had been done to the repu-

[61] Alexander Cowie, *Educational Problems at Yale College in the Eighteenth Century* (New Haven, 1936), pp. 21–25.

[62] Dexter, *Yale Biographies and Annals,* III, 167–68. Clap was on his way toward emptying the college of students. The class that entered in 1766 and graduated in 1770 numbered only 19 at the time of its commencement, as did the class that followed it. These were the smallest graduating classes in 16 years. Over the quarter of a century prior to 1770 graduating classes had had an average of 29 students.

tation of the college under Clap, elected to the presidency a man who was in many ways his antithesis, the Reverend Ezra Stiles of Newport. A graduate of the class of 1746 and a moderate Calvinist, Stiles was a man of broad tolerance and wide interests. He accepted the presidency after a visit with the Corporation during which he obtained from them the promise that they would repeal the religious restrictions enacted in 1753 and attempt as soon as possible to provide permanent professors for the college.[63] Stiles was unalterably opposed to any continuation of the internecine squabbles of Clap's era. "There is so much pure Christianity among all sects of Protestants," he wrote,

that I cheerfully embrace all in my charity. There is so much defect in all that we all need forbearance and mutual condescension. I don't intend to spend my days in the fires of party; at the most I shall resist all claims and endeavors for supremacy or precedency of any sect; for the rest I shall promote peace, harmony, and benevolence. I honor all Protestant churches so far as they are reformed, and even the Church of England as a sister, by no means a mother, church. But I conscientiously give the preference, in my own choice, to the Congregational churches as nearest the primitive standard, and most purified from the corruptions of the Latin church.[64]

Two weeks after his installation the seniors were disputing forensically, "Whether a Toleration of all Religions is beneficial to the State?" [65]

UNITARIANISM AT HARVARD

The period of more than twenty-five years during which Yale was under Clap's domination represents no more than a temporary reversal of the underlying trend toward liberalism in the eighteenth century. In most places theology was affected by an increasing breadth and liberality, whether in the form of Arminianism, emergent Unitarianism, or even Deism. Theology itself ceased to have such an inclusive claim on men's interests, as the growth of commerce, the enlargement of the well-to-do classes, the importation of the ideas and concerns of the European Enlightenment, and the development in America of the absorbing

[63] W. L. Kingsley, *Yale College*, p. 104. Stiles was in a position to make a good bargain. His election was the occasion of an elaborate reconsideration of the relationship of Yale to the Assembly, which reached its fruition in 1792. See Stiles, *Literary Diary*, II, 224–69, *passim*, for the relevant entries.

[64] Quoted by W. L. Kingsley, *Yale College*, p. 104. Stiles, however, accepted the Saybrook platform and promised to teach accordingly.

[65] Stiles, *Literary Diary*, II, 287.

eighteenth-century middle-class passion for pure and applied science, for practical improvements, comforts, and conveniences, broadened enormously the range of intellectual preoccupations. All these things were reflected, on the whole rather promptly, in the colleges themselves. With the exception perhaps of the forward role of Harvard in the growth of a liberal theology, it would be too much to claim that the colleges took the initiative in many of these developments. It is probably nearer the truth to say that the colleges followed closely but at a safe distance; that their leaders were prompt to take an interest in the new concerns of the Enlightenment, but for the most part showed no special daring in pushing them to the forefront.

Necessarily the climate of the Enlightenment brought with it a somewhat greater concern for a free intellectual atmosphere in education. This did not result, to be sure, in the development of any highly self-conscious or formal sanctions for academic freedom for teachers, or in any open pulling and tugging at the inherited system of restraint which was so notable wherever fundamental religious interests were touched upon. But a new degree of latitude seems very slowly to have developed even in the absence of any such formal rationale. *Am Anfang war die Tat:* men exercised a measure of freedom before the formulation of any body of ideas with which they were prepared to challenge the traditional limitations. One can sense this new freedom in reading the history of the colleges in the eighteenth century; one sees some of its evidences in changes in the curriculum, which in most places were instituted by, or at the suggestion of, the presidents and professors themselves. It seems a safe conclusion that where intellectual changes of the magnitude suggested by these curricular innovations took place without being imposed externally by trustees or overseers, a certain amount of vital intellectual initiative had passed to the faculties. What is most impressive, however, is the quietness and gradualness with which the change took place. It was a long, slow advance, characterized by opportunism rather than daring, preceded by a careful reconnaissance of the terrain, and marked by few explosions.

A part of the story of the unfolding of the Enlightenment in America was the growing intrusion into the curriculum of a new interest in the utilitarian and the scientific; another was the change in theology itself, which was slowly and all but imperceptibly being liberalized. Among Anglicans this process took place with perhaps the least excitement, as the writings of latitudinarian theologians who had long been dominant in the more advanced thought of England were imported; but among

Congregationalists and Presbyterians the process was attended by more alarums and excursions, and the development in New England of that theological liberalism which came to be so important for Harvard deserves some attention.

The Puritans, it must be recognized, had begun to delimit and soften Calvinist predestinarianism even before Massachusetts Bay Colony was securely established. Calvin, although he was of course studied by the founding fathers of New England, was not in fact the sole fount of the characteristic Puritan theology. From the beginning the standard work, the one prescribed for study in the Puritan colleges, was William Ames' *Medulla Theologiae,* which had appeared in 1623, sometimes supplemented by his book of casuistry, *De Conscientia* (1632). These works were used until well into the eighteenth century, when they were often supplemented by Johannes Wollebius' *Compendium Theologiae Christianae* (1626). Predominant theological opinion, then, among the New England Congregationalists followed what was known as the Federal, or Covenant, Theology, which was predestinarian with modifications.[66] The Puritans had made an attempt to reduce somewhat the role of the arbitrariness of God by positing that God had voluntarily entered into a covenant with man in which He engaged to abide by certain principles governing salvation. While this view did not abandon the core of the predestinarian position, it had the effect of encouraging men to believe that the terms governing the gift of grace to man were, after all, infused with some principles of order amenable to human reason; and it encouraged them to cultivate whatever seeds of grace they might imagine they found in themselves. It was the first crack, however tiny, in the formidable dikes of Calvinist doctrine. Until the fourth decade of the eighteenth century the Covenant Theology was the only thing that could be spoken of as the orthodox position of New England Congregationalism. Only after the established churches had shown what the New Lights felt to be signs of advanced decay did a return toward orthodoxy take place.

There were doubtless several reasons why this turn to high Calvinism took place, but the one with which we must be most concerned was a reaction against the rise within the Congregational churches of a tendency toward liberal speculation which was generally stigmatized by the name "Arminianism." Now "Arminianism," like the terms "agrarianism" and

[66] The character of New England theology is carefully delineated by Perry Miller in "The Marrow of Puritan Divinity," *Publications of the Colonial Society of Massachusetts,* XXXII (1937), 246–300.

"anarchism" in the nineteenth century and "communism" in the twentieth, was a seventeenth- and eighteenth-century swear word; it is not always correct to conclude that a preacher accused of it by contemporaries actually espoused Arminian doctrines. The number of doctrinal points upon which one might choose to quarrel either with high Calvinism or the Federal Theology was quite large, and it would take the patience of a Harnack to trace in full the tortuous development of theological liberalism in eighteenth-century New England and to assess with any precision the extent to which this or that clergyman was really an Arminian. Understandably the gross evidence is confusing.[67] We have already seen how Increase Mather felt it necessary to take steps to "put down Arminianisme" among the Masters at Harvard in the 1690s; and yet his son Cotton is on record as congratulating the New England Congregational churches in 1726 because not one of their pastors was guilty of this abominable heresy.[68] Only eight years later, nonetheless, Jonathan Edwards was troubled by "the great noise that was in this part of the country, about Arminianism"; and yet a modern student of the subject stoutly insists, concerning the fountainhead of liberal New England theology, that "either deism or Arminianism in Harvard College before the Revolution is a myth." [69]

The confusion derives partly from the fact that much of what was called Arminianism was a shade of belief only a trifle more liberal than the pristine New England orthodoxy—an exploitation, as it were, of the germs of liberalism that could be found in the Covenant Theology itself.[70] The Covenant Theology, with the passage of time, slowly shaded off into Arminianism, just as Arminianism later shaded off into Unitarianism. What really aroused men like Edwards was not so much a clear and classifiable trend toward doctrinal deviation but something far more serious: an unmistakable continuation of that decline in religious morale that had been troubling the pastors of New England for two generations. This was a matter that went beyond doctrine, and was far more palpable.[71] Even

---

[67] The prevalence of Arminianism is minimized by F. A. Christie, "The Beginnings of Arminianism in New England," *Papers of the American Society of Church History,* Second Series, Vol. III (New York, 1917), pp. 153–72.

[68] *Ibid.,* pp. 154–55.   [69] *Ibid.,* p. 159.

[70] Some of the complexities of the problem are illustrated by Conrad Wright in his discussion of "Edwards and the Arminians on the Freedom of the Will," *Harvard Theological Review,* XXXV (October, 1942), 241–61, in which he finds large areas of agreement between Edwards and his opponents.

[71] The significance of this trend and its rather broad relation to Arminianism is assessed by Perry Miller, *Jonathan Edwards* (New York, 1949), pp. 101–26.

among those pastors who did not trouble themselves to challenge the old doctrines, those doctrines themselves had lost their original meanings; and the pulpits of New England—at least in the large seaboard towns and the centers of trade—were being filled with substantial but dull liberal intellectuals like Charles Chauncy, the great-grandson of the seventeenth-century President Chauncy. Such men hobnobbed with the great merchants, defended avowed Arminians if they did not actually join them, enjoyed the works of Tillotson, and put off afternoon services for an hour in order to allow time for the luxurious dinners served by members of their congregations.[72] It was against the social atmosphere that produced such men that the New Lights revolted and the Edwardians protested.

Whatever the efficacy of the protest in the inland counties, it did not check the course of events around Boston. In 1791, when Ashbel Green, who was later to become president of Princeton, visited the Boston Association, the local organization of clerics, he reported that the prayer with which the meeting opened was the only religious event in the course of the meeting.

But, as I understand, they are so diverse in their sentiments that they cannot agree on any point in theology. Some are Calvinists, some Universalists, some Arminians, some Arians, and one at least is a Socinian. How absurd it is for men of such jarring opinions to attempt to unite. How much more con-

[72] See the excellent sketch of Chauncy by Shipton, *Sibley's Harvard Graduates,* VI, 439–67, esp. p. 443. One cannot help but conclude that religion in New England mercantile centers must have reached a stage similar to that treated so disdainfully by Milton, when he discussed in the *Areopagitica* the relations between rich men and eminent divines: "A wealthy man, addicted to his pleasure and to his profit, finds Religion to be a traffic so entangled, and of so many piddling accounts, that of all mysteries he cannot skill to keep a stock going upon that trade. What should he do? fain he would have the name to be religious, fain he would bear up with his neighbors in that. What does he therefore, but resolve to give over toiling, and to find himself out some factor, to whose care and credit he may commit the whole managing of his religious affairs? some Divine of note and estimation that must be. To him he adheres, resigns the whole warehouse of his religion, with all the locks and keys, into his custody; and indeed makes the very person of that man his religion; esteems his associating with him a sufficient evidence and commendatory of his own piety. So that a man may say his religion is now no more within himself, but is become a dividual movable, and goes and comes near him, according as that good man frequents the house. He entertains him, gives him gifts, feasts him, lodges him; his religion comes home at night, prays, is liberally supped and sumptuously laid to sleep, rises, is saluted, and after the malmsey, or some well-spiced brewage, and better breakfasted than he whose morning appetite would have gladly fed on green figs between Bethany and Jerusalem, his Religion walks abroad at eight, and leaves his kind entertainer in the shop trading all day without his Religion." *Areopagitica* (1644; ed. Chicago, 1949), pp. 44–45.

ducive to improvement and to pleasure, that the parties should divide, and that those who are agreed should walk by themselves. Yet this plan I know would be esteemed by them as the effect of bigotry and narrowness of mind; and so they will meet, and shake hands, and talk of politics and science, and laugh, and eat raisons and almonds, and apples and cake, and drink wine and tea, and then go about their business when they please.[73]

As a social occasion, Green remarked, he saw nothing objectionable in the meeting, but for the purposes of church government it was "ludicrous."

Possibly so. This is the comment of a Presbyterian with consistent notions of church government upon a group of latitudinarian Congregationalists who, he thought, had no church to govern. It may also be the reaction of a man who had not yet learned poise in the presence of a difference of opinion and could not entertain two conflicting ideas without acute discomfort. To a modern observer the combination of unity and diversity achieved by the Boston clergy might seem highly desirable; and their ability to prevent doctrinal differences from becoming the causes of internecine squabbling might be regarded as a signal accomplishment of civilized men. As the background for the government of a college, the temper of the Boston clergymen, who were characteristic clerical members of the Overseers, seems wholly admirable; and it may be worth pointing out that the Harvard which reflected their attitudes and those of their sons was soon to go on to some of its highest achievements, while the Princeton of Ashbel Green's regime reached a point that has been described by its historian as "Princeton's Nadir." [74]

Most of the liberal ministers who flourished during the period of change were former students of the first Edward Wigglesworth, who held his divinity professorship for over forty years and lived to see the great majority of the pulpits of Massachusetts and northern New England filled by ministers whom he had trained.[75] In his theology Wigglesworth was hardly more than a moderate liberal whose views corresponded very closely to those prevailing among the more sophisticated clergy; he was considerably less radical, for instance, than Ebenezer Gay, whose ministry at Hingham began five years before Wigglesworth's induction, and

[73] Quoted by James King Morse, *Jedidiah Morse: Champion of New England Orthodoxy* (New York, 1939), p. 36.
[74] The title of Wertenbaker's chapter on Princeton under Green in his *Princeton*, pp. 153–83; cf. the author's comments, pp. 121–22, 160–62, 164, 169–70, 172.
[75] Shipton, *Sibley's Harvard Graduates*, V, 552.

who is usually classified as a pioneer of Unitarianism.[76] But although Wigglesworth opposed Arminianism he refused to join Edwards in a crusade against it; he taught his students that such weighty arguments could be made on both sides of the controversy that mutual charity was clearly in order, and recommended, with admonitions, that they critically read the works of Tillotson.[77] He seems, in short, to have been something of an intellectual diplomat. And if his opinions were not notably advanced for Boston, they were at first well ahead of those of the older ministers who held forth in the rural churches; his intellectual leadership was thus important for the countryside, as had been that of Leverett and Brattle before him.

While there were complaints against Wigglesworth's habit of presenting to students both sides of the controversy rather than hammering home the orthodox position, his long tenure was on the whole untroubled. His position was strengthened by the offer of the Rectorship at Yale; his original five-year appointment under the terms of Hollis' endowment was made more secure, and in later days his financial needs were amply met.[78] Thus the first person in the history of American collegiate education to hold a major professorship can be said to have enjoyed a notable measure of intellectual freedom in his academic post, despite the inauspicious examination that preceded his election. His son, the second Edward Wigglesworth, maintained his father's tradition until 1794, and marked a further step away from the original scheme of Puritan divinity when he dropped Wollebius in favor of the lectures of the liberal English dissenting educator, Philip Doddridge. During this period the leadership of the clerics among the Overseers was in the hands of Jonathan Mayhew, the first openly avowed Unitarian among the clergy, and his friend, Charles Chauncy, who belatedly espoused Unitarianism in 1784.[79] In 1789 the executors of the estate of one John Alford, a Charlestown

[76] Shipton demurs from this classification, *ibid.*, VI, 62; cf. the sketch by Samuel A. Eliot, *Heralds of a Liberal Faith* (Boston, 1910), I, 1–8. W. B. Sprague, in his *Annals of the American Pulpit,* Vol. VIII (New York, 1865), lists Gay as the first Unitarian in an American pulpit. Sprague finds that there were seven preachers who took up their ministries before 1750 who can be called Unitarians, including Gay and Chauncy; there were ten more between 1750 and 1775, and thirty during the last quarter of the century.

[77] Shipton, *Sibley's Harvard Graduates,* V, 549–50, 553.

[78] *Ibid.,* pp. 550–51.

[79] See the somewhat indignant account by Charles Lyttle, "A Sketch of the Theological Development of Harvard University, 1636–1805," *Church History,* V (December, 1936), 301–29.

merchant who had left large sums for charitable purposes upon his death
twenty-eight years before, established the Alford Professorship of Natural
Religion, Moral Philosophy, and Civil Polity. The duties of the incumbent were prescribed by Alford's executors in considerable detail, but in
such broad terms that a Deist could easily have fulfilled them.[80] These
terms would of course be balked at by a modern professor of philosophy,
but in the context of the time they represented a distinct and explicit enlargement of the scope of theology.

The culmination of Unitarian advance came in the years 1804–06,
when Harvard University (so styled after 1780) was taken over by the
Unitarians. David Tappan, the successor of the younger Wigglesworth
and a moderate Calvinist, died in 1803, and for two years the election of
the next Hollis Professor was in doubt. A battle took place between the
liberals and the conservatives in the Corporation in which high feelings
were aroused on both sides. Tappan's ten-year occupancy of the Hollis
Professorship had not been distinguished by any brilliancy of the sort to
reconcile the liberals to the idea of another Calvinist divine, and after
much maneuvering and many heated words the Corporation nominated
the Reverend Henry Ware, against whom it had been objected that he
was not a Trinitarian. The presentation of this choice to the Overseers
was the occasion of a thorough but angry review of the whole question
of the doctrinal commitments of the college. The essence of the conservative position was that the first Thomas Hollis, who had endowed the
professorship, had been a Calvinist and that the provisions of his endowment called for a man of sound and orthodox principles—a phrase
which, even granting Mr. Hollis' famed liberality, surely excluded
Arminians, Arians, and Socinians.[81] The liberals argued that the terms

[80] ". . . . whose principal duty it shall be . . . to demonstrate the existence
of a Deity or First Cause, to prove and illustrate his essential attributes, both natural
and moral, to evince and explain his providence and government, together with
the doctrine of a future state of rewards and punishments; also to deduce and
enforce the obligations which man is under to his Maker, and the duties which he
owes him, resulting from the perfections of the Deity, and from his own rational
nature . . . interspersing the whole with remarks, showing the coincidence between
the doctrines of Revelation and the dictates of reason. . . ." Quincy, *History of
Harvard,* II, 502. This professorship was not filled until 1817, when sufficient funds
had accumulated. It was first occupied by Levi Frisbie.
The earlier benefactions of the second Thomas Hollis, who had done his best
to stock the Harvard library with Unitarian books, also deserve mention. See
Caroline Robbins, "The Strenuous Whig: Thomas Hollis of Lincoln's Inn," *William
and Mary Quarterly,* Third Series, VII (July, 1950), 444 ff.
[81] The best account of the controversy is that of James K. Morse, *Jedidiah Morse,*
Chap. VII; cf. Quincy, *History of Harvard,* II, 284–88, and Samuel Eliot Morison,

"sound" and "orthodox" ought to be construed according to the changing sentiments of the times; by this criterion Ware could be held to qualify. While the liberals were accused of undermining sound faith and planning to convert Harvard into an Arminian university, the conservatives were charged with narrowness and bigotry. The liberals had the majority, and Ware was confirmed. In 1806 Samuel Webber, whose views verged on Unitarianism, was elected president and the Unitarian victory was complete.

Had the victory of the Unitarians simply meant the domination of the university by a new sect as intractable as the old, it would have had little to do with the advance of a free intellectual climate at Harvard. But tolerant principles were far more central to the religious views of the Unitarians than they had been to those of even the moderate Calvinists, and the victory of the Unitarians was a genuine gain for the principle that different shades of belief could coexist under the roof of the same institution. It was much more likely, for instance, that an institution dominated by liberals would choose a Calvinist as its professor of divinity (as Harvard did in the case of Tappan) than that an institution dominated by Calvinists would choose a liberal. Similarly, it was the liberals who stood for a broad and catholic presentation of religious beliefs in the teaching of divinity, while most Calvinists held out for firm indoctrination.

THE SECULARIZATION OF LEARNING

The most significant trend in collegiate education during the eighteenth century was the secularization of the colleges.[82] By opening up new

---

Three Centuries of Harvard (Cambridge, Mass., 1936), pp. 187–91. The conservative argument is expounded at length by Jedidiah Morse, *The True Reasons on Which the Election of a Hollis Professor . . . Was Opposed at the Board of Overseers* (Charlestown, Mass., 1805), esp. pp. 9–12. Morse was combating, as he said, "an opinion now avowed, and becoming too fashionable among us, that the Professor of Divinity should not disclose his own particular religious sentiments to the students, but only place fairly before them all the tenets of the different sects of Christians, with their respective arguments, and leave each student to form his own creed." *Ibid.,* pp. 17–18. That the conservatives were thrown on the defensive during this period may be shown by Morse's subsequent denial that he wished to interfere with "the right of private judgment and freedom of inquiry." *An Appeal to the Public on the Controversy Respecting the Revolution in Harvard College* (Charlestown, Mass., 1814), p. 185.

[82] For the background see Michael Kraus, *Intercolonial Aspects of American Culture on the Eve of the Revolution* (New York, 1928), Chap. IX.

fields for college study, both scientific and practical, by rarefying the devotional atmosphere of the colleges, and by introducing a note of skepticism and inquiry, the trend toward secular learning inevitably did much to liberate college work. Secularization was evident in several ways: in the more commercial and less religious tone of newly founded colleges; in the rapidly rising number of college graduates who went into occupations other than the ministry; and in vital changes in the curriculum, notably the rise of scientific studies and the modification of theology to include freer philosophical speculation.

The relative advancement of secularism in the two gentlemen's colleges founded in the 1750s, Philadelphia and King's, is perhaps less important than the changes in the older institutions. Neither of these colleges achieved during the eighteenth century the importance they were later to have among the institutions of the East Coast. At a time when Harvard's graduating classes had more than forty young men, Yale's more than thirty, Princeton's about twenty, and William and Mary's only a few less, Philadelphia averaged about seven seniors and King's College about five.[83] The reasons for the early failure of these colleges to grow more rapidly are complex; at Philadelphia, at least, stagnation, as E. P. Cheyney has suggested, was the price paid for secularism.[84] Both Philadelphia and King's were ruled by predominantly Anglican boards of trustees, although they had been founded on interdenominational bases; both were afflicted by sharp antagonisms between Anglicans and Presbyterians; and the Presbyterians of the region might well prefer to go to Yale or Princeton. Moreover, the possibility of importing Anglican divines from England made the role of clerical education in these schools less important than it was in the institutions dominated by dissenting bodies, and schools located in cities offered fewer living attractions than those situated in small towns.

However, although in size Philadelphia and King's were hardly comparable to the earlier institutions, educational literature produced in connection with their establishment revealed a temper so different from that shown in the founding of the dissenting colleges as to demand some notice here. Despite the part taken by the Anglican gentry in their organization, and the appointment at both institutions of Anglican divines as

[83] Thomas H. Montgomery, *A History of the University of Pennsylvania from Its Foundation to* A.D. *1770* (Philadelphia, 1900), p. 268.

[84] Edward P. Cheyney, *History of the University of Pennsylvania* (Philadelphia, 1940), p. 177.

heads, the dominant note in the discussions preceding the establishment of these institutions was practical and secular. Franklin's *Proposals Relating to the Education of Youth in Pensilvania* had been notable for its emphasis on civic needs, private careers, and practical goals. In 1753, when the prospects of a college for New York were under discussion, the Reverend William Smith drew up a scheme for an ideal college in which educational aims were set forth unaccompanied by those pious remarks commonly found in statements of purpose by the earlier schools.[85] Citing Tillotson to the effect that knowledge of anything that would not make better men would be knowledge of trifles, he called for the abandonment of study in the tomes of rabbis and schoolmen, metaphysicians and theologians, in favor of studies that would simply produce virtuous and tolerant citizens.[86] He also devoted much attention to the necessity of education in the mechanical arts, to be organized in a separate but related school under the governance of the same trustees.[87]

Probably the most remarkable statement in pre-Revolutionary educational discussions also appeared in 1753 when William Livingston, a New York lawyer and Presbyterian leader, published a series of essays on the proposed King's College in a weekly newspaper, the *Independent Reflector*. These essays, although products of a sharp sectarian conflict, are somewhat different from the writings provoked by the Great Awakening in the sense that they are more concerned with political and less with ecclesiastical matters. Livingston, fearing ultimate educational and religious domination by the Anglicans, cast his argument in the form of a plea for a liberal, nonsectarian college. His intentions were not quite as disinterested as his arguments, for he seems to have been more concerned with making certain that there should be *no* college controlled entirely by Anglicans than with insuring that there would be a liberal college controlled without regard to sect.[88] But what is most significant for our

[85] William Smith, *A General Idea of the College of Mirania,* pp. 9–10.

[86] *Ibid.,* pp. 11–12. "Men blest with such an Education will, in all probability, be good Men of any Protestant Church; nor will they think the different modes of professing the same FAITH, and paying the same HOMAGE to the DEITY, of Consequence enough to occasion the least Dispute, or Breach of Charity, between Fellow-Citizens" (p. 68).

[87] *Ibid.,* pp. 14–15.

[88] Livingston refused to act in the office of trustee of King's College, evidently tendered in order to mollify him and his associates, and despite the fact that its educational practices conformed in some considerable measure to his own prescription he never became reconciled to the institution. He was pleased that he had been instrumental in diverting some support from it and relished the fact that "it makes

purpose is not his intent, but the arguments he chose to employ. That his factional passions should have become transmuted into pleas for disinterestedness is another illustration of those ironic processes by which sectarian zeal finally became translated into an understanding of tolerance. Even though Livingston was making his case from a prejudiced point of view, it remains important that he should have felt it expedient to argue in the terms he chose and that he made his case so clearly.

The true use of education, he began, taking from the outset a secular tack, was "to qualify men for the different employments of life, to which it may please God to call them. . . . [and] to render our youth better members of society." [89] Youthful minds were tender and susceptible to almost any impression, and it was impossible to be too careful in shaping them. The colleges were more important in this than the lower schools, because in colleges the students took a more active role in confirming the ideas presented to them and incorporating them into their personal outlook. Unfortunately the colleges were "generally scenes of endless disputation," but seldom places of "candid inquiry."

The students not only receive the dogmata of their teachers with an implicit faith, but are also constantly studying how to support them against every objection. The system of the college is generally taken for true, and the sole business is to defend it.[90]

It was important to alter this practice of teaching so many things that later had to be unlearned. Unless the constitution and government of the proposed college "be such as will admit persons of all protestant denominations upon a perfect parity as to privilege, it will itself be greatly prejudiced, and prove a nursery of animosity, dissention and disorder." There were so many sects in New York that it seemed certain that the domination of the college by any one of them would draw the animosity of all the others and thus operate to impair its development. In such a state of things, Livingston argued (although he must have known that Episcopalians, however uncomfortably, sent their children to Harvard

---

indeed a most contemptible Figure." Dorothy R. Dillon, *The New York Triumvirate* (New York, 1949), pp. 39–40.

Much new information about the controversial background of King's College may be found in Milton M. Klein, "The American Whig: William Livingston of New York," unpublished doctoral dissertation (Columbia University, 1954), Chaps. IX, X.

[89] Schneider and Schneider, *Samuel Johnson*, IV, 120.
[90] *Ibid.*, p. 122.

and Yale), no children would be sent to the college except those of the sect that controlled it. This would not only damage the institution itself, but would cause many youths who would want higher education to be deprived of it.

Moreover, Livingston said, such a party-college, by spreading only its own ideas, would lead to domination of the entire province by members of a single sect. In any case, it would be commanding support from the legislature at the expense of the whole people while serving only a part.

A public academy is, or ought to be a mere civil institution, and cannot with any tolerable propriety be monopolized by any religious sect. The design of such seminaries [is] entirely political, and calculated for the benefit of society, as a society, without any intention to teach religion, which is the province of the pulpit.

Furthermore, if the college were only founded "on the plan of a general toleration" it would prosper by drawing students from the neighboring provinces where the colleges were church-dominated.[91]

Livingston went on to sketch the outlines of a plan for the kind of college he thought desirable. He opposed a royal charter, warning that the freedom of the college might easily fall victim to some future practitioner of "the tyrannical arts of James," and urged instead that it have an assembly charter. A royal charter would put the trustees of the college out of reach of the people and their representatives, and establish them in a position from which they could propagate their own civil and religious principles by choosing "such persons to instruct our youth, as would be the fittest instruments to extend their power by positive and dogmatical precepts."[92] A college incorporated by an act of the assembly would be in the hands of the people or their guardians, and this would preserve the essential "spirit of freedom."

For as we are split into so great a variety of opinions and professions; had each individual his share in the government of the academy, the jealousy of all parties combating each other, would inevitably produce a perfect freedom for each particular party.[93]

That Livingston did not rely upon the initiative of the faculty itself to produce such freedom in diversity was clear when he expounded his conception of the role of faculty officers:

[91] *Ibid.*, pp. 124–28.   [92] *Ibid.*, pp. 129–35.
[93] *Ibid.*, p. 138; readers will notice the similarity to the rationale of the *Federalist*, Number 10, and the whole theory of balanced government.

Every officer in the college being under the narrow aspect and scrutiny of the civil authority would be continually subject to the wholesome alternative, either of performing his duty with the utmost exactness, or giving up his post to a person of superior integrity.[94]

Like most other writers on education of the period, he meant, when he spoke of a free college, a free college *for students;* his concept of the teacher was simply that of an obedient instrument of the welfare of the students and the community. He assumed without question that teachers would reflect the "positive and dogmatic precepts" of the trustees who chose them. He did not ask whether this was desirable: it was certain to happen, and the way to provide the students with the benefits of diversity and freedom was not to underwrite a free faculty, but to put both the trustees and the faculty under the pressure of so many conflicting elements in the community that they would be forced to accept the community's diversity. Livingston was arguing for a kind of free consensus through a plurality of pressures. This is a defensible model of freedom indeed, but because it assigns to the faculty a purely passive role, it bears little resemblance to the concept of academic freedom with which we are familiar today. It neglects to count the interest of the teachers themselves as within the plurality of legitimate interests.

In offering his positive notions as to how the prospective college should be set up, Livingston specified that no person of any Protestant denomination should be disqualified by virtue of his religion from holding any office in the college; that the choice and removal of the president by the trustees be subject to confirmation by the legislature, so that the head of the college would have greater independence of the trustees in his educational duties than if he were answerable to them alone; that college by-laws be ratified by the legislature, and that the legislative constitution provide for as many details of the government of the college as foresight could make possible; that "no religious profession in particular be established in the college, but that both officers and scholars be at perfect liberty to attend any Protestant Church at their pleasure respectively"; that the prescribed public prayers offered twice daily at the college follow forms all Protestants could subscribe to; that divinity should not be taught at the college, that the corporation be constitutionally barred from electing a professor of divinity and degrees be offered only in arts, medicine and civil law; that

[94] *Ibid.,* p. 139.

the officers and collegians have an unrestrained access to all books in the library, and that free conversation upon polemical and controverted points in divinity, be not discountenanced, whilst all public disputations upon the various tenets of different professions of Protestants be absolutely forbidden; and finally, that disputes among the inferior officers of the college be settled by the trustees, while those of the trustees be settled by the legislature.[95]

Livingston's proposals may be profitably contrasted with Clap's intentions at Yale which, even as he wrote, was on the eve of its severest trials. And yet one cannot help but observe that Livingston, in his zeal to secure a nonsectarian institution, was far from solving his problem in the freest way. His confidence in the superiority of the wisdom of a public legislature to that of private trustees, for instance, has not been borne out by the histories of state and private universities in the United States. His attempt to reduce the religious commitment of the college to vague public prayers held twice a day (and made compulsory for the students) was in itself a liberating suggestion, as were some other religious provisions. But to free the college of sectarianism by barring the teaching of divinity and banning the clash of theologies would be to deprive undergraduates of the chance to consider some of the most important intellectual currents of the eighteenth century, and it seems far inferior to the solution that was gradually emerging at Harvard—i.e., of discussing, not too dogmatically, at least some of the different systems of divinity and presenting the students with differences and choices. The context in which these proposals were presented, however, shows that Livingston, for all his factional zeal, had a good understanding of and an honest belief in the principles of toleration and religious liberty as many men of enlightenment saw them in his time. He simply lacked confidence (and perhaps with reason) that a plurality of religious systems could be taught under one college roof without producing deleterious sectarian bickering; and, being determined that no single profession should dominate the institution, he preferred to go almost all the way toward establishing a secular college. In this fashion sectarian antagonisms tended to modulate themselves in the eighteenth-century climate.[96]

[95] *Ibid.*, pp. 142–46.
[96] Note that even Bishop Madison, the head of the reorganized William and Mary, wrote Ezra Stiles almost thirty years later that the professorship of divinity there had been given up because it was deemed incompatible with a republic. Stiles, *Literary Diary*, II, 447.

At the time that men like Franklin, Smith, and Livingston were writing, piety in the older colleges was declining. A tendency extremely significant for the role of higher education was the precipitate fall in the proportion of undergraduates destined for the ministry. The percentage of future ministers among graduates, which had always been over 50 percent and often over 60 percent in the closing decades of the seventeenth century at Harvard and in the opening decades of the eighteenth at Harvard and Yale together, declined steadily until the early 1740s, when it was around 40 percent. The percentage of future ministers in all but two of the colonial colleges fell from a little over 40 percent in 1751 to about 20 percent in 1791, which represented the nadir for the eighteenth century.[97] The course of Yale's development is illuminating. Among the graduates whose occupations were known to Dexter, ministers vastly outnumbered physicians and lawyers together up to 1777. But in the classes from 1778 to 1805, Dexter found 350 lawyers, 238 ministers, and 94 physicians. In the period after 1792 businessmen, teachers, farmers, and planters appeared in sufficient numbers to warrant separate enumerations.[98] As future ministers increasingly shared the college halls with men destined for other occupations, both the tone and the curriculum of the college changed. The impulse of presidents and professors to catch up with the new currents of thought of the Enlightenment was strengthened by the growing complexity and receptivity of the undergraduate bodies.[99]

Changes in the curriculum bear directly on the origins of academic freedom, for in this sphere the initiative was passing into the hands of the faculties, especially where strong presidents reigned. If we look first at the schools in the Congregational-Presbyterian tradition, we find that

[97] See the table in Bailey B. Burritt, *Professional Distribution of College and University Graduates* (Washington, 1912), p. 75, and the explanation of his sample, p. 74.

[98] Dexter, *Yale Biographies and Annals,* gives a brief statistical résumé of the occupations at the end of each volume. For comparable figures on the shift at Brown between its founding and 1802, see Walter C. Bronson, *The History of Brown University, 1764–1914* (Providence, R. I., 1914), pp. 129, 154; for Princeton from 1761 to 1794, see John Maclean, *History of the College of New Jersey* (Philadelphia, 1877), I, 274–357. There, under President Finley, 45 percent of the graduates became ministers, whereas under Witherspoon 24 percent did.

[99] One good index of the development of the colleges is the change in student intellectual interests. Valuable sidelights on this subject may be found in Edward J. Young, "Subjects for Master's Degree in Harvard College from 1655 to 1791," *Proceedings of the Massachusetts Historical Society,* XVIII (1881), 119–51, and David Potter, *Debating in the Colonial Chartered Colleges* (New York, 1944), Chaps. I, II, III.

Harvard was the first to undergo an important curricular reformation; this occurred during the regime of President Holyoke, 1737–69. While Wollebius was still studied in divinity up to about the middle of the century, he had been dropped by 1759. In 1742–43, the college faculty resolved to use Locke on the human understanding and to use 'sGravesande's natural philosophy, a popular statement of Newtonianism, Isaac Watts' astronomy, and other such works.[100] Yale clung to Wollebius and Ames right up to the time of the Revolution, but these writers were supplemented during the second half of the century by Wollaston's *Religion of Nature Delineated,* so that during that period at least the Yale students could contemplate and compare both the old Federal Theology and the new natural theology. Edwards' *Enquiry into the Freedom of the Will* was also used for a time, but was dropped, evidently because it gave offense. During the last quarter of the century the college studies became thoroughly infused with the influence of Newton and Locke and their popularizers.[101] Princeton took cognizance of the new philosophy almost from the beginning.[102] Princeton was also profoundly influenced, as was Yale and to a lesser degree Harvard, by the textbooks of the English dissenting divine and hymnist, Isaac Watts, who in the reckoning of American Protestants was accounted an important thinker and whose works on astronomy, logic, theology, and philosophy mingled the traditional dissenting theology with the new concerns of the age. Even Watts, however, was alleged to be tainted with the heresy of Arianism, and at Yale the relevant volume of his work did not become available to students for a century after it was received by the library in 1730.[103]

The New York and Philadelphia colleges, whose advantage it was to have been founded in the midst of the Enlightenment, were burdened

[100] Louis F. Snow, *The College Curriculum in the United States* (n.p., 1907), pp. 47–48; Morison, *Three Centuries of Harvard,* p. 89. The only full-length study of the subject, Colyer Meriwether, *Our Colonial Curriculum 1607–1776* (Washington, 1907), is lamentably inadequate.

[101] John C. Schwab, "The Yale College Curriculum, 1701–1901," *Educational Review,* XXII (June, 1901), esp. 4–8; cf. Snow, *The College Curriculum,* pp. 41–45, 79–81; Benjamin Rand, "Philosophical Instruction in Harvard University from 1636 to 1900," *Harvard Graduates' Magazine,* XXXVII (September, 1928), 29–45. See also G. Stanley Hall, "On the History of American College Textbooks and Teaching in Logic, Ethics, Psychology, and Allied Subjects," *Proceedings of the American Antiquarian Society,* IX (April, 1894), 137–74.

[102] For an excellent study of Princeton, see Francis L. Broderick, "Pulpit, Physics, and Politics: The Curriculum of the College of New Jersey, 1746–1794," *William and Mary Quarterly,* Third Series, Vol. VI (January, 1949), pp. 42–68.

[103] Anne Stokely Pratt, *Isaac Watts and His Gifts of Books to Yale College* (New Haven, 1938), pp. 13–14.

with somewhat less of the traditional theological and metaphysical baggage that Harvard and Yale sloughed off. Both, at their beginnings, made rather strong gestures toward supplementing the usual classical studies with many practical subjects, but neither in practice went quite so far. At King's College, presided over by Samuel Johnson, one of the first colonials to perceive the importance of Locke's philosophy and to grow weary of Ames and Wollebius,[104] students were introduced to Whitby and Hutcheson, Grotius and Pufendorf.[105] At Philadelphia Provost Smith drew up a program of studies requiring considerably more science, theoretical and applied, than had been common. His was, Cheyney points out, the first systematic arrangement in America "of a group of college studies not following medieval tradition and not having a specifically religious object." [106] The tenor of his educational program was also shown in the materials recommended for additional reading by the students in their "private hours"—the *Spectator,* the works of Watts, Newton and the Newtonian popularizers, and Locke, Pufendorf, Hutcheson, and others.[107]

The rise of science was the most impressive aspect of curricular changes in the eighteenth century. While less than one tenth of the Harvard curriculum of the seventeenth century had consisted of scientific subjects, the typical curriculum of 1760 gave to them one fifth or more of the students' classroom time.[108] In the sixty years from 1640 to 1700 there had been little advance in the teaching of science at Harvard, but in the quarter of a century after 1725 the two holders of the Hollis Professorship of Mathematics and Natural Philosophy, Isaac Greenwood and John Winthrop, had revolutionized the teaching of science and mathematics and had made of Harvard a center of Newtonianism.[109] The

---

[104] Schneider and Schneider, *Samuel Johnson,* I, 6.

[105] Snow, *The College Curriculum,* pp. 56–60.

[106] Cheyney, *History of the University of Pennsylvania,* p. 82.

[107] Horace Wemyss Smith, *Life and Correspondence of the Rev. William Smith* (Philadelphia, 1879), pp. 58–59, 124–25; for an estimate of the practical significance of this curriculum see Cheyney, pp. 81–87, and for its origins, Theodore Hornberger, "A Note on the Probable Source of Provost Smith's Famous Curriculum," *Pennsylvania Magazine of History and Biography,* LVIII (1934), 370–77.

[108] Theodore Hornberger, *Scientific Thought in the American Colleges, 1638–1800* (Austin, Texas, 1945), pp. 23, 29. The development of science in the colonial curricula is traced in Chap. IV.

[109] On the advance of Newtonian science see Frederick E. Brasch, "The Newtonian Epoch in the American Colonies," *Proceedings of the American Antiquarian Society,* New Series, Vol. XLIX (October, 1939), pp. 314–32. The progress of early Harvard science is the theme of I. Bernard Cohen's *Some Early Tools of American Science* (Cambridge, Mass., 1950).

other colleges made comparable progress. Jefferson's mentor, Dr. William Small, although not a creative scientist of Winthrop's stature, taught science and mathematics inspiringly at William and Mary, while Presidents Clap and Stiles devoted themselves to the advancement of science at Yale.[110] And while neither President Johnson of King's College nor Provost Smith of the College of Philadelphia was able to realize his ambitious plans for scientific and practical studies, their institutions were founded in the midst of a lively interest in the new science. From its very beginning the College of Philadelphia had a science professor, inherited from the Academy that preceded it, while King's College acquired one eight years after the date of its charter. By the beginning of the Revolution six of the eight colonial colleges that were actually open (Rutgers being temporarily defunct) had professorships of mathematics and natural philosophy; and by 1788 all eight were so staffed. While astronomy and physics were the central subjects of study, other sciences were beginning to receive a share of attention, and the subsequent founding of medical schools in association with Harvard, King's, and Philadelphia gave an impetus to the study of botany and chemistry.[111] Considering their size and limited funds, the colleges appropriated generous sums for demonstration equipment and orreries.[112] Trustees were well aware that a good lecturer in science and a spectacular piece of equipment—like the famous orrery made by David Rittenhouse for Princeton—were assets in the reputation of a college. The possession of such items soon began to be mentioned prominently in college promotional literature.

The greatest creative activity in colonial science, of course, took place outside the colleges, being carried on chiefly by gifted amateurs and sponsored most notably by scientific societies.[113] Mathematical education in American colleges had started from too negligible a base to provide good groundwork for advanced study in physics or astronomy, and biology

[110] On Small see Hornberger, *Scientific Thought*, pp. 61–62; on Clap and Stiles, Louis W. McKeehan, *Yale Science: The First Hundred Years, 1701–1801* (New York, 1947), Chap. II.

[111] Medical schools were founded in 1765, 1767, and 1782 at Philadelphia, King's, and Harvard. Cheyney, *History of the University of Pennsylvania*, pp. 96–104; Morison, *Three Centuries of Harvard*, pp. 167–69. For the early development of medical education, see W. F. Norwood, *Medical Education in the United States* (Philadelphia, 1944); for the biological sciences, W. M. and M. S. C. Smallwood, *Natural History and the American Mind* (New York, 1941), Chaps. II, X, and XI. I. B. Cohen, *Some Early Tools of American Science*, Chaps. IV and V, traces early chemistry and biology at Harvard.

[112] Hornberger, *Scientific Thought*, p. 37.

[113] See Ralph S. Bates, *Scientific Societies in the United States* (New York, 1945), Chap. I.

and chemistry were late additions to the curriculum. The names of the outstanding colonial scientists—men like Bartram, Franklin, Logan, Garden, Rittenhouse, and others—are for the most part names of men who were not on college faculties; Winthrop alone among the academic scientists was of comparable stature.[114] But the same thing can be said for the most part about the universities of Europe, which with only a few exceptions had not been important centers for advanced scientific work since the decay of the medieval universities. Considering the university standards of the time, and their limited resources, the record of the colonial colleges is in this respect far from discreditable; and it must also be said of them that unlike the European universities of the seventeenth century they never showed antagonism to the work of the scientific societies.[115]

However one may assess its scientific value, the growth of science teaching had an important effect on the colleges. In all the colleges the first professor of mathematics and natural philosophy was the first professor of a secular subject. Often he was also the first professor whose personal background was secular. While an able professor of science was like an able professor of divinity in the sense that he had something distinctive to bring to the college, something besides mere conformity, he was different in that he introduced the *discovery* of knowledge into the classroom. In education, the study of science, one may admit, is by no means intrinsically or universally a liberating discipline: it can be made as hidebound or formularized as the pedagogue wills. But eighteenth-century science breathed an air of freshness and discovery that seems not to have been lost upon either pupils or professors.[116] Teaching itself was freshened. While in the study of the classical languages recitation from the textbook was almost the sole method of instruction, the science teachers relied in great measure upon lectures, often accompanied by

[114] Rittenhouse, it should be observed, served very briefly on the faculty of the College of Philadelphia, but his most sustained relationship with it was that of trustee. Among those listed by Raymond Phineas Stearns in his "Colonial Fellows of the Royal Society of London, 1661–1788," *William and Mary Quarterly,* Third Series, Vol. III (April, 1946), pp. 208–68, are the names of five American academic men: William Brattle, John Leverett, and Thomas Robie of Harvard, all three of whom were elected after their teaching years were over; Dr. John Morgan, Professor of Medicine at the College of Philadelphia; and John Winthrop. Twenty-two non-academic scientists were elected from the American colonies.

[115] Martha Ornstein, *The Role of Scientific Societies in the Seventeenth Century* (Chicago, 1938), Chap. VIII.

[116] Cohen, *Some Early Tools of American Science,* pp. 12–17.

demonstrations. It may have done the students some good to memorize whole paragraphs of Locke's *Essay concerning Human Understanding;* it seems to have done them more good to be able to ask questions of the professors of natural philosophy.[117] Before the creation of the science professorships the divinity professors were usually the only men of stature on the college faculties who normally did more than check on the students' knowledge of some particular text. Now the undergraduates were exposed also to men of science who had posts of comparable stature and something of their own to impart. While the divinity professors continued to preach to the undergraduates and educate the masters for the ministry, the science professors now spoke from their secular pulpits with authority equal to that of the divines, and often reared the undergraduates in that passion for nature which was so much a part of eighteenth-century religion. Where the college had been in the past directed, even in its science teaching, toward the conservation and inculcation of existing knowledge, the science professors began to acquaint undergraduates with the idea of inquiry, to encourage the feeling that it was the business of the mind to discover things hitherto unknown.

The student of the history of intellectual freedom will observe that the intellectual changes resulting from the development of the Enlightenment in American colleges came about almost completely without incident. A whole world of new ideas was opened to the minds of undergraduates without struggle on the part of the old order, and frequently with the active interest and enthusiasm of governing boards. The only case in which a science teacher seems to have become involved in a controversy over his scientific teachings occurred in 1755. The scientist was John Winthrop, and the resolution of the issue is worthy of note because in this case it was the scientist who took the offensive and because his victory was so complete.

In November, 1755, Boston was shaken by a severe earthquake, which provoked a great deal of speculative literature. Notable among the reactions were a pamphlet by the Reverend Thomas Prince and a lecture given by John Winthrop in the Harvard College chapel. It was Prince's thesis that earthquakes were above all tokens of God's "just Displeasure," a familiar clerical theme. But in addition to giving currency once again to this now obsolescent reaction, Prince ventured to suggest that earthquakes were made more severe around Boston because the town con-

[117] *Ibid.*, p. 15.

tained so many lightning rods. It was his notion (and one not unknown among distinguished scientists at that time) that the severity of earthquakes was increased because the lightning rods drew "the Electrical Substance" out of the air. To erect lightning rods, Prince thought, was blasphemous: "O! there is no getting out of the mighty Hand of God! If we think to avoid it in the *Air,* we cannot in the *Earth.* . . ." Winthrop, provoked by some fallacies in Prince's reasoning, added an appendix to his own published lectures on the earthquake in which he effectively castigated the minister's arguments. When this drew from Prince an amiable but befuddled partial retraction, Winthrop replied with a withering communication which attacked still further the poor preacher's confusions. In the end the minister retreated in total disorder, amid a flurry of phrases in praise of Winthrop's family.[118] This public spanking administered to a cleric by a scientist (and to an Overseer by a professor) is a minor landmark in the intellectual history of New England, a token of the rising prestige of science and the vulnerability of some of the old providential interpretations of nature that had once held undisputed sway. It was not, however, an episode in any "war" between science and religion. Like so many of the Puritan clergy, Prince was himself a well-informed amateur scientist, not an opponent of science as such; he was simply trying to combine scientific with theological explanations in a way that the more rigorous Winthrop would not let pass. He had, moreover, the wit to know that he had been outargued, and the grace to admit it.

What is truly remarkable, indeed, is the absence of a "war" between religion and science during this great period of scientific advance, as well as the atmosphere of freedom in which the new science was introduced into the colleges.[119] In this respect the American colonial colleges compared very favorably with European universities of the period and with some later American institutions in the Darwinian age. All this is not to say that there was no tension between religion and science; all systems of faith are likely to contain tendencies hostile or inhibiting to scientific

[118] See the account of the affair by Eleanor M. Tilton, "Lightning-Rods and the Earthquake of 1755," *New England Quarterly,* XIII (March, 1940), 85–97; cf. Theodore Hornberger, "The Science of Thomas Prince," *ibid.,* IX (March, 1936), 26–42, and the comments by Cohen, *Some Early Tools of American Science,* pp. 127–28.

[119] Cf. Cohen, *Some Early Tools,* p. 127: "During the 18th century at Harvard, as throughout New England, and indeed the rest of America, there was a general freedom from clerical opposition to science."

inquiry, among them an exclusive preoccupation on the part of some persons with the supernatural. But the absence of overt clash, the development of so much positive support for science, may be ascribed in good measure to the fundamental hospitality of Puritanism to scientific inquiry. Many students of Puritanism have commented on its relationship to a high state of working morale in business and industry; this same devotion to work in the Puritan ethos carried over into leisure time and encouraged the spirited pursuit of knowledge in such areas as history and natural science. Diligence in the pursuit of knowledge, like diligence in one's calling, was congenial to the Puritan spirit, for the acquisition of knowledge about God's world was another means of glorifying Him.[120] It is now a familiar fact that in the remarkable creative activity that characterized English science in the seventeenth century, the number of Puritan backgrounds and convictions was far out of proportion to the number of Puritans in the population.[121]

The American Puritans were secure in their conviction that the knowledge of nature, far from undermining religion or contravening the glory of God, could only add to man's sense of the grandeur of His work. "Science was not merely tolerated because faith was believed to be secure, whatever physics or astronomy might teach, but it was actually advanced as part of faith itself, a positive declaration of the will of God, a necessary and indispensable complement to Biblical revelation." [122] In valuing science partly for its revelation of divine power, Increase Mather took quite the same position as Isaac Newton.[123] It is true that the Puritans had, especially in the early days, a strong need to see natural events as divine

[120] While there seems to have been no interference in the substantive teaching of science at Harvard, the Corporation itself did resolve in 1788 that the Hollis Professor of Mathematics and Natural Philosophy "be directed, while he is delivering his Philosophical and Astronomical lectures, to make such incidental reflections upon the Being, Perfections and Providence of God, as may arise from the subjects, and may tend seriously to impress the minds of youth." *Ibid.,* p. 12.

[121] The relation between science and Puritanism is discussed at length by Robert K. Merton, "Science, Technology, and Society in Seventeenth Century England," *Osiris,* IV (1938), 360–632, esp. Chaps. IV, V, VI; see also Richard Foster Jones, *Ancients and Moderns* (St. Louis, 1936), Chaps. V, VI, VII. James Bryant Conant in an essay on "The Advancement of Learning during the Puritan Commonwealth," *Proceedings of the Massachusetts Historical Society,* LXVI (1942), 27–31, points out that there were Puritans and Puritans, and that the ultra-doctrinaire Calvinists seem to have been far less interested in science than the Puritan moderates.

[122] Perry Miller, *The New England Mind* (New York, 1939), p. 211.

[123] See E. A. Burtt, *The Metaphysical Foundations of Modern Physical Science* (London, 1949), pp. 280–99.

symbols, or "providences." But they adapted an ancient and convenient dualistic conception of the universe under which events could be taken as having symbolic and providential significance and yet could be admitted to conform to natural laws.[124] Thus the transition from Puritanism to the dominant teleological defense of Christianity in the eighteenth century was an easy one.

From the very beginnings at Harvard, scientific innovations were viewed by many with enthusiasm and by the rest with tolerance. Although the first generation of undergraduates was taught the astronomy of the ancients, later the Copernican system, which was introduced at least as early as 1659, only ten years in the wake of Oxford, was accepted without fuss even by the orthodox. So conservative a preacher as the Reverend John Davenport of New Haven, presented with a copy of an almanac prepared by a Harvard tutor that gave an exposition of the new astronomy, observed that the work contradicted Scripture, but said of its author, "let him injoy his opinion; and I shall rest in what I have learned, til more cogent arguments be produced then I have hitherto met with." [125] Others took a more positive view: the almanac was approved, for instance, by President Chauncy, and Professor Morison remarks of the Puritan clergy that "instead of opposing the acceptance of the Copernican theory," they "were the chief patrons and promoters of the new astronomy, and of other scientific discoveries, in New England." [126] Even those clerical leaders who have been identified with conservatism or reaction in theology had a consistent record of enthusiasm for science. Increase and Cotton Mather were notable promoters of science—the latter a very courageous one—as were Thomas Clap and Timothy Dwight at Yale. And Jonathan Edwards, far from rejecting the new science, was one of

---

[124] See, for instance, Kenneth Murdock, *Increase Mather* (Cambridge, Mass., 1926), p. 146. Perry Miller, *The New England Mind*, Chap. VIII, discusses the Puritan attempts to synthesize providences and natural uniformity.

[125] Samuel Eliot Morison, "The Harvard School of Astronomy in the Seventeenth Century," *New England Quarterly*, VII (March, 1934), 13. For an estimate of the strength and weakness of early Harvard science, see Morison, *The Puritan Pronaos* (New York, 1936), Chap. X. The relation between American Puritanism and science is discussed briefly in Perry Miller and Thomas H. Johnson, *The Puritans* (New York, 1938), pp. 729–38 and at length by Theodore Hornberger, "American Puritanism and the Rise of the Scientific Mind," unpublished Ph.D. dissertation (University of Michigan, 1934).

[126] "The Harvard School of Astronomy," p. 13; cf. Shipton's observation about the clergy of a later day in "The New England Clergy of the 'Glacial Age,'" *Publications of the Colonial Society of Massachusetts*, XXXII (1937), 37–39, 45–46.

the first in New England to see its significance, and seized upon it to reinforce a revival of Calvinism in a remarkable synthesis of science and theology.[127]

While the leading clerics, then, were highly receptive to science, it does not follow that science was not, in some degree, subversive of the inherited religious outlook. Although most Puritans failed to anticipate it, the rise of science did in the end contribute to the decline of orthodoxy.[128] Ingenious as were the logical reconciliations between natural law and "providences," the greater familiarity with the one weakened concern with the other. While the Calvinist system had put its stress upon God's foreknowledge of everything that man would do and all that would befall him, the progress of science, interpreted as the advancing knowledge of God's laws, gave men greater confidence in their own foreknowledge, so to speak, of what God would do. The difference, although not perceived at first, was ultimately vital. As time went on the tenets of Puritanism passed gradually but easily into the tenets of the Enlightenment, divine providences yielded to natural law, and theology rested more and more upon teleology. Of course, defenders of orthodoxy ultimately realized that the incursions of science had made things more difficult for older forms of religion,[129] but the full force of this realization was not felt until the reaction from the Enlightenment that came in the early nineteenth century.

POLITICS AND REVOLUTION

The political life of the American colonies quickened after 1750 as questions of large historical importance elbowed their way onto the stage. In

[127] Miller speaks of Edwards as "the last great American, perhaps the last European, for whom there could be no warfare between religion and science, or between ethics and nature." *Jonathan Edwards,* p. 72.

[128] Cf. Robert K. Merton, "Science, Technology and Society in Seventeenth Century England," *Osiris,* IV (1938), 438: "The possibility that science, as means toward a religious end, would later break away from such religious supports and in a measure tend to delimit the realm of theological control, was seemingly unrealized. The apparent conflicts between theology and science which arose when scientific findings seemed to disprove various contentions of orthodox theologians occurred later with each extension of scientific inquiry into realms which were hitherto regarded as sacred. . . . the Reformers did not anticipate the full actual consequences of their teachings, consequences which did not coincide with their expectations."

[129] For the beginnings of this realization, see Hornberger, *Scientific Thought in the American Colleges,* pp. 80–85.

the earliest days of the American colleges, politics as a subject of study had its place only as an incidental part of courses in ethics or moral philosophy; but with the development of the eighteenth-century curriculum a large part of such courses was avowedly given over to the broad principles of politics, law, and civil ethics. Students were introduced to the writings of Grotius, Pufendorf, Wollaston, Locke, Hutcheson, and others. In the curriculum itself the studies were directed toward moral and political philosophy rather than to topical problems, and while it is reasonable to assume that the college presidents, who usually offered the relevant courses, used current issues to illustrate general principles, little is known about the details of classroom teaching.[130]

An incident involving Provost Smith at Philadelphia suggests that comments made by a teacher of politics about current issues were most likely to involve him in difficulties if he was at the same time an active figure in political controversies. Smith, who was an ardent champion of the interests of the proprietors in the struggle between them and the Quaker faction, was the object of much criticism in the newspapers, most of it in the form of anonymous letters; his teaching was alleged to be both irreligious and un-Pennsylvanian. The trustees, fearing that these charges would damage the reputation of the college, ordered an investigation in July, 1756. They were soon presented with strong testimony on Smith's behalf signed by the only four members of the senior class who were then present in town. The undergraduates averred that Smith's teaching had been nonpartisan as to the current provincial struggles and that

in the whole Course of his Lectures on Ethics, Government and Commerce, he never advanced any other Principles than what were warranted by our standard Authors, Grotius, Puffendorf, Locke, and Hutcheson; writers whose sentiments are equally opposite to all those wild notions of Liberty that are inconsistent with all government, and to those pernicious Schemes of Government which are destructive of true Liberty.

Moreover, said these young laymen of their clerical preceptor, his teachings embraced both morality and religion.[131]

The committee of trustees charged with the inquiry issued a report which expressed their conception of the problem of biased instruction:

. . . on examination, it must appear to everyone, as it really does to us, that no single Master can, by the Constitution of the College and Academy, carry

130 See Anna Haddow, *Political Science in American Colleges and Universities, 1636–1900* (New York, 1939), Chaps. I–VII.
131 Horace Wemyss Smith, *Life . . . of the Rev. William Smith*, I, 126–27.

on any separate or party-Scheme, or teach any principles injurious to piety, Virtue and good Government, without an evident failure of Duty in the whole Body of Trustees and Masters; the general Scheme of Education being fixed, a part of it assigned to every Master, The Visitations of the Schools by the Trustees monthly, and in the Interim between their Meetings, the Government, the Morals, and the Education of the whole Youth committed to the Faculty, which consists of the Provost, Vice-Provost, and Professors, who have it in charge to examine into and report to the Trustees at their Stated Meetings whatever shall appear wrong in any of the Professors, Masters or Scholars.[132]

The entire government of the college thus being a system of mutual espionage and counterespionage, it seemed that any misdemeanors on the part of the Provost would have become known to the trustees; and having closely examined Provost Smith's record, the committee found him whole. Indeed, having gone to the trouble, they said, of looking into the lecture notes of the four students who were in town as well as receiving their friendly representations about their teacher, they concluded that he had "discharged his Trust as a capable Professor and an honest man," and had given ample evidence "of the goodness of his Principles." [133] Although Smith was thus vindicated, the incident gives illuminating evidence of some of the limitations under which he carried on his work in this closely governed college. His situation, however, was untypical, not only because of the exceptionally intimate government of the college by its trustees but because of the acrimony of Pennsylvania's factional politics and his active role in it. Teachers of politics and ethics elsewhere, who paid the price of remaining aloof from current controversies, seem not to have been similarly troubled by criticism of their teaching.

While faculties do not seem on the whole to have been notable for their daring or importance in political speculations, much effort was made to encourage among the students a keen taste for controversy about political principles. It is no accident that the generation of acute political controversialists that led the pre-Revolutionary colonial agitations were men who had been for the greater part educated in the free and inquiring atmosphere of the colleges.[134] A primary source of vigorous and contro-

---

[132] *Ibid.*, p. 127.   [133] *Ibid.*, p. 127.

[134] See James J. Walsh, *The Education of the Founding Fathers of the Republic* (New York, 1935) which emphasizes the continuity with the scholastic tradition (especially Chap. X). Morison suggests that the schooling of the colonials in dissenting politics may have owed more to their traditional classical studies than to current eighteenth-century writings on politics. *Three Centuries of Harvard,* pp. 135–36.

versial thinking was the student disputations, which offer additional grounds for the conclusion that the undergraduates in these early colleges were freer men than the faculty members. As the eighteenth century wore on there was greater and greater evidence of ardent political argumentation, and many of the recorded theses show that urgently controversial topical questions were argued along with questions of political theory; among them were the value of paper-money issues, the lawfulness of resisting the supreme magistrate, the compact theory of government, the legality (debated after the Stamp Act) of collecting taxes by military force, and the moral propriety of slavery.[135]

An indulgent view was taken of these student exercises in all colleges about which we have sufficient evidence for conclusions. "The young gentlemen," wrote the Reverend Andrew Eliot, a member of the Harvard Corporation, to an English benefactor of the college in the early 1770s,

are already taken up with politics. They have caught the spirit of liberty. This has always been encouraged, but they have sometimes been wrought up to such a pitch of enthusiasm that it has been difficult for their Tutors to keep them within due bounds; but their Tutors are fearful of giving too great a check to a disposition, which may, hereafter, fill the country with patriots; and choose to leave it to age and experience to check their ardor.[136]

This was Harvard; but much the same might have been said at Princeton or William and Mary. The seniors at Yale under Stiles could debate such questions as "Whether polygamy is lawful?" and in 1780, despite the local bitterness excited by a recent British invasion of New Haven, they were freely arguing "Whether America would be more happy as a part of the British Empire, than as an Independ't Republick? or Whether America would be more happy in a subordinate connexion with Great Britain . . . ?"[137] They also debated such moot questions as whether

---

[135] On disputations see Haddow, *Political Science in American Colleges*, Chaps. III, VII; Potter, *Debating in the Colonial Chartered Colleges*, pp. 43–53.

[136] Morison, *Three Centuries of Harvard*, p. 138.

[137] Stiles, *Literary Diary*, II, 434. The diary affords frequent illustrations of the latitude allowed for disputation subjects. Cf. Reuben A. Guild, "The First Commencement of Rhode Island College and American Independence," *Collections of the Rhode Island Historical Society*, III (Providence, 1895), 267–98. Some readers have questioned whether allowing students to debate liberal-sounding issues in theology or politics was actually as liberal as it seemed, since in some instances —say, the lawfulness of polygamy—a ritualistic resolution of the argument on the "correct" side was expected. Even when this objection is taken into account, the intrinsic liberality of the brave effort constantly to rationalize one's conclusions and beliefs must be admitted. So long as *pro forma* debate is allowed, there is always the possibility that the "incorrect" conclusion may become functional to

there should be amnesty for Tories (1783) and whether the Federal Constitution should be ratified (1787). Men of Stiles' stamp evidently realized that even in a time of crisis it is educational wisdom to give free rein to the dissents and questions of eighteen-year-old minds.

The coming of the Revolution led, of course, to many severities and injustices to Loyalists, including some violations of civil liberties. This is in itself a large and important story—no doubt a more important one than the history of the colleges themselves during the revolutionary period—but it involves issues distinct from that of academic freedom. Civil liberties and academic freedom often suffer together from the same causes, but they are not identical. Another of Provost Smith's unhappy experiences provides an excellent case in point. In 1757 his friend (and subsequently his father-in-law), Judge William Moore, became embroiled with the dominant Quaker faction in the Pennsylvania Assembly. Out of this conflict there came a sharply worded counterattack written by him and published by Provost Smith in a German newspaper which Smith had established. Moore and Smith were both charged with libeling the Assembly, and in the course of events were jailed.[138] The incident is pretty clearly a case of political persecution,[139] and as such doubtless marks one of the low points in the history of civil liberties in the province. But oddly enough it turned out to be a landmark in the history of academic freedom; for the trustees of the college, upon hearing that the provost had expressed a desire to continue his classes, and his students a like desire to go on under his tutelage, gave permission to have his classes carried on "at the usual Hours in the Place of his present confinement." For several weeks Smith met his twelve students in his cell in the jail at Sixth and Walnut streets. Later the trustees gave him leave to go to England to carry an appeal from the Assembly to the Crown, which proved to be successful although it brought Smith no redress. Inasmuch as three of the trustees were members of the Assembly and one was a

---

some personal or social interest, and that Arminius' experience of being converted to the view he was engaged to refute may be repeated.

[138] The most ample account from Smith's standpoint is that of Horace Wemyss Smith, *Life . . . of the Rev. William Smith,* Vol. I, Chap. XII. The provost had an opportunity to escape sentence through a retraction, but he told the Assembly: "I cannot make acknowledgements or profess contrition. No punishment which this Assembly can inflict on me would be half so terrible to me as suffering my tongue to give to my heart the lie."

[139] See the detailed critical analysis by William R. Riddell, "Libel on the Assembly," *Pennsylvania Magazine of History and Biography,* LII (1928), 176–92, 249–79, 342–60.

judge who had denied habeas corpus to the provost, the action of that body involved, for some of its members at least, an element of self-denial.[140] As an episode in American academic history it may provide an interesting precedent for the determination of trustees to draw a line of demarcation between educational decisions and political controversy. The Philadelphia trustees did not raise questions about Smith's legal status, but they acted upon the ineluctable fact that it had no bearing upon his competence as an educator.

In nationalist and colonial revolutions college and university students have always played an aggressive part, and to this the American college students were no exception. At the dissenting colleges trustees, faculties, and students were so strongly committed to the patriotic cause from the time the controversies with the mother country became acute that there was little likelihood that any interference with the academic freedom of a patriotic student or professor would occur. As for the few Loyalists on academic faculties, they suffered, when they suffered at all, violations of civil rather than academic liberties, which, serious though they were, fall outside the necessary limits of our story. Most notable of the incidents in this category was the case of Myles Cooper, the second president of King's College and a resolute Loyalist, who would have been tarred and feathered in 1775 if young Alexander Hamilton, then an undergraduate and an activist in the patriotic cause, had not delayed an angry mob long enough to facilitate his escape. Hamilton's conduct, which suggests that he may have learned something about the principles of civil freedom at King's College, saved the president from a humiliating experience but it did not save his post; he was forced to flee to England, where he remained for the rest of his life.[141] A man like William Smith, however, who had been active in the early patriotic movement but could not follow the patriot cause to the point of demanding outright independence, found it possible when his college closed to retire to his country home at the Falls of Schuylkill without molestation.[142] Later he returned to educational administration both in Maryland and Pennsylvania.[143] The Anglican insti-

[140] Cheyney, *History of the University of Pennsylvania,* pp. 107–9.

[141] *A History of Columbia University* (New York, 1904), pp. 46–49; Nathan Schachner, *Alexander Hamilton* (New York, 1946), pp. 41–42. For a similar instance of persecution see E. Alfred Jones, "Two Professors of William and Mary College," *William and Mary College Quarterly,* Second Series, Vol. XXVI (April, 1918), pp. 221–31.

[142] Horace Wemyss Smith, *Life . . . of the Rev. William Smith,* Vol. I, Chap. XXXV.

[143] The only non-Anglican president who got into difficulties was Eleazar Wheelock

tutions themselves not only lost their affiliation with the English church but narrowly escaped losing their private character as well. The reorganization of William and Mary completed the victory of the Virginia laymen over the Anglican faculty. Both King's College and the College of Philadelphia underwent rather complex reorganizations which almost resulted in their having the legal status of state universities governed by combined boards of politicians and denominational representatives. Both drifted back, however, into their old private status.

Aside from the immediate effects of war, invasion, and inflation, and the temporary suspension of most of the colleges, the long-range effects of the Revolution upon higher education were far from favorable. The financial support which the colleges had had from private philanthropy in England was, of course, largely cut off both during and after the fighting. This was something that could be remedied at home; indeed the fact that sixteen institutions of higher education were chartered in America between the end of hostilities and the year 1795 suggests that the American states had resources enough to maintain and extend their system of higher education. Unfortunately they had already begun to scatter their resources. More serious than the financial loss was the fact that the close cultural ties with England, which had so long been a restraining hand on provincialism and sectarian bigotry, were now considerably loosened.[144] Possibly the benefits of this connection would have been lessened in any case after the reaction from the French Revolution began in England. At any rate, the political life of the American states themselves was troubled and often acrimonious from the end of the Revolution until the period of expansion that followed the War of 1812. Had there been a professoriat actively devoted to Republican principles, it is hardly likely that it would have survived the period of the Alien and Sedition laws, during which the major colleges north of Virginia were all committed to Federalism, without yielding many casualties to political persecution.[145]

---

of Dartmouth, but in his case a false and malicious accusation of disloyalty to the revolutionary cause was investigated by local Committees of Safety that not only cleared him but recommended that his accuser give satisfaction for slander. Leon Burr Richardson, *History of Dartmouth College* (Hanover, N.H., 1932), I, 159–62.

[144] Anglo-American cultural relations are treated in detail by Michael Kraus, *The Atlantic Civilization: Eighteenth Century Origins* (Ithaca, N.Y., 1949).

[145] The case of Josiah Meigs is suggestive. Having joined the Yale faculty as Professor of Mathematics and Natural Philosophy under his friend, Ezra Stiles, he became an ardent Republican and found himself completely at odds with Stiles' successor, Timothy Dwight, under whom Yale was imbued with Connecticut Federalism. In order to escape being dropped from the college, he found it necessary at

Despite all the gains that had been made by the emergent academic profession at the close of the eighteenth century, the American colleges had not reached the point at which a professor or tutor could be politically active in ways that did not meet with the approval of his president or board of trustees.

---

one point to make a formal statement of his political beliefs, which was interpreted as a recantation. In his letter to the Yale Corporation he declared that if he were in truth such an "enemy to the constitution and liberties of my country" as he had been alleged to be, it would be the Corporation's duty indeed to throw him out. He was kept in his post in return for making a public statement of his real views, but some two years later, having found the life of an ardent Republican in a Federalist community unbearable, he resigned, and went to the new University of Georgia—"an exile," as his wife put it, "to the backwoods . . . only twelve miles from the Cherokee Indians." Meigs was not attached to his position as president at Georgia ("I long to see the civilized part of the United States once more," he wrote in 1806), and soon fell out with the trustees, whom he denounced as "a damned pack or band of tories and speculators." After his dismissal there, Jefferson gave him jobs as Surveyor General and then Commissioner of the General Land Office. See William M. Meigs, *Life of Josiah Meigs* (Philadelphia, 1887), esp. pp. 38–42, 51–54; Richard Purcell, *Connecticut in Transition* (Washington, 1918), pp. 301–2; Charles E. Cuningham, *Timothy Dwight* (New York, 1942), pp. 198–99; E. M. Coulter, *College Life in the Old South* (New York, 1928), pp. 23–26.

V: THE OLD-TIME COLLEGE
1800–1860

THE GREAT RETROGRESSION

DURING the last three or four decades of the eighteenth century the American colleges had achieved a notable degree of freedom, vitality, and public usefulness and seemed to have set their feet firmly on the path to further progress. The opening decades of the nineteenth century, however, brought a great retrogression in the state of American collegiate education, a decline in freedom and the capacity for growth that universally afflicted the newer institutions and in all but a few cases severely damaged the older ones. While advances had been made in curricula and teaching methods from 1730 to about 1800, the succeeding forty years, despite much educational unrest and considerable experimentation, could show only modest improvements in the best institutions, to be weighed against the inadequate and unprogressive system of collegiate education that was being fixed upon the country at large.[1]

Perhaps the root cause of the retrogression was the pervasive national reaction from the Enlightenment. But one of the primary factors in the backsliding of the collegiate system was that the sponsors of collegiate education, instead of developing further the substantial and altogether adequate number of institutions that existed in 1800, chose to establish new institutions far beyond the number demanded by the geography of the country. Although it was partly a consequence of the physical growth of the young republic and of its feverish local rivalries, this multiplying and scattering of colleges was primarily the result of denominational

[1] Francis Wayland, comparing the pulpit and the bar of the 1840s with those of the revolutionary generation, concluded that intellectual training had considerably deteriorated. *Thoughts on the Present Collegiate System in the United States* (Boston, 1842) pp. 79–80. He attributed this in large part to the severance of educational relations with England after the Revolution, which deprived the cultivated American world of Oxford and Cambridge teachers as well as laymen familiar with English standards. *Ibid.,* p. 78.

sponsorship and sectarian competition. The gains of the colonial colleges had depended in part upon their tendency to break free from the sectarian limitations that men like Thomas Clap would have imposed upon them and their impulse to move into the mainstream of intellectual life.[2] The most advanced educational thinkers of the late eighteenth and early nineteenth centuries hoped that the interdenominational pattern of the later colleges would presage the development of larger, well-financed institutions, basically secular in their mode of operation, where some advanced studies and allied professional education would be available. Instead, the intellectual and religious reaction fostered a host of little institutions in which doctrinal and sectarian considerations were rated above educational accomplishment. Where serious attempts were made to achieve the university ideal, notably in the "state universities" chartered in the South, these attempts were defeated by sectarian rivalries. Throughout the country educators who had carried into the nineteenth century the liberal habits of mind of the eighteenth—men like Samuel Stanhope Smith at Princeton, Asa Messer at Brown, and still later, Thomas Cooper at South Carolina—found themselves out of harmony with their new environment.

From the outset the severely denominational institutions neither aspired to nor pretended to foster academic freedom; and very commonly—although not universally—their teachers lived and worked placidly within this framework. In a certain sense the problem of academic freedom as it is understood in the modern university did not yet exist in these colleges, or existed only in a rudimentary form. This fact itself elicits a few further observations. Perhaps the most significant is that the general absence of what we consider academic freedom was associated in the old colleges with a lack of advanced work, with certain severe limitations upon the colleges' educational achievement and their public value. In this chapter we will attempt to show how really advanced university studies failed for a long period to develop in American education, and, further, that this failure occurred not simply because the old denominational colleges ex-

---

[2] For a short time, to be sure, toward the close of the century, deistic and rationalistic rebellion among undergraduates reached such a pitch that almost everyone familiar with the situation became alarmed. This, of course, was an ephemeral result of turbulent times and heady new ideas. But the reaction that followed it was far from ephemeral. On this aspect of college history see G. Adolph Koch, *Republican Religion* (New York, 1933), Chap. VIII; Vernon Stauffer, *New England and the Bavarian Illuminati* (New York, 1918), Chap. I; Herbert Morais, *Deism in Eighteenth Century America*, pp. 159–63.

isted as an alternative to real universities, but because the same cultural conditions that fostered such colleges operated to stultify the efforts that were made to achieve all the conditions of true university work, including the necessary condition of freedom. The worst thing that can be said of the sponsors and promoters of the old colleges is not that they failed to foster sufficiently free teaching and research in their own colleges, but that when others attempted to found freer and more advanced institutions the denominational forces tried to cripple or destroy their work. In the contemporary American educational system the great universities and leading colleges call the tune, and even the smaller church-related institutions (the heirs of the old denominational colleges) very often share to some degree their ideals of academic freedom. In the denominational era, the small denominational colleges set the pattern, and even the would-be sponsors of universities were hamstrung by that circumstance.

When we speak of American colleges down to 1780 we are speaking only of nine institutions, which varied in size and fiscal strength but which had roughly comparable goals. When we look at the college system in 1799, we find that sixteen more institutions had been added. In this period of nineteen years the area of the country had also grown, however, and such regions as the South Atlantic states, the growing areas of Tennessee and upstate New York, hitherto lacking in such educational centers, had begun to be served. Thus there had been no more than a moderate extension of the earlier system. But when we total the number of colleges in 1830, we find, counting only those that were strong enough to survive, that another twenty-four had been added; and by 1861, it is clear, the situation had gotten completely out of hand, for there were by then an additional 133—a total of 182 *permanent* colleges had been founded throughout the country down to the eve of the Civil War.

This figure itself is enough to give one pause, but it is trifling as compared with the number of colleges founded in the same period that failed to survive. Donald G. Tewksbury has found records of 516 colleges that were established before the Civil War in sixteen states of the Republic, and of those 104, or only 19 percent, survived! [3] The further one looks into the West or South the worse this record becomes. Of 36 colleges founded in New York State, 15 survived. In Ohio it was 17 out of 43; in North Carolina, 7 out of 26; in Missouri, 8 out of 85; in Texas, only 2 out of 40.

[3] Tewksbury, *The Founding of American Colleges and Universities before the Civil War* (New York, 1932), p. 28.

Physically, the great continental settlement of the United States in the pre-Civil War era was carried out over the graves of pioneers; intellectually, over the bones of dead colleges.

The experiences and findings of Philip Lindsley, one of the best educators of the first half of the century, illustrate the process of diffusion and fragmentation that went on in American collegiate education. A graduate of Princeton (1804), Lindsley had preached for a time and served as tutor, professor, librarian, vice-president, and acting president of his alma mater. After declining several presidencies, he finally yielded to the call from Cumberland College, soon to be rechartered as the University of Nashville. It appears that he accepted chiefly because he was attracted by the educational needs and opportunities to be found in the lower Mississippi Valley. He was impressed, when he first went to Nashville in 1824, by the fact that in the immense valley of the lower Mississippi, which had at least a million inhabitants, there was not a single college.[4] But within less than twenty-five years thereafter he found that thirty small, competing institutions had been founded in a radius of 200 miles of Nashville and nine within a radius of 50 miles.[5] Colleges, he protested,

rise up like mushrooms on our luxuriant soil. They are duly lauded and puffed for a day; and then they sink to be heard of no more. . . . Our people, at first, oppose all distinctions whatever as odious and aristocratical; and then, presently, seek with avidity such as remain accessible. At first they denounce colleges; and then choose to have a college in every district or county, or for every sect and party—and to boast of a college education, and to sport with high sounding literary titles—as if these imparted sense or wisdom or knowledge.[6]

Only a few of these denominational schools were equal to good second-rate grammar schools, Lindsley charged, and he scorned their "capacious preparatory departments for A, B, C-*darians* and Hic, Haec, Hoc-*ers*—promising to work cheap; and to *finish off* and graduate, in double quick time."[7] Although Lindsley was able to accomplish a good deal in his years at Nashville, he was perpetually plagued by the competition of these fly-by-night colleges, as was every educator in the newer regions who attempted to maintain serious educational standards.

[4] John E. Pomfret, "Philip Lindsley," in Willard Thorp, ed., *The Lives of Eighteen from Princeton* (Princeton, 1946), pp. 163–64.

[5] Philip Lindsley, *Speech about Colleges Delivered in Nashville on Commencement Day, October 4, 1848* (Nashville, 1848), p. 13.

[6] Philip Lindsley, *Paragraphs . . . from a Baccalaureate Address . . .* (n.p., n.d. [1829]), pp. 17–18.

[7] Lindsley, *Speech about Colleges,* p. 14.

This fragmentation of higher education was devastating in its consequences both for the quality of academic work and the position of the professor, but it was an all but inevitable response to the conditions of American life. The area of the Union was, of course, extensive, and travel was uncomfortable and costly. No doubt a country such as the United States needed a certain geographic dispersion of its colleges and universities. But geography alone hardly accounts for the extreme diffusion and wastefulness of educational effort in the denominational era. Travel in Europe was difficult in the Middle Ages and early modern times, and yet when men were sufficiently moved by a hunger for knowledge they traveled hundreds of miles to sit at the feet of a great master—often, incidentally, bypassing a nearer and lesser university—and wandered from university to university when they thought it would help them. In the American milieu the expense and inconvenience of travel loomed larger in the minds of most parents and students than the quality of the education to be received. Some educators complained bitterly that Americans expected to come by their collegiate education far too cheaply.[8] The cost of traveling a considerable distance to college and back was often higher than the tuition fee. One student who came to Amherst in the 1820s from a distance of 300 miles spent $60 a year in transportation at a time when tuition ran about $25 a year in such colleges and a student could get a year's board for considerably less than $60.[9]

Other popular attitudes militated against concentrating the educational effort in a few colleges: there was the notion that it was better for a young man's morals that he be educated in a country college than reside in the city, and the feeling that the social atmosphere of some of the older colleges and the more recently chartered state "universities" was excessively aristocratic.

The two factors that were far more important than geography in determining that American education should be fragmented were denominational sponsorship of colleges and local pride. The multiplicity of colleges was a product of the multiplicity of Protestant sects compounded by the desire of local bodies, religious or civic, to promote all kinds of enterprises

[8] See Francis Wayland's complaint that despite all the charitable investment in public education, "we cannot induce men to pursue a collegiate course unless we offer it vastly below its cost, if we do not give it away altogether." *Thoughts on the Present Collegiate System*, p. 16. Cf. Albea Godbold, *The Church College of the Old South* (Durham, N.C., 1944), pp. 54–60.

[9] On travel and other expenses, see Clarence F. Birdseye, *Individual Training in Our Colleges* (New York, 1907), Chap. IX.

that gratified local pride or boosted local real-estate values. Counting only those institutions that he classed as permanent, Tewksbury listed 49 institutions founded under Presbyterian auspices, 34 founded by the Methodists, 25 by the Baptists, 21 by the Congregationalists, 14 by the Roman Catholics, 11 by the Episcopalians, 6 by the Lutherans, and 20 by miscellaneous sects; there were as well 21 state institutions, 3 semi-state institutions, and 3 municipal ones.[10]

The denominations not only desired to educate their ministers locally and inexpensively, but wished to keep their co-sectarians in colleges of their own lest they be lured out of the fold. They entered, accordingly, into an intense rivalry to supply every locality with a cheap and indigenous institution that would make it possible for local boys who desired degrees to get them easily.[11] This denominational fervor was supplemented by civic loyalties, the measure of which can be taken by the pall of gloom that sometimes spread over a community at the news that its neighbor was about to become the seat of another country college.[12]

A fact that confronts every student of American educational history is that the American system of collegiate education was qualitatively almost as heterogeneous in the first half of the nineteenth century as it is today, and that the name "college" was given to a multitude of institutions ranging from those that respectably upheld the name of college to some that would not quite honor the title of high school. What was mischievous in all this was the competition that enabled the low-grade institutions, backed by the political strength of denominational sponsors, to offer "college" degrees.[13]

The great retrogression in education which we are considering did not occur only where this vast proliferation of third-rate and fourth-rate col-

[10] Tewksbury, *Founding of American Colleges and Universities,* p. 90; these figures do not allow for the occasional duplication or triplication of sponsorship, which the author has indicated.

[11] The factors in this rivalry are discussed by Tewksbury, *ibid.,* pp. 66–91.

[12] An attitude by no means confined to the West or South. When Amherst was chartered, a panic "seized the public mind and extended to the college" at Williamstown, in the words of its president. "The heavens were covered with blackness; and during the awful syncope that succeeded in vacation, we often looked up and inquired *'Is this death?'* " Leverett Wilson Spring, *A History of Williams College* (Boston, 1917), p. 128. The people of Williamstown had only recently extended themselves to raise over $18,000, a very substantial sum for such a town at the time, to keep Williams College from being moved to Northampton. *Ibid.,* p. 113.

[13] A number of institutions that took the more modest title of academy probably offered a sounder education than the weakest "colleges."

leges was most extreme. It occurred in varying degrees almost universally, although at different times. It tainted the older colleges as well as the new, the East as well as the West and South. It was in good part the outcome of the epidemic of revivals, the rise of fundamentalism, and the all but unchecked ragings of the denominational spirit. Along with revival meetings and a growing counterattack against skepticism came a concerted effort on the part of the Protestant churches to expand their influence and tighten their control over spiritual and intellectual life. New colleges were kept under tight supervision; old ones were infused with new piety. Theological seminaries were founded to train an abler and more combative ministry, and their work was kept free from the corrupting influences of ordinary undergraduate life.[14] Sunday schools, Bible societies, and missions were founded, and the influence of piety was brought into the newly settled regions of the West. The barbarism of the age was softened by humanitarian reforms espoused by the pious. Morals, too, were tightened: dancing, horse racing, card playing, and liquor were frowned upon, and the zealous energy of "temperance" was set in motion. Puritan earthiness and realism

[14] The early history of Andover Theological Seminary, established by Massachusetts Calvinists in 1808 to defend orthodoxy through scholarship, suggests, however, one of the dilemmas confronted by defenders of the Puritan tradition. Wherever orthodoxy wanted to further serious scholarship, it was compelled to make some concessions to the working needs of the scholars, for even under the best of circumstances serious scholarship and absolute rigidity of dogma were incompatible. The leading scholar at early Andover was the great Hebraist, Moses Stuart, who promptly fell under suspicion for his devoted interest in German biblical scholarship, which, the trustees found in 1825, "has evidently tended to chill the ardor of piety, to impair belief in the fundamentals of revealed religion, and even to induce, for the time, an approach to universal skepticism." Daniel Day Williams, *The Andover Liberals* (New York, 1941), p. 17. What was poor Stuart to do? Could he maintain his hard-won eminence in this field without drinking deeply at the fountains of the most advanced scholarship of the time? Although formally orthodox enough, he seems to have concluded that he could not. The Seminary was and ought to be, he said, liberal in its mode of work. "We profess to shrink not from the most strenuous investigation. I am bold to say there is not a school of theology on earth, where a more free and unlimited investigation is indulged, nay, inculcated and practiced. The shelves of our library are loaded with books of Latitudinarians and Skeptics, which are read and studied. We have no apprehension that the truths which we believe are to suffer by such an investigation." Henry K. Rowe, *History of Andover Theological Seminary* (Newton, Mass., 1933), p. 19. Are we not getting close again to the "Averroistic" compromise? One attempts to secure a wide range of freedom for investigation by promising that if one is allowed to range through latitudinarian and skeptical scholarship, probing its arguments and ideas, one will always end with a formal commitment to the proper dogma. That is to say, one wins a certain freedom to philosophize in return for the guarantee that one will ultimately profess the right belief.

gave way to Victorian prudery, as throughout the country the little candles of the Enlightenment guttered or failed.[15] Between 1790 and 1830 the intellectual and moral temper of the country was drastically transformed.

An excellent illustration of the impact of the great retrogression upon enlightened scholarship in an older college is the later career of Samuel Stanhope Smith at Princeton. A graduate of Witherspoon's Princeton, the son-in-law and protégé of the Scottish educator, Smith tempered his piety with a certain amount of speculative boldness and independence of mind.[16] He had been a tutor and professor in the college, and in 1795, after Witherspoon's death, the trustees unanimously elected him to the presidency, an office whose duties he had in fact largely fulfilled for seven years. An outstanding personality, Smith had formulated educational policies that, as Professor Wertenbaker remarks, were far ahead of his time. Had he been given the same magisterial powers that the trustees had allowed his father-in-law, the progress Princeton had long been making might well have gone on. But the tide of trustee sentiment had turned and Smith was treated in a way that would have been unthinkable had he been Witherspoon. Not only did the trustees turn a deaf ear to most of Smith's proposals for improvement, but they began to assert their own powers of government obtrusively and in small matters as well as large. They had grown increasingly concerned with sectarian considerations, particularly with the fight against Episcopalianism. Some of the more eager watchdogs of orthodoxy among them became far more interested in establishing a Presbyterian theological seminary than in maintaining the college, which they anticipated could not be linked in harmony with the seminary and might actually be a rival.[17] A few of the trustees, notably Ashbel Green, became

---

[15] The religious reaction of the early nineteenth century is traced by Merle Curti, *The Growth of American Thought* (New York, 1943), Chap. VIII, and John A. Krout and Dixon Ryan Fox, *The Completion of Independence, 1790–1830* (New York, 1944), pp. 162–75. See also the penetrating comments by E. B. Greene, "A Puritan Counter-Reformation," *Proceedings of the American Antiquarian Society,* New Series, Vol. XLIII (1932), pp. 17–46, and Dixon Ryan Fox, "The Protestant Counter-Reformation in America," *New York History,* XVI (January, 1935), 19–35. For some illuminating comments on the state and influence of American religion in the 1830s see Alexis de Tocqueville, *Democracy in America* (New York, ed. 1912), I, 328–39; II, 488, 510–13.

[16] He had also a capacity for diplomacy that makes him appear sometimes to be two-faced. Compare his very enlightened letters to Jefferson on the relation of sectarianism to education (*The Papers of Thomas Jefferson,* Julian P. Boyd, ed., II [Princeton, 1950], 246–49, 252–55) with his later correspondence with Jedidiah Morse in the Princeton Library manuscript collections.

[17] As one of the leading trustees, Samuel Miller, put it, they wanted "to have the divinity-school uncontaminated by the college, to have its government unfettered,

impatient to get rid of the ill and aging president. Green, who was head pastor at the Second Presbyterian Church in Philadelphia, a figure of much influence in church politics and a leader in the movement for establishing the seminary, took the initiative in undermining Smith's authority. He set a tutor and some of the divinity students to informing on him, and the word was spread about that the President of Princeton had endorsed polygamy, recommended Arminian essays, expressed doubts about the efficacy of baptism, and inspired among the divinity students an open denial of the doctrine of total depravity.[18]

In spite of such molestations, Smith did manage to improve scientific instruction and restore the college after the disastrous fire that destroyed the college hall in 1802. But the usual differences with trustees over student discipline and the decline in enrollment finally led to drastic faculty retrenchment; and at the dawn of the second decade of the century Princeton stood about where it had been thirty years before. The resources of the Presbyterian church were thrown behind the newly founded theological seminary at Princeton, whose clerical trustees soon began to dominate the college. In 1812 the trustees, by suggesting that a vice-president was needed to run the college, succeeded in provoking Smith's resignation; they replaced him with Ashbel Green, who was far less equipped than he to solve Princeton's problems in the new milieu. The college continued to decline under Green and his successor, and might have had to close its doors altogether had it not been rescued by some of its alumni during the 1830s.[19] Thus the institution that had flourished under Witherspoon's direction during the full tide of the Enlightenment was nearly destroyed in the ebb of the great retrogression.

The early history of Dickinson College, another Presbyterian institution, founded in 1783 at Carlisle, indicates that any attempt to repeat Princeton's fortunate experience with Witherspoon was likely to be doomed. Benjamin Rush and the other early trustees made such an attempt

---

and its orthodoxy and purity perpetual"—for all of which a separate establishment seemed to them to be necessary. Samuel Miller, *The Life of Samuel Miller* (Philadelphia, 1869), I, 242; cf. pp. 192, 240–44.

[18] Thomas J. Wertenbaker, *Princeton, 1746–1896* (Princeton, 1946), Chap. IV, is most illuminating on Smith's presidency; cf. Samuel Holt Monk, "Samuel Stanhope Smith," in Thorp, *The Lives of Eighteen from Princeton*, pp. 86–110. For further light on the trustees of the period, see George Adams Boyd, *Elias Boudinot* (Princeton, 1952), and Gilbert Chinard, "A Landmark in American Intellectual History," *Princeton University Library Chronicle*, XIV (Winter, 1953), 55–71.

[19] Wertenbaker, *Princeton*, Chap. VII.

when they brought to Carlisle the Reverend Charles Nisbet, another learned Scot from whom they had no doubt similar expectations. Both Nisbet and the trustees were bitterly disappointed. Some of the reasons were purely personal, but the breach caused by the president's dislocation and his shock at first seeing an American college was made hopelessly wide by the continued interference of the trustees in Dickinson's affairs. Rush, who had plenty of excellent ideas that he was in no wise ready to try to put into practice—among them the belief in a great measure of faculty government [20]—was no less ready than some of the less celebrated trustees to condemn Nisbet; and it was long before the institution achieved any significance. One of the most remarkable episodes in the history of higher education occurred at Dickinson in the years 1799–1801 when, after the students' demand that the entire college course be completed in one year had been denied by the president, the trustees reversed his decision and permitted the travesty.[21] Maladministration by the trustees continued at Dickinson for many years. As late as 1815 the entire faculty resigned in protest, and the college was temporarily closed.

While it was being demonstrated in the opening decades of the nineteenth century that the Princeton tradition could neither be sustained in New Jersey nor reproduced in Pennsylvania, the rest of the colonial colleges were for the most part marking time or actually losing ground. The exceptions were Yale, which was laying the foundations of its scientific eminence under presidents Dwight and Day, and Harvard, which was beginning to achieve the literary stature which was so long to be the source of its reputation. William and Mary, which had never recovered from the removal of the capital from Williamsburg, was hit again by the creation of the University of Virginia, and sank to the level of the small country colleges. The University of Pennsylvania, never altogether prosperous, went through her lowest ebb during the years from 1791 to 1828, when the obtrusions of the trustees upon all facets of college life reached a point that "would have been incredible except for

[20] See his letter to the trustees, October 21, 1786, in *Letters of Benjamin Rush,* Lyman H. Butterfield, ed. (Princeton, 1951), I, 397. "When our professors cease to be qualified to share in the power of the College, it will be proper to dismiss them, for government and instruction are inseparably connected."

[21] Harry G. Good, *Benjamin Rush and His Services to American Education* (Berne, Ind., 1918), Chap. IV. On trustee interference and its consequences, see also James Henry Morgan, *Dickinson College* (Carlisle, Pa., 1933), pp. 131–44.

the testimony of the written records." [22] Until the 1820s Pennsylvania's graduating classes remained pitifully small. Columbia College was described by its trustees, in a petition to the New York legislature in 1814, as "an Object of Curiosity and Remark to Strangers . . . a Spectacle mortifying to its friends, humiliating to the City, and calculated to inspire opinions which it is impossible your enlightened body wish to countenance." [23] It was only in the 1840s that it ceased to present this pathetic aspect, and only in the post-Civil War period that the effects of the trustee changes of the late 1850s were sufficiently felt to lay the groundwork of its modern distinction in American education. Rutgers carried on in the state of half-existence that had characterized it almost from the beginning. In 1816 it was for the second time closed for lack of funds, and it did not reopen for nine years.[24] Brown under the presidency of Asa Messer, who served from 1802 to 1826, fared better than most of its sisters, but even there the president eventually ran into trouble with the trustees for his Unitarian opinions; after several years of harassment by his religious opponents in the community and the Corporation, he resigned.[25]

At Dartmouth, the last of the colonial colleges, there began a quarrel that was destined to have an important effect on the history of higher education in the United States. The school had been founded and maintained during its earliest days by the immense exertions of Eleazar Wheelock, and its presidency had been bequeathed by him to his son John. This singular dynastic procedure had aroused little comment or objection, and for some years the Wheelock autocracy continued unmolested by the trustees or the community precisely because the college itself was an institution of such little significance that no one who lacked the personal stake of the Wheelocks cared to contend for it. But by 1814 Dartmouth had become a thriving country college with a faculty of three professors and two tutors, a well-regarded little medical department, and students drawn from all the states of New England.[26] Toward

[22] Edward P. Cheyney, *History of the University of Pennsylvania* (Philadelphia, 1940), p. 178; see his Chap. V for a general account of this period.
[23] *A History of Columbia University, 1754–1904* (New York, 1904), p. 100.
[24] William H. S. Demarest, *A History of Rutgers College, 1766–1924* (New Brunswick, N.J., 1924), pp. 242–44, 277–78; as late as the 1840s the graduating classes usually had fewer than twenty students. *Ibid.*, p. 343.
[25] Walter C. Bronson, *The History of Brown University, 1764–1914* (Providence, R.I., 1914), pp. 186–92.
[26] Leon B. Richardson, *A History of Dartmouth College* (Hanover, N.H., 1932), Vol. I, Chap. V.

the closing years of John Wheelock's administration began a quarrel whose central issue was whether the college was to remain under the control of the Wheelock dynasty or to be governed by its trustees. Although there seem to have been no serious theological or political differences between Wheelock and the trustees, the conflict took on a political character because the president's cause was opportunely espoused by the local Democratic politicians while the Federalists generally stood by the trustees.[27] In 1816, the Democrats, who had captured the legislature, passed a law modifying the Dartmouth charter and changing the institution from a college to a "university." The college trustees refused to accept the change, and for more than a year both the old college and the new university functioned side by side in Hanover until the propriety of the legislation was finally passed upon by the Supreme Court in the famous Dartmouth College Case. The Court, of course, decided in favor of the college, and the university was disbanded. This decision, which occupies a celebrated place in the history of American constitutional law for its sweeping protection to corporations and encouragement to corporate business, was of comparable importance in the history of American higher education; it offered to the founders of private colleges the assurance that once they had obtained a charter from a state legislature they were secure in the future control of the institution.

Although the proliferation of small colleges was already well under way in 1819, the Dartmouth College decision provided a secure legal base for the host of private and denominational colleges that were about to emerge.[28]

As the American educational system expanded throughout the West and South, the most pervasive influence upon its character was the denominational affiliations of the small colleges and the struggle of these institutions and the churches that supported them against the larger nonsectarian or intersectarian "universities" or colleges that occasionally appeared. This struggle took on a somewhat different aspect in the

[27] *Ibid.,* Chap. VII; for the relation of the controversy to local politics, see William G. North, "The Political Background of the Dartmouth College Case," *New England Quarterly,* XVIII (June, 1945), 181–203.

[28] Tewksbury, *Founding of American Colleges and Universities,* pp. 64–66. The most valuable documentary source on the case is Timothy Farrar, *Report of the Case of the Trustees of Dartmouth College against William H. Woodward* (Portsmouth, N.H., 1819), which contains the opinions and arguments in both the Superior Court of New Hampshire and the Supreme Court. Of particular interest here is Daniel Webster's argument that college presidents and professors have freeholds in their offices. See pp. 269–72.

Southern states, especially those of the seaboard, than it did in the West. In the South several state universities were chartered at a time when the liberal thought of the Enlightenment was still widely current, especially among planter and merchant aristocrats, and when denominational colleges had not yet taken a foothold. There the story, as we shall later show, is one of persistent struggles between sectarian forces and the emerging church colleges on one side and the educationally more ambitious state institutions on the other. In the West the denominational colleges, except, notably, in Michigan, generally took root quickly and were often established by the time the state universities were chartered; and here the principal type of institution before the Civil War was represented by such private colleges as Illinois, Kenyon, Antioch, Knox, Beloit, Denison, Shurtleff, De Pauw, Wabash, and Lawrence. The dominant educational influences were those of the Presbyterians and Congregationalists, who, despite gestures toward union, did not always get along too well. Western educators carried with them preconceptions derived from such eastern schools as Yale, Princeton, Dartmouth, Union, Amherst, and Williams. Many of them also brought the Puritan temper which in the pre-Civil War period so often found its expression in reform agitations. Thus, while sectarian controversies and repressions were by no means absent from the Western colleges,[29] some of the most interesting academic controversies arose out of abolitionism. The implications of these will be treated later. But

[29] Among educators whose work was hampered by sectarian pressures was Horace Mann, president of Antioch College from 1852 to 1859. E. I. F. Williams, *Horace Mann: Educational Statesman* (New York, 1937), Chap. XV, and George A. Hubbell, *Horace Mann in Ohio* (New York, 1900), esp. pp. 48–50. Good accounts of sectarian influences upon Middle Western colleges are given in Frederick C. Waite, *Western Reserve University: The Hudson Era* (Cleveland, 1943), and Charles H. Rammelkamp, *Illinois College* (New Haven, 1928). Sectarian influences on the state university are discussed by Wilfred Shaw, *The University of Michigan* (New York, 1920), Chaps. III and IV; Andrew Ten Brook, *American State Universities* (Cincinnati, 1875), pp. 209–10, and Merle Curti and Vernon Carstensen, *The University of Wisconsin* (Madison, Wis., 1949), I, 87 ff. One of the more notable academic controversies in the region, however, was chiefly administrative —that aroused by the dismissal of President David Bates Douglass from Kenyon. See George Franklin Smythe, *Kenyon College: Its First Century* (New Haven, 1924), Chap. XIV; D. B. Douglass, *Statement of Facts and Circumstances . . .* (n.p., 1844), and *Further Statement of Facts and Circumstances . . .* (Albany, 1845); *Reply of Trustees of Kenyon College . . .* (Philadelphia, 1844). For controversies at a New England college involving the removal of an Episcopalian and a Universalist, see Richardson, *History of Dartmouth*, II, 446–52, and Benjamin Hale, *Valedictory Letter to the Trustees of Dartmouth College* (n.p., 1835); "Alumnus," *Professor Hale and Dartmouth College* (n.p., n.d.); *Remarks on a Pamphlet Entitled "Professor Hale and Dartmouth College"* (n.p., n.d.).

first it is necessary to look at the old college as a whole and attempt to understand some of the internal institutional factors bearing upon intellectual freedom.

THE OLD COLLEGE SYSTEM

"It is, sir, as I have said, a small college,—and yet there are those who love it," declaimed Webster in the bathetic peroration to his famous argument in the Dartmouth College Case. As the institutions of the world went, Dartmouth was no doubt a small college; but on the American educational scene it was a giant whose graduating classes had in recent years run close in size to those of Harvard and well above those of Yale. On the scale by which Dartmouth could be reckoned a small college there were none but small colleges in the United States, and there were to be none but small colleges for more than a generation to come. As late as 1839, if we may judge from the loosely gathered and poorly reported statistics of the period, the average college would be most closely represented by a school like Randolph-Macon, with its 98 students, the modal college by Kenyon and Waterville (later Colby), with their 55 students apiece; while Dartmouth, which had very promptly recovered from the ill effects of its litigation, was still second in size among undergraduate bodies, with 321 students.[30]

Size, of course, is not to be taken as the primary key to the quality of an educational institution. But there is such a thing as a college so excessively small as to be unable to afford adequate standards. Certainly, in the absence of a generous endowment, the faculty maintained by a college of 50 or 75 students could hardly be a distinguished one, nor could it be very lavishly maintained. Such a factor as size, which bears on the quality of the college education, also has much to do with problems of academic freedom and government; for these problems have an important relation to the growth of the faculty body. Larger faculties

[30] For figures on undergraduates, medical students, professors and other instructors, total graduates, and library volumes in 93 institutions in 1839 see *American Quarterly Register,* XIII (August, 1840), 110–16. At that time the leading ten colleges, each of which had over 150 undergraduates, were in this order: Yale, Dartmouth, Princeton, University of Virginia, Harvard, Union, Brown, Amherst, College of South Carolina, Bowdoin. Bacon College in Harrodsburg, Kentucky, claimed 203 students, which would put it in this group, but its claim to be a genuine college, even by the American standards of the time, is dubious.

tended to have more self-government and to be more self-assertive. Prospering colleges could defend freedom more readily than poverty-stricken ones shuddering at every gust of criticism that might cost them a few students or a handsome benefaction. Other things being equal, then, it was the larger and more prosperous institutions that had the greater power to protect dissent. Hence the small size and impoverished character of the American college is a major part of our story.

By 1839 some faculties had, to be sure, grown to a respectable size for the time. Harvard was most imposing, with twenty-one professors and two tutors, followed by Yale with sixteen professors and seven tutors, Dartmouth with an aggregate faculty of fifteen, and Transylvania, New York University, Hampden Sydney, Union, and Columbia, each of which had from ten to thirteen.[31] The representative faculties, again, were those of the smaller institutions: Randolph-Macon, say, with its six professors, or Waterville with five professors and one tutor, or Kenyon with six professors and one tutor. By and large the humble tutor was disappearing in favor of more permanent and august teachers labeled "professors" or occasionally "instructors." [32] In the country at large tutors were outnumbered by men in the other teaching categories by more than six to one, and the colonial conditions that had made faculty government impossible because of the youth and impermanence of teachers were gone.

To found a great many small colleges rather than to build up a modest number of larger ones meant to fill the country with precarious little institutions, denomination-ridden, poverty-stricken, keeping dubious educational standards, and offering little to teachers in freedom or financial rewards. The evidence is overwhelming that during the de-

[31] These figures include teachers in medical departments or other divisions who offered little or no instruction to regular undergraduates. Omitted are eight Catholic colleges which had a somewhat different way of reckoning faculty members, often counting "the novices and younger members of the Order . . . [as] professors and officers of the college." Francis Patrick Cassidy, *Catholic College Foundations and Development in the United States, 1677–1850* (Washington, 1924), p. 25. Teaching by priests with pastoral duties was supplemented by the work of lay faculty members. *Ibid.,* pp. 85–86. Thus a college like St. Mary's, with only 70 students in 1839, had 25 persons attached in some way to its instructional staff.

[32] Harvard began to recognize the justice of advancing tutors early in the regime of President Kirkland, when the principle was adopted that a tutor must be advanced to a college professorship, with increased compensation, after six years of satisfactory service. Josiah Quincy, *The History of Harvard University* (Cambridge, Mass., 1840), II, 354.

nominational era a great proportion of the schools in the United States that called themselves "colleges" were in fact not colleges at all, but glorified high schools or academies that presumed to offer degrees. As the president of the University of Georgia told his trustees in 1855, the American people were generally satisfied with the *name* of a college, and sought for their sons not so much an education as a degree.[33] Americans and Europeans alike who were familiar with the educational systems of the Continent and England tended to agree that American colleges characteristically (not at their worst) were rather more like the German *Gymnasium,* the French *lycée,* or the English public school than like either the university or college of these countries.[34] It should be borne in mind, too, that the colleges were trying to handle student bodies with a considerably wider age range than the student bodies of our own time. Students were on occasion admitted into some institutions at the age of thirteen or fourteen, although the better institutions were successfully raising the compulsory age level for entering freshmen to sixteen.[35] Since it was not at all uncommon for men in their twenties to begin

[33] Alma Pauline Foerster, "The State University in the Old South," unpublished Ph.D. dissertation (Duke University, 1939), pp. 242–43.

[34] The evidence on this point is too voluminous to cite. See, however, *Journal of the Proceedings of a Convention of Literary and Scientific Gentlemen. . . . October, 1830* (New York, 1831), *passim.* In 1858 F. A. P. Barnard spoke of "the grade of the German gymnasium—which is precisely our grade of today," and an immigrant German professor declared, perhaps more accurately, "Our colleges, compared to the learned institutions of Germany, occupy a place between the gymnasia and universities, being generally similar to the three highest classes of the gymnasia and comprehending, also, some of the studies of the university." Richard J. Storr, "Academic Overture: The American Graduate School . . . ," unpublished Ph.D. dissertation (Harvard University, 1949), pp. 272, 304. Page references are to this version; a shorter version has been published as *The Beginnings of Graduate Education in America* (Chicago, 1953). Henry P. Tappan, *A Discourse . . . on the Occasion of His Inauguration . . . December 21st, 1852* (Detroit, 1853), p. 37. Schmidt, *The Old Time College President,* pp. 102–5, is illuminating on educational standards.

[35] Birdseye, *Individual Training in Our Colleges,* Chap. III; trends in the last half of the nineteenth century are discussed by W. Scott Thomas, "Changes in the Age of College Graduation," *Popular Science Monthly,* LXIII (June, 1903), 159–171. The factor of age explains much of the disciplinary problem. "They admit into college, children of 13 and 14 years," wrote Thomas Ruffin, Jr., to his father from Chapel Hill in 1843, "and the consequence is that they are compelled to reduce the standards of scholarship in order to get them through. The [student] Societies are a humbug for their members have not the sense, it cannot be expected that they should have at their age, to keep them straight, and there are some here really so young that they do not know how to take care of themselves." Quoted by Foerster, "The State University in the Old South," p. 262. Cf. John Fulton, *Memoirs of F. A. P. Barnard* (New York, 1890), pp. 163–64.

college in order to gain advancement in the professions, the colleges were dealing with a very large spread in the ages of undergraduates that added to the acuteness of their disciplinary problems.[36]

While the system of American higher education in effect in the pre-Civil War period offered studies of considerable variation in quality, the American college, in structure and government, was for the most part the same everywhere. Even those institutions that were called "universities," whether private or state, consisted, at the core, of a college, and often had no more than the core. It sufficed for the time that the founders were enamored of the name university, and therefore adopted it; or that they intended ultimately to establish a genuine one; or that there was appended to a college—this was the most frequent circumstance—a medical department. Occasionally there was also instruction in law, or there was an associated theological seminary; but most education for the law, ministry, and medicine was unfortunately dissociated from a genuine university structure and carried on either in separate schools (which for law and medicine were generally very poor and venal), or informally by individual practitioners.[37] Even the state universities were notably different from the huge organizations of the present day. American universities bore no resemblance to the great German universities that were beginning to inspire the admiration of almost all the great educational reformers. In some respects the American colleges resembled the English colleges from which they stemmed; but while the English colleges clustered at the great university centers, the American colleges were scattered.[38] Like the English university colleges, the American colleges aimed to be residential, an aim which they achieved wherever they

[36] See Wayland, *Thoughts on the Present Collegiate System* (Boston, 1842), p. 31; F. A. P. Barnard, *Letters on College Government* (New York, 1855), pp. 58–60. On the role of student discipline in academic government see below, Chap. VI.

[37] Wayland noted the existence, in addition to 101 colleges, of 39 theological seminaries, 10 law schools, and 31 medical schools. *Thoughts on the Present Collegiate System*, p. 8. For early medical education see Abraham Flexner, *Medical Education in the United States and Canada* (New York, 1910), Chap. I; for the law, Alfred Z. Reed, *Training for the Public Profession of Law* (New York, 1921), and Willard Hurst, *The Growth of American Law* (Boston, 1950), Chap. XII; for theology, Robert L. Kelly, *Theological Education in America* (New York, 1924), Chap. I.

[38] For some comparative comments by a student familiar with both Yale and Cambridge, see Charles A. Bristed, *Five Years in an English University* (New York, 1874), pp. 19–23, 445–515; see also the critical comments by Francis Bowen in *North American Review*, LXXV (July, 1852), 47–83, 75–80.

had the means for buildings. But they differed profoundly from the English colleges in their academic achievement, for they could expect much less from students in the way of secondary preparation and cultural background, and they were equipped to carry their students a much shorter part of the way toward profound knowledge or serious scholarship.[39] One of the most serious obstacles to university development in the United States was the fact that higher education had no organic relation to careers in civil service and diplomacy, as it had in England and some continental countries. Thus the spoils system and "democratic" rotation in office deprived American higher education of much of the potential importance of university work, while lax standards of professional training in medicine and law hurt it from another side.

The standard college curriculum was the program of classical-mathematical studies inherited from Renaissance education. To enter upon it at most institutions the student needed some minimal competence in Latin, Greek, and mathematics, requirements to which geography, history, English grammar and composition, algebra, and geometry were widely added during the decades from 1800 to 1870.[40] At college these attainments were supplemented by much further reading in standard Latin and Greek writers; mathematics up to plane and spherical trigonometry and analytical geometry; a smattering of mechanics, optics, and astronomy; some chemistry, botany, and biology (and geology if the college was fairly advanced and not overawed by the book of Genesis); and varying amounts of rhetoric, ethics, logic, metaphysics, political economy, history, and constitutional or legal lore.[41] Although the standard course took four years, it was not uncommon for the well-prepared academy student or a student who had been privately tutored to enter at a level above the freshman class.[42]

[39] Perhaps the crux of the difference rested here: "The Englishman's tardiness of development is in a great measure intentional. He is kept back to take a good start. He leaves [preparatory] school at the period of life when the American leaves College." Bristed, *Five Years in an English University,* p. 465.

[40] See Edwin C. Broome, *A Historical and Critical Discussion of College Entrance Requirements* (New York, 1902).

[41] On the curriculum see R. Freeman Butts, *The College Charts Its Course* (New York, 1939), and William T. Foster, *Administration of the College Curriculum* (Boston, 1911). For a brief contemporary characterization, see Wayland, *Thoughts on the Present Collegiate System,* pp. 32–42.

[42] Unfortunately the college too often repeated a large part of the work of a good academy, adding at first very little. Wayland, *Thoughts on the Present Collegiate System,* p. 108. Cf. Bristed, *Five Years in an English University,* p. 19: "During the first year I did little but read novels and attend debating societies. . . .

While there was much dissatisfaction with the old college curriculum among educators and many attempts at reform were made, it was not until the university era that the prescribed classical curriculum really broke down. Educational reformers argued that the common course of studies was too rigid, that a large measure of election should be introduced, that alternative scientific programs should be set up, and that the community demanded greater concessions to practical and vocational needs and less liberal education. While much of this argument was undoubtedly well advised, it seems also true that those social classes that commonly sent their sons to college were not as wholeheartedly attracted to experimentation as educational reformers implied, and that those who called upon the colleges to reform gave them inadequate support when they tried to do so. One of the most ardent and capable of the reformers, Francis Wayland of Brown, admitted as much in 1842 when he remarked that the colleges that had yielded to public demands by enlarging or altering their requirements had not been supported well enough to sustain the reforms: "And thus have we been taught that the public does not always know what it wants, and that it is not always wise to take it at its word." [43]

So much damage was done in later years to the cause of liberal education when the educational reformers finally got their way, threw out the prescribed curriculum, introduced the elective "system," and ultimately cluttered up undergraduate education with a mass of trivial "practical" courses, that the modern historian of education may in reaction be tempted to sentimentalize the old college and overestimate its value.[44] Since we have many strictures to make on the old college as a center of free thought or professional gratifications for its teachers, it is only just to say in passing that at or near its best it was very far indeed from a negligible agency of education. Men of considerable intellectual distinction came in reasonable numbers from its halls. It tried seriously to

This is the case with most boys who enter well prepared at a New England College; they go backwards rather than forwards the first year."

[43] Wayland, *Thoughts on the Present Collegiate System,* p. 13.

[44] For an account of some of the difficulties caused by the dissolution of the old curriculum see George W. Pierson, "The Elective System and the Difficulties of College Planning, 1870–1940," *Journal of General Education,* IV (April, 1950), 165–74. The faculty of Yale College, in their famous defense of the standard curriculum, understood one thing that was for long forgotten in American education: "There are many things important to be known, which are not taught in colleges, because they may be learned anywhere." *The American Journal of Science and Arts,* XV (1829), 308.

cultivate both the minds and the characters of its students. Its classical curriculum exposed them to great writers, great ideas, and fine expression. It encouraged articulate writing and thinking, and indicated that these abilities were to be put to work in civic as well as private affairs. It introduced its students to the problems of philosophy and theology. By inculcating serious application to mental, if not always intellectual, work, it does seem to have bred in its students a capacity for persistence and effort that modern education frequently fails to produce. It was not entirely lacking in inspiring teachers, who left a lifelong impress on their students. Perhaps most important of all, its student literary clubs and debating societies acquainted young men, who had perhaps had very little other contact with the life of the mind, with the fact that ideas and civic problems and literary values were proper objects around which men might associate. It rubbed the raw edges off many a country boy, taught him to write and talk and wonder, and sent him into life with advantages he could have found nowhere else.[45]

And yet when all these things have been said it must be added that the old college had grave failings as an instrument for the development of both students and teachers. Many contemporaries, in and out of the colleges, saw this. Many prescriptions for remedying the deficiencies of the old college were offered. Altogether too many of these stemmed from a persistent dissatisfaction with the prescribed classical curriculum. What was wrong with the curriculum, however, was not, as so commonly argued then and now, that it was a classical or a prescribed curriculum, for just such a curriculum had long contributed enormously to the rearing of the best minds in Western society. What was really wrong with the old college was that this curriculum was more often than not drably and unimaginatively taught. What was wrong was not that it still emphasized the classics so heavily—had not that great generation of superbly educated American leaders of the late eighteenth century been reared on the same classical writers?—but that it trained no good classi-

45 For some evaluations see Carl Becker, *Cornell University: Founders and the Founding* (Ithaca, N.Y., 1943), pp. 16–22; Walter P. Rogers, *Andrew D. White and the Modern University* (Ithaca, N.Y., 1942); Richard Hofstadter and C. DeWitt Hardy, *The Development and Scope of Higher Education in the United States* (New York, 1952), Chap. I and pp. 53–56; Schmidt, *The Old-Time College President,* pp. 146–49. The old college is defended by George F. Whicher in his preface to William Gardiner Hammond, *Remembrance of Amherst* (New York, 1946), pp. 1–18. There is an excellent account of contemporary dissatisfactions with the system in Storr, "Academic Overture," *passim.*

cists, that it reduced the study of classics to grammar and linguistics, that it usually failed to convey the spirit of the cultures of antiquity, that it often failed, indeed, even to teach very much Latin.[46]

Thus while the curriculum bore the brunt of the criticism, the great failure of the old college probably lay less in its course of studies than in its pedagogy and its pedagogues. The root of the matter was that most teaching was carried on by the recitation method—what one Harvard professor described as "the humble and simple, old-school, tedious business of recitation." [47] The job of the student was to address himself to a text, memorize it or master a translation, and reproduce it in class to the best of his ability, while the job of the instructor was to see that he got it right. While some advanced subjects were taught by lectures, and science courses at their best required some demonstrations, recitation was the true base of the old college's pedagogy, and this the students found tiresome and the faculty stultifying. The average teacher was closely bound to the text and had to spend the greater part of his time ascertaining whether the student had done his work. This left him no time to plan his own course, no incentive to add to his knowledge, for, as Wayland observed, "He already knows more than he has the opportunity to communicate." [48] This system dulled the minds of students and blunted the edge of faculty scholarship; and such well-educated students as the colleges turned out were usually triumphs of the human spirit over bad methods.

From the point of view of instructors, the lean monotony of the recita-

[46] Cf. Edward Everett in 1817: "It fills me with indignation that a person may pass through all our schools, academies and colleges, without being taught to speak a Latin sentence. . . . But our poor schoolmasters and preceptors and tutors are not to blame, they cannot teach what they never learned." Orie Long, *Literary Pioneers: Early American Explorers of European Culture* (Cambridge, 1935), p. 71. Cf. *Life, Letters, and Journals of George Ticknor* (Boston, 1877), I, 363.

[47] Storr, "Academic Overture," p. 6.

[48] Wayland, *Report to the Corporation of Brown University on Changes in the System of Collegiate Education* (Providence, 1850), p. 19. Cf. Wayland's *Thoughts on the Present Collegiate System*, pp. 84–86. Samuel Eliot Morison points to the case of the gifted Hellenist, Cornelius Conway Felton: "He was only a cog in the Quincy machine. He conducted recitations for at least twelve hours a week of the three upper classes, in alphabetical sections, and could not escape the requirement to hear and grade them on lessons from prescribed texts. It was not until the Class of 1852 entered College [Felton had then served for 23 years] that the Greek department had sufficient staff to permit Professor Felton to lecture once a week for half the year." *Three Centuries of Harvard* (Cambridge, Mass., 1936), p. 263. Cf. the experiences of Longfellow related in James Taft Hatfield, *New Light on Longfellow* (Boston, 1933), pp. 66, 82–83.

tion system was but one failing of a profession that was hardly professionalized. To become a college teacher required only a B.A. degree plus a modest amount of more advanced training, perhaps in theology. College teachers, although they might at the beginning of their careers earn slightly more than a fledgling in some other profession, soon lost ground by comparison. New England professors earned from $600 to $1,200 a year in the 1840s, but the former figure was more common in the country as a whole; on the eve of the Civil War salaries of $1,000 were more customary.[49] A good private instructor, not to speak of men in other professions, could earn a great deal more. Moreover, there was no system of rewards for competence; salaries were commonly inflexible, there was no system of raises, no hierarchy of promotion; once installed, the professor was treated much the same whether he was an eminent success or a substantial failure as a teacher.[50] Although a professor usually held office indefinitely on good behavior, his tenure depended upon usage and had no legal status: he could be fired at will by the governing board; in many institutions a hearing was not required.[51] Since there was no system of graduate education, no advanced work to look forward to, and no pecuniary reward for distinction in scholarship, the professor tended to settle into the groove of the recitation system and the policing of the students in which he was frequently required to join at much expenditure of time and energy and sometimes at the cost of humiliation.[52]

Those teachers whose energies led them to additional effort were tempted into literary work unconnected with their colleges or with schol-

[49] Although low in relation to some of the opportunities in business and the professions, this is not as low as it may seem. A highly skilled worker like a watchmaker or printer could earn a little over $600 a year in 1860 if he had a full year's employment. Thus the professor earning $1,000 a year in 1860 had a higher relative standing compared with a skilled worker than would the average professor today, when annual earnings in the two groups are about on a par. This, of course, does not apply to top professorial salaries today. Nor would it in 1860, when the highest salaries were about $2,000.

[50] It should also be noted that the dependence of the small college on tuition fees gave faculties a pecuniary ground for consenting to lower academic standards in order to entice more students.

[51] For the situation of the professor see Wayland, *Thoughts on the Present Collegiate System*, pp. 25, 26–27, 59, 62–76, 84–86, 136–37.

[52] Francis Lieber, one of the best-paid professors in the United States during his stay at South Carolina College, was once overheard to exclaim, after plunging over a pile of bricks on a nocturnal excursion after some aberrant students, "Mein Gott! All dis for two tousand dollars!" Frank Freidel, *Francis Lieber* (Baton Rouge, La., 1947), p. 140.

arship. But even had they been determined to carry out advanced work, the library of the typical college forbade it. When George Ticknor was at Göttingen in 1816 he noted with envy that while at Harvard there were twenty professors and fewer than 20,000 volumes, there were at the German university forty professors and more than 200,000 volumes. A taste of scholarly life under German conditions, Ticknor thought, would be enough to arouse the Cambridge professors to permanent discontent with their lot.[53] Such was the situation at Harvard, whose library was far better stocked than any other. By 1839, when Harvard had 50,000 volumes, there was only one other institution (Yale, with 27,000) that had more than half as many, and only sixteen that had more than 10,000 apiece. College libraries with as few as 1,000 volumes were by no means rare [54] at the time when Ticknor was building a personal library of 13,000 books.[55]

The absence of professional standards and rewards had its compensations from the standpoint of the individual teacher. Precisely because his profession required so little preparation beyond the B.A. degree and because it was so ill compensated both in money and in intellectual satisfactions, he was not as much attached or committed to it as is the modern teacher. If he was excessively troubled by his duties or by some administrative controversy, he could resign and go into some other walk of life more readily and easily than the modern professor. The transition to the law or the ministry was commonly not difficult, and business opportunities were many. An ex-professor might easily better his financial condition by opening a private academy.

In college teaching itself, moreover, new opportunities were multiplying in the expanding college system; and the antebellum college teacher, unlike his successor of today, did not face anything resembling a national code of political orthodoxy. One is impressed in reading over the histories of the early colleges by the readiness which which teachers and presidents at the smaller and less stable institutions turned in their resignations, accepting without apparent reluctance or anxiety the severance of a connection to which the modern professor will cling

[53] Orie Long, *Literary Pioneers,* p. 13. Cf. Wayland, *Thoughts on the Present Collegiate System,* p. 128: "The means do not exist among us for writing a book, which in Europe would be called learned, on almost any subject whatever." Cf. Godbold, *Church College of the Old South,* pp. 79–81, on libraries in small colleges.

[54] *American Quarterly Register,* XIII, 110–16.

[55] C. C. Jewett, "Statistics of American Libraries," in *Fourth Annual Report . . . of the Smithsonian Institution . . . during the Year 1849* (Washington, 1850).

desperately at the cost of many sacrifices.[56] However, these mitigating circumstances, which provided outlets for many spirited individuals, were unfortunate for the profession as a whole. The least enterprising and self-assertive, often the least able, members of an inferior faculty were those most likely to remain docile in their jobs under intolerable pressures. Any profession is in a bad way when its members can seek freedom most effectually by leaving it. The absence of mature professionalism contributed, as did denominationalism, fragmentation, and poverty, to the inadequacies of the old-time college. Professors suffered, but their students and the community often bore the greater share of the loss.

Changes, however, were beginning to take place in the management of the better colleges and in the status of scholarship. From the days of Ticknor's *Wanderjahre* and Jefferson's devotion to the projected University of Virginia, hardly a year went by in which some reform or experiment was not either proposed or quietly pushed forward. Many of these changes merely pointed to the debasement of liberal education by utilitarian studies that was to come in a later age. Others had genuine value for the students or the teachers.

Not the least of these changes was the slow transfer of college management from the hands of trustees through the presidents and into the faculty bodies. This process, which began in the larger and better institutions, seems indeed to have been closely related to the size of the faculties and the complexity of the colleges themselves. Trustees had long been in the habit of meeting either once a year (at commencement) or once a term.[57] Since this frequency was plainly insufficient for the

[56] Colleges were often chronically so near disaster that presidents or professors felt a moral obligation to resign when they became unpopular lest they bring upon their school its death blow. What is most interesting, in comparison with the attitude of the modern professoriat, is the absence of the feeling that their professional competence gave them any right to cling to their jobs. The general feeling seems to have been that strong criticism *obliged* them to resign. A man like Benjamin Hedrick was thought to be exceptionally willful and stubborn because he refused to resign his post at the University of North Carolina under pressure, and forced the trustees to fire him.

[57] On the role and function of trustees, see Wayland, *Thoughts on the Present Collegiate System*, pp. 43–62, 151–56. The history of academic government and of the transit of some governmental powers from trustees to faculties has never been written. It is for the most part ignored by Charles F. Thwing in his standard *History of Higher Education in America* (New York, 1906). The old college era is slighted in such studies as Samuel Katzin, "A Comparative Study of the Problem of Control

purposes of college management, the handling of details of policy was often delegated to committees of trustees, while individual members of boards on occasion exercised their right of visitation. Unfortunately this system seems often to have resulted in the settling of all but plenary powers upon committees composed of those trustees residing closest to the college—a principle of selection that might favor the most limited and provincial members and exclude the more sophisticated men of affairs. Thus the typical college was under the governance of a self-perpetuating board of absentee gentlemen, predominantly laymen but generally selected with an eye to their sectarian affiliations, who held their offices for life but were generally too busy to undertake the detailed management of the institution under their charge. Of necessity immense discretion had to be placed in the hands of the president, who was usually an ex-officio member of the board and by far its most important officer.

The situation of the president *vis-à-vis* his board and his faculty had somewhat changed since the days when faculties consisted predominantly of young tutors. In the colonial period it had not been too difficult for the strong president to overwhelm such a faculty—and even in the first half of the nineteenth century this doubtless remained the situation in the smallest colleges. But it was not in the larger ones. It was one thing for a president to sit down with one or two professors and a few tutors, and quite another to meet with a body of from six to ten or more professors, many of whom were men of some distinction and all of whom were likely to be approximately his peers in age and scholarship. As presidents came on occasion to be drawn from the ranks of the faculties rather than the ministry, they entered their offices with greater knowledge of the professors' problems. From being the spokesman of the board to the faculty, the president tended to become more the intermediary between the board and the faculty, obliged to find a substan-

in the Administration of Higher Education in the United States and Europe," unpublished Ph.D. dissertation (New York University, 1931), and Omer Stewart Williams, "Democracy in Educational Administration," unpublished doctoral dissertation (Northwestern University, 1940). See, however, W. H. Cowley, "The Government and Administration of American Higher Education: Whence and Whither?" *Journal of the American Association of Collegiate Registrars,* XXII (July, 1947), 477–91; George Bogert, "Historical Survey of Faculty Participation in University Government in the United States," in John D. Russell, *Emergent Responsibilities in Higher Education* (Chicago, 1946), pp. 107–18.

tial measure of harmony in both bodies in order best to carry out his work.[58] More and more, in the better institutions, the will of the faculty was something that had to be taken into account.

The history of the first beginnings of faculty participation in governing decisions has not yet been written. Since the early eighteenth century Harvard has had, in addition to the Corporation and the Overseers, a third body commonly called the "Immediate Government." This is, actually, the faculty sitting as a body to exercise those discretionary powers that were left to it by the Corporation.[59] How large and important the role of that body was before 1810 is doubtful; but under the presidency of John Thornton Kirkland (1810–28) the government of the College was left substantially in the president's hands and he showed an increasing reliance on his growing faculty. In the years 1823–25 an attempt was made by some spirited members of the faculty to revive the claim that the teachers alone were entitled to seats on the Corporation. Like Nicholas Sever's move more than a century before, this was doomed to failure, but it stimulated a thorough review of the process of college government. Although this movement was probably the most self-assertive act undertaken by any college faculty in the period, it was not based upon a desire to challenge the general powers of an absentee governing board. Indeed, the resident instructors, who had become irritated by some of the intrusions of the Corporation, were simply objecting to the presence of such a third body standing between themselves and the Overseers, and they strategically suggested that the Corporation, in addition to usurping functions that were properly their own,

[58] See John G. Palfrey's estimate of the president-faculty relationship in 1840: "The relation of the head of a college to the immediate associates of his cares is not without its delicacy. They are his equals, yet his inferiors; his inferiors, as sustaining individually a less share in the common responsibility, and subject in some respects to his supervision; his equals, as called by the public voice to be connected with him in the administration of a great public interest, as belonging to the same rank in society, and as his fellow-citizens of the commonwealth of letters. If they have a right to be where they are, they have a right to be treated with consideration and respect; and such undoubtedly needs to be the spirit of the intercourse maintained with them, if it concerns the public that their places should not cease to be attractive to such men as the public service requires." *A Discourse on the Life and Character of the Reverend John Thornton Kirkland* (Cambridge, Mass., 1840), p. 29. Cf. Andrews Norton, *Remarks on a Report of a Committee of the Overseers of Harvard College . . . Read May 4, 1824* (Cambridge, Mass., 1824), pp. 6–7.

[59] As early as 1708 there is evidence that the faculty of Harvard College acted on occasion as a body separate from the Corporation. In 1725 it began to keep records of its proceedings. Quincy, *History of Harvard*, I, 278–79, 391.

had also usurped the proper prerogatives of the Overseers.[60] Since the Corporation, however, was the dynamic agent in University government, its control by the faculty would have made a signal difference in the control of Harvard. In the light of the all but inevitable failure of the faculty claim, its true significance lies in the degree of self-consciousness on the part of the faculty that it showed, and the confidence with which it asserted the value of a large measure of self-government.[61] To collect as large and as able a faculty as that of Harvard in the 1820s was to invite faculty challenges to the inherited dominance of the colleges by nonresidents.

More influential than events at Harvard in American college government as a whole was the transition toward faculty participation at Yale under the regime of Jeremiah Day (1817–46). Coming to the presidency with many years of professorial experience behind him, Day adopted the practice of discussing and deciding all questions connected with college policy in a meeting of the assembled faculty. By the end of his regime a strong precedent had been established that even the Corporation should not take action without the recommendation or assent of the instructors. The principle that a new professor or other officer connected with instruction should not be appointed without the consent of his future colleagues seems to have been observed with particular scrupulousness.[62]

[60] Cf. Professor Andrews Norton in his *Speech Delivered before the Overseers of Harvard College . . . February 3, 1825* (Boston, 1825), p. xxi, and *Memorial to the . . . Overseers of Harvard* (Cambridge, Mass., 1824), presented by the members of the faculty, p. 20. For an account of the controversy, see Quincy, *History of Harvard*, II, 338–53. See also Edward Everett, *A Letter to John Lowell* (Boston, 1824); *Report of a Committee of the Overseers of Harvard College on the Memorial of the Resident Instructors* (n.p., 1825); [Andrews Norton], *Remarks on a Report of a Committee of the Overseers of Harvard College . . . Read May 4, 1824* (Cambridge, Mass., 1824); George Ticknor, *Remarks on Changes Lately Proposed or Adopted in Harvard University* (n.p., 1825); *Remarks on a Pamphlet Printed by the Professors and Tutors of Harvard University . . . by an Alumnus of That College* (Boston, 1824); *Further Remarks on the Memorial of the Officers of Harvard College by an Alumnus of That College* (Boston, 1824).

[61] Cf. Professor Norton: "Every one would be struck with the absurdity of entrusting the concerns of a mercantile body to those who were not merchants, or of an agricultural society to those who were not agriculturists; and the absurdity would be greatly enhanced, if the gentlemen who received the trust were, at the same time, so separated from the establishment which it was their business to govern, as to render it impossible for them to acquire any practical knowledge of its concerns." *Speech . . . February 3, 1825*, p. 22.

[62] William L. Kingsley, ed., *Yale College: A Sketch of Its History* (New York, 1879), I, 126–27; cf. George W. Pierson, *Yale College*, Chap. VII. On the early recognition of tutors as a part of faculty government at Yale, see Fulton, *F. A. P. Barnard*, pp. 65–66.

By 1830, at least the better Eastern colleges were following the practice of having new faculty members chosen upon the recommendation of the faculties.[63] In a great many places, however, this prerogative was still exercised by the president alone.

In 1837 the Reverend Jasper Adams, an Episcopalian who was at the time chaplain and professor of geography, history, and ethics at the military academy at West Point, and who had been for more than ten years an extremely successful president at Charleston College, delivered a lecture at Worcester which stated very effectively the more advanced thinking among academic administrators of the period. Although Adams pointed out that the legal status of faculty-trustee relations was an altogether cloudy one, he had a clear theory of his own as to what these legal and moral relations should be. Faculties were like quasi-corporations, grafted on the essential corporate bodies composed of trustees; they were, in any coherent conception of the nature of a college, the administrative body of such an entity, just as the trustees were its legislative body.[64] The purpose of a college, he said, was not simply to be incorporated, but rather to be incorporated in order that it might gather together a learned faculty and offer instruction. Since the assembling of the faculty was the end in view, to make the faculty subordinate to the trustees was "to reverse the usual order of things, to subvert first principles, to exalt the means above the end, instead of making them subordinate to the accomplishment of the end." [65] In the public mind the

[63] *Journal of the Proceedings of a Convention of Literary and Scientific Gentlemen,* pp. 79–86. Cf. Wayland in 1842: "But it may be asked, . . . how are appointments made. . . . Generally, I believe, upon the recommendation of the faculty. . . . Inasmuch as the Board to which this duty specially appertains, is unable to devote to it the attention which its importance usually demands, they [i.e., the faculty] are commonly obliged to perform an office which does not properly [i.e., legally] belong to them. . . . Thus they really nominate and the corporation appoint. But since where there is a good understanding between the parties, their nomination is almost always confirmed, they may be considered as in fact filling their own vacancies, and making their own appointments." *Thoughts on the Present Collegiate System,* p. 66. Wayland, it should be remarked, was most familiar with the better institutions, and even in these he had observed some sad violations of this practice. *Ibid.,* p. 67. On problems involved in faculty appointments, see pp. 67–75.

[64] Jasper Adams, "On the Relation Subsisting between the Board of Trustees and Faculty of a University," *American Institute of Instruction, Lectures . . . at Worcester, Mass., August, 1837* (Boston, 1838), pp. 144–46. Cf. Henry Davis, *A Narrative of the Embarrassment and Decline of Hamilton College* (n.p., 1832). For a later protest against the power of trustees see J. F. Jackson "American Scholarship," *The Knickerbocker,* XXVIII (July, 1846), 9–10.

[65] Adams, "On the Relation . . . between the Board of Trustees and Faculty," p. 147.

faculties inevitably got the credit or blame for the success or failure of instruction and discipline; hence they must be permitted to select their own means, agents, and associates, if they were not to be charged with responsibility without power.[66] Trustees should therefore not attempt to direct the instruction and discipline of the college.[67] The relation of the faculty member to the trustees, said Adams, is not that of a workman to his employer; it is rather like that of the lawyer to his client or the minister to his congregation—a relation in which the person retained has certain special skills, experiences, and qualities that put him in a position to advise and in a sense to direct the man who retains him.[68]

Generalizing from the experience of American colleges, Adams pointed out that "no college in this country has permanently flourished, in which the trustees have not been willing to concede to the faculty, the rank, dignity, honor, and influence, which belong essentially to their station." Contrariwise, "those colleges have been most flourishing, in which the instruction and discipline have been most exclusively committed to their faculties." The historical instances of obtrusive trustee interference in college management were all instances of failure.[69] Adams concluded by suggesting a functional allocation of powers: to the trustees should go the right of original organization under the college charter, the original choice of the faculty, the right of removal "for just and adequate cause," the right of managing institutional funds, and the duty of acting as the patrons and protectors of the faculty; to the faculty should go the determination of the course of study, including the choice of textbooks, and the right to decide all internal matters of instruction, discipline, and administration.[70] Perhaps the most impressive of Adams' remarks were his historical generalizations. His legal and moral observations were persuasively put, and in pointing out that those who expected to found colleges of repute that would survive and flourish must expect

[66] Cf. also Andrews Norton, *Speech . . . February 3, 1825,* p. iii.

[67] Adams, "On the Relation . . . between the Board of Trustees and Faculty," pp. 147–48.

[68] *Ibid.,* pp. 148–49.

[69] *Ibid.,* pp. 150–51. Cf. Norton, *Speech . . . February 3, 1825,* p. 13: "Every literary institution among us, other things being equal, has flourished in proportion as the government of it . . . has been virtually intrusted to the resident instructors." Trustees on occasion contributed in important ways to the management and reformation of colleges. The important point here is that they invariably failed when they tried to make themselves responsible for details of discipline and education.

[70] *Ibid.,* pp. 155–58. For a successful appeal by a president for enlarged faculty powers, see Fulton, *F. A. P. Barnard,* p. 204–5.

to delegate large powers to their faculties or fail, he was simply generalizing the whole experience of American academic life. For the main historical reason for the emergence of delegated faculty government within the framework of the plenary legal powers of the trustees was that complete trustee government had universally failed, while a division of powers among trustees, president, and faculty had in many cases conspicuously succeeded.[71]

PRESBYTERIANS AND PARTISANS

By the end of the eighteenth century and the beginning of the nineteenth the idea of freedom for the college or university scholar had received a rough formulation deriving from the ideals of toleration and religious liberty and the intellectual liberalism of the Enlightenment. In the first decades of the new century, as we have seen, there were beginning to appear institutional changes that laid the primitive basis for the development of academic freedom. The idea of freedom had won acceptance among at least a limited portion of the enlightened lay public, and it had also aroused enemies. Hence in the era of the old college we find something that had been absent before: a more or less continuous struggle, flaring up now in one place, now in another, for a freer atmosphere in education.

There can be found no better illustration of the extent to which the ideal of freedom had evolved among enlightened laymen than in the educational theory and practice of Thomas Jefferson; and no more helpful clues are available to its limitations, both in thought and in the American realities, than Jefferson's own compromises with the ideal and the difficulties he encountered in trying to realize that ideal at the University of Virginia.

Jefferson wanted to be remembered chiefly for three among his many achievements, each associated with the history of liberty: the Declaration of Independence, the Virginia Statute for Religious Freedom, and his work in the establishment of the University of Virginia. This institution,

---

[71] It should be noted also that stagnation and episodes of maladministration could bring about faculty rebellions. See, e.g., Samuel Eliot Morison, "The Great Rebellion in Harvard College, and the Resignation of President Kirkland," *Publications of the Colonial Society of Massachusetts*, XXVII (1932), 54–112; Theodore F. Jones, ed., *New York University* (New York, 1933), pp. 45–52; E. M. Coulter, *College Life in the Old South* (New York, 1928), pp. 254–63. For additional factors bearing on academic government see below, Chap. VI.

which he once referred to as "the hobby of my old age," [72] would be based, he said, "on the illimitable freedom of the human mind. For here we are not afraid to follow truth wherever it may lead, nor to tolerate any error so long as reason is left free to combat it." [73] This university, for which Jefferson worked so many years before it was finally opened in 1825, was to represent the realization of those reforms he had failed to effect at his own college, William and Mary, in 1779. It was to embody his faith in education, his taste in architecture, his love of science, his tolerant and unsectarian views, his political liberality. It was also to pioneer in the spread of the university idea in this land of colleges. Most of the changes which were to sweep over American education almost two generations after Jefferson's death were clearly foreshadowed in his plans for the university of his native state. There were to be eight schools altogether, including schools of law and medicine. The best available professors were to be secured, and they were to be sought abroad as well as at home, at whatever risk of criticism from provincials and chauvinists. They were to be paid ample salaries. They were to give lectures, not merely preside over recitations. The students, who (with a few exceptions) would not be allowed to enter until the age of sixteen, would be somewhat more mature than those at most American colleges, and they would not be bound by the prescribed curriculum: they were to choose among schools and select their own course of studies.[74] They would be governed by disciplinary rules more generous than those then in fashion, and they would exercise a distinct measure of self-government. Professors would have relatively secure, although not absolute, tenure. Moreover, there would be democracy within the faculty: an inoffensive rotating chairmanship would replace the customary university presidency, after the fashion of the rotation of the rectors in the German universities.[75]

[72] *Writings* (P. L. Ford, ed., New York, 1892–99), X, 174.

[73] *Writings* (H. A. Washington, ed., Washington, 1853–54), VII, 196. Cf. *Writings,* Ford, ed., X, 174: ". . . the illimitable freedom of the human mind to explore and to expose every subject susceptible of its contemplation."

[74] Although Jefferson was one of the curricular reformers who not only advocated an elective system but also encouraged a certain amount of utilitarianism in the curriculum, he did not belong to the barbarian wing of educational reform; he assigned to the classics a central role in a liberal education. Philip A. Bruce, *History of the University of Virginia* (New York, 1920), I, 54; see pp. 1–44 for Jefferson's views and their impress on the University. Cf. Roy Honeywell, *The Educational Work of Thomas Jefferson* (Cambridge, Mass., 1931), and Orie Long, *Thomas Jefferson and George Ticknor: A Chapter in American Scholarship* (Williamstown, Mass., 1933).

[75] Honeywell, *Educational Work of Thomas Jefferson,* pp. 99–100. Professors

Like William Livingston, Jefferson proposed above all to avoid the blighting influence of sectarianism by having no school or professorship of divinity, an omission which brought down upon him the expected accusations from sectarians and old political foes. To his mind the primary function of a university was not to engender piety but to foster knowledge in all its branches; and while knowledge of religion and theology, as knowledge in an historical and philosophical sphere of inquiry, was important, he hoped to escape the traps of sectarian antagonism by committing the university to no sect while respecting all. An early recruit to the faculty was advised that he and his colleagues would be expected to stay clear of sectarian doctrines.[76] Jefferson hoped to appease the sects by inviting them to establish their own separate little schools and professors in the vicinity of the university, offering their students the opportunity to attend its lectures and share its facilities. "And by bringing the sects together, and mixing them with the mass of other students, we shall soften their asperities, liberalize and neutralize their prejudices, and make the general religion a religion of peace, reason and morality." [77] The sects, however, were implacable. Not until the eve of the Civil War did one of them consider responding to this suggestion. In the interim they were often active in their hostility, and as Jefferson wrote in 1820, the serious enemies of the university were "the priests of the different religious sects, to whose spells on the human mind its improvement is ominous. . . . The Presbyterian clergy are the loudest; the most intolerant of all sects, the most tyrannical and ambitious. . . . They pant to reestablish by law the holy inquisition which they can now only infuse into public opinion." [78]

In one important respect Jefferson's philosophy of academic liberty was deficient and inconsistent: for all his fine and deeply felt rhetoric about

---

were to be removable only for cause and upon a vote of two thirds of the Visitors. Jefferson pointed out to one prospective appointee that the high character and liberal ideas of the Visitors amounted in effect to a guarantee of tenure. *Ibid.*, pp. 98–99.

[76] Francis Walker Gilmer, while searching for teachers abroad, told one: "Allay your fears . . . about religion. Far from requiring uniformity, we scrupulously avoid having clergymen of any sort connected with the University, not because we have no religion but because we have too many kinds. All that we shall require of each professor is that he shall say nothing about the doctrines which divide the sects." Bruce, *History of the University of Virginia*, I, 369.

[77] *Writings*, H. A. Washington, ed., VII, 267.

[78] Honeywell, *Educational Work of Thomas Jefferson*, p. 154. See Bruce, *History of the University of Virginia*, II, 361–80, for the post-Jeffersonian religious development of the university.

the illimitable freedom of the human mind he could not transcend the tendency, almost universal in his time, to subordinate intellectual freedom in some considerable measure to considerations of partisan politics. As early as 1800, observing with alarm "the general political disposition [i.e., Federalist] of those to whom is confided the education of the rising generation," he had consoled himself with the thought that the common sense of parents would remedy it and had doubted that any more drastic remedy was admissible.[79] This concern with the possible role of a higher education, monopolized by his political opponents, in indoctrinating students, grew with the years. By the time the University of Virginia was in the making he was actively concerned that Virginians were leaving their native state for schools like Princeton and Harvard where they might be expected, he thought, to imbibe the principles of Northerners on such issues as the Missouri question.[80] In the year of the university's opening he wrote to a fellow trustee that while they ought not to presume, like trustees elsewhere, to prescribe textbooks in the sciences, still there was one branch of knowledge "in which we are the best judges, in which heresies may be taught, of so interesting a character to our own State and to the United States, as to make it a duty in us to lay down the principles which are to be taught"—the field of government.[81] To James Madison he wrote in 1826 that "In the selection of our law professor we must be rigorously attentive to his political principles"; for he believed that while the Coke-Littleton tradition had made good Whigs, ardent for the liberties of Englishmen, the coming of Blackstone had made a generation of Tories. "If we are true and vigilant in our trust," he continued, "within a dozen or twenty years a majority of our own legislature will be from one school, and many disciples will have carried its doctrines home with them to their several states and will have leavened the whole mass." [82] Thus, in the sphere of politics in which his emotions were deeply engaged, Jefferson was as determined that the university should be an agent of ex parte indoctrination as his enemies, the Presbyterians, were in their sphere. Leaving all other subjects to the determination of the professors, he was bent on propagating principles of law and government that were consistent with the truth as it was understood by the enlightened Republican

[79] *Writings,* H. A. Washington, ed., VII, 455.
[80] *Ibid.,* VII, 202; cf. p. 204. Unlike many later Southerners, however, he would never have ruled out Northern professors. He was very eager to get Ticknor for literature and Bowditch for mathematics.
[81] *Ibid.,* VII, 397.   [82] *Ibid.,* VII, 433.

Virginia gentry.[83] Had he been confronted with this inconsistency, he would doubtless have answered that his preference for Whig indoctrination was a preference for indoctrination in the principles of freedom itself, and hence not of a comparable order of stringency with the tenets of his foes. He might have said too—and correctly—that the fundamental bias of American collegiate education had long been so much in the hands of Federalists and sectarians that in tipping the balance the opposite way in one institution he was only redressing it. Nonetheless it is true that even Jefferson, the most enlightened lay educator of his time, had not thoroughly thought out the intensely perplexing problems of freedom in education; and that if he was remarkably libertarian in other areas he was in politics still an unwitting exponent of the kind of partisanship in education that, practiced by the Federalists, had impelled the Jeffersonian Meigs to leave both Yale and the University of Georgia.

To explain why so many of Jefferson's high hopes for his university were not fulfilled would be to explore at length the entire cultural milieu in which it was founded.[84] But there were three primary obstacles to a free and flourishing system of higher education in the ante-bellum era that revealed themselves in the early story of the University of Virginia. One, the incubus of slavery and sectional antagonism, which was vaguely foreshadowed by Jefferson's anxiety about the Northern education of Virginians, we will account for later. It remains here to explore the consequences of the other two, the sectarian animus, particularly with regard to the leading role of the Presbyterians, and the blighting effects of acts proceeding from civic and political motives of a far more urgent and demanding sort than the political partisanship Jefferson exhibited.[85]

In social terms the struggle over intellectual freedom during the early decades of the nineteenth century was one between the liberal gentry,

[83] Bruce, *History of the University of Virginia*, I, 327–29. See also Gordon E. Baker, "Thomas Jefferson on Academic Freedom," *Bulletin*, AAUP, XXXIX (Autumn, 1953), 377–87.

[84] The legislature never supported the university with the generosity which would have been necessary if many plans were to have been realized. Blighted by poverty only slightly less acute than many of its sisters', the university secured a faculty which was able, but not of that "first grade of science" Jefferson had hoped for. The rotating chairmanship proved onerous to many of the professors and had to be given up after twenty years. While control of students was perhaps a little more lenient than in many institutions, this did not eliminate the usual student disorders, and the university enjoyed the dubious distinction of having a faculty member murdered by an undergraduate during a riot.

[85] For further comment on the way in which denominational considerations entered into the college system, see below, Chap. VI.

generally representing in the South and West the principles of Jeffersonianism and the waning afterglow of the Enlightenment, and the ardently sectarian clergy, whose appeal reached wider but often less influential strata of the population. The hope of the liberals usually rested in institutions fostered by state legislatures and established upon a broad base of public responsibility, while the sectarians placed theirs in small denominational colleges.[86] In the South and Southwest, the liberals attempted to capitalize upon the fact that the state institutions were chartered before a system of private colleges had taken root. Such institutions as the University of Georgia (chartered 1785), the University of North Carolina (1789), the University of Tennessee (chartered as Blount College, 1794), and the South Carolina College (1801), later the University of South Carolina, were launched before the tide of Enlightenment thought had receded and in advance of the establishment of the denominational schools, while even Jefferson's University of Virginia, chartered in 1819, was not too late to benefit by the guidance of the declining generation of liberal aristocrats.

In promoting public institutions, most of the liberal educationalists seem to have been moved by no desire to promote an aggressive secularism or skepticism, but simply by a desire to advance the cause of higher education without getting ensnared in sectarian controversy. This was a goal easier to aim at than to achieve, and in the long run none of the state institutions maintained a secular atmosphere. Until the post-Civil War period not one of them grew to true university stature. While the sectarians were not strong enough to prevent such institutions from being founded and maintained, they did help to keep them from flourishing. Probably more important to the cause of freedom than all the individual cases of interference was the fact that sectarianism checked the growth of those internal institutional factors in the colleges that make for free and advanced scholarship.

It was a difficult path that the sponsors of nonsectarian education had to tread. To be neutral among the various sects was to keep clergymen of zealous denominational commitments out of professorships and presidencies, to forswear the teaching of divinity, and to avoid compulsory religious exercises with sectarian content—all of which left the institution

[86] For an excellent account of the state university idea see Curti and Carstensen, *The University of Wisconsin*, Vol. I, Chap. I; for the eighteenth-century background, Allen O. Hansen, *Liberalism and American Education in the Eighteenth Century* (New York, 1926).

vulnerable to charges of godlessness. To mollify one religious group by appointing clerical professors or a clerical president from its ranks was to heighten the competitive animosity of the others.[87]

Of all the churches, the Presbyterians were by far the most vigilant and censorious, as men like Jefferson, Thomas Cooper, Horace Holley, and Francis Lieber painfully learned. The history of collegiate education in the South and West is in a large measure the history of struggles in which that church played a central part.[88] This is not to say that there were no liberal Presbyterian educators in the Witherspoon tradition,[89] nor is it to say that the record of the Presbyterians was unambiguous, for they nourished education with one hand while throttling it with the other. But their vigorous role in sectarian controversies was a matter of common observation by contemporaries. The Episcopalians and Unitarians, who tended to be aristocratic and latitudinarian, drew fire from the Presbyterians on both counts. The Methodists and Baptists, although in most places far more numerous than the Presbyterians, were not nearly as interested or competent in the educational sphere.[90] The Presbyterians possessed an ardent concern for dogma, a rigorous spirit, a consistent interest in education, and a tight system of church organization. Their members were solid citizens of the middle and upper-middle classes whose place in the social structure enabled them to wield political influence far out of proportion to their numbers.[91] To staff a college in the South almost in-

[87] For the struggle between state universities and denominational colleges see Foerster, "The State University in the Old South," Chap. IV; Godbold, *Church College of the Old South,* Chap. V; Luther L. Gobbel, *Church-State Relationships in Education in North Carolina since 1776* (Durham, N.C., 1938).

[88] Jefferson concluded that the planners of his University of Virginia could get along with the Methodists, Baptists, and Anglicans of the Old Dominion, but that the Presbyterians were "violent, ambitious of power, intolerant in politics as in religion and want nothing but license from the laws to kindle again the fires of their leader John Knox." Foerster, "The State University in the Old South," pp. 221–22. C. Harve Geiger, *The Program of Higher Education of the Presbyterian Church in the United States of America* (Cedar Rapids, Iowa, 1940), treats informatively but indulgently of the Presbyterian record.

[89] For the effects of this tradition see Donald R. Come, "The Influence of Princeton on Higher Education in the South before 1825," *William and Mary Quarterly,* Second Series, Vol. II (October, 1945), pp. 359–96.

[90] The dogmatism of Presbyterians was hardly more imposing as an obstacle to educational development than the anti-intellectualism and educational indifference common among Baptists and Methodists in the ruder communities of the West. See Curti, *The Growth of American Thought,* pp. 268–70.

[91] On the social recruitment of the churches see H. Richard Niebuhr, *The Social Sources of Denominationalism* (New York, 1929). Such differences were embodied

evitably meant to turn to the Presbyterians for professors and presidents; but it was a fortunate institution that did not find them on occasion too vigilant in matters of doctrine or too provocative to the other sects.

A problem second only to the intrusions and failings of sectarianism was the rising spirit of political partisanship and the social hostilities that raged in the United States from about 1820 to the Civil War. The development of the democratic spirit in the years before and during the Jackson administration had complex results. It was attended by a vogue of humanitarianism and reform as well as an assertive mood of equalitarianism. One of its great contributions to American life was to make available to broader masses of people a free public education at the grammar-school level. In the field of collegiate education its consequences were far less favorable. One of the dominant popular motives was the passion for equalizing opportunity, which manifested itself in the political sphere by the cry for general suffrage, rotation in office, and the "democratization" of many political forms, and in economic life by the attempt to destroy all kinds of monopolies and privileges.[92] Whatever the benefits of this movement in such areas, its consequences for professional and higher education tended to be deleterious because the hostility to privilege and caste, the desire for opportunity, became in these fields a disdain for authority and excellence and *expertise* of all kinds. The public mood encouraged informal training of lawyers, doctors, and, in the popular denominations, ministers. It became far easier than it had been in the more stratified society of the eighteenth century for a young man who began life without money or family to apprentice himself to a lawyer and "read law" in his office; for a future physician to take a brief course in a commercial private medical school unconnected with university or hospital, or to serve an apprenticeship to a practitioner; for a pious lad to qualify without theological training for the ministry in an evangelical sect. Not only professional schools but colleges could thus be by-passed.[93] And if the well-to-do still preferred to employ conventional educational methods out of a sense of status or respect for knowledge, they were vulnerable to the

in an amusing piece of Protestant folklore: "A Methodist is a Baptist who wears shoes; a Presbyterian is a Methodist who has been to college; an Episcopalian is a Presbyterian who lives off his investments."

[92] For an interpretation of this aspect of Jacksonian democracy see Richard Hofstadter, *The American Political Tradition* (New York, 1948), Chap. IV.

[93] See Hofstadter and Hardy, *Development and Scope of Higher Education*, pp. 71–73, 82–84.

charge of aristocratic leanings. Even within the colleges, Francis Wayland noted, the old practice of assigning academic rank to students at commencement had often been "dropped like a polluted thing" because administrators were "awed by the hoarse growl of popular discontent." [94]

The most formidable manifestation of popular democratic sentiment was the widespread idea that the state universities were agencies for the rich that simply served to perpetuate and aggravate class distinctions. In fact, the early state universities, unlike those of today, did not offer free tuition, and generally they were patronized chiefly by the sons of the wealthy. Again and again their development and support were opposed before the public, to the great delight of promoters of sectarian colleges, on the ground that they required the taxing of the poor to educate the children of the rich. The situation of the state university of Georgia (then called Franklin College) is illustrative: it was forever under the accusation that it was an institution for the rich, but this very allegation was used to prevent placing at its disposal the funds necessary to create a system of scholarships that would have mitigated the charge.[95] This was an insoluble dilemma so long as the masses remained disdainful of education as an end in itself and so long as higher education was unnecessary to professional and vocational advancement.

The centers of aristocratic culture were far more generous in fostering higher education than were the regions in which popular democracy enjoyed a more unqualified reign. Thus such leading institutions as Harvard, the University of Virginia, and South Carolina were fostered by local aristocracies; and just as mercantile Boston sponsored a more liberal institution than the relatively democratic province of Connecticut, so the planters whose culture centered at Charleston produced a more liberal college than the more democratic states of Georgia and North Carolina. Likewise, as Howard Beale has pointed out in his *History of Freedom of*

[94] Wayland, *Thoughts on the Present Collegiate System,* p. 40; cf. pp. 92–93. Wayland compared this with the respectful evaluation of university distinctions in England. *Ibid.,* pp. 38–40. Not everywhere, however, did this dislike of academic rank win out. Many colleges kept it, and in elementary schools it persisted into the 1900s.

[95] See the excellent discussion in Coulter, *College Life in the Old South,* Chap. IX. For the popular hostility to the state institutions, see also pp. 130, 221–30. Cf. Daniel Walker Hollis, *University of South Carolina,* Vol. I: *South Carolina College* (Columbia, S.C., 1951), pp. 5, 6, 130; Foerster, "The State University in the Old South," pp. 61–62, 210 ff.; Kemp Battle, *History of the University of North Carolina, 1789–1868* (Raleigh, N.C., 1907), I, 132, 138, 142, 146–49, 332, ff.; Gobbel, *Church-State Relationships in Education . . . since 1776,* pp. 37n., 55.

Teaching in American Schools, Jeffersonian democracy (which was aristocratic in its leadership) was "anti-theological and liberal," while Jacksonian democracy, which was profoundly popular, was "pious and intolerant." [96] None of this should be taken to imply that those who stood in the democratic tradition were invariably hostile to freedom in higher education, while aristocrats were invariably tolerant. What does seem true is that the most enlightened aristocracies had a considerably better record than the most militantly democratic communities.

The principle had not been generally accepted on either side of the political fence—had not even been vigorously formulated and fought for by those most concerned—that the politics of a college president or professor ought to be considered irrelevant to his competence. To appoint a prominent professor or president whose politics were outspokenly opposed to the dominant politics of his own trustees was a rare thing and one that did not make for an easy tenure. To appoint one whose views, however congenial or acceptable to trustees, challenged those of the community, was to subject an entire institution to sniping.[97] It was a refreshing thing when the Jeffersonian trustees of South Carolina College elected a New Englander and a strong Federalist like Jonathan Maxcy to the presidency of that institution in 1804, and it was something of a landmark in American educational history when trustee Wade Hampton, urged to vote for a politically more congenial officer, retorted, "I know of no necessary connection between politics and literature." [98] The implications of this remark, made by a man considered to be perhaps the richest planter of his time, go as far beyond Jefferson as Jefferson himself would have gone beyond his predecessors. Hampton was expressing a rare attitude, but one still rarer where the populistic spirit was stronger.

The classic case in which the denominational spirit and popular level-

[96] Howard K. Beale, *A History of Freedom of Teaching in American Schools* (New York, 1941), p. 87; see Chap. III of that work for a discussion of the impact of evangelicalism and democracy on freedom.

[97] Foerster, "The State University in the Old South," Chap. VII, discusses in detail the relation of the political views of presidents and professors to the development of their institutions.

[98] *Ibid.,* p. 395; cf. Hollis, *South Carolina College,* p. 34. Foerster ("The State University in the Old South," pp. 104 ff.) concludes that the liberal attitude taken toward South Carolina College was attributable to the South Carolina aristocracy and its domination of the state legislature. North Carolina Federalists, however, were less tolerant. David Ker, the first presiding professor at Chapel Hill, felt it prudent to resign in 1796 because his religious liberalism and his Republicanism had made him unpopular. Battle, *University of North Carolina,* pp. 66, 100–101.

ing combined to destroy the work of a liberal educator may be found in
the experience of Horace Holley at Transylvania University in Lexington,
Kentucky.[99] Early Kentucky was, of course, largely under the influence
of Virginians. The intellectual and political inheritance of the liberal Kentucky leadership was that of the Jeffersonians. Religious indifference was
widespread among all classes in the state at the close of the eighteenth
century, but indifference or skepticism was particularly common among
the educated upper classes, who were known to have in their libraries
works by such writers as Paine, Hume, Godwin, Condorcet, Voltaire,
Rousseau, Volney, and Erasmus Darwin. The battle for the control of
education in Kentucky in the early nineteenth century took the form of a
fight between this liberal gentry and the Presbyterian clergy. Even before
the establishment of Transylvania University in 1799, a seminary that
preceded it had see-sawed between the control of the Presbyterians, who
had been instrumental in founding it, and the liberals.[100] By 1805 the
Presbyterians seemed to have gained control of the institution, but they lost
ground in the state during the period of the War of 1812, partly because
many prominent Presbyterians opposed the war in a region in which it was
pre-eminently popular, and partly because their pretensions to power
alarmed other denominations. Having only a small proportion of the
state's total population, they were confronted with a serious problem
in diplomacy, and the effects they were able to achieve in the educational sphere are a remarkable commentary on their cohesiveness and
power. At the close of the war the liberals, inspired by a growing sense
of the need for professional men educated at home and desirous of
building a local institution to compensate for the economic decline of
Lexington, made a concerted effort to recapture and revive the university,
which had vegetated under Presbyterian domination. In 1817, by exerting
legislative pressure, they forced the trustees to elect Horace Holley as
president after a vigorous campaign to oust his predecessor.

At the time of his election Holley, the offspring of a well-to-do Con-

---

[99] The following account is based very closely on Niels H. Sonne's excellent
study, *Liberal Kentucky, 1780–1828* (New York, 1939). See also Thomas D. Clark,
A History of Kentucky (New York, 1937), and F. Garvin Davenport, *Ante-Bellum
Kentucky* (Oxford, Ohio, 1943).

[100] An English-born Unitarian preacher, Harry Toulmin, armed with recom-
mendations from Jefferson and Madison, had been chosen to preside over this
institution in 1794, and had been impelled to resign by the hostility of Federalists
and Presbyterians. A professor at the university had also been forced to resign by
the pressure of opinion among liberal students. Sonne, *Liberal Kentucky,* Chap. II.

necticut family and a graduate of Timothy Dwight's Yale, was the minister of the Unitarian South End Church in Boston and a member of Harvard's Board of Overseers. He was also a convinced Federalist—a fact which did not disturb his Jeffersonian sponsors in Kentucky, as they were seeking, above all, a promising educator who was free of the limitations of provincial religion.

An able preacher, a man of the world, and a man of versatile mind, Holley brought to Lexington the precise qualities needed for the promotion of an institution of learning. "I aim," he promised, "to be liberal without indifference, moderate without coldness, rational without skepticism, evangelical without fanaticism, simple without crudeness, natural without licentiousness, and pious without the spirit of exclusion or intolerance." [101] Within a few years he took an institution which the trustees had reduced to a condition in which the entire course was offered in one year and fashioned it into a small but valuable university with an arts college, a creditable law school, and a medical college that was rapidly acquiring fame. The teaching staff included such men as Constantine Rafinesque, Judge Jesse Bledsoe, and the celebrated Dr. Daniel Drake. A traveler passing through Lexington in 1819 commented with approval on the fact that Transylvania's professors were "chosen purely for their talents, without an requirement of unanimity of religious opinion. . . . eminently calculated for their respective positions. . . . This institution promises to be in the moral world what the sun is in the natural world." [102] By 1823 Transylvania had achieved a national reputation and was drawing students from fourteen states.

When Holley arrived at Transylvania he was greeted cordially by members of all denominations except the Presbyterians, to whom no Unitarian would have been acceptable. The greeting accorded him was abundant testimony to the importance that was attached, quite realistically, to the leadership of a distinguished educator. Holley's very ability to fulfill the expectations of those who hoped to build a cultural center at Lexington increased the opposition of the Presbyterian clergy. Having begun to snipe at him even before his arrival, they continued to make intermittent criticisms throughout his early years there. In 1823 they opened a concerted campaign of criticism through pamphlets and the press, the goal of which was to discredit his work in the eyes of the public. Although they themselves were a tiny part of the state's total population, the Pres-

[101] Sonne, *Liberal Kentucky*, p. 168.   [102] *Ibid.*, pp. 171–72.

byterians argued that since Holley was a member of a minority sect the
popular will was being ignored at Transylvania. Thus they skillfully transmuted the issue from one of choice between a nonsectarian state university and a sectarian one to an issue of minority rule versus the popular
majority.[103] Then they drummed up a barrage of ingenious charges against
the person of Holley. He held Sunday parties, at which music was played.
He encouraged students to study on the Sabbath. Because he had said that
education might be an asset to a religious life, he was charged with having
held that it was necessary to be educated to go to heaven. He was accused
of denying human depravity and of asserting that the Devil is not a real
personage. "Will you," asked one critic, "pay the President of a university
to laugh and brow-beat your sons out of the little religion which they may
possess?" [104] The graduates and the faculty rallied to Holley's defense,
denied the false charges, and tried to convey a sense of Holley's distinction as a teacher and administrator,[105] but it soon became clear that the
Presbyterian clergy had succeeded in making the control of the university
a live political question once again by stigmatizing it as infidel and aristocratic.

On purely religious grounds the Presbyterian attack was formidable
enough, but it was much heightened by current economic discontents. A
depression, followed by a sharp political conflict over banking and currency policies, had split Kentucky between a conservative party and the
party of debtors. Transylvania University was doubly affected: its income
was sharply cut at the same time that criticisms of its "aristocratic" bias
were heightened by social conflicts. It was forced to raise tuition at the
very moment when the cries were loudest that it favored the rich. Holley's

[103] *Ibid.*, pp. 197–99. The early historians of Transylvania noted that the Presbyterians, "numbering but six tenths of one per cent of our [Kentucky] population in
1820, or being about one in every hundred and sixty, exerted a greater influence than
all the other religious denominations on our educational institutions." Robert and
Johanna Peter, *Transylvania University* (Louisville, 1896), p. 127n. The affiliated
members of all sects, as recorded in the estimates, amounted to only a fraction of
the state's population. Presbyterians were, however, outnumbered at least ten to
one by Baptists and Methodists. See Robert H. Bishop, *An Outline of the History
of the Church in the State of Kentucky* (Lexington, 1824), pp. 306–7.

[104] *Ibid.*, p. 205.

[105] The faculty proposed a scheme, designed to mollify the denominations, according to which the pastors of the Methodist, Presbyterian, Episcopalian,
Baptist, and Roman Catholic churches should share in rotation the task of preaching
in the college chapel. This plan was accepted by the trustees and endorsed by
members of seven religious denominations, including the Presbyterian, but the
intransigence of a few Presbyterian ministers and an indiscretion of Holley's blocked
it. *Ibid.*, pp. 232–34.

past allegiance to Federalism was recalled, and he was charged with living luxuriously. The Jacksonian newspaper, the *Argus,* turned on the university, and finally the popular politician, Governor Joseph Desha of the Relief Party, attacked it as a hotbed of aristocracy that had ceased "to unite the confidence and affections of the people," and urged that more money be spent instead on the common schools. Actually there is more than a suspicion that the attack was motivated by the desire of many politicians to secure the accumulated literary fund, ordinarily earmarked for the university, for the construction of turnpikes.[106] Holley resigned in 1827, and before long the institution went into a decline from which it never recovered.[107] Thus the attempt to transplant into the hinterland the idea of the secular state university broke upon the rocks of popular hostility and the *odium theologicum.*

Sectarian considerations were less important and the democratic impulse considerably more so in the ousting of Henry P. Tappan from the presidency of the University of Michigan in 1863. Tappan was one of the outstanding educators in the country and one of the most advanced educational theorists. But he made no friends among the other denominations by his attendance at the Presbyterian church, while he lost the support of the Presbyterians themselves for not being a notably good churchman. He also offended the growing temperance movement by serving wine. But the dominant charge against him, the one that brought upon him attacks by the *Detroit Free Press* that were echoed by the Democratic press of Michigan, was the charge that he was "aristocratic," Eastern, foreign, and Prussian, that he espoused "the follies of a rotten aristocracy over the sea." His interest in adapting the Prussian university system to the State of Michigan, his affecting the title of Chancellor, his Eastern birth and accent, his cultivated manners, counted against him in many quarters and after a long press campaign brought into office a Board of Regents thoroughly hostile to him. In spite of his remarkable services he was unceremoniously ousted.[108]

---

[106] Thomas D. Clark, *A History of Kentucky,* pp. 315–16.

[107] For its subsequent history see James F. Hopkins, *The University of Kentucky* (Lexington, Ky., 1951), pp. 33–43.

[108] See Charles M. Perry, *Henry Philip Tappan* (Ann Arbor, 1933), pp. 195–211, Chaps. XII, XIII; for a full review by Tappan of his own connection with and achievements at the University of Michigan, see University of Michigan, *Regents Proceedings, 1837–1864* (Ann Arbor, 1915), pp. 1119–66. For a balanced comment on the situation, see Andrew D. White, *Autobiography,* I, 278–81. Cf. Wilfred Shaw, *The University of Michigan* (New York, 1920), pp. 45–55.

It is extremely doubtful that popular democracy was any more inclined than sectarian zeal to pay respect to the independence of the academic man or the academic institution. The case of Francis Bowen at Harvard in 1851 is evidence of the impatience of the popular side with an outspoken ultraconservative. Bowen, who was editor of the *North American Review* and who was destined to be one of the most able and productive academic scholars of his time, was chosen in 1850 by the Corporation to be McLean Professor of Ancient and Modern History. He had already taught for a term when his nomination came before the Overseers for confirmation. There it struck a snag. For two reasons Bowen was unpopular among the coalition of Democrats and Free-Soilers that had recently come into power: he had defended Daniel Webster's famous Seventh of March speech in favor of the Compromise of 1850, and he had attacked Louis Kossuth and the cause of Hungarian independence. Now at this time Harvard was under criticism in Massachusetts for all those reasons for which a good university might expect to suffer at the hands of an anti-intellectualistic democracy.[109] The Calvinists still disliked it for its religious liberalism, the Democrats for its Federalist-Whig traditions, the reformers for its alleged indifference to such issues as slavery (in spite of the fact that several of its professors were active Free-Soilers), and the popular editorialists because it was "aristocratic" and offered a rounded liberal education instead of courses that would help young men to become better farmers or merchants.[110]

Bowen, in defending the most unpopular act of Webster's political life, affronted one of the most profound strains of New England feeling. He was strategically far more vulnerable, however, for his sharp attack on Kossuth. At the time American jingoism had taken the form of a bumptious espousal of certain nationalist movements elsewhere, and Hungarian independence was all the rage among nationalistic Democrats. Bowen poured cold water over this enthusiasm by pointing out, in a well-documented if acidulous essay, that Hungarian independence involved the

---

[109] As Morison remarks, "What the New England democracy wanted in the period 1820–60, and even later, was not a liberal college, or a university, but a sectarian college, where sons would be reared in their fathers' beliefs, and obtain a Bachelor's degree in the shortest time, at the cheapest rate." *Three Centuries of Harvard,* p. 257.

[110] For the Bowen case and its background see Morison, *Three Centuries of Harvard,* pp. 286–93, and the same author's "Francis Bowen, an Early Test of Academic Freedom in Massachusetts," *Massachusetts Historical Society Proceedings,* LXV (February, 1936), 507–11.

persecution by the Magyars of millions of Slavs, Slovaks, Rumanians, and Germans. He further charged, in his characteristically cranky way, that American sympathy for the Hungarians had been drummed up by "a small *clique* of these infidel socialists, mostly refugees from Europe, who have obtained command of a few penny newspapers, and are endeavoring through their means to exercise the system of *terrorism* here which they practised on a large scale in the old world." [111] While the defense of Webster probably caused the greater animus against Bowen, his comments on Magyar independence were more easily used against him.[112] Although his professional competence was unquestioned, he was rejected by the preponderant ex-officio members of the Overseers, who were Free-Soilers and Democrats. However, the Board of Overseers was in the process of being reconstituted that very year. A legislative act of 1851 removed most of the ex-officio members, and in 1853 the new board made Bowen Alford Professor of Natural Religion, Moral Philosophy, and Civil Polity, a post in which he served until 1889. The case helped to persuade the friends of Harvard that the welfare of the university would be better served if power to elect the Overseers could be transferred from the Legislature, in whose hands it was left by the Act of 1851, to its alumni. This change was finally brought about in 1865.[113]

SLAVERY AND ABOLITION

The besetting moral problem of American political life from 1830 to the close of the Civil War, the issue which the colleges, for all their timidity, could not stay entirely clear of, was slavery. During these decades the slavery controversy caused more commotion and more proscriptions on college campuses than any other issue.

Open discussion of the slavery issue was all but impossible in the South after 1835 because that section had become almost of one mind on the subject, and it was exceedingly difficult in the North because that section

[111] [Francis Bowen], "The Rebellion of the Slavonic, Wallachian and German Hungarians against the Magyars," *North American Review*, LXXII (January, 1851), 240.

[112] "Every now and then," said Bowen, "a good-natured friend in the country sends me a copy of the *Worcester Spy*, or some other rural sheet, in which I am called a 'Russian Serf,' a 'college professor of despotism,' a 'hired slave of the Boston aristocracy,' or some other pleasant and high-sounding designation." Morison, "Francis Bowen," p. 509.

[113] Edward C. Elliott and M. M. Chambers, *Charters and Basic Laws of Selected American Universities and Colleges* (New York, 1934), pp. 218–21.

was so bitterly divided between friends, sympathizers, and descendants of the Southerners on one side and reformers stemming from the Puritan or evangelical traditions on the other. As a result, while there were many colleges so committed to proslavery views that nothing but a whole-hearted defense of slavery would be tolerated, and a few colleges committed entirely to abolitionism or free-soil beliefs, there seem to have been very few colleges in which all ranges of opinion could be found on the faculty.[114]

Berea College in Kentucky and Illinois College in Jacksonville, Illinois, offer rare examples of schools committed to antislavery existing in pre-dominantly hostile territory. Berea was founded in 1855 in Berea, Ken-tucky, as an openly abolitionist institution by the Reverend John Gregg Fee, a graduate of Lane Seminary. In 1859, when Fee was in the East raising money for the college, a somewhat garbled report of one of his speeches in which he was said to have endorsed John Brown's activities (he had actually praised Brown's spiritual consecration) caused an up-rising against the members of the college, who were forced to flee across the Ohio River. Fee returned to Kentucky in 1863 and restored the col-lege, which he served until 1901.[115] The situation of Illinois College was somewhat easier. It was established in a territory settled heavily by mi-grants from the South and predominantly Southern in its social com-plexion. However, the school's trustees as well as its faculty stemmed from the New England Congregational tradition and its immediate locale, Jacksonville, was a New England outpost. Its faculty was always out-spokenly antislavery, despite the fact that this attitude cost the college a great deal in both students and benefactions and stirred many press attacks in Illinois and Missouri. Although some members of the faculty were probably inspired to tone down their antislavery enthusiasm by concern for the position of the college, at least one was active in the underground

---

[114] Even Harvard, which had several organizers of the Free Soil party on its faculty, dropped Karl Follen, the refugee scholar, in 1835 after the appearance of his *Address to the People of the United States* on the subject of slavery; but in the light of Harvard's liberal policy toward professors it seems clear that Follen's abolitionism was far less vital in his dismissal than his inability to get along with the strong-minded President Josiah Quincy. On this point Morison (*Three Centuries of Harvard*, p. 254) is at odds with Kuno Francke's sketch of Follen in the *Dictionary of American Biography*. See also George W. Spindler, *Karl Follen* (Chicago, 1917); Eliza Cabot Follen, *The Works of Charles Follen* (Boston, 1842), I, 343 ff.

[115] On Fee see his *Autobiography* (Chicago, 1891); John A. R. Rogers, *Birth of Berea College* (Philadelphia, 1903), and Edwin R. Embree, "A Kentucky Crusader," *American Mercury*, Vol. XXIV (September, 1931).

railway system; and at one point the college refused to take disciplinary action against students who were involved in "stealing" Negroes from their masters.[116] That this college survived and even exerted a certain unmeasurable influence on the antislavery movement throughout Illinois was a testament to the determination of its trustees and faculty and an illustration of the possibilities of institutional resistance to community pressure. But to persist at all took courage. One of the faculty members received an anonymous letter warning that Missouri freeholders were planning to kidnap or assassinate him and destroy the college. "I would not consent," wrote President Julian Monson Sturtevant in 1844, "to suffer what I have suffered on that subject in the last seven years, and am still suffering, for any other consideration than the most imperious sense of duty." [117]

In the South the border states, notably Kentucky, showed the largest hospitality to dissent on the slavery issue, especially in the mountainous area, where slavery was unpopular. At Centre College in Danville President John C. Young, a Northerner by birth, wrote a pamphlet in 1836 advocating gradual emancipation, introduced a clause in the proposed state constitution of 1849–50 providing gradual emancipation, and twice emancipated groups of his own slaves. Perhaps because he was a slave-owner and a moderate who resisted the claims of extreme abolitionists, Young continued to preside, in spite of these deviations, over a successful institution, which was prospering at the time of his death in 1857. The more radical James G. Birney and another abolitionist professor, however, were dropped from the same institution.[118] Another Northern-born president, Howard Malcolm of Georgetown College in Kentucky, felt compelled to resign by the criticism aroused by his voting for an emancipation candidate to a constitutional convention.[119] In Tennessee a slave-owning professor, Nathan Greene of Cumberland University, managed as late as 1858 to express an old-fashioned Jeffersonian opposition to slavery without calling for immediate abolition. A professor of law with a distinguished career as a jurist, he was a widely respected figure, and was not removed from his post despite attacks in the press.[120]

[116] Rammelkamp, *Illinois College,* Chap. V; see the same author's "Illinois College and the Anti-Slavery Movement," *Transactions of the Illinois State Historical Society for the Year 1908* (Springfield, Ill., 1909), pp. 192–203.

[117] Rammelkamp, "Illinois College and the Anti-Slavery Movement," p. 202. Cf. J. M. Sturtevant, *An Autobiography* (New York, 1896), Chap. XV.

[118] Clement Eaton, *Freedom of Thought in the Old South* (Durham, N.C., 1940), p. 201; article on John Clarke Young in the *Dictionary of American Biography.*

[119] Eaton, *Freedom of Thought in the Old South,* p. 202. [120] *Ibid.,* p. 207.

Up to about 1830 it was still possible to criticize the slave system in the South. The inheritance of the Jeffersonian generation, which had thought of slavery as an evil that must in good time somehow be eliminated, was still faintly alive, although the cotton empire had already reached such dimensions as to make it clear to a realistic observer that such an immense vested interest could not be unseated without social upheaval. During the 1830s, with the growth of the abolition movement and the increasing defensive commitment of the cotton-growing South to slavery, the mind of the South rapidly closed. The entire intellectual energies of the section, so far as public matters were concerned, were given to the moral justification of slavery and its defense in the political arena. Intellectual and spiritual considerations that interfered with this defense had somehow to be shoved out of view. Intolerance and repression with widespread ramifications in almost every area of thought developed on the base of the proslavery argument.[121] It was the tragedy of the South that while the blacks were enslaved by the whites, the whites were enslaved by slavery.

Such little glimmers of latitude in opinion as might be found were no more than tiny sparks glowing through the general darkness that descended upon the intellectual life of the South after 1835. As one of the University of Virginia professors wrote in a pamphlet published anonymously in Boston in 1857, "a funeral pall" had been drawn over rational discussion of the issue, anyone who held critical views, once openly expressed, now whispered them in confidence, and "No person can safely reside in the South who is suspected of liberal views on the subject of slavery." [122]

The history of Francis Lieber's residence at South Carolina College, the most liberal institution in the deeper South, offers a case in point. He had not been by any means a militant abolitionist, but even his theoretical repugnance to human bondage had to be kept under wraps to make possible his two decades in South Carolina. Lieber found himself in a dilemma: because he longed to get out of the Carolina milieu, which he found thoroughly uncongenial on several grounds, he had to avoid ap-

---

[121] On the fate of freedom in the old South see *ibid.,* esp. Chap. VIII, "Academic Freedom below the Potomac." An illuminating commentary on the Southern experience is that of W. J. Cash, *The Mind of the South* (New York, 1941); see also Virginius Dabney, *Liberalism in the South* (Chapel Hill, N.C., 1932), and Howard Beale, *History of Freedom of Teaching,* Chap. V.

[122] Eaton, *Freedom of Thought in the Old South,* p. 206.

pearing to some of his Northern friends as an apologist for slavery; but in Carolina his silence on the subject at a time when Southern academic men were expected to be outspoken on behalf of slavery, was taken as a sign of secret abolitionist sentiments. So the eminent Professor Lieber, who wrote big encyclopedic books on political ethics and civil liberty, remained uneasily silent about the great problem of political ethics in his own time. Even his nationalism was unpopular in the particularist environment of South Carolina, and his religious sentiments also had to be kept quiet. He was driven to emphasizing perhaps far more than he otherwise would have done the central point of agreement between his own and the Carolina philosophy—his belief in free trade. Essentially an opportunist,[123] aspiring to the presidency of the college, to which his scholarly eminence gave him a strong claim, he tempered his life and work to the prevailing winds, but when his chance finally came in 1855 he was defeated in favor of a mediocre Presbyterian professor of mathematics. Lieber resigned in anger, and although there was great protest among his friends and admirers, the trustees did not ask him to reconsider his action. He left, jobless, for New York, where in 1857 he accepted a more satisfactory professorship at Columbia College.[124]

During the 1850s the attempt to insulate the mind of the South quickened, Northern textbooks were on occasion proscribed, and the president of a Southern university might easily find himself under intense criticism for appointing a Northerner to a professorship. Chancellor F. A. P. Barnard of the University of Mississippi, a Northerner by birth who had spent more than twenty years laboring in the vineyards of Southern higher education, found himself unable to keep in step with Southern mores in 1859–60, when he accepted the testimony of a Negro slave girl who had charged assault against a student. Such testimony was not accepted in any Southern court, and for voting for the student's suspension, Barnard became vulnerable to the charge, originating in the faculty itself, that he was unsound on the slavery question. A slaveholder himself, without sympathy with any shade of antislavery sentiment, Barnard was investigated thoroughly by the Board of Trustees, who in the end pronounced their

[123] See, however, the eloquent and prophetic open letters that he planned to address to Calhoun but evidently never published. See *The Life and Letters of Francis Lieber,* Thomas Sergeant Perry, ed. (Boston, 1882), pp. 228–37, for selections, and the comments of Freidel, *Francis Lieber,* pp. 238–42.

[124] For Lieber's position at South Carolina see Freidel, *Francis Lieber,* esp. Chaps. VII, X, XI, XII, and Hollis, *South Carolina College,* Chap. X.

confidence in his ability, integrity, and fitness for his position "increased rather than diminished." [125]

Probably the most celebrated academic-freedom case arising out of the slavery issue was that of Professor Benjamin Sherwood Hedrick at the University of North Carolina. The prevailing level of Southern responses in the mid-fifties is illustrated by this case. Hedrick was a native of the state and had been educated at the university; but he came from a social class that commonly had reservations about slavery as the base of the aristocracy, and he had spent some time at Harvard. Following tradition, the young professor of chemistry had been a Democrat, but in 1856, when the Republican party first offered a national ticket, rumors got about that he favored it. The *North Carolina Standard,* a local Democratic paper of much influence, declared that the nascent Republican party was a subversive organization, "incompatible with our honor and safety as a people." [126] An outcry was directed against Hedrick, to which his only answer was a statement of his Jeffersonian reasons for opposing the extension of slavery and his support of Fremont, the Republican candidate. He denied that his students would be subjected to free-soil indoctrination. His candid statement of his ideas, however, aggravated the outcry against him. The faculty repudiated his views, the students burned him in effigy, and the press throughout the state demanded his resignation. Refusing to resign, he was soon dismissed by the trustees. The sole member of the faculty who had supported him, the subsequently famous scholar Henry Harrisse, also became unpopular among the faculty and left not long after because of disciplinary controversies.[127] The supreme irony in the Hedrick case was that there was no Fremont ticket in North Carolina, and the professor's support of him was purely a matter of sentiment.

No doubt there were very few native Southerners in academic posts in 1856 who would have cared to challenge the South's peculiar institution

---

[125] Fulton, *F. A. P. Barnard,* pp. 246–51.

[126] James G. de Roulhac Hamilton, "Benjamin Sherwood Hedrick," *James B. Sprunt Historical Publications,* Vol. X, No. 1 (1910), p. 8. This work provides a documentary history of the case.

[127] On Harrisse see Henry Vignaud, *Henry Harrisse* (Paris, 1912). "You may eliminate all suspicious men from your institutions of learning," Harrisse proclaimed at this time, ". . . . but as long as people study, and read, and think among you, the absurdity of your system will be discovered and there will always be found some courageous intelligence to protest against your hateful tyranny. Close your schools, suppress learning and thought, you have nothing else to do in order to be faithful to your principles, and it is the only means which remains to you of continuing the struggle with some chances of success." Eaton, *Freedom of Thought in the Old South,* p. 205.

or the mores connected with it. They would have sworn that to be unable with impunity to espouse "lunatic" notions like Hedrick's was no real deprivation of liberty.[128] They had, in short, subjective freedom on this issue. But there is no condition more dangerous to a community than subjective freedom of this kind without objective freedom. By the 1850s the South had lost its ability to take realistic stock of social issues. While the absence of freedom in its halls of learning was only one of the symptoms of this loss, it was a token of a severe general intellectual paralysis. The cost to the South, to the nation at large, from the incapacity of Southern leadership to take a more liberal and rational view of the immense problems arising out of slavery and the sectional conflict, was tremendous. The history of the ante-bellum South is a cogent illustration of the principle that the maintenance of intellectual freedom is not of concern to the intellectual classes alone, but is of central importance to all members of the community.

In the North the situation was better but far from ideal. Northern society was too pluralistic to be unified around one ideal and one code of thought on the slavery question. In many Northern institutions a philosophical exploration of the moral aspects of slavery appears to have been allowed so long as it did not lead to agitation. Northerners distinguished sharply between those who condemned slavery abstractly on moral grounds or proposed gradual or ultimate emancipation, and the "immediatist" abolitionists of the more radical school who engaged in politics outside the classroom. The latter were on occasion silenced,[129] although the tendency seems to have been toward a larger measure of freedom during the 1840s and after, when antislavery sentiment grew in strength, gained a modest amount of support from the respectable classes, and proved itself to be a political force to reckon with. Although a student abolitionist society was suppressed by the faculty of Amherst in the early 1830s, such organizations generally survived without difficulty in the colleges of the Northeast.[130] In the Northwest, where the streams of New

[128] Cf. the *Raleigh Register:* ". . . the Professor evinced more zeal than judgment on the subject, and . . . the Lunatic Asylum might become a fit receptacle for all such characters, if, upon examination, they should be found to be monomaniacs on the subject of the Presidency." Hamilton, "Benjamin Sherwood Hedrick," p. 34.

[129] For instance, a professor was discharged from the University of Michigan because he endorsed the "higher law" doctrine. Shaw, *The University of Michigan,* pp. 41–42; University of Michigan, *Regents Proceedings, 1837–1864,* p. 502.

[130] A brief general account of Northern college controversies may be found in Russel B. Nye, *Fettered Freedom: Civil Liberties and the Slavery Controversy, 1830–1860* (East Lansing, Mich., 1949), pp. 85–93.

England and Southern culture mingled, there were sharper controversies.[131] On those campuses where trustees as well as faculty members were of some variety of abolitionist persuasion, colleges could survive community pressures and a large measure of freedom of utterance and action was protected, although the preference of most colleges was for complete silence on the subject. Such institutions as Illinois College, Franklin College and Oberlin College in Ohio, and New York College were open centers of abolitionism. In a few cases, discriminations were actually practiced against men who were anti-abolitionist. At Franklin College President Joseph Smith lost his post because he was not an abolitionist, and Judge Edward Greely Loring was dismissed from a lectureship in Harvard Law School because in his capacity as a federal judge he had enforced the fugitive slave law in a famous case. In the midst of the tensions of the Civil War, President Nathan Lord of Dartmouth, who had long been an ardent and crusty defender of slavery as a divine institution, was driven to resign because, as the local Congregationalists put it, widespread criticism had aroused "a popular prejudice against [the college] arising from the publication and use of some of his peculiar views touching public affairs." [132]

In sum, while a number of Northern colleges were in a sense "aboli-

---

[131] For such controversies, in addition to the works cited by Nye and Beale, see Robert S. Fletcher, *A History of Oberlin College* (Oberlin, Ohio, 1943), Vol. I; Wilbur Greeley Burroughs, "Oberlin's Part in the Slavery Conflict," *Ohio Archeological and Historical Society Publications,* XX (1911), 269–334; Frederick Clayton Waite, *Western Reserve University: The Hudson Era* (Cleveland, 1943), pp. 94–103; Sydney Strong, "The Exodus of Students from Lane Seminary to Oberlin in 1834," *Papers of the Ohio Church History Society,* IV (1893), 1–16; James H. Rodabaugh, "Miami University, Calvinism, and the Anti-Slavery Movement," *Ohio State Archeological and Historical Quarterly,* XLVIII (January, 1939), 66–73; Charles H. Rammelkamp, "The Reverberations of the Slavery Conflict in a Pioneer College," *Mississippi Valley Historical Review,* XIV (March, 1928), 447–61; Shaw, *The University of Michigan,* pp. 41–42; University of Michigan, *Regents Proceedings, 1837–1864,* p. 502.

[132] Leon B. Richardson, *A History of Dartmouth College* (Hanover, N.H., 1932), II, 510, see also pp. 511–12. Although the trustees of Dartmouth had neglected to act upon the suggestion that Lord be removed, they had in effect censured him by dissociating themselves and the faculty from his views. He abandoned his office without hesitation, but not without a vigorous protest against the right of the trustees "to impose any religious, ethical or political test upon any member of their own body or any member of the College Faculty, beyond what is recognized by the Charter of the Institution or express Statutes or stipulations conformed to that instrument. . . . For my opinions and my expressions of opinion on such subjects [as Biblical ethics] I hold myself responsible only to God, and the constitutional tribunals of my country, inasmuch as they are not touched by the Charter of the College or any express Statutes or stipulations."

tionist colleges" and thus contributed much to the moral agitation over slavery, the academic culture of the Northern states did not make a striking contribution to a rational discussion and sober exchange of views on the possible solutions of the slavery question. In part this was a product of their traditional curricular practices and their neglect of advanced sociological inquiry. But in greater part it must be attributed to the absence of sufficient freedom and detachment. The Northern colleges were on the whole much freer than those of the South so far as this issue is concerned. But for the most part Northern academic freedom on the slavery issue seems not to have gone much beyond the possibility that a professor might discuss the moral question of slavery in an abstract way; or that a determined board of trustees and faculty could sustain an abolitionist school in a friendly, or at times even an unfriendly, social atmosphere. No doubt it was better to live in a society with both abolitionist and nonabolitionist colleges than in one in which only anti-abolitionist colleges were possible, and in this sense the North had the advantage. But to have institutions dedicated not merely to ideological and moral agitation but to research, discussion, and inquiry, in which faculty members were free to follow their minds to such ends as the search for truth would take them—to have, in short, institutions capable of making some contribution to the analysis and solution of the issues—this was a state of academic development that not even the North was able to achieve.

This is not to say that academic freedom on the slavery issue would in itself have educated a generation of leaders capable of avoiding secession and war, but simply that the state of the colleges was symptomatic of a more general state of mind that ultimately led to disaster. The suppression of academic discussion was a token of a more general and more important suppression of thought and criticism that in the end took the entire subject out of the sphere of discussion and into the realm of force. The breakup of the American union and the resort to war is perhaps the best instance in our history of the principle that societies that imagine themselves unable to meet the costs of free discussion are likely to be presented with a much more exorbitant bill.

THE IDEA OF ACADEMIC FREEDOM

The modern idea of academic freedom has been profoundly affected by the professional character of the scholar, by the research function and scientific conceptions of the search for truth, and by the manifold services, aside from teaching students, that are rendered to the community by the great university. These things were largely absent from the American colleges of the pre-Civil War era. The academic man was only beginning to be really professional. The university as it exists today, or as it then existed in Germany, had not yet appeared except in a very few places, and even in those on a very small scale. The intellectual life of the colleges was not profoundly affected by the sciences until the Darwinian era. And finally, the organic relation between university and community that so often gives the modern educator a talking point in appealing for funds or defending free inquiry was only vaguely foreshadowed by the time of the Civil War, for the early colleges had no more than a modest relation to the professional life of the country and hardly any relation at all to its science, technology, business, or agriculture.

This does not mean that an ideal of academic freedom was altogether lacking among educators and laymen of the ante-bellum period, or that there were no widely accepted sanctions that could be invoked. Indeed, the first major history of an American university, Josiah Quincy's history of Harvard, published in 1840, closed with an eloquent appeal for educational freedom.[133] The conceptions of religious toleration and religious liberty which had been so vigorously fought for during the seventeenth century and so widely accepted during the age of the Enlightenment, although weakened as a consequence of the Protestant Counter Reformation, were still ideals widely accepted in America. The English tradition of civil liberty, quickened in America by the Revolution and embodied in the Bill of Rights, was also a factor relevant in a broad way to academic life. The constitutions of the states, as well as the charters of the colleges, bore testimony to this dual inheritance of religious and civil freedom.

Of course neither civil liberty nor religious liberty is identical with academic freedom. Both of these are more inclusive rights than academic freedom, for they affect the lives of all citizens directly; academic freedom is an immediate concern chiefly of the teacher in his professional capacity. However, both of these more inclusive rights are at points broadly analogous to academic freedom, and together they pro-

[133] Quincy, *History of Harvard,* II, 444–46. See also Quincy's *Speech . . . before the Board of Overseers . . . February 6, 1845* (Boston, 1845). For a stirring appeal for intellectual freedom against "ecclesiastical prescription," see Henry P. Tappan, *University Education* (New York, 1851), pp. 36–43.

vided the historical matrix of the concept of academic liberties. Long before college presidents and professors used the phrase "academic freedom" they were invoking the spirit of tolerance, the right of conscience, freedom of speech or the press, the clauses in college charters against religious discrimination.

For the most part, the concept of academic freedom as it is usually expressed today had not received a clear formulation in the ante-bellum period. The usual strategy for the college president or professor who was subject to pressure because of his acknowledged opinions was to appeal to sanctions that had received their clearest expression in the fields of religion or politics. Most commonly it was religion. In fact academic freedom first appeared in the guise of religious liberty for professors. There was a rough analogy between the interdenominational college and the political state in which official religion had been disestablished, just as there was between the more easy-going denominational colleges and the state which had a religious establishment but practiced toleration. So long as most colleges had a denominational affiliation, it was all but impossible for any educator to assert with success his *right* to be judged on his competence alone without regard to his religious opinions; but he might manage to persuade many men that it would be *expedient* not to stand too firmly on doctrinal grounds. Most often this expedience consisted in the political or economic necessity to conciliate opposing sects; occasionally it involved the welfare of the educational institution. Where, however, an institution was to be formally free of denominational commitments, as with the state universities, a formidable case might be made on the grounds of constitutional rights alone. And where trustees were deeply concerned to develop an institution of real university stature, the consideration of institutional welfare alone could become an asset to emergent academic freedom. Where men of great talents were urgently wanted, their religious convictions would be overlooked.

The stage to which the idea of academic freedom had developed in the ante-bellum period may be analyzed by reference to two celebrated cases, the Cooper case at the College of South Carolina and the Gibbs case at Columbia. In the first of these, the most articulate and advanced rationale for academic freedom to be expressed by any American in that period was formulated by a college president in the face of community pressure and was sustained by the trustees. In the second, the victim himself was altogether silent; but the relationship of religious freedom to university development was given mature and impressive consideration by minority members of the Board of Trustees, whose views were destined, in the not too distant future, to become the predominant ones.

South Carolina College, at the time Thomas Cooper took over its presidency in 1820, was one of the best colleges in the United States. Cooper himself was one of the most distinguished men in American academic life.[134] Born in England in 1759 and educated at University College, Oxford, Cooper had come in 1794 to the United States, where he practiced law and medicine and engaged in polemics on behalf of the emerging Jeffersonian party. In many ways his life had been dedicated to the principle of freedom of discussion,[135] and he went to South Carolina with the history and temperament of an inveterate controversialist. He had been ineligible to take a degree at Oxford because of his unwillingness to sign the Thirty-nine Articles. He had left England because he felt that the reaction that followed the French Revolution was disastrous for freedom of expression, and had turned away from France itself because he was disgusted with the Revolutionary Terror. He thus came to America, which he considered a haven of freedom, as a self-exiled refugee. In 1800 he had been convicted in a celebrated case for violation of the Sedition Law—the result of his attacks on the Federalists—for which he had been fined and sentenced to six months in prison. Afterwards he served for seven years as a state judge in Pennsylvania, an office which came to him as a reward for his services to Republicanism and from which he was removed on charges of arbitrary conduct. Tired of politics, and alienated from the popular democracy to which he had long been devoted, Cooper turned to teaching and taught briefly at both Dickinson College and the University of Pennsylvania. Through Jefferson's friendship and patronage he had been elected to the faculty of the University of Virginia, but the Presbyterians made it impossible for him to occupy the position, and he went instead to South Carolina. Cooper had so often been at the center of some controversy in which freedom of expression was central that his choice as a professor, and im-

---

[134] For Cooper's life and relations with South Carolina College see Dumas Malone, *The Public Life of Thomas Cooper* (New Haven, 1926), and Hollis, *South Carolina College,* Chaps. V and VI.

[135] See for instance his essay, "The Right of Free Discussion," appended to the second and third editions of his *Lectures on the Elements of Political Economy* (Columbia, S.C., 1829 and London, 1831).

mediately afterward as president, was testimony to the spirit of liberalism in which the college at Columbia was then conducted.

In philosophy Cooper was a materialist, in religion a Deist, in church politics a militant anticleric, in civil politics a conservative and a patriotic South Carolina separatist. He defended slavery, taught a laissez-faire political economy that accorded with the interests of the South Carolina planters, espoused nullification in the famous constitutional controversy, and in general made himself so congenial to the ruling class of the state, which cared more about cotton than it did about the Trinity, that his religious views were long tolerated. Given a free hand by friendly trustees, he served the college well. "He enriched the curriculum, raised the entrance requirements and the academic standards, retained a competent faculty, handled disciplinary problems adequately, and enjoyed the continued financial support of the legislature." [136]

As a consequence of his outspoken opposition to Calvinism and his sharp attacks on the Presbyterian clergy, Cooper was under criticism from the beginning of his administration. As early as 1822 he triumphantly survived an investigation of the college. By 1830–31, however, the president, now past seventy, was more vulnerable than in his earlier years. To his clerical enemies were now added the forces of the South Carolina unionists, who resented his support of nullification. He had recently published two anonymous pamphlets, one of which attacked the principle of a hired clergy and the other the essential doctrines of Calvinism. In 1831 he published his translation of François J. V. Broussais' book on insanity, De l'Irritation et de la folie (1828), in which Cooper proclaimed his confidence in the triumph of materialism and even asserted that materialism was the doctrine of Christ and His apostles. The new provocations precipitated a pamphlet war which ended in one of the most important academic freedom cases of the period. The details of this case, which has been more than once carefully studied and retold, need not detain us here, but Cooper's self-defense deserves special attention as the most elaborate justification of academic freedom in the ante-bellum period.

The pamphlet war led to a movement in the legislature to unseat Cooper on the grounds that he had assailed the religious views of a large portion of the people and thus damaged the college, that he had interfered with the religious opinions of the students, taught them doctrines

---

[136] Hollis, *South Carolina College*, p. 97.

offensive to parents and guardians, and had sneered at the observance of the Sabbath, at public prayers, and at certain religious sects. A few of these charges, especially those bearing on his teaching, Cooper denied, but his essential argument was that the charges, being based upon his religious views, dealt with matters of which the legislature could not constitutionally take cognizance. Thus the greater part of Cooper's argument was a legal one. His chief sanction was a provision of the state constitution guaranteeing "the freedom of the press, and the freedom of religious belief and profession without discrimination or preference." [137]

Considerably more interesting to the modern student of academic freedom than Cooper's strictly legal argument are some of his broader historical observations linking academic freedom to religious freedom and freedom of the press, and some more specific observations bearing on the professional needs of the teacher. In the attempt to remove him Cooper thought he saw "a continuation of the warfare that has taken place from the very earliest period of letters to the present day." The friends of truth had always tried "to open wide the doors of free inquiry," knowing no other way to arrive at truth but through fair and free discussion, while there had always been civil and ecclesiastical rulers opposed to such freedom who had tried to curtail it by invoking positive law against heresy and sedition.[138] Cooper saw in the Constitution of the United States the first successful attempt to break down this coalition against freedom, and remarked that he had come here believing it a settled matter in the United States that "actions only and not opinions, were the proper objects of legal control." [139] Having had to wage one fight for freedom of the press against the Sedition Law, Cooper found himself now waging another against the power of the clergy. His opponents, he believed, wanted to interdict freedom of the press and discussion of all matters bearing on clerical interests, to es-

[137] *The Case of Thomas Cooper. . . . Submitted to the Legislature and the People of South Carolina, December 1831* (Columbia, S.C., 1831), p. 3. Elsewhere Cooper pointed out the inconsistency of withholding rights within the college that were supposed to prevail elsewhere in the state. "So, I may profess what I please in South-Carolina, but not in the South-Carolina College! Where is it laid down that the boundaries of South-Carolina do not include the College?" *Dr. Cooper's Defense before the Board of Trustees* (Columbia, S.C., 1832), p. 15. The logic of this argument is an excellent illustration of the influence of civil and religious freedom on the development of academic freedom.

[138] *The Case of Thomas Cooper*, Preface, pp. iii–iv.

[139] Cooper was mistaken on this point. The matter has not yet been settled.

tablish the right of the legislature to interfere in religious matters, to establish a religious test for the president of the college, and to broaden clerical influence in politics.[140] In truth neither the legislature nor the trustees, as its agents, had any right to inquire into the religious beliefs of any officers of the college. Not only did the constitution and their oaths forbid them, but the "interminable disputes and sectarian manouvrings" which such investigations would bring, not to speak of the hypocrisy that it would encourage among candidates for college offices, "ought to restrain them for attempting to do so." [141]

But, it had been argued, the unpopularity of the president's opinions had been doing harm to the college. What if they be so unpopular that many people would refuse to send their sons? To this Cooper gave an answer that went far beyond the usual legal considerations and anticipated in many ways modern sanctions for academic freedom. In part his case was purely factual: he was able to show that despite unfavorable economic conditions the reputation of the college had risen, and attendance had gone up.[142] But he also countered the charge by reference to other principles whose validity was borne out by the history of many denominational colleges and state institutions. The college was not a theological seminary. "Students are sent here to acquire useful knowledge, not sectarian theology." No religious denomination of students could be excluded. If a member of some particular sect were to be president, the prejudices of the other denominations might as easily be aroused against him as against a man committed to no denomination. If prejudice were rampant enough, it could thus harm the college under any president. In fact the good repute of the president as a scholar was more valuable to the development of the institution than any matters bearing on his opinions.[143]

Probably the most strikingly modern-sounding phrases uttered by Cooper came in connection with his attempt to say what might and might not reasonably be required by the trustees (and by implication the legislature) of the teacher. They ought not, he said, go beyond

requiring that he shall treat those questions only that are connected with the subject of his lecture, and that he shall treat them fairly and impartially.

[140] *Ibid.*, pp. 2–3.   [141] *Ibid.*, p. 11.   [142] *Ibid.*, pp. 19–21.
[143] *Ibid.*, pp. 14–15. To allow college policies to be governed by those parents who would not send their sons to the institution because of the opinions of its president, Cooper argued, would be to sacrifice the college to some of the more ignorant men in the community. *Ibid.*, p. 16.

If doubts bearing on the subject are concealed and not discussed, the students will have reason to complain of injustice. The difficulties which a professor is forbidden to approach will remain on their minds, and they will depart unsatisfied with half knowledge and doubts unsolved. They have a right to expect from their professor no concealment, no shrinking from unpopular difficulties, but a full and honest investigation, without suppression or disguise.

Whatever temporary advantage may result from a timid suppression of truth, or a compliance with unreasonable dictation, it is of great consequence to the permanent reputation of this College that students shall come here with the expectation of being taught fully, impartially, and honestly, whatever they are required to learn: and that they should leave this College with the impression that they have actually been thus honestly taught: any impression that their teachers are directed or inclined to avoid difficulties, because they are unpopular, or to suppress or conceal doubts that must arise hereafter, or any timid manouvring in the mode of teaching, may serve the purpose of a narrow minded caution, but it is not fair; and therefore it does not become the reputation of this College or its professors.[144]

Here was an argument derived squarely from the internal necessities of the teaching profession itself, from the relation between teacher and student, and not from such formal externals as contracts, charters, or constitutions. While it formed but a small portion of Cooper's whole argument it represents a distinct advance in the concept of academic freedom.

Although Cooper denied many of the charges concerning his indoctrination of the students, he did acknowledge that in the teaching of geology he had refused to accept the book of Genesis, and here again he stood firmly on professional and intellectual grounds. The whole subject of Mosaic geology, he asserted, was "so intertwined with the present state of the science, and so absolutely necessary to be settled, that the consideration of it is unavoidable." To this any competent man would agree, he said. Benjamin Silliman, who disagreed with Cooper on the religious issues involved, had used the Mosaic account: were his ideas not to be examined? "The book of Genesis," said Cooper firmly, "was not composed to teach either Astronomy or Geology; nor has it been directed as a College text book for these sciences." [145] Here, where treat-

---

[144] *Ibid.,* p. 16.

[145] *Ibid.,* pp. 19, 40. The essential arguments delivered to the legislature were repeated in *Dr. Cooper's Defense before the Board of Trustees,* but occasional appeals to the nullifying sentiments of the trustees were added, as were references to other victims of persecution for opinion, including Aristides, Socrates, Jesus, Servetus, Galileo, Locke, Buffon, and others. See esp. pp. 3, 6, 7, 12–13.

ment of the subject seemed necessary in the light of the internal needs of science, he would indeed persist in raising questions bearing upon Scripture, putting professional and scientific considerations above expediency.

It is perhaps significant that the boldest and most advanced argument for academic freedom to be made in the United States during the pre-Civil War period should have been made by a man in his seventies. While Cooper was, seen from our vantage point, ahead of his times, from the standpoint of his contemporaries he was behind them. For Cooper was a figure out of the Enlightenment bringing eighteenth-century ideals of civil, religious, and intellectual liberty to the support of academic freedom in the age of the great retrogression. Cooper deserves to be remembered for the link he tried to forge between the ideals of the Enlightenment and those of the university era. But in his own day he was hardly successful. Although his trustees, commissioned by the legislature to investigate Cooper, did so with the result that he was vindicated and retained, the publicity given to his views by the case hurt the college so badly that he was forced to resign a few years later, along with his entire faculty. The charges of his clerical enemies could be met with argument, but to the drastic shrinkage in the student body that followed the case there was no answer.

If the Cooper case belonged to the old conflict between Enlightenment ideals and sectarianism, the Gibbs case, which occurred more than twenty years later, anticipated, despite its unfavorable outcome, the future victory of the university idea over sectarian limitations. Indeed the fact that Columbia, as a great university, eventually emerged from the somnolent day school for New York boys that it was at the time of Gibbs' nomination for a professorship is in good part attributable to the repercussions of the Gibbs controversy. The Gibbs case shows how well some trustees were aware, as others were soon to become, of the fatal implications of sectarian narrowness for university development. Where Dr. Cooper had battled over broad religious and ideological principles, the progressive wing of the Columbia trustees was more concerned with the practical considerations involved in making a university out of a college. In both cases sectarian bigotry was the enemy, but the arguments were different.

At the time of the Gibbs case, Columbia, then about to observe its centennial, was still a small, nonresidential college, catering annually to about 140 students, chiefly from New York City, and governed by a tradition-minded body of trustees referred to by the great diarist, George Templeton Strong, who had recently joined it, as "the Board of Incurables." [146] The case probably would never have occurred, and certainly would have been of slight importance, had it not arisen from the urgent desire of a small group of trustees, notable among them Samuel B. Ruggles, an alumnus of Yale, a New York lawyer, real estate investor, and man of affairs, to make the modest little college a real university, "a broad, comprehensive seat of learning, science, and art." [147] When Professor James Renwick's retirement from the professorship of Natural and Experimental Philosophy and Chemistry in 1853 gave the reformers an opportunity for an opening move, they nominated as Renwick's successor Wolcott Gibbs, who was then teaching at the Free Academy which later became the College of the City of New York. Gibbs was an outstanding chemist who had studied with Liebig at Giessen and with other great European chemists. He was known and recommended by the most distinguished scientists in the United States.[148] But Gibbs was also by family inheritance a Unitarian, and a fierce prejudice still existed in many quarters against members of that denomination. The Columbia Board of Trustees, which was predominantly Episcopalian and included six clergymen of three denominations, reflected this prejudice with greater zeal than did the New York community at large.[149] After much maneuvering and discussion, Gibbs was rejected by a narrow vote in favor of another, far less promising candidate, Richard McCulloh. Although the Columbia charter forbade religious tests for trustees or officers, and some anti-Gibbs trustees publicly denied that their votes against him were decided by his Unitarianism, the *in camera*

[146] *The Diary of George Templeton Strong,* Allan Nevins and Milton Halsey Thomas, eds. (New York, 1952), II, 37. This work is a major source on the case, esp., II, 136–76, and *passim.* See also the searching analysis by Milton Halsey Thomas, "The Gibbs Affair at Columbia in 1854," unpublished M.A. thesis (Columbia University, 1942), and Daniel G. Brinton Thompson, *Ruggles of New York* (New York, 1946), Chaps. V, VI, and X.

[147] Samuel Ruggles, *The Duty of Columbia College to the Community, and Its Right to Exclude Unitarians from Its Professorships of Physical Science. . . .* (New York, 1854), p. 17.

[148] See the letters from such men as John W. Draper, Benjamin Silliman, James D. Dana, Joseph Henry, Louis Agassiz, and others, in *Report of the Select Committee Appointed to Examine into the Affairs of Columbia College* (Albany, 1855), State of New York, Senate Document No. 67, pp. 103–25.

[149] For an analysis of the Board of Trustees see Thomas, "The Gibbs Affair," pp. 36–58.

proceedings of the meetings made it clear that his religion was the real cause of his rejection.[150]

The case became a matter of public controversy, commanding the interest not only of the alumni but the local press as well. All the secular papers except the New York *Herald* took Gibbs' side, while the alumni by an overwhelming vote resolved to condemn the "spirit which would make a particular religious belief a test of fitness for a Professorship of Physical Science" as intolerant, unjust, inconsistent with the charter and the public character of the institution, and highly injurious to its best interests.[151] The most outstanding document of the Gibbs case was a powerful pamphlet written by Ruggles and Strong and published under Ruggles' name, which argued the case for university reform and religious liberalism in terms which at a few points go beyond the conventional arguments of the period. Ruggles linked the bigotry of the anti-Gibbs trustees with the backward character of the college in a manner which shows how intimately connected in his own mind were his fight for Gibbs and his idea for the development of a metropolitan university. He argued that the trustees had a duty to the community to meet its largest educational needs, and that their failure to give New York a university was the outcome not of insufficient means, but of insufficient imagination. He compared Columbia with Göttingen—which had also been founded under King George II in another of his dominions, but which had grown to a great university during the hundred years Columbia had slept—and with Yale, which by maintaining and encouraging Day and Silliman, at an annual cost of no more than four thousand dollars, had put Columbia to shame.[152] Gibbs, Ruggles maintained, was neither an infidel nor a proselytizing Unitarian, but a highly competent scholar and teacher, whose religious views had never been intruded into his teaching at the Free Academy. He was the victim of the "composite intolerance" of the Episcopalians, Presbyterians, and Dutch Reformed members of the board who, unable to agree among themselves in matters of dogma, had nevertheless established a factitious standard of heresy simply to exclude Gibbs.[153] It had been widely argued by the

[150] See *The Diary of George Templeton Strong,* Vol. II, esp. pp. 146–47.
[151] Thomas, "The Gibbs Affair," p. 104.
[152] Ruggles, *The Duty of Columbia College to the Community,* pp. 11–13.
[153] Ruggles was himself an observing Episcopalian, as was his ally, Strong, who considered Gibbs' religious views nonsensical. The real passion of these men was not religious libertarianism, liberal though they were, but the development of a university.

opposition that since exclusion from an office is not a punishment, it was therefore not punishing a man for heresy to decide him unfit on religious grounds. "This common-place of intolerance," said Ruggles in a significant passage, "has long been abandoned. Our criminal law recognizes exclusion from office as one of the penalties of crime." And here, by such exclusion, although we no longer impose legal punishment for heresy "we do in fact punish, quite as severely—in another mode— by professional, civil, and social degradation." [154] In these remarks Ruggles pierced the obscurantism of formal reasoning to assert the realities of social life. He was concerned about the possibility that if Gibbs were formally branded as heretical he might be stigmatized everywhere and driven out of professional life, and after him a whole train of Unitarians who were eminent in science, letters, and politics.[155] (While this fear was not unreasonable, Ruggles did not reckon with the healthy pluralism of American society. Gibbs in fact went on to a distinguished career at Harvard as Dean of the Lawrence Scientific School, and in 1873 was awarded an LL.D. degree at Columbia by unanimous vote of the trustees.) [156] Like Cooper, Ruggles indicated that he placed the internal and professional demands of the teacher's position above sectarian interests when he declared that even if Columbia College were an organ of the Episcopal Church, pure and simple, it would still be the duty of the trustees to pick the best man of any faith as its professor of chemistry because the principles of chemistry were irrelevant to denominational theology.[157]

The immediate results of the Gibbs controversy were not of especial importance. The college lost the potential services of one of the country's outstanding scientists, to receive instead those of a vastly inferior scholar and a sadistic teacher.[158] Such bitter feelings were aroused among trustees and alumni that Columbia's centenary observations had to be set aside. An investigation by the state Senate was procured by the pro-Gibbs faction, but the committee of inquiry was forced to conclude

[154] Ibid., pp. 33–34.   [155] Ibid., pp. 37–39.

[156] Ironically, McCulloh, who was elected in his stead, resigned from Columbia in 1863 and took a commission in the Confederate army—an action that so enraged the same trustees who had appointed him that they denounced him as a traitor and ingrate, and voted his expulsion from the faculty.

[157] Ibid., pp. 34–35. Cf. Strong: "His duties will not carry him into contact with transcendental physics. And I cannot think that talking to boys about NO_3 and CHO_2 and Fer Cy Ka has any connection (for practical purposes) with theological truck. . . ." Diary, II, 141.

[158] On this point see Thomas, "The Gibbs Affair," p. 132.

that while individual trustees may have violated their trust, the corporation as a whole could not be found to have violated the antidiscriminatory terms of its charter.[159]

The long-run consequences of the affair were momentous for Columbia. As Ruggles' biographer remarks, it "acted as a powerful stimulus to the trustees," [160] and all through the next quarter of a century plans, discussions, and inquiries were afoot for university development. It is hardly an exaggeration to say that Columbia University arose out of the case. The progressive trustees and alumni were invigorated, and one may hazard the conjecture, in the light of the preponderance of pro-Gibbs sentiment in the community and among the alumni, that some of the more conservative trustees were sufficiently shamed to be thrown on the defensive. The reforming trustees now began to emphasize with more success what Jefferson had long ago understood when he proposed to acquire wholesale a faculty from one of the Scottish universities for the University of Virginia: that to develop a university one must begin by winning the battle for scholars of repute and meet their terms and needs, and that these include certain prerogatives and freedoms. "All that can be done in the first instance," suggested George Templeton Strong, when plans for expansion were under consideration in 1856, "is to employ professors of great repute and ability to teach, and to invite (if necessary to *hire*) students to learn: *confiding everything, at the outset, to the control of the teachers,* finding out, by degrees, what we want, and feeling our way towards a code of rules, step by step." [161] Strong's statement on the central importance of the professors is one of the most notable of the ante-bellum period:

It seems certain that we shall effect nothing lasting or important except by and through teachers of the first order and the highest repute. They are not merely necessary to the vigor of the Institution but conditions of its existence. Whether the experiment succeed or fail depends mainly on their presence or absence. With professors of respectable mediocrity or a little above it, a College will languish, but may subsist indefinitely. But a University cannot be planted and long sustained in life without professors of splendid name and

[159] *Report of the Select Committee* . . . , pp. 8–12.

[160] Thompson, *Ruggles of New York,* p. 90; cf. Thomas, "The Gibbs Affair," p. 140; note also Strong's remark, in a moment of discouragement: "Another Gibbs controversy must be got up, or the College will doze off for another hundred years . . ." *Diary,* II, 376.

[161] "Statement of George T. Strong, Esq.," in *Statements, Opinions, and Testimony Taken by the Committee of Inquiry Appointed by the Trustees of Columbia College* (New York, 1857), pp. 19–20. Italics added.

ability, especially in a community where such institutions are unknown and where general mediocrity of attainment and aspiration is the obstacle to be removed and the evil to be remedied. If they be obtained, the Academic system we establish for them, even if prematurely and unwisely settled, will do little harm. They must be diligently sought, and, like founders of Universities in all ages, we shall probably be obliged to seek them beyond (as well as within) the limits of our own country and language.[162]

In a statement like this, one sees intimations of the great university developments that lay not far in the future; and in the premium Strong placed on the able professor one sees a foreshadowing of those prerogatives that had to be given to the leaders of the teaching profession before great universities could be founded. Thus the soundest educational reformers of the period—those who proposed not to chop up or debase the existing curriculum so much as to supplement it by plans for systems of more advanced study—walked hand in hand with those who had a perception of the professor's need for dignity and freedom. The time was not far in the future when a college president could proclaim to the American community what the founders of the first European universities had understood from the beginning: "Professors are sometimes spoken of as working for the college. They are the college." [163]

[162] *Ibid.*, p. 20. For comparable statements on the need for professors of such caliber see Long, *Literary Pioneers*, p. 166; Sonne, *Liberal Kentucky*, p. 145; Morison, *Three Centuries of Harvard*, pp. 326–27.

[163] President Paul Ansel Chadbourne in his inaugural address at Williams College, 1873. Spring, *History of Williams College*, p. 234.

Part Two

THE AGE OF THE UNIVERSITY

by WALTER P. METZGER

VI: THE OLD REGIME AND THE EDUCATIONAL REVOLUTION

Between the years 1865 and 1890 a revolution in American higher education took place. Ideas that had been debated in pre-Civil War journals—the elective system, graduate instruction, scientific courses—became educational realities. New mansions of learning, more imposing than any the nation had seen, were built at Cornell, Johns Hopkins, Clark, Stanford, and Chicago; new towers were added to Harvard, Columbia, Yale, and Princeton, to Wisconsin, Michigan, and Illinois. Along with the establishment of new institutions and the renovation of old went the adoption of new academic goals. To criticize and augment as well as to disseminate the tradition-at-hand became an established function—a great departure for a system that had aimed primarily at cultural conservation. To serve the whole community in its vast variety of needs became a creditable aspiration—an important innovation for a system that had served mainly the limited needs of the learned professions. The institutional setting, the educational objective, and the meaning and status of academic freedom are, as we have seen, intimately connected. Inevitably, therefore, during this quarter-century, the problem of academic freedom was as drastically revised as its context.[1]

Every revolution is born in an old regime, and every old regime, while it clings to exalted ideals, is undermined by prosaic events. This was true of the university revolution and of the old regime from which it sprang, the denominational college. Founded by evangelical fervor, the denominational college allied Christian piety and humanistic study against the skeptical rationalism of the Enlightenment. A center of culture on crude frontiers, it endeavored to endow a haphazard society

---

[1] To point out that the connection between the institutional setting and the ideal of academic freedom has not been adequately studied for this period is to call attention once more to the vast untilled areas in the historiography of this subject. The work that comes closest to filling the gap is Howard K. Beale's *A History of Freedom of Teaching in American Schools* (New York, 1941).

with religious truths and values. Taking it all in all, the denominational institution was not by any means unsuccessful in these difficult undertakings. But like all other old regimes, the denominational college in the period between 1800 and 1860 faced two commonplace problems with which it could not cope—the problem of internal disorder and the problem of financial insolvency. In attempting to resolve these problems, it developed practices and devices that only weakened its authority and cohesion. The need to check constant student disorder led to the growth of faculty (as opposed to trustee) control over discipline and instruction. The effort to offset mounting deficits resulted in the organization of alumni into collegiate philanthropic associations. By a paradoxical turn that was not without parallel or precedent, the remedies proved harmful to the regime which they were intended to fortify. The first remedy, by diffusing responsibility, in time destroyed the college's unitary purpose. The other, by summoning secular support, in time weakened its religious aspirations. And neither completely solved the basic problems which were, in the last analysis, symptoms of the college's failure to answer the needs of society. The story of academic freedom under the old regime can be plotted in terms of these paramount ideals, these unresolvable problems, and these self-defeating remedies.

THE EDUCATIONAL IDEALS OF THE OLD REGIME

The American college in the first half of the nineteenth century was centered in tradition. It looked to antiquity for the tools of thought, to Christianity for the by-laws of living; it supplied furniture and discipline for the mind, but constrained intellectual adventure. Like most institutions anchored to tradition, the ante-bellum college [2] was also paternalistic and authoritarian. In honoring the past and depreciating the pres-

---

[2] We use "ante-bellum" to denote all the colleges in the period between 1800 and 1860; "denominational" to denote all except the state universities.

[3] Whatever concessions were made in the curricula to modern languages, modern sciences and modern history, disdain for the interests and achievements of the present was deeply characteristic of this philosophy. Noah Porter wrote: "We hold the opinion very earnestly that upon the retention and successful regulation of classical study more than upon any single feature of the college economy hangs the question for this country whether we shall continue as a people to respect and honor what is noble in the past or shall give ourselves up to the unsteady and often mistaken guidance of the unreflecting and uninstructed present." *The American Colleges and the American Public* (New Haven, 1870), p. 273.

ent,[3] it drew the doubtful conclusion that age best imparts its wisdom when youth surrenders its style. Students took prescribed courses and recited their lessons by rote; professors acted like schoolmasters, drillmasters, and prisonkeeps. The dreary assumptions of American pedagogy in this period were hardly touched by the romantic mood of transcendentalism, or by the democratic faith of Jacksonianism. Despite the triumph of the ideal of perfectibility in the outer world of affairs, the academy lived in the inexorable presence of Sin, which only mental exertion and piety were presumed to temper or expiate. "Man is born free and is everywhere in chains," and its gentler Emersonian equivalent, "Whoso would be a man, must be a nonconformist," were never the cardinal mottoes of these colleges. The theory of collegiate education was perfected by Yale and Princeton—Phoenicias of the educational world—and was disseminated in their academic colonies through their graduate sons. Whether one reads the *Yale Report* of 1828 or Noah Porter's *The American Colleges and the American Public* (published in 1870), one encounters a consistent spirit and argument: the preceptive importance of religion, the disciplinary advantage of the classics, and above all, the waywardness and immaturity of youth that called for precepts and discipline.[4]

This triad of assumptions—traditionalism as an educational goal, "stamping in" as a pedagogical method, the contumacy of youth as a major expectation—effectively stifled the desire for academic freedom in the ante-bellum colleges. First of all, the emphasis on traditional subject matter and mechanical drill discouraged comment from the professor's rostrum on the burning issues of the day. To this there was one exception: the course on moral philosophy, which had replaced moral theology as the science of conduct at the end of the eighteenth cen-

[4] "Original Papers in Relation to a Course of Liberal Education," *American Journal of Science and Arts,* XV (January, 1829), 297–351; Porter, *American Colleges,* p. 98 and *passim.* The former was establishing policy, the latter desperately defending it; hence the differences in overtone and emphasis. The first report was not so concerned about the fate of religion in the colleges, resting in the assurance that it was secure; Porter, writing after Darwin, was apprehensive.

There is a great body of literature on these two important educational papers. A concise statement and analysis covering the *Yale Report* from the progressive point of view can be found in R. Freeman Butts, *The College Charts Its Course: Historical Conceptions and Current Proposals* (New York, 1939), pp. 118–25. A point of view more sympathetic to conservatism may be found in the section on Noah Porter in George W. Pierson's history of Yale, *Yale College: An Educational History, 1871–1921* (New Haven, 1952), pp. 57 ff.

tury.[5] This course—and its later offshoots, constitutional history,[6] political philosophy,[7] and political economy [8]—dealt with some of the problems of active life, particularly when they were taught by the college president.[9] But moral philosophy was a dessert for seniors, to be taken only after the less appetizing studies of Greek verbs, syllogistic logic, and English grammar; and it was the ingenious or conscience-driven tutor who could insinuate living problems while drilling in the *Graeca Majora*. More than this, the college with rigid standards for student piety also had rigid conventions for professorial propriety. While the colleges were custodians of student morals, professors had to be exemplars of good behavior. As long as students lived under parental rules, professors had to dwell close to or in the colleges in order to be able to enforce them.[10] Despotism limits the despot: the other aspect of parental power is the burden of parental responsibility. Freedom, aca-

[5] L. L. Bernard and J. S. Bernard, "A Century of Progress in the Social Sciences," *Social Forces,* XI (May, 1933), 488–505.

[6] The publication of the various national and state constitutional documents fostered the development of this subject after 1825. Treatises on law and government gradually increased in number to accommodate the growing number of courses in constitutional law and constitutional history.

[7] The two outstanding works in the field of political philosophy were Francis Lieber's *Political Ethics* (1838) and Frederick Grimke's *Nature and Tendency in Free Institutions* (1848).

[8] Chairs in this subject were established at Columbia College in 1817 and soon afterward at the College of South Carolina, Dickinson College, and William and Mary. It was taught by such prominent men as John McVickar of Columbia College, Thomas Cooper of the College of South Carolina, Henry Vethake of Dickinson (later of the University of Pennsylvania), Thomas R. Dew of William and Mary, and George Tucker of the University of Virginia. Such issues as the tariff, money, currency, and banks were touched on.

[9] Gladys Bryson, "The Comparable Interests of the Old Moral Philosophy and the Modern Social Sciences," *Social Forces,* XI (October, 1932), 19–27; George P. Schmidt, *The Old Time College President* (New York, 1930), pp. 108–45.

[10] That the residential requirement rankled is seen in Edward Everett's unhappiness over his forced seclusion at Cambridge. After his sojourn in Germany, he dearly wished to stay in the more congenial and intellectually stimulating atmosphere of Boston and to go to Cambridge only for his classes. Ticknor, as a very special dispensation, had won that privilege. But in 1822 the Overseers of Harvard, voting on Everett's application, decided that "it would be highly detrimental to the interests of the University to depart from the ancient usage of requiring the constant residence of those professors, whose offices, from the nature of them, are essentially connected with the necessary studies of the undergraduates." Everett remained at Harvard, chafing at this restriction, until his election to Congress ended his connection with the college. Paul Revere Frothingham, *Edward Everett: Orator and Statesman* (Boston, 1925), pp. 72–75. Undoubtedly the majority of American professors would have considered Cambridge the epitome of sophistication compared with the isolated hamlets in which their own colleges were situated.

demic or otherwise, requires a private sphere where prescriptive codes do not apply, and the discipline of the ante-bellum college was the eternal foe of privacy.

The temper of this age was factious and zealous: public issues like those of Republicanism vs. Federalism, abolitionism vs. slavery, free trade vs. protectionism, were fraught with an almost religious emotion. It is thus the more remarkable that academic cases in this period were rarely joined over questions of intramural utterance. When, for example, Professor Benjamin Hedrick of North Carolina was dismissed in 1856 for supporting Fremont, he was not accused of having aired his views in class; [11] Francis Bowen, rejected by the Harvard Board of Overseers, presumably for articles favoring the compromise of 1850 and opposing Magyar independence, was not charged with the crime of trying to convince his students.[12] To be sure, the colloquies of the classroom are almost as scantily recorded as the dialogue of the confessional, whereas a speech or published essay is in the public ear or eye. Nevertheless, one gets the impression that the teacher *qua* teacher was far less willing to engage in controversy than the teacher *qua* citizen, and that this was in part related to the colleges' educational norms. The contentious Thomas Cooper of South Carolina College, a firebrand of anticlericalism, repeatedly swore that he had not in any way tried to influence the religious opinions of his students.[13] President Robert Hamilton Bishop of Miami University, while fighting within the councils of the Presbyterian church against the institution of slavery, tolerated but would not join the antislavery society on campus.[14] The Amherst faculty, opposed to abolition but favoring the settlement of Negroes in Africa, felt it "inexpedient" to allow students to organize either abolitionist or colonization societies.[15] Francis Lieber, privately a staunch opponent of slavery,

[11] Kemp P. Battle, *History of the University of North Carolina, 1789–1909* (2 vols.; Raleigh, 1912), I, 654–59. See also Clement Eaton, *Freedom of Thought in the Old South* (New York, 1951), p. 203.

[12] Samuel Eliot Morison, "Francis Bowen, An Early Test of Academic Freedom in Massachusetts," *Proceedings of the Massachusetts Historical Society,* LXVI (February, 1936), 507–11.

[13] Dumas Malone, *The Public Life of Thomas Cooper, 1783–1839* (New Haven, 1926), p. 338.

[14] James H. Rodabaugh, "Miami University, Calvinism and the Anti-Slavery Movement," *Ohio State Archaeological and Historical Quarterly,* XLVIII (1939), 66–73.

[15] Claude M. Fuess, *Amherst, the Story of a New England College* (Boston, 1935), pp. 110–11.

granted in a letter to Calhoun that he had no right "to use my chair for propagandism of specific and personal views." [16]

How closely connected were professorial and student freedoms was demonstrated by one academic-freedom case in this period. In 1833 an antislavery society was formed at Lane Theological Seminary in Cincinnati by students and a number of the faculty. The board of trustees, composed of solid businessmen and some clergymen, banned this society, stating that "education must be completed before the young are fitted to engage in the collisions of active life." This was a standard reaction of trustees to student initiative in the realm of ideas: what made the statement inappropriate, however, was the fact that the "young" in this case happened to be rather old—thirty of these seminarians were over the age of twenty-six. Nor were they of mood or mind to accept the stricture of the trustees. "Free discussion, being a duty," they announced, "is consequently a right, and as such, is inherent and inalienable. It is *our* right. It *was* before we entered Lane Seminary; privileges we might and did relinquish; advantages we might and did receive. But this *right* the institution 'could neither give nor take away.' " After firing this broadside, the students removed in a body to Oberlin, where they won the concession that their faculty (which included a professor who had been dismissed from Lane) would supervise them without interference from the trustees.[17] Unfortunately, this case was altogether atypical. Elsewhere students were more likely to rebel against the food served in Commons than against the repression of freedom of speech. A mass boycott of this kind, reminiscent of the medieval universities, was never to be repeated. And the moral that it taught—that *Lehrfreiheit* and *Lernfreiheit* were closely related—was not one that the parent-professors of the college would quickly learn or wish to apply.

In short, the current assumptions of educational psychology stymied free discussion in the classroom and discouraged bold intellectual excursions. On the one hand, since the college student was regarded as morally deficient or immature, the college teacher had to render a firm decision on all the normative issues he raised. The weight of this responsi-

[16] Joseph Dorfman and Rexford G. Tugwell, "Francis Lieber: German Scholar in America," *Columbia University Quarterly*, XXX (1938), 169. Also, Frank Freidel, *Francis Lieber: Nineteenth Century Liberal* (Baton Rouge, 1947), pp. 115–43.

[17] Robert S. Fletcher, *A History of Oberlin College* (Oberlin, Ohio, 1943), I, 150–78.

bility kept the instructor from venturing very far from received and safe opinions. On the other hand, the college student was also regarded as intellectually innocent and impressionable—an assumption that had a close if paradoxical affinity to the supposition that he was totally depraved. Great care had to be taken lest, by some irreverent remark, he be misguided by his teachers and led astray. The college in America could not be a market place of ideas so long as it regarded its students as both gullible and perverse. For the conclusion is inescapable: if students are both iron and clay, it is wasteful or it is rash to treat them to controversy.

SCIENCE UNDER THE OLD REGIME

We have touched upon the demand for academic freedom in the area of classroom instruction; we have now to see that the demand for academic freedom was just as slight in the area of research. In this area, however, another set of inhibitions operated, as can be seen when we consider the status of scientific studies in the ante-bellum colleges.

It has already been pointed out that the curriculum of the American colleges had never been closed against the sciences, despite the dominance of classical subjects and the ruling interest in religion.[18] That religion and science could coexist within Protestantism had been demonstrated as early as 1642, when President Dunster of Harvard made provision for a course in astronomy, and it was reaffirmed by the increasingly large place assumed by physics, chemistry, and geography in the Harvard curriculum of the next century and a half.[19] It is true that the intense scientific interests of the Enlightenment, as reflected in the curricula of the University of Pennsylvania and King's College, were not sustained in the era of religious reaction. Yet even in the early nineteenth century, mineralogy, chemistry, geology, botany, and zoology made their way into many courses of study; [20] "natural philosophy" and "natural history" were taught in the most orthodox centers; [21] Amherst and Union pioneered in offering

---

[18] See Chap. IV.

[19] Theodore Hornberger, *Scientific Thought in the American Colleges, 1638–1800* (Austin, Texas, 1945).

[20] Louis Franklin Snow, *The College Curriculum in the United States* (New York, 1907).

[21] For an example of the potpourri of subjects covered in the typical natural philosophy course, see James Renwick's text, *Outlines of Natural Philosophy* (New York, 1826). At Columbia Renwick taught mechanics, ballistics, hydrostatics, climatology, meteorology, electricity, optics, and astronomy—all in a half-year

parallel courses in science and classics; [22] Timothy Dwight, champion of Christianity against all that smacked of heresy, put Benjamin Silliman, Sr., in the chair of chemistry at Yale.[23] After 1840, scientific courses began to be differentiated and considerable specialization was allowed. By no means, then, was the college curriculum of the early nineteenth century as archaic and as rigid as later reformers thought it had been, nor was science as under-represented as its votaries usually claimed.

But the significant fact is that, with exceptions made for a few unusual institutions and men, the addition of scientific studies to the curriculum did not bring about a free flowering of scientific research. Instruction was didactic and catechetical, or else demonstrations were used merely to cause wonder or to amuse.[24] Scientific speculation was diverted either to natural theology, where the conceptual framework was given, or to survey, classification, and invention, where the conceptual content was slight. Science, in short, was integrated into the disciplinary and conservational goals of the college, and if there was gain in knowledge organized and seen whole, there was no gain in intellectual friction.

Three factors blighted the courage and imagination of college science in the ante-bellum period. First, and least important, was the emphasis on utility and practicality which was general at that time. In the eighteenth century the "promotion of useful knowledge" had not been by any means

---

sequence. For the subjects covered in natural history, see W. and M. Smallwood's discussion of William Dandridge Peck's "Lectures on Natural History" in *Natural History and the American Mind* (New York, 1941), pp. 302 ff. Peck lectured on botany, ornithology, ichthyology, and entomology at Harvard.

[22] George P. Schmidt, "Intellectual Crosscurrents in American Colleges," *American Historical Review*, XLII (October, 1936), 46–67. Fuess, *Amherst*, p. 99.

[23] Charles E. Cuningham, *Timothy Dwight, 1752–1817* (New York, 1942), pp. 198 ff.

[24] This is exemplified by the retarded development of laboratory techniques in teaching and research. Russell H. Chittenden summarizes the state of experimentalism in the colleges in the year 1845: "The study of the physical and natural sciences in the United States, at this date, was exceedingly simple and very elementary in character. It was confined to undergraduates, for graduate students were practically unknown at that period, and was limited to textbook work, supplemented by lectures and some demonstrations. Laboratories, as we know them today, did not exist and consequently there were no opportunities for the pursuit of scientific studies by the method which alone will give satisfactory results. . . . Indeed it is probably not far from the truth to state that some, and perhaps many, of the professors of science in the early years of their appointment had never done experimental work." *History of the Sheffield Scientific School of Yale University, 1896–1922* (2 vols.; New Haven, 1928), I, 25–26. See also John F. Fulton, "Science in American Universities, with Particular Reference to Harvard and Yale," *Bulletin of the History of Medicine*, XX (July, 1946), 97–110.

the sole justification for scientific studies. In the pansophist ideal of the American Philosophical Society, in the encyclopedic interests of men like Benjamin Rush, David Rittenhouse, and Benjamin Franklin, in the speculative materialism of Cadwallader Colden, Joseph Priestley, and Thomas Cooper, one finds an interest in nature as law side by side with an interest in science as technique.[25] It was only after 1830 that a truly rigorous practicality was demanded. The Jacksonian transformation of American society—the decline of aristocratic standards, the liberation of entrepreneurial energies, the conquest of the open continent, the growth of a new business class—made profits and efficiency, the foes of intellectual curiosity, predominant social values.[26] It was then that charities and benefactions went primarily toward the useful sciences: toward hospitals rather than medical laboratories, toward engineering rather than basic physics. It was then that government subsidies favored the more exploitable sciences—geological surveys were preferred to studies of geological theory; engineering at the Military Academy was subsidized, rather than science at the National Institution for the Promotion of Science.[27]

Up to a point, the ante-bellum colleges were able to resist these utili-

[25] The practical interests of the Enlightenment have been overemphasized. A genuine concern with theory and basic research was there, overlaid perhaps by the optimistic faith that all truths had ultimate and important applications. See I. Bernard Cohen, "How Practical Was Benjamin Franklin's Science?" *Pennsylvania Magazine of History and Biography,* LXIX (October, 1945), 284–93; Richard H. Shryock, "American Indifference to Basic Science during the Nineteenth Century," *Archives Internationales d'Histoire des Sciences,* V (1948), 50–65; Harold A. Larrabee, "Naturalism in America," in *Naturalism and the Human Spirit* (New York, 1944), pp. 331–38; Richard H. Shryock, "Factors Affecting Medical Research in the United States, 1800–1900," *Bulletin of the Chicago Society of Medical History,* V (July, 1943), 7.

[26] Not until about 1900 did the implications of basic research for technology become more apparent to business leaders. Bernal's sharp antithesis between science as a contemplative art and science as an instrumental art, and his dictum that "the history of science shows that both the drive which led to scientific discoveries and the means by which those discoveries were made were material needs and material instruments," underplays the importance of abstract thought in both the motivation and application of science. J. D. Bernal, *The Social Function of Science* (London, 1939), p. 6.

[27] The interest of the states in subsidizing surveys was almost entirely given to prospecting and the opening up of exploitative possibilities, rather than in the discovery of guiding principles. See Charles S. Sydnor, "State Geological Surveys in the Old South," in David Kelley Jackson, ed., *American Studies in Honor of William Kenneth Boyd* (Durham, N.C., 1940), pp. 86–109. Exceptions should be noted: Lardner Vanuxem's stratigraphical correlations (South Carolina) and William Barton Rogers's study of the formation of the Appalachian chain (Virginia). See George P. Merrill, *The First One Hundred Years of American Geology* (New Haven, 1924).

tarian pressures. They had too much of the Aristotelian contempt for common industrial pursuits to turn themselves into schools of applied science.[28] In some of the Eastern colleges engineering courses were added, but Harvard's example of applying a gift for a school of engineering toward a school of general science (1847),[29] and the widespread retention of the term "natural philosophy" in the titles of scientific professorships,[30] are indications of the genteel aversion to technology that persisted throughout this period.

But the colleges did succumb to practicality in their preference for scientific teaching over scientific research. Just as the clinical demands on the medical doctor retarded original research in that profession, so the pedagogical and monitorial demands on the college scientist withered his interest in investigation. Required to live in a world of "dorms" and early-morning chapel, the college scientist was far removed from the professional climate of the scientific societies. Since academic honors hinged on his work as a teacher, he lacked the energy and time for that systematic investigation which, rather than occasional observation, is the method of scientific research. Indeed the idea had a certain currency among college officials that research was positively harmful to effective teaching. As late as 1857, a committee of the Columbia College Board of Trustees pointed to the fact that three professors "wrote books" as a possible cause of the low state of the college.[31] It cannot, of course, be contended that the Princeton of Joseph Henry, Albert B. Dod, and Stephen Alexander, the Yale of Silliman, Olmsted, and Dana, the Harvard of Agassiz and Gray, were antipathetic to research. Yet even these institutions, which after 1840 forged far ahead of all others in America in the study of the physical and natural sciences, invariably placed teaching first. In 1869, Charles W. Eliot, the new president of Harvard, declared that his institution did not possess, "with the single exception of the endowment of the Observatory

[28] Madge E. Pickard, "Government and Science in the United States: Historical Background," *Journal of the History of Medicine,* I (April, 1946), 254.

[29] Samuel E. Morison, *Three Centuries of Harvard* (Cambridge, Mass., 1936), pp. 279–80.

[30] Thus Silliman was professor of chemistry and natural philosophy and Denison Olmsted was professor of natural philosophy and astronomy at Yale; Gurdon Saltonstall was professor of mathematics and natural philosophy at Alabama (1831–33); in 1837 F. A. P. Barnard occupied a chair of "mathematics, natural philosophy and astronomy" at the same institution; Hitchcock at Amherst was professor of natural theology and geology. See Howard Mumford Jones, *Ideas in America* (Cambridge, Mass., 1944), p. 283n.

[31] Frederick Paul Keppel, *Columbia* (New York, 1914), p. 7.

. . . a single fund primarily intended to secure to men of learning the leisure and means to prosecute original researches," and that "the prime business of American professors in this generation must be regular and assiduous class teaching." [32] The dictum was not to be obeyed—a new era of college and university science was about to begin—but the priority Eliot gave to teaching reflected prevailing conditions.

More important than the practical bent of college science in limiting its range of speculation was the doctrinal moralism of the colleges. We use this phrase as a caption for the discussion of two assumptions which, if not often explicitly acknowledged, were seldom in this period controverted.

The first assumption was that character was a function of belief. "To say a man is an Infidel," wrote Timothy Dwight the elder, "is understood of course as a declaration that he is plainly an immoral man." [33] The logic was St. Paul's essentially: anyone who was "faithless" in religion was, beyond doubt and by definition, "faith-less" in all other affairs. That this assumption is still maintained in certain secular universities of our own day becomes readily apparent if one substitutes the word "disloyal" for the word "faithless." In both cases it is assumed that a man who believes certain things cannot be fit for his office: the premises force the conclusion, and the disparities that actually exist between a man's belief and his behavior are not taken into account. This assumption, however, had even greater force and wider appeal in the ante-bellum period (where a paternal interest in morals was combined with a vital concern for creed) than it has today. Then it was applied to professorial appointments in such a way as to exclude religious nonconformists, even where open religious tests were impolitic or forbidden. Timothy Dwight barred from the Yale Medical School one of the leading medical practitioners of the time, Dr. Nathan Smith, until the latter recanted his doubts of the truth of divine revelation.[34] The Presbyterians in Virginia kept Thomas Cooper out of the state university by attacking the chronic intemperance which they thought could safely be inferred from his resolute religious skepticism.[35] In short, where belief is the main clue to character, creed can become a

[32] Charles W. Eliot, "Inaugural Address," in *Educational Reform: Essays and Addresses* (New York, 1898), p. 27.

[33] Timothy Dwight, *The Duty of Americans at the Present Crisis* (New Haven, 1798).

[34] Cuningham, *Timothy Dwight,* pp. 216–19.

[35] Malone, *Public Life of Thomas Cooper,* pp. 240–41.

test for employment, not on the mean ground of sectarianism, but rather on the high ground of righteousness.

More particularly damaging to the interests of science was the second tenet of doctrinal moralism, the assumption that an idea was warranted and verified by proof of its moral advantages. This kind of moral pragmatism thoroughly imbued the thinking of scientists in the ante-bellum colleges. It was seen in the attitude of Benjamin Silliman, Sr., the so-called "Nestor of American science," when he took exception to the theories of James Woodhouse, a pioneer American chemist. Silliman thought Woodhouse's theories were incorrect because they could have impious and harmful consequences. Particularly did he object to the "levity and ridicule" with which Woodhouse treated "the idea that the visitations of the yellow fever might be visitations of God for the sins of the people." Woodhouse should not have forgotten that "physical causes [of disease] may be the moral agents of the Almighty." [36] In reviewing Robert Chambers's *Vestiges of the Natural History of Creation,* an adumbration of the theory of evolution, Professor Albert B. Dod, the Princeton mathematician, wrote "we trust it would be deemed an ample refutation of any system to show clearly that it was atheistic in its essential character." [37] Again, the tendency to subject ideas to the test of their moral results can be discerned in many quarters today. The language of invective has somewhat changed—now the refutation is deemed ample if a system can be called "socialistic," "communistic," "globalistic," or "subversive." Nevertheless, it would appear that the ante-bellum colleges, with their clear-cut Christian convictions, had a more certain grasp of the moral advantage to be looked for and of the doctrines that would bring that reward.

Last among the restrictions on speculation under which ante-bellum science worked were the substantive limitations of natural theology. After 1820, once materialism and Deism had declined, science and theology entered an intellectual *détente,* using as their formula of peace the Paleyan doctrine of "design." This doctrine was able to satisfy both scientific and clerical interests: the former, by sanctioning the empirical study of natural phenomena; the latter, by assigning to natural events a providential, supernatural cause. In the rhetoric of amity that developed, the word "harmony" was constantly used, though not in the same sense as before. Among the philosophers of the Enlightenment, "harmony" had usually

[36] George P. Fisher, *Life of Benjamin Silliman* (2 vols.; New York, 1866), I, 101.
[37] Thomas J. Wertenbaker, *Princeton, 1746–1896* (Princeton, N.J., 1946), p. 233.

signified the uniformity and regularity of nature, the universality of reason, the moral and intellectual likeness of all the members of the human race. To the Deists, representing one element of the thought of the Enlightenment, it also denoted opposition to the special creeds that were dividing the major religions.[38] "Harmony," in the language of ante-bellum science, had different denotations. It meant that Christian revelation agreed with all the conceptions of reason, that the ethical principles of Sinai were borne out in natural law, that the words in the Book of Genesis agreed, when correctly interpreted, with the evidence in the strata of rocks. Nature not only revealed a wondrous plan from which God's intelligence and benevolence could be inferred—this the Enlightenment had not denied; but now Nature was also considered to give evidence of the miracles on which the Christian eschatology was built.

One result of the prevalence of this commodious doctrine of design was that sacerdotal and scientific lines could be easily crossed: ministers could take up science, in the time-honored Mather tradition; [39] scientists could deliver religious sermons based on natural texts.[40] From the point of view of the present, this halcyon accommodation of naturalism to supernaturalism appears as the calm before the storm—or, perhaps, to the positivistic mind, the dark night before the dawn.[41] Darwinism was to loose all the latent antagonisms in the doctrine of design, cleaving it into a

[38] Arthur O. Lovejoy, "The Parallel of Deism and Classicism," in *Essays in the History of Ideas* (Baltimore, 1948), pp. 78–98.

[39] Some of the leading professional clergymen who were also teachers of science in this period were Edward Hitchcock, president of Amherst (1845–54), Congregationalist, geologist and paleontologist; Chester Dewey, professor of mathematics and natural philosophy at Williams College (1810–27), Congregationalist, also professor of chemistry and natural sciences at the University of Rochester (1850–61); Benjamin Hale, professor of chemistry at Dartmouth (1827–35), president of Geneva (Hobart) College (1836–58), Episcopalian, also a geologist and mineralogist; Charles Cogswell Upham, professor of mental and moral philosophy at Bowdoin (1824–67), Congregationalist, psychologist. There is unfortunately no career-line study of clerical personnel in science to answer some of the fundamental questions that this crossing of interests raises—for example, the reason for the large number of Congregationalists, the social and personal motivations that led them to their interest in natural science, the influence of their biases on the teleological flavor of American science.

[40] This was a common practice of scientists in England and America. See the lives of Faraday, Sir David Brewster, William Whewell, Sir Charles Bell, James D. Dana, William Maclure, Louis Agassiz, Benjamin Silliman, Asa Gray.

[41] In his survey of the first century of American education in 1876, Daniel C. Gilman found that "hostility toward scientific pursuits or toward scientific instruction has never in this country been manifested to any noteworthy extent by the religious part of the community or by theological teachers." "Education in America, 1776–1876," *North American Review,* CXXII (January, 1876), 224.

dogma of supernatural election and an hypothesis of natural selection, into a theory of providential intervention and a theory of divine concurrence. But God the Designer and God the Governor become sharply differentiated only when science and theology are at odds. In this period, science worshiped both the active and the passive God.

The accommodation to theology did not, to be sure, work consistently to the disadvantage of scientific thought. For example, the Christian version of design gave the science of geology a sanctuary from attack and a mantle of respectability. By dwelling on the "harmony of [God's] word with the visible creation," Silliman was able to answer the fundamentalist objections of Moses Stuart of Andover Theological Seminary.[42] By insisting that each harvest of fact gleaned from nature corroborated the working of Providence, James Dwight Dana effectively combatted the prejudices against science felt by obscurantist theologians like Tayler Lewis.[43] Had they not quieted qualms and disarmed opposition, it is doubtful that American scientists in the ante-bellum period could have pushed geology as far as they did. Methodologically, geology differed from the older sciences in that it sought the laws of natural development. It raised the question of how things came to be, and not the question, much safer for religion, of how things function as they are. Substantively, geology dealt with events definitively described in Scripture: it was the first science organized to deal not only with the work but with the word of God. With such a jurisdiction and such a basic point of view, geology was a potential threat to theology, natural and revealed. The fact that this threat called up in the scientists new talents for rationalization and compromise does not cancel the significant advances made. Always desiring to answer the interpretative problems of geology in a way least offensive to the Mosaic cosmogony, Silliman nevertheless had the integrity to turn to the anti-Biblical Vulcanist theory of earth-formation when the factual basis of the Neptunist theory of the diluvian crisis seemed to have been destroyed.[44] Eager to keep the peace between

[42] See Moses Stuart, "Remarks on a 'Critical Examination of Some Passages in Genesis 1,'" *American Journal of Science,* XXX (1836), 114–30; Fisher, *Life of Benjamin Silliman,* II, 132–60.

[43] Tayler Lewis, *The Six Days of Creation, or the Scriptural Cosmology* (Schenectady, 1855); James D. Dana, "A Review of Six Days of Creation," *Bibliotheca Sacra,* XIII (January, 1856), 80–129, and XIV (July, 1857), 461–524. See also Agassiz' approval of Dana's rebuttal in Daniel C. Gilman, *The Life of James Dwight Dana* (New York and London, 1899), p. 324.

[44] Dirk J. Struik, *Yankee Science in the Making* (Boston, 1948), pp. 300–301. For comparable developments in England, see Charles Coulston Gillispie's instructive book, *Genesis and Geology* (Cambridge, 1951), *passim.*

science and religion, Edward Hitchcock had the courage to abandon the literal interpretation of the Bible. "The facts of science, rightly understood," he wrote in 1851, "should not contradict the statements of revelation, correctly interpreted." [45] Thus, when "rightly understood," geology furnished irrefutable proof of the late appearance of man, the immutability of species, and the special providences of God, and so backed up both revelation and design at the most significant points. On the other hand, when "correctly interpreted," the Pentateuch was a figurative version of geological truth, and science should construe its metaphors. Thus, the six demiurgic days should be considered spans of geological time, and the ecumenical flood, disputed by science, should be reinterpreted as a local deluge.[46] Even Lyell, whose uniformitarian theory ruled out miraculous intervention in the whole domain of inorganic development, received a hearing in America,[47] though the most popular theories, down to the Darwinian era, were those of Cuvier, whose catastrophist hypothesis of the earth's formation squared more completely with the Biblical account.[48]

But the advance of geological science was the heaviest strain that the theological compromise would endure. As far as biology was concerned, scientists were timid in their generalizations, not out of positivistic caution, but out of concern for moral consequence and because of their theological preconceptions. As Arthur O. Lovejoy persuasively argues, the main proofs of organic evolution, except for the explanatory key of natural selection, were accessible in the writings of Lamarck, St. Hilaire, and, particularly, Robert Chambers.[49] Fifteen years before Darwin, Chambers had marshaled the evidence in favor of the theory of evolution: the general harmony between the theory of evolution and the rest of scientific thought, particularly uniformitarian geology; the presence in animals of rudimentary organs; the paleontological evidence of increasingly complex organisms appearing in succeeding epochs. Yet the scientific fraternity mercilessly attacked his theory when it appeared in 1844. To concede that everything was adapted for use and nothing for beauty and perfection, to

[45] Edward Hitchcock, *The Religion of Geology* (Boston, 1851), p. 4.
[46] *Ibid., passim.*
[47] Struik, *Yankee Science,* pp. 302–3; W. N. Rice, "The Contributions of America to Geology," *Science,* XXV (1907), 161–75.
[48] C. Wright, "The Religion of Geology," *New England Quarterly,* XLI (1941), 335–38.
[49] Arthur O. Lovejoy, "The Argument for Organic Evolution before 'The Origin of Species,'" *Popular Science Monthly,* LXXV (November and December, 1909), 499–514, 537–49.

give over the realm of life to blind chance and mechanical law, would have imperiled the Paleyans' conceptions. To relinquish the anthropomorphic God would have jeopardized the structure of faith on which morality presumably rested.[50] The recoil of scientific thought from such hazards threw it back upon the less plausible theory of repeated acts of "special creation," upon a series of miracles separated by long intervals of time. Here providentialism and moral purpose maimed academic science at a critical juncture of thought.

From the foregoing we conclude that academic freedom in investigation was diminished not by the action of forces alien and antipathetic to science, but by the inhibitions present within science itself. Rationalistic historians like Draper and White, who later presented the relation of science and religion or science and theology as one of inherent and recurring antagonism, missed or misread the ante-bellum record.[51] When Benjamin Silliman, Sr., the arch-exponent of the theological compromise, appended to a geology textbook an orthodox account of Creation,[52] when Professor John McVickar, in a perfect illustration of one tenet of doctrinal moralism, declared that "what religion reproves as wrong, Political Economy rejects as inexpedient," [53] when Louis Agassiz failed to draw what now seems the obvious evolutionary implication from his biogenetic law,[54] they were not making gestures to conformity, with *eppur si muove* spoken under the breath. The weapons which a frightened theol-

[50] There were, to be sure, non-theological reasons for rejecting Chambers—his mysticism, occasional inaccuracies, and other lapses from scientific propriety. But, as Lovejoy demonstrates, many of the weaknesses in the logic and evidence of Chambers' book that called forth biting attack from the scientists were also present in Darwin's work. At least the hypothesis, if not the particular rendering of it, should have been accepted, but scientists damned the author and his idea. Lovejoy, "The Argument for Organic Evolution," pp. 502, and *passim*.

[51] John William Draper, *History of the Conflict between Religion and Science* (New York, 1874); Andrew Dickson White, *A History of the Warfare of Science with Theology* (2 vols.; New York, 1896).

[52] Cf. Silliman's supplement to *An Introduction to Geology* by Robert Bakewell, first American ed. (New Haven, 1829), pp. 3–126. In the second edition Silliman went further, entitling his supplement "Consistency of the Discoveries of Modern Geology with the Sacred History of the Creation and the Deluge" (1833). Thomas Cooper attacked this attempt at conciliation as ruinous to science; see *On the Connection between Geology and the Pentateuch* (Boston, 1833).

[53] Gladys Bryson, "The Emergence of the Social Sciences from Moral Philosophy," *International Journal of Ethics*, XLII (April, 1932), 311.

[54] In his "Essay on Classification" in the first volume of the *Contributions to the Natural History of the United States* (Boston, 1852), Agassiz adumbrated a theory that later became known as the biogenetic law. "The changes which animals undergo during their embryonic growth coincide with the order of succession of

ogy employs to defend its static ideas—such weapons as censorship, heresy trials, economic sanctions, excommunication—were not used against ante-bellum scientists. The absence of open conflict was not owing simply to the unprovocative character of scientific thought. It testified also to the acceptance by the religious of scientific inquiry as an essential social good, to the growing deference to the authoritative pronouncements of science, and to the general confidence that the court of nature would always sustain the vital pronouncements of religion. It was not until Darwin forced science to accept the transmutation theory that the necessary limits of scientific inquiry, the proper sources of authority, and the tribunal role of nature became matters of basic controversy.

PIETY WITHOUT PARTISANSHIP?

To what degree was the demand for academic freedom—both in instruction and in investigation—affected by the proselytizing purpose of the ante-bellum colleges? To what extent was religious orthodoxy also sectarian in character? In their official pronouncements the Protestant colleges invariably claimed to be religious but not sectarian. Credibility was lent to this claim by the all but total absence of religious tests for students,[55] the occasional charter proscriptions against religious tests for faculties,[56] and the frequent absence of formal ecclesiastical control.[57] But the test

---

the fossils of the same type in past geological ages." The astounding thing is that Agassiz could enunciate such a principle and yet oppose Darwinism so vehemently.

[55] Of the 19 state and 32 private institutions studied by Elliott and Chambers, 10 state and 16 private colleges were in existence during the middle period. A perusal of these twenty-six charters reveals not a single reference to the right or intention to disqualify students on religious grounds. Edward C. Elliott and M. M. Chambers, *Charters and Basic Laws of Selected American Universities and Colleges* (New York, 1934), *passim*. On the other hand, 4 private institutions (Columbia, Princeton, Brown, Knox) and all public institutions covered by Elliott and Chambers provide in their charters that *no* such test shall be imposed. There is good reason to believe that this is a representative sample of the charter provisions on student entry at this time.

[56] Elliott and Chambers (*ibid.*) show that 4 state and 6 private institutions of the 26 ante-bellum colleges they covered had charter prohibitions against the imposition of religious tests for faculties. In their list, Yale alone provided for the administration of a religious oath to the faculty in its charter of incorporation.

[57] The Congregationalists relied mainly on sympathetic association with their colleges rather than formal control. The Congregational Society for the Promotion of Collegiate and Theological Education at the West favored the autonomy of individual colleges, preferring to promote Congregational ideals through financial aid.

is not so much the selection of students—where the chronic debt and desire for fees were mitigating factors [58]—as the selection of teachers; not so much the promises and ideals of the charters—which were political documents designed to allay the suspicions of hostile denominations [59] —as the motive for college establishment, the style of the college's religious ritual, the flavor of the college's instruction. Judged on these latter points, and excluding the special cases of Harvard, Pennsylvania, Union, and certain state universities in the early part of this period, the ante-bellum colleges substantiate the aphorism that piety without partisanship is easier to praise than practice.

The enormous expansion of denominational colleges in the first half of the century was impelled by a variety of motives. The founders were animated by the desire to bring the word of God and the chance of salvation to the heathen frontier, to counteract the infidelities and heresies spawned by the Revolution and the Enlightenment, to educate citizens for the duties imposed by the broadening franchise, to open professional careers to youths in the isolated hinterland, to extend the benefits of a liberal education. But certainly one of the most powerful and sustained of their motives was the aggrandizement of sect. The separation of church and state after the Revolution did not bring about the separation of church and college. On the contrary, disestablishment, by ending the monopolistic position of favored religions, opened the educational field to fiercer sec-

The Presbyterians also maintained very lax control through their Board of Education until 1883, when the constitution of the central Board of Aid provided that every college receiving aid be organically connected with the church, or else provide by charter that two-thirds of its board of control should be members of the church. On the other hand, the polity of the Lutherans, Baptists, and Methodists favored ecclesiastical control over the institutions receiving aid from the church. See Paul M. Limbert, *Denominational Policies in the Support and Supervision of Higher Education* (New York, 1929).

[58] See Chap. V.

[59] Despite the large number of colleges founded in this period, hardly a single college charter was passed by a state legislature without popular or sectarian opposition. As a result, a good deal of political maneuvering and verbal camouflaging went on. The Georgia Baptists, for example, with unusual candor, wanted to call their college "The Baptist College of Georgia." They found it more politic to settle for a less provocative name, Mercer University. Albea Godbold, *The Church College of the Old South* (Durham, N.C., 1944). Seldom in the charters were the sectarian attachments of the original self-perpetuating board pointed out. For example, Princeton's charter designated twelve Presbyterian ministers and eleven laymen, of whom only two were Quakers and one was an Episcopalian, without explicitly consigning that institution to Presbyterian control. See Willard W. Smith, "The Relation of College and State in Colonial America," unpublished Ph.D. dissertation (Columbia University, 1949).

tarian competition. In the East, where in colonial times the colleges of the established churches had reigned supreme—in Virginia, Massachusetts, Connecticut, New Hampshire, and New York—statehood and disestablishment allowed the pent-up demand for rival colleges to find unrestrained expression.[60] In the West, particularly when the evangelistic sects saw the need for a trained as well as consecrated ministry, the churches fell to the task of college-building with a militant missionary zeal. As imperialistic as the nations in the field of politics were the churches in the field of education. There was the same promoting of wares and searching for markets, the same carving of spheres in semicivilized domains, the same multiplying of jurisdictions. Except for the Congregationalists and Presbyterians, who collaborated (with mounting tension) in the establishment of ten colleges in a Plan of Union that lasted from 1801 to 1852, each denomination worked separately, adding to its own dominion, serving the one God and the particular creed.[61]

The proselytizing of colleges for their sects was rarely admitted or openly condoned. In a typical utterance, the board of trustees of Congregationalist Marietta College declared that "the essential doctrines and duties of the Christian religion will be assiduously inculcated, but no sectarian peculiarities of belief will be taught." [62] But the scope of the verb "to teach" and the definition of the adjective "sectarian" were very ambiguous. Like all the new denominational colleges of the period, Marietta, emulating the early colonial colleges, was founded "mainly to meet the demands for competent teachers and ministers of the Gospel." [63] The number of college graduates going into the ministry between 1816 and 1840 was greater than the number going into any other profession. By one estimate, one third of the graduates entered upon clerical careers in the peak period, 1836 to 1840; [64] the ratio of ministerial to other

[60] See G. Bush, *History of Education in Massachusetts* (Washington, D.C., 1891), pp. 225–79; G. Bush, *History of Education in New Hampshire* (Washington, D.C., 1898); Thomas Le Duc, *Piety and Intellect at Amherst, 1865–1912* (New York, 1946), pp. 1–5.

[61] See Chap. V for a fuller treatment of the post-Revolutionary expansion of the denominational college system.

[62] Charles F. Thwing, *A History of Higher Education in America* (New York, 1906), p. 231.

[63] *Seventh Report* of the Society for the Promotion of Collegiate and Theological Education at the West (1850), p. 61; quoted in Donald G. Tewksbury, *The Founding of American Colleges and Universities before the Civil War* (New York, 1932), p. 83.

[64] According to Burritt's combined statistics for the professional distribution of college graduates in thirty-seven representative colleges and universities, the per-

professional careers was estimated in 1857 as one in four for the Congregational colleges.[65] In addition, indigent preministerial students were heavily subsidized by church organizations. Although in time these new denominational colleges differentiated their theological courses from the rest of the curriculum, not until the end of the period, when the development of separate theological schools was well under way [66] and the proportion of ministerial candidates in the general student body had dropped to as low as one in five,[67] did these colleges lose their seminarial look. Nor was indoctrination confined to the classroom. Use was made of symbol and association: the halls and streets bore the names of the prophets and martyrs of the church.[68] Use was made of ritual and ceremonial: Sunday service and morning devotions were cast in the style of the sponsoring sect.[69] Sometimes two creeds were recognized in worship and ritual, as when the Princeton board in 1802 voted to print "copies of the Westminster Shorter Catechism and that of the Episcopal

---

centage of graduates going into the ministry did not dip below 50 until 1720, except for the 1661–1695 period. From 1721–1745 it held to around 40 percent and dropped until it reached the low point of 20.8 percent in 1791–1795, when it was overtopped by the law. A gradual rise thereafter brought it up to 32.8 percent in the 1836–1840 period. Bailey B. Burritt, "Professional Distribution of College and University Graduates," *Bulletin of United States Bureau of Education,* XIX (Washington, D.C., 1912), 74–83, 142–44.

[65] C. Van Rensselaer, "Commencement Address at Carroll College" (1857), in *Pamphlets on College Education* (Columbia University Library), Vol. VII, No. 9, p. 387.

[66] The establishment of professional schools of theology which were independent of colleges began in the second half of the eighteenth century. In the early nineteenth century, Andover Theological Seminary and Princeton Theological Seminary attained positions of real importance. At Harvard, divinity studies were separated from the college and organized into a distinct school in 1819. The Yale Divinity School was organized in 1822. By 1876, there were 113 seminaries. Still, until the middle of the nineteenth century, many schools preferred to retain the close relation between theological training and the liberal arts. Robert Kelly, *Theological Education in America* (New York, 1924).

[67] Burritt, "Professional Distribution of College and University Graduates," p. 75.

[68] Viz., Emory College, named for a bishop of the Methodist Church, its streets commemorating the names of Wesley, Asbury, and Coke. Godbold, *Church College of the Old South,* pp. 62–63.

[69] Yale was strict. Under Dwight, it denied students the right to attend Episcopalian services, though this permission had been granted under President Clap forty years before. Harvard allowed students to worship at the nearby churches, Brown made provision for Jews to consecrate their Sabbath. But in effect the freedom to worship elsewhere was limited. Traveling off the campus was not encouraged by college authorities; for convenience, if not because of other pressures, students generally accepted the devotional forms of the college. See Samuel Eliot Morison, *Three Centuries of Harvard,* p. 88; Walter C. Bronson, *History of Brown University, 1764–1914* (Providence, R.I., 1914), pp. 98–99.

Church." [70] Furthermore, though religious revivals were encouraged on behalf of an undifferentiated Christian piety, the lists of conversions suggest that the Spirit was likely to visit in the sectarian garb of the college.[71] At all events, parents who sought to keep their sons in the family faith had no difficulty in determining on which side the colleges were "neutral." Cheyney notes that in the first decades of the century, Philadelphia Presbyterians showed a marked preference for Dickinson and Princeton, Philadelphia Lutherans for Franklin, Philadelphia Anglicans for Columbia and William and Mary; the local and more convenient, but truly nonsectarian, University of Pennsylvania was by-passed.[72]

One manifestation of the sectarian spirit was seen in the employment of the faculty. Nine times out of ten, the college president was a minister,[73] and ministers in academic posts were usually ordained in the sponsoring church. Schmidt tells us that "there was no religion of the college president as such; he rather reflected the theological views of the denomination in which he held membership and whose interest he served." [74] On the affiliations of professors, the statistics are less conclusive because they are less complete and accessible. Our survey of the faculty rosters of Harvard, William and Mary, Miami, Oberlin, Lafayette, Princeton, and Middlebury for the period 1800 to 1860 indicates that about 35 per cent of the total were clergymen, which again strongly suggests sectarian choice.[75] The variations among these institutions suggest further that sects with a congregational structure were less able to impose this criterion

[70] This was the way the board interpreted a faculty resolution to allow students "to make choice of the Catechism of that denomination to which he belongs." John Maclean, *History of the College of New Jersey* (Philadelphia, 1877), II, 50–51.

[71] Thus the religious revival that hit Princeton in 1848 brought 25 conversions, of which 18 were to the Presbyterian Church (the sponsors), 6 to the Episcopalian (at Princeton, the minority church, recognized as such), and only 1 to the Methodist. Maclean, *History of the College of New Jersey,* II, 20.

[72] Edward P. Cheyney, *History of the University of Pennsylvania* (Philadelphia, 1940), pp. 176–77.

[73] Schmidt, *The Old Time College President,* pp. 184–86.

[74] *Ibid.,* pp. 187–88.

[75] This percentage was compiled from S. J. Coffin, *The Men of Lafayette, 1826–1893* (Easton, Pa., 1891), pp. 23–33, 113–20, 125–29; *Catalogue of Miami University, 1809–1892* (Oxford, Ohio, 1892), pp. xiii–xxii; *Third and Fourth Triennial Catalogues for Miami, 1840* and *1843; Annual Circulars for Miami, 1847,* pp. 55, 58, 59; Edgar J. Wiley, *Catalogue of the Officers and Students of Middlebury College . . . 1800–1915* (Middlebury, Vt., 1917), pp. ii–xix, xxvii–xxix, xxx–xxxv; Maclean, *History of the College of New Jersey,* II; *The History of the College of William and Mary from Its Foundation, 1660–1874* (Richmond, 1874), pp. 80–81.

than those with a synodal structure.[76] We also conclude that sectarian affiliation was a qualification for professors when subject-competence was not, and that subject-competence was not of prime importance when professors had to "double on the brass" in tiny tutorial orchestras. Thus Unitarian and cosmopolitan Harvard boasted in 1831 a heterogeneous interdenominational faculty—six Unitarians, three Roman Catholics, one Lutheran, one Episcopalian, one Quaker, and one Sandemanian; of them all, only the professor of divinity was required to pass a creedal test.[77] Baptist Brown also prided itself on its broad-minded choice of faculty.[78] At the other extreme, however, Presbyterian Miami in 1831 had three professors, all of them Presbyterian divines.[79] Presbyterian Pittsburgh College, closer to the mean in size if somewhat advanced in urbanity, in 1831 had four ordained Presbyterian ministers and one Catholic priest out of a faculty of five.[80]

The politics of sect intruded even upon the nominally neutral ground of the state universities. Twenty-one state universities struggled to survive in the ante-bellum period.[81] To the more militant sects these universities seemed designed to seduce young minds for either Satan's or Caesar's purposes. Treating them either as prizes to be fought for and won, or as enemies to be countered and destroyed, the churches placed their agents on state boards of trustees or else built competing colleges. The aggressiveness of the sects stymied the growth of the state universities throughout the period.[82] For varying periods of time North Carolina,

[76] See Chap. V, "Presbyterians and Partisans."

[77] Morison, *Three Centuries of Harvard*, p. 242.

[78] Bronson, *History of Brown University*, pp. 100–1.

[79] W. L. Tobey and W. O. Thompson, *Diamond University Volume: Miami University* (Oxford, Ohio, 1899), pp. 192–98.

[80] Agnes Lynch Starrett, *Through One Hundred and Fifty Years* (Pittsburgh, 1937).

[81] These, with their dates of founding, were Georgia (1785), North Carolina (1789), Vermont (1791), Tennessee (1794), Ohio (1802), South Carolina (1805), Miami (1809), Maryland (1812), Virginia (1816), Alabama (1821), Indiana (1828), Delaware (1833), Kentucky (1837), Michigan (1837), Missouri (1839), Mississippi (1844), Iowa (1847), Wisconsin (1848), Minnesota (1851), Louisiana State (1853), California (1855). The names are those in use today; the dates of founding are approximate. See Tewksbury, *Founding of American Colleges and Universities*, pp. 133–207. Several of these universities began as church institutions and lost their sectarian connections.

[82] Control of the board of trustees by certain denominations was easier to acquire and hold when these boards were self-perpetuating than when they were under state control. When originally founded, North Carolina, Delaware, Vermont, Transylvania, Tennessee (Cumberland and East Tennessee Colleges), Miami, Indiana (Vincennes), Mississippi, and California (College of California) had private

Tennessee, Vermont, Kentucky, Transylvania, Miami, Indiana, and Alabama universities fell under the direct influence and control of particular sects.[83] The universities of Missouri, Mississippi, and Michigan bowed to the pressure of several competing denominations.[84] The universities of Georgia, Ohio, Missouri, and Iowa, among others, were stunted by the competition of rival denominational colleges.[85] In the northeastern states and in six of the southern and western states, ecclesiastical opposition prevented the birth of state universities until after the Civil War.[86]

The state universities were not indifferent to religion. From their beginnings, they adopted the practices of religion in education—Bible classes, daily prayers, compulsory chapel, revivalism.[87] That they did not neglect the spiritual welfare of students may be deduced from the backgrounds of their presidents and professors who, in the ratio of one in three, were also recruited from the ministry.[88] Even Jefferson's plan for the University of Virginia, which went further along the road to secularism than

boards of trustees, which encouraged one sect, usually the Presbyterians, to take hold from the start. After the Dartmouth College case, however, the state usually inserted in the charter its right of revision. After prolonged battles, control ultimately came to rest in the hands of the state.

[83] See D. H. Gilpatrick, *Jeffersonian Democracy in North Carolina, 1789–1816* (New York, 1931), p. 129; L. S. Meriam, *Higher Education in Tennessee* (Washington, D.C., 1893), pp. 20–61, 63–105; G. Bush, *History of Education in Vermont* (Washington, D.C., 1900); Niels H. Sonne, *Liberal Kentucky, 1780–1828* (New York, 1939), pp. 160–261; G. W. Knight and J. R. Commons, *The History of Higher Education in Ohio* (Washington, D.C., 1891), p. 34; David D. Banta, "History of Indiana University," in *Indiana University, 1820–1920: Centennial Memorial Volume* (1921), pp. 103–7.

[84] E. Mayes, *History of Education in Mississippi* (Washington, D.C., 1899), pp. 25–117; Wilfred Shaw, *The University of Michigan* (New York, 1920), p. 40; Jonas Viles, *University of Missouri* (Columbia, Mo., 1939), p. 23.

[85] E. M. Coulter, *College Life in the Old South* (Athens, Ga., 1928), Chap. VIII; Knight and Commons, *Higher Education in Ohio*, p. 23, 55–58; Viles, *University of Missouri*, Chap. III; L. F. Parker, *Higher Education in Iowa* (Washington, D.C., 1893), Chap. IX.

[86] Tewksbury, *Founding of American Colleges and Universities*, pp. 169–74.

[87] Earle D. Ross, "Religious Influences in the Development of State Colleges and Universities," *Indiana Magazine of History*, XLVI (December, 1950), 343–62.

[88] Ross, "Religious Influences," p. 349; Curti and Carstensen, *The University of Wisconsin* (Madison, Wis., 1948), pp. 17–19; Coulter, *College Life in the Old South*, p. 19. Between 1804 and 1860, for example, four out of eight presidents of South Carolina College were ministers; ten out of thirty-eight professors were ministers. M. LaBorde, *History of the South Carolina College* (Charleston, S.C., 1874), pp. 527–28 and *passim;* Edwin L. Green, *A History of the University of South Carolina* (Columbia, S.C., 1916), p. 210 and *passim.* Between 1800 and 1860, two out of North Carolina's three presidents and nine out of its twenty-nine professors were ministers. Battle, *History of the University of North Carolina,* I, 51–54, 67–72, 79–80.

any other, permitted a definite amount of "released time" so that students might worship with their own pastors, offered the university's facilities for the use of outside divinity schools, and instructed the professor of ethics to emphasize religious values. Only because he feared sectarian controversy did Jefferson forbid formal instruction in theology, the appointment of clerical professors, and any form of sectarian control. Yet this measured secularism earned for Virginia the sobriquet of "godless" and the immoderate hatred of the militant sects throughout the antebellum era.[89] It was not the irreligion of the universities but their *politique* attitude toward sect that aroused the wrath of the churches.

In this connection too the churches disavowed any narrow sectarian purposes. Indeed, they often claimed that they were acting in behalf of a true nonsectarian policy. Again, it was a question of definition, not one of conscious deception. In the semantics of the religious, it was not sectarian to teach the immortality of the soul, the infallibility of the Bible, or even the existence of the Trinity, provided no pronouncements were made on such truly divisive points as the sanction for voluntary baptism. Conversely, however, it was sectarian—in a "Socinian," Unitarian, or Deistic way—to consider any of these basic Christian postulates open to serious question. Arguing, therefore, that an open mind was a sectarian position, the churches turned the tables on their enemies. The Horace Holley case, referred to above,[90] is an interesting case in point. The Presbyterian Church in Lexington, Kentucky, forced the dismissal of Transylvania's president because he had proved himself to be "violently sectarian." He had indoctrinated students, wrote the editor of the *Western Luminary,* a Presbyterian organ in Kentucky, in a religion "whose confession of faith is to have no confession, and whose sectarianism is to despise all sects." [91] Nor did sectarianism masquerade as its opposite only through a play on words. It was persuasively argued that the only way to stop the abuse of religious favoritism was to distribute faculty chairs in the state universities among the denominations in proportion to their

[89] Philip Alexander Bruce, *History of the University of Virginia* (5 vols.; New York, 1920–22), III, 133–47. Professor D. H. Hill, in his inaugural address as Professor of Mathematics of Davidson College, called the University of Virginia while under Jeffersonian principles "a terror to the land, a curse to the cause of education, in fact a nursery of crime and vice." Godbold, *Church College of the Old South,* p. 15.

[90] See Chap. V.

[91] Robert Peter and Johanna Peter, *Transylvania University, Its Origin, Rise, Decline, and Fall* (Louisville, Ky., 1896), p. 141.

respective strength in the community. This reversal of the Reformation rule, *cuius regio eius religio,* would, it was maintained, be in line with American democratic practice. A state with a large Baptist population should no more be required to have only Congregationalist teachers than a state with a predominance of Democrats should be forced to have only Whig representatives. Responding to this argument, the University of Virginia, having hired with Jeffersonian indifference a Catholic and a Jew, was compelled to right the balance by adding a militant Presbyterian clergyman.[92] Where no sect had clear domination, the nonsectarian course was presumed to lie in an equal division of the spoils. Accepting the premise that sectarianism disappears when a variety of sectarians are brought together, the University of Michigan for years pursued a policy of even-handed injustice, and named a minister of a different sect to each of its professorships.[93]

State constitutions gave little protection to the universities where sectarianism was at high tide. The constitutional provision against *any* religious test for professors could be interpreted in practice to sanction a *different* religious test for each academic office.[94] The "wall between church and state"—a barbed fence when the state tried to nullify a private church-college charter [95]—was a trampled hedge when the churches undertook to dominate the state universities.

For all this, the oppression of sect was not complete nor did it go unchallenged. The anguish and glory of Protestant separatism is that it covets intellectual solidarity but creates intellectual diversity. For one thing, the interchurch rivalry that built the colleges was often continued in the form of intramural conflict for the control of the colleges. Of the forty-nine colleges controlled by the Presbyterians in the ante-bellum period, three fell into the hands of the Methodists; three became state universities; seven fell to the Congregationalists; one began as Anglican, tarried briefly with the Presbyterians, and finally turned independent; one began as a semi-state institution, was associated with the Presbyterians, and was taken over by the Baptists; eight by slow degrees moved into virtual independence; and one (Transylvania) endured the vertiginous experience of passing from the control of the Baptists to the Episcopalians to the

[92] Bruce, *History of the University of Virginia,* III, 133–35.
[93] Shaw, *University of Michigan,* p. 40.
[94] Banta, "History of Indiana University," pp. 72–73.
[95] See *Trustees of Dartmouth College* vs. *Woodward* ("The Dartmouth College Case"), *4 Wheaton 514, 712* (1819).

Presbyterians to the Methodists to the Disciples of Christ.[96] Moreover, the schismatic conflict between the Old and the New Light Presbyterians, and the fission of the church into northern and southern branches, brought further intramural conflict to the twenty-six schools that remained in the Presbyterian fold.[97] Designed as shrines to particular truths, the denominational colleges were often embarrassed by a succession of creeds.

These conflicts for control, so threatening to the life and educational continuity of the colleges, set off flashes of rebellion against the denominational system as a whole. The close association of Miami University with the Presbyterians involved it in the fratricidal strife that split this church in the decade of the 1830s. Recognizing that theological controversy was harmful to church and college alike, President Robert Hamilton Bishop fought for unity in the church and for a liberal spirit in the college.[98] At Illinois College, J. M. Sturtevant, a sincere religionist and one of the original Illinois Yale Band, was so incensed by the inquisitions of the Presbyterian Synod into the teaching at his college that he became a vocal opponent of "the passion, the prejudice, the bigotry" of denominationalism in education.[99] In one article, he wrote:

We do not affirm that ecclesiastical governments so conditioned are bad; we do not affirm that they may not accomplish useful and important ends. But we do affirm that they cannot be stable. They must be constantly liable to the rise of minorities, whose views and feelings are in irreconcilable conflict with those of the ruling majority; and whenever this does happen, convulsion and disruption must and do ensue. . . . The tendency of sect [is] . . . to reduce all our Colleges to feebleness and starvation, by multiplying them beyond the demands and necessities of the community . . . [This spirit of sect] elevates minor denominational peculiarities into tests of fitness for the highest and most dignified stations; it tends to fill our most important chairs of instruction with men of inferior talents and attainments, because they are supposed to be right in the matter of denomination, and thereby to impair the efficiency of the Institution in the discharge of its appropriate function.[100]

Decades before Charles W. Eliot proclaimed that "a university cannot be built upon a sect" and made this the guiding principle of the post-

[96] Tewksbury, *Founding of American Colleges and Universities,* pp. 91–102.
[97] R. E. Thompson, *History of the Presbyterian Church in the United States* (American Church History Series, Vol. VI [New York, 1895]).
[98] James H. Rodabaugh, "Miami University," pp. 66–73.
[99] Charles Henry Rammelkamp, *Illinois College, A Centennial History: 1829–1929* (New Haven, 1928), pp. 119–26; J. M. Sturtevant, *An Autobiography* (New York, 1896), pp. 188, 198–99, 245–49.
[100] "Denominational Colleges," *The New Englander,* XVIII (February, 1860), 82.

Civil War era, opposition to sectarianism gathered head within the denominational colleges themselves.

DISORDER AND DEFICIT

We have seen that the educational ideals of the old regime—its traditionalism, authoritarianism, paternalism, doctrinal moralism, and sectarianism—depressed the demand for freedom in two areas of academic expression, instruction and inquiry. The word "depressed" (rather than "suppressed") is chosen in this context advisedly. Freedom thrives on desire and desire on opportunity; and these ideals were an effective prophylactic against the passion and incitement to be free. But educational ideals are not the whole of academic existence, nor are they the only institutional factors relevant to our theme. The college is not only a place where formal teaching and learning go on; it is also a unit of government, an economic entity, a congeries of social relationships. How it functions in these roles influences those opportunities for intellectual conflict, those expectations of indulgence, those inclinations to self-assertion, that kindle the demand for freedom. Seen in the light of these diverse functions, the ante-bellum college was not characterized only by indoctrination and compliance. Throughout the period there was student agitation against the rules, discontent in the faculty with its status and role, and—pushing the colleges toward reform—a hovering, nagging poverty. In sum, two forces were dialectically opposed in the ante-bellum colleges. The first was a conception of education that tended to make the college a monolithic institution. The second—of increasing power as time went on—was an intramural spirit of revolt and reform which, in challenging authority in a system fundamentally authoritarian, acted as one of the agents which eventually destroyed that system.

There is a strong impression among academic men today that fewer and weaker powers are being delegated to them by trustees now than formerly, and that there has been a regression from a Golden Age of faculty self-government to a present state of subservience. We were once "cleric, now we are clerical," says Professor Jacques Barzun, in a witty but mistaken epigram. Actually, in their conventional relations with trustees, faculties were in an inferior position and at a disadvantage all through the seventeenth and eighteenth centuries; in the early nineteenth century a nadir seems to have been reached. In the latter period the system of control by a nonresident board, carried over from the colonial colleges, evolved into an instrument of academic government that was officious, meddlesome, and often tyrannical. One finds the trustees of colleges prescribing the work of the classroom, writing the laws of student government, shaping the curriculum, subjecting the private lives of teachers to scrutiny and espionage. Take the obsessional interest in minutiae exhibited by the board of trustees at Princeton in the early nineteenth century. "When a committee of the board came to examine the faculty's 'minutes'," writes one historian of early Princeton,

it sternly reported that the pages of the minute book were not numbered, that in one place a date was wanting, that there were instances of grammatical construction which it thought incorrect. . . . Worse than all this, however; it was learned that one tutor had been away on a trip, that another had entertained friends in his room . . . all of which showed a great want of proper discipline.[101]

It is doubtful that the most intrusive board of trustees today would ever display toward its faculty so marked an attitude of contempt. Nor was this a unique example: Pennsylvania's board rivaled Princeton's in its concern for petty details,[102] and the trustees of Hamilton and Lafayette were not far behind in their disregard for faculty judgment.[103]

In accounting for this state of affairs it is not enough to conclude that this is how a theocracy always functions, that the ministerial mind turned the colleges into pastorates and made close surveillance a duty. As a matter of fact, clergymen rarely predominated on the early nineteenth-century boards of control,[104] and officiousness was a habit of

[101] Varnum Lansing Collins, *Princeton* (New York, 1914), pp. 116–17.

[102] Cheyney, *University of Pennsylvania*, p. 178.

[103] Joseph D. Ibbotson and S. N. D. North, eds., *Documentary History of Hamilton College* (Clinton, N.Y., 1922), pp. 181, 185, 193, 195–226; David Bishop Skillman, *The Biography of a College* (2 vols.; Easton, Pa., 1932), I, 172–78.

[104] Beard claims in *Rise of American Civilization* that clergymen dominated these boards (New York, 1942), II, 470. Schmidt controverts this with his random figures. "Up to 1861, the records list thirty-three clergymen and forty-three laymen [at Williams]. . . . The totals for Union college in 1861 were nineteen clerical and forty-eight lay representatives. . . . The corresponding figures for Amherst in the same year were twenty-four and thirty-eight." Schmidt, *The Old Time College President*, p. 51. Further figures support our contention that laymen usually predominated. The thirty-six charter trustees of Lafayette College were all nonclergymen; between 1830 and 1860, thirty-three were clergymen and forty-six were nonclergymen (Coffin, *Men of Lafayette*). At Middlebury there were seventeen clergymen and fifteen laymen between 1801–1829, twenty-five clergymen and twenty-three laymen between 1830 and 1860 (Wiley, *Catalogue of the Officers and Students of Middlebury College*). At Miami, between 1824 and 1829, ten were clergymen, fourteen were

boards that were almost or entirely nonclerical.[105] Greater emphasis, it would appear, should be given to the status relationships then existing in the colleges. In dealing with the men of large affairs who sat on the governing boards, the president, the professors, and the tutors were often hopelessly outclassed. As in colonial times, the tutor was a functionary to whom deference was never generously paid, and it was only gradually that he was to make his exodus from the nineteenth-century college scene.[106] The professor was not held in much higher regard; dependent on student fees and yet the inquisitor of student morals, he took on the uncertain authority and something of the status of the nursemaid. Most damaging to faculty prestige was the decline in the caliber of the president who, as an ex-officio member of the board of trustees, as the guardian of campus religiosity, and as the head of the college faculty, held a strategically powerful position. While the screen of orthodoxy was tightly woven, it served to keep from the presidency the celebrated, the independent, the truly top-notch man.[107] Powerful personalities like Josiah

---

not; between 1830 and 1836, sixteen were clergymen and seventy were not (*Catalogue of Miami University, 1809–1892*). Finally, McGrath, studying thirteen private institutions—Williams, Wabash, Knox, Yale, Pennsylvania, Princeton, Dartmouth, Lafayette, Amherst, Wesleyan, Hamilton, Lawrence, and Beloit—concludes with the statement that 39.1 percent of the trustees in the year 1860 were clergymen. Earl J. McGrath, "The Control of Higher Education in America," *Educational Record*, XVII (April, 1936), 259–72. Of course, all this does not mean that clergymen were not an enormously important element.

[105] One example is provided by the Board of Trustees at the University of Virginia, which despite Jefferson's democratic leanings kept very close control on faculty doings. "The professors were under as close supervision in the work of the classroom as the students themselves. The chairman of the Faculty was expected to report: (1) how often each instructor had failed to lecture as required; (2) how frequently he had neglected to question the members of his class; (3) how much time was consumed by him in delivering lectures and making his examinations; and (4) how often he had omitted sending in his class report to show the number of his pupils' absences, and the degree of their attention and progress." There were no clergymen on this board. Bruce, *History of the University of Virginia*, II, 132.

[106] In the eastern colleges there was a gradually diminishing proportion of tutors to total faculty between 1820 and 1850. At Harvard, Yale, Columbia, Williams, Union, Hamilton and Amherst, tutors were 30 percent of the whole in 1820, 27 percent in 1830, 25 percent in 1840, 23 percent in 1850. The gradual decline is significant, and represents an important though gradual shift in status relationships and potentialities. The western colleges had fewer tutors than the eastern, and the tradition of the celibate young tutor did not take strong hold there. For figures, see those prepared especially by the New York Public Library for Clarence F. Birdseye, *Individual Training in Our Colleges* (New York, 1907), p. 135.

[107] There were a few notable exceptions: Dwight of Yale (1795–1817), Jeremiah Chaplin of Colby (1820–1833), John Kirkland of Harvard (1810–1829), Joseph Caldwell of North Carolina (1804–1812, 1817–1835), Eliphalet Nott of Union (1804–1866).

Meigs of Georgia and Horace Holley of Transylvania were compelled to resign; giants like John Witherspoon of Princeton and William Smith of Pennsylvania were succeeded by less able and more tractable men; the first two decades of the century found Amherst, Bowdoin, Columbia, Dartmouth, Vermont, and Williams in an interregnum between important presidents. In the dialogues of power that always go on between laymen and professionals, the president's voice can be decisive. When it is loud and clear, it can "cleave the general ear"; too often, alas, it is whispery; in this period, it was, with very few significant exceptions,[108] almost inaudible.

Gradually, by a step forward here and a short gain there, in the course of the next decades the college teacher was elevated from the position of a powerless subaltern to the status of an executive officer in the realm of discipline and instruction. What improved the situation was not any widespread adherence to some overarching principle of professorial autonomy. Rather, the factor that seems to have been crucial in furthering reform was the prosaic and commonplace, but disquieting and relentless, problem of the lack of student discipline. Never have the colleges had so many rules for students and so much student unruliness as in the ante-bellum period. Coulter, in his *College Life in the Old South,* presents some of the laws of the University of Georgia that frustrated student joy:

If any scholar shall be guilty of profaneness—of fighting or quarreling—if he shall break open the door of a fellow-student—if he shall go more than two miles from Athens without leave from the President, a Professor or a Tutor,— if he shall disturb others by noisiness, loud talking or singing during the time of study,—if he shall ring the Bell without order or permission—if he shall play at billiards, cards or any unlawful game—if he shall associate with vile, idle or dissolute persons, or shall admit them into his chamber,—if he shall instigate or advise any student to a refractory stubborn behavior—he shall for either of those offenses, be punished by fine, admonition, or rustication, as the nature and the circumstances of the case may require.

Then, there were laws against more serious offenses, which were gravely enumerated: keeping dogs, robbery, fornication, forgery, striking an instructor, fiddling on Sunday, and defacing the walls with indecent figures. Finally, "Whereas the laws of the College are few and general" [sic],

---

[108] See Franklin B. Dexter, "An Historical Study of the Powers and Duties of the Presidency of Yale College," *Proceedings of the American Antiquarian Society,* New Series, Vol. XII (1897), pp. 27–42.

in cases not covered, the faculty might proceed at their discretion![109] Unfortunately, for every law to break, there was a febrile adolescent lawbreaker. A semester unmarred by expulsions was memorable in college annals; a chapel that escaped vandalism enjoyed a most unnatural quiet. The chief instrument of student aggression—the firecracker—was part of standard student equipment; the ivied halls would shake to the reverberations of explosions. Needless to say, the safety-valve of college sports had not yet been invented; the effective cajoleries of the kindly dean had not yet appeared; to maintain a system of too much government in an undergoverned society was the task the college set for itself, and the task was truly insuperable.

To be sure, adult authority would always reassert itself against prank and rebellion. An institution so dedicated to discipline engendered dedicated disciplinarians. The offenders would be rounded up; the president would be solemn and severe; the faculty would constitute itself the high court and mete out appropriate punishment. But peace was easier to restore than the faculty's equanimity. These multitudinous acts of student exuberance or irritation—always defined as acts of irreverence or defiance—struck like so many arrows at professorial complacency. Not only did student dismissals damage the reputation of the college and threaten it with financial ruin; not only was the professor's image of himself as remote and benevolent impaired by sorties against students in the night; but these outbreaks invariably brought down on the teachers' heads a plague of trustees, who disrupted the normal course of pacification. Should the trustees, like those at Hamilton College, recognize student petitions of grievance, then students could play the distant authority against the local tyrants with a skill that made discipline impossible.[110] Or should the trustees, like those at Transylvania and Brown, be divided on sectarian lines, then student insubordination might actually be encouraged by one faction of the trustees in order to discredit the other.[111] More common, if hardly less disserviceable, were the trustees who assiduously offered advice though they were out of touch with the situation. Thus the trustees of Princeton, descending into its riotous at-

[109] Coulter, *College Life in the Old South,* pp. 60–62. For other listings of student laws, see Bronson, *History of Brown University,* pp. 153 ff.; Wertenbaker, *Princeton,* pp. 132–214.

[110] Henry David, *A Narrative of the Embarrassments and Decline of Hamilton College* (1832).

[111] Sonne, *Liberal Kentucky,* pp. 88–89; Bronson, *History of Brown University,* pp. 188–89.

mosphere in 1817, counseled the use of civil force against the students to maintain order, a course that outraged the parents, violated academic traditions, and damaged Princeton's reputation for decades.[112]

This dual hazard of student disobedience and trustee interference led to demands by the faculties for greater self-government.[113] The demand was for partial autonomy, not for total independence. Though the plans for reform differed in detail from college to college, they were consistent in this one vital point. No European gild of scholars, autonomous in all its concerns, was envisioned by these reformers of the early and middle nineteenth century. No serious attempt was made to alter the charter so as to shift legal control to professors. The management of funds, the selection and appointment of the chief executive, the preparation and approval of budgets—which all lay within the province of English and Scottish professors—were powers neither sought by American faculties nor tendered by American trustees.[114] Even at Harvard, where a final and unsuccessful move to seat the faculty on the Corporation was made in 1825, the presence of the Board of Overseers was always protection against complete faculty self-rule.[115] The main effort was directed toward convincing the trustees to delegate to the faculty power over education and discipline; toward developing, as it were, a limited faculty *imperium* within a trustee *imperio*.

On this theme each ante-bellum college, tied to its own traditions and past mistakes, worked its own variation. Great powers were yielded to the faculty at Yale, where a line of strong presidents since Thomas Clap had never been interrupted, and where the Corporation had learned from the senior Dwight to respect the authority of the president.[116] In the regime of Dwight's successor, the less majestic and more democratic Jeremiah Day, the president undertook to share his powers with leading

[112] Collins, *Princeton*, pp. 131–32; Maclean, *History of the College of New Jersey*, II, 168–70; Wertenbaker, *Princeton*, p. 109.

[113] This is an unwritten chapter in the various histories of American higher education, partly because of the pre-eminent interest in curricular change and little else. Charles F. Thwing, who is concerned with the wider institutional aspects (he actually devotes a chapter in his history to the financing of the denominational college) almost ignores the informal power relationships in the college. See *A History of Higher Education in America* (New York, 1906). The several doctoral dissertations on this subject tend to slight the denominational era.

[114] For example, the charters of Yale and Knox colleges were issued almost a century apart, yet the changes in the powers of their respective boards were insignificant. Elliott and Chambers, *Charters and Basic Laws*, pp. 283–86, 588–93.

[115] Morison, *Three Centuries of Harvard*, pp. 224–38.

[116] Yale University, *Sketches of Yale College* (New York, 1843), p. 56.

members of the faculty. Not only initiative in making curricular changes and undivided power over disciplinary cases, but the right to approve all new appointments, was conceded to the faculty. So firmly was this tradition planted that in 1871 a Yale president could claim that "with scarcely an exception, no law has been passed, no officer appointed, unless after full consultation and exchange of views between the boards of control and of instruction.[117] Princeton's trustees, unable to cope with financial failure and student unruliness, turned for guidance to Professor John Maclean, whose plan for higher salaries, an expanded curriculum, and alumni contributions they passively adopted. The success of this plan set a precedent for their dependence on faculty initiative, and thereafter the power to establish as well as to execute policy flowed to the side of the faculty.[118] Elsewhere, down through the years, the trustees relinquished numerous powers: the power to revise, unaided, the course of study;[119] to control student admissions;[120] to undertake systematic classroom visitations;[121] to conduct the final oral examination—their last affectation of scholarship. This functional separation of power ranks with the establishment of lay control and the bureaucratization of personnel practices as one of three important milestones in the development of American academic government.

Still the problem of student discipline remained—the rock which even the sanguine Jefferson dreaded as he charted the course for his university.[122] That the faculty was allowed to use its discretion did not mean that it would use its discretion wisely. Doubtless most teachers in the

[117] Pierson, *Yale College*, p. 134.   [118] Collins, *Princeton*, pp. 140 ff.
[119] The revision of the statutes of the University of Mississippi was designed to give the faculty control over educational policy (1856). Prior to that time, they had been framed so as to put the most minute affairs under the discretion of the trustees, "including even such matters as the ringing of the college bell and the arrangement of the hours of recitation." President Barnard argued: "You have appointed us because we are professional teachers and you believe we understand our business; you have prescribed the broad outlines of our work, and we have undertaken to do the work on those lines. Now, if you are to direct the details of the work at every step, you will succeed no better than you would succeed if you were to direct the engineers of the Mississippi Central in the same way. Our professional knowledge and experience will be set aside and rendered useless, and our whole work will probably be badly botched." John Fulton, *Memoirs of Frederick A. P. Barnard* (New York, 1896), pp. 204–5.
[120] Fletcher, *History of Oberlin*, I, 178.
[121] See W. H. Cowley, "The Government and Administration of Higher Education: Whence and Whither?" *Journal of the American Association of Collegiate Registrars*, XXII (July, 1947), 477–91.
[122] Letter to Ticknor (1820), Thomas Jefferson, *Writings* (Washington, 1890), XV, 455.

ante-bellum period remained convinced that the traditional approach to student discipline was best, and regarded the disciplinary problem as the problem of how to make discipline more rigid. Some sought more ascetic laws or a tighter system of espionage, or else worked laboriously at marking up merits and demerits of conduct, as though the whole issue could be resolved into a simple and inexorable arithmetic.[123] Others settled on one cause of disobedience—infidelity—and sought one primary remedy—to extricate fallen students with the hoists of evangelical religion.[124] But there was also a growing minority that attacked the faulty methods of teaching and the uninspiring content of instruction. A small contingent of Americans who had studied at German universities came home to insist that power was better exercised over subjects than over subject schoolboys, that a contribution to philology was far more significant than a contribution to student manners, that the whole emphasis of the college should be shifted from discipline to scholarship.[125] Those who read the works of Fellenberg, Pestalozzi, and that new and exciting theorist, Herbert Spencer, were turning to the view that dull recital did not sublimate the aggressions, that gerund-grinding did not occupy the attention, that prescribed courses did not satisfy the interests of the average boy at college—and that there was the heart of the problem.[126] And, as the period drew to a close, such reformers as Francis Wayland spoke in a native idiom of how the conventional curriculum no longer answered the problems of real life, and of how only a more vocation-centered offering could meet the needs of undergraduates.[127]

Thus the problem of student discipline stirred up doubts on some

[123] See Francis H. Smith, *College Reform* (Philadelphia, 1851). Smith worked out a disciplinary system that defined every duty and punished its negligence with demerit marks. Henry James in his biography of Eliot called this kind of discipline a system wherein "a docile but stupid lamb might outrank a superior scholar who was caught in a good many pranks." *Charles William Eliot* (Boston and New York, 1930), I, 38.

[124] One means was the promotion of revivals in the sectarian colleges of the South. Though they upset college routine, sometimes for a week or more, they were encouraged by college officials. Godbold, *Church College of the Old South*, p. 70.

[125] See Chap. VIII for an analysis of the German contribution to American higher education.

[126] See Chap. VII for an analysis of Spencer's theory of education and its influence on American educational reform.

[127] See Wayland's *Thoughts on the Present Collegiate System in the United States* (Boston, 1842); *Report of the Corporation of Brown University* (1850).

of the most fundamental issues. Was it irreligion or faulty instruction that made students ill-tempered and disobedient? To what extent was doctrine the source and touchstone of morality? If few, perhaps, contended that religion was irrelevant to good morals, some were coming to see that religion was insufficient for good morals. After all, if the University of Virginia had disciplinary problems while under Jefferson's "godless" tutelage, so had those near-by citadels of the faith, Randolph-Macon and Washington colleges.[128] Observing the spectacle of cows in the chapel of the highly Presbyterian LaGrange College, F. A. P. Barnard, president of the state University of Mississippi, concluded that if his institution was less "godly," it was nevertheless better disciplined.[129] The carousing and dissipation that Andrew Dickson White encountered while a student at Geneva College, an institution under "direct Christian influence," must have suggested to him that free thinking and free drinking were not necessarily connected.[130]

As pressing as the problem of disorder, and perhaps even more far-reaching in its effects, was the problem of financial distress. The eastern colleges in the first three decades of the nineteenth century, and the western colleges throughout the period, were poor—but this word does not fully convey their plight. Material undernourishment is an endemic ailment of all academic bodies. Even the richly provided universities of the golden nineties complained of this condition. But whereas theirs was the emaciation of bodies in too-rapid growth, the ante-bellum colleges were atrophied organisms, living at a low ebb. So small was their scale of operations that the slightest shift of fortune was enough to determine life or death. In 1827, Princeton's treasury showed a deficit of $753, not an heroic debt in modern terms, but one that made her reduce the salaries of two professors to what must have been below subsistence level.[131] Twice Rutgers lapsed into the status of an academy for want of funds; [132] once Amherst's income was so low that her professors worked without salaries in order to keep her alive.[133] The western colleges fared worse

[128] Richard Irby, *History of Randolph-Macon College* (Richmond, Va., 1898), pp. 112–13.

[129] Fulton, *Memoirs of Frederick A. P. Barnard,* pp. 203–4.

[130] Andrew D. White, *Autobiography* (New York, 1922), I, 18–19.

[131] Wertenbaker, *Princeton,* p. 170.

[132] William H. S. Demarest, *A History of Rutgers College, 1766–1924* (New Brunswick, N.J., 1924), pp. 184–271.

[133] George Whicher, ed., William Gardner Hammond's *Remembrance of Amherst: An Undergraduate's Diary, 1846–1848* (New York, 1946), p. 10.

and for a longer time.[134] Their high mortality rate is eloquent of their protracted, inescapable poverty.[135] Undoubtedly the hostility to change that was part of the character of the ante-bellum colleges can be attributed to inadequate means. Change meant expansion, expansion meant expense, and theirs was a destitute economy. A scholastic and tradition-bound curriculum was, aside from its other supposed virtues, decidedly cheap.

Put in commercial terms, low sales, inadequate capital, and high operating costs tell the story of these financial failures. In relation to the growth in population, the percentage of college enrollments declined all through the period. In New England in 1826 the proportion of students in college to the population was one in 1,513; in 1855, one in 1,689; in 1869, one in 1,927.[136] At the same time, endowment did not keep pace with the rising cost of education. For the eastern colleges the starvation time in endowments was the period from 1800 to 1830. The loss of carefully nurtured nest eggs in the inflation of the American Revolution,[137] the drying up of English sources of philanthropy after independence,[138] the parsimony of the state legislatures,[139] all worked

[134] In 1871 eight eastern colleges—Amherst, Bowdoin, Dartmouth, Harvard, Middlebury, Vermont, Williams, and Yale—had four times the endowment of eighteen western colleges—Beloit, Berea, College of California, Carleton, Heidelberg, Illinois, Iowa, Knox, Marietta, Oberlin, Olivet, Pacific Union, Ripon, Wabash, Western Reserve, Wilberforce, and Wittenberg. See George F. Magoun, "Relative Claims of Our Western Colleges," *Congregational Quarterly*, XV (January, 1873), 49–75.

[135] Tewksbury, *Founding of American Colleges and Universities*, p. 28.

[136] Taking his figures from President Barnard's reports, Charles Kendall Adams concluded that "the sad fact stares us in the face that the training which has long been considered essential to finished scholarship has been losing ground from year to year in the favor of the people." "The Relation of Higher Education to National Prosperity," Phi Beta Kappa address, 1876, in Northrup, Lane, and Schwab, eds., *Representative Phi Beta Kappa Orations* (Boston and New York, 1915), pp. 160–61.

[137] Colleges such as Harvard, which had Federalist sentiments and had been fortunate enough to have speculated in state and federal paper, recouped their losses in the Hamiltonian windfall, but Princeton invested every penny in United States loan certificates on which the government defaulted in 1782. Morison, *Three Centuries of Harvard*, pp. 157–58; Wertenbaker, *Princeton*, pp. 66–67.

[138] Jesse B. Sears, *Philanthropy in the History of American Higher Education* (Washington, D.C., 1922), p. 22.

[139] The years in which the eastern colleges received their last cash endowments or subsidies from the state were Harvard, 1824; Yale, 1831; Dartmouth, 1809; Columbia, 1819; Hamilton, 1846; Union, 1804; Geneva, 1846; Pennsylvania, 1844. Princeton, Rutgers, and Brown never received grants or appropriations. Vermont received no grants or appropriations but was allowed the remission of a small debt in 1852. Frank W. Blackmar, *The History of Federal and State Aid to*

to reduce the colleges' productive assets to pitiable figures. After a century of existence Columbia's income from all sources was less than two thousand dollars a year.[140] In 1817, Princeton's yield from income-bearing assets was a mere $1,500.[141] As late as 1831, after 130 years of private and public beneficence, Yale's receipts from all sources, including tuition, were slightly less than twenty thousand dollars.[142] The western colleges were even less solvent. The poverty of their frontier communities, the competition of the state universities, which had first claim on the public purse, the fluctuations in the values of land on which their endowments were based, the strain on denominational resources caused by their proliferation, gave them a tenuous hold on life. For the first quarter-century of its life, Illinois College (founded 1835) subsisted more on fervor than funds. Its initial capital was some fourteen thousand dollars and several hundred acres of land, taxable but for a long period unsalable. A subscription of $100,000, the result of its president's fund-raising mission in the east, was repudiated in the crash of 1837. The faculty, sent east to ask alms, returned empty-handed. By 1843, the pay of its professors was in arrears, its debt had mounted to $25,000, and its property was heavily mortgaged. Only the aid of the Society for the Promotion of Theological and Collegiate Education kept Illinois College alive until the late fifties, when secular philanthropy and gifts from alumni pushed it over to the side of solvency. Nor was it able in its time of troubles to seek a more auspicious re-establishment elsewhere. Saddled with debts and chattels, this mendicant college, unlike the poor medieval university, was immobilized by its poverty.[143]

Here again, the remedy prescribed for the problem shook authority out of its settled grooves. One main resource was available and it was used—the sympathy and largesse of the alumni. As individuals, college graduates had always been interested in the welfare of their alma maters. Attachment to class and college had been fostered by the small numbers of students, the close living, and the class unity that characterized the old-time colleges; time and the worse restraints of adult life dimmed

---

Higher Education in the United States (Washington, D.C., 1890). However, other sources of income were made available to the colleges by the states; for example, exemption from taxation, land endowments, and the right to hold lotteries. See Thwing, *History of Higher Education in America,* pp. 328–30.

[140] Thwing, *History of Higher Education in America,* p. 326.
[141] Wertenbaker, *Princeton,* p. 120.
[142] Sears, *Philanthropy in Higher Education,* p. 37.
[143] Rammelkamp, *Illinois College,* pp. 82–244.

the memory of sophomoric repression. But it was not until the nineteenth century [144] that this sentimental concern was organized, capitalized, and set to earning dividends. Between 1827 and 1853, Princeton, Williams, Rutgers, Pennsylvania, Harvard, Amherst, and Brown, which together had half the total number of all alumni alive in 1829,[145] organized alumni associations.[146] The idea spread to the newer colleges of the Middle West, where organization of alumni associations followed close upon the establishment of colleges.[147] Similarly, the midwestern state universities endeavored to organize their graduating classes and to keep alive their sense of sodality.[148] Results were observable from the start, particularly in the Atlantic Seaboard colleges, whose alumni were relatively numerous and wealthy. Yale's and Princeton's sons tendered large sums in subscription drives.[149] Harvard received spectacular bequests from Christopher Gore and Abbott Lawrence, as well as aid from its organized alumni.[150] These transfusions revivified these colleges, and they quickly forged ahead of all competitors. Columbia, on the other hand, not having founded her alumni organizations until 1854, remained in the doldrums of deficit until almost the end of the period.[151]

Originally, the purposes of alumni organizations were convivial and philanthropic—to renew the friendships of youth and to provide a viable endowment. For a time, the college authorities successfully resisted sporadic attempts by the alumni to secure an official place in college councils. Not until 1865, after a long struggle, did the Harvard alumni obtain the right to elect the members of the Board of Overseers; [152] not until 1872 did the Yale alumni supersede the six state senators on the Corporation and challenge clerical control; [153] not until 1900 did Princeton's alumni secure seats on the board of trustees.[154] But long before they secured formal recognition as a law-giving as well as a fund-raising group, the alumni influenced the course of educational policy.

[144] Except at Yale, where the records of class organization date back to 1792. Wilfred B. Shaw, "The Alumni," in Raymond A. Kent, ed., *Higher Education in America* (New York, 1930), p. 657.

[145] *American Quarterly Review,* I (April, 1829), 224–55.

[146] Shaw, "The Alumni," pp. 658–59.

[147] *Ibid.,* p. 658.   [148] *Ibid.,* p. 659.

[149] Thwing, *History of Higher Education in America,* p. 325.

[150] *Ibid.*   [151] *Ibid.*

[152] John Hays Gardiner, *Harvard* (New York, 1914), pp. 296–98, 301.

[153] Bernard C. Steiner, *History of Education in Connecticut* (Washington, D.C., 1893), pp. 178–79.

[154] Collins, *Princeton,* p. 249.

Status-wise, the alumni were at least on a par with the trustees. Social deference did not have to be paid to any group by an alumni association like Harvard's, whose first officers were John Quincy Adams; Joseph Story, justice of the Supreme Court; Edward Everett, governor of Massachusetts; John Pickering, president of the American Academy; Horace Binney, member of Congress; Lemuel Shaw, chief justice of the Massachusetts Supreme Court; Leverett Saltonstall, member of Congress; Nathaniel L. Frothingham, overseer and fellow of the American Academy; Peleg Sprague, judge of the United States District Court and United States Senator; Benjamin R. Curtis, afterward judge of the Supreme Court.[155] The very presence of so distinguished a group made the faculty feel accountable to another will than that of the trustees. In some cases the alumni and the faculty made common cause against the conservative book-balancers on the board of trustees.[156] At Princeton, the result of faculty-alumni collaboration in the 1830s and 1840s was the transfiguration of Old Nassau, founded to raise up men for the gospel ministry, into a school that excelled in science and modern languages, that hired scholars rather than mere pious pedagogues, that already glimpsed its future as a university.[157] Its thought became secularized, slowly, almost imperceptibly. In 1812 the Princeton trustees, choosing a teacher, had recommended him as "pious, prudent and highly respectable," and then had mentioned his attainments in mathematics and natural philosophy. Twenty years later, scholarship was the major requirement, and Joseph Henry could write to Maclean that his prime goal in accepting an appointment at Princeton was to win "the reputation of a man of science." [158] With the help of the alumni, the needs of the nation started to replace the needs of the church.

The organization of the alumni produced effects that often were not premeditated. Graduate loyalty was often attached, then as well as now, to infantile or regressive projects. No doubt the main objective of the alumni was to preserve the old college they had known, not to submerge

---

[155] Gardiner, *Harvard,* pp. 304–5.

[156] This, of course, depended on a spirit of reform existing within the faculty. In certain cases the faculty resisted the lay interests of the alumni which threatened their vested interests in the classical subjects. In 1872, the Dartmouth faculty joined with the president and the trustees to beat down a request of the alumni that they be seated on the board of control to hasten educational reform. See Richard T. Ely, *Ground Under Our Feet* (New York, 1938), pp. 29–30.

[157] Wertenbaker, *Princeton,* pp. 215–55.

[158] *Ibid.,* pp. 153, 220.

her identity in a large university. No doubt they were, on the whole, more inclined to build a new chapel than to build a new scientific school. But their very presence was an incentive to experimentation. Knowing that the generosity of the alumni would catch up with him, Silliman the younger organized a school of science at Yale before he had acquired an endowment for it. In time, the alumni responded handsomely. When they did, the exclusiveness of the college that had been their pride, the homogeneity of the college that had won their praise, were in part destroyed. The Silliman school, which was differentiated from the college proper, required no compulsory prayers, no compulsory chapel, no compulsory hours of study. Its students, more mature than the average undergraduate, worked on their own in the laboratories, and its professors were guides, not goads, to learning. Soon there were Yale men who knew chemical laws but did not know Latin hexameters, and it was not less upsetting to staid tradition that these students did not receive the same liberal-arts degree awarded other Yale graduates.[159]

The breeding ground of institutional change is the sense of institutional failure. Student disorder and chronic poverty created grave inner doubts about the value of the education offered and led men to question the proposition that sound doctrine breeds sound morals. The organization of the alumni and the growth of faculty autonomy opened certain of these "strongholds of ancient prescription" to lay interests and liberal ideas. These changes in the roles of alumni and faculty were, to be sure, undirected movements; the old system was still substantially intact. The purposeful construction of a new system awaited the social and intellectual changes of the postwar period. It should not, however, be forgotten that the great builders of that period—Gilman, White, Eliot, Barnard—were schooled in the ante-bellum college. Not only did they acquire a sharp distaste for the old rigidities; they were inspired by its stirrings toward reform. And it should not be forgotten that it was, after all, Ticknor, not Eliot, who first suggested the elective system at Harvard; Silliman, not Hadley, who first breached the intrenched positions of Greek and Latin at Yale; Wayland, not White, who offered the first large-scale plan for a vocationalized higher education.

By 1860 the signs were pointing to a drastic revision of the goals of the college system. The growing emphasis on scholarship, the questioning of old pedagogical assumptions, the enlarging scale of philanthropy,

[159] Chittenden, *History of the Sheffield Scientific School*, I, 49–50.

were converting the larger colleges into institutions geared for research. At the same time, as the result of deeper social forces at work, the "conserving" function of the college no longer loomed so large. The unhinging of moral certainties by urban living, the fading out of the evangelical impulse, the depersonalization of human relations in the process of industrial expansion, were destroying that integral vision, that firm and assertive credulity, required of institutions devoted to conservation. Two other forces were to consummate this shift from "conserving" to "searching" in the universities of postwar America. The first was to be the powerful impact of Darwinism, which would unlock the creative potential of American academic science. The second was to be the influence of the German university, whose scholarly lore and academic traditions Americans admired and adapted. By 1860, the American colleges stood at the verge of a new outlook; two or three decades later, they would possess it fully.

The shift from conserving to searching portended great changes in the conception of academic freedom. As long as conserving was the foremost ideal, academic freedom was a freedom *for,* not *in,* the colleges. The conserver, taken as an ideal-type within the ranks of the men of knowledge, regards the knowledge inherited from the past as the seasoned wisdom of the race or the afflatus of God. As priest, he celebrates it; as scholastic, he systematizes it; as fundamentalist, he applies it, reverencing *ipsissima verba.* The pre-Civil War academic, by filling all three roles, maintained a certain intellectual autonomy—a freedom and isolation as a member of the community of the educated. In a New World, peopled by the uprooted, he kept alive a respect for traditions. In a democratic society, tending to be plebiscitarian in taste as well as in politics, he resisted the attempts of public whim and vulgarity to depreciate the college education. A good part of his opposition to a more secular university and a more vocationalized curriculum stemmed from his desire to protect very fragile values from the crush of a rough society. He sought the freedom not to acquiesce in the philistinism of his age.

This was the contribution of our academic conservers. But it is also in the character of the conserver to submit to the ideas he protects, and this is his major defect. The pre-Civil War college teacher considered the fundamental questions settled, the great truths possessed and funded and waiting only to be drawn upon. Alas, his fundamental questions, answered too didactically, were often empty of educational significance. Subjected to the parochialism of the denominational college, his great truths were transformed into dogmas. Screened for piety and correct belief, he was more alarmed by the attacks of outside parties than by the smothering influence of his own. His demand for freedom in instruction and investigation was, as a consequence, unemphatic and occasional: in a prisonhouse of one's own making, there are few incentives to escape.

The advent of the searcher into academic life reversed the relationship and relative importance of outer and inner freedoms. Characteristically, the searcher regards accumulated knowledge as no more than lore and hypothesis, as fallible as the men who made it. He may be the religious reformer, who strips the veil of mystery from arcane symbols; the artist, who rebels against the academy's official vision; the philosopher, who seeks a new starting point for thought. In the new university that was about to be born, the searcher was most often to wear the vestments of the scholar, seeking facts upon which to base new interpretations of the past; the social scientist, distinguishing what is myth and what reality; the physical and natural scientist, applying a disciplined test to current theories. The cultural autonomy of the college would matter less to the college teacher in these roles. Imbued with German ideals of scholarship, he would hope to contribute to progress by knowing more and knowing it more exactly, not by holding fast to values and a sense of the totality of things. Believing that progress was a social law, he would not only assume that tradition was mere opinion and experience, but that opinion improves as society ages and that experience grows stale with senescence. Without truths to speak for or purposes to defend, the new university would incline toward utility, and jeopardize its initiative and independence in order to answer client needs.

But these weaknesses were to be paid for by new strengths. The academic searcher was to develop arguments for freedom *within* the university that had not been strong before. Armed with the assumption that truth was something progressively to be discovered and provisionally held, he was to attack the presence of sectarianism in American higher education. By appealing to scientific methods of verification, he was to shift the emphasis from results to procedures in the warranting of belief. By introducing German methods of teaching and the German ideal of academic freedom, he was to attack those parental controls that curbed teacher and student alike. Finally, his prolonged apprenticeship, his specialized training, and his close ties with workers in his field, were to enable him to develop a professional *esprit* that would shield him against coercive administrators.

VII: DARWINISM AND THE
NEW REGIME

POLITICAL REVOLUTIONS, we are told, have certain traits in common. They are engendered by a series of events that inflame a segment of the population and reveal the injustice of the rulers. They are inspired by an ideology of resentment against those in positions of authority. They invoke the name (even as they transform the sense) of vital, though often dormant, human freedoms. The American academic revolution, foreshadowed in the ante-bellum period and fomented in the era of Darwin, reveals roughly analogous traits. The dismissals and harassments of teachers of evolution were the inflammatory events. The attack upon religious authority in science and education was the ideology of resentment. Freedom for academic inquiry, for which a new rationale was developed, was the freedom that was invoked. Under headings provided by this analogy, we shall analyze the decisive influence of Darwinism on academic thought and institutions.

INFLAMMATORY EVENTS

By any reckoning, the acceptance of Darwinism by American scientists was remarkably rapid. Darwin had surmised, with characteristic shrewdness, that the "young and rising naturalist" would be more receptive to his views than the men of the older generation who had staked their reputations on the special-creations theory.[1] And this was true. No sooner did the *Origin of Species* appear in 1859 than the younger scientists fell to work to test its hypotheses, fill in its gaps, and prove its prophecies.[2] But the great biologist had underestimated, with a

[1] Charles Darwin, *On the Origin of Species by Means of Natural Selection* (London, 1859), p. 417.
[2] Particularly Charles C. Abbott, William A. Hyatt, E. D. Cope, George B. Goode, William K. Brooks, Burt G. Wilder, O. C. Marsh, David S. Jordan, A. E. Verrill, A. S. Packard. The detailed work done in zoology to prove evolution is

humility that was also characteristic, his ability to convince older scientists, once their preconceptions had been challenged. To be sure,
Louis Agassiz never did come around to accepting the mutability of
the species, although he retreated from his first contention that Darwinism was "a scientific mistake, untrue in its facts, unscientific in its
method, and mischievous in its tendency" to the view that Darwin had
used "scientific methods" but had claimed more than was warranted
by the facts.[3] Nevertheless, awesome as was Agassiz' authority, and
important as it was in delaying the complete acceptance of evolution
by American scientists,[4] it did not deter his colleague Asa Gray from at
once championing Darwin's ideas—and this was the Gray who once had
written that the fixity of species "has been settled by human observation." [5] Much against Darwin's expectations, James Dwight Dana, the
inheritor of Benjamin Silliman's professorial chair and theological convictions, slowly gave his assent.[6] More quickly, Jeffries Wyman, in
the twilight of his career, and Joseph Leidy, at the height of his fame,

---

summarized in Edward S. Morse, "Address," *Proceedings of the American Association for the Advancement of Science*, XXV (1877), 137–76.

[3] "Professor Agassiz on the Origin of Species," *American Journal of Science and
Arts*, XXX, Second Series (July, 1860), 142–55; Louis Agassiz, "Evolution and
the Permanence of Type," *Atlantic Monthly*, XXXIII (January, 1874), 94.

[4] See Bert J. Loewenberg, "The Reaction of American Scientists to Darwinism,"
American Historical Review, XXXVIII (July, 1933), 687–93.

[5] Asa Gray, "Explanation of the Vestiges," *North American Review*, LXII
(April, 1846), 471. The first review by Gray of Darwin's book was cautiously
favorable. "The Origin of Species by Means of Natural Selection," *American
Journal of Science and Arts*, XXIX (March, 1860), 153–84. "Under the circumstances," he wrote to Darwin, "I suppose I do your theory more good here, by be-
speaking for it a fair and favourable consideration, and by standing non-committed
as to its full conclusions, than I should if I announced myself a convert; nor could
I say the latter, with truth." Letter of Gray to Darwin, January 23, 1860. Francis
Darwin, ed., *The Life and Letters of Charles Darwin* (New York, 1898), II, 66.
Subsequent articles in the *Atlantic Monthly* (July, August, October, 1861) revealed that Gray had become a complete convert, though one more interested in
squaring evolution with natural theology than in merely proving the empirical
adequacy of the hypothesis.

[6] Darwin did not expect his friend Dana to be convinced. In a letter to the Yale
scientist in 1863, Darwin wrote that he did not suppose that "with your strong
and slowly acquired convictions and immense knowledge, you could have been
converted. The utmost that I could have hoped would have been that you might
possibly have been here or there staggered." Daniel C. Gilman, *Life of James
Dwight Dana* (New York, 1899), 315. The 1870 edition of Dana's *Manual of Geology* considered the attempt to prove evolution as "vain"; the 1874 edition considered
evolution a conclusion "most likely to be sustained by further research" though man
was exempted from its laws; the final edition of the *Manual* (1895) put man in
the evolutionary process. Loewenberg, "The Reaction of American Scientists to
Darwinism," pp. 700–701.

cast in their lot with Darwinism.[7] The response of American scientists was more affirmative than that of the French (Darwin's candidacy for membership in the French Academy was at first rejected), more immediate than that of the English (not until twenty years after the appearance of the *Origin of Species* did Cambridge, Darwin's university, award him an honorary degree).[8] By contrast, the American Philosophical Society awarded Darwin honorary membership as early as 1869, and the gesture was soon repeated by other American societies.[9] By 1873, the year of Agassiz' death, the theory of evolution was no longer a disputed hypothesis within the American scientific community, though some scientists entertained strong doubts as to whether natural selection was the major evolutionary agent,[10] and a few were reluctant to place man in the evolutionary process.[11] When one considers the prolonged enthronement of the miracle-working God in organic science, the enormous pre-Darwinian resistance to the theory of transmutation, the entrenchment of the Aristotelian-Christian doctrine of fixed forms and final causes, fifteen years of scientific inquest were a very brief period of doubt.

But it happened that, as scientific doubts subsided, religious opposition rose. At first, the spokesmen of orthodox religion were mostly content to attack the new theory as grossly hypothetical or untrue. Remembering the fate of Lamarck and St. Hilaire, they were confident that science would refute what appeared to be a new perpetration of old errors.[12] When, however, it became increasingly clear that science

[7] Burt G. Wilder, "Jeffries Wyman, Anatomist: 1814–1874," in David Starr Jordan, ed., *Leading American Men of Science* (New York, 1910), pp. 193–94. "The Joseph Leidy Centenary," *Scientific Monthly,* XVIII (June, 1924), pp. 422–36.

[8] *Popular Science Monthly,* II (March, 1873), 601. *Atlantic Monthly,* XXX (October, 1872), 507–8.

[9] Thomas Huxley, "On the Reception of the 'Origin of Species,'" in Francis Darwin, ed., *Life and Letters of Darwin,* II, pp. 538–41.

[10] Under Edward Drinker Cope there arose a neo-Lamarckian school—misnamed because the school stressed the direct action of the environment on organic structure (which had been denied by Lamarck) as well as the effects of use and disuse. See Cope, *The Origin of the Fittest* (New York, 1887). A neo-Darwinian school, consisting of the American followers of August Weismann, emphasized natural selection exclusively, which had never been Darwin's position. See George Gaylord Simpson, *The Meaning of Evolution* (New Haven, 1949).

[11] A respectable though not authoritative view, propounded by St. George Mivart and Alfred Russel Wallace, alleged the discontinuity between sentient and rational forms of life. St. George Mivart, *On the Genesis of Species* (New York, 1871); Alfred Russel Wallace, *Criticism of the Descent of Man* (New York, 1871).

[12] Cf. Heman Lincoln, "Development vs. Creation," *Baptist Quarterly,* II (July, 1868), 270; W. C. Wilson, "Darwin on the Origin of Species," *Methodist Quarterly Review,* XLIII (October, 1861), 605–25.

would return a favorable verdict, and when, furthermore, Darwin bluntly declared that his theory included man, the pitch of opposition rose and was sustained for several decades.[13] In this chapter we shall enlarge upon the character of the religious opposition to Darwin. Suffice it for the moment to say that it too diminished in time. In the 1880s, certain religious leaders came to see that science would not be swerved from its course by clamor and vituperation, and that the rigid opposition of the churches would serve to isolate them, insulate them, and destroy their ancient power.[14] The fading appeal of the Protestant churches for the working masses in the cities underscored the need for change, for some concession to the times.[15] Hence, one group of theologians, taking their cue from the compromises effected during the controversy over geology, endeavored to prove that the Biblical text supported the evolution of animals, and that the whole process of evolution was another indication of design.[16] A second group went further and undertook a thorough revision of theology in the light of evolutionary science. Applying Darwin's laws and Spencer's optimism to a wide range of Christian dogma, they maintained that sin was not a falling from grace but the heritage from man's brutal ancestry, that revelation was not a visitation from above but the product of developing reason, that God's will does not work from outside nature, but works through nature immanently.[17] In the eighties such doctrines were still regarded by the orthodox as abominable theological heresies. By the last decade of the nineteenth century, however, many religious spokesmen, especially in the Northeast, had crossed over to evolution on just such causeways of rationalization.[18] Talk of conflict between

[13] An analysis of the trends in religious opposition to Darwinism can be found in Windsor Hall Roberts, "The Reaction of American Protestant Churches to the Darwinian Philosophy," unpublished Ph.D. dissertation (University of Chicago, 1936).

[14] There had, of course, been moderates in the religious camp from the beginning. See S. R. Calthrop, "Religion and Evolution," *Religious Magazine and Monthly Review*, L (September, 1873), 193–213.

[15] Arthur M. Schlesinger, Sr., "A Critical Period in American Religion," *Proceedings, Massachusetts Historical Society*, LXIV (June, 1932), 423–47.

[16] See James McCosh, *The Development Hypothesis: Is it Sufficient?* (New York, 1876); Arnold Guyot, *Creation or The Biblical Cosmogony in the Light of Modern Science* (New York, 1884).

[17] See Henry Ward Beecher, "The Sinfulness of Man," in *Evolution and Religion* (New York, 1885), p. 81; Lyman Abbott, *The Evolution of Christianity* (New York, 1893), pp. 112 ff.

[18] The turn of opinion in the Northeast is neatly exemplified by the articles that appeared in a popular journal, the *North American Review*. In 1860, the magazine published Francis Bowen's violently antagonistic review of Darwin's book ("Dar-

science and religion was then discounted in the very journals that had cried it up a decade or two before.[19] By the end of the century, antievolutionism had lost its place in serious theology,[20] though it remained astonishingly strong as part of a folkish fundamentalism.[21]

How may we account for the hostility of the religious community to this new development in biology? The modern ear, jarred by fundamentalist idioms, may hear only the accent of unreason. That some of Darwin's critics were shallow and ignorant is certainly true. On one obtuse level of criticism, for example, some of Darwin's opponents foreshortened the steps in the process of evolution and described it as "the tendency of favourable varieties of turnips to become men," or as the theory that "man, having first been a tadpole, became a monkey, and then wore off his tail by sedentary habits." [22] Others, exhibiting a kind of phylogenetic snobbery, seemed to think that Darwin had libeled the race by discovering simian rather than seraphic ancestors.[23] Still others, not grasping the distinction between probable and demonstrative reasoning, thought the absence of fossil remains linking man with the other primates completely disproved evolution.[24] But ignorance

---

win on the Origin of Species," XC [April, 1860], 474–506). In 1868, Francis E. Abbot, reviewing Spencer's *Principles of Biology,* attacked the special-creation hypothesis (CVII [October, 1868], 378). In 1870, C. L. Brace, in an article entitled "Darwinism in Germany," lauded Darwin's "incomparable carefulness and diligence" (CX [April, 1870], 284–99). Finally, Chauncey Wright's three articles appeared in defense of Darwin, Darwinism, and the Darwinian method of inquiry, "Review of Wallace's Contributions to the Theory of Natural Selection," CXI (October, 1870), 282; "Review of Darwin's Descent of Man," CXIII (July, 1871), 63–103; "Evolution by Natural Selection," CXV (July, 1872), 1–30.

[19] William North Rice, a geologist and an eminent Methodist layman, had castigated the clergy in the 1870s for their unmovable opposition to Darwinism. In 1891, Rice reported that "now and then . . . some theological Rip Van Winckle attempts the old Sinaitic thunders in denunciation of the essential atheism of evolution; but his utterances are regarded by his brethren in the church not with sympathy, but with amusement or mortification." "Twenty-five Years of Scientific Progress," *Bibliotheca Sacra,* L (January, 1893), 27–28.

[20] Frank H. Foster, *The Modern Movement in American Theology* (New York, 1939), p. 160.

[21] Stewart G. Cole, *The History of Fundamentalism* (New York, 1931), *passim.*

[22] Cited in *The Index,* Vol. III, Supplement (April 13, 1872), p. 3; see, also, Sidney Ratner, "Evolution and the Rise of the Scientific Spirit in America," *Philosophy of Science,* III (January, 1936), 108–9.

[23] "Modern Atheism," *The Southern Review,* X (January, 1872), 121–58.

[24] Frederick Gardiner, "Darwinism," *Bibliotheca Sacra,* XXIX (April, 1872), 240–89; "Darwinianism," *American Quarterly Church Review,* XXI (January, 1870), 524–36.

alone would not have attached so much passion to these objections. At the core of the religious resistance, making it hard and bitter and giving it desperate strength, was not so much ignorance as fear. "Nothing is more evident," wrote the Andover theologian, William J. Tucker, "than that a certain sense of fear . . . has begun to seize the heart of our generation. We are literally afraid of the world in which we live." [25] The fact was that while Darwin had labored to make the natural world intelligible and pellucid, to many of the men of his generation he had rendered that world cold and repellent, and they fought to keep it safe from his negations.

Generally speaking, two eventualities were feared: the annihilation of spirit and the destruction of moral sanctions. Darwin's extension of natural law to organic life, following upon its extension to the heavens and to the history of the earth, seemed to exclude divine and ideal ends from the whole theater of existence. Until vitalism and finalism were reconstructed in evolutionary terms, it did not seem that any of the old truces between spirit and matter, purpose and law, could survive under Darwin's influence. The idea of the evolution of the species cut straight under the belief that all living things attain a preordained form; the idea of the evolution of the species through chance variations refuted the belief in divine contrivance; the idea of the evolution of man through chance variations destroyed all hope of spiritual favor. By thus denying spirit, Darwin was thought to doom the whole moral economy based on salvation and retribution. For, in a world where man was mere matter, a being perhaps ultimate but not unique, the ideas of immortality and redemption were errors based on delusions. In a world directed by impersonal force, insensible to the suffering through which it achieved blind goals, prayer and propitiation were wasted on a void. In a world that was lawful through and through, and not susceptible to miracles, the mission and the message of Christ could not have been supernaturally decreed. If in such a world values were to have any meaning or pertinence at all, this could only be achieved by seizing on brute existence and calling it ideal—a course that the popular Herbert Spencer was taking, to the destruction of transcendental ethics and all absolute good. As though this were not enough, Biblical scholarship had come on the scene to complete the unholy work.

[25] Quoted in Daniel Day Williams, *The Andover Liberals: A Study in American Theology* (New York, 1941), p. 46.

Just as the evolutionists linked man with lesser organisms, so the anthropologists linked Scripture with heathen fable. Where Darwin put God beyond the frontiers of nature, the critics of the Bible put His word in the limbo of myth. Who, then, could look on theories that turned Christianity into a mere quotation, theology into an erroneous physics, the universe into something soulless and friendless, and not call these doctrines false, their perpetrators anathema?

This was the psychological background for the attack upon evolution in the colleges. Inevitably, as science was converted to evolution and the curriculum was converted to science, the heresies broached by Darwin bid for academic acceptance. This was inevitable and not at first far-reaching, but in the catastrophic vision of the faithful, where small things loomed as great and innocuous acts as enormities, the attempt to teach evolution seemed part of a devilish plot. Determined efforts were made in the sixties, seventies, and early eighties to hold the line of education by the tactic of exclusion where possible, by threats and tirades where necessary. Synods gave warnings to trustees and trustees instructed presidents to reject the applications of Darwinians. Attacks in the local pulpits, alarms in the religious press, were employed to make colleges toe the mark and professors mend their ways. Once again, a battle of ideas became a battle for the schools.

Because the religious reaction was intense, the colleges experienced difficulties; because the religious reaction was also variable, the colleges experienced rebellion. Had a policy of excluding the proponents of evolution been uniformly applied, it is very possible that deviants would never have appeared to disturb the peace of the academy. If professors could always have known the penalties, they might never have been willing to run risks. But the fact was that academic policy was not consistent and the wages of heresy were not always known. Whether evolutionists would be hired or not depended on a number of factors: the strength of the college's tie to a church or sectarian sponsor; the rigidity of the religious creed binding trustees and staff; the importance of science and scientists in the college's scheme of education; the ambition of college leaders to defend their institution's reputation. In general, the theological seminaries practiced exclusion more rigidly than the state universities, the colleges under close church governance more consistently than those whose church connections were looser. But even in a theological seminary, a Woodrow or Smyth could gain admittance, and even in a church-dominated college, a Winchell could be engaged. Moreover, the religious forces did not agree on the kind of teaching they should proscribe. Lacking ecclesiastical unity, Protestants could not be consistent in their policies, positions, and plans. Some thought it dangerous mischief to teach evolution even as an hypothesis; others were roused to action only when it was taught as the truth. In certain places, any sort of evolutionary exegesis would incur the wrath of the religious; in others, a barrier would be erected solely around the field of philosophy. Furthermore, there was a division in religious councils as to the possibilities of reconciliation: in certain places the old faith was to be kept pure, free from any foreign admixture; in other places it might be combined with some of the findings of science. In fostering academic friction, uncertainty is as important as repression. In a situation where the margin of safe divergence is obscure, the pale of orthodoxy undiscernible, the penalties of heresy unpredictable, the cautious man will blunder and the man of moderation will be martyred. One of the consistent and significant features of these academic-freedom cases was that the participants were temperate evolutionists who, in the course of events, were trapped into conflict with authority and were surprised into suffering for the cause.

The clearest illustrations of this can be found in the cases that arose in the theological seminaries.[26] In these institutions a large proportion of the faculty was cut to the denominational pattern; the purposes of instruction were creedal, the interest in science undeveloped. This was particularly true in the southern theological seminaries. John M. Mecklin, who knew the southern seminaries in this period at first hand, described them as living in "peaceful monastic seclusion" untroubled by the new discoveries of science. Their mental outlook, he wrote, was "not essentially different from that of Bernard and the monks of Clairvaux. It was naively assumed that this orthodox point of view coincided

[26] Valuable secondary works on these and all the academic-freedom cases involving Darwinism are few. The chief source of information is Andrew Dickson White's *A History of the Warfare of Science with Theology* (New York, 1896), and every subsequent treatment of these cases has followed at least the valuable leads of these volumes, if not their biases. This work's compilation of cases and use of not readily available newspaper materials are invaluable, but its simple Manichean interpretation, suggested by the militant title, leaves much to be desired. Supplementary to this work are Bert J. Loewenberg, "The Impact of the Doctrine of Evolution on American Thought," unpublished Ph.D. dissertation (Harvard University, 1933), and Howard K. Beale, *A History of Freedom of Teaching in American Schools* (New York, 1941), pp. 202–7.

with the truth." [27] Yet even these schools for ministers, in their conservative southern setting, were not consistent enough in their demands to eliminate all uncertainty.

In 1857 the Presbyterian Theological Seminary in Columbia, South Carolina, established "The Perkins Professorship of Natural Science in Connexion with Revelation, the design of which shall be to evince the harmony of science with the records of our faith, and to refute the objections of infidel naturalists." [28] The controlling synods chose for this task a Presbyterian minister who had studied science under Agassiz and had received a Ph.D. from Heidelberg. For twenty-five years James Woodrow labored to fit the odd-shaped pegs of science into the existing holes of theology, and his long tenure may be taken as evidence that he was thought to have succeeded.[29] Meanwhile, however, Darwin had appeared on the scene to complicate the problem of apology. The suspicion arose that the professor had accepted evolution, and that, in holding to this theory as his standard, he had reversed the fitting process and was now attempting to adapt theology to his scientific beliefs. Requested by the seminary's board in 1884 to expound his views on evolution, Woodrow replied that he accepted the "divine inspiration of every expression which [the Bible] contains"; that he thought, however, that the Bible had nothing to say on the mode of man's creation; that where it did speak in contrary terms, as in the story of the origins of Eve, he was willing to reject evolution.[30] As Woodrow expected, the Board of Directors was appeased by an approach to evolution that let the Bible decide its applications. But the governing Synod declared Woodrow out of bounds by that small but all-important fraction of belief which sets sectarians apart. The issue, resolved one group in the South Carolina Synod, did not hinge on whether "the said views of Dr. Woodrow contradicted the Bible in its highest and absolute sense, but upon the question whether they contradict the interpretation of the Bible by the Presbyterian Church in the United States." [31] The

[27] John M. Mecklin, *My Quest for Freedom* (New York, 1945), pp. 60, 61.

[28] Marion W. Woodrow, ed., *Dr. James Woodrow as Seen by His Friends* (Columbia, S.C., 1909), p. 13.

[29] Woodrow's conflict with the obscurantists in his church preceded this crisis. See Thomas Cary Johnson, *The Life and Letters of Robert Lewis Dabney* (Richmond, Va., 1903), pp. 339–49.

[30] James Woodrow, "Address on Evolution," delivered May 7, 1884, to the Alumni Association of the Columbia Theological Seminary. In Marion Woodrow, *Dr. James Woodrow*, pp. 617–45.

[31] White, *History of the Warfare . . .* , I, 317.

Board of Directors yielded to pressure, and Woodrow was dismissed for fostering the kind of compromise it was the duty of his office to promote.[32]

The southern seminary was not the only place where trials and ordeals for vague infidelities were endured. In 1886, the Board of Visitors of the Andover Theological Academy (Congregational), which by charter was charged with the task of admonishing or removing professors for heterodoxy,[33] tried five members of the faculty for defection from the Andover Creed. As a result, one of the accused, Professor Egbert C. Smyth, Brown Professor of Ecclesiastical History and President of the Faculty, was dismissed. The defendants had not been entirely unaware that they had been earning the displeasure of the Visitors. For some years their teachings had been subjected to mounting criticism in the church. According to the most orthodox theologians, Calvinism was based on the absolute trustworthiness of Scripture, the inherent sinfulness of man, the certainty of future punishment. The Andover professors, using the *Andover Review* as their organ, had accepted the higher criticism of the Bible, the doctrine of natural evolution, and the dogma of probation after death for those who had never known Christ.[34] But these did not seem to them gross enough divergences to warrant indictment and trial. After all, their heresies, in any large view, were marginal, and their tenure of office had been long. In no vital respect did they disavow the fundamental dogmas of Calvin. Certainly they had always opposed the aberrant views of the Unitarians and the agnosticism of such evolutionists as Spencer. *Progressive Orthodoxy,* the title of one of their books, was the proper name for their position. Moreover, when appointed to their positions, they had reserved the right to interpret the Andover Creed in accordance with their consciences, and had not been disturbed for doing so—Smyth for as long as twenty-five years. The fact that the trustees sided with

[32] A similar case occurred at the Southern Baptist Seminary at Louisville, Kentucky, where in 1879 Professor Crawford H. Toy was expelled for expounding advanced Biblical criticism. This came after a ten-year incumbency. Charles C. Torrey, "Crawford H. Toy," *Dictionary of American Biography,* XVIII, 621–22; *National Cyclopedia of American Biography,* VI, 94.

[33] William J. Tucker, *My Generation* (Boston and New York, 1919), p. 186. Tucker, one of the defendants in the trial, gives the clearest picture of the Andover controversy. See also Henry K. Rose, *History of Andover Theological Seminary* (Boston, 1933), pp. 168–79.

[34] Daniel Day Williams, *The Andover Liberals,* gives an excellent presentation of the New Theology as promulgated at Andover; pp. 64–83, and *passim.*

the accused at the trial,[35] and the fact that the Visitors dismissed only Egbert Smyth, though his colleagues shared his opinions, reveal the divided and unpredictable character of the orthodox attack. As it happened, the case had a happy outcome. The Visitors' decision was appealed and set aside in the Supreme Court of Massachusetts and Smyth was restored to his position.[36]

The Winchell affair at Vanderbilt presents another variation on the same theme. A large gift from Commodore Vanderbilt in 1873 converted Central University in Nashville, Tennessee, from a school for the training of ministers to a large, multipurpose university. Under the terms of the gift the institution retained an ecclesiastical system of control: the bishops of the Methodist church comprised the Board of Supervisors, and Bishop Holland N. McTyeire was named permanent president of the trustees.[37] The addition of wealth to evangelical zeal had the effect of broadening perspectives. Desiring to make this university supreme among the institutions of the region, and possessing a money endowment unmatched in the impoverished South, McTyeire engaged eminent men for his faculty, among them the able Alexander Winchell, an avowed, though conservative, evolutionist. It was logical to assume that once ambition had opened the gates to an evolutionist, ambition would thereafter protect him. No doubt this was Winchell's assumption when in 1878 he wrote a tract on the pre-Adamite origin of man.[38] The argument, based on the assumption that Negroes were racially too inferior to have stemmed from the Biblical Adam, had appeared in southern race mythology before.[39] The book was liberally sprinkled with reverent allusions to the scientific truth of Scripture. Winchell, moreover, was not yet ready to concede that the law of evolution included man, and he always believed that the law of evolution but administered the will of the Maker.[40] Yet even these conciliatory

[35] The arguments of the complainants and the defendants can be found in *Arguments on Behalf of the Complainants in the Matter of the Complaint against Egbert C. Smyth* (Boston, 1887); *The Question at Issue in the Andover Case* (Boston, 1893); *The Andover Heresy: Professor Smyth's Argument, Together with the Statements of Professors Tucker, Harris, Hincks and Churchill* (Boston, 1887).

[36] *Egbert C. Smyth* vs. *Visitors of the Theological Institution in Phillips Academy in Andover, 154 Massachusetts Reports, 551–69 (1892).

[37] Edwin Mims, *History of Vanderbilt University* (Nashville, Tenn., 1946), pp. 32–33.

[38] Alexander Winchell, *Adamites and Preadamites* (Syracuse, 1878).

[39] For a systematic discussion of this point see William Sumner Jenkins, *Pro-Slavery Thought in the Old South* (Chapel Hill, N.C., 1935), pp. 254–75.

[40] Alexander Winchell, *The Doctrine of Evolution: Its Data, Its Principles and*

ideas proved offensive to the faithful. Religious journals, one of them under the editorial direction of the dean of Vanderbilt's Biblical Department, accused Winchell of attempting to destroy the truths that were given in the Gospel.[41] In the face of this criticism, the President's ambition quickly surrendered to caution. Winchell was dismissed, under circumstances that again reveal the incalculable consequences of nonconformity. We quote Winchell's published account in full:

Forty-five minutes before the hour appointed for my late lecture at the University on "Man in the Light of Geology," I met Bishop McTyeire casually, and he embraced the opportunity to introduce a business which caused me extraordinary surprise. He said, in effect:

"We are having considerable annoyance from the criticisms which are passed by our people on some of your positions in matters of opinion, and it is likely to increase."

"What positions?" I asked.

"The positions taken in your pamphlet on Adamites and Pre-Adamites. Our people do not believe those things; they object to evolution."

"But," said I, "evolution is not professed in that pamphlet; there is not a single position in it which is not generally accepted, save the opinion that perhaps the black races are older than the white and brown."

"Well, our people are of the opinion that such views are contrary to the 'plan of redemption.' "

"The redemption of man," I replied, "could as well operate retroactively from Christ to races older than Adam, as from Christ to Abraham or Adam."

"I am not offering any objections myself," replied the Bishop, "but our people are complaining and the University will suffer, and I thought, perhaps, you might relieve us of our embarrassments. The Board," he continued, "will be in session in a few minutes, and they will meet again, after your lecture."

"I am unable to understand you. I think you exaggerate the complaints. Besides, the complaints are groundless."

"Well," said the Bishop, "the St. Louis *Advocate* has been hostiling the subject, and you know what the attitude of our *Advocate* has been."

The latter mention aroused equal surprise and indignation; for only a few days previously the Bishop, in a lengthy and confidential interview, which of course I am not at liberty to report, had made statements—revelations—to me, such that I did not expect to see Dr. Summers' perversions and insinuations turned to my disadvantage at the hand of a high official occupying an inside position. I reminded the Bishop of what he had said in the conversation with a view to inducing me to remain till commencement and deliver a

Its Theistic Bearings (New York, 1874), lectures delivered at Drew Theological Seminary, December, 1873; *Reconciliation of Science and Religion* (New York, 1877), p. 144; "Grounds and Consequences of Evolution," *Sparks from a Geologist's Hammer* (Chicago, 1881), p. 332.

[41] Mims, *History of Vanderbilt University,* p. 100.

lecture. "And you, yourself," I added, "proposed that I should lecture on Evolution."

"That is true," he replied, "for I wanted you to have an opportunity to put yourself right."

He did not explain whether he wished me to recant, or assemble [sic] or avow and defend my belief.

Referring again to the two discontented newspapers, he said, "These are feathers—straws."

"A great University ought to know how to withstand feathers and straws," said I.

"But they are likely to become stones," added the Bishop.

"These complaints are puerile," I continued. "They are themselves misconceptions of the facts, and they are prompted by bigotry. There has been no attempt to disprove the positions of my pamphlet. Besides that, I have not been heard; I have had no opportunity to explain or defend."

On repeating his request that I would relieve the Board of an embarrassment, I declared that I did not understand his meaning, and he then explained that he thought I might considerately "decline a reappointment."

"Are professors subject to annual appointment?" I asked.

"Well, yes; special professors are," he replied.

"No," said I, with indignation and scorn, "I will not, on such grounds, decline a reappointment. If the Board have the manliness to dismiss for cause, and declare the cause, I prefer they should do it. No power on earth could persuade me to decline. But the action which you foreshadow will be unjust and oppressive, as well as discrediting to the University. It will recoil upon its authors."

"We do not propose to treat you as the Inquisition treated Galileo," said the Bishop.

"But what you propose is the same thing," I rejoined. "It is ecclesiastical proscription for an opinion which *must be settled by scientific evidence.*" [42]

In the older eastern colleges, the cases arising over evolution formed a somewhat different pattern. Here religion and science had lived together in better accord. Steeped in irenic traditions, these colleges proved to be far more receptive to evolutionary ideas. Gradually, without fanfare, Darwinists were appointed to their expanding departments of science. In 1880, the roster at Yale included such evolutionists as O. C. Marsh in paleontology,[43] Addison Emery Verrill in zoology,[44]

[42] Letter of Alexander Winchell to the Nashville *Daily American,* June 16, 1878. The italics are in the text. The Library of Congress newspaper collection.

[43] Marsh was a distinguished advocate of the evolution of all life from simple forms, and his thoroughgoing evolutionism admitted no exceptions. "To doubt evolution to-day is to doubt science and science is only another name for truth." *Proceedings of the American Association for the Advancement of Science,* XXVI (1877), 212. "One of the main characteristics of this epoch is the belief that *all*

Sidney Irving Smith in zoology and comparative anatomy,[45] and James Dwight Dana in geology; [46] at Brown there was Alpheus Spring Packard, a neo-Lamarckian entomologist; [47] at Princeton, though Cope's application was refused,[48] Arnold Guyot in geography,[49] Charles A. Young in astronomy, and Cyrus Brackett in physics [50] were evolutionists to some degree. At Harvard, the oldest college, which was becoming under Eliot also the greatest, every naturalist on the staff—Gray, Hagen, Goodale, Whitney, Shaler, James, Farlow, Faxon, and the younger Agassiz—accepted the theory of mutability.[51] To be sure, the pace of acceptance was not everywhere rapid: in 1880, the Reverend Mr.

---

life, living and extinct has been evolved from simple forms. Another prominent feature is the accepted fact of the *great antiquity of the human race.*" Presidential Address, *Proceedings of the American Association for the Advancement of Science,* XXVIII (1879), 33. Winchell had been dismissed only a year before for saying what Marsh could say with complete impunity. Indeed, even at Nashville, Marsh was bold enough to say in 1877 that "every sensible man is an evolutionist." Mims, *History of Vanderbilt University,* p. 60. In paleontology, Marsh's reconstruction of the development of the horse through geologic ages was acclaimed by Darwin as the best support of his theory that had appeared since the *Origin of Species.* Charles Schuchert and Clara Mae Le Vene, *O. C. Marsh, Pioneer in Paleontology* (New Haven, 1940), p. 247.

[44] See Wesley R. Coe, "Addison Emery Verrill," National Academy of Sciences, *Biographical Memoirs,* XIV (1929), 39; Wesley R. Coe, "A Century of Zoology in America," *A Century of Science in America* (New Haven, 1948), pp. 410–12.

[45] "An eager disciple of the then controversial Darwinian theory of Evolution, he sought for verification of this hypothesis in all he saw around him." Wesley R. Coe, "Sidney Irving Smith" in National Academy of Sciences, *Biographical Memoirs,* XIV (1929), 8.

[46] See p. 321n.

[47] With Cope and Hyatt, Packard founded the Neo-Lamarckian school of evolutionary thought. *Popular Science Monthly,* LXVII (May, 1905), 126–27. Packard's textbooks for high school and college students declared for evolution. See *First Lessons in Geology* (Providence, R.I., 1882), and *Zoology for High Schools and Colleges* (New York, 1880).

[48] In 1873, Cope failed to receive consideration for a newly created chair in natural science. His impression was that this was because of his pronounced views on evolution, but there is no factual proof that this was so. Benjamin Marcus, "Edward Drinker Cope," in Jordan, ed., *Leading American Men of Science,* p. 335.

[49] "While adopting the law of development and applying it to all history, still [he] believed that true species came into existence only by divine act. In his later years, as his work on 'Creation' shows, he was led to accept, though with some reservation, the doctrine of evolution through natural causes. He excepted man, and also the first of animal life." James Dwight Dana, "Arnold Guyot," National Academy of Sciences, *Biographical Memoirs,* II (1886), 334.

[50] There is nothing in their textbooks that would reveal acceptance of evolution, but it was claimed in the *Popular Science Monthly* that they were evolutionists "without reserve." "Scientific Teaching in the Colleges," *Popular Science Monthly,* XVI (February, 1880), 558.

[51] *The Index,* XI (March 4, 1880), 112–13.

Chadbourne, President of Williams, held forth against evolution in the college's only course in biology;[52] Amherst did not offer a course on evolution until 1897.[53] Taken as a group, however, these colleges were not proscriptive in the area of science: their scientists could find facts in Darwin's favor and not be denounced as unclean. Yet even here there was an area where ideas collided. This was the vague and indeterminate zone where science impinged on philosophy. It fell to the clerical presidents to try to police that zone, and friction arose when they laid down the rule: "Evolution so far but no further."

We are able to describe the attitudes of these pivotal figures, the eastern college presidents, on the basis of a questionnaire addressed to nine of them in the year 1880.[54] The question they were asked was whether they allowed it to be taught that "man, at least so far as his physical structure is concerned," was evolved from irrational animals. The answer they gave was "No!" and the reasons they gave are instructive. Several referred to the lack of evidence for such a sweeping hypothesis. The Reverend Julius H. Seelye, President of Amherst, wrote:

So long as the notion that man is evolved from the monkey has not a single fact to rest upon, and is in flat contradiction to all the facts of history, I think we may leave it with the sciolists. . . . This college does not yet teach groundless guesses for ascertained truths of science.[55]

[52] Cf. Paul Ansel Chadbourne, *Lectures on Natural Theology* (New York, 1867), and *Instinct, Its Office in the Animal Kingdom and Its Relation to the Higher Powers in Man* (New York, 1872).

[53] The catalogue of 1884–85 said: "While one special aim of the department is to furnish the student of medicine with a broad foundation for his future studies, its general aim is to lead every student to a careful examination of the laws which govern the structure, actions and occurrence of all living forms" (p. 32). The catalogue of 1897–98 went further: "The evolution of the Animal Kingdom. In this course the student traces, *as far as possible* [our italics], the line of evolution leading from the protozoon to man" (p. 52). The catalogue of 1900–1901 completely accepted evolution: "Zoology 2a. The evolution of lower invertebrates. 2b. The evolution of higher invertebrates and of vertebrates. 2c. The evolution of man" (p. 62).

[54] The presidents polled were Noah Porter of Yale, Martin Brewer Anderson of Rochester, James McCosh of Princeton, William Cassaday Cattell of Lafayette, Julius H. Seelye of Amherst, Eliphalet Nott Potter of Union, Paul Ansel Chadbourne of Williams, Samuel Gilman Brown of Hamilton, Ezekiel Gilman Robinson of Brown. Taken by the orthodox and vigilant *New York Observer,* the poll was designed to disprove the assertion that the evolution of man was taught in the colleges. The presidents of Harvard, Pennsylvania, and Johns Hopkins were not polled, for the probable reason that these presidents would not have given the desired answers. For commentary on the liberal side, see *The Index,* IX (March 4, 1880), 112–13.

[55] *Ibid.,* p. 112.

On the same tack, President Samuel Gilman Brown of Hamilton declared that

the doctrine of the "evolution of man from irrational animals" has never to my knowledge, been taught at Hamilton College. I trust it never will be till it has been proved true, as in my judgment it has not been, and I do not think it ever will be.[56]

The modern commentator cannot help observing that while these presidents paid their respects to the data, they ignored the verdict of science; that whereas they wished to put alien doctrines to test, they artfully or credulously supposed that their own assumptions were true. Others relied on the arguments of doctrinal moralism. The Reverend William Cassaday Cattell of Lafayette declared:

I have never known of any of my colleagues expressing either in private or in the classroom, the opinion referred to. . . . We are keenly alive to the danger from what is manifestly the infidel *trend* of the views generally held by evolutionists. It is a great relief to me to know that there is such a cordial acceptance of the old faith, which it has been the tendency or avowed aim of these materialistic teachers to destroy." [57]

And the Reverend James McCosh of Princeton replied:

I teach that man's soul was made in the image of God, and his body out of the dust of the ground. I do not oppose development, but an atheistic development.[58]

This was a half-way covenant that Francis Abbot called an "oil-and-water mixture of miracle and law." The two conventional arguments of the religious opposition were the pseudoscientific "not proven" and the theological "infidel trend."

Neither argument would pacify or convince the evolutionists on the faculties of institutions governed by antirevolutionists. Both arguments invited contradiction: the first through different readings of the record, the second through denials of the charge. The Porter-Sumner case at Yale in the late 1870s illustrates the point that once evolution had been accepted in the commerce of academic ideas, no selective blockade or embargo could thereafter easily be enforced. Hostilities began at Yale in 1879 when President Noah Porter demanded that Sumner abandon the use of Spencer's *Study of Sociology* as a textbook. Yale's venerable president had no objection to the teaching of evolution in the field of

[56] *Ibid.*   [57] *Ibid.* (Italics in the text.)   [58] *Ibid.*

natural science; [59] but he saw a great difference between Darwin's scientific synthesis of variation, adaptation, and selection and Spencer's philosophical trinity of matter, environment, and force. The difference, as he saw it, lay primarily in the implications of each for theistic religion. Porter wrote to Sumner:

The freedom and unfairness with which it [Spencer's book] attacks every Theistic Philosophy of society and of history and the cool and yet sarcastic effrontery with which he assumes that material elements and laws are the only forces and laws which any scientific man can recognize, seem to me to condemn the book as a textbook for a miscellaneous class in an undergraduate course.[60]

This pronouncement took Sumner by surprise. Porter had appointed Sumner to his post in 1872 over considerable religious opposition.[61] Spencer's works had been used in Porter's classes, and though there they became foils for Christian doctrine,[62] their use in other classes had not been proscribed. It would seem, wrote Sumner in reply, that "the use of Spencer's books is a privilege of the President and his use of them does not . . . constitute a precedent for anybody else; but I confess that this view of the matter never suggested itself to me." [63] Here again the unpredictable character of the religious riposte made prudence all but impossible. On the other hand, it is doubtful that the arrogant and opinionated Sumner would have taken the prudent course even if he had known it. To him, Porter was identified with a group that was opposing everything modern in education, from the elective system to alumni representation.[64] As a minister of the Episcopal church, Sumner had fought to liberalize theology and to correct the follies of sectarianism.[65] In Spencer, Sumner found scientific support for his rigid ethic of self-reliance and his strenuous belief in *laissez faire*.[66] A

[59] Schuchert and Le Vene, *O. C. Marsh*, pp. 238–39. Porter was no obscurantist in religion. He was opposed to fanaticism and pietistic fervor, and to sectarian bickering in missionary work. See Walter James, "Noah Porter," unpublished Ph.D. dissertation (Columbia University, 1951).

[60] Harris E. Starr, *William Graham Sumner* (New York, 1925), pp. 346–47. Starr's account of this controversy is indispensable.

[61] Cornelius Howard Patton and Walter Taylor Field, *Eight O'Clock Chapel, A Study of New England College Life in the Eighties* (Boston and New York, 1927), p. 102.

[62] Henry Holt, *Garrulities of an Octogenarian Editor* (Boston and New York, 1923), pp. 306–7.

[63] Starr, *William Graham Sumner,* p. 361.

[64] *Ibid.,* p. 75.   [65] *Ibid.,* p. 114.

[66] See William Graham Sumner, *What Social Classes Owe to Each Other* (New York, 1883).

powerful controversialist, a strong personality, a man who became a tradition at Yale while he lived and the idol of a cult after his death, Sumner was a formidable adversary for even a president of Yale.[67]

Sumner's defense was contained in a letter which he circulated to the faculty and the members of the Yale Corporation. He did not undertake to defend the merits of Spencer's book in any serious way— "what could be gained by an argument about that question? Where should it be carried on? Who wants to hear it?" The essential issue, as he saw it, was whether a professor who was competent enough to be allowed to teach should teach without restraint from religious taboos. In pitching his answer on this level Sumner wrote neither an *apologia pro vita sua* nor a brief for evolutionary philosophy, but an important document of academic freedom.

Sumner's arguments were directly opposed to those offered by the nine clerical college presidents. First of all, he rejected the *ad hominem* test so dear to the doctrinal moralists:

Mr. Spencer's religious opinions seem to me of very little importance in this connection, and, when I was looking for a book on sociology, the question whether it was a good or available book in a scientific point of view occupied my attention exclusively. Neither did I take into account the horror of Spencer's name, which, as I have since learned, is entertained by some people. If I had known of it, however, I should not have thought that it was a proper consideration to weigh much in the question which presented itself to me.[68]

Nor, said Sumner, was the argument that sociology was undeveloped as a science in any sense sufficient or compelling:

Pres. Porter affirms that sociology is inchoate and tentative. So is psychology; so are many new developments of physics, biology and other sciences. To object to what is inchoate and tentative is to set up a closed canon of human learning.[69]

Above all, he would not concede that any part of science should be quarantined:

His [Porter's] position was that the students might better get no sociology than run the risk of getting agnosticism in getting sociology, and he even seems to maintain that they might better get no sociology than get it from a book by Spencer. I resisted this and maintained that they should have sociology anyhow, from the best means available, and I would not submit to a restraint the

[67] Biographical material on Sumner may be found in Sumner's autobiographical sketch in *A History of the Class of 1863 of Yale College* (New Haven, 1905).

[68] Starr, *William Graham Sumner,* pp. 358–59.   [69] *Ibid.,* p. 360.

motive of which was consideration for metaphysical and theological interests.[70]

The immediate outcome was a draw. The Corporation, aware of Sumner's powerful support in the faculty and in a segment of the public press, refused to accept his resignation. On the other hand, Sumner did withdraw the text, claiming that its usefulness had been impaired by the publicity the contest had received. But one may agree with Harris E. Starr that, in the long run, the laurels rested with Sumner. Sumner "made his fight, and thereafter every professor at Yale who was devoted to truth rather than tied to dogma had greater confidence and courage." [71]

Except for Harvard,[72] the older eastern colleges in the early eighties

[70] *Ibid.*   [71] *Ibid.,* p. 369.

[72] Harvard was the first college to provide a lectureship for the exposition of evolutionary thought, this being John Fiske's course on "The Positive Philosophy" delivered during the academic year 1869–70 and again in 1870–71. It was a measure of the change brought about by the election of Charles W. Eliot to the presidency in 1869, for eight years before, as an undergraduate, Fiske had been threatened with expulsion from Harvard for lecturing to his schoolmates on Comtism. See John Spencer Clarke, *The Life and Letters of John Fiske* (Boston and New York, 1917), I, 231–35. Spencer wrote to Fiske: "That eight years should have wrought such a change as to place the persecuted undergraduate in the chair of lecturer is something to wonder at, and may fill us with hope, as it must fill many with consternation." Clarke, p. 356. A good deal of doubt, however, appears as to why Fiske, who had received a temporary appointment as instructor in history and then as assistant librarian, failed to receive a permanent professorship at Harvard. Clarke writes that the publication of Fiske's lectures in the New York *World* immediately produced a "wave of bitter objurgation and denunciation" in the "religious and a portion of the secular press" in protest against "Harvard's Raid on Religion." Many writers have subsequently followed Clarke in assuming that there was a great religious outcry over Fiske's lectures. Our own investigation of contemporary newspapers does not support that assumption. There is no defense of Fiske or mention of the attack in the New York *World* in the year those lectures were given, which surely would have been the case had that paper's favorite author been attacked. There is no mention of it in the New York *Tribune* (Nov. 13 to April 1, 1869–70) or the New York *Times* (Nov. 13 to Feb. 1, 1869–70). No reference to the Fiske lectures appears in the New York *Evangelist,* a Presbyterian weekly (Nov., 1869 to Feb. 10, 1870), or in the orthodox New York *Observer* (Nov., 1869 to March, 1870). The Boston newspapers are equally negative.

It is true that the Harvard University Board of Overseers had religious objections to Fiske. According to Clarke, when Fiske was nominated to his instructorship in history, "the orthodox element in the Board of Overseers, chafing under the steady progress of President Eliot's liberalizing policy, was roused to opposition, and vigorous protest to Fiske's confirmation was promptly made. It was openly charged that Fiske was a pronounced atheist, and the more dangerous because of his learning and ability. It was alleged that the Board had gone to the extreme limit of toleration in confirming him as Lecturer on Philosophy; to go further and sanction his occupancy of the chair of History, even temporarily, would be an insult to all the traditions of the college" (p. 374). But there are cryptic aspects in the Board's

were still provincial and religious in tone. They had not yet entered on their careers as universities. Although they swallowed, even stomached, evolution, it was not truly to their taste. By contrast, two secular private universities established after the Civil War—Cornell and Johns Hopkins—were broad and free in design. By their charters' terms and their founders' wishes they were nonsectarian institutions.[73] To their presidents and faculties evolution was not gall and wormwood, but everyday nourishing fare.[74] Cornell's students learned about evolution from President Andrew Dickson White in history, from Burt G. Wilder in biology, and, somewhat later, from Edward Titchener in psychology.[75] President Daniel C. Gilman of Johns Hopkins appointed Newell Martin, a disciple of Huxley, as professor of biology, and invited Huxley himself to speak at the university's opening ceremonies.[76] But there were limits to tolerance here too. Generally, evolution could thrive in the open, and doctrinaire Darwinists were safe, but scholarly critics of religion, or materialists in philosophy, were not. The weakness and strength of these universities lay in their newness and secular approach. More worldly than the New England colleges, they were less sure of themselves in the world; more openly committed to tolerance, they lacked a tradition of dissent; more secular in outlook and spirit,

---

attitude too. Clarke states that "broad-minded clergymen" like James Freeman Clarke supported Fiske, yet a letter by J. F. Clarke on file in President Eliot's correspondence, dated February 5, 1870, objects to Fiske on the grounds that his espousal of the positive philosophy of Auguste Comte disqualified him for instructional duties at Harvard. (Letter of David W. Bailey, secretary of the Harvard Corporation, to the author, January 28, 1953.) Furthermore, the Board at this time carried Fiske's nomination through despite the opposition, which would suggest that Fiske's subsequent failure to obtain a permanent position did not stem exclusively from religious considerations.

[73] Cornell's charter provided that "persons of every religious sect or of no religious denomination, shall be equally eligible to all offices and appointments." Carl L. Becker, *Cornell University: Founders and the Founding* (Ithaca, N.Y., 1943), p. 93. For Johns Hopkins' antisectarianism, see Fabian Franklin, *The Life of Daniel Coit Gilman* (New York, 1910), pp. 184, 186, 219–22.

[74] See Walter P. Rogers, *Andrew D. White and the Modern University* (Ithaca, N.Y., 1942), p. 79; Daniel Coit Gilman, "The Sheffield Scientific School," in *University Problems* (New York, 1896), pp. 113–14.

[75] For a discussion of Burt G. Wilder's contribution to evolution, see J. H. Comstock, "Burt Green Wilder," *Science,* LXI (May 22, 1925), 531–33. For Andrew Dickson White's, see C. K. Adams, "Recent Historical Work in the Colleges and Universities of Europe and America," *Papers, American Historical Association,* IV (January, 1890), 39–65; for Edward Titchener's work, see Edwin G. Boring, *The History of Experimental Psychology* (New York, 1929), pp. 402–13.

[76] Daniel Coit Gilman, *The Launching of a University* (New York, 1906), p. 20; Franklin, *Life of Gilman,* pp. 220–21.

they were not chafed by the Puritan conscience that would brook no outer restraint.

Thus, in the early eighties, the trustees of Johns Hopkins turned down a liberal English minister, James Ward, presumably because he was not orthodox enough for their chair in philosophy.[77] In 1877, Cornell refused to reappoint the philosopher Felix Adler, whom President White had secured to lecture on Hebrew and Oriental literature. Returning from graduate studies abroad, Adler had given lectures that, in the words of an editorial in the Cornell *Review,* were "calculated to develop in young minds, at least, strongly rationalistic views." [78] When he went so far as to suggest to a public audience that some of the central doctrines of Christianity were discoverable in other religions as well, he was roundly attacked in the local religious press. The university authorities warned him to desist, and at the end of his three-year appointment did not again offer him a place.[79] Since Adler's lectureship had been supported by the funds of an outside philanthropist, Vice-President Russel tried to make it appear that the trustees had not objected to Adler but to the donor's control over nominations.[80] White gave a different account, implying that Adler voluntarily withdrew.[81] But a letter from Russel to Adler, written toward the end of the latter's term, shows that the actual reason was the administration's faintness of heart:

You are surprised at my silence about your chances of returning here. One who walks a very narrow path over which he can safely guide his charge ought not to be very talkative. My charge is this university. Besides my children I have no other interest. Truth and Liberty will take care of themselves, their triumph is secure, but an institution may be injured irreparably, and no such great injury can befall it as a collision with either Truth or Liberty. Should one who guides it expose it to such a chance? . . . True wisdom, it seems to me, forbids my bringing on a contest where victory would not be of greatest importance, but where defeat would be lasting injury. This is the reason why I said nothing to you about returning on a new engagement. Had I the power I would make such an engagement, for I believe that your lectures here did nothing but good.[82]

[77] J. Mark Baldwin, *Between Two Wars: 1861–1921* (Boston, 1926), I, 118.
[78] Article in the New York *Times,* May 21, 1933.
[79] Rogers, *Andrew D. White,* p. 77.
[80] Letter of William C. Russel to Joseph Seligman, May 5, 1877. Furnished by Professor Horace L. Friess of Columbia University.
[81] Andrew Dickson White, "An Open Letter," April 5, 1877. Reproduced in *The Index,* VIII (June 21, 1877), 292–93.
[82] Letter of William C. Russel to Felix Adler, March 12, 1877. Furnished by Horace L. Friess of Columbia University.

Ironically, Russel was dismissed by the trustees four years later, for reasons that are still obscure, but which may have had to do with his own (as Lyman Abbott charged) "pronounced nonreligious convictions." [83]

All together, these incidents had a shattering effect on the colleges' inner harmony and poise. Formerly, the presidents had played the rebel, and their ethos of resignation had usually shortened the part. Now the role was taken by professors who, though reluctantly, played it lustily and at length. Winchell told his story to the papers; Smyth and friends fought their case in court; Sumner wrote a letter to his colleagues that was by former standards insubordinate. Disaffection, in becoming a movement, shunned the usual disguise.

Behind this break in the convention of acquiescence one perceives a shift in the faculties' groups of reference—that is, the groups toward whose judgment they were oriented, by whose values and demands they were controlled. Customarily, professors had deferred to their trustees. To be sure, long before the fight for evolution, the wisdom of the trustees had been challenged in the sphere of classroom teaching and control. Trustees had ceased to be the source of expert judgment on problems relating to technique. But they had not lost their moral authority over the wider sphere of deportment. As elders of the church and shepherds of the fold, they had the minister's and the prelate's prestige. As they were in close contact with the college community, their influence was personal and direct. Generally, in the ante-bellum era, the trustees ruled *de jure* as in fact. But their blunders in the conflict over Darwinism squandered this inheritance of respect. Their policy of repression, since it wavered, was seen by professors as caprice, and no rule can keep its moral nimbus when it seems to be a fickle changing thing. Again, the waverings of their policy of repression gave professors the courage to dissent, since there was always another college to go to should home grounds prove at any time unsafe. In addition there now appeared a new group of reference which rivaled and replaced the trustees. One result of the Darwinian crisis was that it brought together like-minded teachers—scientists, scholars, and philosophers— who believed in evolution and who developed new standards of conduct from their interaction and mutual support. To dissent, in their frame of reference, was not to be disloyal or obstructive, but to light a

[83] Rogers, *Andrew D. White,* p. 157.

beacon of reason in a fog of orthodox fears. Professors on trial for their opinions thus spoke to a larger jury than the one which adjudged their tenure. In fighting for scientific freedom, Winchell addressed not only his employers, but also his cohorts outside; he failed before the Methodist board, but he reached his allies and friends, and there was the greater reward. Nor did this shift in the axis of allegiance bring only intangible satisfactions. The evolutionists, scattered throughout the profession, were in a position to give concrete help, so that the victims of religious repression often improved their statuses and careers. Winchell received an appointment to a chair at the University of Michigan; Woodrow was eventually appointed to the presidency of the University of South Carolina; Crawford Toy was the recipient of a first-class position at Harvard. The other aspect of alienation from the trustees was a broader academic connection that encouraged and rewarded dissent.

The significance of the academic-freedom cases lies not only in the professorial attitudes they illustrated but in the public reaction they caused. These trials over matters of belief, with their openly inquisitorial spirit, their solemn invasions of privacy, their blatant idealizations of sect, were notoriously inept. The spectacle of a trial at Andover to decide whether the "Universal Atonement" claimed by the Andover professors agreed with the "General Atonement" in the Creed—agreement, not truth, being the issue—was a revival of a kind of heresy-hunt the age was confident it had outgrown.[84] To a people in search of solidarity after years of fratricidal war, a Presbyterian standard for Gospel, exclusively and coercively applied, seemed almost as perverse and as factious as a Methodist brand of mathematics or a Baptist rendition of Greek.[85] Attempts to put a good face on these actions (at which sophisticated secularists would have been successful) were defeated by the artless exultation of sectarians whenever they tasted success. Thus,

[84] "Heresy" trials occurred in the churches as well as in the colleges. In 1883, W. Heber Newton, a prominent Episcopalian clergyman, was indicted but not prosecuted. *The Nation,* XXXVIII (February 28, 1884), 179. Another Episcopalian minister, Howard MacQueary, was condemned by an Episcopalian council in 1891 for his *Evolution of Man and Christianity.* See "Intellectual Liberty," *Popular Science Monthly,* XXXVIII (April, 1891), 844. In 1898, however, when Arthur Cushman McGiffert, a Presbyterian minister, wrote a book that advanced opinions contrary to the Westminster Confession, the Assembly of the Presbyterian Church merely made it a question of honor as to whether he should withdraw from the church. It was a tacit admission that the heresy trial had become inappropriate. Loewenberg, "The Impact of the Doctrine of Evolution," p. 268.

[85] See the compilation of northern and southern newspaper opinion in Marion Woodrow, *Dr. James Woodrow,* pp. 646–720.

when the president of Vanderbilt tried to justify his ousting of Winchell by citing the need to retrench,[86] his more ingenuous coreligionists gave the underlying reason away. "The university has afforded us intense gratification by its recent action," declared the Tennessee Conference after Winchell's dismissal.

This is the age in which scientific atheism, having divested itself of the habiliments that must adorn and dignify humanity, walks abroad in shameless denudation. . . . But our university alone has had the courage to lay its young but vigorous hand upon the man of untamed speculation and say: "We will have no more of this. . . ." [87]

To call the religious and conciliatory Winchell a "man of untamed speculation" was to add the mistake of hyperbole to the sin of naiveté of mind. Liberal opinion took this as the cue for its counterattack. Vanderbilt University, wrote the editor of the *Popular Science Monthly,* "follows the exploded precedents of past centuries, and puts forth its power to muzzle, repress, silence and discredit the independent teachers of scientific truth." [88] Winchell was compared with Galileo. Something musty and medieval seemed to emanate from the scene of these purgations, something altogether out of keeping with the forward movement of the age.[89] In this new age of enlightenment, intellectual coercion meant regression; in this age of automatic progress, regression was a cardinal sin. The chief benefit and utility of these cases, therefore, was that they stuck in the craw of the public. Even before the phrases of academic freedom had become common American catchwords, these infringements on academic freedom came to be regarded as anachronisms.

Finally, the evolutionary cases spurred a fresh assault on sectarianism in the colleges. Heretofore, sectarian control had been attacked on financial grounds as inadequate, or on administrative grounds as unstable. Now it lay open to attack as the foe of scientific advance.[90] By reveal-

[86] See Hunter Dickinson Farish, *The Circuit Rider Dismounts: A Social History of Southern Methodism, 1865–1900* (Richmond, 1938), pp. 295–98.

[87] As reported in an editorial, "Vanderbilt University Again," *Popular Science Monthly,* XIV (December, 1878), 237.

[88] "Religion and Science at Vanderbilt University," *Popular Science Monthly,* XIII (August, 1878), 493.

[89] *The Index,* IX (July 11, 1878), 325.

[90] Thus Andrew Dickson White linked denominationalism to ancient oppressions of thought: "Here we have survivals of that same oppression of thought by theology which has cost the modern world so dear; the system which forced great numbers of professors, under penalty of deprivation, to teach that the sun and planets revolve

ing the intolerance of sectarian minds, the incompetence of clerical trustees, the excesses of religious authority, these widely noticed cases hastened secular reform. They did so, however, only because the intellectual ground was being prepared. An ideology of resentment against religious authority, emerging from the crucible of the Darwinian debate, was effectively undermining the philosophical supports of sectarianism. We turn now to explore the main ideas in that ideology.

THE ATTACK UPON RELIGIOUS AUTHORITY

The attack of the evolutionists upon religious authority was not a "war between science and religion." However certain it appeared to their opponents that atheism was their goal and the anti-Christ their collaborator, the evolutionists' mood was conciliatory. To be sure, most of the evolutionary scientists thought Darwin had delivered the *coup de grâce* to the main tenets of natural theology. No longer did they accept literally the Adamite version of creation. No longer did they resort to Paley's arguments. To maintain that the usefulness of natural organs proved God's existence, prevision, and moral aim seemed an anthropomorphic mistake fit for a cruder day. But it was still very much a matter of argument among them as to whether science, having overthrown certain tenets of natural theology, had also liquidated its concerns and biases. There were evolutionary positivists, like Chauncey Wright, who staunchly maintained that science should no longer be concerned with matters beyond factual description.[91] They believed that science should answer *hypotheses non fingo* to every question of spiritual meaning, cosmic purpose, and final ends. Their unwillingness to combine science with natural theology was shared by Darwin himself. As presented in the *Origin of Species,* the metaphor of natural selection was a principle for ordering facts, not an ethical or ontological law.[92] But other evolutionists still were eager to salvage the

---

about the earth; that comets are fire-balls flung by an angry God at a wicked world; that insanity is a diabolic possession; that anatomical investigation of the human frame is sin against the Holy Ghost; that chemistry leads to sorcery; that taking interest for money is forbidden by Scripture; that geology must conform to ancient Hebrew poetry." White, *History of the Warfare . . . ,* I, 318–19.

[91] Gail Kennedy, "The Pragmatic Naturalism of Chauncey Wright," *Studies in the History of Ideas* (New York, 1935), pp. 484 ff.; Philip P. Wiener, "Chauncey Wright's Defense of Darwin and the Neutrality of Science," *Journal of the History of Ideas,* VI (January, 1945), 19–45.

[92] See Francis Darwin, ed., *Life and Letters of Charles Darwin,* pp. 274–86.

intellectual estate of natural theology. Spencerians like John Fiske believed that science could disclose the plan and purpose of the universe, provided that in adhering to law it disclosed a master plan, an immanent purpose.[93] Still others, like William James, holding scientific laws merely probable, thought that the "will to believe" could resuscitate faith and religion.[94] There were, in addition, conservative theists like Asa Gray who still saw the hand of Providence working in mysterious ways, and more pantheistic scientists like Joseph Le Conte who ascribed the unpredictable products of evolution to a spiritual force in nature.[95] Truly, evolution proved compatible with a wide diversity of religious beliefs.[96]

Similarly, the evolutionists' attack upon religious authority over education was not an attack upon religion *per se*. The evolutionists who became university presidents—Charles W. Eliot, Andrew Dickson White, Daniel C. Gilman, and David Starr Jordan—could be considered irreligious only by narrow orthodox standards. To be sure, they were hostile to the religious bias that prevented acceptance of Darwin, and they opposed sectarian control of colleges. But each was loyal to what he considered the core-beliefs of religion, though that core might be practically devoid of dogma. Eliot's evolutionism led him to a conception of God as a glorious "Transcendent Intelligence," [97] and the quality of his piety was not strained. "He who studies Nature," he wrote in justifying his early choice of a scientific career, "studies the thoughts and works of God. God is revealed in His works as well as in His word, and he who reverently contemplates the works, worships

[93] John Fiske, *The Idea of God as Affected by Modern Knowledge* (Boston, 1886), pp. 95–96, and *passim*.

[94] William James, *The Will to Believe* (New York, 1903). See, also, Ralph Barton Perry, *The Thought and Character of William James* (2 vols.; Boston, 1935), II, 207–44.

[95] Asa Gray, *Natural Science and Religion* (New York, 1880); Joseph Le Conte, *Evolution: Its Evidence and Its Relation to Religious Thought* (New York, 1894).

[96] We still await a full-scale treatment of the conciliations of science and religion undertaken by the evolutionary scientists. Valuable articles have appeared, notably Sidney Ratner, "Evolution and the Rise of the Scientific Spirit in America," *Philosophy of Science*, III (January, 1936), 104–22; Bert J. Loewenberg, "The Controversy over Evolution in New England," *New England Quarterly*, VIII (June, 1935), 232–57; Loewenberg, "Darwinism Comes to America, 1859–1900," *Mississippi Valley Historical Review*, XXVIII (December, 1941), 339–68; Herbert W. Schneider, "The Influence of Darwin and Spencer on American Philosophical Theology," *Journal of the History of Ideas*, VI (January, 1945), 3–18. See also Edward A. White, *Science and Religion in American Thought: The Impact of Naturalism* (Stanford, 1952).

[97] Henry James, *Eliot*, I, 318.

as truly as he who reads the word." [98] For all his reputation for rationalism, Andrew Dickson White firmly believed in the Scriptural plan of salvation.[99] David Starr Jordan scorned the atheist, and though his God was more like Spencer's Great Unknowable than the Christian personal God, he used consecrated phrases to describe Him—the "power that made for righteousness," that which "transcends humanity." [100] Perhaps there was something genteel and colorless about the religion of these educators, perhaps something underdeveloped and oversimple; but they were not, as their religious enemies made them out to be, godless, faithless, unmindful of the need of worship.

But this is not to say that all the ideological conflicts were apparent, and that none of them was real. For the great Darwinian debate was richer in significant issues than any in the American annals of disputation. It went far beyond the substantive problem of whether evolution was true, and far beyond the psychological problem of how to hold to acquired science while retaining birth-right beliefs. Touching on the nature and sanctions of authority, the methods and problems of verification, the standards of scientific debate, the Darwinian controversy eventually implicated all that was problematic in the area of human judgment. The philosophy of science, the psychology of learning, the metes of intellectual freedom, all entered the purview of this controversy. In consequence there was not *a* war, but many particular wars: a war between two kinds of men of knowledge—the clerical and the scientific; between two sorts of educational control—the sectarian and the secular; between two fundamental ways of knowing—the authoritarian and the empiricist; between two basic approaches to instruction —the doctrinal and the natural. We can summarize these conflicts by saying that science and education joined forces to attack two major objectives—the authority of the clergy and the principles of doctrinal moralism—and that one of the effects of this coalition was the hastening of academic reform.

ANTI-CLERICALISM IN SCIENCE AND EDUCATION

In Chapter VI we noted that in the days before Darwin, the Protestant pastor and the scientific worker had usually walked in step. One

---

[98] *Ibid.,* I, 64.　　　　　　　　　　　[99] Rogers, *Andrew D. White,* p. 83.
[100] Edward McNall Burns, *David Starr Jordan: Prophet of Freedom* (Stanford, 1952), p. 189.

reason for their rapport was the effect of the Protestant spirit and heritage upon the office of the minister. Opposed to any priestly exclusiveness, the Protestant minister shared the intellectual interests of his communicants. Because he was outside the infallible Church, he had to buttress religious doctrine with the facts and theories of science. Quite often, as we have seen, he dabbled in science himself. But, paradoxically, once Darwin caused a parting of the ways, these same clerical Protestant attitudes only served to widen the breach. Because he was close to the views of his congregation, the Protestant minister tended to reflect its unenlightened ideas and give voice to its unreasoning fears. In a sense, therefore, clerical anti-Darwinism became the spearhead of popular anti-intellectualism. Worse yet, since he could trade on his scientific reputation, the Protestant minister felt no qualms in challenging expert opinion, in searching the scientific literature for anti-revolutionary testimony, in declaring with pontifical assurance that Darwin was factually wrong. What made clerical anti-Darwinism so imprudent, so powerful, and also so resented was that it carried the fight against evolution into the court of science itself.[101]

The reaction of the evolutionists was to attack the competence of the clergy to judge the issues of science. Huxley's retort to Bishop Wilberforce at the 1860 meeting of the British Association for the Advancement of Science became a favorite anecdote and then a legend of American scientific anticlericalism. "Is it on his grandfather's or his grandmother's side that the ape ancestry comes in?" the fatuous Bishop had inquired. Huxley had been unsparing in his reply: "If there were an ancestor whom I should feel shame in recalling, it would be a man . . . who, not content with success in his own sphere of activity, plunges into scientific questions with which he has no real acquaintance." [102] This moral was soon recited by native Huxleys.[103] The clergy

[101] Selectively, the Protestant ministers quoted from the scientist Richard Owen to prove natural selection ineffective; from the scientist Quatrefois to prove the species in nature immutable; from the scientist St. George Mivart to prove Darwin in error at many points. See Loewenberg, "The Impact of the Doctrine of Evolution," p. 268.

[102] Various eyewitnesses to this colloquy have presented different accounts. The version quoted above can be found in Henshaw Ward, *Charles Darwin: The Man and His Warfare* (Indianapolis, 1927), pp. 313–15.

[103] We have relied heavily on the *Popular Science Monthly,* a crusading journal of evolution, and on *The Index,* the organ of the Free Religious Association. While these journals were on the "left" in the evolution controversy, they are of inestimable value for the accounts of a wide range of events and opinions contained in their

are not competent to make scientific judgments, wrote John **Trow-**bridge in the *Popular Science Monthly*.

Ministers who are only general readers in science can have no conception of the scientific spirit which comes through investigation. There is a cultivated interest which arises only from familiarity with methods, processes, and instruments. A minister lives apart from the seething turmoil and progress of the scientific world; and, if he should attempt to dispute with innovators, he will meet the same fate as any comparative recluse who attempts to dictate to the world from his retirement.[104]

Not only occupational, but mental and temperamental disabilities, were charged against the clergy. The clerical mind, wrote Francis Abbot, editor of *The Index,* can never accept the fact of its own fallibility.[105] The clerical mind, wrote David Starr Jordan, is irrevocably committed to untestable assumptions.[106] The key argument of the disciples of evolution was that science and religion, while not necessarily different as to content, were quite separate as spheres of competence.[107]

Like the doctrine of design in an earlier day, the doctrine of scientific competence was one of the large and influential ideas that have altered the course of intellectual history and the historical relations of intellectuals. It took the form of two theories: a theory of the scientific elite, in which the function of competence was judicial; and a theory of scientific procedure, in which the function of competence was methodological. Both can be found in the writings of Francis E. Abbot, the leader of the Free Religion movement. Opposed both to the transcendentalists, who relied mainly on private illumination, and the Biblical fundamentalists, who sought a fixed and infallible authority, Abbot pro-

---

pages. *The Index* was published from 1870 to 1886; cf. Stow Persons, *Free Religion* (New York, 1947), pp. 85–90. The *Popular Science Monthly* was launched in 1867 and continues to the present day.

[104] John Trowbridge, "Science from the Pulpit," *Popular Science Monthly,* VI (April, 1875), 734–35.

[105] Francis E. Abbot, "Authority in Science and in Religion," *The Index,* III (Dec. 20, 1871), 412.

[106] David Starr Jordan, "The Church and Modern Thought," *Overland Monthly,* XVIII (1891), 392.

[107] This argument was presented by so conservative a scientist as St. George Mivart, an English Catholic, whose book arguing for psychogenesis in evolution was placed on the Roman Catholic Index, and who, in arguing for the right of science to decide matters within its province, was excommunicated. In an article entitled "Modern Catholics and Scientific Freedom," printed in *Nineteenth Century,* Vol. XVIII (July, 1885), Mivart argued that the past blunders of the Church in scientific matters disqualified it to be the supreme arbiter in scientific affairs and that even loyal Catholics might refuse to submit to its decisions (pp. 35–36).

posed that a "tribunal of science" be created—a court of trial and appeal for the provisional determination of truths. On it, would sit the leading authorities of science; to it, the problems of science would be submitted; from it, a "consensus of the competent" would be derived; by it, the world would be purged of imposture by continuing applications of *expertise*. The idea of a scientific tribunal was, of course, an old and vulnerable one—a Baconian dream easily rebuffed by realities. But the idea that the competence of scientists was exclusive and that their judgment for the moment was authoritative—this was a formidable conception, and it endured in the ideology of science.[108]

Competence, to Abbot, did not rest merely on acquired skill and knowledge; it also was dependent upon the discipline of the scientific method. "I vindicate," he wrote, "the rights of the human intellect as the sole *discoverer* of truth; I maintain the unique and exclusive claim of the scientific method as the sole *organon* of its discovery." [109] To Abbot there was nothing recondite about the scientific method: it was ordinary thinking corrected and refined by caution. It began, as he understood it, with facts—not with innate ideas or intuitions; it proceeded through hypothesis and deduction—through the pure operations of reason; it ended in verification—in the empirical test of conclusions; it submitted to public inspection—to the verification of others. It differed from other ways of knowing: from the ways of faith, intuition, and authority. It accepted no prerequisite beliefs from faith, no untestable propositions from intuition, no final decrees from authority.

These two conceptions of competence were in some ways closely related. The judicial competence of the scientist depended upon his ability to perform the operations of the scientific method; the methodological competence of the scientist depended upon the use of his acquired knowledge in perceiving and formulating problems. On the other hand, in certain ways, the two conceptions of competence were opposed. In the one—the conception of the "wise men"—competence was depicted as uncommon, antecedent, and adjudicative; in the other—the theory of the "wise means"—competence was depicted as more common, projective, participative. The first conception set the scientist apart

[108] Francis E. Abbot, "A Tribunal of Science," *The Index,* IX (June 6, 1878), 270; "The Individual at the Bar," *ibid.,* X (April 17, 1879), 186–87; *ibid.,* X (Dec. 25, 1879), 613.

[109] Francis E. Abbot, "The Scientific Method in Religion," *The Index,* VIII (March 22, 1877), 136.

from other men: he was an oracle who spoke truthfully and to the profit of those who heard him; he was an esoteric specialist comprehensible only to his kind. The other drew the scientist closer to the run of men: he was the exponent of their artisan interest in facts and causes and effects; he represented their moral interest in detachment and in mental candor. Those who were concerned with the relations of science to the common life would find it difficult to strike a balance between these two notions of competence. But however this may be, both notions upheld the claim that scientists were exemplary men of knowledge, and this is their significance for our theme. Both discounted the qualifications of the priest to control the dominion of knowledge. Both asserted that cultivation rather than consecration, accomplishments rather than observances, skill and method rather than piousness, accredited the man of knowledge. Not before the Darwinian controversy did scientists present so pre-emptive and imperious a claim to gnostic superiority.[110]

These anticlerical, panscientific notions soon found expression within the colleges, where the position of the Protestant minister was undergoing changes. No longer did he address a student body bent on emulating his career. Whereas in 1830 the proportion of ministers among the graduates of Harvard, Yale, and Princeton had been one in three, by 1876 the proportion had dropped to one in thirteen.[111] There had been a time when the only systematic professional training in America had been for the ministry. Lawyers and doctors had learned their trades as apprentices, and scientists had practically trained themselves. By the 1880s the universities were taking over the professional and preprofessional training of doctors and lawyers,[112] and a trend toward

[110] This assertiveness, of course, did not stem only from the discoveries of evolution, but also from the refutation by science of religious conceptions in psychology and anthropology. The development of experimental psychology, by connecting psychic phenomena to the functioning of the nervous system, refuted spiritualistic theories; the development of pathological psychology, by connecting mystic phenomena to the unconscious, took from the former their supernatural character; the development of historical and ethnological studies, connecting religion to the solemn moments in collective life, undermined classic notions of the origin of religion. See Antonio Aliotta, "Science and Religion in the Nineteenth Century," in Joseph Needham, ed., *Science, Religion and Reality* (New York, 1926), pp. 154–55.

[111] Charles W. Eliot, "On the Education of Ministers," *Princeton Review,* LIX (May, 1883), 340–56.

[112] For example, of the 156 medical schools in existence in 1900, 86 were founded between 1876 and 1900. The real boost in medical standards, however, did not take place until after Abraham Flexner published his report on medical education in

specialized training in the sciences was going on apace.[113] Even the classics departments were becoming less congenial haunts for clergymen, as philological and historical scholarship cast a shade over classical discipline. The passage from the pulpit to the classroom, once a natural and unremarkable event in a clergyman's career, now seemed less warranted; with the decline in enrollment of divinity students it was less necessary, and with the development of lay scholarship it was more strange. In this propitious setting, a movement was begun to rid the colleges of the symbols and the presence of clerical power.

In the attack upon clerical control, no argument figured more prominently than the contention that the clergy were incompetent in science. Professor F. W. Clarke of the University of Cincinnati scored the situation that allowed "almost any decayed minister, seeking an asylum" to beat an American Laplace in a race for a professorship.[114] The *Nation* was of the opinion that "clergymen were no longer *par excellence* the learned men of the community" and that "the increased demands of the natural sciences in the universities call for an amount of administrative talent and experience which ministers rarely possess." [115] Charles W. Eliot believed that the clergy, with their fixation on creed and rigidity of belief, had never learned to practice or respect the scientific method. The scientific spirit of inquiry, wrote Eliot,

seeks only the fact, without the slightest regard to consequence. . . . The achievements of scientific inquirers, animated by this spirit of sincerity and truth, have been so extraordinary within the past sixty years . . . that the educated world has accepted it as the only true inspiration of research. . . . No other method of inquiry now commands respect. . . . Protestant theologians and ministers must rise to that standard, if they would continue to command the respect of mankind.[116]

Medical Education in the United States and Canada, Bulletin 4, Carnegie Foundation for the Advancement of Teaching (1910).

[113] By 1880, Johns Hopkins, California, Pennsylvania, and Rutgers boasted six teachers in science apiece, and Harvard had as many as fourteen. Nicholas Murray Butler, ed., *Monographs on Education in the United States,* II (Albany, N.Y., 1900), 3–42.

[114] F. W. Clarke, "American Colleges versus American Science," *Popular Science Monthly,* IX (August, 1876), 472.

[115] Rogers, *Andrew D. White,* p. 80.

[116] Charles W. Eliot, "On the Education of Ministers," pp. 345–46. Eliot did not, as did some of his contemporaries, despair of winning the ministers over to the scientific method; consider his reorganization of the divinity school at Harvard on a nondenominational and, as he saw it, "scientific" basis. See William J. Potter, "Theology at Harvard," *The Index,* X (April 24, 1879), 198–99; Eliot, *Annual Report,* 1878–79.

Educational anticlericalism and scientific anticlericalism, feeding on the same ideas, were part of a single movement.

The outcome—if we can apply such a word to a campaign that knew no instant of victory or article of capitulation—was the disappearance of the clergy as an academic force. Earl McGrath, in a well-known study, gives a statistical picture of the exodus of clerical trustees from the nation's private colleges. In 1860–61, 39.1 percent of the members of the boards of 15 private institutions were clergymen; by 1900–1901 the percentage had dropped to 23 percent, and clergymen were outnumbered for the first time by lawyers and businessmen; by 1930–31, the percentage had dwindled to 7.2 percent.[117] At Harvard, 7 of the 36 governors (Overseers and Fellows) were clergymen in 1874–75; in 1894–95 only one was. Between 1884 and 1926 the number of clergymen on the board of trustees at Amherst was reduced by half, at Princeton by two thirds, and at Yale by 60 percent.[118] The secularizing of the office of the president—a traditional benefice of the clergy—took longer to accomplish. Harvard appointed its first lay president, Eliot, in 1869; Yale did not follow until 1899, with Arthur T. Hadley. Cornell and Johns Hopkins began with lay presidents, but Princeton, Amherst, and Dartmouth did not appoint lay presidents until the twentieth century. Oberlin did not unfrock the presidency until 1927. In certain of the larger institutions the exit of the cleric coincided with the entry of the scientist. President Gilman of Johns Hopkins was a geographer, Eliot of Harvard a chemist, Hall of Clark a psychologist, Jordan of Stanford a biologist, Hadley of Yale an economist, Wilson of Princeton a political scientist. But the apostolic succession of the scientist was far from automatic or assured. More often than not, the seats vacated by the clergy fell to incongruous occupants—politicians, businessmen, lawyers, professional administrators, and, later, generals—whose competence in science or educational administration seemed at times extremely doubtful.

[117] Earl McGrath, "The Control of Higher Education in America," *Educational Record*, XVII (April, 1936), 259–79.

[118] The trustees of these institutions were identified through the *Dictionary of American Biography*, the *National Cyclopedia of American Biography*, *Who Was Who in America, 1897–1947*, and from school catalogues, where the designation of "Rev." or "D.D." was taken as fully descriptive. It could not be determined whether about 10 percent of the members of these boards were clergymen.

THE ATTACK UPON DOCTRINAL MORALISM IN SCIENCE AND EDUCATION

The notion of competence was not the only ideological product of the Darwinian debate. Equally important was the rejection in science and in education of the tenets of doctrinal moralism. It will be recalled that, as a standard of reliability, doctrinal moralism was the view that veracity was a function of faith, that only the believer could be believed. As a criterion of verification, it held that the truth of any idea was determined by its envisioned moral consequences. The religious opponents of evolution were unbridled in their use of both tenets. No theist could believe in evolution, wrote Enoch Fitch Burr, lecturer on the scientific evidence of revealed religion at Amherst, because evolution was "founded by atheism, claimed by atheism, supported by atheism." [119] To a Catholic writer, the theory of evolution, since it "opens the gate to the free indulgence of passion . . . cannot be a sound one; for no sound system produces such fruit, and from the fruits one comes to know the tree." [120] Again and again, the orthodox churchmen "refuted" evolution by casting aspersions on its proponents or by predicting its evil effects.

The use of doctrinal moralism as a standard of reliability infuriated the evolutionists. "Charges of 'heresy,' 'infidelity,' or 'atheism' are beside the question," insisted one writer in the *Popular Science Monthly*. "If a theory in astronomy, in geology, in physics, chemistry or biology, is in doubt, let it be judged on its own evidence." [121] A scientific work, the evolutionists held, should not be judged by the character of its author, but should stand clear and dissociated, held to account only for itself. Moreover, the charge of faithlessness was not only irrelevant, but, if recklessly and indiscriminately applied, was also insubstantial. When Andrew Dickson White was vilified as an atheist for keeping the works of Channing, Renan, and Strauss in his library, the inanity of the argument was clear enough; when Louis Agassiz was accused by a clergyman of preaching "atheism and Darwinism," the dangerous inaccuracy of the name-calling device was even more clearly

[119] Enoch Fitch Burr, *Pater Mundi, or the Doctrine of Evolution* (Boston, 1873), II, 14.

[120] F. S. Chatard, "Darwin's Mistakes," *Catholic World*, XXXIX (June, 1884), 292.

[121] *Popular Science Monthly*, IX (July, 1876), 328.

exposed.[122] "Denounce the thought or the word as much as you please," wrote Francis Abbot,

but if you denounce the thinker because of his honest thought, you are a tyrant to the extent of your power—all the worse if you quote morality and religion to justify your tyranny. . . . Show the theory to be false, and you have proved it be injurious; turn aside from the theory to denounce the theorizer, and even if you succeed in overwhelming both with odium, you have won the victory by a cruel, false and wicked trick, which will yet return to plague the inventor.[123]

In scientific criticism, the dissociation of the man from his work became a cardinal principle.

Subtler, more profound, and less consistent objections were raised against the use of doctrinal moralism as a method of verification. One significant rebuttal was offered by the astronomer and mathematician Chauncey Wright.[124] In seeking to clarify scientific debate, Wright opposed both the use of inflammatory words that had entered from the side of theology and the use of metaphysical generalizations that had entered from the side of philosophy. He argued for rules that would "demand of the criticism . . . the same judicial attitude that is demanded of the investigation." [125] This devoted apostle of Darwin and Mill demanded that every subjective element be eliminated from scientific concerns. Knowledge becomes objective and science comes into its own

when it ceases to be associated with our fears, our respects, our aspirations—our emotional nature; when it ceases to prompt questions as to what relates to our personal destiny, our ambitions, our moral worth; when it ceases to have man, his personal and social nature, as its central and controlling objects.[126]

In short, science must seek the "true"—the conformity of ideas to reality—and not the "good"—the conformity of reality to ideals.[127] He drew a distinction between the "scientific mind," which holds rigidly "to the truth of things, whether good or bad, agreeable or disagreeable,

---

[122] Andrew Dickson White, *Autobiography,* I, 424.

[123] Francis E. Abbot, "Argument and Denunciation," *The Index,* III (April 20, 1872), 125.

[124] See Philip Wiener, *Evolution and the Founders of Pragmatism* (Cambridge, Mass., 1949), pp. 31–69.

[125] "Evolution by Natural Selection," in *Philosophical Discussions* (New York, 1877), p. 170.

[126] "The Philosophy of Herbert Spencer," *loc. cit.,* p. 49.

[127] "Natural Theology as a Positive Science," *loc. cit.,* pp. 40–41.

admirable or despicable," and the " 'philosophical habit of mind,' trained in the school of human life, . . . viewing and interpreting nature according to its own dispositions." [128] Here, then, was one answer to the argument that the ethical consequences of an idea were its primary test of truth. Rather, thought Wright, science and ethics—the "true" and the "good"—belonged in separate and incommensurable categories.

Wright articulated the ideas of the practicing scientist. His precept— objectivity—was the fetish of the laboratory and the field. Refusing to see in the succession of events an ideal or dramatic tendency, he exalted piecemeal research. Assuming the ethical and metaphysical neutrality of science, he supported the scientist's austere craving for "the disenchantment of the world." [129] But few evolutionary philosophers took joy in his icy neutrality, his self-denying ordinances, his divorce of contemplation from desire.[130] A rift, opened by temperamental differences, was expanded by philosophical disagreements. Wright's metaphysical neutrality of science was to James a derogation of metaphysics, to Peirce an emasculation of science.[131] To Dewey, the ethical neutrality of science meant the surrender of the issues of ethics to fixed authority and outmoded sanctions.[132] Though these philosophers shared Wright's disdain for verbal solutions and emotional appeals in debate,[133] they did not be-

[128] "Evolution by Natural Selection," *loc. cit.*, p. 196.

[129] See Max Weber, "Science as a Vocation," in Logan Wilson and William L. Kolb, eds., *Sociological Analysis* (New York, 1949), pp. 5–16.

[130] See Perry, *Thought and Character of William James*, I, 522.

[131] Though James was close to Wright on many philosophical points—both were empiricists and both opposed the gospel of evolutionism as presented by Spencer and Fiske—James would not take Wright's "anti-religious teaching" which he labelled "philosophical nihilism." Perry, *Thought and Character of William James*, Vol. I, Chap. XXXI. See Charles Peirce, "What is Pragmatism?" *Monist*, XV (1905), 161–81; Charles Hartshorne and Paul Weiss, eds., *Collected Papers of Charles Peirce* (6 vols.; Cambridge, Mass., 1935), VI, 33.

[132] A recurrent idea in Dewey's works, which perhaps appears most clearly in a much later work, *The Quest for Certainty: A Study of the Relation of Knowledge to Action* (New York, 1929), pp. 40 ff.

[133] There is no doubt that the standard of empirical adequacy that Wright espoused was also adhered to by his evolutionary opponents. Even in so improbable a place as the writings of John Fiske, we find a vigorous defense of the empirical test in science. Take Fiske's statement that "the truth of any proposition, for scientific purposes, is determined by its agreement with observed phenomena, and not by its congruity with some assumed metaphysical basis" (*Cosmic Philosophy*, I, 272), and his castigation of Agassiz for having intruded his "preferences" into scientific debate. "A scientific inquirer has no business to have 'preferences' . . . . What matters it whether we are pleased with the notion of a monkey ancestry or not? The end of scientific research is the discovery of truth, and not the satisfaction

lieve that the cognitive and moral interests of the scientist could or should be dissociated. Whereas Chauncey Wright, starting from the logic of Mill and the methods of Darwin, emphasized the disciplined, objective, mirroring aspects of knowing, William James, using as a basis the ethics of Mill and the functional psychology of Darwin, emphasized the conative, purposive, active aspects of knowing. From this other corner of the evolutionary camp—one that may loosely be called pragmatist—came another reply to the canons of doctrinal moralism.

On the surface, as principles of verification, pragmatism and doctrinal moralism had much in common. Both assumed that the truth of an idea was disclosed in some way by its consequences. Both denied that cognition existed as an end in itself, or that science should be divorced from human purposes. But here the resemblances ended. For pragmatism took the significant step of divorcing morality from doctrine and rooting it in changing experience. Thus, whereas in doctrinal moralism the "good" was absolute and unconditional, in pragmatism the "good" was plural and contingent. Whereas the former accepted new theory if it agreed with an older stock of beliefs, the latter accepted new theory if it resolved an ongoing human problem. Whereas the former regarded the existing stock of beliefs as inviolable and eternal, the latter regarded accepted beliefs as guides to problem-solving action, always subject to revision, required to work and give satisfaction or else to relinquish their title.

Thus the assault on doctrinal moralism was mounted on two major premises—the ethical neutrality of science and the experimental status of ethics. We need not, for our immediate purpose, dwell on the tensions between practicing science and scientific philosophy that these different premises point to. For the moment, their significance may be said to lie in the preferences and aversions they shared. Differing as to whether truth was something found or made, both asserted that truth was temporary, growing, and contingent, not permanent, static, and absolute. Differing as to whether values were a subject matter for science, both agreed that values were not disclosed by the properties of antecedent reality or by knowledge supernaturally established. Differing as to scope

---

of our whims or fancies, or even of what we are pleased to call our finer feelings. The proper reason for refusing to accept any doctrine is, that it is inconsistent with observed facts, or with some other doctrine which has been firmly established on a basis of fact." "Agassiz and Darwinism," *Popular Science Monthly,* III (October, 1873), 697. But the difference between Wright and Fiske was that the latter was confident that *his* major preference—cosmic benevolence—had been proved beyond doubt inductively.

of inquiry, both assumed that no belief was so inherently valuable as to be immune to the tests of inquiry. Both, in short, were profoundly hostile to the fundamental axioms of religious authority.

Again we find the evolutionists in education preaching on much the same text. Nowhere had the assumptions of doctrinal moralism been more firmly fixed than in the American college. Yet in the seventies and eighties, as a reflection of the impact of evolution on educational psychology, an attitude hostile toward these assumptions came to prevail even here. Where the philosophers of science sought to clarify terms and to avoid logomachic argument, the philosophers of education sought to prevent the teacher from inculcating verbal abstractions. Where the positivists in science urged the scientist to be ethically neutral, the secularists in education urged the teacher to be doctrinally neutral. Where the pragmatists in science based values on utility and experience, the pragmatists in education did very much the same thing. Here, again, in animus and assumption, education and science were allied.

As a sign of the changing times, England, once the cradle of academic classicism, produced Herbert Spencer, the great philosopher of these new trends in education, and Thomas Huxley, their major publicist. In the United States, Edward L. Youmans and Charles W. Eliot were Huxley's and Spencer's important advocates. Spencer made his mark on the educational world with four essays written between 1854 and 1859 which were compiled in a volume called *Essays on Education*.[134] Huxley put his epigrammatic style into the service of Spencer's ideas in the public forum here and in England.[135] Youmans, the editor of the *Popular Science Monthly,* of more than fifty volumes of the "International Science Series," and of an influential book entitled *The Culture Demanded by Modern Life,* gave Spencer a wide American audience.[136] Eliot served

[134] The book was first published in the United States in 1861. References in the following pages are the Everyman's Library edition published in 1910 in New York. An interesting analysis of Spencer's educational theory is provided by Elsa Peverly Kimball, *Sociology and Education: An Analysis of the Theories of Spencer and Ward* (New York, 1932).

[135] Volume Three of his *Collected Essays* contains some of Huxley's leading addresses (New York and London, 1914).

[136] For Youmans' work in popularizing the ideas of Spencer, see John Fiske, "Edward Livingston Youmans," *A Century of Science and Other Essays* (Boston and New York, 1902), pp. 61–95; H. G. Good, "Edward Livingston Youmans, A National Teacher of Science," *The Scientific Monthly,* XVIII (March, 1924), 306–17. The contributors to *The Culture Demanded by Modern Life* were a galaxy of the scientific stars of that time: John Tyndall, Arthur Henfrey, Thomas Huxley, James Paget, Michael Faraday, W. B. Hodgson, Herbert Spencer, F. A. P. Barnard,

the cause with numerous addresses and articles [137] and used his position at Harvard to put the theory into practice. One need not go beyond the works of this talented quadrumvirate to perceive the main lines of the argument, though an enormous polemical literature reveals the interest the dispute aroused.

The plea of these thinkers for a scientific education was the springboard for their attack on doctrinal moralism. The case for a scientific education was consummately argued by Spencer in his essay "What Knowledge Is of Most Worth?" "Worth," to this worthy successor of Bentham, was equated with usefulness, and his essay was a persuasive disquisition on behalf of practical training. To Spencer, the leading kinds of human activities, in their order of importance, were those that administered to self-preservation, those that secured the necessaries of life, those whose end was the care of offspring, those which were involved in the maintenance of good citizenship, and lastly, those which gratified taste and feeling. These, thought Spencer, were the activities that education should cultivate, the first most, the last least. The current emphasis on the ornamental studies was in inverse relation to need, he thought, and had little articulation with life.[138] But education should prepare for life, the curriculum should be as broad as life—which meant that the subjects that were concerned with life should receive primary consideration. To Spencer, the sciences, natural and social, pre-eminently filled the bill. They enabled man to survive, to manufacture, to guard against disease, to produce fit offspring. They equipped him for the tasks of civic life and even furthered the creative arts. With prophetic insight, Spencer foresaw the day when science would conquer the curriculum.[139]

In his effort to give science the highest credentials, Spencer did not disdain the disciplinary goals and faculty psychology of the classicists. He and his followers were not loath to claim that science sharpened the judgment, inculcated many virtues, flexed the muscles of memory.[140] But this derivative psychology, placed in a new context of evolutionary naturalism, lost all its old authoritarian associations. Since mind was a phe-

---

Justus von Liebig, and Youmans himself. (International Science Library, Akron, 1867).

[137] For some of Eliot's more famous addresses and articles, see *Educational Reform* (New York, 1898).

[138] *Essays on Education*, p. 32.   [139] *Ibid.*, p. 44.

[140] Thomas Huxley, "Scientific Education," *Collected Essays*, pp. 127–28; Youmans, *The Culture Demanded by Modern Life*, p. 6.

nomenon of nature and its growth an evolutionary process, the content and the method of teaching must conform to the laws of the mind's development. Since all evolutionary movement was a progressive integration of matter, the course of effective teaching must go from the simple to the complex. Since instincts, tropisms, and propensities played a vital role in survival, student interest and desire must be consulted and engaged in teaching. Like Rousseau, the evolutionists drew a sharp distinction between a "natural" and an "artificial" education. The natural way in education was to put mind into contact with fact through all of the intaking senses, to let thought be the reflective result of direct and immediate experience. The artificial way was merely to transmit words, to funnel truths into passive receptacles. And the natural way, to these evolutionary naturalists, was doubly blessed: first, because nature was good and guaranteed human perfectibility; second, because control of nature was good, and insured competitive success.

The ultimate goal of these educators was to shift the center of gravity from the teacher to the student. Nowhere was this more apparent than in their approach to moral education, a field that had so long been preempted by parental wish, adult restraint, and the imposing "shalt nots" of the Decalogue. Character development, Spencer and his followers agreed, was the primary objective of every system of education. It was their opinion, however, that this result could not be achieved by a prescribed adherence to creed, but only by adherence to the laws of Nature when those laws were inductively discovered. For Nature was the supreme instructor in the art of moral conduct. Her disbursement of pleasures and pains was in relation to man's obedience to her laws, and obedience to natural laws was the essence of moral action. Her punishments and rewards were just, because they were exactly proportionate to the offense; they were fair, because they were invariant effects of causes; they were instructive, because they followed immediately upon the act. To train the individual to cope with nature and her requirements was the meaning of "education"—the *leading out* of the mind. "Important as may be the mental preparation for dealing with certainties," wrote Youmans, "it is still more important to prepare for uncertainties; to ignore this, arrests education at an inferior stage and but ill prepares for the emergencies of practical life." [141] To eliminate mediate authority was

[141] Youmans, "Mental Discipline in Education," *The Culture Demanded by Modern Life,* p. 36.

to foster individual responsibility and the courageous assumption of risks.

These doctrines were accepted in the colleges, not immediately, not in all areas, and not all at once, but they were accepted conclusively. In helping them take effect—whether in the curriculum, in the classroom, or in the chapel—one institution, Harvard, was always in the vanguard. Under Eliot, the free choice of subjects by students was officially and almost fully allowed. Between 1872 and 1894, subject requirements were abolished for all classes of students except the freshmen, who had to endure the coercion of one required course in English and one in a foreign language.[142] Other colleges followed suit, without, however, going quite so far. Between 1875 and 1886, Amherst more than tripled the number of electives in the junior and senior year; at Yale 50 percent of the courses for juniors and 80 percent of the courses for seniors were made elective; Brown, Dartmouth, and Williams took long strides in the same direction.[143] In 1901, a survey of ninety-seven institutions showed that the elective system had penetrated 70 percent of the program of thirty-four, 50 to 70 percent of twelve, less than 50 percent of fifty-one.[144] In the teaching of the sciences, Eliot was one of the first to champion laboratory methods—i.e., first-hand observation and experiments by students.[145] By 1899, James B. Angell could proclaim that "the method of scientific instruction has been revolutionized. In the last half century no more important step in education has been taken than in the universal introduction of the laboratory methods." [146] In other subjects, the technique of rote recitation was replaced by lecture and discussion—at Harvard by 1880, according to its president's report.[147] The statutes and laws of Harvard College, which had grown harsh and picayune, were pruned to a mere five pages and made considerably more forbearing.[148] At many other institutions the same reforms were accomplished.[149] In

[142] See Samuel Eliot Morison, "College Studies, 1869–1929," in *Development of Harvard University*, pp. xxix–l.

[143] George Herbert Palmer, "Possible Limitations of the Elective System," *Andover Review*, VI (December, 1886), 581.

[144] E. D. Phillips, "The Elective System in American Education," *Pedagogical Seminary*, VIII (June, 1901), 206–30.

[145] Eliot wrote a chemistry textbook with Francis H. Storer that "caused a revolution in the teaching of elementary chemistry by making it a laboratory subject in the United States." James, *Eliot*, I, 164.

[146] James B. Angell, "The Old College and the New University," in *Selected Addresses* (London, 1912), pp. 136–37.

[147] Morison, *Three Centuries of Harvard*, p. 347.

[148] James, *Eliot*, I, 242.

[149] Walter C. Bronson, *The History of Brown University, 1764–1914* (Providence,

the establishment of voluntary worship, Harvard far outdistanced contemporary institutions of her type. In 1886, compulsory chapel—that ancient combination of a ritual observance and a penal system—was abolished at Harvard.[150] In the other private eastern colleges, however, compulsory chapel remained—at Dartmouth until 1925, at Yale until 1926, at Williams until 1927. Princeton commuted the obligation to informal Sunday discussion classes in 1932.[151] Despite the unevenness of change, the authoritarian method everywhere fell on the defensive, and at most important points gave way.

The exodus of clerical trustees, the eclipse of authoritarian norms, the evisceration of the traditional course, doomed the collegiate system that had prevailed in America for centuries. But yet, with that hardihood and unconscious tenacity that age imparts to old forms, church-controlled institutions did not die or disappear from the scene. In 1906, the Carnegie Foundation for the Advancement of Teaching, set up to provide retirement allowances for professors in private, nonsectarian colleges, initially labeled only fifty-one institutions as completely nondenominational.[152] Sectarian control was maintained in a variety of ways. Though all colleges were open to all students without restriction as to creed,[153] 109 were re-

R.I., 1914), pp. 404–20; Thomas J. Wertenbaker, *Princeton, 1746–1896* (Princeton, N.J., 1946), pp. 315–19.

[150] Morison, *Development of Harvard University,* pp. li–lviii.

[151] *Ibid.,* p. lviin. The *Dartmouth College Catalogue* for 1895–96 provided that "Prayers are conducted by the President each week-day morning. . . . All undergraduate students are required to be present," or might attend other churches (p. 112). First provision for voluntary attendance is to be found in the *Dartmouth College Catalogue* for 1925–26, p. 14. See also, Leon B. Richardson, *History of Dartmouth College* (2 vols.; Hanover, N.H., 1932), II, 780. The *Yale Catalogue* for 1924–25 provides that "attendance at the daily and Sunday chapel services is required of all freshmen. Exemption from this requirement is granted for the Sunday services. . . ." (p. 105). The next year's catalogue omits all mention of that requirement. The *Princeton Catalogue* for 1893–94 required all undergraduates to attend morning prayers, and gave permission to attend elsewhere "on special occasions" and on "application to the president" (p. 148). By 1907–8 this had become a twice-a-week requirement, with "at least one half of the Sunday Chapel services each quarter" required (p. 321); by 1915–16, the twice-a-week requirement was dropped; finally, by 1932–33, it was announced that "[a] service of worship is held in the chapel each Sunday morning at eleven o'clock. For those who object to required attendance at a religious service, an alternative is offered in the form of an informal discussion class on Sunday evenings" (p. 222).

[152] The Carnegie Foundation for the Advancement of Teaching, *First Annual Report of the President and Treasurer* (1906), p. 28. Hereafter these documents are referred to as *First Annual Report, Second Annual Report,* and so on.

[153] There were still, on the other hand, examples of students required to attend a specified church in the neighborhood: Olivet, Park, and Wake Forest Colleges were cited. *Second Annual Report* (1907), p. 46.

ported as still requiring all or part of the trustees to belong to a specified sect. Formal creedal restrictions on teachers were rare, though there were instances of this as well. The Carnegie Foundation listed 200 institutions that were either owned outright by a church (these were largely the Roman Catholic colleges and universities) or whose boards of trustees were elected by a governing body of the denomination. In certain places, only the right to nominate trustees was vested in an organ of the church; in others, only the right to confirm them. Control was exercised by church assemblies, by high ecclesiastical officers, or by subsidiary or allied corporations.[154] These were only some of the varied designs of the formal machinery of control. The Carnegie Foundation did not enumerate, nor did it exclude, colleges merely in sympathy with a church.[155]

But numbers did not tell, nor the forms of control describe, the decline and attenuation of American academic sectarianism. In many of these institutions, the control of the church was barely nominal, a mechanical adherence to form which convention had managed to preserve and lethargy alone defended.[156] In many places, church control was an incubus which the college was attempting to throw off, or which it endured merely because the charter made remedial action difficult.[157] In few institutions was it reckoned a positive, necessary good. When the Carnegie Foundation inquired as to "whether denominational connection or control ministers to the religious or intellectual life," the respondents in the denominational colleges declared "almost without exception that such connection played little, if any, part in the religious or intellectual life of the student body." To the question whether such a connection improved the organization of the college the answer was "almost universally" couched in the negative.[158] How meaningless was the sectarian form is indicated by the alacrity with which certain colleges proclaimed their independence and revised their charters and by-laws in order to receive the Foundation's benefits. Bowdoin gave up a lucrative sectarian endowment in order to be eligible for membership in the Foundation. Drake University and

---

[154] *Ibid.*, pp. 42–50.

[155] It is difficult to ascertain how many were in sympathetic and traditional association. The College Board of the Presbyterian Church rated 471 colleges and universities denominational in 1911, using this broader standard. The figure may be too high considering the over-generous definition of "college" that denominational rating boards used. W. S. Plumer Bryan, *The Church, Her Colleges and the Carnegie Foundation* (Princeton, N.J., 1911), p. 57n.

[156] *First Annual Report* (1906), p. 49.

[157] *Second Annual Report* (1907), p. 60.　　　　[158] *Ibid.*, pp. 53–54.

Drury College quickly abolished all tests and conditions. In four years, twenty institutions qualified under the Foundation's rules; after that, in a change of policy, the Foundation required contributions from participants and the process of conversion slowed down.[159] To be sure, several hundred colleges remained sectarian despite these blandishments. But they were marginal institutions, financially, educationally, intellectually. Sectarian colleges are still with us today. But generally they are in the lag, not in the forerank of history, serving as illustrations of the disparities in American education.

A NEW RATIONALE OF ACADEMIC FREEDOM

In interpreting the history of ideas, the belief that nothing under the sun is ever new competes with the Heraclitean doctrine that nothing in the world is abiding. It is with qualifications, therefore, that we conclude that a "new" rationale of academic freedom grew out of the Darwinian debate. For example, we conclude that science invested the theory of academic freedom with a special conception of truth and a formula for tolerating error. But this should not be taken to mean that these ideas came altogether unanticipated upon minds totally unprepared. An academic preference for truth and an academic attitude of tolerance predated the articulation of these ideas and insured their ultimate success. Similarly, we conclude that the concept of scientific competence gave the faculties new leverage against misuses of administrative power. But it would be a mistake to assume that the merits of an argument for competence had never before been grasped by academics: we have seen that the medieval masters used it, as did certain American college presidents, in prescientific contexts. Lastly, we conclude that the assimilation of the values of science made academic freedom an ethic, an affirmative moral position, and not merely a negative condition, the absence of overt restraint. Even so, the morality of science did not denote a complete transvaluation of existing values, nor should we count, in the derivation of this ethic, the two thousand years since Socrates as a barren and insignificant age. Without the canons of evolutionary science, we contend, the modern rationale of academic freedom would not exist. But this does not imply that, for science or academic freedom, yesterday was the common date of birth.

With this *caveat* in mind, we shall proceed briefly to explore the three

[159] *Third Annual Report* (1908), pp. 12–29.

contributions of science: the formula for tolerating error; the limitation upon administrative power; the set of positive values.

THE FORMULA FOR TOLERATING ERROR

All justifications for intellectual freedom rest upon a conception of the nature of truth which implies a reason for tolerating error. A concise review of some of the older formulas may help to illuminate the contribution of science. As we have seen,[160] it had been argued in the past that since truth is consistent with itself, the new discoveries of reason will but confirm the dogmas of faith and close the breach against error. Or, that, since only certain beliefs have import for salvation, the rest, however erroneous, carry no penalty of sin. Or, again, that though the truth is already known and needs no further corroboration, the persecution of error is inexpedient since it hardens men in their mistakes. Or, once more, that truth, being invincible and unmistakable, can never be defeated by error, since "who ever knew Truth put to the worse, in a free and open encounter?" The evolutionists devised another formula. To them, all beliefs are tentatively true or tentatively false, and only verifiable through a continuous process of inquiry. Embodying this idea, the modern rationale of academic freedom has become more categorical than any of its predecessors: all seeming errors must be tolerated, for what is truth is never fully known and never finally knowable.

At the same time, the emphasis on disciplined inquiry set important limits to the permissible tolerance of error. The evolutionists' formula did not level every opinion to equal value. It held that every claim to a discovery of truth must submit to open verification; that the process of verification must follow certain rules; that this procedure is best understood by those who qualify as experts. Hence, academic freedom does not theoretically justify all kinds of intellectual nonconformity, but only that kind of nonconformity that proceeds according to rules; not any private belief, but that kind of private belief that allows itself publicly to be tested; not a perfect competition of ideas, but rather an imperfect competition, to which certain opinions come enhanced with a special professional warranty. In this respect, it makes fewer allowances for vagaries of opinion than do, say, the doctrines of Milton and Mill. In the modern theory, though no conclusion is unchallengeable, the method for arriving at conclusions is prescribed.

---

[160] See above, Chap. I, "The Idea of Toleration"; Chap. IV, "The Secularization of Learning"; Chap. V, "The Idea of Academic Freedom."

LIMITATIONS UPON ADMINISTRATIVE POWER

The prerogative of judging the fitness of professors is lodged by established usage in college boards of trustees; consequently, the institutional aspect of the struggle for academic freedom has turned on whether and to what extent trustees should exercise their prerogative. Since the Darwinian era, the argument for limitation has effectively made use of the notion of scientific competence. When one hears it argued that the professional standing of a professor can only be established by experts, that these experts must be chosen from among his professional peers, that the general consensus of peers is the highest available wisdom in such matters, the argument for judicial competence is called to mind. Sometimes the argument for methodological competence is heard, as, for example, when a professor's dismissal is protested on the ground that the trustees had an inadequate knowledge of the facts, that they admitted prejudiced testimony, or that they were swayed by irrelevant considerations. Again, it would be unwise to exaggerate the novelty of these arguments. They also reflect an affection for "due process"—for basic rules of fair play—that is as old as the common law. Nevertheless, it is also clear that the argument for scientific competence, used in the Darwinian debate as an answer to clerical presumptuousness, has been turned to useful account as a reply to trustee presumption.

These arguments have had a practical effect. They have been implemented by innumerable faculty committees on appointment, tenure, and promotion; by occasional faculty hearings to determine the fitness of a colleague; and by a standing committee of investigation set up by the American Association of University Professors. This investigating committee, composed of professors, investigates complaints over dismissals, seeks out the relevant data, evaluates *ex parte* evidence, and publishes the results of its findings.[161] There is a striking parallel between its operations and assumptions and those upheld by the Darwinian advocates of scientific competence.

THE MORALITY OF SCIENCE

Finally, the rationale of academic freedom has been endowed with certain fundamental values, values not original to science, but implicit in scientific assumptions and inherent in scientific activity. Such values as tolerance and honesty, publicity and testifiability, individuality and co-

[161] See Chap. X.

operativeness, have been part of the scientific bequest. Two other values deserve particular emphasis. The scientific criterion of reliability—the dissociation of a scientific work from the beliefs and associations of its author—has bestowed on academic freedom the value of universalism. By universalism is meant the elimination of particularistic criteria— creedal, racial, or national—in judging the merits of a work, and the elimination of unearned advantages—connections, rank, and caste—in considering the merits of a man. The second value is that of neutrality, an interest in disinterestedness that is deeply ingrained in science. By assimilating the value of universalism, academic freedom has come to signify the brotherhood of man in science that is akin in aspiration to the brotherhood of man in God. Attempts to foist upon the academic community an American or a Presbyterian science, or a class or color yardstick in appointments and promotions, are thus infringements of academic freedom. By acquiring the value of neutrality, academic freedom has come to stand for the belief that science must transcend ideology, that professors must renounce all commitments that corrupt the passion for truth. Attempts to suborn professors by pay or other preferences, attempts by professors themselves to hold departments to a particular "line," are thus infringements of academic freedom. As the symbol and the guardian of these two values, academic freedom has come to be equated not only with free intellectual activity, but with an ethic of human relations and an ideal of personal fulfillment.

We should not interpret these changes in the colleges and in the rationale of academic freedom as evidences of a law of progress. Leaving the cocoon of religious authority, the colleges did not emerge at once into sunlit freedom. Taking over the concepts of science, the rationale of academic freedom was not thenceforth complete and unambiguous. In the next chapter, when we examine the last stage in the educational revolution—the building of the graduate school on the model of the German university—we shall see that the new university in some ways compromised the independence of the academic. We shall see—by comparing American academic freedom with German *Lernfreiheit* and *Lehrfreiheit*—that the principles of neutrality and competence were susceptible to restrictive interpretations. The paradox of revolutions—and here our analogy holds too—is that the freedom in the name of which they conquer is often gravely endangered by the new conditions they create.

VIII: THE GERMAN INFLUENCE

THE FULL STORY of the contacts between the American university and the German university has never been told.[1] Fully treated, it would reveal, first of all, a relationship of one-sided dependence. More than nine thousand Americans studied at German universities in the nineteenth century. Through these students, through the scores of Americans who knew Germany from books and an occasional *Wanderjahr,* through German expatriates teaching in American colleges, the methods and ideals of the German university were transported into this country.[2] The story of this contact would also show the effects of cultural selection. America took from German sources only that which fitted her needs, only that which was in harmony with her history. In a certain sense, the German academic influence, powerful as it was, reinforced rather than initiated native American tendencies toward change. Before 1850, for example, comparatively few American candidates for academic posts followed the trail to Göt-

[1] This is a wide gap in American historiography. There is only one study that attempts directly to relate the German and the American universities: Charles Franklin Thwing, *The American and the German University, One Hundred Years of History* (New York, 1928). While this book has the virtue of regarding the German impact comprehensively, taking into account institutional, personal, and scholarly influences, it is skimpy on details and superficial in analysis. John A. Walz, *German Influence in American Education and Culture* (Philadelphia, 1936), is a little essay too thin to justify its title. B. A. Hinsdale, "Notes on the History of Foreign Influences upon Education in the United States," *Report of the Commissioner of Education,* I (1897–98), 610–13, gives a list of the names of American students at Göttingen, Halle, Berlin, and Leipzig, a valuable but unfortunately incomplete listing. On the over-all impact of German culture on the United States, there are several studies of tangential value. Albert B. Faust, *The German Element in the United States* (New York and Boston, 1909), is a two-volume compendium of bits of information that overstresses the German contribution to American culture. Orie W. Long, *Literary Pioneers* (Cambridge, Mass., 1935) is an excellent study of literary influences, and contains much that is illuminating on the reaction of Everett, Bancroft, Cogswell, Ticknor, Longfellow, and Motley to the German university. Two studies of the American magazines' reaction to German literature contain bibliographical references pertinent to this theme: Scott H. Goodnight, "German Literature in American Magazines Prior to 1846," and Martin H. Haertel, "German Literature in American Magazines, 1846 to 1880," both in *Bulletin of the University of Wisconsin Philology and Literature Series,* IV (1908).

[2] Thwing, *The American and the German University,* p. 41.

tingen blazed by Ticknor and Bancroft.[3] Of those who went, a disproportionate number were graduates of atypical Harvard.[4] The denominational college was neither eager for German-trained scholars nor ready
for German-trained scholarship. German theology was too skeptical, German philology too specialized, German *Wissenschaftslehre* too strenuous.[5]
It was not until a German degree offered advantages to career chances at
home—which is to say, it was not until the American college had already
grown more secular, specialized, and intellectually ambitious—that the
great exodus of American scholars began. It must be assumed, therefore,
that the increase in the number of Americans going to Germany in the
second half of the nineteenth century—the figures are roughly 200 before
1850 and go up to 2,000 in the peak decade of the 1880s—tells as much
about the pace of indigenous change as about the growth of our cultural
debt.[6]

Finally, the story would reveal the effects of cultural modification. The
Germany seen through American eyes was bound to be, in part, a figment
of American preconceptions. Brought into contact with our own ideals

[3] Harold S. Jantz objects to the traditional view that the publication of Mme.
de Staël's *De l'Allemagne* in this country in 1814 and the pioneer activities of the
Göttingen Four were America's first introduction to German culture and the German university. See "German Thought and Literature in New England, 1620–1820,"
Journal of English and Germanic Philology, IV (1942), 1–45. But his evidence
hinges on the interests of a few scholars of particularly broad reading and not on
those of the mass of American college graduates, whose interest in English culture
was dominant before 1820.

[4] Hinsdale, "Notes on the History of Foreign Influences," pp. 610–13; William
Goodwin, "Remarks on the American Colony at Göttingen," *Proceedings of the
Massachusetts Historical Society,* XII, Second Series (1897–99), 366–69.

[5] Particularly was there a great reluctance to admit German-trained theological
students into the colleges. George Bancroft, though he was provided with a three-
year scholarship by the Harvard Corporation to become a philologist and Biblical
critic, felt that he had to make his Christian invulnerability to German skepticism
quite clear to his Harvard sponsors. Writing to President Kirkland of Harvard in
1819, he assured him that he had nothing to do with German theology except
insofar as it was merely critical. "Of their infidel systems I hear not a word: and
I trust I have been too long under your eye, and too long a member of the Theological Institution under your inspection to be in danger of being led away from the
religion of my Fathers. . . . I say this explicitly, because before I left home I
heard frequently expressed fears, lest I join the German school." Long, *Literary
Pioneers,* pp. 114–15. A folkish fear of German theology remained long past the
midpoint of the century. In 1863, William Graham Sumner, deciding to acquire
a German theological training, was thought by his family to do so with considerable
risk to his immortal soul. Harris E. Starr, *William Graham Sumner* (New York,
1925), p. 56. Similarly, George Sylvester Morris' family feared for his orthodoxy
when he decided to go to Germany in 1866. R. M. Wenley, *The Life and Works of
George Sylvester Morris* (New York, 1919), p. 115.

[6] Thwing, *The American and the German University,* p. 42.

and on our own ground, German academic ideals were bound to be greatly altered. The analysis that follows covers briefly only two of many German contributions—the ideal of academic research, and the ideals of *Lernfreiheit* and *Lehrfreiheit*. But even this incomplete account of a complex cultural connection illustrates the three-fold process of dependence, selection, and modification.

ACADEMIC RESEARCH

The conception of a university as a research institution was in large part a German contribution. In this country, the meaning of "university" had been depreciated and obscured by an inflation of institutional claims. Before the mid-century, the word "university" variously denoted: (1) a college with at least one professional school attached to it, such as the University of Pennsylvania or Harvard University; (2) simply a state-controlled institution of higher learning, such as the University of Georgia and the University of North Carolina; (3) a state-controlled institution with one or more professional schools which also offered a wider assortment of elective courses, such as the University of Virginia; (4) any college that aspired to be grand, as did numerous institutions in the South and West.[7] Neither the word nor the thing it referred to encompassed the activity of research. As long as the techniques of research could be self-taught, as long as private libraries could keep pace with the growth of knowledge, there was no cause for a Franklin to seek a professorship, for an Emerson to soliloquize before schoolboys, for a Jefferson, an Irving, or a Motley to try didactically to reproduce his kind. The adoption of research as an academic function awaited changes in the conditions of inquiry—the vast extension of empirical knowledge and the refinement in the techniques of investigation; the overcoming of academic resistance; and, very important, a greater familiarity with the German university which, in the nineteenth century, was a model for reformers and a spur.

[7] Daniel C. Gilman, first president of Johns Hopkins, tells in his memoirs of a dignitary who visited Yale and introduced himself as "chancellor of the University." " 'How large a faculty have you,' asked Dominie Day. 'Not any,' was the answer. 'Have you any library or buildings?' 'Not yet,' replied the visitor. 'Any endowment?' 'None' came the monotonous and saddening negative. 'What have you?' persisted the Yale President. The visitor brightened as he said, 'We have a very good charter.' " *Launching of a University* (New York, 1906), pp. 5–6. For a brief account of the evolution of the word "university" in American academic life, see Carnegie Foundation for the Advancement of Teaching, *Second Annual Report of the President and Treasurer* (1907), pp. 81–85.

The German universities had not always been famed as research institutions. For two centuries following the Reformation they had been little more than agents of the prescribed theology, drowsy centers of scholasticism, branches of the state bureaucracy. Leibnitz' refusal to accept a position at a German university is one indication of their lack of appeal for scholars.[8] That they forged ahead of all others in the nineteenth century and became the cynosures of richer and older institutions was the result of many factors, among which two—their peculiar structural advantages and the revival of academic philosophy—deserve our special notice.

In organization the German universities in the late eighteenth and early nineteenth centuries were stronger than the clustered colleges of Oxford and Cambridge and the independent technical and professional schools that emerged in France after the Revolution.[9] First of all, the German universities had retained the philosophical faculty in its old medieval conjunction with theology, law, and medicine. Thus they had been, even in their darkest days, something more than theological seminaries or professional schools. Secondly, the relegation of preparatory courses to lower schools, the abandonment of the communal student life in *Bursen* and colleges, the gradual rise in the age of entering students, liberated the German professor from most parental responsibilities. There was less danger, where the student-teacher relation was an *entente cordiale* and not a forced alliance, that the presence of students would spoil the inspiration of searchers; there was a greater chance, in the freer devotion of mind to mind, for the habit of discipleship to be reborn. Thirdly, the German universities were the possessions and the pride of the several territorial states—which, if not an unmixed blessing, at least allowed them to benefit from the princely penchant for display.[10] Finally, the development of a civil bureaucracy and the adoption of the Roman law in the

[8] See Paul Farmer's excellent but all too brief essay on this break between academic and intellectual life in Europe, in "Nineteenth Century Ideas of the University: Continental Europe," Margaret Clapp, ed., *The Modern University* (Ithaca, N.Y., 1950), pp. 3–24.

[9] See Stephen d'Irsay, *Histoire dès universités françaises et étrangères des origines à nos jours* (2 vols.; Paris, 1933–35), II, 168–77; John Theodore Merz, *A History of European Thought in the Nineteenth Century* (4 vols.; Edinburgh and London, 1907–14), Chap. I: "The Scientific Spirit in France."

[10] Friedrich Paulsen, *The German Universities: Their Character and Historical Development* (New York, 1895), pp. 57–64; Paulsen, *The German Universities and University Study* (New York, 1906), pp. 44–46, 137–39. The debt of this section to Paulsen is very large.

German states in the eighteenth century created a need for officials with university training. Even the nobility had to study the new jurisprudence in order to maintain its supremacy in the German bureaucracies—and this did much to enhance the power and the prestige of the German professor and the university.[11]

The flowering of German philosophy came in the eighteenth and early nineteenth centuries. The history of universities provides no example of a philosophical movement so academic in origin (unless it be the development of Scottish common-sense realism at Edinburgh and Glasgow); [12] the history of philosophies hardly recounts a phase so thoroughly academic in flavor. Whereas French Encyclopedism and the English Enlightenment flourished outside the universities, their German counterpart was well ensconced at Göttingen from the year of its founding (1737), at Halle after the reinstatement of Christian Wolff by Frederick the Great in 1740, at Königsberg during the glorious reign of Immanuel Kant (1755–1797).[13] Long before romantic idealism infiltrated the French and English universities, it prospered under Fichte and Schelling at Jena, and under Fichte, Hegel, and Schelling at Berlin. It is worth noting that whereas the great philosophers of England, from Bacon to John Stuart Mill, were men of affairs, the great figures in the heroic age of German philosophy were academic men. From this circumstance may be traced both the glory of English philosophy and the grandeur of the German university.

The philosophical revival revitalized the universities by redefining the idea of searching. Under the long-reigning scholastic system, to philosophize had meant to explain dogma, to deduce its consequences, and to demonstrate its validity: searching, within this confine, was an act of ratiocination. To philosophize, according to the philosophical rationalists, was to submit all belief, even the very conditions of knowledge, to the verification of reason: with them, searching became an act of intellectual criticism.[14] With the rise of German idealism, searching was defined as a positive act of creation: to philosophize, in Fichtean terms, was to find

[11] Paulsen, *German Universities and University Study,* pp. 119–21; W. H. Bruford, *Germany in the Eighteenth Century: The Social Background of the Literary Revival* (Cambridge, 1935), p. 251.

[12] See Gladys Bryson, *Man and Society: The Scottish Inquiry of the Eighteenth Century* (Princeton, N.J., 1945).

[13] Frederick Lilge, *The Abuse of Learning: The Failure of the German University* (New York, 1948), Chaps. I and II. Lilge is a good antidote to the idyllic view of the German university presented by Paulsen.

[14] Immanuel Kant, *Der Streit der Fakultäten* (Königsberg, 1798), Rossmann ed. (Heidelberg, 1947), pp. 21–26.

the content of reality through the very activity of thought.[15] In part, this apotheosis of mind was compensation for the German's failure in action. It helped make amends for defeats on the field of battle to seek spiritual and moral goals in a sphere that was free from contingencies. It was to counteract the materialism of French philosophy that the Idealists sought a suprasensual reality behind the screen of perceived appearances. In addition, deep religious aspirations, evidenced in disguised religious symbols, were met by this abstruse metaphysics. Fichte's selfless scholar may be identified with the celibate priest; the intellect conscious of the Absolute, with the mystic union of man with God; the search for philosophical truth, with the quest for religious certainty.[16] Each of the several schools of idealism was like a militant church whose creed was revealed to its founder. To these academic philosophers, the search for truth was not an occupation, but a calling—a transcendent necessity, a requirement for salvation.

The hegemony of philosophy in the German universities broke down in the 1820s and 1830s with the introduction of the natural and experimental sciences. For decades a war of methods was fought between the scientists, who sought to explain nature through quantitative measurement and careful observation, and the speculative philosophers of Schelling's school, who regarded nature as knowable through a priori schemes, more or less intuitively derived. With the success of Johannes Mueller's pioneer work in physiology, the wide acclaim given to Liebig's chemical laboratory, the popularity of Alexander von Humboldt's lectures on natural science, the victory of the methods of science was assured. After 1840, intense specialization, rigid objectivity, the mustering of footnoted evidence, became the hallmarks of German scholarship. But the philosophic spirit was not rooted out of academic thought by these empirical procedures. The idealistic mood lingered over the German universities long after it was severed from the circumstances of its origin. Nineteenth-century German scholarship, even when it exhibited the most painstaking empiricism, was polemical and subjective. "In no other country," Santayana has written, pointing to this characteristic,

has so large, so industrious and (amid its rude polemics) so co-operative a set of professors devoted itself to all sorts of learning. But as the original motive was to save one's soul, an apologetic and scholastic manner has often

[15] J. G. Fichte, "Bestimmung des Gelehrten," *Nachgelassene Werke,* III, 183–93.
[16] See George Santayana's brilliant analysis of this philosophy in *Egotism in German Philosophy* (New York, 1940), Chaps. I and II.

survived: the issue is prejudged and egotism has appeared even in science.
. . . If the controlling purpose is not political or religious, it is at least "philosophical," that is to say, arbitrary. . . . Hence a piece of Biblical or Homeric
criticism, a history of Rome or of Germany, often becomes a little system of
egotistical philosophy, posited and defended with all the parental zeal and
all the increasing conviction with which a prophet defends his supernatural
inspirations.[17]

The very notion of *Wissenschaft* had overtones of meaning utterly missing
in its English counterpart, *science*. The German term signified a dedicated,
sanctified pursuit. It signified not merely the goal of rational understanding, but the goal of self-fulfillment; not merely the study of the
"exact sciences," but of everything taught by the university; not the study
of things for their immediate utilities, but the morally imperative study of
things for themselves and for their ultimate meanings.[18]

The German university undertook to train as well as to maintain its
scientists and scholars. The lecture, through which the results of new
research was transmitted, replaced the old medieval *praelectio,* the exposition of canonical texts.[19] The seminar, which once had been the means
for training acolytes in the art of disputation, became, along with the
laboratory, a workshop of scientific practice. Working in the vineyard of
knowledge side by side with his master, the student learned the methods
of his discipline and undertook his own investigations.[20] Gradually, as
the faculty of philosophy grew in size and importance, this technique was
extended to the other professional faculties. The joining of teaching and
research gave the four-part German university a distinctive purpose and
character. To a large extent, though not entirely, it arrested the tendency
of theology to seek antecedent certainties, of law to become the study
of procedures, of medicine to become exclusively clinical.[21] Not pastors

[17] *Ibid.,* pp. 17–18.
[18] See John Theodore Merz's discussion in *A History of European Thought in the
Nineteenth Century,* pp. 90, 168–74, 170n, 172n.
[19] Herbert Baxter Adams, "New Methods of Study in History," *Johns Hopkins
University Studies in Historical and Political Science* (Baltimore, 1884), II,
64–65.
[20] See Rudolph Virchow, Rectorial Address, "The Founding of the Berlin University and the Transition from the Philosophic to the Scientific Age," in *Annual
Report of the Board of Regents of the Smithsonian Institution* (Washington, D.C.,
1896), pp. 685 ff.
[21] One exception to this was to be found in theological instruction in the Catholic
faculties. Religious compromise had provided for parallel Catholic and Protestant
faculties of theology at Bonn, Breslau, Strasbourg, and Tübingen, and Catholic
theology faculties at Freiburg, Munich, Münster, and Würzburg. The presence in a
university of a faculty over which the Roman Catholic Church exercised a con-

but theologians, not lawyers but jurists, not practitioners but medical scientists, were the desired products. The German university was not a place where anyone could study anything, nor was it a place, despite the practical preparations demanded by state examinations, where the interest in practice was predominant. Technological training in nineteenth-century Germany, by no means neglected, was usually made available in separate schools and institutes; basic courses and tool subjects, by no means disregarded, were offered in the efficient *Gymnasien.* This indifference to vocational ambition, this insistence on disinterested research, created a gulf between the spirit of the university and that of everyday life. Like an independent spiritual order, the German university trained its own personnel, held novitiates to its own standards, and kept the secular world at a certain remove.

To these radiant ideals and great accomplishments, many Americans reacted enviously, and with contempt for their own institutions. "What has heretofore been the idea of an University with us?" wrote the young Henry Wadsworth Longfellow while a student at Göttingen in 1829. "The answer is a simple one:—Two or three large brick buildings,— with a chapel, and a President to pray in it!" How inferior was this to the Göttingen idea "of collecting together professors in whom the spirit moved—who were well enough known to attract students to themselves, and . . . capable of teaching them something they did not know before." [22] As the Gilded Age approached, contrasts of this sort became more and more common. Reform-minded intellectuals, unhappy in the universe of Ulysses Grant, yet sharing its spirit of expansionism, held up the achievements of the German university as indictments of American education. To Benjamin Apthorp Gould, the noted Harvard astronomer, it was intolerable that America, like Rome, should have to send her sons abroad for intellectual nourishment. [23] The reviewer of Noah Porter's book on American education compared the German *Gelehrte* with the

---

trolling influence both in appointments and dogma was a source of friction throughout the nineteenth century. The argument against removal to separate institutions relied on the fear of communal divisionism in Germany and on the hope, not unwarranted, that the scientific method would penetrate Catholic theology too. See Max Müller, *Die Lehr- und Lernfreiheit: Versuch einer systematisch-historischen Darstellung mit besonderer Berücksichtigung der französischen, deutschen und schweizerischen Verhältnisse* (St. Gallen, 1911), pp. 191–200.

[22] Long, *Literary Pioneers,* p. 166.

[23] Benjamin A. Gould, "An American University," *American Journal of Education,* II (September, 1856), 289.

American professor, and found the native product to be "a nondescript, a jack of all trades, equally ready to teach surveying and Latin eloquence, and thankful if his quarter's salary is not docked to whitewash the college fence." [24] Almost all of those destined to become presidents of the great new universities compared the frowsiness of Alma Mater with the charms of the foreign Lorelei. Andrew Dickson White, as a student at the University of Berlin, saw his "ideal of a university not only realized, but extended and glorified," and resolved to "do something" for American education.[25] Three decades later, Nicholas Murray Butler savored the matchless knowledge of German scholars at the same institution, and acknowledged that it "left an ineffaceable impression of what scholarship meant, of what a university was and of what a long road higher education in America had to travel before it could hope to reach a place of equal elevation." [26] James Burrill Angell, Charles W. Eliot, Daniel Coit Gilman, and Charles Kendall Adams were also in this company of future college presidents who admired Germany.[27] In America's continual rediscovery of her cultural inferiority, the German paradigm played a conspicuous part.

Before the 1850s, those who turned to German universities for inspiration were more impressed by the advancement and specialization of their teaching than by their commitment to scholarly research.[28] It was the elementary quality of American collegiate education that discouraged Joseph Green Cogswell at Harvard and made him leave to found his little *Landschule* at Northampton, Massachusetts.[29] It was the thorough-

---

[24] "The Higher Education in America," *Galaxy,* XI (March, 1871), 373.

[25] Andrew Dickson White, *Autobiography* (New York, 1922), I, 291.

[26] Nicholas Murray Butler, *Across the Busy Years* (New York, 1935), I, 126.

[27] See James Burrill Angell, *Reminiscences* (New York, 1912), p. 102; Henry James, *Charles W. Eliot,* I, 136–37; Gilman, *Launching of a University,* p. 275; Charles Foster Smith, *Charles Kendall Adams, A Life-Sketch* (Madison, Wis., 1924), pp. 12–13. See also, S. Willis Rudy, "The 'Revolution' in American Higher Education, 1865–1900," *Harvard Educational Review,* XXI (Summer, 1951), 165–69.

[28] For example, the primary object of George Ticknor's projected reforms at Harvard in 1825 was to provide for a wider range of subjects, an elective choice of subjects, lectures instead of recitations. This admirer of the German universities did not try to make Harvard over into an institution of research. See George S. Hilliard, *Life, Letters and Journals of George Ticknor* (Boston, 1877), I, 358; George Ticknor, *Remarks on Changes Lately Proposed or Adopted at Harvard University* (Boston, 1825). The early attempts to found graduate schools envisioned advanced studies, but rarely the deliberate encouragement of research. Richard F. Storr, "Academic Overture," unpublished Ph.D. dissertation (Harvard University, 1949).

[29] *Life of Joseph Green Cogswell* (Cambridge, Mass., 1874), p. 134; Joseph Green Cogswell, "University Education," *New York Review,* VII (1840), 109–36.

ness of the German system that drew high encomiums from the Reverend Henry E. Dwight, son of the Yale president, who wrote a widely reviewed book about Germany in 1829.[30] Not until after the middle of the century was the German ideal of academic research approved for emulation. Henry P. Tappan's *University Education* (1850), perhaps the first full-length book by an American author dealing exclusively with advanced studies, was one of the earliest attempts to define a university as a place where, among other things, "provision is made for carrying forward all scientific investigation." [31] The tendency to regard the university from the point of view of the scholar as well as of the student became marked in the next few decades. The object of the German university, wrote James Morgan Hart, in the first extensive study of the German university published in this country, is the "ardent, methodical, independent search after truth in any and all its forms, but wholly irrespective of utilitarian applications." [32] Research, under academic auspices, he argued, breathed life into the university. It attracted men of outstanding abilities, not pedagogues and disciplinarians. It gave students a genuine concern for matters of the mind.[33] This belated recognition of Germany's real glory points up the factor of cultural selection. Cultural goods can only be imported into friendly markets, and before 1850 our canons of education were not receptive to the idea of academic research.[34]

[30] Henry E. Dwight, *Travels in the North of Germany* (New York, 1829), p. 175 and *passim*.
[31] Henry P. Tappan, *University Education* (New York, 1850), pp. 43–45, 68. See, also, Alexander D. Bache, "A National University," *American Journal of Education,* I (May, 1856), 478.
[32] James Morgan Hart, *German Universities: A Narrative of Personal Experience* (New York, 1878), p. 264.
[33] *Ibid.,* pp. 257, 338–55.
[34] Without attempting the almost impossible task of providing a full bibliography, the following arguments for research as an academic function are worthy of mention: George S. Morris, "University Education," in *Philosophical Papers of the University of Michigan* (Ann Arbor, 1886–1888), Series 1–2, pp. 8–9; many addresses by Daniel C. Gilman, including his "Inaugural Address" (1876), in *University Problems in the United States* (New York, 1898), pp. 18–19; David Starr Jordan, "The Building of a University" in *The Voice of the Scholar* (San Francisco, 1901), p. 28; Jordan, "Inaugural Address" (1891) in David Weaver, ed., *Builders of American Universities* (Alton, Ill., 1950), p. 356; F. W. Clarke, "American Colleges versus American Science," *Popular Science Monthly,* IX (August, 1876), pp. 467–74; Charles Phelps Taft, *The German University and the American College* (Cincinnati, 1871), p. 23; Francis A. March, "The Scholar of Today," in Northrup, Lane, Schwab, eds., *Representative Phi Beta Kappa Addresses* (New York, 1915), pp. 112–23; John W. Hoyt, "Address on University Progress," delivered before the National Teachers' Association, 1869, in *National University Pamphlets,* (Columbia University Library), pp. 6–79. Opposition to the idea of searching as an academic function was voiced by many traditionalists; they did not, however,

In time, however, the old assumptions were challenged and were cast aside. In the centennial year of the nation's independence, Johns Hopkins University, the first university in America based on the German model, opened its doors. The aim of this university, said Daniel Coit Gilman when he assumed the duties of the presidency, was "the encouragement of research; the promotion of young men; and the advancement of individual scholars, who by their excellence will advance the sciences they pursue, and the society where they dwell." [35] Suiting action to his words, he appointed a small but eminent faculty, giving it time and freedom for research, and assembled a small but remarkable group of graduate students, giving them incentives for scholarly work; and the names of these men —James J. Sylvester, Henry A. Rowland, Herbert B. Adams, Henry C. Adams, Josiah Royce, Thorstein Veblen, Woodrow Wilson, Richard T. Ely, John Dewey—are the best testimonials of his success.[36] Aptly was this university called the Göttingen at Baltimore. Of fifty-three professors and lecturers on the roster in 1884, nearly all had studied at German universities, and thirteen had been awarded the doctoral degree.[37] Johns Hopkins adopted the lecture, the seminar, and the laboratory, and brought teachers and students together in close and congenial association. What it called the graduate school was the equivalent of the German faculty of philosophy—broad in its range of specialties, nonutilitarian in its objectives, devoted to the tasks of research. And the spirit was German too: "One longed," wrote Josiah Royce, "to be a doer of the word, and not a hearer only, a creator of his own infinitesimal fraction of a product, bound in God's name to produce it when the time came." [38]

Inspired by Johns Hopkins, fifteen major graduate schools or departments were established by the end of the nineteenth century.[39] Decade by

---

unite on any one argument. Some opposed the German emphasis on self-discipline and argued for the older notion of mental discipline, see "The American Colleges versus the European Universities," Nation, XXXIV (Feb. 16, 1882), 142–43, 143–44. Some continued to fear the irreligion of German education, see L. H. Atwater, "Proposed Reforms in Collegiate Education," Princeton Review, X (July, 1882), 100–120. Others defended the classical subjects and the prescribed curriculum; see Andrew F. West, A Review of President Eliot's Report on Elective Studies (New York, 1886).

[35] Gilman, University Problems, p. 35.

[36] John C. French, A History of the University Founded by Johns Hopkins (Baltimore, 1946), p. 41 and passim.

[37] Thwing, The American and the German University, p. 43.

[38] Josiah Royce, "Present Ideals of American University Life," Scribner's Magazine, X (September, 1891), 383.

[39] W. Carson Ryan, Studies in Early Graduate Education (New York, 1939), pp. 3–14.

decade, the output of American degrees of doctor of philosophy increased almost geometrically. Before 1861 not a single doctorate had been awarded by an American institution; in 1890, 164 such degrees were conferred; in 1900, more than twice that number.[40] In 1871, the total number of postgraduate students in American institutions was 198; by 1890, the number had risen to 2,872.[41] Whatever these figures reveal as to the crowding of the graduate schools and the lowering of standards and results, their chief import is the evidence they give of the thorough domestication of the ideal of academic research.

Rarely, however, does an ideal undergo a drastic change of scene and remain intact in form or spirit. Original meanings are lost in new ideological surroundings; new implications are acquired in strange institutional settings. In practice, America transformed, even as she borrowed, the notion of academic research. Americans did not approach the task of building universities as did the French: no minister of education, like Jules Ferry, could cast our institutions into one comprehensive system: the molding forces were public and private, local and national, lay and professional. Americans did not build their universities with the logical consistency of the Germans: for various reasons no sharp lines separated colleges from graduate schools, or technical from intellectual concerns. In answering the question: "What should the new university be?" every need clamored for satisfaction, every craft hoped for inclusion. Our postwar institutions of higher learning were therefore not merely motley, but mongrel; not only different from each other in size, quality, independence, and sophistication (which was a familiar American pattern), but eclectic in their character and purposes (which on the whole was something new). In calling attention to this fact we do not imply, as do certain critics of the American university, that consistency is a supreme educational good.[42] It may well be that diversity is a sign of effectiveness, that consistency can only be bought at the price of real vitality. But it does appear that our eclecticism was responsible for a confusion and ambivalence in the rela-

---

[40] Walton C. John, *Graduate Study in Universities and Colleges in the United States* (Washington, D.C., 1935), pp. 9, 19.

[41] *Report of the Commissioner of Education,* 1872, pp. 772–81; *Report of the Commissioner of Education,* 1890–1891, II, 1398–1413.

[42] Critics of American higher education have made much of its hodge-podge character. See, particularly, Abraham Flexner, *Universities: American, English and German* (New York and London, 1930); Robert Maynard Hutchins, *The Higher Learning in America* (New Haven, 1936); Jacques Barzun, *Teacher in America* (Boston, 1945), pp. 253–319; Carnegie Foundation for the Advancement of Teaching, *Second Annual Report of the President and Treasurer* (1907), pp. 76–97.

tion of the university to its publics which affected in turn the spirit and goals of academic research.

It was apparent to certain reformers that colleges and universities were not only different, but essentially incompatible, institutions. In a famous manifesto of the university movement, John W. Burgess, the Columbia political scientist, argued that the college was an educational anomaly, unable to become a university and unwilling to become a *Gymnasium;* and that therefore it should cease to exist.[43] G. Stanley Hall wanted to make Clark University into a "school for professors," designed for original research and instruction of the highest grade, without the encumbrance of an undergraduate department.[44] But this drastic excision of the college did not and indeed could not take place. Sentiment overruled logic, and sentiment is always the main conduit of academic financial support. The alumni and friends of the older colleges were willing to pay to see them exalted, not destroyed, by graduate schools. The state universities would not take so "undemocratic" a step as to differentiate intellectual interests. Even the brand-new universities—Johns Hopkins, Clark, Chicago, Stanford—retained, or (as in the case of Clark) in time acquired, an undergraduate division, either out of deference to local sentiment, or because of a lack of qualified graduate students, or out of a sheer obsession with size. As a consequence the parental assumptions of higher education were never dispelled. Comparing the aims of college educators in 1843–76 with those in 1909–21, one writer has demonstrated the persistence of "morality and character" as basic collegiate values, while the greater attention given in the later period to "civic and social responsibility" was a kind of secular substitute for piety.[45] The existence of the college on university grounds perpetuated a residual belief in the immaturity of academic students, and as their age at the time of entry mounted, their putative age of in-

[43] John W. Burgess, *The American University: When Shall It Be? Where Shall It Be? What Shall It Be?* (Boston, 1884), p. 18. Burgess had returned from the seminars of Droysen and Von Gneist to teach survey courses in history at Amherst College. Amherst in the 1870s was still a denominational college of the parental type, and Burgess' attempt to introduce a graduate seminar along German lines met with severe opposition. With higher hopes, he had then turned to Columbia University, only to find that this richer and less pious institution, located in a center of American sophistication, was also opposed to research. Though eventually he was able to establish a graduate school in political science, the lesson he learned was that the collegiate spirit was antipathetic to graduate research. John W. Burgess, *Reminiscences of an American Scholar* (New York, 1934), pp. 138–90.

[44] Ryan, *Studies in Early Graduate Education,* p. 48.

[45] Leonard V. Koos, "College Aims Past and Present," *School and Society,* XIV (Dec. 3, 1921), 500.

nocence was increased. In the public mind, the American university was not clearly defined as a center of independent thought, an agent of intellectual progress; it was also, perhaps primarily, a school of preparation for minors, a substitute parent for the young.[46]

The combination of technical and intellectual interests in each university was also a wedlock of incompatibles. The emergence of the university coincided with the growth of industrialism, urbanism, agricultural commercialism, and corporate enterprise. Dynamic and growing, the machine society needed technical skill to run it, scientific knowledge to improve it, managerial experience to organize it, engineering competence to give it cost advantages. The land-grant colleges were the most famous product of the industrial movement in education. Set up under the terms of the Morrill Act (1862), they reflected the activities of leaders of scientific agriculture, of advocates of a free public education, of politicians free with public lands.[47] As teaching organizations, the land-grant colleges purveyed the abundant and complicated "know-how" that American industry was acquiring. As research organizations, they emphasized the applied sciences—the "better-ways-of-doing"—that American culture was geared to accept. The significant point, however, is not that land-grant colleges and graduate schools coexisted, for each served its own area of need; the significant thing is that they coexisted in the same institutions. In the original disposition of the land-grant fund, agricultural and mechanical arts colleges were added to ten existing universities; ultimately some of the independent land-grant colleges increased their size and added to their purposes by taking on graduate schools.[48] Cornell University, the perfect example of the academic crossbreed, was a land-grant college, a Germanized graduate school, a private university, a liberal arts college.[49] Eclecticism could be achieved, however, in institutions which did not include a land-grant

[46] See Richard H. Shryock's interesting discussion of this point in "The Academic Profession in the United States," *Bulletin,* AAUP, XXXVIII (Spring, 1952), 37 ff.

[47] The best analysis of the industrial movement in education is provided by Earle D. Ross, *Democracy's College: The Land-Grant Movement in the Formative Stage* (Ames, Iowa, 1942), pp. 1–45; Merle Curti and Vernon Carstensen, *The University of Wisconsin, 1848–1925* (Madison, Wis., 1949), Vol. I, Chap. I; Frank T. Carlton, *Education and Industrial Evolution* (New York, 1913); Philip R. V. Curoe, *Educational Attitudes and Policies of Organized Labor in the United States* (New York, 1926), pp. 61, 88, 95–98.

[48] Ross, *Democracy's College,* pp. 68–86.

[49] Walter P. Rogers, *Andrew Dickson White and the Modern University* (Ithaca, N.Y., 1942), pp. 90–123 and *passim.*

college. The University of Chicago, sharing the imperious spirit of the Standard Oil tycoon who was its patron, served both practical and intellectual interests from the outset: it was a community center for the popular diffusion of knowledge, a great institution for scientific and scholarly research, a workshop of practical engineering, a center for professional training, and an undergraduate college.[50]

As a result, the American university united two divergent conceptions of research. In the one view, research was an activity to be initiated and directed from within the university. The searcher was to be independent, not only with respect to his conclusions, but to his choice of an area of work. To fill the gaps in knowledge that continuing inquiry revealed, to conduct investigations as the logic of a discipline directed— these were to be the functions of academic inquiry. Practical results might be forthcoming, but inquiry should be allowed to push against any of the frontiers of knowledge, and not merely along that border where material benefits were promised. Fundamentally, this was the graduate school's conception of research.[51] Adopting the methods of the German seminar and laboratory, it favored an unremitting quest for facts, a strenuous objectivity, the reconstruction of past events "as they actually happened." [52] With the constant development of new specialties, the graduate-school scholar tended to submit his work to a small group of the *cognoscenti* upon whose recognition and approval his professional advancement depended. Moreover, like the German faculty of philosophy, the graduate school preserved its cultural independence by training its own personnel. Not entirely by design,[53] the Ph.D. in America

[50] Thomas W. Goodspeed, *A History of the University of Chicago* (Chicago, 1916), p. 26.

[51] See Daniel C. Gilman, "The Future of American Colleges and Universities," *Atlantic Monthly,* LXXVIII (August, 1896), 175–79; G. Stanley Hall's statement in *Clark University, 1890–1899, Decennial Celebration* (Worcester, Mass., 1899), p. iii, for contemporary expressions of this view of graduate research.

[52] For the German influence on this version of research, see Herbert B. Adams, "New Methods of Study in History," *Johns Hopkins University Studies in Historical and Political Science,* II (1884), 94; Adams, *The Study of History in American Colleges and Universities* (Washington, D.C., 1887); Edward A. Ross, *Seventy Years of It* (New York, 1936), pp. 37–38; Ray Stannard Baker, ed., *Woodrow Wilson: Life and Letters* (New York, 1927), I, 174–75; Carl Murchison, ed., *A History of Psychology in Autobiography* (Worcester, Mass., 1930), I, 2–4, 102–7, 301–10, 450–52; II, 214–20. Paul Shorey, "American Scholarship," *The Nation,* LCII (May 11, 1911), 466–69; C. M. Andrews, "These Forty Years," *American Historical Review,* XXX (January, 1925), 225–50.

[53] The hope of some of the founders of the graduate school that it would also train men for the higher ranks of government was disappointed by the slow development

turned out to be marketable mostly in the type of institution that conferred it, or in the colleges ranking immediately below. But unlike the
German faculty of philosophy, which was *primus inter pares* and spiritual leader of the other faculties, the graduate school in the American
university was only one of a heterogeneous group of divisions. In the
other schools and departments, research was often geared to external
and ulterior purposes. The Agricultural College, for example, took its
cues for research from the problems of the agricultural community, often
from the requests of the Dairyman's Association or the local horti-
cultural society.[54] The departments of commerce, the schools of engineering, the schools of business administration, tended to perfect the skills
required by the industrial and business community. In this second view,
research was a public service that originated in a client's need and
ended in a client's satisfaction.

It would be a mistake to conclude that, compared with the German
university, our hybrid university possessed and offered no advantages.
From the standpoint of science there was much to be said for keeping
open the channels between pure and applied research. From the standpoint of social policy it could be argued that there was something intrinsically good about a system that did not draw tight distinctions between one kind of interest and another, one kind of student and
another, one kind of inquiry and another. And we shall see that, from
the standpoint of academic freedom, one of the cues taken from the
workaday world by university scholars was a bolder demand for civil
liberty. Yet it is no less true that our eclecticism carried penalties.
It blurred the public's picture of what a university was and ought to
be. Like Hamlet's cloud, it appeared in the shape of a camel, or a
weasel, or a whale. Some saw in that indistinct image a refuge for
recondite thought; others perceived a public station, catering to all
comers. Each delineation of the university carried a different interpretation of its rights. As a culturally autonomous gild, the university was
independent of all social groups and stood above the clash of their in-

---

of the civil service and the superiority of the study of law as a threshold to political
careers. Nor, as originally planned, did the graduate schools fill the higher echelons
of journalism, business, and secondary education, once these functions were taken
over by special graduate institutions after the turn of the century. See Richard
Hofstadter and C. De Witt Hardy, *The Development and Scope of Higher Education in the United States* (New York, 1952), pp. 57–100.

[54] An excellent analysis of community initiative in the research projects of the "Ag"
college can be found in W. H. Glover, *Farm and College: The College of Agriculture of the University of Wisconsin* (Madison, Wis., 1952).

terests; as a serviceable folk institution, it was the instrument of all social groups and dared not rasp the interests of constituents. The members of the university did not relieve this confusion. In undertaking to perform a variety of services, the university engaged many teachers to whom unqualified freedom of inquiry was not desirable or not germane. In the university, searchers, the seekers for truth wherever it led, hobnobbed with technicians, who were the purveyors of *ad hoc* techniques, and craftsmen, who were the executors of someone else's designs. In a faculty composed of accountants, home economists, sociologists, military scientists, physicists, physicians, physical educationalists, fashion designers, marketing experts, and mining engineers, there could be no unified sense of the need for academic freedom, no united front against attacks on university independence, no sure definition of the university.

LEHRFREIHEIT AND LERNFREIHEIT

All through the nineteenth century, but particularly after the establishment of the Empire, German scholars boasted of their academic freedom and brought it to the attention of the scholarly world. And the scholarly world, in the habit of paying homage to the German universities, agreed that freedom was triumphant there, the proof and cause of their superiority. In recent times, it is worth noting, the reality of this vaunted freedom has been sharply questioned. With the recent capitulation of the German universities to pseudo-science and the totalitarian state, doubt has arisen as to whether, at any time in the pre-Hitler period, they had ever truly been free. It is pointed out that professors as civil servants had been subject to a special disciplinary code; that under the Kaisers, Social Democrats, Jews, and other minorities had been discriminated against in appointments; that on most questions of national honor and interest (witness the performance of the German professors during the First World War), the academic corps had docilely taken its place in the chauvinistic chorus.[55] It is also pointed out that the German universities were state universities in an undemocratic state,

---

[55] See E. Y. Hartshorne, "The German Universities and the Government," *Annals of the American Academy of Political and Social Science,* CC (November, 1938), 210–12; Louis Snyder, "German Universities Are on the March Again," *Prevent World War III,* XIV (April–May, 1946), 28–30; R. H. Samuel and R. H. Thomas, *Education and Society in Modern Germany* (London, 1949), pp. 114–15; Frank Smith, "Presidential Address, Association of University Teachers," *Bulletin, AAUP,* XX (October, 1934), 383–84; Paul R. Neureiter, "Hitlerism and the German Universities," *Journal of Higher Education,* V (May, 1934), 264–70.

dependent upon the uncertain good will of the minister of education and on a dynasty far more autocratic than the constitutional forms reveal.[56] Granting all this to be true, however, there remains the question of what was the basis of the boast that the German universities were free.

Two factors point to the answer. The first is the greater independence enjoyed by the universities under the Empire than at any time before. The Reformation had fixed the universities in the theology of the territorial ruler. Though test oaths for students had been abolished in the Protestant universities during the eighteenth century, and speculative philosophy and theological skepticism had flourished at the expense of orthodoxy, it was not until complete separation of church and state was achieved under the Hohenzollerns that the universities were finally free from church control.[57] Likewise punitive action by the state became comparatively rare after unification. The German states lost much of their cameralistic urge to regulate everything directly. The territorial oaths and religious tests in force in the seventeenth century, such as the official resolution of the University of Marburg in 1653 to ban Cartesian philosophy,[58] the capricious absolutism of the eighteenth century, revealed in Frederick William I's expulsion of Christian Wolff and the

---

[56] For the activities of the high-handed Friedrich Althoff, head of the Prussian Ministry of Education (1897–1907), see Friedrich Paulsen, *An Autobiography* (New York, 1938), pp. 361–69; Ulrich Wilamowitz-Moellendorff, *My Recollections, 1848–1914* (London, 1930), pp. 300–303. The case of the Berlin *Privatdocent* Leo Arons, who was deprived of the *venia legendi* by the Prussian authorities over the pointed objections of the Berlin philosophical faculty, suggests the power that could be exercised by the throne. *Die Aktenstücke des Disziplinarverfahrens gegen den Privatdocenten Dr. Arons* (Berlin, 1900), gives the essential documents in the case. For late 19th century infringements of the faculty's control over *Privatdocenten*, see William C. Dreher, "A Letter from Germany," *Atlantic Monthly,* LXXXV (March, 1900), 305.

[57] Except for the seven Roman Catholic theological faculties, where the appointment of professors, under the religious compromise, had to receive the sanction of the bishop of the diocese.

[58] Similarly at Jena in 1696, the unanimous consent of the faculty was required before a teacher might point out Aristotle's mistakes. Frequently, it was the sovereign who gave distinguished scholars protection against the gild oaths and narrow-mindedness of professors. For example, Karl Ludwig, Elector Palatine, invited Spinoza in 1673 to his University of Heidelberg, where the latter was guaranteed every freedom of philosophical instruction, hedged only by the Elector's expectation that he would not disturb the established religion. The Great Elector, Frederick William of Brandenburg, proposed that all scholars oppressed in their homelands assemble in one of his cities—a plan that did not materialize. See G. Kaufmann, *Die Lehrfreiheit an den deutschen Universitäten im neunzehnten Jahrhundert* (Leipzig, 1898).

reprimand of Kant by Prime Minister Wollner,[59] and the repressive censorship of the early and middle nineteenth century, exemplified by the Carlsbad Decrees and the dismissal of the Göttingen Seven,[60] all seemed part of an inglorious but forever finished past. The provision in the Prussian Constitution of 1850 that "science and its teaching shall be free" epitomized the more permissive attitude of the new order. Finally, the German universities were not directly affected by public opinion under the Empire. Public opinion in general never reached the degree of crystallization, organization, and articulation that it achieved in England, France, or the United States. Like the army, the universities belonged to the state, which protected them against local and sectarian pressures.

The German system of control allowed the universities considerable corporate autonomy. The states drew up the budgets, created new chairs, appointed professors, and framed the general scheme of instruction. But the election of academic officials, the appointment of lecturers or *Privatdocenten,* and the nomination of professors were powers enjoyed by the faculty.[61] No lay board of control was interposed between

[59] On the charge that he was encouraging desertion in the army with his fatalistic philosophy, Christian Wolff was run out of Halle on forty-eight hours' notice under pain of the halter (1723). Frederick the Great (1740–86) had no real sympathy for German scholarship, though he reinstated Christian Wolff and was tolerant in religious and intellectual matters. After his death, there was a sharp reaction. A royal decree restricted freedom of teaching and publication in 1788; it was under the authority of this edict that Kant was reprimanded by Prussian Minister Wollner for having used his philosophy "for the purpose of distorting and deprecating several basic teachings of the Holy Bible and of Christianity." Lilge, *The Abuse of Learning,* p. 7.

[60] Military defeat and the great spiritual revival of Prussia in the early nineteenth century brought the brief flowering of German liberal humanism. As Secretary of the Department of Education and Religion in the Prussian Ministry of Education, Humboldt secured the abolition of censorship for scholarly, scientific, and literary works in 1809–10. But with the general reaction that came with the Congress of Vienna, a system of espionage and repressive control was established over the universities. The Carlsbad Resolutions of 1819 provided for strict censorship and a curatorial system to control the universities. During this period of reaction, seven professors at Göttingen, led by Dahlmann, refused to swear allegiance to a new and less liberal constitution in 1837 and were dismissed. There were other dismissals: Mommsen from Leipzig, David Strauss from Tübingen, Maleschott and Kuno Fischer from Heidelberg. See Robert B. Sutton, "European and American Concepts of Academic Freedom, 1500–1914," unpublished Ph.D. dissertation (University of Missouri, 1950), pp. 177 ff.

[61] The federal nature of the German Empire allowed for a certain amount of variation in the forms of state control. In Prussia, the faculty submitted the names of three men to the king to fill vacancies in professorial chairs; the king

the ultimate authority of the state and the plenary powers of the professors. No elaborate administrative structure was required; no office of the president was established. Each faculty was presided over by a dean elected by and chosen from that faculty; each university was represented by a rector chosen from and elected by the whole professorial corps. The German universities were state institutions, but the combination of governmental restraint, cultural isolation, limited professorial co-option, and elected administrators gave them the appearance of self-governing bodies.[62]

The German definition of academic freedom offers the second clue. When the German professor spoke of academic freedom,[63] he referred to a condition summed up by two words: *Lernfreiheit* and *Lehrfreiheit*. By *Lernfreiheit* he meant the absence of administrative coercions in the learning situation. He referred to the fact that German students were free to roam from place to place, sampling academic wares; that wherever they lighted, they were free to determine the choice and sequence of courses, and were responsible to no one for regular attendance; that they were exempted from all tests save the final examination; that they lived in private quarters and controlled their private lives.[64] This freedom was deemed essential to the main purposes of the German university: to forward research and to train researchers. By *Lehrfreiheit*, the German educator meant two things. He meant that the university professor was free to examine bodies of evidence and to report his findings in lecture or pub-

---

usually, but not invariably, chose one of them for the position. On the other hand, Prussia granted the faculty full right to appoint *Privatdocenten* (until the passage of the *Lex Arons*, 1898, which made the minister of education the final court in the disciplining of lecturers). In Bavaria, the king granted the *venia legendi* to all university teachers; in Saxony, Württemburg, and Mecklenburg-Schwerin, the consent of the minister of instruction was necessary.

[62] See, for a good short résumé in English of the structure of university control in Germany, "The Financial Status of the Professor in America and in Germany," *Bulletin*, Carnegie Foundation for the Advancement of Teaching, II (1908), 66.

[63] Actually, the literal translation of academic freedom, *akademische Freiheit*, usually denoted *Lernfreiheit* alone. See J. G. Fichte, "Ueber die einzig mögliche Störung der akademischen Freiheit," in *Sämtliche Werke*, VI, 449–76; Hermann von Helmholtz, "Ueber die akademische Freiheit der deutschen Universitäten," in *Vorträge und Reden* (2 vols.; Braunschweig, 1884), II, 195–216. When the Germans referred to freedom of teaching, or what in current American usage is called academic freedom, they used the term *Lehrfreiheit* or *akademische Lehrfreiheit*. Viz., Friedrich Paulsen, "Die akademische Lehrfreiheit und ihre Grenzen: eine Rede *pro domo*," *Preussische Jahrbücher*, XCI (January–April, 1898), pp. 515–31.

[64] See Helmholtz, "Ueber die akademische Freiheit," pp. 195–216.

lished form—that he enjoyed freedom of teaching and freedom of inquiry. This, too, was thought to follow from the searching function, from the presumption that knowledge was not fixed or final, from the belief, as Paulsen put it, that *Wissenschaft* knew no "statute of limitation," no authoritative "law of prescription," no "absolute property right." [65] This freedom was not, as the Germans conceived it, an inalienable endowment of all men, nor was it a superadded attraction of certain universities and not of others; rather, it was the distinctive prerogative of the academic profession, and the essential condition of all universities. Without it, no institution had the right to call itself a "university." [66] In addition, *Lehrfreiheit,* like *Lernfreiheit,* also denoted the paucity of administrative rules within the teaching situation: the absence of a prescribed syllabus, the freedom from tutorial duties, the opportunity to lecture on any subject according to the teacher's interest. Thus, academic freedom, as the Germans defined it, was not simply the right of professors to speak without fear or favor, but the atmosphere of consent that surrounded the whole process of research and instruction.

The German's pride in these two freedoms can be attributed in part to the status they conferred and to their significance as patriotic symbols. To the university student, coming from the strict and formal *Gymnasium,* *Lernfreiheit* was a precious privilege, a recognition of his arrival at man's estate. To the university professor, extremely sensitive to considerations of social esteem, *Lehrfreiheit* was a dispensation that set him apart from the ordinary civil servant. In a nation still aristocratic and feudalistic in its mores, caste considerations thus underlay the loyalty to academic freedom.[67] In addition, *Lern-* and *Lehrfreiheit* had patriotic associations. They were identified with the national revival. The renewal of student peregrinations in the eighteenth century symbolized the breakdown of territorial exclusiveness and the growth of national consciousness. The University of Berlin, dedicated to academic freedom, was a phoenix that had arisen from the ashes of military defeat. The denial of academic freedom in the Metternich era had been the work of Catholic dogmatism, Protestant particularism, petty absolutism—all enemies of a united Reich.[68] Moreover, after unification, academic free-

[65] Paulsen, *The German Universities and University Study,* p. 228.
[66] Paulsen, "Die akademische Lehrfreiheit," pp. 515–31.
[67] For analysis of social structure in nineteenth-century Germany, see Ernst Kohn-Bramstedt, *Aristocracy and the Middle Classes in Germany* (London, 1937).
[68] See Paulsen, *German Universities and University Study,* pp. 36–67, 227–62;

dom was thought to atone for the lack of political freedoms and to prove the special virtue of the Fatherland.[69] The romantic nineteenth century was given to equating freedom and nationality, but it was a peculiarity of German thought that it made academic freedom one of the major terms in this equation.

The German conception of academic freedom, reflecting the philosophical temper of German academic thought, distinguished sharply between freedom *within* and freedom *outside* the university. Within the walls of academe, a wide latitude of utterance was allowed, even expected. With Fichte's heroic scholar as their model, university professors saw themselves, not as neutral observers of life, but as the diviners and spokesmen of absolutes, as oracles of transcendent truths. In the normative sciences particularly, "professing" in Germany tended to be the presentation with aggressive finality of deep subjective convictions. Among certain professors, to be sure, there were proponents of a more restrained and cautious conception. In 1877, in the heat of the Darwinian controversy, Rudolph Virchow, the great German pathologist, argued that unproved hypotheses should never be taught as true, that professors should stay within their spheres of competence, that they should consult the *consensus gentium* before expressing possibly dangerous beliefs.[70] But in a famous reply to Virchow, Ernst Haeckel, the biologist, contended that no line between objective and subjective knowledge could or ought to be drawn, that science advances only through the open clash of wrong and correct opinions, that the obligation of the professor to adhere to indubitable facts or to defer to existing opinion would relinquish the field of education to the religious infallibilists.[71] The leading theorists [72] of academic freedom in this period adhered to the latter position—Max Müller of St. Gallen, Georg Kaufmann, von Helmholtz, Friedrich Paulsen. Reasoning from ration-

Virchow, "The Founding of Berlin University," p. 685; Fichte, "Ueber die einzig mögliche Störung der akademischen Freiheit," *Sämtliche Werke,* VI, 451–76.

[69] Helmholtz, "Ueber die akademische Freiheit," p. 214.

[70] R. Virchow, *Freedom of Science in the Modern State.* Discourse at the Third Meeting of the 50th Conference of the German Association of Naturalists and Physicists, Munich, 1877 (London, 1878), pp. 8, 22–24, 41, 49–50.

[71] Ernst Haeckel, *Freedom of Science and Teaching* (New York, 1889; first printing 1878), pp. 63 ff.

[72] Max Weber was an exception. See "Die Lehrfreiheit der Universitäten," *Hochschul-Nachrichten,* XIX (January, 1909), 89–91. Weber argued for neutrality on normative issues, insisting, however, that the professor be the judge of his own transgressions.

alistic or idealistic premises, they believed that the only alternative to the presentation of personal convictions was the prescription of authoritative dogma, that the only alternative to polemical controversy was the stoppage of academic inquiry. Recognizing that there were dangers in subjective and polemical teaching, they thought there were adequate safeguards in the freedom and maturity of the student, who was neither captive nor unprimed. As Paulsen put it:

The content of instruction is not prescribed for the academic teacher; he is, as searcher as well as teacher, attached to no authority; he himself answers for his own instruction and is responsible to no one else. Opposite him is his student with complete freedom to accept or to reject; he is not a pupil but has the privilege of the critic or the improver. There is only one aim for both: the truth; only one yardstick: the agreement of thought with reality and with no other outside authority.[73]

To Helmholtz,

Whoever wants to give his students complete conviction about the accuracy of his statements must first of all know from his own experience how one wins conviction, and how one does not. Thus he must have had to know how to struggle for this by himself when no predecessor had yet come to his aid; this means that he must have worked on the boundaries of human knowledge and conquered new realms for it. A teacher who imparts convictions that are not his own is sufficient for students who are to be directed by authority as the source of their knowledge, but it is not for such as those who demand a foundation for their conviction down to the very last fundamentals. . . . The free conviction of scholars is only to be won if the free expression of conviction on the part of the teacher, freedom of teaching, is assured.[74]

But outside the university, the same degree of freedom was not condoned. Though quite a few German professors played prominent political roles in the nineteenth century, and a number of these—notably Mommsen and Virchow—were outspoken critics of Bismarck, it was not generally assumed that *Lehrfreiheit* condoned or protected such activities. Rather, it was generally assumed that professors as civil servants were bound to be circumspect and loyal, and that participation in partisan politics spoiled the habits of scholarship. Even so firm a libertarian as Paulsen held that

the scholars cannot and should not engage in politics. They cannot do it if they have developed their capacities in accordance with the demands of their calling. Scientific research is their business, and scientific research calls for

[73] Paulsen, "Die akademische Freiheit," p. 517.
[74] Helmholtz, "Ueber die akademische Freiheit," pp. 208–9.

constant examination of thoughts and theories to the end of harmonizing them with the facts. Hence those thinkers are bound to develop a habit of *theoretical indifference* with respect to the opposing sides, a readiness to pursue any other path in case it promises to lead to a theory more in accordance with the facts. Now every form of practical activity, and practical politics particularly, demands above everything else a determination to follow *one* path that one has chosen. . . . Political activity . . . produces a habit that would prove fatal to the theorist, the habit of *opportunism*.[75]

A university teacher who violated this canon by working for the Social Democratic Party (a legal party after 1890) might find the temporal power rigid and severe. The removal of Dr. Leo Arons, *Privatdocent* at the University of Berlin, for having delivered speeches for the Social Democratic Party is a case in point. The Prussian Minister of Education declared, in removing him, that every teacher "must defend the existing order against all attacks." [76] The philosophical faculty of Berlin had admonished Arons some years before "to cease from such agitation . . . as may bring . . . the good name of the university into obloquy." [77] When, however, their power to discipline the *Privatdocenten* was infringed upon by the Prussian Minister, they defended Arons and demanded that he be retained. Their verdict, which was overruled, contained the statement that university professors "were not strictly comparable to other officials" and that they should enjoy "a wider realm of utterance." But they did concede that professors were not "free and independent citizens," and that professors were obliged, as members of state institutions, to adhere to a special code of decorum.[78] What was noticeably missing from their statement was any assertion that professors, as citizens, enjoyed an uninfringeable right to freedom of extramural speech. The issue was debated on the ground of prerogative, not on the ground of civil liberty.

In this dichotomy between freedom within and freedom without, we perceive, in transmuted form, some of the classic dualities in German philosophy. The assumption that there were two realms of professorial existence—the one, within the university, the realm of freedom; the other, outside the university, the realm of legal compulsion—suggests Kant's division of the noumena and the phenomena, of the world of

---

[75] Paulsen, *German Universities and University Study,* pp. 255–56.
[76] *Die Aktenstücke . . . gegen den Privatdocenten Dr. Arons,* p. 12.
[77] *Ibid.,* pp. 18–19.   [78] *Ibid.,* pp. 16–17.

free will and the world of causal necessity. The limitation of freedom to the inner realm suggests Luther's formula of spiritual freedom combined with temporal obedience. And the injunction that the scholar withdraw from the sphere of practical matters to the anchorite's world of contemplation suggests Fichte's distinction between the true student and the false one, between him who is dedicated to truth and him who seeks selfish advantage.

The American reaction to the German universities' concept of academic freedom again shows striking evidences of dependence, selectivity, and modification.[79] Dependence appeared from the days of the first expatriates, when the freedom of the German professor in theological affairs gripped the attention and won the admiration of Americans. Ticknor wrote from Göttingen:

No matter what a man thinks, he may teach it and print it; not only without molestation from the government but also without molestation from publick opinion. . . . The same freedom in France produced the revolution and the same freedom in England would now shake the deep foundations of the British throne—but here it passes as a matter of course. . . . If truth is to be attained by freedom of inquiry, as I doubt not it is, the German professors and literati are certainly on the high road, and have the way quietly open before them.[80]

Considerably cooler to the skepticism and impiety of the Göttingen theologians, George Bancroft also marveled at the fact that

the German literary world is a perfect democracy. No man acknowledges the supremacy of another, and everyone feels himself perfectly at liberty to

[79] We have uncovered only one article that deals with this aspect of the impact of German ideals: Leo L. Rockwell, "Academic Freedom—German Origin and American Development," in *Bulletin*, AAUP, XXXVI (Summer, 1950), 225–36. Scattered references to *Lehrfreiheit* and *Lernfreiheit* abound, but no attempt has been made to follow their career in American thought, and sometimes the one is confused with the other, as for example by Morison in his *Three Centuries of Harvard* (p. 254), when he gives the false impression that it was freedom of teaching and not the freedom of learning that first appealed to the Harvard reformers. The bulk of the material bearing on this question must be sought in autobiographical statements. Autobiographical information is unreliable, however, first on the general ground that it is subject to faulty memory and prejudiced interest, and second on the particular ground that during and after the First World War, American academic opinion changed from admiration of to hostility toward the freedoms of the German university, so that an opinion expressed at the later date may be a distortion of the author's first impression.

[80] Ticknor to Jefferson, October 14, 1815, quoted in Orie W. Long, *Thomas Jefferson and George Ticknor: A Chapter in American Scholarship* (Williamstown, Mass., 1933), pp. 13–15.

follow his own inclinations in his style of writing and in his subject. . . . No laws are acknowledged as limiting the field of investigation or experiment.[81]

Decades later, William Graham Sumner, no Germanophile, paid tribute to the freedom and courage of the German scholar in an area designated as sacrosanct in America:

I have heard men elsewhere talk about the nobility of that spirit [the seeking of truth]; but the only *body* of men whom I have ever known who really lived by it, sacrificing wealth, political distinction, church preferment, popularity, or anything else for the truth of science, were the professors of biblical science in Germany. That was precisely the range of subjects which in this country was then treated with a reserve in favor of tradition which was prejudicial to everything which a scholar should value.[82]

After the Civil War, when theological freedom under university auspices no longer occasioned surprise, American economists, psychologists, and philosophers sang the praises of German freedom. "The German University is to-day the freest spot on earth," wrote G. Stanley Hall, the psychologist; [83] the German university made him "free intellectually, free spiritually," attested Paul Russell Pope, professor of German at Cornell; [84] "we were impressed in the German university by a certain largeness and freedom of thought," said Richard T. Ely, speaking for himself and for other founders of the American Economic Association.[85]

Since the propensity of Americans to acknowledge that others are free is not usually great, we are led to seek the reason for the lavishness of this praise. As far as the earlier enthusiasts are concerned, the reason may lie in the fact that most of them attended the freest of the German universities, Göttingen and Berlin. This was not by chance: at these universities they did not have to take the religious oaths that would have

[81] Bancroft's journal and notebook, March, 1819, in Long, *Literary Pioneers*, p. 122.

[82] "Sketch of William Graham Sumner," *Popular Science Monthly*, XXXV (June, 1889), 263. See also Philip Schaff, *Germany: Its Universities, Theology and Religion* (Philadelphia, 1857), pp. 48, 146–51.

[83] G. Stanley Hall, "Educational Reforms," *Pedagogical Seminary*, I (1891), 6–7.

[84] Thwing, *The American and the German University*, p. 63.

[85] Ely, "Anniversary Meeting Address," *Publications*, American Economic Association, XI (1910), 77. "The American Economic Association took a stand at its organization for entire freedom of discussion. We were thoroughly devoted to the ideal of the German university—*Lehrfreiheit* and *Lernfreiheit*; and we have not hesitated to enter the lists vigorously in favor of freedom when we have considered it endangered" (p. 78).

tried their consciences at the South German Catholic universities or at the universities of Oxford and Cambridge.[86] In addition, it should be recalled that most of the Americans who went to Germany throughout the century were young men who were suddenly projected into an older and more permissive culture than their own. Temperament decided how this situation would be used, but we can assume that it would be an American in whom the asceticism of Calvin and the prudishness of Victoria were deeply and ineradicably ingrained who would resist the blandishments of the carefree German Sabbath, the *Kneipe* in the afternoon, and perhaps an innocent, initiating love affair. Biography and autobiography are not very revealing on this score, but it is not unlikely that many an American small-town boy shared, with G. Stanley Hall, a sense of deliverance from "the narrow, inflexible orthodoxy, the settled lifeless *mores,* the Puritan eviction of joy." "Germany almost remade me," the president of Clark University wrote in his candid autobiography. "It gave me a new attitude toward life . . . I fairly revelled in a freedom unknown before." [87] To an unmeasurable degree, the German university's reputation rested on the remembrance of freedoms enjoyed that were not in any narrow sense academic. Needless to say, this did not diminish its reputation.

"To the German mind," wrote James Morgan Hart, "if either freedom of teaching or freedom of learning is wanting, that institution, no matter how richly endowed, no matter how numerous its students, no matter how imposing its buildings, is not . . . a *University.*" [88] If one were to single out the chief German contribution to the American conception of academic freedom, it would be the assumption that academic freedom, like academic searching, *defined* the true university. This simple though signally important idea fastened itself upon American academic thought. It became an idea to which fealty had to be expressed. It took hold in the rhetoric of academic ceremonials, a rhetoric that,

[86] See Goldwin Smith, *A Plea for the Abolition of Tests* (Oxford, 1864). Not until 1854 was the requirement of the student's submission to the Thirty-nine Articles of the established church remitted for the degrees of Bachelor of Arts, Law, and Medicine at Oxford; not until 1856 was it remitted at Cambridge. Test oaths for fellowships were not removed until 1871 and other religious restrictions not until 1882. See John William Adamson, *English Education, 1789–1902* (Cambridge, 1930), Chaps. III, VII, XV.

[87] G. Stanley Hall, *Life and Confessions of a Psychologist* (New York, 1923), pp. 219, 223.

[88] Hart, *German Universities,* p. 250.

for all its flamboyance, tells much about underlying assumptions. Charles W. Eliot in his 1869 inaugural address decked this idea with memorable words:

A university must be indigenous; it must be rich; and above all, it must be free. The winnowing breeze of freedom must blow through all its chambers. It takes a hurricane to blow wheat away. An atmosphere of intellectual freedom is the native air of literature and science. This university aspires to serve the nation by training men to intellectual honesty and independence of mind. The Corporation demands of all its teachers that they be grave, reverent and high-minded; but it leaves them, like their pupils, free.[89]

Not since Jefferson had an academic leader acclaimed academic freedom so aphoristically and from so high a tribunal. But where Jefferson's tribute to the "illimitable freedom of the human mind" spoke for a waning hope, Eliot's words were harbingers of a mood that would thoroughly conquer. Again and again, high-placed figures in the academic world gave this idea their support. Gilman, at his inauguration, asserted that freedom for teachers and students was essential to a true university.[90] Andrew Dickson White, commenting on the Winchell case, declared that "an institution calling itself a university thus violated the fundamental principles on which any institution worthy of the name must be based." [91] William Rainey Harper of Chicago spoke these glowing words:

When for any reason, in a university on private foundation or in a university supported by public money, the administration of the institution or the instruction in any one of its departments is changed by an influence from without, when an effort is made to dislodge an officer or a professor because the political sentiment or the religious sentiment of the majority has undergone a change, at that moment the institution has ceased to be a university, and it cannot again take its place in the rank of universities so long as there continues to exist to any appreciable extent the factor of coercion. . . . Individuals or the state or the church may found schools for propagating certain special kinds of instruction, but such schools are not universities, and may not be so denominated.[92]

Nor did these hosannas swell from the throats of reformers alone: a president of a small church-related college, a trustee to whom Ricardo

[89] Charles W. Eliot, "Inaugural Address," *Educational Reform* (New York, 1898), pp. 30–31.
[90] Gilman, "Inaugural Address," *University Problems,* p. 31.
[91] Andrew Dickson White, *History of the Warfare of Science with Theology* (New York, 1896), I, 315.
[92] University of Chicago, *President's Reports,* 1892–1902, p. xxiii.

was the last word in economics, an alumnus proud of his university's achievement at games, were also willing choristers.[93]

It need hardly be said that a gap existed between these words and their implementation. Early in his regime, Charles W. Eliot told a professor to omit a doctrine offensive to Boston businessmen from his projected book, or else erase any reference to his Harvard connection from the title page: the Harvard president was to regret his arbitrary imposition.[94] Andrew Dickson White's understanding of the principle of tenure was so underdeveloped when he took office that he proposed an annual scrutiny of the performance of each professor by the trustees, with dismissal to follow upon a sufficient number of unsatisfactory ballots.[95] White's discreditable role in the Adler case has already been recounted. William Rainey Harper's statement on behalf of academic freedom was preceded some years before by the dismissal of the economist Edward W. Bemis on what appeared to be ideological grounds.[96] And many a eulogy to academic freedom was followed by a contradictory recitative proclaiming the absolute right of trustees to hire and fire whomsoever they pleased.[97] Nevertheless, the idea that academic freedom was part of the definition of a university was new and consequential. It was a norm from which the distance to practice could be measured. It was a belief which, in entering the ambit of good form, more easily won advocates and an audience. It was an ideal that elevated academic freedom from an undefined and unconscious yearning to a conscious and declared necessity of academic existence.

[93] See Julius Hawley Seelye, "The Relation of Learning and Religion," Inaugural Address as President of Amherst College, 1877, in Weaver, ed., *Builders of American Universities,* pp. 181–82; Judge Alton B. Parker, "The Rights of Donors," *Educational Review,* XXIII (January, 1902), 19–21; Thomas Elmer Will, "A Menace to Freedom: the College Trust," *Arena,* XXVI (September, 1901), 255.

[94] Charles W. Eliot, *Academic Freedom,* Address, Phi Beta Kappa Society (Ithaca, N.Y., 1907), p. 13. This address also appeared in *Science,* XXVI (July 5, 1907), 1–12, and *Journal of Pedagogy,* XX (September–December, 1907), 9–28.

[95] "Report of a Committee on Appointment of Faculty" (1867), in Rogers, *Andrew Dickson White,* pp. 161–64. The plan was never put into effect.

[96] For discussion of this case, see Chap. IX.

[97] Thus D. B. Purinton: "It is the business of any board of trustees to see that every instructor under its charge has absolute freedom to investigate truth in his department and to promulgate the results of his careful and deliberate investigation." BUT: "In case the published doctrines of an instructor in a state institution are plainly subversive of the state, of society or good morals, the trustees cannot sustain the instructor in such doctrines. . . . Whether a given doctrine is or is not thus subversive in character, is a question to be decided by the trustees themselves." "Academic Freedom from the Trustees' Point of View," *Transactions and Proceedings,* National Association of State Universities, VII (1909), 181–82.

The contribution to the development of academic freedom in America made by German-trained scholars was more than oratorical. From the nineties to the First World War, a good proportion of the leaders and targets in academic-freedom cases had studied in Germany: Richard T. Ely, E. Benjamin Andrews, Edward A. Ross, John Mecklin, J. McKeen Cattell.[98] Others—E. R. A. Seligman, Arthur O. Lovejoy, and Henry W. Farnam—worked on behalf of embattled colleagues.[99] Eight of the thirteen signers of the 1915 "Report on Academic Freedom" of the American Association of University Professors had studied in Germany: Seligman, Farnam, Ely, Lovejoy, U. G. Weatherly, Charles E. Bennett, Howard Crosby Warren, Frank A. Fetter.[100] Some of the leaders in the fight for professorial self-government were German university alumni: Cattell, Joseph Jastrow, and George T. Ladd.[101] That the attitudes of these prominent professors were formed solely by their sojourn abroad is not, of course, certain. It is possible that their very prominence, combined with their interest in the threatened social sciences, placed them in the forefront of battle. But it is not too fanciful to see also in their remarkable showing a pattern of withdrawal-and-return wherein American scholars, temporarily abandoning their world and drawing courage from alien springs, returned to dispense their inspiration.

This much we take to be the direct German contribution. But evidence of selection and modification can also be perceived. The 1915 "Report on Academic Freedom" of the AAUP opened with the statement that " 'academic freedom' has traditionally had two applications—to the freedom of the teacher and to that of the student, to *Lehrfreiheit* and *Lernfreiheit*." [102] This was a gracious acknowledgment of the influence the Germans exerted. When, however, one reads further in that classic

[98] See Chaps. IX and X for discussions of these cases.

[99] Seligman supported Ely when the latter was attacked at Wisconsin, was the chairman of the committee of the American Economic Association that investigated the Ross dismissal, and took a leading part in the formation of the AAUP. Arthur O. Lovejoy was one of those who resigned from the Stanford faculty in protest against the dismissal of Ross and Howard, and was a leading theorist on the subject of academic freedom. Henry W. Farnam was one of the economists who investigated the Ross case. All three, as noted, took part in the framing of the 1915 Report.

[100] See Chap. X for a discussion of the founding of the AAUP.

[101] See J. McKeen Cattell, *University Control* (New York and Garrison, N.Y., 1913), pp. 6–8; Joseph Jastrow, "The Administrative Peril in Education," *ibid.*, p. 321; George T. Ladd, *ibid.*, p. 31.

[102] *Bulletin,* AAUP, I (December, 1915), 20.

document, it soon becomes apparent that the American conception was no literal translation from the German. The idea had changed its color, its arguments, and its qualifications in the process of domestication. All the peculiarities of the American university—its inclusion of a college, its eclectic purposes, its close ties to the community—and all the peculiarities of American culture—its constitutional provision for free speech, its empiricist traditions, its abundant pragmatic spirit—contributed to a theory of academic freedom that was characteristically American.

One obvious difference was the dissociation of *Lernfreiheit* and *Lehrfreiheit* in the American pattern of argument. "It need scarcely be pointed out," wrote the authors of the 1915 report, "that the freedom which is the subject of this report is that of the teacher." [103] The frame of reference had not always been so limited. Indeed, before the nineties, "academic freedom" had alluded primarily to student freedoms, particularly the freedom to elect courses. In 1885, when Dean Andrew F. West of Princeton wrote an article asking "What Is Academic Freedom?" he answered: the elective system, scientific courses, voluntary chapel attendance. [104] But once the battle for elective courses had been won, and attention came to be focused on the collision of social ideologies that was leading to faculty dismissals, the phrase came to be applied to professorial freedoms, to the producer rather than the consumer in education. The new reference became fixed in the nineties, when, at the nearest hint of a violation of professorial freedom, "academic freedom" and *Lehrfreiheit* were invoked, as though merely to sound the phrases had a certain incantational value. [105] In 1899, when Professor Albion W. Small of Chicago wrote an article entitled "Academic Freedom," he made no mention of student freedoms. [106] After that date, only one of

[103] *Ibid.*

[104] Andrew F. West, "What Is Academic Freedom?" *North American Review,* CXL (1885), 432–44.

[105] Seligman wrote Ely: "I was very much disturbed reading in the papers that they have appointed a committee at Madison to investigate your teaching. I had thought that in our State Universities, if anywhere, 'Lehrfreiheit' would be respected." (August 13, 1894; Ely Papers, Wisconsin State Historical Society). H. H. Powers wrote to Ely: "Our 'Lehrfreiheit' [is] sharply challenged." (Oct. 4, 1892; Ely Papers). H. P. Judson offered his congratulations to Ely on the successful outcome of his trial, "in the interest of 'lehrfreiheit' of which every university should be jealously regardful." (Sept. 3, 1894; Ely Papers).

[106] Albion W. Small, "Academic Freedom," *Arena,* XXII (October, 1899), 463–72.

the important documents of academic freedom linked *Lernfreiheit* with *Lehrfreiheit;* this was Charles W. Eliot's 1907 Phi Beta Kappa address. Under the heading of "Academic Freedom," the septuagenarian Harvard president included the student's freedom to choose his studies, to refuse to attend chapel, to compete on even terms for scholarships, and to choose his own friends, as well as the professor's freedom to teach in the manner most congenial to him, to be free from harassing routines, to enjoy a secure tenure, and to receive a fixed salary and a retirement allowance.[107] But this catholic approach was exceptional.

A close reading of Eliot's Phi Beta Kappa address provides the reason for the subordination or exclusion of student freedoms in later definitions. Eliot's discussion of *Lehrfreiheit* was almost entirely given over to administrative issues: to the hazardous relations of professors with nonprofessional boards of trustees, to the friction between professors and dictatorial presidents. He made a point of the fact that "so long as . . . boards of trustees of colleges and universities claim the right to dismiss at pleasure all the officers of the institutions in their charge, there will be no security for the teachers' proper freedom," that "it is easy for a department to become despotic, particularly if there be one dominant personage in it." [108] The status of the American professor in the university organization presented a unique set of problems. He was an employee of a lay board of control; he was not, as in Germany, a civil servant of the state or, as in England, a director in a self-governing corporation. Further, he was governed by an administrative hierarchy which possessed the power to make important decisions; not by officials elected from the professors' ranks, as in Germany and England, or by a Ministry of Education removed from the scene, as in Germany. To resolve the anomaly of being at one and the same time an employee and a scientific researcher, to cope with the problem of maintaining spontaneity in a highly bureaucratized system—these problems absorbed the interest of American theorists. Faced with the task of adorning, democratizing, and protecting the academic job, they lost sight of the goal of *Lernfreiheit*. The focus of the problem of academic freedom in this country became institutional, not primarily educational.

Another difference between the American and the German theories of academic freedom lay in their arguments for the defense of the independence of the university. German theorists leaned on the protective

---

[107] Eliot, *Academic Freedom.*   [108] *Ibid.,* pp. 2, 4.

power of the state and on traditional gild prerogatives. Neither of these was meaningful on the American scene. Here government by trustees not only prevented professorial independence, but encouraged the widespread notion that professors were incapable of self-government. The state was an unreliable mainstay. The tradition of local sponsorship in American education made federal intervention—assuming that it might have improved the position of the university—impossible. The courts were unwilling to upset decisions of the administrative authorities save when these clearly conflicted with the university's charter. To appeal to state legislatures was hazardous, since their members were so often no better disposed toward intellectual freedom or academic independence than were trustees or private pressure groups. Thus, American theorists, unable to appeal with practical effect to the lawmakers or the courts, yet searching for some authority which could be used to check continual encroachments, appealed to the will of the whole community. They asserted that all universities, private or state, belonged to the people as a whole; that the trustees were merely public servants, the professors public functionaries, the universities public properties. Hence, regardless of legal provisions for control, to treat the universities as though they were private possessions, to tie them to a particular faith or ideology, to bend them to the interest of a class or sect or party, was to violate a public trust. At this point, American theorists faced a further problem. What if, as so often happened, the public should consent to the violation of that trust? What if crusading newspapers or patriotic groups, presuming to speak for the whole community, should try to warp the university toward their particular goals? American theorists had to maintain that the real public interest was not the same as the public opinion of the moment. Indeed, from Tocqueville to Lippmann, no group was more critical of the workings of public opinion in democracy than the theorists of academic freedom.[109] In America, where the university presented such diverse and irreconcilable aspects, academic freedom was too new an idea to arouse patriotic feelings, too exclusive to prompt mass support. In sponsoring the public interest, therefore, American theorists were sponsoring something that transcended all the current and ephemeral forms of its expression. Like Rousseau, they found the true will and need of the public to lie not in

[109] See Eliot, *Academic Freedom*, p. 2; Arthur T. Hadley, "Academic Freedom in Theory and Practice," *Atlantic Monthly*, XCI (March, 1903), 344.

the public's own transient notions, but in something more nebulous and abstract. They fell back in the last resort upon a *mystique* of the general will.[110]

We come to the heart of the difference when we compare the American and German conceptions of inner and outer freedom. We need not assume that the lines of each were exactly drawn in order to assert that the areas they covered were incongruous. The German idea of "convincing" one's students, of winning them over to the personal system and philosophical views of the professor, was not condoned by American academic opinion. Rather, as far as classroom actions were concerned, the proper stance for American professors was thought to be one of neutrality on controversial issues, and silence on substantive issues that lay outside the scope of their competence. Innumerable statements affirmed these limitations. Eliot, in the very address that so eloquently declared that the university must be free, made neutrality an aspect of that freedom:

Philosophical subjects should never be taught with authority. They are not established sciences; they are full of disputed matters, open questions, and bottomless speculations. It is not the function of the teacher to settle philosophical and political controversies for the pupil, or even to recommend to him any one set of opinions as better than any other. Exposition, not imposition, of opinions is the professor's part. The student should be made acquainted with all sides of these controversies, with the salient points of each system; he should be shown what is still in force of institutions or philosophies mainly outgrown, and what is new in those now in vogue. The very word "education" is a standing protest against dogmatic teaching. The notion that education consists in the authoritative inculcation of what the teacher deems true may be logical and appropriate in a convent, but it is intolerable in universities and the public schools, from primary to professional.[111]

The norm of competence was neatly summarized in President Harper's convocation address, cited above:

A professor is guilty of an abuse of his privilege who promulgates as truth ideas or opinions which have not been tested scientifically by his colleagues in the same department of research or investigation. . . .

A professor abuses his privilege who takes advantage of a classroom ex-

110 Cf. "Preliminary Report of the Joint Committee on Academic Freedom and Academic Tenure," *American Economic Review,* Supplement, V (March, 1915), 316; Thorstein Veblen, *The Higher Learning in America* (New York, 1918), *passim;* and Arthur O. Lovejoy, "Anti-Evolution Laws and the Principle of Religious Neutrality," *School and Society,* XXIX (Feb. 2, 1929), 137–38, for different approaches to this argument.
111 Eliot, "Inaugural Address," *Educational Reform,* pp. 7–8.

ercise to propagate the partisan views of one or another of the political parties.

A professor abuses his privilege who in any way seeks to influence his pupils or the public by sensational methods.

A professor abuses his privilege of expression of opinion when, although a student and perhaps an authority in one department or group of departments, he undertakes to speak authoritatively on subjects which have no relationship to the department in which he was appointed to give instruction.

A professor abuses his privilege in many cases when, altho shut off in large measure from the world and engaged within a narrow field of investigation, he undertakes to instruct his colleagues or the public concerning matters in the world at large in connection with which he has had little or no experience.[112]

These were not merely the cautious constructions of conservative elements in education. If they were narrowly interpreted by certain members of boards of trustees to prevent professors from criticizing the social order,[113] if they were invoked by university presidents to justify disciplinary action against nonconformist professors,[114] they were also upheld by liberal professors like Howard Crosby Warren and John Dewey,[115] and by progressive college presidents like Alexander Meiklejohn of Amherst.[116] The liberal wing of the academic community, like

[112] University of Chicago, *President's Report* (December, 1900), p. xxiii.

[113] For an example of how conservative trustees interpreted these limitations, see Judge Alton B. Parker, "The Rights of Donors": "With the indoctrination in the minds of students of such social, political, economical or religious ideals as tend to subvert the purpose of the founders or directors of the chair he occupies, or which can have reference only to a more or less distant, revolutionary future, the professor and university should have nothing to do" (p. 21).

[114] For statements of conservative university presidents making use of the narrow code of propriety for this purpose, cf. William Oxley Thompson, "In What Sense and to What Extent Is Freedom of Teaching in State Colleges and Universities Expedient and Permissible," *Transactions and Proceedings,* National Association of State Universities, VIII (1910), 64–78; D. B. Purinton, "Academic Freedom from the Trustees' Point of View," pp. 177–86; Nicholas Murray Butler, "Is Academic Freedom Desirable?" *Educational Review,* LX (December, 1920), 419–21; Butler, "Concerning Some Matters Academic," *Educational Review,* XLIX (April, 1915), 397; Herbert Welch, "Academic Freedom and Tenure of Office," *Bulletin,* Association of American Colleges, II (April, 1916), 163–66.

[115] John Dewey, "Academic Freedom," *Educational Review,* XXIII (January, 1902), 1–9; Howard Crosby Warren, "Academic Freedom," *Atlantic Monthly,* CXIV (November, 1914), 691. One article has been uncovered which expresses the spirit of German academic freedom in the classroom: Josiah Royce's "The Freedom of Teaching," *The Overland Monthly,* Vol. II, New Series (September, 1883), pp. 237–38. "Advanced instruction aims to teach the opinions of an honest and competent man upon more or less doubtful questions. . . . Honesty . . . requires that as a teacher of doctrines the instructor should be free to teach what doctrines he has been led freely to accept." Compare with the statements of Eliot and Harper above.

[116] Alexander Meiklejohn, "Freedom of the College," *The Atlantic Monthly,* CXXI (January, 1918), 88–89.

every other, still believed that college students were in constant danger of mental seduction by their teachers. The old fear that students were easy prey to heretical doctrine became the new fear that students had but fragile defenses against subtle insinuation of "propaganda." [17] The norms of "neutrality" and "competence" constituted a code of fair practices in ideas, and as such won assent from all sides.

Of course, the roots of these norms went deeper still. "Neutrality" and "competence" describe not only the limits of American academic freedom, but the very temper of American academic thought. They reflect, in the first place, the empiricist bias of that thought. Even in the ante-bellum period the main accent of American philosophy, sounded by the Scottish school, was empirical, realistic, commonsensical.[118] No invading Napoleon in that period forced our professors to seek refuge in thought against disturbing realities. The transcendental philosophy, the American version of German idealism, generally could not breach the academic barrier. Its intuitionism was opposed by our clerics, lest each man disclose his own religion and become unto himself a church; its idealism was resisted by our philosophers, lest mind or nature be deified, and atheism or pantheism result.[119] With the advent of the university, the triumph of science-oriented philosophies deepened the commitment to empiricism. Kant and Hegel had a brilliant revival, yet their luster was dimmed somewhat by the more effulgent light of evolutionary pragmatism and positivism. Most Americans who went to study in Germany in this period took home the methods of her seminars and laboratories, but left the *Anschauung* of idealism behind. To this empiricist heritage, one must add the influence of Darwinism on American academic thought. In Germany, the first success in the attack upon religious authority was achieved by philosophy; in America, as we have seen, the hold of religious authority was broken by the advocates of science. The empiricist heritage fostered the belief that facts must be the

---

[117] An interesting contemporary analysis of the norm of neutrality can be found in Paul S. Reinsch, "The Inner Freedom of American Intellectual Life," *North American Review,* CCI (May, 1915), 733–42.

[118] James McCosh, "The Scottish Philosophy as Contrasted with the German," *Princeton Review,* LVIII (November, 1882), pp. 326–44.

[119] See Ronald Vale Wells, *Three Christian Transcendentalists: James Marsh, Caleb Sprague Henry, Frederick Henry Hedge* (New York, 1943), for an analysis of the limited appeal of transcendentalism in the ante-bellum colleges; for orthodox expressions of hostility to transcendentalism, see Francis Bowen, "Transcendentalism," *Christian Examiner,* XXI (January, 1837), 371–85, and "Locke and the Transcendentalists," *Christian Examiner,* XXIII (November, 1837), 170–94.

arbiters between competing notions of truth, thus strengthening the standard of neutrality; that universal and synthetic speculation must give way to specialized knowledge, thus promoting the standard of competence. The Darwinian influence, as we have noted, fostered the belief that certainty was as alien to inquiry as immutability was to the processes of life (neutrality); that the right to pass judgment on scientific questions was reserved tò those who possessed special credentials (competence). The German and American theories of intramural freedom thus reflected different philosophical traditions.[120]

These theories, it should be emphasized, were concerned with norms for intramural utterance, for the utterances of professors in their role as teachers. Outside the university, for professors in their civil roles, the American norm was more permissive than the German, because it reflected a stronger social and constitutional commitment to the idea of freedom of speech. The connections between free speech and academic freedom are many and subtle. One thing is clear as far as their historical linkages are concerned: the advance of the one has not automatically produced a comparable advance of the other.[121] We have seen, for example, that academic freedom scored victories in which freedom of speech did not share. The masters of the North European medieval uni-

[120] One notes that the partisanship, dogmatism, and metaphysics of German professors frequently repelled the American student; often this was the single stain of disapproval in his otherwise generous endorsement. Ticknor reacted unfavorably to the "spirit of philosophical vehemence" that he observed among German professors. (Hilliard, *Life, Letters, and Journals of George Ticknor,* p. 97). G. Stanley Hall observed that the professors of philosophy in Germany "seemed to be almost mouthpieces of the Divine. Some of them claimed to ignore all other authors and to lecture only upon their own ideas or discoveries, to demonstrate God—as though He had been waiting all these years to have the honor of this proof conferred upon Him—or they established the reality of the world as though it depended upon their ratiocination" (*Life and Confessions,* p. 212). Nicholas Murray Butler condemned von Treitschke for giving "scant attention to the teaching of the history of Europe and Germany, altho his chair was supposed to deal with these subjects. What von Treitschke really did was to make lectures on the history of Europe and of Germany the vehicle for the very effective and emphatic expression of his own personal opinions on men and things in the world about him. . . . There is something to be said for the policy of making academic teaching effective by relating it to present-day interests and problems, but there is nothing to be said for turning academic teaching into an exercise in contemporary journalism." "Concerning Some Matters Academic," *Educational Review,* XLIX (April, 1915), 397.

[121] This point does not appear often in the literature of academic freedom, probably because it is strategic to identify academic freedom, a comparative stranger to our loyalties, with reverenced constitutional rights. For one of the earliest clear-cut distinctions between the two, see Arthur T. Hadley, "Academic Freedom in Theory and Practice," p. 157.

versities won a measure of philosophical freedom without like benefits being conferred on the laity; Halle and Göttingen in the eighteenth century were islands of intellectual freedom amid seas of petty despotism; Imperial Germany was far less free in the political sphere than in the sphere of academic education. Conversely, freedom of speech has made gains while academic freedom stood still. Thus, the abolition of the Alien and Sedition laws coincided with the expansion of denominational colleges and the sectarianizing of the state universities. One may therefore conclude that the two freedoms develop independently for different reasons, or that they are causally related to a common long-term factor, such as the diffusion of political power or the growth of the habit of tolerance.[122]

Nevertheless, it can also be demonstrated that, under certain favorable conditions, these two freedoms do affect one another directly, and that the secure position of the one may improve the position of the other and deepen and broaden its meaning and potency. Free speech was protected in America; the post-bellum university presented the favorable conditions. First, the university granted its teachers the time to engage in outside activities: it removed the old residence requirement, it ended the boarding-house vigil. Secondly, the university appointed men whose interests were not engrossed by campus duties. It brought in the professional scholar, whose works were appraised by other specialists; it brought in the new-style president, a man of wide affairs; it brought in the technical expert, available for outside consultation. Thirdly, the university professor began to give up the quiet retreat of moral philosophy for the more worldly concerns of social science. This movement was accelerated by a fourth development, the rise of the philosophy of pragmatism, which sanctioned the application of the trained intelligence to the varied problems of life. For these reasons, the American university professor, much more than his German counterpart, functioned in the arena of social and political action.[123] In that arena, he demanded the prerogative of free speech that was given to other citizens. There he felt that he had the right to express his opinion even on controversial subjects, even on matters outside his scholarly

[122] Thus, the universities of France lost their autonomy when the Crown asserted its unqualified authority, and the fate of both freedoms under the totalitarian system is well known.

[123] See the report of Committee G, "Extra-collegiate Intellectual Service," *Bulletin*, AAUP, X (May, 1934), 272–86. Surveying 42 articles and books, the report showed overwhelming approval of professors who engaged in extramural activities.

competence. There academic freedom became an aspect of the struggle for civil liberty.

And it was precisely in that arena that the greatest amount of academic friction was generated. The attempt to assimilate the doctrine of free speech into the doctrine of academic freedom aroused hostility in certain quarters. It seemed to demand a special protection for professors when they engaged in the rough give-and-take of politics. To argue that the institutional position of professors should not be affected by what they said as citizens was to urge immunity for them from the economic penalties that may repay unpopular utterances— the dwindling of clients, the boycott of subscribers, the loss of a job. Such a demand for immunity, exceeding anything provided by the constitutional safeguard of free speech, going even further than the "free-market" conceptions of the great philosophers of intellectual liberty,[124] was bound to strain the less tensile tolerance of American trustees and administrators. A barrage of argument was touched off by this demand. In its favor, professors and certain presidents mustered methodological arguments: "ideas must be tested in action," [125] the function of philosophy "is to clarify men's ideas as to the social and moral strifes of their own day"; [126] administrative arguments: "If a university or college censors what its professors may say . . . it thereby assumes responsibility for that which it permits them to say . . . a responsibility which an institution of learning would be very unwise in assuming"; [127] pedagogi-

[124] Thus Milton, in fighting for free speech and publication against public censorship, did not argue that social penalties were inadmissible. There is, moreover, in his picture of free intellectual competition the suggestion that ostracism or worse will ultimately repay the purveyor of falsehood. "And though all the winds of doctrine were let loose to play upon the earth, so Truth being in the field, we do injuriously, by licensing and prohibiting, to misdoubt her strength. Let her and Falsehood grapple; who ever knew Truth put to the worse in a free and open encounter: Her confuting is the best and surest suppressing. . . ." *Areopagitica* (Regnery edition, pp. 58–59). John Stuart Mill's *On Liberty* addressed itself to the tyranny of the majority rather than the tyranny of the state, and in it the pregnant statement occurs that "in respect to all persons but those whose pecuniary circumstances make them independent of the good will of other people, opinion, on this subject, is as efficacious as law; men might as well be imprisoned, as excluded from the means of earning their bread" (Regnery edition, p. 39). But Mill did not say that this immunity belonged to any particular body of men, but to all men, or to a minority of one, against the despotism of numbers.

[125] See John Dewey, *Democracy and Education* (New York, 1916), pp. 76–77 and *passim.*

[126] John Dewey, *Reconstruction in Philosophy* (New York, 1920), p. 26.

[127] A. Lawrence Lowell, "Report for 1916–17," in Henry Aaron Yeomans, *Abbott Lawrence Lowell* (Cambridge, Mass., 1948), p. 311.

cal arguments: what young men need "are not hermit scholars, but active zealous citizens, with opinions to express upon public questions, and power to express them." [128] The answering volleys were usually, but not exclusively, returned by presidents and trustees. They too used methodological arguments: when a teacher enters politics, he acts "as a partisan and [loses his] place as a judge and an unbiased individual"; [129] administrative arguments: "to use this institution and the funds so contributed for a purpose foreign and contrary to the ideas both of the contributors and of the whole community, and appropriate them to the propaganda of the exceptional ideas of a single individual, is a perversion of public trust"; [130] pedagogical arguments: the professor who uses his university position as "an object of political purpose" destroys his educational effectiveness.[131] And the salvos resound to this day.

The second source of friction was the closely allied problem of professional ethics in the public forum. Despite the invocation of the right of free speech, it was generally conceded by the academic fraternity that professors reached a limiting line of professional propriety long before they approached the boundary of libel, slander, or sedition. But where was that line to be drawn? Was it proper for a professor to run for political office or to work actively for a political party? The academic community spoke with two voices on this point.[132] Was it proper for a professor publicly to criticize the actions of a colleague or a superior? In this most bureaucratically controlled of all the professions, it was not easy to decide where free speech left off and insubordination began. Was the professor's relation to his trustees analogous to the relation of the judiciary to the executive power? The analogy was useful in suggesting that the trustees could not remove their appointee at will, but it was a two-edged sword, for it also suggested that professors were

[128] Editor's Table, *New England Magazine,* XVII, New Series (September, 1897), 126; cf. Edward P. Cheyney, "Trustees and Faculties," *School and Society,* II (Dec. 14, 1915), 795. Also, W. H. Carpenter, "Public Service of University Officers," *Columbia University Quarterly,* XVI (March, 1914), 169–82.

[129] Letter of President Frank L. McVey of the University of North Dakota to Professor Joseph L. Lewinsohn, in "The Participation of University Professors in Politics," *Science,* Vol. XXXIX, New Series (1914), pp. 425–26.

[130] "Free Thought in College Economics," *Gunton's Magazine,* XVII (December, 1899), 456.

[131] Letter of President McVey, in "The Participation of University Professors in Politics," p. 426.

[132] See U. G. Weatherly, "Academic Freedom and Tenure of Office," *Bulletin,* Association of American Colleges, II (April, 1916), 175–77.

bound by the staid public ethics of judges.[133] Again, the conflict between free speech and professional ethics created a storm center which has never lifted.

AN AMERICAN CODE

We can best summarize what has preceded by quoting more extensively from the classic 1915 Report of the Committee on Academic Freedom and Tenure of the American Association of University Professors. How representative of faculty opinion this report may have been is an open question. It was strictly a product of professorial thinking; college and university presidents and deans were explicitly banned from membership in the AAUP in its early years. The authors, being among the most illustrious, were perhaps not the most representative members of the profession. Seven of the thirteen members were social scientists, and may have reflected the bias of their disciplines. Still, the report has great value for synopsis and reference. It was not the product of haste or improvisation, nor was it an angry answer to some galvanic injustice. Many of the ideas contained in the report had been adumbrated by its authors in previous articles or can be traced back to a preliminary report of a joint conclave of economists, political scientists, and sociologists which was written a year before.[134] It created a widely favorable impression. One comment in the press hailed it as "the most comprehensive, general declaration of principles regarding academic freedom that has ever appeared in this country." [135] The United States Commissioner of Education called it "one of the most valuable contributions of the year to the discussion of educational policy," and the Bureau of Education distributed thousands of copies.[136] It was the basis for the statement of the principles of academic freedom and tenure endorsed

[133] For the academic debate over the use and limitations of the analogy of the judiciary, cf. John H. Wigmore, "An Analogy Drawn from Judicial Immunity," *The Nation*, CIII (Dec. 7, 1916), 539–40; Arthur O. Lovejoy's rejoinder, "Academic Freedom," *The Nation*, CIII (Dec. 14, 1916), 561; Wigmore's counter-reply, in *The Nation*, CIII (Dec. 14, 1916), 561–62. The debate was waged intensively in the succeeding decades. Cf. Raymond Buell, Letter to the New York *Herald Tribune* (June 17, 1936); Lippmann's rejoinder, Letter to the New York *Herald Tribune* (June 20, 1936); Walter E. Spahr in defense of Buell's position, Letter to the New York *Herald Tribune* (June 29, 1936).

[134] "Prefatory Note," 1915 Report, *Bulletin*, AAUP, I (December, 1915), 17.

[135] *Current Opinion*, LX (March, 1916), 192–93.

[136] *Report of the Commissioner of Education* (1916), I, 138.

in subsequent years by the Association of American Colleges, representing college administrative officers, and the American Association of University Professors.[137] One modern commentator has properly called it "a landmark in the development of the teaching profession." [138]

ACADEMIC FREEDOM AS AN INDISPENSABLE ATTRIBUTE OF A UNIVERSITY

The Committee tied academic freedom to three requirements—the needs for academic research, adequate instruction, and the development of experts for public service. Some of their arguments closely resembled those of the Germans. "In the earlier stages of a nation's intellectual development, the chief concern of educational institutions is to train the growing generation and to diffuse the already accepted knowledge." It was only slowly that the purpose of conservation gave way to that of searching. More and more, "the modern university is becoming . . . the home of scientific research." Now, in all the domains of knowledge, in natural science, in social science, in religion and philosophy, the chief condition of progress "is complete and unlimited freedom to pursue inquiry and publish its results. Such freedom is the breath in the nostrils of all scientific activity." [139]

Such freedom is no less important to the teacher. No man can be a successful teacher, wrote the framers of the report, who does not enjoy the respect of his students, and this respect will not be forthcoming if the confidence of students in his intellectual integrity and courage is impaired. Helmholtz would have endorsed the following:

It is not only the character of the instruction but also the character of the instructor that counts; and if the student has reason to believe that the instructor is not true to himself, the virtue of the instruction as an educative force is incalculably diminished. There must be in the mind of the teacher no mental reservation. He must give the student the best of what he has and what he is.[140]

The third justification for academic freedom was more originally American. Reflecting the mood of Progressivism, the authors also believed that the modern university should aim to develop experts to help solve the complex problems of society. The professor can only be of use

---

[137] Robert P. Ludlum, "Academic Freedom and Tenure," *Antioch Review*, X (Spring, 1950), 25.
[138] *Ibid.*, p. 19.   [139] *Bulletin*, AAUP, I (December, 1915), 27–28.
[140] *Ibid.*, p. 28.

to the legislator and the administrator if his conclusions are disinterested and his own.[141]

UNIVERSITY INDEPENDENCE AND THE GENERAL WILL

With the *legal* supremacy of the boards of trustees the professors who wrote the report did not quarrel: but legal power, to them, was not equivalent to moral duty. As they saw it, the moral obligations of university trustees were two. Where trustees were bound by their charters to propagate specific doctrines, they should be completely candid about it. The public should not be misled into thinking that the school is searching for truth when in fact it is communicating dogma. In all other cases, the trustees were trustees for the public, and "they cannot be permitted to assume the proprietary attitude and privilege, if they are appealing to the general public for support." If the basis of academic authority was public, the nature of the professor's calling was no less so. Any assumption that the professors were employees of the governing board was gratuitous and insupportable.

The responsibility of the university teacher is primarily to the public itself, and to the judgment of his own profession; and while, with respect to certain external conditions of his vocation, he accepts a responsibility to the authorities of the institution in which he serves, in the essentials of his professional activity his duty is to the wider public to which the institution itself is morally amenable.[142]

To nail down this point, the Committee used the analogy of the relationship between the executive and the judiciary, albeit (one gathers from the text) with some trepidation lest the analogy be misused.

So far as the university teacher's independence of thought and utterance is concerned—*though not in other regards*—the relationship of professor to trustees may be compared to that between judges of the Federal courts and the Executive who appoints them. University teachers should be understood to be, with respect to the conclusions reached and expressed by them, no more subject to the control of the trustees, than are judges subject to the control of the President, with respect to their decisions.[143]

But the authors of the report did not confuse the public with its political representatives, or the public will with contemporary opinion. To rely wholly on the government was dangerous:

[141] *Ibid.,* pp. 21–22.   [142] *Ibid.,* pp. 22–23, 26.
[143] *Ibid.,* p. 26. Italics supplied.

Where the university is dependent for funds upon legislative favor, it has sometimes happened that the conduct of the institution has been affected by political considerations; and where there is a definite governmental policy or a strong public feeling on economic, social, or political questions, the menace to academic freedom may consist in the repression of opinions.[144]

Similarly, public opinion, which was apt to regard any departure from convention with suspicion, was a weak staff on which to lean. Rather, the university

should be an intellectual experiment station, where new ideas may germinate and where their fruit, though still distasteful to the community as a whole, may be allowed to ripen until finally, perchance, it may become a part of the accepted intellectual food of the nation or of the world.[145]

The public for which the trustees acted and to whom the professors were responsible was an abstraction called "posterity."

THE NORMS OF NEUTRALITY AND COMPETENCE

On the assumption that freedom is never absolute and unqualified, but entails limits and obligations, the Committee gave its clear approval to the norms of neutrality and competence.

The liberty of the scholar within the university to set forth his conclusions, be they what they may, is conditioned by their being conclusions gained by a scholar's method and held in a scholar's spirit; that is to say, they must be the fruits of competent and patient and sincere inquiry, and they should be set forth with dignity, courtesy and temperateness of language.

This did not mean that the teacher had to hide his opinions under a mountain of equivocal verbiage. But he should

be a person of fair and judicial mind; he should, in dealing with such [controversial] subjects, set forth justly, without suppression or innuendo, the divergent opinions of other investigators; he should cause his students to become familiar with the best published expressions of the great historic types of doctrine upon the questions at issue; and he should, above all, remember that his business is not to provide his students with ready-made conclusions but to train them to think for themselves.[146]

The committee's opposition to oracular and dogmatic teaching rested in large part on the supposed immaturity of students:

In many of our American colleges, and especially in the first two years of the course, the student's character is not yet fully formed, his mind is still rela-

144 *Ibid.*, p. 31.   145 *Ibid.*, p. 32.   146 *Ibid.*, pp. 33–34.

tively immature. In these circumstances it may reasonably be expected that the instructor will present scientific truth with discretion, that he will introduce the student to new conceptions gradually, with some consideration for the student's preconceptions and traditions, and with due regard to character-building.

The teacher must especially be on guard against

taking unfair advantage of the student's immaturity by indoctrinating him with the teacher's own opinions before the student has had an opportunity fairly to examine other opinions upon the matters in question, and before he has sufficient knowledge and ripeness of judgment to be entitled to form any definitive opinion of his own.[147]

Again, the assumption was that university education is adolescent education, and that the young mind yields to the imprint of ideas as easily and uncritically as wax.

FREEDOM OF SPEECH FOR EXTRAMURAL UTTERANCE

The Committee spoke boldly on the general principle of free extramural utterance. In their extramural utterances, the Committee contended, it is not desirable that scholars should be bound by the norms of neutrality and competence. It is not desirable that they be debarred "from giving expression to their judgments upon controversial questions, or that their freedom of speech outside the university should be limited to questions falling within their own specialties." Nor is it proper that they be prohibited "from lending their active support to organized movements which they believe to be in the public interest." [148] But the Committee also recognized that professors were saddled with the obligation of discretion incumbent upon professional persons. "It is obvious that academic teachers are under a peculiar obligation to avoid hasty or unverified or exaggerated statements, and to refrain from intemperate or sensational modes of expression." And this led to the vexing question of whether professors should be allowed to work for a political party or run for political office. As one of its members later revealed, the Committee was divided between those who took the view that scholarship and partisan action were not antipathetic, and those who held to the German position that political partisanship was incompatible with objective inquiry.[149] The Committee could only express its indecision. On the one hand, it wrote,

[147] *Ibid.*, p. 35.   [148] *Ibid.*, p. 37.
[149] See the statement of U. G. Weatherly in "Academic Freedom and Tenure of Office," pp. 175–77.

it is manifestly desirable that . . . teachers have minds untrammeled by party loyalties, unexcited by party enthusiasms, and unbiased by personal political ambitions; and that universities should remain uninvolved in party antagonisms.

On the other hand,

it is equally manifest that the material available for the service of the State would be restricted in a highly undesirable way, if it were understood that no member of the academic profession should ever be called upon to assume the responsibilities of public office.[150]

On this inconclusive note, the 1915 report closed.

The scheme of the 1915 report, like that of this chapter, was analytical rather than historical. But it did make one historical reference which leads us back to a sequential treatment of our subject. The authors of the report noted that the character of the infringements of academic freedom had changed in the last few decades:

In the early period of university development in America the chief menace to academic freedom was ecclesiastical, and the disciplines chiefly affected were philosophy and the natural sciences. In more recent times the danger zone has been shifted to the political and social sciences.

The present problem, as the Committee saw it, was that every question in the political, social, and economic fields affected the private interests of class, and that,

as the governing body of a university is naturally made up of men who through their standing and ability are personally interested in great private enterprises, the points of possible conflict are numberless. When to this is added the consideration that benefactors, as well as most of the parents who send their children to privately endowed institutions, themselves belong to the more prosperous and therefore usually to the more conservative classes, it is apparent that . . . pressure from vested interests may . . . be brought to bear upon academic authorities.[151]

More calmly and judiciously than some of their professorial contemporaries, the members of the Committee gave support to the thesis that wealth was an academic malefactor, and that a particular class was opposed to academic freedom. This is the thesis we must now evaluate, and we shall do so by turning to the Populist period in which the thesis was born.

[150] *Bulletin*, AAUP, I (December, 1915), 38.   [151] *Ibid.*, pp. 29–31.

IX: ACADEMIC FREEDOM AND BIG BUSINESS

CONFRONTATION

IN THE FINAL DECADES of the last century, the leaders of American business began to support our universities on a completely unprecedented scale. Before that period, old mercantile wealth, with its tradition of patronage, had had only modest resources for philanthropy, while new industrial wealth, with ever-growing resources, had been bent on unceasing acquisition and had not learned the great virtue of giving. Thus it is recorded that the largest single gift to an American college before the Civil War was Abbott Lawrence's $50,000 to Harvard.[1] An institution like Amherst College, to take another example, had been founded on $50,000, assembled from small contributions.[2] Weighed in the scale of big-business philanthropy, these sums seem almost negligible. Johns Hopkins University received $3,500,000 from a Baltimore merchant and capitalist; Leland Stanford Junior University received $24,000,000 from the estate of the California railroad king; the University of Chicago received $34,000,000 from the founder of the Standard Oil Company.[3] The foundation came to supplement the endowment as a method of bestowing gifts. Among the early foundations assisting the colleges and universities in some way were the General Education Board, founded in 1902 by John D. Rockefeller, with assets of $46,000,000; the Carnegie Corporation, founded in 1911, with assets of $151,000,000; the Commonwealth Fund, founded in 1918 by Mrs. Stephen V. Hark-

---

[1] Charles F. Thwing, "The Endowment of Colleges," *International Review,* XI (September, 1881), 259.

[2] *Ibid.,* p. 260.

[3] Daniel Coit Gilman, *The Launching of a University* (New York, 1906), p. 28; Orrin L. Elliott, *Stanford University, the First Twenty-five Years* (Stanford, 1937), p. 251; Thomas W. Goodspeed, *A History of the University of Chicago* (Chicago, 1916), Appendix I, p. 487.

ness, with assets of $43,000,000.[4] Truly, the new men of wealth organized their philanthropies as grandiosely as they organized their businesses.

Inevitably, the increase in the size of gifts changed the relations of donor to recipient. Borrowing a term from economic history, one may say that the givers became entrepreneurs in the field of higher education. They took the initiative in providing funds and in deciding their general purposes. William Rainey Harper wrote in 1905 that "in the case of 90 percent of the money given to a large institution the initiative is taken by the donor, and not by the university concerned." [5] This was a reversal of the procedure that had been in effect before the Civil War, when college presidents sued for alms on the basis of needs which they determined. But passive roles did not suit the new men of wealth. It was Jonas Gilman Clark, not G. Stanley Hall, who made the decision to found a new university at Worcester; Clark hired Hall to carry out his ideas.[6] It was Leland Stanford, not David Starr Jordan, who conceived the project at Palo Alto.[7] It was (to take a crowning example) Andrew Carnegie who decided to give retirement pensions to professors, and this without their prior solicitation.[8] Sometimes, depending upon inclination, these donors were also active in determining educational policies. Before the Civil War, businessmen did not usually earmark their gifts for specific educational projects. Abbott Lawrence's gift for an engineering school at Harvard was an exception, but it is interesting to note that President Everett thwarted the intention of the donor by converting the school into a department of natural science.[9] To compare Everett's treatment of Lawrence with Clark's treatment of Hall is to compare the power of $50,000 with the power of several millions of dollars, and to compare the independence of a well-established college with the servility of a young university dependent on the benevolence of one man. In Hall's autobiography we find that the president

---

[4] Ernest V. Hollis, *Philanthropic Foundations and Higher Education* (New York, 1938), pp. 303–6.

[5] William R. Harper, *The Trend in Higher Education* (Chicago, 1905), p. 178.

[6] Calvin Stubbins, "Biography of J. G. Clark," *Publications of the Clark University Library*, I (April, 1906), 138–76.

[7] David Starr Jordan, *The Days of a Man* (New York, 1922), pp. 268–69.

[8] See letter of Andrew Carnegie to the trustees of the Carnegie Foundation (April 16, 1905). In *Annual Report of the Carnegie Foundation for the Advancement of Teaching* (Washington, D.C., 1906), pp. 7–8.

[9] Samuel Eliot Morison, *Three Centuries of Harvard* (Cambridge, Mass., 1936), p. 279.

was forced to break contracts at the orders of the founder, to reduce the scale of salaries because the founder wished to economize, to add an undergraduate college to what he had hoped would be a graduate institution, because the founder willed it so.[10] The antagonisms between Hall and Clark were not in any sense typical. More common was a harmonious association like that of Andrew D. White and Ezra Cornell, and more common still was an obsequious attitude like that of David Starr Jordan toward Mrs. Jane Stanford.[11] But Hall's story does exemplify the passage of academic initiative to the great providers who had come upon the scene.

The change in the occupational background of trustees measures the growing power of the business element in education. Whereas wealth and a talent for business had once been considered virtues in trustees, now they were thought to be prerequisites. The increase in income and endowment brought new problems of balances and budgets, of property investment and management, of the husbanding and parceling of resources, with which businessmen were presumed to be familiar. As a result, a trusteeship in a large university became, along with a listing in the Social Register, a token of business prominence and of pecuniary qualification. Charles and Mary Beard did not exaggerate when they wrote that "at the end of the century the roster of American trustees of higher learning read like a corporation directory." [12] In 1865, Ezra Cornell could boast of the representative composition of the board of the university that bore his name. Aside from ex-officio members representing the locality and the state, it included, he said, three mechanics, three farmers, one manufacturer, one merchant, one lawyer, one engineer, and one "literary gentleman." [13] By 1884, the Cornell Board of Trustees included five bankers, three lawyers, two manufacturers, two judges, and one editor.[14] Among the new arrivals was Henry W. Sage, the owner of the largest lumber business in the world at that time.[15] By 1918, new prizes had been added: Andrew Carnegie;

[10] G. Stanley Hall, *Life and Confessions of a Psychologist* (New York, 1923), pp. 225–57.

[11] Carl L. Becker, *Cornell University: Founders and the Founding* (Ithaca, N.Y., 1943), p. 118.

[12] Charles A. Beard and Mary R. Beard, *The Rise of American Civilization* (New York, 1927), II, 470.

[13] Becker, *Cornell University,* Document 11.

[14] In several cases, the occupations of trustees fall into more than one category.

[15] "Henry W. Sage," *National Cyclopedia of American Biography,* IV, 478.

Charles W. Schwab, president of Bethlehem Steel; H. H. Westinghouse, chairman of the board of the Westinghouse Company; and others of the top business elite.[16] This trend was observable elsewhere. In a study of twenty private and state universities, McGrath found that 48 percent of the members of the boards of trustees were businessmen, bankers, and lawyers in 1860; in 1900, 64 percent belonged to those occupational categories.[17] The great anomaly of American higher education—that laymen dominate the domain of professionals—had become more patent than ever.

But the line between business and scholarship was not crossed from one side alone. Under the stimulus of a newly awakened interest in the workaday world and its problems, professors in the social sciences began to focus on the institutions by which society was organized and its activities maintained. The trend in the field of economics was toward historical and statistical analysis, and away from the speculative search for logically consistent systems. This was the period when E. R. A. Seligman wrote his studies of public finance; when Taussig wrote his *Tariff History;* when Henry Carter Adams wrote "The Relation of the State to Industrial Action"—all of them evidence of their authors' departure from the belief that life could be deduced from first principles.[18] This was the period when Ely wrote about labor and socialism and actually took these subjects seriously, proving that economics could be something more than conventional conservative apologetics.[19] Moreover, this was the period when the American Economic Association, in defiance of the edicts of Manchester, took its stand against *laissez faire,* and called upon the nation's economists to play a part in the shaping of public policy. In sociology, no less than in economics, the desire to take hold of realities was apparent and pervasive. "Pure" sociology—both Ward's and Sumner's—gave support to social programs; "applied" sociology—the other large division of the field—was little more than the art of social betterment.[20] By 1901,

[16] *Register of Cornell University, 1918–19,* p. 8.

[17] Earl McGrath, "The Control of Higher Education in America," *Educational Record,* XVII (April, 1936), 264.

[18] Joseph Dorfman, *The Economic Mind in American Civilization* (New York, 1949), III, 167, 245–57, 264–71.

[19] Richard T. Ely, *Ground under Our Feet* (New York, 1938), pp. 309–23.

[20] In announcing that a chair in sociology had been established, the Columbia Faculty of Political Science justified it by proclaiming: "it is becoming more and more apparent that industrial and social progress is bringing the modern commu-

hardly a college did not promise, under the heading of "sociology," a course on "the city and its problems," or "defectives, delinquents and dependents," or "socialism, its history and philosophy," or "the methods of social reform." [21] Finally, in the newest of the new social sciences—political science—the attention of scholars was given to political and administrative reform.[22] Throughout the field of the social sciences, the concern with public problems sought legitimation and expression.

More than anything else, it was the sense that the world was out of joint that gave rise to this new academic worldliness. By long habituation, Americans had become accustomed to social change: to the movement of rootless populations, to an economy permanently in flux. But the changes that came late in the nineteenth century were changes in the rhythm of change, upheavals in social relations, and they challenged settled assumptions. The traditional morality of individualism and the traditional injunction to get rich had produced an undisciplined wealthy elite that thought itself mightier than the laws and threatened democratic institutions. The classical world of small business and the classical law of competition had given birth to gargantuan trusts that were ruining or enveloping their rivals and were rigging the machinery of the market. Worst of all, the appearance of persistent poverty—hunger in the granary of the world, class war in the classless society, despair in the land of opportunity—put all our social shibboleths on trial.

This discomfiture of old ideologies helped vitalize American social science. It was not that our social scientists agreed on policies and programs. But there was one identifying bias that social Darwinists like Sumner and Darwinian socialists like Veblen, that gold-standard partisans like Laughlin and silver-standard partisans like Ross, that high-tariff advocates like Patten and low-tariff advocates like Walker, all

---

nity face to face with social questions of the greatest magnitude, the solution of which will demand the best scientific study and the most honest practical endeavor." Frank L. Tolman, "The Study of Sociology in Institutions of Higher Learning in the United States," *American Journal of Sociology,* VIII (July, 1902), 85; see, also, Albion W. Small, "Fifty Years of Sociology in the United States (1865–1915)," reprinted in the *American Journal of Sociology,* Index to Vols. I–LII (1947), pp. 187 ff.

[21] Tolman, "The Study of Sociology," pp. 88–104.

[22] Anna Haddow, *History of the Teaching of Political Science in the Colleges and Universities of the United States, 1636–1900* (New York, 1939).

significantly shared. This was the fundamental belief, of ancient lineage but of new allure, that science applied to society could alleviate social crises and remedy social problems. A number of invidious comparisons were used in support of this belief. It was thought that other groups were bound to ideology, but that social scientists were ideology-free. Other panaceas were looked upon as fanciful; the prescriptions of social science were presumably based on facts and social laws.[23] The distinguishing badge of competence that natural scientists wore was claimed by social scientists by right of direct descent.[24]

Thus big businessmen and professors came into fateful contact. The former supported the university and took command of its organ of government, the latter surveyed society and tried to sway its course: two spheres of action and interest, formerly far apart, drew close and overlapped. It was not immediately apparent, nor was it at any time inevitable, that this confrontation would be hostile. If there is truth in the popular antithesis between the "doers" and the "thinkers" of the world, there were also, in this case at least, substantial reasons for friendship. For one thing, some of the more articulate big businessmen, even of that parvenu generation, were fond of expressing admiration for the life of study and research. The contrary notion notwithstanding, the large contributors to the universities were usually not of that philistine crowd that undervalued the wisdom in books, or thought it far more edifying to meet a payroll than to meet a class. A philanthropist like Andrew Carnegie romanticized the life of intellectuals. He held up their "higher satisfactions" and "indifference to material possessions" as examples for the wealthy to follow; he consorted with writers and philosophers. Not every philanthropist was a Carnegie, yet the theme in his "Gospel of Wealth"—that the province and office of wealth was the diffusion and advancement of culture—proved strangely attractive to men whose one goal had been accumulation and who were themselves extravagantly uncultivated.[25] For all

[23] Cf. Lester F. Ward, *Applied Sociology* (Boston, 1906), pp. 5–6, 28–29; *Glimpses of the Cosmos* (New York, 1913–18), III, 172; IV, 11; Albion W. Small, *General Sociology* (Chicago, 1905), pp. 36–37.

[24] John Lewis Gillin, "The Development of Sociology in the United States," *Papers and Proceedings of the American Sociological Society,* XXI (1926), 1–6.

[25] Andrew Carnegie, "Individualism and Socialism," in *Problems of Today* (New York, 1908), pp. 121–39; "Wealth," *ibid.,* p. 35; "Variety and Uniformity," *ibid.,* p. 145. Cf. John D. Rockefeller, *Random Reminiscences of Men and Events* (New York, 1909), p. 166; Sarah K. Bolton, *Famous Givers and Their Gifts* (New York, 1896), pp. 108–28.

their quirks and vulgarities, the tycoons of Fifth Avenue and Newport were closer to the patricians of Beacon Street than to the business gentry of Main Street. Besides, the patrons of the university received from the academic world the ornate courtesies of gratitude.
They did not enter academe as intruders; they were welcomed into
the realm and escorted to its high places by its very grateful inhabitants. Within the academic fraternity, to cultivate the good will of
donors was a highly approved activity, betokening fine public spirit. To
offend the bearer of gifts was an action sometimes defined as the deep-
est disloyalty and treachery. Cordiality was thus demanded of professors by the most compelling of motives—self-interest and the desire for social approval.

In the light of these reasons for friendship, it is particularly surprising that sharp antagonisms developed over the issue of academic freedom. Yet almost from the moment of confrontation, the picture of
the business patron as an enemy of academic freedom took form in the
minds of professors. This began in the middle eighties, when Professor Henry Carter Adams was dismissed from Cornell for having
delivered a pro-labor speech that annoyed a powerful benefactor.[26]
The picture acquired lurid colors in the nineties, when such cases occurred in profusion, and when the victims, unlike Adams, would not
suffer the blow in silence. In this period, it derived a certain plausibility
from the Populist suspicion that big business supported the universities only to further its own interests, and that the attacks upon academic freedom were part of a plutocratic plot. In the Progressive
period and beyond, the picture was colored and defined by another belief—that the values of the factory and the counting house were injurious to the values of research, and that the attacks upon academic freedom were the results of this basic disaccord. We have no way of
measuring the popularity of the theses of "conspiracy" and "cultural incompatibility" among professors. It is probable that professors of social
science were generally more hostile to businessmen than were professors
of business administration. Undoubtedly, in every department, there was
a minority of critics and crusaders who were more outspoken than the

[26] See E. R. A. Seligman, "Memorial to Former President Henry Carter Adams,"
American Economic Review, XII (September, 1922), 405; R. M. Wenley, Lawrence
Bigelow, and Leo Sharfman, "Henry Carter Adams," *Journal of Political Economy,*
XXX (April, 1922), 201–11. Letter of Henry C. Adams to E. R. A. Seligman,
February 27, 1901, in Seligman Papers, Columbia University.

rest. But there can be no doubt that the image of the businessman as a malefactor became a potent academic stereotype. In the martyrology of wronged professors and the demonology of oppressive trustees, the businessman acquired, in the space of a few short decades, a conspicuous and infamous place.

A reappraisal of these beliefs is in order. How valid were the theses of conspiracy and cultural incompatibility? This question, we are aware, impinges on current ideological controversies. But we shall try to abstain from the present contest between "neo-conservatives" and "New Dealers," and from the provocative use of such terms as "Robber Barons" and "free enterprise." Our reasons for holding aloof are several. For one thing, it is doubtful whether high-order generalizations about the social role of big business can be deduced from these materials. Attitudes toward academic freedom are too specific for broad extrapolation. In this very circumscribed play, many facets of behavior are discrete: a man can give and give and be a villain, or be ungenerous with his purse and still a saint. Then, again, we deface the meaning of history by interlineating it with current knowledge. How the third generation of Rockefellers comports itself should not place a lien on our judgment as to how the founder of that house behaved. But most of all, we must let the evidence speak for itself, a difficult thing at best, yet hardly possible if we defend inclusive theories. Hence, in the following sections, we shall examine certain pre-World War academic freedom cases and certain trends in academic government with the modest ambition of putting two specific theses to a test.

THE THESIS OF CONSPIRACY

In 1901, Thomas Elmer Will, erstwhile professor and president of Kansas State Agricultural College, listed the academic-freedom cases that had occurred during the preceding decade. As he described them, they were all of the same ugly pattern: a professor had espoused reform, or had criticized the social order, and had thereupon been summarily dismissed. This, he wrote, was the story behind the dismissal of Dr. George M. Steele, president of Lawrence College, for leanings "toward free trade and greenbacks" (1892); the dismissal of President H. E. Stockbridge of North Dakota Agricultural College for "political" reasons (1893); the trial of Richard T. Ely, professor of economics at

Wisconsin, for heretical social and economic writings (1894); the dismissal of Docent I. A. Hourwich of the University of Chicago for participating in a Populist convention (1894); the dismissal of Edward W. Bemis, economist, from the University of Chicago, for championing antimonopoly views (1895); the dismissal of James Allen Smith, political scientist, from Marietta College for "antimonopoly teaching" (1897); the attack upon President E. Benjamin Andrews of Brown University for having promulgated views favorable to free silver, and his eventual resignation (1897); the dismissal of John R. Commons, economist, from Indiana University because of his economic views (1896), and the withdrawal of support from his chair at Syracuse University for the same reason (1899); the removal of Frank Parsons and Bemis from the Kansas State Agricultural College because of their "positions on economic questions" (1899); the forced resignation of President Henry Wade Rogers from Northwestern University for his opposition to imperialism (1900); the dismissal of Edward A. Ross from Stanford University for his opinions on silver and coolie immigration.[27] With this list, Will called the role of most of the well-known liberals in academic life at that time.

To Will, the cause of these attacks upon academic freedom was entirely self-evident. All academic-freedom cases were, he believed, the results of inevitable clashes between free disinterested inquiry and self-seeking vested interest. Formerly, this conflict had taken the form of a war between science and theology; now it was openly displayed as a war between science and wealth. Science is bent on telling the truth without favor. But the truth, dispassionately told, was what "the industrial monarchy" dared not and would not tolerate. It knows that "free investigation is all that is necessary to expose the rottenness of the existing economic system." Accordingly, "with the arrogance equalling that of the slave power, our plutocracy has issued its edict that the colleges and universities must fall into line." "Hence the inevitable conflict." [28] In the folklore of Populism, the three assumptions in this argument—that free inquiry exposes social evils and is therefore inherently reformistic, that big business dreads such exposure and is therefore incorrigibly intolerant, and that therein lies the cause of

[27] Thomas Elmer Will, "A Menace to Freedom: The College Trust," *Arena,* XXVI (September, 1901), 254–56.
[28] *Ibid.,* pp. 246–47.

infringements of academic freedom—gained wide acceptance.[29] And many later historians, pondering the cases that arose in the nineties, have also accepted these assumptions, though often not in their Populist frame.[30]

The first step in a reappraisal of this thesis is to ask: Was Will's catalogue of the cases accurate, was it complete and inclusive? In one case—that of George Steele—it is very likely that Will was in error, for Steele resigned in 1879, and his last presidential report suggests that he did so voluntarily.[31] In three other cases—those of Stockbridge, Hourwich, and Rogers [32]—the desolate wastes of the trustees' minutes reveal nothing that supports Will's contention, and without a statement from the participants there is nothing to go on, save the contention itself.[33] In another case—that of Commons—the evidence is entirely

[29] Charles A. Towne, "The New Ostracism," *Arena*, XVIII (October, 1897), 433–51; Edward W. Bemis, "Academic Freedom," *The Independent*, LI (August 17, 1899), 2196–97; Edward A. Ross, *Seventy Years of It* (New York, 1936), p. 64.

[30] Cf. Russel B. Nye, *Midwestern Progressive Politics* (East Lansing, Mich., 1951), pp. 154–55; Eric F. Goldman, *Rendezvous with Destiny* (New York, 1952), pp. 100–104; Arthur M. Schlesinger, *The Rise of the City* (History of American Life Series, X, 1933), pp. 227–29; Howard K. Beale, *A History of Freedom of Teaching in American Schools* (New York, 1941), pp. 227–34.

[31] Steele's last annual report, dated April 7, 1879, reviewed the course of his presidency which had lasted fourteen years, and referred to his onerous duties as financial agent which had cost him a considerable sum of money. "The reasons for my resignation are implied in the present situation of the College. I feel that the time has come for a movement which I do not feel that I have the ability or energy to conduct with any assurance of success. I am confident that someone else can, and that it is my duty, as well as yours, to heed the indications of God's providence in the premises." Letter of H. A. Brubaker, Librarian, Lawrence College, to the author, October 7, 1953.

[32] The librarian of North Dakota Agricultural College reports that many of the records of the trustees and of the president's office have been destroyed, and those that are available are not informative. Letter of H. D. Stallings to the author, January 13, 1954.

The University of Chicago archives reveal nothing about Hourwich or his dismissal: his name was simply dropped from the *Annual Register*. The trustees' minutes merely record the resignation of I. A. Hourwich, Docent, on February 1, 1895.

The only published material on Rogers' resignation in the Northwestern University archives is a letter of resignation, dated June 12, 1900. Whatever antagonism there might have been between Rogers and his board was masked by conventional politeness: "The time has come when in my judgment it is best for me to retire. . . . In thus terminating our official relations, I desire to express my grateful appreciation of the kindness you have always shown me in all our personal and official relations."

[33] The inference that Rogers was dismissed for his opposition to American policy in the Philippines was drawn from the bitter attack upon him in the press. See "The Menace to Free Discussion," *The Dial*, XXVI (May 16, 1899), 327. An article in

ex parte.[34] In the remaining six cases, however, there is a good deal of evidence to support Will's basic charges. Materials that have since come to light—the Ely correspondence, the Seligman letters, the Jameson papers [35]—show that in each of these cases the expression of personal opinion which was repugnant to officious conservatives led to the professor's undoing. It is true that Ely, compelled to defend his opinions, was vindicated and retained,[36] and that Andrews, asked to withhold his views, was not dismissed when he refused to do so.[37] Nevertheless, these six authenticated cases make it abundantly clear that the decade of the nineties— so curiously and inappropriately called "gay"—had seen the rise of a new kind of heresy defined as economic nonconformity.

But there are other genuine cases, not listed on Will's famous roster, in which the demand for economic conformity arose from the Populist "left." The career of J. Allen Smith provides an example of the bipartisan nature of intolerance. The author of a liberal dissertation on the money problem and a supporter of William Jennings Bryan

---

the Elgin (Ill.) *News,* November 8, 1895, may give some basis for assuming that Hourwich was dismissed for his opinions. "Chicago University seems to be singularly unfortunate in its professors of political economy. Following the lead of the old school writers of free trade, they not only teach their heresies but go a step further and champion the pernicious doctrines of socialism and populism. Prof. Bemis was 'resigned' for that cause, and now Dr. Isaac Hourwich is debarred from teaching because he is an 'avowed socialist, an infidel, and a sympathizer with the people's party.' The last count is not so bad, because every man has a right to his political convictions, but no self-respecting institution should retain for an hour among its lecturers one who holds such dangerous opinions as Dr. Hourwich. While the prompt action of President Harper saved the university from serious harm, he should be warned against nominating men to professorships till their fitness is fully ascertained." Mr. George Kennan Hourwich, the son, conveyed to the author his impression that President Harper had warned his father to give up politics or his post, but another member of the family denies that this had ever happened.

[34] John R. Commons, *Myself* (New York, 1934), pp. 50–68. To an earlier request to examine the Syracuse material, the librarian of Syracuse reported that the material could not be made available. S. R. Rolnick, "The Development of the Idea of Academic Freedom in American Higher Education," unpublished Ph.D. dissertation (University of Wisconsin, 1951), p. 169. To this writer the author of the forthcoming history of Syracuse University, reports that he was unable to discover "ground for assuming he was dismissed." Letter of Professor W. F. Galpin to author, November 20, 1953.

[35] The Ely papers are in the Wisconsin State Historical Society, Madison, Wisconsin. A microfilm of the letters bearing on academic freedom cases is in the Columbia University Special Collections. The Seligman letters are in the Columbia University Special Collections. The Jameson papers are in the possession of Dr. Leo Stock, Research Historian, Carnegie Institution, Washington, D.C.

[36] A discussion of the Ely case may be found on pp. 425–36.

[37] The best discussion of the Andrews case is Elizabeth Donnan's "A Nineteenth-Century Cause Célèbre," *New England Quarterly,* XXV (March, 1952), 23–46.

in the election of 1896, Smith was fired from Marietta College by a board of trustees dominated by Charles G. Dawes, a wealthy partisan conservative.[38] When, however, Smith applied for a university position in the West, he discovered that there monometallism was the heresy and free silver the orthodox creed. The Populist president of the University of Missouri proposed to make room for a true believer by firing a gold-standard professor; Smith saw the moral equivalence between this and Marietta's action, and would not accept the offer. Ideological considerations figured in his next appointment nevertheless. The Populist presidents of Kansas State Agricultural College and the University of Washington offered Smith jobs; he accepted the Washington offer.[39] The tendency in both parties was for like to seek out like.

The vicissitudes of the Kansas State Agricultural College are further proof that the conservatives did not sin alone. In 1894, the Board of Regents, then under the control of a Populist majority, decreed that "the principles maintained by the advocates of land nationalization, public control of utilities, and reform of the financial or monetary system shall be fairly stated and candidly examined . . . without bias or prejudice."[40] For this purpose, Thomas Elmer Will, a doughty champion of reform causes, was appointed professor of economics, thus insuring an "unprejudiced" examination in behalf of Populism, an "unbiased" statement against Republicanism. In 1896, the state-wide victory of Democrats and Populists resulted in a thorough reorganization of the college. All contracts with the faculty were at once terminated, and the president was forced to resign. Many of the professors were rehired, but the presidency and the department of economics were taken as Populist prizes.[41] Will was elevated to the presidency; Edward W. Bemis, expelled from Rockefeller's Eden in Chicago, was made professor of economics; Frank Parsons, reform crusader, was made professor of

[38] See "The Case of Professor James Allen Smith," *The Industrialist,* XXIII (September, 1897), 180, which effectively scotches the argument of the Marietta authorities that they were moved by financial considerations. It was the nation's, rather than the college's, finances that were uppermost in their minds, for the places of the dismissed professors were very quickly filled.

[39] Eric F. Goldman, "J. Allen Smith: The Reformer and His Dilemma," *Pacific Northwest Quarterly,* XXXV (July, 1944), 198 ff.

[40] Julius T. Willard, *History of the Kansas State College of Agriculture and Applied Science* (Manhattan, Kansas, 1940), p. 96. Willard gives most of the documents relevant to this case.

[41] George T. Fairchild, "Populism in a State Educational Institution, the Kansas State Agricultural College," *American Journal of Sociology,* III (November, 1897), 392–404.

history and political science.[42] A faculty organ, *The Industrialist,* became the spokesman for the party of reform.[43] The Populization of the college lasted for only three years. In 1899, by another turn of the wheel of politics, the Republicans returned to power. This was the occasion for partisan reprisal from the "Right." Abruptly, Will, Bemis, and Parsons were dismissed, and Kansas State was once more restored to sound conservative economics. In judging the actions of the Populist board, Bemis had written to his friend Ely that the Regents "were not really violating academic freedom." When he reflected upon the Republicans' purge, however, Bemis wrote that "there can be no doubt whatever that the present dismissals . . . were entirely for political reasons in order to prevent the possible development among the students and in the state at large of a point of view different from that usually favored by the donors to private universities and colleges." [44] The beam was always in the other's eye.

According to the thesis of conspiracy, there were certain essential conditions for and one effective cause of the curtailment of academic freedom. A liberal professor, pursuing his science; a conservative board, dominated by business—these were the necessary conditions. An antagonistic trustee or an imperious patron—this was the efficient cause. A closer look at two of Will's cases offers a test of this theory of causation. Richard T. Ely and Edward W. Bemis were economic infidels to about the same degree. Both subscribed to the "new" economics and rejected the immutability that had been claimed for laissez-faire doctrines. Both looked to the power of the state as the guardian of the general welfare; both looked upon the study of economics as a way of defending public interests.[45] And both were meliorists in social reform and gradualists in social action, rejecting the anarchist's method

---

[42] The course of events at Kansas State Agricultural College can be traced in notices of *The Outlook.* See LVI (May 15, 1897), 144, and (May 29, 1897), 240–41; LVII (September 4, 1897), 10, and (September 25, 1897), 209. On Parsons, see Arthur Mann, "Frank Parsons, The Professor as Crusader," *Mississippi Valley Historical Review,* XXXVII (December, 1950), 471–90; Benjamin O. Flower, "An Economist with Twentieth Century Ideals," *Arena,* XXVI (August, 1901), 157–60.

[43] *The Industrialist,* in the years of Will's presidency, gives an excellent picture of the one-sidedness of the faculty's point of view. See Vols. XXIV–XXV.

[44] Letter of Bemis to Ely, October 3, 1897, in Ely Papers: Bemis' statement, June 10, 1899, in Ely Papers.

[45] Cf. Sidney Fine, "Richard T. Ely, Forerunner of Progressivism, 1880–1901," *Mississippi Valley Historical Review,* XXXVII (March, 1951), 599–624; Edward W. Bemis, "A Point of View," *Biblotheca Sacra,* LIII (January, 1896), 145–51.

and the socialist's total panacea.[46] Yet each, when taken to task, was treated and judged very differently. Ely, attacked for his heterodox views, was tried, acquitted, and vindicated; Bemis, attacked for his heterodox views, was dismissed without formality. The comparison automatically suggests that there existed a greater variety of factors, and more complex initial conditions, than were dreamed of in Populist philosophy.

In 1894 Ely, director of the University of Wisconsin School of Economics, Politics and History, was tried by a committee of the Regents for believing in "strikes and boycotts, justifying and encouraging the one while practicing the other." His accuser was Oliver E. Wells, superintendent of public instruction and an ex-officio member of the board. Ely was alleged to have threatened to boycott a local firm whose workers were on strike; to have said that a union man, no matter how dirty and dissipated, was always to be employed in preference to a nonunion man, no matter how industrious and trustworthy; to have entertained and advised a union delegate in his home. Ely's books, Regent Wells went on to charge, contained "essentially the same principles," provided a "moral justification of attack upon life and property," and were "utopian, impracticable or pernicious." [47] Given the hysteria of the times, the authority of the Regent, and the public nature of the charges, Ely's position was gravely jeopardized. With conservative lawyers and businessmen sitting on the board and on the trial committee, Ely and his supporters feared the very worst. Their fears, however, proved to be unfounded. The trial resulted not only in Ely's exoneration, but in a declaration in favor of academic freedom that

[46] Ely's conservativism appears in his "Fundamental Beliefs in My Social Philosophy," *Forum*, XVIII (October, 1894), 173–83. Bemis presented his views in a letter to President Harper, which he wrote when he learned that he was suspect. "Having been informed today on second hand but apparently trustworthy authority that some of the authorities (trustees, I assume) of our University are displeased with what they suppose has been my attitude in this great RR strike, I write to correct any possible false reports. I wrote a letter to Mr. Debs, just before the strike, urging him, for I knew him slightly, not to have the strike. Then when all the trade unions were considering the propriety of a general strike in the city, I spent several hours in trying to dissuade the leaders of some of the unions. . . . In every way have I tried to calm the troubled waters while making use of the opportunity to urge upon employers a conciliatory Christ-like attitude." Letter of Bemis to Harper, July 23, 1894, in Harper Papers, University of Chicago Archives.

[47] Letter of Oliver E. Wells to *The Nation*, LIX (July 12, 1894), 27. Theodore Herfurth, *Sifting and Winnowing: A Chapter in the History of Academic Freedom at the University of Wisconsin* (Madison, Wisconsin, 1949), p. 8.

one historian of the University has called the "Wisconsin Magna Charta" [48] and that Ely hailed as "the strongest defense of freedom of instruction which was ever issued authoritatively from an American University." [49]

As Regents of a university with over a hundred instructors supported by nearly two millions of people who hold a vast diversity of views regarding the great questions which at present agitate the human mind, we could not for a moment think of recommending the dismissal or even the criticism of a teacher even if some of his opinions should, in some quarters, be regarded as visionary. Such a course would be equivalent to saying that no professor should teach anything which is not accepted by everybody as true. This would cut our curriculum down to very small proportions. We cannot for a moment believe that knowledge has reached its final goal, or that the present condition of society is perfect. We must therefore welcome from our teachers such discussions as shall suggest the means and prepare the way by which knowledge may be extended, present evils be removed and others prevented. We feel we would be unworthy of the position we hold if we did not believe in progress in all departments of knowledge. In all lines of academic investigation it is of the utmost importance that the investigator should be absolutely free to follow the indications of truth wherever they may lead. Whatever may be the limitations which trammel inquiry elsewhere we believe the great State University of Wisconsin should ever encourage that continual and fearless sifting and winnowing by which alone the truth can be found.[50]

At the very same time, Edward W. Bemis, one of Ely's former students, ran afoul of the authorities at the University of Chicago. He had delivered a speech against the railroad companies while the Pullman strike was going on, and had declared:

If the railroads would expect their men to be law-abiding, they must set the example. Let their open violation of the inter-state commerce law and the relations to corrupt legislatures and assessors testify as to their past in this regard. . . . Let there be some equality in the treatment of these things.[51]

The speech was reported in the press, and in certain Chicago circles it was considered nothing short of seditious. The president of the University, William Rainey Harper, was quick to express his displeasure.

Your speech . . . has caused me a great deal of annoyance. It is hardly safe for me to venture into any of the Chicago clubs. I am pounced upon from

[48] J. F. A. Pyre, *Wisconsin* (American College and University series, New York, 1920), p. 292.
[49] Letter of Ely to Henry D. Lloyd, December 24, 1894, in Ely Papers.
[50] Herfurth, *Sifting and Winnowing*, p. 11.
[51] Letter of Bemis to Ely, August 13, 1894, in Ely Papers.

all sides. I propose that during the remainder of your connection with the University you exercise very great care in public utterance about questions that are agitating the minds of the people.[52]

But it was already too late for repentance. At the end of the academic year, Bemis was dropped without a trial or an open specification of charges.

Contemporary opinion was greatly divided as to the causes of Bemis's dismissal. Ely, Ross, and Commons had no doubt that Bemis had been sacrificed on the bloody altar of Mammon.[53] Harper and Albion W. Small, head of the Sociology Department, were just as insistent that Bemis had been removed for incompetence.[54] One cannot judge motives from so far a remove, or take sides with complete assurance. But the timing of the dismissal and the self-incriminating letter of the President make the assumption highly plausible that a quiet or conservative Bemis would not have lost his position.

[52] *Ibid.*

[53] Ross wrote to Bemis: "I see that the issue between you and the Gas Trust University has become a national affair. I feel certain that the storm of public indignation while it may come too late to benefit you this year will react in your favor and ultimately more than compensate you for the treatment received by the University. I have known the tendencies there but have always tried to treat the University in a liberal spirit, but from now on I vow that I shall never recommend the economic, political or sociological departments of the University of Chicago to any student. . . . The Chicago concern has forfeited all right to the name and dignity of a University till it falls under other control." September 5, 1895, in Ely Papers. Ely wrote to Hamilton Mabie, the editor of *The Outlook:* "I will say, at once, that it is my firm conviction that Professor Bemis who is stronger than any man they now have in the department of economics, would be a member of the faculty of the University of Chicago in good standing had he not held the views which he entertains." August 24, 1895, in Ely Papers. However, Allan Nevins reports, in his biography of Rockefeller, that Ely in later years changed his mind and told him in 1939 that this was not a *bona fide* academic freedom case. *John D. Rockefeller* (New York, 1940), II, 263–65.

[54] Small insisted in letters and in articles that Bemis's dismissal had nothing to do with the doctrines he espoused. He attempted to explain away Harper's letter as follows: "It should be noted that President Harper's request that Mr. Bemis should exercise care in his statements was not made with reference to any utterances which Mr. Bemis was making in university work or in a university extension lecture, but in an outside capacity before a promiscuous audience. This was, as already intimated, at a time when agitation of any kind was universally regarded as imprudent. It should also be noted that President Harper did not even then take issue with Mr. Bemis on any 'doctrine' but that he requested him to be careful about making untimely and immature statements." Small's press statement on Bemis, October 18, 1895, in Ely Papers. The explanation is almost as damning as the action it seeks to explain. Small's exclusion of extramural utterance from the meaning of academic freedom was a truncated view of that principle and represented surrender on what to the pro-Bemis group was precisely the vital issue. His failure to grasp the intimidating overtones of Harper's letter was a quibble or a deliberate evasion.

Puzzled by the discrepancy in their treatment, Ely and Bemis searched for the key to explain it. Their conclusion, colored by the suspicion of conspiracy, was that the crucial factor in each case was the degree of big-business domination that existed in their respective institutions. Ely believed that state control of the University of Wisconsin minimized the influence of wealth. "Some of the Germans have a theory that society is tyrannical and that the state is an organ of freedom. This was illustrated in my case; the state protected me from the attacks of private persons." By contrast, he thought, a private university must pay court to its sources of support and need not publicly account for its actions.[55] Bemis believed that the pressure of local corporations was particularly strong at Chicago because of the University's crass commercial spirit. Pointing to the conservative Laughlin and the timorous Albion W. Small as key examples, he asserted that Chicago had established a "line" agreeable to those business interests; from this no professor could ever deviate and hope to keep his position.[56]

None of these interpretations adequately covers the facts. In the light of current and subsequent attacks on academic freedom in state universities, Ely's diagnosis was not perceptive, certainly not prophetic. The shaky tenure of faculties in the state universities was exemplified by the mass dismissals that occurred at Kansas State.[57] Even at Wisconsin, practice lagged behind principle, as Edward A. Ross discovered when he was reprimanded by the Board of Regents in 1910 for having announced to a class that the anarchist Emma Goldman would give a public lecture in Madison.[58] Ely's diagnosis is also refuted by later evidence compiled by Committee A of the American Association of University Professors from 1915, the year of its founding, to

[55] Letter of Ely to Henry D. Lloyd, December 24, 1895, in Ely Papers.

[56] At first Bemis blamed Rockefeller for his dismissal, but later thought that the manager of the Gas Trust of Chicago was the really sinister influence. Letter of Bemis to Ely, January 12, 1895, in Ely Papers. Nevins offers rather convincing proof that Rockefeller did not impose his economic views on the university, though he did intervene in theological matters. Nevins, *Rockefeller*, II, 259–62. The charge that the Gas Trust opposed Bemis and was responsible for getting him removed was made by George H. Shibley and denied by President Henry P. Judson of the University of Chicago before a House of Representatives Committee in 1914. See Rolnick, "Development of the Idea of Academic Freedom," p. 142.

[57] At the State University of Iowa in 1887, Democratic politicians led a movement to remove 3 Republican professors who were prohibitionists. In 1893 the Regents of West Virginia University dismissed the entire faculty including the President. Rolnick, "Development of the Idea of Academic Freedom," pp. 108, 116.

[58] Herfurth, *Sifting and Winnowing*, pp. 14–31.

1947. In that period, the Committee reported on 73 violations of academic freedom, of which 37, or more than half, occurred at state universities.[59] Bemis's explanation also leaves much to be desired. It does not explain, for example, why Professor Charles Zeublin, a socialist, was retained in the Department of Sociology;[60] how that congenital nonconformist, Thorstein Veblen, managed to survive at Chicago for as long as fourteen years;[61] why Harper put E. J. James, a defender of bimetallism and labor unions, at the head of the Extension Division the year after Bemis departed;[62] and why Bemis had been appointed in the first place, since his views had always been well known.[63] Plainly, one must search for additional factors.

One of these factors was the role of the presidents at Wisconsin and Chicago. From the start, Wisconsin's president, Charles Kendall Adams, supported Ely and his cause. It does not appear that his reasons were primarily ideological, for he was much more conservative than Ely; nor that they were based on administrative principles, for he had often offended professors with tactless and high-handed actions.[64] More likely, his reasons were personal—he happened to be fond of this young

[59] These figures are based on a statistical analysis of the AAUP Bulletins from 1915 to 1947, Vols. I–XXXIII.

[60] Zeublin was appointed in 1892 as instructor, was promoted to the rank of assistant professor in 1895, to the rank of associate professor in 1896, and to the rank of full professor in 1902. He resigned in 1908 to become editor of the *Twentieth Century Magazine*. *National Cyclopedia of American Biography*, XIV, 454–55.

[61] Oddly enough, J. Laurence Laughlin was Veblen's protector at Chicago. Laughlin had been a thorn in Bemis's side, and Bemis had always attributed his hostility to ideological differences. Yet, in 1903, when Veblen directly contradicted Laughlin's credit theories in an article, Laughlin arranged to have the article published. Largely through Laughlin's offices, Veblen took on most of the duties of managing editor of the *Journal of Political Economy* and was promoted to assistant professor in 1900, though he did not attract undergraduates as a teacher and though Harper was critical of his personal life. Alfred Bornemann, *J. Laurence Laughlin* (Washington, D.C., 1940), pp. 26–28.

[62] "Personal Notes, University of Chicago," *Annals of the American Academy of Political and Social Science*, VII (January, 1896), 78–86; "Personal Notes, University of Chicago," *Annals of the American Academy of Political and Social Science*, XVII (March, 1901), 318–21.

[63] In an exchange of letters with Laughlin, Bemis had made it very clear where he stood on such things as government ownership of telegraph, the tariff, immigration restriction, child labor laws, and the currency question. Laughlin had agreed that he would have the liberty of expression he demanded. Letter of Bemis to Laughlin, February 27, 1892, in Harper Papers.

[64] Waterman T. Hewett, *Cornell University: A History* (New York, 1905), I, 198; Jessica Tyler Austen, *Moses Coit Tyler* (New York, 1911), pp. 249, 250, 253, 264; Merle Curti and Vernon Carstensen, *The University of Wisconsin, 1848–1925* (Madison, Wis., 1949), II, 576–77.

professor and to detest the Regent who accused him. At any rate, all through the hectic summer of 1894, while Ely was preparing his defense, Adams offered him comfort and sage advice. At the trial, he submitted a testimonial in Ely's behalf. There are indications, too, that he wrote the text of the "sifting and winnowing" statement.[65] With the president staunchly at his side, Ely was spared the disconsolate feeling of being forsaken by the parent, of which institutional authority is a symbol. And Adams's word carried weight: a patriarchal figure in the world of scholarship, an intimate of men of affairs, he was an incalculably valuable ally. By the same token, the forceful and domineering Harper was an extremely powerful antagonist. In all his dealings with Bemis, he was uncharitable, curt, and uncandid. Had he so desired, he might have defended the right of professors to speak as freely as other citizens; instead, he accepted the right of other citizens to curb the speech of professors. Had he been scrupulous, he would have given Bemis a chance to answer the charges against him; had he been kind, he would not have hinted to the press that those charges were utterly damning.[66] There is no mistaking Harper's animus, but controversy still beclouds his motives. A generous interpretation would have it that he was confronted with an incompetent professor and handled the problem ineptly. Perhaps the more accurate view would be that he was obsessed with the grandoise dream of a rich and great university, that to make that dream a reality he wished to stay in the good graces of his patrons, and that with this objective in view a talkative professor in the Extension Division was carelessly considered expendable. But it is clear that in both cases—can one not say, in most cases?—the president held the key to the outcome.

Still another differentiating factor was the professional position of

[65] The elder Robert LaFollette assumed that Chynoweth, the chairman of the investigating committee, wrote the text. Robert M. LaFollette, *Autobiography* (Madison, Wis., 1913), p. 29. But Ely was certain that Adams was the author. Letter of Ely to Edwin S. Witte, June 5, 1942, in Ely Papers.

[66] Bemis wrote to Ely: "If I had evidence of Harper's directly attacking me the way would be plain, but he is likely to speak well of my character and work but shrug his shoulders and express the hope to other presidents. 'Try him. I hope you will like him (or get along with him) better than we did.' Such 'damning with faint praise' and the natural action of trustees I now think were what Pr't H. had in mind when he said, 'If we say we did not like you (i.e., he explained, did not like my personality), you cannot get a college place in America.' " September 24, 1895, in Ely Papers. This, however, was exactly what Harper was saying surreptitiously to the press. See letter of Harper to Arthur T. Edwards, editor of the *Northwestern Christian Advocate,* August 1, 1895, in Harper Papers.

the defendants. Before coming to Wisconsin, Ely had taught for eleven years at Johns Hopkins, at a time when its fame was unrivaled. No teacher in America had had a more brilliant group of graduate students, nor could any boast more devoted disciples. Among them were Frederick Jackson Turner, at the time of the trial, professor of history at Wisconsin; David Kinley, professor of political economy at Illinois; Charles Homer Haskins, professor of history at Wisconsin; H. H. Powers, professor of economics and sociology at Smith; William A. Scott, associate professor of political economy at Princeton; Edward A. Ross, professor of economics at Stanford; John R. Commons, professor of economics at Indiana; Albion W. Small; Albert Shaw, editor of the *Review of Reviews;* John H. Finley, president of Knox College; and George P. Morris, associate editor of the *Congregationalist.*[67] "These," said Ely, "are my jewels." [68] They were, indeed, priceless assets. Scott, Turner, and Kinley masterminded Ely's defense; Shaw, Warner, and Morris gave him a sympathetic press; Shaw, Small, Turner, and Kinley were character witnesses at the trial. Their agitation aroused the entire profession; social scientists everywhere rallied to Ely's defense.[69] They made the Regents aware that Ely was not an isolated individual, but a powerful academic force. They made the Regents aware of what the Regents tended to overlook, that the bonds of obligation were mutual, that if the professor was dependent on the institution for a salary and a platform, the institution was indebted to the professor for his popularity and renown.[70] As a factor in the trial and the acquittal, the importance of Ely's status cannot be overestimated.

[67] Many who had not studied formally under Ely expressed their debt to him. Among these were Frederick C. Howe, LaFollette, and Theodore Roosevelt. See Howe, *The Confessions of a Reformer* (New York, 1925), p. 28; Ely, *Ground under Our Feet,* pp. 216, 277–79.

[68] Ely's Chautauqua Statement, August 14, 1894, in Ely Papers.

[69] So confirmed a conservative as the Harvard economist Charles Dunbar, who had refused to join the American Economic Association because it was too radical, became one of Ely's supporters. Letter of W. J. Ashley to Ely, August 23, 1894, in Ely Papers. Albert Bushnell Hart, the Harvard historian, was in Paris when the case broke, and was so out of touch with academic sentiment that, almost alone among the nation's important academic men, he wrote a letter to the press condemning Ely. When he returned and could gauge the situation, he apologized to Ely. Letter of A. B. Hart to Ely, September 7, 1894, in Ely Papers.

[70] Thus, one of Ely's friends, Professor Jerome L. Raymond of the University of Chicago, wrote to a Wisconsin Regent: "I cannot imagine a greater loss to the University of Wisconsin than the loss of his ministrations. His reputation is not only national, but international. While you have him at Madison, you have the foremost department of Economics in this country. Scour the country throughout and you

By contrast, there can be no doubt that Chicago had less need of Bemis than Bemis had of Chicago. Though not an insignificant figure, Bemis was still on a low rung of fame and not yet rich in disciples. Since he was a teacher in the university's Extension Division, his institutional status was not high. Presumably—and this was a commercial consideration that counted at the University of Chicago—he did not attract enough students to cover the cost of his appointment.[71] Largely at Ely's instigation, many members of the profession took an interest in Bemis and his plight—but not with the same enthusiasm that they showed in Ely's behalf and usually with reservations or a certain condescension. Bemis, wrote Hamilton Mabie to Ely,

is a perfectly guileless, straight-forward and honest man,—industrious, conscientious and well up on his work; but . . . he lacks any notable personal power and is devoid of that contagious element which wins people from the platform and often in the classroom. . . . A year ago when your fight came on you had solid ground under your feet. I do not think Bemis has.[72]

Bemis lacked the personal and professional resources that might initially have averted the attack or else might have won the engagement.

A third difference lay in the extent to which Ely and Bemis put their theories into action. For all his talk of the need for concrete reform, Ely's criticisms of the social order tended to be general, not specific; hortatory, not programmatic.[73] For all his warm humanitarianism, he made no intimate contact with the multitude. "Only twice in my life," he once wrote, "have I ever spoken to audiences of working men, and I had always held myself aloof from agitations as something not in my province—something for which I am not adapted." [74] Replying to the charge by Regent Wells that he *had* acted on his sympathies for labor, he issued a categorical denial. This author of a friendly history of the labor movement denied, at his trial, that he had ever entertained a walking delegate in his home, that he had ever counseled workers to strike, that he had ever threatened an anti-union firm with a boycott, or

---

could not get a man who would do so much to attract students of Economics to Madison." Letter of Raymond to H. D. Dale, August 13, 1894, in Ely Papers.

[71] See Small's press statement, October 18, 1895, in Ely Papers.

[72] Letter of Mabie to Ely, October 4, 1895, in Ely Papers.

[73] There were occasional exceptions in his writings. See his attack on the Pullman Company in "Pullman: A Social Study," *Harper's New Monthly Magazine*, LXX (February, 1885), 452–66.

[74] Letter of Ely to Amos P. Wilder, July 22, 1894, in Ely Papers.

that he had ever favored the principle of a closed shop.[75] Were these charges true, Ely wrote, they would "unquestionably unfit me to occupy a responsible position as an instructor of youth in a great University." [76] These were the words of a very academic reformer.

Of all who wrote to congratulate Ely, Bemis alone perceived that he had won the particular case, but had relinquished a vital principle. "That was a glorious victory for you," he wrote. "I was sorry only that you seemed to show a vigor of denial as to entertaining a walking delegate or counseling strikers as if either were wrong, instead of under certain circumstances a *duty*." [77] This was the difference between them: Bemis was not only a partisan of, but an active party to, the fight for underdog causes. Bemis, wrote H. H. Powers to Ely, "is a moderate man in his views but he has unquestionably taken a vigorous stand in favor of 'doing something about it.' It is his very efficiency in this line that has made him so obnoxious to interested parties." [78] "I have no doubt," wrote Ely to Mabie,

[that] Professor Zeublin is quite as brave as Dr. Bemis but the nature of the work is such that he does not feel called upon to deal specially with the gas question, street car corporations, etc. Dr. Bemis is not by any means radical, but he happens to take interest in one or two lines of scientific work which appear to be particularly dangerous.[79]

These comments are very illuminating. They point to the significant fact that, in a secular milieu, professors ran greater risks by threatening concrete interests than by doubting accepted ideologies. Not disbelief alone, but disbelief when applied to gas rates, was what most aggrieved the business community. The subsequent careers of Ely and Bemis bear out the importance of this point. Ely survived (and in good part renounced) his spoken and written heresies.[80] He remained in a full state of academic grace for the rest of his life, taking a post at Northwestern in 1925 and one at Columbia in 1937. Bemis became an aca-

---

[75] *Transcript of the Ely Trial,* p. 19, in Ely Papers.
[76] Ely's Chautauqua Statement, August 14, 1894, in Ely Papers.
[77] Letter of Bemis to Ely, October 4, 1894, in Ely Papers.
[78] Letter of H. H. Powers to Ely, November 14, 1895, in Ely Papers.
[79] Letter of Ely to Hamilton W. Mabie, August 24, 1895, in Ely Papers.
[80] Ely became increasingly conservative as time went on. He became Director of the so-called Institute for Research in Land Economics and Public Utilities (an organization heavily subsidized by the National Association of Real Estate Boards and the public utilities companies) which was accused by labor organizations of pleading in its sponsors' interest. See Laura P. Morgan, "The Institute of Politics and the Teacher," *American Teacher,* XII (November, 1927), 12–14.

demic Ishmael, with a reputation as a partisan and a malcontent that he never was able to live down. Except for his brief and ill-starred tenure at Kansas State, he received no further academic appointments.[81] The trustees of the republic of learning could inflict on this kind of miscreant the terrible retribution of neglect.

Finally, in listing the factors that differentiate these cases, the personality, power, and standing of Ely's chief accuser must be mentioned. The idea of a trial, it should be noted, originated with the Regents, not with Ely and his friends. The latter had many misgivings about it. They were afraid that a trial in those troubled times would not be conducted with respect for the rights of the defendant.[82] They feared that a trial over matters of belief would mark a return to old inquisitional habits, that Wisconsin would go the way of Andover. "It has been reserved for the University of Wisconsin," wrote a writer in the *Dial,*

to offer the first example, to our knowledge, of a trial for heresy in which theology has no part. To hale a public teacher of science before an investigating committee, for the purpose of examining his opinions . . . is a procedure so novel, and, we may add, so startling, that one may well pause to consider its significance, and the possible consequences of an extension of the principle thus involved.[83]

But the trial was intended to serve a purpose that Ely and his supporters did not suspect. At the start of the proceedings the Committee decided not to consider in evidence any of Ely's writings that did not bear directly on doctrines taught in class. It was reluctant, it declared, to censor books in the library or to indulge in the insidious sport of quoting passages out of context.[84] This decision proved fatal to the case of the accuser, for none of the other charges, as it turned out, could be substantiated. Wells walked out midway through the proceedings, objecting to the limitations that had been placed on the scope of the inquiry. After this, the Committee reversed its decision,

[81] From 1901 to 1909, Cleveland's reform mayor, Tom L. Johnson, made use of Bemis's practical talents by appointing him superintendent of the water department. From 1913 to 1923, Bemis was a member of the advisory board of the Valuation Bureau of the Interstate Commerce Commission. "Edward W. Bemis" (obituary), New York *Times,* September 27, 1930.

[82] Letter of William A. Scott to Ely, July 21, 1894. Letter of Frederick Jackson Turner to Ely, August 4, 1894, in Ely Papers.

[83] "The Freedom of Teaching," *The Dial,* XVII (September 1, 1894), 103.

[84] *Transcript of the Ely Trial,* p. 22, in Ely Papers.

and allowed Ely to read from his writings any extract that he chose! Plainly, the Committee was on the side of the professor, and the reason is not hard to find. Regent Wells was cordially disliked and distrusted. He had tangled with his colleagues before, and had earned a reputation as a troublemaker. He was a Regent only ex officio, and had been elected to his office only because of a freakish Democratic victory in a normally Republican state. And he had completely isolated himself by going over the heads of the Regents, by giving his charges to the public press, and by implying that the university condoned Ely's teachings and was an accessory to his sins. Therefore, the ulterior purpose of the trial was to discredit this enemy of the tribe, who had infiltrated its high council. In the old theological trials—as in certain congressional hearings that were to come at a later day—accuser and investigator were one. In the Ely trial at Wisconsin, the accuser stood accused.

Thus, in the concrete instance, the professor's fate was decided by a number of non-ideological factors. Admittedly, however, these two cases do not shed much light on the role of the business patron. At Wisconsin, the attack upon academic freedom was undertaken by a bungling, small-town teacher; the defense of academic freedom was made by a committee of the Regents composed of a city banker, a wealthy doctor, and a small-town lawyer. At Chicago, the attack was probably inspired by certain local big-business men. There are, however, two other cases that exhibit in a clear and unmistakable way the attitudes of business leaders. One was the case of Edward A. Ross at Stanford, the other the case of John S. Bassett at Trinity, which occurred in 1903. Both Ross and Bassett were members of institutions that were dependent on a single rich sponsor. Both were sharply attacked for speaking unpopular opinions. Ross was eventually dismissed, the victim of his patron's intolerance; Bassett was retained, the beneficiary of his patron's indulgence. Again, the comparison suggests complexities not embraced by the theory of class malevolence.

Under the provisions of the founding grant of Stanford University, the functions of the trustees were exercised solely by the Founders.[85] The death of Leland Stanford in 1893, and the assumption of full

---

[85] A board of trustees took over the power of the Founder when the charter was amended by Mrs. Stanford in 1903. Jane Lathrop Stanford, *Address on the Right of Free Speech,* April 25, 1903, pp. 3–6.

authority by his wife, converted this unusual oligarchy into a still more unusual matriarchate. Into the university built in memory of her son the strong-willed, emotional Mrs. Stanford poured all of her abundant energy. When, in the infancy of the institution, the Stanford estate was tied up in probate court, she contributed her personal income—even sold her personal possessions—to keep the University alive.[86] So well mothered, the infant institution survived, and very soon waxed strong. But universities must, like children, pay a price for filial dependence. Both kinds of organisms must be independent to mature, and both must be mature to be free. Stanford University became the victim of the commanding meddlesome love which an unbridled maternal instinct thrusts upon an only child.

It was not long before the professors found this motherly embrace oppressive. In 1898, Professor H. H. Powers, a popular teacher in political science, delivered a speech on religion which Mrs. Stanford happened to hear.[87] Intensely devout, the "Mother of the University" was shocked by its heretical sophistication.[88] As imperious as she was generous, she demanded that Powers be removed. The founding grant vested the power of dismissal in the hands of the president, and this power could be exercised at will, since all professors were on annual appointment. In David Starr Jordan, a well-known zoologist, an advocate of evolution, a pioneer in the university movement, the faculty had a president who well understood the danger of permitting lay preconceptions of propriety to interfere with academic expression. Unfortunately, the faculty also had, in David Starr Jordan, a president who was compelled by a sense of obligation and by his own sycophantic personality to defer to the wishes of the Founder. Agreeing with the one side, but subservient to the other, he was completely miscast in the role of mediator between the faculty and Mrs. Stanford. In this instance, he

[86] The story of the crisis of the infant Stanford University is graphically told in Elliott, *Stanford University*, pp. 251–308. The Ross case is discussed in this volume with unusual candor and fullness.

[87] The speech, as far as we know, was not recorded. Powers' version of it is as follows: "I offended Mrs. Stanford by an address of a somewhat philosophical religious character which I delivered at the request of a student organization. Mrs. S. whom I had never seen was there and was much offended by my pessimism and heterodoxy which it is needless to say she did not understand." Letter of H. H. Powers to Ely, January 14, 1898, in Ely Papers.

[88] See Bertha Berner, *Mrs. Leland Stanford, An Intimate Account* (Stanford University, 1935), for a chatty, adulatory biography written by Mrs. Stanford's personal secretary, which gives unintended evidence of the latter's naiveté.

pleaded that Powers should be retained and spoke of his valuable services; but yet, when the Founder refused to be moved, he did not challenge her verdict. In 1898, Powers was forced to resign, the first of a very large brood that soon was to be disinherited.

Edward A. Ross was exactly the man to ignite this situation. Fresh from Ely's seminar, fired by liberal causes, convinced that the aim of big business was to throttle social criticism, Ross had come to Stanford almost spoiling for a fight. "As secretary of the American Economic Association," Ross wrote many years later in his autobiography,

I had gained an inside view of the growing pressure on economists and resolved that I for one would be no party to this fooling of the public. I would test this boasted "academic freedom"; if nothing happened to me others would speak out and economists would again really count for something in the shaping of public opinion. If I got cashiered, as I thought would be the case, the hollowness of our rôle of "independent scholar" would be visible to all.[89]

With bravery that verged on bravado, Ross said and did just those things that would put him in the Founder's eye. At a time when the conservative community thought Eugene V. Debs the incarnate devil, Ross publicly defended him; in a university that had been founded by a railroad Republican whose ventures had depended on free labor, he advocated municipal ownership of utilities and a ban on Oriental immigration. At a time when most economists were for McKinley and gold, he wrote a tract in favor of free silver that was used by the Democratic party. Perhaps Leland Stanford, had he been alive, would have tolerated the iconoclasm of this professor. There was something of the iconoclast in Stanford, too, as witness his bill for fiat money that he proposed while a member of the Senate.[90] But his wife had all the prejudices of her class, and they had been hardened by her ignorance into absolutes. "When I take up a newspaper . . . and read of the utterances of Professor Ross," she wrote to Jordan,

. . . and realize that a professor of the Leland Stanford Junior University, who should prize the opportunities given him to distinguish himself among his students in the high and noble manner of his life and teachings before them, thus steps aside, and out of his sphere, to associate himself with the political demagogues of this city, exciting their evil passions, drawing distinctions between man and man, all laborers and equal in the sight of God, and literally plays into the hands of the lowest and vilest elements of socialism,

[89] Edward A. Ross, *Seventy Years of It* (New York, 1936), pp. 64–65.
[90] George T. Clark, *Leland Stanford* (Stanford, 1931), pp. 459–61.

it brings tears to my eyes. I must confess I am weary of Professor Ross, and I think he ought not to be retained at Stanford University.[91]

For several years, Jordan interceded with the Mother on behalf of the erring child. He argued that Ross's scholarship was impeccable, his teaching in the classroom judicious, his personal life unimpeachable. He called Ross (it was a eulogy he was later to regret) a "wise, learned and noble man, one of the most loyal and devoted of all the band" at the University.[92] At the same time, he entreated Ross to use restraint. To hold him in rein, he transferred him from the Department of Economics to the Department of Sociology.[93] As a desperate last step, he prevailed upon Ross to write the patroness directly and present his side of the case.[94] All of these efforts came to nought. Mrs. Sanford was adamant:

All that I have to say regarding Professor Ross, however brilliant and talented he may be, is that a man cannot entertain such rabid ideas without inculcating them in the minds of the students under his charge. There is a very deep and bitter feeling of indignation throughout the community . . . that Stanford University is lending itself to partisanism and even to dangerous socialism. . . . Professor Ross cannot be trusted, and he should go.[95]

Jordan was aware that his own prerogative was invaded by the implacable stand of the Founder.[96] It can be argued that this awareness made his ultimate capitulation more blameworthy. But cowardice never had better reasons. Had Jordan threatened to resign, Mrs. Stanford would no doubt have held her ground; had Jordan carried out his threat and taken the faculty with him, the University might well have expired. In Jordan's scale of judgment, the institution outweighed the individual: the value of the institution's existence was preponderant over other academic values. In 1900, Ross was forced to resign.

[91] Elliott, *Stanford University*, p. 340–41. [92] *Ibid.*, pp. 346–47.
[93] Letter of Ross to Frank Lester Ward, April 25, 1897; reprinted in Bernhard J. Stern, "The Ward-Ross Correspondence, 1897–1901," *American Sociological Review*, XI (October, 1936), 594.
[94] Even Ross succumbed to the mood at Stanford and expressed his filial loyalty. "I have completely identified myself with the University you founded. I have devoted my whole soul and strength to the glory of Stanford, trusting that Stanford would look out for me. . . . Mrs. Stanford, I do not want to stay unless you can give me that degree of confidence which I deem my just due for faithful service, and without which I can do no good work here. I am loyal to you, and out of reverence for you as the Mother of this University will conform to your wishes in every way I can. I will do everything but sacrifice my self-respect . . ." Elliott, *Stanford University*, p. 343.
[95] *Ibid.*, pp. 343–44. [96] *Ibid.*

For Ross a silent retreat was unthinkable; it would have defeated the purpose of his rebellion. Hence, the day after he was dismissed, he issued a statement to the press and made the "Ross Case" public property. The statement was skillfully composed to show that there had been a clear-cut violation of academic freedom. Quoting from Jordan's own letters, Ross depicted the president as a victim unwilling to become a martyr. Playing on the Westerner's fear of the "Oriental menace," he implied that his speech on coolie immigration was the primary cause of his downfall. Appealing to academic opinion, he invoked the argument of scientific competence.

I cannot with self-respect decline to speak on topics to which I have given years of investigation. It is my duty as an economist to impart, on occasion, to sober people, and in a scientific spirit, my conclusions on subjects with which I am expert. . . . It is plain, therefore, that this is no place for me.[97]

By this time, academic-freedom cases, particularly those that involved wealthy donors, had become matters of national interest. Ross's charge was headlined in the newspapers throughout the land. By this time, too, a sizable public had been conditioned to accept such a charge at its face value. A large number and variety of journals took the side of the dismissed professor and condemned the Stanford authorities. Some of these journals, like the *Outlook,* had been schooled by a decade of suspicion to see conspiracy everywhere afoot.[98] Others, like *Gunton's Magazine,* had always defended the right of "academic management" to fire any of its employees, but happened to agree with Ross that Oriental immigration should be checked.[99] Ross's partisans ranged from the New York *Evening Post,* now atoning under a new editor for its illiberal views in the Ely case, to the Republican San Francisco *Chronicle,* which bore a grudge against the Southern Pacific.[100] For all sorts of reasons, protest welled in every section of the country.

When colleges were religious institutions, the expulsion of professors for their opinions often went unextenuated and undisguised. Sophistry and self-deception were not then basic to the art of administration.

[97] Ross, *Seventy Years of It,* pp. 69–72.
[98] Editorial, "Freedom of Teaching Once More," *Outlook,* LXVI (November 24, 1900), 727–28.
[99] *Gunton's Magazine,* XX (April, 1901), 367–69.
[100] New York *Evening Post* (February 23, 1901); San Francisco *Chronicle* (November 15, 16, 17, 21, 24, 25, 27, and 29; December 16 and 23, 1900; February 18, 1901). In Bancroft Library, University of California.

This was not a sign of moral superiority: candor comes easily to those who feel they have committed no wrong and who seek only parochial approval. The Stanford authorities, however, were too committed to academic freedom and too sensitive to public opinion to tell the unvarnished truth. They would not admit to themselves that Ross had been punished for heresy; they could not admit to others that his heresy had been detected by the donor. A sense of guilt and a concern for reputation made them seek their justification in the oldest source of absolution—the imperfections of the victim. The need to do this was not lost even on Mrs. Stanford, whose dim comprehension of what she had done was later tinctured by misgivings. In 1903, in turning over the management of the university to a board of trustees, she denied that her objection to Ross had been based on his political opinions. He had had, she averred, perfect freedom to express his views in class. But he had violated the fundamental canon that no professor should use his position for electioneering or for participation in political campaigns. He had been dismissed because he had compromised the neutral position of the university.[101] Jordan let it be known that Ross had not been "the proper man for the place." Ross had been "slangy and scurrilous" in discussing current issues, and he had revealed an unscrupulous character by appealing to the public and divulging family secrets.[102] It may well be that Mrs. Stanford sincerely believed that she had preserved a precious neutrality, and it may well be that Jordan sincerely expected devotion even from a professor who had been ejected from the clan. But the fact remains that in 1896 fifty members of the Stanford faculty had endorsed McKinley without incurring the charge of "partisanism," and that Jordan had warmly defended Ross's character before the denouement.[103]

The argument of neutrality and the charge of moral turpitude did

---

[101] Stanford, *Address on the Right of Free Speech, passim.*

[102] Ross was also accused of attacking Stanford's business methods. This he completely denied. It is not beyond doubt, however, that he did not use the Southern Pacific Railroad as an illustration of the sharp practices of business. See "Still Deeper in the Mire," San Francisco *Chronicle,* November 17, 1900, in Bancroft Library, University of California.

[103] Among the signers of letters praising McKinley and attacking the Democratic standard-bearer in a two-page advertisement in the San Francisco *Chronicle* were 17 of the 37 professors and associate professors of the Stanford Academic Council who later justified Jordan's dismissal of Ross. See San Francisco *Chronicle,* September 27, 1896, pp. 27–28, in Bancroft Library, University of California. See, also, *Science,* New Series, Vol. XIII (May 10, 1901), p. 751.

not convince several Stanford professors. After Ross resigned, Professor George E. Howard took up the torch of rebellion. He declared, in a signed statement to the press, that

the summary dismissal of Dr. Ross for daring in a frank but thoroughly scientific spirit to speak the simple truth on social questions is . . . a blow aimed directly at academic freedom, and it is, therefore, a deep humiliation to Stanford University and to the cause of American education. The blow does not come directly from the founder. It really proceeds from the sinister spirit of social bigotry and commercial intolerance which is just now the deadliest foe of American democracy.[104]

The addition of Howard to the *dramatis personae* changed the whole tenor of the play. For where Ross was headstrong and brash, Howard, who was twenty years his senior and a member of the first Stanford faculty, was known to be circumspect. When Mrs. Stanford successfully put pressure on Jordan to expel this outspoken professor also, a chain reaction was produced. In all, seven professors presented their resignations in protest: Frank Fetter, professor of economics; Arthur O. Lovejoy, associate professor of philosophy; Morton A. Aldrich, associate professor of economics; William Henry Hudson, professor of English; Henry B. Lathrop, professor of rhetoric; Charles N. Little, professor of mathematics; and David E. Spencer, associate professor of mathematics. Ross was jubilant: "Stunning news from the Pacific Coast, isn't it?" he wrote to Ely. "So far $12,000 of annual salary has been voluntarily renounced in protest against Mrs. Stanford's action. That's vindication!" [105] A socialist organ saw the most individualistic of exploited laborers finally developing class-consciousness.[106] This conclusion was premature, for the majority of the faculty remained loyal to Jordan. But it was true that never before had an American faculty demonstrated so great a sense of internal solidarity and so rebellious and courageous a spirit.

Equally unprecedented—and even more momentous—was the decision taken by economists, at the thirteenth meeting of the American Economic Association in 1900, to launch an investigation of the Ross case. With this decision, the first professorial inquiry into an academic-freedom case was conceived and brought into being—the predecessor,

[104] Elliott, *Stanford University,* pp. 361–62.
[105] Letter of Ross to Ely, January 19, 1901, in Ely Papers.
[106] "College Class-Consciousness," *International Socialist Review,* I (1901), 586–87.

if not directly the parent, of the proceedings of Committee A of the AAUP. It is doubtful that the "thirty or forty" economists who met that December in Detroit and appointed a committee of inquiry were conscious of the historical importance of the tactic they were devising. Perhaps there were some who did reason that the secular sophistication of administrators now rendered their explanations unreliable, that the greater complexity of the "cases" made disinterested fact-finding essential, that only independent outsiders could safely undertake such inquiries, that only the professor's peers possessed the competence to evaluate the issues.[107] But doubtless many acted on the spur of the moment and the case, impelled by Ross's personal popularity (he had been secretary of the Association, was the son-in-law of Lester Frank Ward, and was part of Ely's entourage), by the flagrancy of Mrs. Stanford's actions (they alarmed diehard conservatives no less than automatic liberals),[108] and by the flimsy excuses of Jordan (which promised easily to be exposed and to reveal a "case" of unparalleled transparency).[109]

Owing to either their lack of long-run objectives, or to their inexperience in these matters, the organizers of the committee made two serious tactical mistakes. First of all, out of the desire not to involve absent members, they did not use the aegis of the Association, but met as an informal body. This laid them open to the charge of lacking official authority and of not being truly representative. The fact that they constituted a large proportion of the members then attending the Detroit sessions, and the fact that they appointed to the committee of inquiry three highly reputed conservatives, did not erase the public impression that the entire investigation was ex parte.[110] Furthermore, the scope of the inquiry was too narrowly conceived. The committee sought

[107] Professor Sidney Sherwood of Johns Hopkins suggested to Ely at this time that a professional association should seize the opportunity to "investigate and report on the general subject of *Lehrfreiheit*" in order to "challenge public attention and create a method by which the professions might work unitedly." Letter of Sherwood to Ely, December 22, 1900, in Ely Papers.

[108] Even Albion W. Small, who had written an article flatly denying that donors infringed academic freedom, was nettled by Mrs. Stanford: "The Dowager of Palo Alto" he wrote to Ely, "has captured the booby prize, with no competition in sight." Letter of November 24, 1900, in Ely Papers.

[109] Letter of Ely to Seligman, June 7, 1901, in Seligman Papers.

[110] Taking this line, several journals refused to take seriously the conclusions of the committee. See *Science,* New Series Vol. X (March 8, 1901), pp. 361–62; *Dial,* XXX (April 1, 1901), 221–23.

the answer to one question—"What were the reasons which led Mrs. Stanford to force Professor Ross's resignation?" [111] In making this foray into feminine psychology, it lost sight of the significant questions that lay beyond the issue of motives: whether it was healthy for a university to be bound by the wishes of one person, however noble her intentions; whether it was good for the community as a whole for philanthropists to make donations to institutions which they then controlled as though they were private properties; whether it was helpful to the science of economics to shun, under the rubric of nonpartisanship, all subjects on which people were divided; whether it contributed to academic freedom to keep professors on year-to-year appointments.

The attempt to uncover motives encountered formidable difficulties. Powerless to subpoena witnesses, without the standing that would secure cooperation, the committee relied on voluntary testimony, which it acquired mainly through letters. This was not an efficient method for probing the inner recesses of the administrative mind. The committee did not even approach Mrs. Stanford—it did not suppose that she would admit its right to interfere in her affairs. With Jordan, the committee was more hopeful. "May we inquire," asked Seligman, the chairman, "whether there are other reasons than those mentioned for the resignation of Professor Ross, and may we hope that, if such other reasons exist, you may be disposed to communicate them to us." [112] Jordan replied that a faculty committee "in possession of the facts" would answer the committee's questions. But the letter of the faculty committee was as patronizing and laconic as any a college president might have written. "In reply," wrote Professors Branner, Stillman, and Gilbert of the Stanford faculty,

we beg to say that the dissatisfaction of the University management with Professor Ross antedated his utterances on the topics you refer to. His removal was not due primarily to what he published, said or thought in regard to coolie immigration or in regard to municipal ownership. We can assure you furthermore that in our opinion his removal cannot be interpreted as an interference with freedom of speech or thought within the proper and reasonable meaning of that expression. These statements are made with a full knowledge of the facts of the case. [113]

[111] "The Dismissal of Professor Ross," *Report of a Committee of Economists* (1901), p. 3.
[112] Letter of Seligman, Farnam, and Gardner to Jordan, December 30, 1900, in *Report of a Committee of Economists,* Appendix, p. 9.
[113] Letter of J. C. Branner, J. M. Stillman, and C. H. Gilbert to Seligman, Farnam, and Gardner, January 14, 1901, *ibid.,* p. 11.

The economists were not willing to take this judgment on faith, even from a faculty committee. They wrote to Jordan again, and received this pontifical reply:

[I do not] consider it expedient or proper to go into a discussion of extracts from my letters or conversations or my statements or alleged statements, or those of others, as published in the newspapers. . . . It will be necessary for you to assume my knowledge of all the facts.[114]

With this pronunciamento, the correspondence came to a close.

The report of the committee had to disclaim any definite knowledge of motives. But it concluded, nevertheless, that the official explanations of why Ross was dismissed were spurious or unsupported by the evidence. It concluded further that there *was* evidence to show that Mrs. Stanford's objections were based, at least in part, on Ross's utterances and beliefs. As it did not indulge in sweeping generalizations, the report did not explicitly support the theory of the conspiracy of big business.[115] But the indictment of Mrs. Stanford—backed as it was by the signatures of eighteen professors high in the Who's Who of social science—gave those who accepted the theory implicit and impressive confirmation.[116] Because of its narrow focus, the report did not mention the many peculiarities of the case—the incapacities of the university's patroness, the dependence of the university, and the absence of such counteracting forces as an effective, long-standing tradition, a stalwart university president, or a functioning board of trustees. Instead, it gave a picture of capitalist aggression which was unrelieved by the tints of personality and circumstance.

The case of John S. Bassett, which occurred in a different setting, shows the business patron in a different light. In 1894, when Bishop John C. Kilgo became its president, Trinity College in Durham, North Carolina, was an impecunious denominational college; in 1910, when Kilgo retired, it could boast a larger endowment than any other Southern college.[117]

---

[114] Letter of Jordan to Seligman, Farnam, and Gardner, February 7, 1901, *ibid.*, pp. 14–15.

[115] *Ibid.*, p. 6.

[116] Those who joined the authors in signing the document were John Bates Clark, Richard T. Ely, Simon H. Patten, Franklin H. Giddings, Davis R. Dewey, Frank W. Taussig, Henry C. Adams, Richmond Mayo-Smith, William J. Ashley, Charles H. Hull, Henry C. Emery, Henry R. Seager, John C. Schwab, Sidney Sherwood.

[117] The best treatment of Trinity College's history can be found in Paul Neff Garber, *John Carlisle Kilgo* (Durham, N.C., 1937). This may be supplemented by Robert H. Woody's "Biographical Appreciation of William Preston Few," in *The Papers and Addresses of William Preston Few* (Durham, N.C., 1951), and John Franklin Crowell, *Personal Recollections of Trinity College, North Carolina, 1887–1894* (Durham, N.C., 1939).

It owed its growth and good fortune to the generous benefactions of the Duke family, and it was bound, like Stanford, by a silver cord of obligation. President Kilgo, who had once been a Populist, became a defender of gold and the tobacco trust, which led one unfriendly wit to say that the old motto of the college, "Eruditio et Religio," had been extended by the influence of the Dukes to read "Eruditio et Religio et Sugario et Cigarro et Cherooto et Cigaretto et Kilgo." [118] But Durham was not Palo Alto. The Dukes, who were unabashed Republicans and leaders of the industrial "New South," were a suspect minority in the region, despised by social conservatives as the foes of white supremacy, feared by agrarian reformers as monopolistic exploiters of the poor.[119] Moreover, Trinity College, retaining its Methodist identity, was not ruled by a single oligarch, but by a board of ministers and businessmen. There was another difference, too: Kilgo belonged to the school of self-righteous preacher-presidents, and not to the newer tribe of public-relations experts. A champion of unpopular causes (he opposed the state university and took a liberal view of the Negro problem), he, and with him Trinity College, did not seek to be universally beloved.[120]

In 1903, John S. Bassett, the editor of the *South Atlantic Quarterly* and a professor of history at the college, made himself a target of attack by writing an article on the Negro problem. A wave of lynchings, disfranchisements, and Jim Crow laws had come in the wake of Southern Populism, and Bassett tried to calm the troubled waters with an appeal to sense and understanding. The Southerner should realize, wrote Bassett, that there are wide differences among Negroes, and that a man like Booker T. Washington, although atypical of the race, was "all in all the greatest man, save General Lee, born in the South in a hundred years." [121] The Southerner should realize that the Negro was becoming "too intelligent and too refined" to accept an inferior position, and that, to avert costly racial conflict, the white man must adopt "these children of Africa into our American life." The Southerner should realize that unscrupulous

[118] Garber, *John Carlisle Kilgo*, p. 226.
[119] The attack upon the Dukes by local conservatives and reformers is described in Josephus Daniels, *Editor in Politics* (Chapel Hill, N.C., 1941), pp. 116–18, 232–33, 426–38; Aubrey Lee Brooks, *Walter Clark, Fighting Judge* (Chapel Hill, N.C., 1944), pp. 102–28.
[120] See Luther L. Gobbel, *Church-State Relationships in North Carolina since 1776* (Durham, N.C., 1938), pp. 132–71; Garber, *John Carlisle Kilgo*, pp. 43–83.
[121] John S. Bassett, "Stirring Up the Fires of Race Antipathy," *South Atlantic Quarterly*, II (October, 1903), p. 299.

elements had seized upon the Negro issue and had awakened "a demon in the South" merely for political advantage.[122] The Negro problem, Bassett declared, cannot be solved by violent aggression and intimidation, but by the infusion of a spirit of conciliation into the hearts of Southern whites. Himself a son of the South, Bassett thought he could speak these unpleasant truths to his kith and kin with complete impunity.[123]

But he had struck a painful nerve of the sensitive Southern conscience. The article was greeted at once with calumnious abuse. Josephus Daniels, publisher of the Democratic, reform-minded Raleigh *News and Observer,* led the attack. The University of Chicago, he wrote, is not "the only institution which harbors freaks who rush into absurd statements and dangerous doctrines—statements which, if true, damn the State of North Carolina, and doctrines which, if carried out, would destroy the civilization of the South." He trusted that the professor would issue a full retraction; otherwise, he added ominously, "let us not anticipate the feeling that Southern people must entertain for a man who can give utterance to such opinions." Almost every hamlet journal and village gazette, playing to its groundlings, devised some new invective. The Lumberton *Robesonian* called him an utter fool; the Greensboro *Telegram* thought he was insane; the Greenville *Eastern Reflector* considered him subversive and incendiary. The Littleton *News Reporter* thought he aimed at a chair at Tuskegee; the Henderson *Gold Leaf* suggested that he was currying favor in the North.[124] The demand arose that Bassett be summarily dismissed, as though to take the professor's scalp would refute the ideas under it. Though Bassett held a doctorate from Johns Hopkins University and was the leading historian of the state,[125] his article was thought to prove its author unfit for his post.[126] Only because he was unpopular, the argument was advanced that he had lost his usefulness to the college. When local pressures mounted, and a boycott of the college was threatened, Bassett submitted his resignation.

But in the Trinity College situation, counterpressures could be registered. Eminent North Carolinians, sojourning in the North and re-

[122] *Ibid.,* p. 304.

[123] For commentary on the writing of this article, see Wendell H. Stephenson, "The Negro in the History and Writing of John Spencer Bassett," *North Carolina Historical Review,* XXV (October, 1948), pp. 427–41.

[124] Garber, *John Carlisle Kilgo,* pp. 244–60.

[125] Bassett had already published his *Regulators of North Carolina, Slavery and Servitude in the Colony of North Carolina, Anti-Slavery Leaders in North Carolina,* and *Slavery in the State of North Carolina.*

[126] Garber, *John Carlisle Kilgo,* pp. 252–53.

flecting its cultural perspective, were in touch with the Dukes and the trustees. Fifteen alumni, now students at Columbia University, petitioned the trustees not to fire Bassett, lest the "national reputation" of Trinity College be impaired.[127] Walter Hines Page, whose brother was a member of the trustees, saw the issue as one of academic freedom, and so presented it to Benjamin N. Duke:

> As to the correctness or incorrectness of the opinion he expressed in his article that has given offense, that is a question of no importance. But it is of the highest importance that a professor from Trinity College should be allowed to hold and express any rational opinion he may have about any subject whatever.[128]

And a powerful counterpressure built up within the college itself. Kilgo put his whole strength behind Bassett's defense. He addressed the board with a sermon on the virtues of Christian tolerance. Using religious rather than scientific rhetoric, he warned the trustees that the dismissal of Bassett would be a terrible blow to the college. It would "enthrone a despotism which the world thought was dead a thousand years ago"; it would commit Trinity to "the policies of the inquisition"; it would repudiate "the spirit and doctrines of the Methodist Episcopal Church, South." [129] He was prepared to resign if the board disregarded his urging. Not only Kilgo but every faculty member on the premises signed a petition for Bassett, and wrote a letter of resignation to be acted upon if the trustees were to fail them.[130] Undoubtedly, this unprecedented unanimity in the Trinity faculty was Kilgo's achievement. He gave them the moral support without which few would have dared to be bold; he urged no strategy of compromise to tempt them with safer options; he spared them the need to conspire, with its accompanying feelings of guilt.

The trustees voted 18 to 7 to keep Bassett on the faculty. Their decision was accompanied by a statement which was written by the Dean of the College. Though they disagreed with Bassett's opinions, the trustees took their stand for vindication on the ground of higher principles. They were, they declared, "unwilling to lend ourselves to any tendency to destroy or limit academic liberty, a tendency which has, within recent

---

[127] Petition of Bruce R. Payne and 14 others to Southgate, November 21, 1903, in Trinity College Papers, Duke University Library.

[128] Letter of Page to Benjamin N. Duke, November 13, 1903, in Trinity College Papers, Duke University Library.

[129] Garber, *John Carlisle Kilgo,* pp. 269–73.

[130] See "Memorial from the Faculty to the Trustees," December 1, 1903, *South Atlantic Quarterly,* III (January, 1904), 65–68.

years, manifested itself in some conspicuous instances." Extramural freedom of expression was included in their definition of academic freedom:
"We cannot lend countenance to the degrading notion that professors in
American Colleges have not an equal liberty of thought and speech with
all other Americans." They used social, political, and religious arguments
(not, it should be noted, scientific ones) to justify their view. Society
must learn that the evils of intolerance and suppression are infinitely worse
than the evils that folly can cause. "We believe that society in the end
will find a surer benefit by exercising patience than it can secure by yielding
to its resentments." Politically, it was important that "rights which were
bought with blood and suffering must not now be endangered for want
of patience, tolerance and a noble self-restraint." Finally, "Trinity College
is affiliated with a great church whose spirit and doctrines are tolerant
and generous, and a due regard for the teachings and traditions of this
Christian society requires us to exercise our judgment in harmony with
its spirit and doctrines." [131] These were memorable phrases, and they
became notable additions to the *belles-lettres* of academic freedom.

The religious tone of the document would lead one to suppose that
the ministers on the board, rather than the business elements, were the
main supporters of Bassett. But the opposite was true. Five of the seven
voting against Bassett were ministers in the Methodist Church, one was
a United States Senator, and only one was a local businessman—the
banker J. F. Bruton.[132] On the Bassett side, four ministers were aligned
with twelve bankers and industrialists. The businessmen who voted for
Bassett included James H. Southgate, head of the largest insurance firm
in the state and a director in a Durham bank; [133] William G. Bradshaw,
managing director of the largest furniture manufacturing company in
the South at that time; [134] Edmund T. White, president of the Bank of
Granville and a director in the Erwin Cotton Mills; [135] William R. Odell,
owner of one of the largest textile manufacturing plants in the state; [136]
James A. Long, director of the Lynchburg and Durham Railroad and

[131] "Trinity College and Academic Liberty: The Statement of the Trustees,"
South Atlantic Quarterly, III (January, 1904), 62–64.
[132] *National Cyclopedia of American Biography,* XXXVI, 129.
[133] Samuel A. Ashe, et al., *Biographical History of North Carolina* (Greensboro,
N.C., 1905), II, 410–16.
[134] *Ibid.,* III, 28–31.
[135] Archibald Henderson, ed., *North Carolina: The Old North State and the New*
(Chicago, 1941), III, 129–30.
[136] Ashe, *Biographical History,* II, 1325–27.

president of the Roxboro Mills.[137] And not least, Benjamin N. Duke, the patron, voted in Bassett's favor. Did he do so because he saw the attack on Bassett as an indirect attack on himself, his interests, and his patronage? Would he have done so had Bassett been accused of favoring silver or socialism? Motives are obscure in this as in every case. What is indisputable is that the patron stood foursquare for tolerance, and refused to pander to prevailing prejudice. Duke was reported to have said to Kilgo:

This man Bassett maybe has played the fool and oughtn't to be on the faculty, but he must not be lynched. There are more ways of lynching a man than by tying a hempen rope around his neck and throwing it over the limb of a tree. Public opinion can lynch a man, and that is what North Carolina is trying to do to Bassett now. Don't allow it. You'll never get over it if you do.[138]

In the Avesta of academic freedom, some patrons wore the cloven hoof, but others, it has clearly been recorded, joined the side of the angels.

Though our samples have been arbitrarily chosen, there is enough in the foregoing cases to indicate some of the flaws in the thesis of conspiracy. First of all, like all simplistic explanations, it lacked the social and psychological dimensions that the complexity of situations calls for. It omitted many significant factors—the disposition of the president, the professional status of the accused, the standing of the accusers—that may decide the fate of professors. It omitted many other significant factors—the geographical location of the college, its particular ideals and traditions, its receptivity to various pressures, the power and personality of the patron—that may determine the role of the businessman. It did not draw basic distinctions between different kinds of professorial heretics, such as theorists and activists; or between different kinds of business patrons, such as those who shared the biases of their community and those who were themselves nonconformists; or between different kinds of pressure from business, such as that which originated from patrons and trustees and that which originated from outside. Secondly, like all highly partisan theories, it falsely ascribed to one faction—in this case, to economic conservatives—a uniquely sinister role. But we have seen from the cases we have examined that virtue was not monopolized by "liberals" and that guilt was very widely distributed. The Wisconsin charter of academic freedom, the Trinity College statement, and the economists' report on

[137] *Ibid.*, III, 231–36.
[138] Robert H. Woody, "Biographical Appreciation of William Preston Few," pp. 40–41.

the Ross case, were not framed by liberal reformers, but by men of conservative leanings. Kilgo, Adams, and Seligman, no less than Ely, Ross, and Will, were in the vanguard in the battles for freedom. Indeed, one of the significant aspects of the cases of this period was the blurring of ideological lines within the academic profession, and the mustering of united support for professors under attack. This *tu quoque* theme can be applied to the infringements of academic freedom as well. In the altercations at Kansas State Populists were not morally superior to Republicans. There was little to choose between the attitudes of Mrs. Stanford, conservative, and those of Josephus Daniels, reformer. The weakness in the theory of conspiracy—and perhaps, too, the source of its psychological vitality—is that it projects the foibles of man onto particular men who are few, recognizable, and isolable. The germ of truth in the thesis of conspiracy is that power is conducive to evil. Devil theories of history are rarely categorically false, particularly when the devils they delineate are men who are very rich, who have taken controlling positions, and who are accustomed to being obeyed. But power may be a function of numbers, as well as a function of wealth; and power may be curbed and chastened by the safeguards of tradition and form.

THE THESIS OF CULTURAL INCOMPATIBILITY

The fear of conspiracy usually flourishes in times of social anxiety. When men face social problems too new for settled habits to control and too complex for current knowledge to explain, they will ascribe them to the work of outside agents—to the jealousy and malice of the gods, or to the intrigues of hostile strangers. But men abandon demonic explanations when, having lived with their problems awhile, they have lost their terror of them. In periods of confident reform, they will look upon social problems merely as functional disorders which intelligence is competent to correct; in periods of intellectual alienation, they will consider social problems rather as organic defects which satire best can expose. It was not by chance, therefore, that the thesis of conspiracy was exceedingly popular in the overwrought decade of the nineties. In the Progressive period that followed, and in the decade after the Great Crusade, the thesis of conspiracy lost favor, though it never disappeared from stock. By those devoted to good causes, a more profound analysis was desired on which to base a program of reform; by those who cultivated disillusion, a more sweeping hypothesis was required to give scope to satirical commentary. The thesis of cultural incompatibility was, therefore, more in keeping with the temper of these times. Critics of the period looked to the culture of capitalism, rather than to the machinations of capitalists, as the source of academic evils. They saw the threat to academic freedom arising in certain habits and values, not in wicked intentions; they condemned the businessman's ethos, not his malice prepense.

Thorstein Veblen's *The Higher Learning in America* (published in 1918, but written in the preceding decade) was the prototype and most effective presentation of this thesis. With his penchant for dramatic abstraction, Veblen constructed a polarity between the culture of science on the one hand and the culture of business on the other. At the one pole were the scientists who, under the "impulsion and guidance of idle curiosity," sought the "profitless quest of knowledge." Veblen considered their curiosity "idle" because it ignored considerations of expediency; he considered their knowledge "profitless" because it was unconcerned with self-advantage. At the other pole, and newly arrived, were the businessmen on the governing boards and the businessmen in academic dress assigned to the presidents' chairs. Not intentionally, but owing to habits of thought conditioned by their occupations, they have foisted on American universities their crude, utilitarian outlook; their parasitical, predatory tactics; their ethos of "quietism, caution, compromise, collusion and chicane." [139] Unwittingly, they have turned what should have been mansions of learning into what tend to be ordinary business establishments. Under their dominant aegis, the universities of the nation have adopted the hierarchical gradation of staff common to business management; the techniques of salesmanship and promotion native to competitive enterprises; and they have reduced American professors to the status of business hirelings. To Veblen, each of these businesslike features acted as a subtle restraint on the academic freedom of professors. First of all, the bureaucratization of the university served as a convenient method for controlling the faculty from above. Secondly, the promotional activity of the university put a premium on intellectual acquiescence. Thirdly, the reduction of the scholar to the status of an employee destroyed his self-respect and narrowed his freedom of action.[140]

[139] Thorstein Veblen, *The Higher Learning in America* (New York, 1918), p. 70.
[140] Of the vast literature that gives expression to this kind of anti-business animus, the following may be regarded as a representative sample: Robert C. Angell, *The Campus* (New York, 1928), pp. 215–18; John E. Kirkpatrick, *Academic Organi-*

Each part of Veblen's indictment contained an element of truth and yet conveyed an erroneous impression. Acutely, he discerned that the trend toward bureaucratization was transforming the university's personnel, structure, and behavior. This change was already evidenced in the army of academic functionaries—the deans, directors, registrars and secretaries—who had come upon the scene to manage the affairs of the university. It was evidenced in the organization of the faculty into a graded hierarchy of ranks, within which passage was controlled by a series of official promotions.[141] It was evidenced in the writing of rules that defined the rights and obligations of professors and trustees.[142] It marked, though it did not cause, the end of an academic era in which the college had been a community and the faculty a body of peers. That this bureaucratizing tendency brought with it new problems and new dangers no one can deny. Perceptively, Veblen caught the strain that bureaucracy introduces between the university's interest in efficiency and its interest in creative thought. There was (and continues to be) the danger that the ponderous apparatus of administration would deaden the spirit of the university by burdening it with procedures and tying it to routines. There was (and continues to be) the danger that the standard of efficiency, made the measure of all things, would rate scholarship only by its quantity, personality only by its docility, services only by their cost.[143]

But to ascribe these changes to business was very far from the mark. Certain practices of the business corporations—particularly those of office management and finance—were, it is true, adopted by the universities. But this in turn was a symptom of certain basic conditions that business and education shared. For one thing, the drive toward rational efficiency was stimulated by the problem of size. The modern university

---

zation and Control (Yellow Springs, Ohio, 1931); Scott Nearing, "The Control of Public Opinion in the United States," School and Society, XV (April 15, 1922), 421–22; "Report of the Committee on Academic Freedom and Tenure," Bulletin, AAUP, IV (February–March, 1918), 20-23; Frank L. McVey, "Presidential Address," National Association of State Universities, as quoted in Bulletin, AAUP, X (November, 1924), 87–88; Robert Cooley, "A Primary Culture for Democracy," Publications, American Sociological Society, XIII (December, 1918), 9.

[141] See A. B. Hollingshead, "Climbing the Academic Ladder," American Sociological Review, V (June, 1940), 384–94.

[142] See C. R. Van Hise, "The Appointment and Tenure of University Professors," as quoted in Science, XXXIII (February 17, 1911), 237.

[143] The effects of bureaucratization on academic life have been examined by Logan Wilson, The Academic Man: A Study in the Sociology of a Profession (New York, 1942), pp. 60 ff., 80 ff.; Charles H. Page, "Bureaucracy and Higher Education," Journal of General Education, V (January, 1951), 91–100.

was complex: the various specializations it embraced, the multiple functions it assumed, could only be joined and coordinated through ganglions of administration. The modern university was large: the multitudes of students it enrolled, the vast numbers of teachers it engaged, rendered relationships impersonal. The modern university, it was said, was too much infatuated with size. But "bigness" in America was not only the businessman's idol: it was worshiped, even while it was cursed, by every social element seeking to improve its position. Size was the key to reputation, size was the emblem of power, in a sharply competitive society strewn across a vast continent. Hence, "Big Business" was matched by "Big Labor"; in time "Big Government" came; it could not have been expected that "Big Education" would tarry.

Moreover, it should not be overlooked that a strong impetus toward bureaucratization arose from the ranks of professors, partly in response to the growing competition for placement. Between 1890 and 1900, the number of college and university teachers in the United States increased by fully 90 per cent.[144] Though the academic market continually expanded, a point of saturation, at least in the more attractive university positions, was close to being reached. At the opening of the University of Chicago, for example, the academic world was treated to the depressing spectacle of thousands of men applying to Harper for a job, most of them without prior introductions.[145] The law of supply and demand did not spare the academic market: as the number of available teachers increased, their bargaining power diminished; as more job-hunters came on the scene, job-holders felt less secure. Under these competitive conditions, the demand for academic tenure became urgent and those who urged it became vociferous. And the demand for academic tenure was, after all, a demand for rules and regulations—for contractual definitions of function, for uniform procedures for dismissal, for definite standards for promotion based on seniority and service—in short, for the definiteness, impersonality, and objectivity that are the essence of bureaucratism. Again, the underlying cause of the coming of bureaucracy was not merely the emulation of business methods, but the desire for security in the job which was also exemplified in the fight for civil service in government and for rules of seniority in industry.

Nor were these bureaucratic features necessarily inimical to academic

[144] *Bulletin,* United States Department of Interior, Biennial Survey of Education 1928–30 (Washington, D.C., 1932), number 20, p. 18.
[145] Goodspeed, *The University of Chicago,* pp. 134–36.

freedom. Instinctively, Veblen was repelled by the automatism of bureaucracy; uncritically, he assumed that bureaucracy served the purposes of tyranny. But rule by bureaucratic directive must be judged in the light of its alternative, which is rule by discretionary choice. There can be no doubt that the establishment of tenure by rank instead of by constant ingratiation and the fixing of salaries by schedules instead of by individual negotiation made professors more independent, more confident, and more willing to take risks.[146] As for the despotic uses of bureaucracy, here too judgment must follow an examination of the system that had existed. The decline, with the growth of bureaucracy, in administrative meddling with minutiae and in presidential rule by caprice is not the kind of obsolescence that the lover of freedom should deplore. At the same time, it is perfectly true that, insofar as bureaucratic administration can never be fully achieved, in every opening for discretion there lies also an opening for tyranny. Again, it is perfectly true that the rules are not self-enforcing and that where there is the will to circumvent them, that will can find a way. The rules are not the thing wherein one catches the conscience of the president. Tenure by rank can be negated by overlong periods of probation, by refusal to make promotions, or by that "judicious course of vexation" that compels professors to resign. Salary by schedule can be subverted by a range of salaries within each grade, assigned to the various recipients with a malicious partiality. But this is merely to say that the bureaucratic organization, like other forms, requires implementation by men who are loyal to its standards and spirit.

In theory, the bureaucratic system is adaptable to autocratic or democratic procedures. Given a hierarchical order, policy can still be determined at the lowest bureaucratic level—the level of the department—instead of at the apex.[147] Given a chain of command, the wishes of the faculty can still be effected through representation on the board of trustees or through control of higher appointments.[148] In practice, the academic

[146] The idea that eccentricities were better tolerated under the personalistic government of the old college than in the bureaucratized university has had much play in academic circles. Thus John Dewey: "The old-fashioned college faculty was pretty sure to be a thorough-going democracy in its way. Its teachers were selected more often because of their marked individual traits than because of pure scholarship. Each stood on his own. . . . All that is now changed." "Academic Freedom," *Educational Review,* XXIII (January, 1902), 12–13.

[147] "Report of Committee T," *Bulletin,* AAUP, XXIII (March, 1937), 224–28.

[148] See W. A. Ashbrook, "The Organization and Activities of Boards Which Control Institutions of Higher Learning," unpublished Ph.D. dissertation (Ohio State University, 1930).

bureaucracy functions in a situation that combines autocracy and democracy in varying degrees and ways. Cornell University can be cited as an example of a university at the democratic extreme. In 1917–18 Cornell was the only institution out of 100 public and private colleges and universities that allowed for faculty representation on the board of trustees, was one of the 10 institutions that provided for faculty nomination of deans, was one of the 27 institutions that gave professors the formal right to participate in the determination of educational policy.[149] Cornell was atypical, as was the institution where all important decisions were handed down through channels from above and where the faculty whiled away its time voting on academic trivia.[150] In 1940, the typical college or university was one that had no definite system for facilitating exchange of opinion between the faculty and trustees or regents, that did not provide a definite procedure whereby the faculty might consult the board of control in the choice of a president, a dean, or departmental chairman, but that did provide for the consultation of department heads with reference to all departmental budgetary needs. As a group, state universities had more faculty participation in budgetary procedures in 1940 than had the total group; women's colleges had a significantly larger amount of faculty-trustee cooperation and faculty participation in appointments, promotions, and dismissals; while the teachers colleges, in general, were more autocratic in their administrative procedures. Interestingly enough, the large endowed universities with graduate schools, where bureaucratization was most complete, were more democratic in their usages than was the total group.[151]

The emphasis on bureaucratization changed the direction of the struggle for academic freedom in this country. The fight for academic freedom became as a result a fight for precautionary rules, for academic legislation, not merely one in which the battles were *ex post facto* attempts to rectify injustices. For good and for ill, academic freedom and academic tenure have become inseparably joined. The good results are many. Too often, the attempt to achieve vindication after a professor has been dismissed is little more than a posthumous inquest: it is the better part of wisdom to look for and devise preventives. Too often, the issues of an academic-freedom case are obscured by the idle question of motives: tenurial rules provide a standard whose infraction is more easily demon-

---

[149] "Report of Committee T," *Bulletin,* AAUP, VI (January, 1920), 23–30.
[150] Logan Wilson, *The Academic Man,* p. 76.
[151] "Report of Committee T," *Bulletin,* AAUP, XXVI (April, 1940), 171–86.

strable. The danger, however, is that in fighting on the line of intramural law, professors may tend to abandon the line of social principle. With the emphasis on "firing" rather than on "hiring," the temptation is to make academic freedom coterminous with the security of professors in the gild, rather than with the social necessity of assembling independent men whatever their range of dissent.[152]

At no point did Veblen's irony go more deeply than when it penetrated the promotional zeal of the American university president. His depiction of the university president as a merchandiser of good will, as a "Captain of Erudition," was one of those clever caricatures that succeed by apt exaggeration. The Eliots, Harpers, Whites, and Butlers were indeed a new variety of their species, far more like the Rockefellers of their time than like the clergymen-presidents of the generation that preceded them. White's consolidation of capital to build a large university finds its illuminating parallel in the business activities of Morgan and United States Steel. Harper's piratical raid on the faculty of Clark University was indeed, as David Riesman remarks, an academic "Chapter of Erie." [153] Like their business contemporaries, they were superlative drummers in their trade; by dignified effrontery and persuasive skill they acquired patronage and support, and increased the power of their "firms." They were even more adept than their business contemporaries in drawing favorable publicity—to their universities by periodic celebrations and by conspicuous buildings and grounds, and to themselves by a relentless round of speech-making and ceremonializing. Veblen thought the influence of these presidents on the freedom of the university was harmful in the extreme. Along with their advertiser's skill went, he thought, all of the advertiser's timidities. The aphorism of expedience, that the customer is always right, became, he thought, the cardinal motto of the university. A conformity to current prepossessions, a sedulous attention to amenities, an acceptance of things as they are—these were inescapable by-products when businessmen ran universities and universities were run as businesses.

Yet, though here the shaft of irony in Veblen's work went deep, it also went astray. That the presidents in this era sometimes equivocated and often played it safe, that they seldom inspired their faculties to high courage and bold ventures, may be taken without question as true. But

[152] See, for the relationship of academic tenure to academic freedom, Henry M. Wriston, "Academic Freedom," *The American Scholar,* IX (Summer, 1940), 339 ff.; "Tenure: A Symposium," *ibid.,* IX (Autumn, 1940), 419 ff.

[153] David Riesman, *Thorstein Veblen* (New York, 1953), p. 102.

to blame this on their adoption of business attitudes is to make the dubious assumption that timidity and acquiescence were new in the presidential character. If, however, the liegemen of the Lord were more intrepid than the captains of erudition, if they were more finely attuned to the idea of academic freedom, history has not recorded it. Indeed, it was a romantic and erroneous assumption that gallantry could not accord with a business interest and competence. The peaks of presidential valor reached in the business age exceeded any of the preceding era. Among those in the presidential chair who have sacrificed assets for ideals, none can compare with Lowell, who reputedly turned down a $10,000,000 bequest offered to Harvard in 1914 on condition that a professor be dismissed.[154] In the way of united action, there is nothing to compare with the Andrews case, when Eliot, Gilman, and Seth Low united to defend a colleague who was assailed by his board of trustees.[155] Moreover, it is important to bear in mind that if these modern presidents were "salesmen," by the same token they were also energetic missionaries. In mediating between the two worlds, the leading figures of this group—the Eliots, Harpers, and their like—brought university ideals to business, as well as business ideals to the university. They were, as we have seen, leaders in the fight for evolution and in the promulgation of German ideals; no victory in the record of the educational revolution neglects to record their names. They promoted not merely the externals, but the spirit of the university: not merely its spurious side-shows, but its intrinsic love of knowledge, its interest in research, its concepts of academic freedom. These ideals might well have languished had these academic men of the world not carried the gospel to the Gentiles. Let it be conceded that there were presidents of lesser rank whose minds were more completely Rotarian. Yet even they were an educative force, if only by reiterating simple platitudes in the course of academic rituals. The thesis of cultural incompatibility saw the businessman corrupting academia, never academia enlightening the businessman. But the fact was that these two contrasted cultures, through the mediation of the presidents, passed in a two-way flow.

Veblen's third charge against the business culture—that it reduced professors to the rank of hired hands—is one that bears more extensive examination. The truth at the core of this indictment is that lay academic government is a kind of ink-blot test in the interpretation of which men

[154] Henry Aaron Yeomans, *Abbott Lawrence Lowell, 1856–1943* (Cambridge, Mass., 1948), pp. 314–17.
[155] Elizabeth Donnan, "A Nineteenth-Century Academic Cause Célèbre," p. 41.

may project preconceptions. A board of trustees could be likened by churchmen to a vestry, by politicians to a governmental agency, by businessmen to a corporation directorate. It took a certain sophistication not to make these identifications, not to suppose, for example, that a president was but a general manager in charge of operational details, or that a professor, because he was hired and paid by the board of trustees, was therefore its private employee. This sophistication was lacking among many business trustees and many business spokesmen. When President Andrews of Brown University voiced sentiments that affronted the trustees and potential donors, one newspaper was of the opinion that "he was only a servant; and a servant must do as his employers wish, or quit their service." [156] One trustee of Northwestern University, a patent lawyer and an officer of the Western Railroad Association,[157] presented this dictum:

As to what should be taught in political science and social science, they [the professors] should promptly and gracefully submit to the determination of the trustees when the latter find it necessary to act. . . . If the trustees err it is for the patrons and proprietors, not for the employees, to change either the policy or the personnel of the board.[158]

This was not an adventitious or atypical comment: when George H. Shibley in 1900 polled the trustees at Chicago, Columbia, Princeton, Yale, Johns Hopkins, Pennsylvania, and American University, he found that the opinion of the trustees whom he interviewed agreed almost unanimously with that of the Northwestern trustee.[159] Perhaps in the intervening years, trustees have grown so sophisticated that they do not now often express such views; but it will not be maintained that they have also become so wise that they do not, on occasion, act upon them.

Again, however, it is important to point out that the businessmen on boards of trustees did not depart from academic tradition. From earliest times, the assumption of American trustees was that professors were employees, and the only way in which the post-Civil War period differs from what went before was that in the later period the professors were more disposed to question the theory, to use professional pressures to mitigate it, and to seek redress in the courts. To be sure, when professors

[156] St. Louis *Globe-Democrat* (July 30, 1897), quoted in Will, "A Menace to Freedom," p. 251.

[157] Northwestern University, *Alumni Record of the College of Liberal Arts* (Evanston, Ill., 1903), pp. 75, 82, 89–90.

[158] Quoted in George H. Shibley, "University and Social Questions," *Arena,* XXIII (March, 1900), 293.

[159] *Ibid.,* p. 295.

took questions of tenure to court, the decisions were mostly unfavorable. This helped to create the impression that the business ideology had taken control of the bench even as it had captured the university. But that impression was mistaken to this extent—the mood of the courts had not changed on the fundamental issues. Before the Civil War, the argument that professors were officers of the corporation with a permanent right to their positions was twice rebuffed in the courts. On the other hand, in the post-Civil War period, professors themselves pressed the view in the courts that they were mere employees of the trustees. Once more, it is a specious reading of the record to say that American professors fell from a pristine high estate.[160]

A brief review of the cases bearing on the legal status of professors in America may supply the historical depth that was missing from Veblen's analysis. The fate of the argument for the "freehold" provides our most suggestive clue. In 1790, in the case of *The Reverend John Bracken* vs. *The Visitors of William and Mary College,* John Taylor of Caroline argued in the Virginia Court of Appeals that professors had a freehold in their office, in which they had tenure for life, and of which they could not be deprived without a hearing and a show of cause. In English common law, the freehold originally designated a holding in land by a freeman in return for homage and services to the lord; later, it designated a tenure in a saleable office to which there were attached rights to collect fees from the public—e.g., a clerkship of a court.[161] Taylor applied this artifact of the common law to the office of the teacher in several ways. He argued that professors had an interest in the landed estates of the corporation. He pointed to the fact that the masters of William and Mary College voted for the college's representative in the Assembly, and thus had, as it were, a political equity in their jobs. He also spoke ambiguously of the "judicial" complexion of the master's office. If Taylor's reasoning was not altogether clear, the gist of his argument was plain. "The Visitors seem wholly to have mistaken their office. They seem to have considered themselves as the incorporated society; and the president and masters as an appendage upon them"—that is, they believed themselves to be employers and the president and professors mere employees. "But the president and masters

---

[160] We take issue on this point with J. E. Kirkpatrick, who has argued that the contractual, employee status of professors was a phenomenon of the post-Civil War period. See *Academic Organization and Control,* pp. 189–201.

[161] Richard B. Morris, "Freehold," *Encyclopedia of the Social Sciences,* VI, 461–65; W. S. Holdsworth, *A History of English Law* (Boston, 1922), I, 247–49.

were a lay corporation, having rights, privileges and emoluments, of which they could not be deprived; at least, without some form of trial." [162]

John Marshall was the attorney for the Visitors in this case, and his arguments against the freehold doctrine have a very modern ring. Marshall denied, first of all, that professors had any share in the property of the corporation. "This is a private corporation. The persons who compose it have no original property of their own, but it belongs to the corporation. There would seem to be no principle on which this College should be placed in a different class of corporations from all other colleges." The estates of the college

are the gift of the founder. They are his voluntary gift. To this gift he may annex such conditions as his own will or the caprice may dictate. Every individual, to whom it is offered, may accept or reject it; but, if he accepts, he accepts it subject to the conditions annexed by the donor. The condition annexed in private corporations is, that the will of the Visitors is decisive.

Marshall denied, secondly, that professors were appointed for life, pointing out that this was not provided for in the charter or statutes. Thirdly, he denied that the courts had the general right to review the acts of a governing body. "If . . . the Visitors have only legislated on a subject upon which they have the right to legislate, it is not for this court to enquire, whether they had legislated wisely or not." Finally, he denied that the professor who brought suit was entitled to a hearing, though he argued this on the narrow ground that Mr. Bracken had not been arraigned for misconduct (that is, he was not deprived of his office by a judicial act), but had been dismissed because the office was declared nonexistent (that is, he was deprived of his office by a legislative act).[163] The Court, without rendering an opinion, voted in the Visitors' favor on the merits of the case.

The second example of the use of the freehold argument was Webster's plea in the Dartmouth College case (1819). By an interesting historical coincidence, Marshall, then Chief Justice of the United States Supreme Court, was the presiding judge. Here the argument took a somewhat different form than it had taken in the Bracken case, for Webster was not defending the interests of professors against the trustees, but the interest of the trustees against a legislature which had repealed the Dartmouth charter and had changed the composition and powers of the college's board without the latter's consent. Hence, Webster admitted that professors were accountable to the trustees, who could hire and fire them for

[162] 3 *Call* 587.   [163] 3 *Call* 592, 595, 598.

good cause. But, he contended, the legislature, by appointing persons other than trustees to exercise this power over professors, had deprived the professors of their "freeholds." "All the authorities," said Webster, "speak of the fellowships in colleges as freeholds, notwithstanding the fellows may be liable to be suspended or removed, for misbehavior, by their constituted visitors." This was rhetoric: if all the authorities said so, Taylor would have won the Bracken case; indeed, if any authority said so, Webster would probably have cited it, something he conspicuously did not do. Instead of legal backing, Webster gave his position strong sentimental support:

No description of private property has been regarded as more sacred than college livings. They are the estates and freeholds of a most deserving class of men; of scholars who have consented to forego the advantage of professional and public employments, and to devote themselves to science and literature, and the instruction of youth, in the quiet retreats of academic life. Whether, to dispossess and oust them; to deprive them of their office, and turn them out of their livings; to do this, not by the power of their legal visitors, or governors, but by acts of the legislature; and to do it without forfeiture and without fault; whether all this be not in the highest degree an indefensible and arbitrary proceeding, is a question of which there would seem to be but one side fit for a lawyer or a scholar to espouse.[164]

Marshall ignored the argument altogether and based his decision in favor of the college on the obligation of contract clause.[165] The freehold argument was rarely heard from again.[166] The argument had never been accepted in an American court of law, and all that can be said for its standing in pre-Civil War legal thought is that it possessed enough plausibility to encourage attorneys to make use of it.

One historic pre-Civil War case set the precedent for judicial restraint in reviewing the actions of trustees that was to prevail in the later period. In 1827, after a trial, the Visitors of Phillips Academy in Andover removed James Murdock from his professorial chair. Murdock claimed that the articles of charge were not sufficiently definite and particular, and he challenged the statutory right of the Visitors to dismiss a professor when-

[164] 17 *United States Reports* 584.

[165] As for the relevance of the freehold argument in Webster's brief, compare Albert Beveridge's statement that Webster was "laying the foundation for his . . . reasoning on the main question" with David Loth's opinion that Webster took "the most blatant excursion into subjects not involved." *Life of John Marshall* (New York, 1919), IV, 240; *Chief Justice John Marshall* (New York, 1949), p. 293.

[166] It cropped up again in the minority decision of Judge Dent in *Hartigan* vs. *Board of Regents of West Virginia University*, 49 *West Virginia* 14 (1901).

ever in their judgment there was "sufficient cause." The Supreme Court of Massachusetts, to which appeal was brought as provided for in the statutes, declared that it was for the officers of the institution to decide whether the "gross neglect of duty," which it said had been adequately demonstrated, warranted dismissal. The Court would only review the case to see that the accused had his common-law right to a fair hearing. The Court did imply, on the other hand, that a professor was a good deal more than an employee: "We hold that . . . no man can be deprived of his office, which is valuable property, without having the offense with which he is charged, 'fully and plainly, substantially and formally described to him.' " [167] But this notion did not last out the Civil War period. In the case of *Union County* vs. *James* (1853), the Pennsylvania courts declared that a professor was an employee and not an officer of the corporation, and was subject to taxation as such.[168]

In certain post-Civil War cases, the professors themselves were the ones to claim the status of employees, seeking contractual protections against the abolition or vacation of their offices by legislatures or trustees. When a Missouri law of 1859 declared certain professorial offices vacant in the state university, a professor unsuccessfully challenged its constitutionality on the ground that it impaired the obligation of contract. In support of his case, the professor, B. S. Head, offered the argument that

although the university may be a public corporation, the professors therein are not public officers; that they are mere servants for hire, with whom contracts for service may be made, and which are binding upon the corporation; that they have a vested right and legal property in their salaries and offices, of which they can be divested only by legal proceedings; that a contract for such service, at a fixed salary, and for a stipulated period, is as much within the purview of the constitutional provision which prohibits the violation of contracts by the passage of a law.[169]

Again, in *Butler* vs. *Regents of the University* (1873), a professor sought to establish himself as an employee in order to sue for the recovery of salary which the Regents of the University of Wisconsin had resolved no longer to pay. The judge upheld the professor, if not the larger interests of professordom, by declaring:

[167] *James Murdock, Appellant from a Decree of the Visitors of the Theological Institutions of Phillips Academy, in Andover,* 24 *Mass. Reports* (7 Pick) 303 (1828).

[168] *Union County* vs. *James,* 21 *Penn State Reports* 525 (1853).

[169] *B. S. Head* vs. *The Curators of the University of the State of Missouri,* 47 *Missouri Reports* 220 (1871).

We do not think that a professor in the university is a public officer in any sense that excludes the existence of a contract between himself and the board of regents that employed him. . . . It seems to us that he stands in the same relation to the board that a teacher in a public school stands with respect to the school district by which such teacher is employed; and that is purely in a contract relation.[170]

In another case, the court, holding that the professors *were* public officers, declared that the legislature could pass a law abolishing a professorial office without violating the Constitution.[171] On the other hand, when professors sought *quo warranto* and *mandamus* actions, which are available only to public or private officers, then they were willing to argue that they were *not* employees.[172]

The notion that professors had declined in the law from the status of officers to that of hired hands was fictitious. Where the professors sustained heavy losses was not in the definition of their status, but in the impairment of the protections of contract which came about through judicial

[170] *Butler* vs. *The Regents of the University,* 32 *Wisconsin Reports* 124 (1873).

[171] *Vincenheller* vs. *Reagan,* 69 *Arkansas Reports* 460 (1901).

[172] *Quo warranto* is a proceeding to determine the right to the use or exercise of a franchise or office and to oust the holder from his enjoyment, if his claim is not well founded. Thus, in *C. S. James* vs. *Phillips* (1 *Delaware County Reports* 41 [1880]), a professor of the University of Lewisberg, who had been dismissed by the trustees without a trial, obtained a writ of *quo warranto* against his successor. The Supreme Court of the State of Pennsylvania overruled the issuance of the writ, saying: "No authority is given to issue the writ against a mere servant, employee or agent of the corporation. It was therefore incumbent on the relator [James] to show that the professorship . . . is a corporate office, and that he was unjustly and illegally removed therefrom. . . . The mere creation of a professorship does not endow it with a fixed term of existence or give its incumbent a term either for life or good behavior. Corporate offices are such only as are expressly required by the charter. The professorship in question is manifestly not one of that character." *Phillips* vs. *Commonwealth ex rel. James,* 98 *Penn. State Reports* 394 (1881).

A writ of mandamus may be issued to compel proper authorities to enact or enforce the laws or to perform a specific duty imposed on them by the law. In the absence of other adequate remedies, mandamus is a proper remedy to restore a person to the possession of a public office from which he had been illegally removed. Thus, when Professor Kelsey of the New York Post Graduate Medical School sought to compel the trustees to reinstate him through mandamus, the Appellate Division of the New York State Court denied the writ: "His application, so far as the mandamus is concerned seems to be based upon the notion that the position of a professor in the defendant's college is in the nature of an office, and that it is the province of mandamus to reinduct him into that office and keep him there. This is an erroneous view, both of the relator's true position and of the office of the writ. The college is a private corporation, and its professors and instructors are simply professional men appointed to serve the institution in a particular manner." *The People of the State of New York ex rel. Charles B. Kelsey* vs. *New York Post Graduate Medical School and Hospital,* 29 *Appellate Division* 244 (1898).

interpretation of state statutes and through "escape clauses" in by-laws and contracts. After the Civil War, the courts were called upon to decide whether state statutes vesting discretionary power to dismiss professors in the regents nullified the tenurial protections of contracts.[173] In 1878, in the case of *Kansas State Agricultural College* vs. *Mudge,* the court refused to make the governing board so supreme and irresponsible that it could violate any agreement it entered into with professors. The court then declared:

While the legislature intended to confer upon the board of regents extensive powers, yet it did not intend to confer upon them the irresponsible power of trifling with other men's rights with impunity. And making the regents responsible for their acts does not in the least abridge their powers. It only tends to make them more cautious and circumspect in the exercise of their powers.[174]

In time, however, a different interpretation came to prevail, and the trustees and regents, unless the statutes provided to the contrary, were empowered to dismiss professors at will. In *Gillan* vs. *Board of Regents of Normal Schools* (1894) the court held that a board of regents could remove a professor without a trial of charges.[175] In *Devol* vs. *Board of Regents of the University of Arizona* (1899), the court held that "when the legislative Assembly gave the board of Regents power to hire and dismiss employees . . . they did not grant to the board the power to bind themselves, or to bind others . . . by a contract different from that which was prescribed by statute." [176] In *Hartigan* vs. *Board of Regents of West Virginia University* (1901), the court denied that it had the right to exercise judicial review of the judgment of a board. "Is the Board of Regents to do as it pleases, without control, erroneous as its actions may be? Yes, so far as the courts are concerned." [177] In *Ward* vs. *The Regents of Kansas State Agricultural College* (1905), the court decided that the statute authorizing the regents to remove any professor "whenever the interests of the college required" became a condition for the employment of a professor, overruling all contractual provisions to the contrary.[178] With few exceptions,[179] the sanctioning of arbitrary and unilateral dis-

---

[173] See Edward C. Elliott and M. M. Chambers, *The Colleges and the Courts* (New York, 1936), p. 81.

[174] 21 *Kansas Reports* 223.   [175] 88 *Wisconsin* 7.

[176] 6 *Arizona Reports* 259.   [177] 49 *West Virginia Reports* 14.

[178] 138 *Federal Reporter* 372.

[179] *State Board of Agriculture* vs. *Meyers,* 20 *Colorado App.* 139 (1904). Also, *Matter of Kay* vs. *Board of Higher Education* (The "Bertrand Russell Case"), 173 *Misc. Reports* 943, 18 *N.Y.S.* (2d) *Sup. Ct.* (1940).

missal came to represent the law. Private institutions were also affected
by this animus of the courts. At Drury College, where the by-laws contained an explicit provision against sectarian tests for the faculty, a
professor was dismissed for donating a book on theosophy to the library.
In *Darrow* vs. *Briggs* (1914), the court held that the action of the trustees
was permissible under the contractual clause that allowed it to dismiss
professors "when the interest of the college shall require it." [180] It was
not to a new status, but to a more helpless state, that the law reduced
American professors.

And yet the ineffaceable fact remains that professors did feel that
they had been socially and institutionally demoted. If this feeling was not
altogether warranted, it was not for that reason less poignant; if it was
based on a poor historical judgment, it was still a significant historical
fact. It is all very well to point out that, as far as income is a social de-
nominator, professors in 1893 had an average income 75 percent higher
than that of clerical workers, 75 percent higher than that of Methodist
and Congregationalist ministers, 300 percent higher than that of industrial
laborers.[181] Though the inflation that set in after 1900 cost them dearly,
even so, in the decade of the 1920s, the income of professors was higher
than that of social workers, ministers, journalists, and librarians.[182] It is
all very well to point out that at no time in the past had professors been
consulted by government so frequently, or for so wide a range of projects,
as in the era before the First World War and during the war itself.[183]
One can also point to the fact that, of the Ph.D.'s graduated from seventeen major institutions between 1884 and 1904, one out of three was
mentioned in *Who's Who* and in *American Men of Science;* [184] that as late
as 1910 academic scientists were still mostly recruited from the homes of
clergymen, farmers, and well-to-do businessmen of native American or
northern European stock—that is, from highly regarded social and ethnic

[180] 261 *Missouri Reports* 244.

[181] John J. Tigert, "Professional Salaries," Address before the Association of
American Colleges, in *School and Society*, XV (February, 25, 1922), 208; Paul
H. Douglas, *Real Wages in the United States, 1890–1926* (New York, 1930), pp.
382, 386, 392.

[182] Harold F. Clark, *Life Earnings in Selected Occupations in the United States*
(New York, 1937), p. 6. Cf. also, Viva Boothe, *Salaries and the Cost of Living in
Twenty-seven State Universities and Colleges, 1913–1932* (Columbus, Ohio, 1932).

[183] See Charles McCarthy, *The Wisconsin Idea* (New York, 1912).

[184] Gregory D. Walcott, "Study of Ph.D.'s from American Universities," *School
and Society*, I (January 9, 1915), 105.

elements.[185] Yet still there was profound dissatisfaction and the deep-seated feeling among professors that their profession had lost caste. To this, no doubt, the presence of the big businessmen contributed, but not in the manner indicated by the thesis of cultural incompatibility. The addition of a new wealthy extreme to the range of classes in America seemed to depress and demote all the others. Compared with the enormous returns that accrued to business, the professor's emoluments seemed small. Compared with the high adventure of finance and the epics of industrial derring-do, his existence seemed drab. Compared with the honors heaped on the practical men, the distinctions accorded the thinking men seemed grudging and picayune. The illusion of a paradise lost was viewed against a perceptual field of sharp contemporary social contrasts.

[185] J. McKeen Cattell, "Families of American Men of Science," *Popular Science Monthly,* LXXXVI (May, 1915), 504–15.

X: ORGANIZATION, LOYALTY, AND WAR

THE ESTABLISHMENT of the American Association of University Professors in 1915 is significant both as a culmination and as a beginning. It was the culmination of tendencies toward professorial self-consciousness that had been operating for many decades. It was the beginning of an era in which the principles of academic freedom were codified, and in which violations of academic freedom were systematically investigated and penalized. To analyze the movement that brought about the establishment of the AAUP is to capture the flavor of American academic life in the period between the turn of the century and the First World War. To examine the activities and achievements of the AAUP since its establishment is to view the main outlines of the problems of academic freedom in the twentieth century. Finally, to explore the difficulties that the AAUP encountered during the First World War is to introduce some of the complications and predicaments that academic freedom encounters today.

THE ESTABLISHMENT OF THE AAUP

Why did the AAUP appear so late in the story? Looking back, one can discover several occasions which might have brought it into being but which somehow did not do so. One might suppose that the Darwinian crisis, in challenging the academic patriotism that espouses "my institution, right or wrong," would have given rise to a professorial union. Nevertheless, the 1860s and 1870s passed without a serious attempt at organization. One might suppose that the alarums and excursions of the Populist period would have led to a defensive alliance of professors. But, though several professors suggested united action and the economists set up an investigating committee in the Ross case, no permanent organization was established.[1] The fifteen-year hiatus between the setting up of the econ-

[1] Thomas E. Will had written to Ely that there was a need "to form some kind of association for mutual defense and protection," and Sidney Sherwood of Johns

omists' investigating committee and the constitution of Committee A of the AAUP cannot entirely be explained by a scarcity of academic-freedom cases.[2] While there was a falling off in the number of cases in that period, there were enough of them to whet the anxiety of professors—take, for instance, the several well-publicized cases in the South, particularly the Bassett case; the Peck and Spingarn cases at Columbia University; the rumors of pressure against liberals and radicals at the University of Pennsylvania; and, of the thirty-one cases handled by Committee A in the first two years of its existence, those which had been incubating for a rather long time.[3] The inertia of the professors seems all the more curious when one remembers that other professionals in America, notably the lawyers and the doctors, were banding together in this period to protect their special interests.

One must seek the reason for delay in the factors that divided the professorial community and militated against the development of united opinion and action. One of these factors was the conditions of scholarly work. Factories, offices, and mines are places of socialization; but libraries, laboratories, and classrooms seclude the academic worker and turn him to his own resources. Nevertheless, the doctors and the lawyers were able to overcome the disadvantages of their self-sufficiency. Perhaps more unique and important in delaying professional organization were the institutional and disciplinary barriers that cut across the professorial community. In America, academic matters tended either to be handled parochially by each individual institution (in the absence of a ministry of education or a unifying educational tradition, each institution was a law unto itself), or else nationally by one or another of the learned societies (which often embraced specialists who were not professors). The different

---

Hopkins had suggested to Ely that a professional organization to investigate academic freedom cases was needed. The idea was in the air, but nothing was done to effect it. Letter of Will to Ely, October 15, 1895; letter of Sherwood to Ely, December 22, 1900, in Ely Papers.

[2] Stanley Rolnick makes this assumption in "The Development of the Idea of Academic Freedom and Tenure in the United States, 1870–1920," unpublished Ph.D. dissertation (Wisconsin, 1952), pp. 237, 284.

[3] For cases arising in the South, see Leon Whipple, *The Story of Civil Liberty in the United States* (New York, 1927), p. 320; Carrol Quenzel, "Academic Freedom in Southern Colleges and Universities," unpublished Master's thesis (University of West Virginia, 1933). For the situation at Pennsylvania, see Edward P. Cheyney, *History of the University of Pennsylvania, 1740–1940* (Philadelphia, 1940), pp. 367–69. For the conflicts of Peck and Spingarn with President Butler, see Horace Coon, *Columbia: Colossus on the Hudson* (New York, 1947), pp. 122–25; Columbia *Alumni News*, II (May 18, 1911), 548.

standards and merits of "colleges" and "universities," the medley of abilities and personalities blanketed by the title of "professor," the gradations of experience and repute signified by different academic ranks, all induced caste divisions.[4] Most important, there was a deep aversion among academic men to entering into an organization whose purposes smacked of trade unionism. The idealism of the profession, built on the rhetoric of service and sustained by psychic compensations, eschewed any activity that had material gain as its main object. The ideology of the profession, claiming to transcend all ideology, did not countenance permanent commitments even to an organization for self-help. The dignity of the profession, fashioned on a genteel code of manners, was opposed to the tactics of the pressure group.[5] And over and above all this, there was the fear of administrative reprisal, and a certain inertness and timidity which the academic mind had acquired through years of ivied isolation.

In the decade prior to the establishment of the AAUP, many of these barriers were broken down. Part of the work of demolition was accomplished by a force that had long been active—the appeal to collective effort inspired by the ideals of science. In discussing the aims of the AAUP in his 1922 presidential address, E. R. A. Seligman paid his re-

[4] See Henry Pritchett, "Reasonable Restrictions upon the Scholar's Freedom," *Publications of the American Sociological Society,* IX (April, 1915), 152.

[5] The further problem of whether professors should join labor unions has agitated the profession from that day to this. Against such affiliation, it was maintained that teachers serve the public; that, unlike labor, pecuniary gain is not their main object; that the strike and other labor tactics of intimidation are indefensible for teachers; that traditions must be interpreted and passed on without bias; that the competitive situation which defines the essential function of a trade union does not exist in the academic calling, where teachers and trustees are both custodians of the public interest. Cf. W. C. Ruediger, "Unionism among Teachers," *School and Society,* VIII (November 16, 1918), 589–91. C. E. Myers, "Should Teachers Affiliate with the AFL," *School and Society,* X (November 22, 1919), 594–97; A. O. Lovejoy, "Teachers and Trade Unions," *Educational Review,* LX (September, 1920), 108–19; and more recent comments, Arthur O. Lovejoy, "Professional Association or Trade Union," *Bulletin,* AAUP, XXIV (May, 1938), 410–15; Samuel P. Capen, "The Teaching Profession and Labor Unions," *The Management of Universities* (Buffalo, 1953), pp. 56–63. On the other side, it has been argued that there can be no protection of professional ideals without improvement in the teacher's economic security; that boards of trustees are allied with business; that the conditions of teaching are indeed like those of labor; that the AFL does not have a class ideology; that the unwillingness to join with labor is evidence of academic snobbery; that unions are a democratic force. Cf. Bird Stair, "The Unionizing of Teachers," *School and Society,* X (December 13, 1919), 699–703; Harry A. Overstreet, "Should Teachers' Organizations Affiliate with Organized Labor," *Survey,* XLIII (March 13, 1920), 736–37; John Dewey, "Why I Am a Member of the Teacher's Union," *American Teacher,* XII (January, 1928), 3–6.

spects to those persisting ideals. "Loyalty to our institution is admirable," he declared,

but if our institution for some unfortunate reason stands athwart the progress of science, or even haltingly follows that path, we must use our best efforts to convince our colleagues and the authorities of the error of their ways. . . . In prosecuting this end we need both individual and collective effort. The leisure of the laboratory and of the study count for much; but almost equally important is the stimulus derived from contact with our colleagues.[6]

"The progress of science"—there was a vibrant tocsin to arouse the most sluggish professors.

Another slow-working factor was the constant tension between administrators and faculties. Of particular importance in building camaraderie among professors was the conflict over the question of who should speak for higher education. Trustees, presidents, and deans assumed that they had the right to act as its spokesmen, and the editors of professional journals did nothing to challenge that assumption. It began to gall professors that the public identified the voice of the presidents of the universities with the voice of the profession itself, that the league of university presidents should call itself the "Association of American Universities." Prior to the establishment of *School and Society* in 1915, which coincided with the publication of the first *Bulletin* of the AAUP, only one of the educational journals—Cattell's *Science*—registered professorial opinion that was critical of the operations of the university. At a time when professors were attacking businessmen in the popular press,[7] *Education* (founded 1881) had published before 1914 only three articles (and those laudatory) on the academic role of businessmen, and *Educational Review* (founded 1891 and under the editorship of Nicholas Murray Butler) did not print a clear-cut attack on the businessman until 1906.[8] Nor was the university a place where professors felt free to criticize their superiors. Evidence of this feeling of constraint can be found in the debate held in

[6] E. R. A. Seligman, "Our Association—Its Aims and Accomplishments, *Bulletin,* AAUP, VIII (February, 1922), 106.

[7] Claude C. Bowman, *The College Professor in America* (Philadelphia, 1938), pp. 173–74.

[8] In *Education,* these articles were by Howard A. Bridgman, "Clark University," X (December, 1889), 239; an editorial on the Ross case unfriendly to Ross, XXI (January, 1901), 307; an editorial on the "Peabody Fund," I (March, 1881), 329. William Cranston Lawton's "The Decay of Academic Courage" was the first highly critical article on the businessman to appear in the *Educational Review* (XXXII [November, 1906], 395–404), and it was quickly answered by J. H. Canfield's article of the same title (XXXIII [January, 1907], 1–10).

the early stages of the founding of the AAUP on the question of whether college and university presidents were to be admitted into the organization. In opposing their admittance, Professor Bloomfield of Johns Hopkins University made the suggestive remark that "this is the first opportunity we have had of being ourselves." [9] When it was proposed that presidents be allowed to speak but not to vote, Cattell moved to amend the proposal by asking that the presidents have the right to vote, but not the right to speak.[10] Another professor expressed the fear that professors would be outvoted by administrators because the former could not afford the expense of attending the meetings, whereas administrators would have their expenses paid by the institution.[11] In the end, it was decided that "no administrative officer who does not give a substantial amount of instruction shall be eligible for membership." [12] This was not to be a company union. The professors sought a platform for their own opinions, a journal for their own ideas, an organization that they would control.

The movement toward an association of professors was pushed forward by more immediate factors as well. One of these was the spirit and ideology of Progressivism. Professors, no less than politicians, caught the epidemic fever for reform. Opposition to boss rule in the cities had its counterpart in opposition to trustee rule in universities; certain instruments advocated by political reformers—the initiative, the primary, the referendum—were advocated as well by professors to make academic government more responsible. Cattell used Progressive ideas when he wrote that "no one believes that a city should be owned by a small self-perpetuating board of trustees who would appoint a dictator to run it, to decide what people could live there, what work they must do and what incomes they should receive. Why should a university be conducted in that way?" [13] Several universities took action in response to this kind of criticism. In 1916, on the basis

[9] H. Carrington Lancaster, "Memories and Suggestions," *Bulletin,* AAUP, XXVI (April, 1940), 220.

[10] Letter of Arthur O. Lovejoy to Gaynor Pearson, March 3, 1947, in Gaynor Pearson, "The Decisions of Committee A," unpublished Ed.D. dissertation (Teacher's College, Columbia University, 1948), p. 28.

[11] Lancaster, "Memories and Suggestions," p. 220.

[12] *Bulletin,* AAUP, II (March, 1916), 20. The eligibility rules of the Association did not bar all administrators. If at least half of the work of administrators was in teaching or research, they could be elected to membership. When an active member of the Association accepted an administrative position, he could continue as an associate member. Ralph E. Himstead, "The Association: Its Place in Higher Education," *Bulletin,* AAUP, XXX (Summer, 1944), 464.

[13] J. McKeen Cattell, *University Control* (New York and Garrison, N.Y., 1913), p. 35.

of answers to a questionnaire sent to college administrators, Stephen Duggan concluded that in filling vacancies on boards of private institutions there had been a trend away from co-option toward granting alumni representation (notably at Ohio Wesleyan and Pennsylvania), for presidents to consult heads of departments in matters of appointment, promotion, and tenure (Illinois, Reed, Kansas), for permanent heads of departments to be replaced by temporary chairmen (Harvard, Yale, Chicago, Illinois).[14]

But it was widely believed in this period that reform was too slow and scanty. This is apparent from the reaction to Cattell's plan for university government which he first proposed in 1906. Cattell did not see much point in tinkering with the old machinery; he preferred a new design. He would have had the university corporation include all the professors of the university, all its officers and alumni, and all the members of the community who wished to pay dues to belong. The corporation would elect the trustees, whose primary duty would be to care for the institution's property. The professors would elect the president, whose salary would not be larger, or position more dignified, than their own. The professors would be selected by the department and the university senate, subject to the veto of the trustees.[15] Having invited comment on his plan from American scientists, Cattell received 299 replies. The reaction to his proposal was not unanimous. Some did not agree with the spirit of the changes he advocated; others suggested alterations in details. A few cautioned against the parties and political intrigues that might result from such democratic innovations; a few emphasized the sterility of faculty deliberations and the personal animus and contentiousness that they assumed characterized faculty self-government. But the great majority of Cattell's respondents did agree that the powers of the trustees should be limited and faculty control much increased. Roughly 85 percent were on the side of change: an indication that on this issue a real consensus of opinion had been formed.[16] The logical next step in this Progressive age was a league for better government to realize such schemes for reform.

[14] Stephen P. Duggan, "Present Tendencies in College Administration," *School and Society,* IV (August 12, 1916), 233–34.

[15] Cattell, "University Control," *Science,* XXIII (March 23, 1906), 475–77.

[16] Cattell, *University Control,* pp. 23–24. The questionnaire was sent to Cattell's friends and acquaintances, and the figures may be biased on that account. On the other hand, they were sent to men in the natural sciences who, being generally favored by university governors, were probably not as opposed to the existing system as, say, their colleagues in the social sciences.

Progressivism also abetted the movement to standardize the theory and practice of academic freedom and tenure. Just as economists began to see the social costs of unregulated business enterprise, so professors began to see the liabilities of an uncoordinated academic system. As far as academic freedom was concerned, there was a wide diversity of opinion with respect to its principles and scope, and a wide diversity of practices with respect to its protection and aid. For other ambiguous freedoms, like those of speech and the press, the courts provided clarification. But there were practically no legal dicta on academic freedom as such.[17] In other institutions, custom fostered fixed standards; but the transformation of our universities had been too recent to allow tradition to regulate policy. Hence, in the hope of introducing some semblance of order, three learned societies collaborated in 1913 to formulate general rules of academic freedom and tenure. A joint committee, composed of members of the American Economic Association, the American Sociological Society, and the American Political Science Association, labored for a year to solve the thorny problem of principles.[18] At the end of its deliberations, it was compelled to conclude that the "subject bristled with complexities of such a character that [the committee] feels itself in a position at present to make only a preliminary report." On the issue of academic freedom, the committee was in doubt as to whether universal rules should apply to colleges as well as universities, to the teachers of immature as well as of advanced students, to men who pronounce on matters outside their subjects as well as to those who stay within their competence, to extramural as well as intramural utterances. It also could not decide where the line of propriety should be drawn: "Can freedom of speech be permitted to cover self-exploitation or mere desire for notoriety?" On the subject of tenure, it posed but could not answer such questions as whether a professor should be virtually irremoveable, as in the Continental universities; whether distinctions should be drawn "between a college and a university teacher, between an officer of higher grade and one of low grade, between

---

[17] To this day, the phrase "Academic Freedom" is not listed separately in the *Legal Digests* or in *Words and Phrases*. A recent survey of academic-freedom cases concludes that "the courts do not appear to have passed upon causes of dismissal raising direct questions of academic freedom at the university level." Thomas I. Emerson and David Haber, eds., *Political and Civil Rights in the United States* (Buffalo, 1952), p. 890.

[18] The members were eight professors and one journalist who were generally recognized as authorities in the field: Seligman, Ely, Fetter, Weatherly, Lichtenberger, Pound, Judson, Dealey, and Herbert Croly.

an officer of long standing and one of recent tenure"; whether there ought to be a trial before every dismissal; whether the reasons for dismissal should ever be suppressed, even in the supposed interest of the individual involved.[19] Plainly, one conference was not sufficient. What was needed was a continuous inter-disciplinary effort to clarify basic principles, and to build, out of case materials, a set of academic rules that would give to future thought some clear direction.

Finally, one striking incident drove home the need to perfect a machinery of investigation in academic-freedom cases.[20] In 1913, the high-handed orthodox Presbyterian president of Lafayette College forced the resignation of John M. Mecklin, an outspoken liberal philosopher.[21] Following the precedent established in the Ross case, Mecklin told his story (which he picturesquely entitled the victory of Calvin over Servetus [22]) to the two professional societies in which he was enrolled—the American Philosophical Association and the American Psychological Association. These associations appointed an investigating committee. Unfortunately, the precedent of the Ross case was followed all too closely: the attempt to elicit information from President Warfield met with the same evasive arrogance that President Jordan had displayed fourteen years before. The mild-mannered question, "May I express the hope that you will be good enough to let the committee have, from yourself personally, some more specific statement in regard to certain facts in the case," was answered by "I trust you will pardon me if I say that your committee has no relation to me personally which would justify my making a personal statement to you with regard to these matters." The committee roundly scored this official overbearance, which was all too common in the ruling echelons of academia:

[19] *Preliminary Report of the Committee on Academic Freedom and Academic Tenure* (December, 1914), pp. 1–6, 7.

[20] Cf. H. W. Tyler, "Comments on the Address by Dr. Capen," *Bulletin,* AAUP, XXIII (March, 1937), 204.

[21] Lafayette College in the period of Mecklin's tenure (1905–13) was facing in two directions: toward its early nonsectarian idealism and toward the orthodox high Calvinism of Princeton Seminary and its autocratic president. The desire to have the best of both worlds created great confusion as to what could be taught at the college. Mecklin's philosophical relativism, his interest in the philosophy of pragmatism, and his teaching of evolution led the president to demand his resignation. After his dismissal, Mecklin went to the University of Pittsburgh, where another kind of battle over economic philosophy was making academic freedom tenuous. In 1920, Mecklin took a chair at Dartmouth College. John M. Mecklin, *My Quest for Freedom* (New York, 1945), pp. 129 ff.

[22] *Ibid.,* p. 164.

The attitude thus assumed does not seem to this committee one which can with propriety be maintained by the officers of any college or university towards the inquiries of a representative national organization of college and university teachers and other scholars. We believe it to be the right of the general body of professors of philosophy and psychology to know definitely the conditions of the tenure of any professorship in their subject; and also their right, and that of the public to which colleges look for support, to understand unequivocally what measure of freedom of teaching is guaranteed in any college, and to be informed as to the essential details of any case in which credal restrictions, other than those to which the college officially stands committed, are publicly declared by responsible persons to have been imposed. No college does well to live unto itself to such a degree that it fails to recognize that in all such issues the university teaching profession at large has a legitimate concern.[23]

This was a lusty rebuke and well deserved, but it also underscored the inability of the learned society to muster enough power and prestige to persuade administrators to cooperate with it.

These, then, were some of the forces that worked toward professorial solidarity in the first decade and a half of the twentieth century. Yet, powerful as they were, it is doubtful that they would have produced a viable organization had the initiative not been taken by a few movers and shakers, by a few professors who, academically, had "arrived." The first call for a conference looking toward the formation of a national association was issued by eighteen full professors of Johns Hopkins University. It was addressed to the faculties of the nine leading institutions of the country, and seven of them—Clark, Columbia, Cornell, Harvard, Princeton, Wisconsin, and Yale—responded by sending delegates. The first meeting, at the Johns Hopkins Club, was an assemblage of academic notables. John Dewey and J. McKeen Cattell represented Columbia; Charles E. Bennett and E. L. Nichols, Cornell; Maurice Bloomfield and A. O. Lovejoy, Johns Hopkins; Edward Capps, E. M. Kammerer, and H. C. Warren, Princeton; C. S. Minot, Harvard.[24] These delegates, in turn, established a committee on organization, consisting of a select group of thirty-four, which included new stars, among them Roscoe Pound and W. B. Munro of Harvard, William E. Dodd of Chicago, Frank Thilly and

[23] Report of the Committee of Inquiry, "The Case of Professor Mecklin," *Journal of Philosophy, Psychology and Scientific Method*, XI (January, 1914), 70–81. Warfield was dismissed by the Lafayette trustees two weeks after the adoption of the Committee's report.
[24] *Science*, New Series, Vol. XXXIX (March 27, 1914), p. 459.

Alvin S. Johnson of Cornell.[25] Finally, when the organization had been mapped out, invitations were extended to "persons of full professorial rank whose names appeared on the lists of distinguished specialists prepared for the committee in each of the principal subjects." [26] This invitation was accepted by 867 professors in 60 institutions, who thus became charter members of the AAUP. The elitist inspiration and composition of the organization were reflected in the membership clause of the first constitution adopted, which provided that "any university or college teacher of recognized scholarship or scientific productivity who holds and for ten years has held a position of teaching or research" was eligible.[27] The membership base was only gradually broadened: in 1920, the required period of service in teaching or research was reduced to three years; in 1929, junior membership for graduate students was provided, with the right to attend the annual meetings but not to vote. The AAUP was not, as at first envisioned, "one big union for all," but a union of the aristocrats of academic labor.

It may be taken as a commentary on the prudence, the idealism, and the crochets of the American professoriate that, despite the eminence of the founders, quite a few prominent men had reservations about joining. J. E. Creighton of Cornell wrote to Lovejoy that

one or two of our most prominent men whose names we should especially like to get were anxious to know of what is involved in the proposal. They were impressed by the names of the J. H. U. signers; but wanted some assurance that the idea behind the movement was not that of attacking the existing condition of affairs in any destructive or antagonistic spirit.[28]

At the second meeting of the Association, Charles A. Beard, without his knowledge, was nominated for membership.[29] Two years later, when he was asked to remit his dues, Beard wrote to the secretary: "I beg to say that, to the best of my knowledge and belief, I have never joined the Association. I regarded it as a futile enterprise when it was begun, and the results have confirmed my suspicions." [30] Men of the caliber of

[25] Pearson, "Decisions of Committe A," p. 22.

[26] A. O. Lovejoy, "Organization of the American Association of University Professors," *Science,* New Series, Vol. XLI (January 29, 1915), p. 154.

[27] *Bulletin,* AAUP, I (March, 1916), 20.

[28] Letter of J. E. Creighton to A. O. Lovejoy, May 23, 1913, in Pearson, "Decisions of Committee A," p. 21.

[29] Letter of H. W. Tyler to Beard, June 21, 1917, in Seligman Papers.

[30] Letter of Charles A. Beard to H. W. Tyler, June 16, 1917, in Seligman Papers.

Barrett Wendell and Albert Bushnell Hart did not immediately join,[31] and W. T. Councilman of the Harvard Medical School justified his refractoriness with this comment:

The matter does not interest me. I am opposed to anything that savours of organization or the formation of societies of any sort. The modern habit of organization I regard as a pernicious form of activity. The present unfavorable conditions of university life will finally be remedied not by organization but by the refusal of capable men to enter into it.[32]

The academic bohemian, the conservative, and the radical all were wary. Still, the membership rolls showed continuous growth. Within six months, the Association had 1,362 members representing 75 institutions; by January, 1922, it had 4,046 members from 183 institutions.[33]

Because of the suspicion that the Association aroused in the profession it sought to serve and the hostility it incurred from the general public, the major effort of the leaders of the AAUP in the early years was to win respectability. A bellicose attitude toward trustees, a militant stand on academic freedom, any of the usual postures of the trade union, would have alarmed and repelled the great majority of American professors. Accordingly, the original conference call issued by the Johns Hopkins professors contained only a few references to academic freedom or to what might be called "unfair labor practices." The main goals of the association appealed to professors as professional men, not as employees.[34] Dewey, in his address to the committee on organization, scotched the idea that the investigation and punishment of infractions of academic freedom would preoccupy the attention of the Association:

I do not know of any college teacher who does not hold that such infringement, when it occurs, is an attack on the integrity of our calling. But such cases are too rare to even suggest the formation of an association like this. . . . In any case, I am confident that the topic cannot be more than an incident of the activities of the association in developing professional standards.[35]

But on this score the philosopher did not possess the gift of prophecy. The Association was astounded and disheartened by the calls that came from all over the country to lend its assistance to professors in their unequal

[31] Pearson, "Decisions of Committee A," p. 24. Hart was listed on the AAUP rolls in 1921.
[32] Letter of Councilman to Lovejoy, December 4, 1914, in Pearson, "Decisions of Committee A," p. 24. Councilman was listed on the AAUP rolls in 1921.
[33] *Bulletin,* AAUP, II (April, 1916), 3–4; *ibid.,* VIII (January, 1922), 51.
[34] *Ibid.,* II (March, 1916), 12.
[35] Thilly, "American Association of University Professors," p. 200.

struggles with administrators. Distress signals came from the University of Utah, where seventeen professors resigned in protest when one of their colleagues was unceremoniously dismissed; from the University of Colorado, where a law professor believed he had been fired for testimony given before a government commission; from Wesleyan University, where a professor believed he had been removed because of anti-Sabbatarian remarks delivered at a nearby club; from the University of Pennsylvania, where Scott Nearing, in a case that achieved great notoriety, was removed from the Wharton School; from the University of Washington, where three professors had been discharged.[36] However much the founders wished to devote themselves to long-run constructive tasks befitting a professional society, they could not evade the fact that professors in trouble looked to them as to a grievance committee, as their long-sought avenging arm. "To have failed to meet the demands," Dewey commented later, "would have been cowardly; it would have tended to destroy all confidence in the Association as anything more than a talking body. . . . The investigations of particular cases were literally thrust upon us." [37]

The pressure on the Association resulted in a bifurcation of its interests and activities. Even as Committee A on Academic Freedom and Academic Tenure was set to work to fashion general principles for the guidance of the profession, special investigative subcommittees were sent scurrying over the country, hearing professorial complaints, investigating actual conditions, writing up reports. Thus, on the one hand, the AAUP tried to function as an agency of codification, fixing its sights on the larger aspects of academic freedom and other professional problems. On the other hand, it had to function as an agency of group pressure, investigating cases and imposing penalties in response to immediate demands. To the historian of the AAUP and the profession, the long-term efforts of the Association may stand out as its greater contribution. But there

[36] "Report of the Committee of Inquiry on Conditions at the University of Utah," *Bulletin, AAUP*, I (July, 1915); "Reports of Committees concerning Charges of Violation of Academic Freedom at the University of Colorado and at Wesleyan University," *ibid.*, II (April, 1916); "Report of the Committee of Inquiry on the Case of Professor Scott Nearing of the University of Pennsylvania," *ibid.*, II (May, 1916); "Report of the Sub-Committee on the Case of Professor Joseph K. Hart of the University of Washington," *ibid.*, III (April, 1917).

[37] John Dewey, "Presidential Address," *Bulletin*, AAUP, I (December, 1915), 11–12. Such was the pressure on Committee A that three cases had to be referred to the learned societies: one, arising at Dartmouth College, to the American Philosophical Association; one, at Tulane University, to the American Physiological Society; one, at the University of Oklahoma, to the American Chemical Society. *Ibid.*, p. 18.

can be no doubt that, because of its immediate involvement in institutional conflicts, the Association became stamped, in lay and professional circles alike, as an organization of professorial defense. In the ensuing years, whatever else it accomplished, the reputation of the AAUP was to hinge on its successes and failures in recognizing and rectifying abuses.

ACHIEVEMENTS: THE AAUP AS AN AGENCY OF CODIFICATION

The first attempt of the AAUP to work out the scope and limits of academic freedom was Committee A's Report on Academic Freedom and Academic Tenure of 1915, the general philosophy of which we examined in a previous chapter. Briefly, its fundamental premises were that academic freedom was a necessary condition for a university's existence; that trustees occupied the position of public officials discharging a public trust; that the only exception to this was when they served private propagandistic purposes, in which case those purposes ought to be made explicit; that in the classroom professors were limited by the norms of neutrality and competence; that outside the university professors had the same right as any other citizens to freedom of utterance and action, limited only by the obligation to observe professional decorum. These ideas were not militant or extreme. The Report emphasized the unassailably respectable if somewhat bromidic point that there were no rights without corresponding obligations, that academic freedom was not academic license. It strained for balance in its judgments. In chiding those trustees who regarded professors as their employees and the university as their own private property, it also took account of the tradition that sanctioned this point of view, and of the restrictions imposed by the charters. Noting the malfeasance of certain wealthy donors and trustees, it also called attention to the danger of political pressure from popular movements of reform.

But the report contained more than generalities; it offered practical proposals as well. And it was over its specific demands, rather than its philosophical principles, that the major battles with academic trustees and administrators were to be fought. Its practical proposals had two main objectives. The first was to place some limitation on the trustees' prerogative to fire teachers. Quite tentatively, the Committee suggested that aberrant opinion should never be grounds for dismissal. It recognized, however, that differences in traditions and local conditions made it difficult to apply uniform substantive limitations. But it held that the procedural limitations could and should be uniform. At this point, the Committee made one of its most controversial proposals: it suggested trials under faculty auspices.

Every university or college teacher (at the rank of associate professor or above) should be entitled, before dismissal or demotion, to have the charges against him stated in writing in specific terms and to have a fair trial on those charges before a special or permanent judicial committee chosen by the faculty senate or council, or by the faculty at large.

At such trial the teacher accused should have full opportunity to present evidence, and if the charge is one of professional incompetency, a formal report upon his work should be first made in writing by the teachers of his own department and of cognate departments in the university, and if the teacher concerned so desire, by a committee of his fellow specialists from other institutions appointed by some competent authority.[38]

The second objective of these practical proposals was to provide security and dignity in the academic job through definite rules of tenure:

In every institution there should be an unequivocal understanding as to the term of each appointment. . . .

In those state universities which are legally incapable of making contracts for more than a limited period, the governing boards should announce their policy with respect to the presumption of reappointment in the several classes of position, and such announcements, though not legally enforceable, should be regarded as morally binding.[39]

Academic freedom was the end: due process, tenure, and establishment of professional competence were regarded as necessary means.

These practical proposals were indicative not only of how much professors had come to rely on bureaucratic safeguards, but also of how much the views of these particular professors reflected their elite position. On every count, the proposals embodied a double standard to distinguish between academic men of high and low estate. Whereas teachers above the level of instructors were to be entitled to one year's notice of dismissal, instructors were only to be entitled to warning three months before the close of the academic year. Whereas those of the rank of associate and full professors were to be entitled to a judicial hearing, it was to be sufficient that the faculty approve the dismissal of anyone below that

[38] "Report," Committee on Academic Freedom and Academic Tenure, *Bulletin, AAUP,* I (December, 1915), 41–42.
[39] *Ibid.,* p. 41.

grade. Whereas all above the grade of instructor were to have permanent tenure after ten years' service, nothing was said about when trustees had to decide to promote or remove instructors. Tenure was identified with rank, but no length of service was specified to insure promotion to rank.[40] Perhaps these distinctions were not entirely the result of the oligarchic character of the Association. In 1915, the ratio of senior to junior officers in American institutions of higher learning was much larger than it subsequently became, particularly after the Great Depression, when cheap academic labor to serve in lower ranks was relatively easy to procure. But it was a weak architectural plan that embellished only the upper floors, and omitted provision for an orderly access to them.

The antagonism and misrepresentation that greeted the AAUP code were the best proofs that it was needed. An editorial writer for the New York *Times* wrote:

Academic freedom, that is, the inalienable right of every college instructor to make a fool of himself and of his college by . . . intemperate, sensational prattle about every subject under heaven, to his classes and to the public, and still keep on the payroll or be reft therefrom only by elaborate process, is cried to all the winds by the organized dons.[41]

Nor did certain academic governors show greater sapience than this journalist. Chancellor Day, who in 1895 had allegedly ejected John R. Commons from the University of Syracuse, observed:

If the professor has the right to give up his position because of his conscience and conviction, what about the right of the trustees to consult their consciences and convictions? Have they not as much right to act by their consciences as he has? Have they not the right to act according to their best judgment after securing all the facts?

This equation of the right to extinguish opinion with the right to express it drew an exasperated response from John Dewey:

It is bad enough when such insults to scholarship and scientific preparation come from a man in the street. It is literally appalling when they come from the head of a university, for, acted upon, they mean the death of American scholarship.[42]

One of the most significant reactions was that of the Committee on Academic Freedom and Tenure of Office of the Association of American

---

[40] *Ibid.*, pp. 40–41.
[41] "The Professors's Union," quoted in *School and Society*, III (January 29, 1916), 175.
[42] "Is the College Professor a 'Hired Man'?" *Literary Digest*, LI (July 10, 1915), 65.

Colleges, an organization of college presidents also founded in 1915. Without undertaking to debate the philosophical assumptions of the AAUP Report, the presidents' committee dismissed its practical proposals as presumptuous. "No way has yet been found," it asserted pontifically, "to play the 'cello or the harp and at the same time to direct the orchestra." The Committee seemed to feel that it had a better right to speak for professors than the AAUP, which, it observed, excluded from its membership the key men of the universities—the presidents—and a large number of academic teachers "who . . . may be doing work of as much importance as the members of the Association." The Committee was of the opinion that "a man who is truly dedicated to teaching is likely to recognize the importance of the division of functions and usually does not wish to participate, except in the most general way, in administration." Making the best of existing conditions is "more alluring to the right-minded man than a more general, more diffuse and more distracting distribution of privileges." [43] The Committe resorted to the argument perennially used by conservatives—the basic solidarity of all interests.

At the same time, the Committee was of the opinion that should this solidarity be endangered by a professor too obtuse to recognize it, the only appropriate course of action was for the professor to resign. It thought institutional harmony far more important to academic life than formal procedural protections. That, in order to preserve harmony, it would be just as appropriate for a trustee to resign, did not cross the minds of these executives:

A man who accepts a position in a college which he has reason to believe is a Christian institution and who, further, may properly infer that the canons of good taste forbid, perhaps, the asking when the contract is made, of intimate personal questions about his own religious belief, can scarcely assume that freedom of speech includes either the right privately to undermine or publicly to attack Christianity. The man called to the average college which believes in monogamy as essential in the upbuilding of student character can scarcely expect the college to submit to a long judicial process in tardily effecting his release if he openly states and on inquiry admits that he believes in free love.

Incompatability of temperament in an educational institution is as serious a problem as in marriage; and since no right-minded corporation will make a contract for life with a new teacher, divorce in a college would seem to be open to few objections provided it be done decently and in order.[44]

[43] "Report," Committee on Academic Freedom and Tenure of Office, *Bulletin,* Association of American Colleges, III (April, 1917), 49–50.

[44] *Ibid.,* p. 51.

The analogy of a marriage was vulnerable: it opened interesting possibilities of a suit for breach of promise or perhaps an award of something corresponding to alimony until the professor was able to rewed.

On the subject of tenure, the presidential committee had this to say:

[The Committee] would gladly leave to professors the determination of the professional standing of their fellows. But there is a bigger question and that is: Shall any association of university professors compel a corporation to retain in office for an indefinite time one who is manifestly unfit for that particular place . . . ? [45]

Of course, the AAUP had proposed no such thing. It had gone to pains to suggest a procedure by which the "manifestly" unfit could be discharged; it insisted only that this unfitness be made "manifest" to competent authorities. Nor did it propose that the AAUP should rate the qualifications of professors. The animus that produced such a gross distortion hardly needs underscoring.

If the claim that professors and administrators had identical interests needed any refutation, it was supplied by the following remarks with which the presidents embellished their report:

Since your Committee regard it as their duty to speak frankly, they would like to add that there are enough cases known to the educational world in which executives have saved institutions from scandal, graft and other grave perils by prompt action, even at great personal risk. . . .[46]

[Trustees] must do the best they can, giving a sense of security to teachers, but at the same time not unmindful that rarely does a teacher give the institution which he serves any sense of security or consider the larger interests of an institution if he has a chance to go to a wider field of usefulness at a greater salary. In fact, many an educational position is used—no one will deny—as a stepping stone to self-promotion, sometimes shamelessly.[47]

There are certain other cases which almost every institution has now and then to manage in which what a trustee of Cornell once called "vexels" or mischief-makers can break the continuity of an institution and set back for years its best interests. The very fact that "vexels" know that some excellent men in responsible positions sometimes advise that at any cost colleges get on with so-called impossible persons, is a distinct encouragement never given in a well-organized corporation to mischief-makers to retard administrative processes.[48]

The presidents' committee seemed to regard the AAUP Report as a revolutionary dictate rather than as a serious attempt to solve a profes-

[45] *Ibid.*, p. 54.   [46] *Ibid.*, p. 53.
[47] *Ibid.*, p. 55.   [48] *Ibid.*, p. 51.

sional problem. A document less distinguished for grammar or common sense than the presidents' report could hardly have been composed.

Interestingly enough, within six years the attitude of the AAC college presidents toward the AAUP Report took a complete turn. Perhaps the softening of animosities was the result of the cooperation between the two organizations during the country's involvement in the war. Another reason for the change may have been the reconstitution of the AAC's academic freedom committee, which, by 1922, had come under the able chairmanship of Dean Charles N. Cole of Oberlin, and had acquired C. F. Thwing, president of Western Reserve University, a noted historian of education, and William J. Hutchins, president of Berea College, the father of Robert Maynard Hutchins.[49] Certainly, credit must also be given to the merits of the AAUP Report, which loomed as a massive contribution compared with the efforts of its critics. At any rate, the leaders of American higher education proved to be educable. In its 1922 report, the AAC's Academic Freedom Commission referred graciously to the work of the AAUP as "significant and highly important." It went on to accept almost every argument that the AAUP Report had made. On the basic principles of academic freedom, it agreed that teaching should be free, and should be limited only by the requirements of neutrality and competence; that teachers acting or speaking outside the university had the right "to precisely the same freedom and the same responsibility as attach to all other persons, subject only to the necessity of protecting the good name and the welfare of the college against serious injury." [50] More remarkable was the wide area of agreement on faculty participation and tenure. The Commission agreed that all appointments and terminations of contracts should be made in conference with the departments concerned, and "might well" be approved by a faculty committee or the faculty itself. Reflecting the attitudes of the late war, the Commission declared that gross immorality or "disloyalty" were grounds for summary dismissal. But in all other cases, and

in all cases where the facts are in dispute, the accused teacher should always have the opportunity to be heard in his own defense by all bodies that pass

[49] The old committee was composed of Herbert Welch, President of Ohio Wesleyan; Lyman P. Powell, President of Hobart; William F. Slocum, President of Colorado; Robert J. Kelly, President of Earlham; and Alexander Meiklejohn, President of Amherst. Other members of the 1922 committee were H. M. Gage, President of Coe, and Roy C. Flickinger, President of Northwestern.

[50] "Report," Commission on Academic Freedom and Academic Tenure, *Bulletin,* AAC, VIII (March, 1922), 100.

judgment upon the case. In the trial of charges of professional incompetence, the testimony of scholars in the same field, either from his own or from other institutions, should always be taken.[51]

Tenure, after an unspecified period of probation, should be long-term, indefinite, or permanent; timely notice of dismissal should be given; the precise terms and expectations of every appointment should be stated in writing. The difference between the AAC and the AAUP had narrowed to details: the AAC added another reason for immediate dismissal without trial, namely financial exigency making drastic retrenchment necessary; and it omitted reference to some of the precise guarantees of due process that the AAUP Report had included.[52]

In its early years, the AAUP had been reluctant to join with the presidential organizations to formulate a code of academic freedom. "Standing alone and united," wrote Frank Thilly, the third president of the Association,

our influence is great; as one unit in a divided, perhaps hostile, group we are apt to lose our force. . . . At present we are slowly winning a battle here and there. . . . Might not an unsuccessful conference with the united representatives of our friend, the enemy, lead to a solid front against us? . . . Somehow I cannot help but feel that we shall be stronger if we do not entangle ourselves in foreign alliances, even though our progress may be slow.[53]

That this caution was justified at the time is amply supported by the first report of the AAC. But the concessions of the second AAC report disarmed the professors. After much preliminary negotiation, the American Council on Education called a conference in 1925 which was attended by representatives of the American Association of University Women, the American Association of University Professors, the Association of Governing Boards, the Association of Land Grant Colleges, the Association of Urban Universities, the National Association of State Universities, the Association of American Colleges, and the Association of American Universities. With only slight textual changes, the AAC's 1922 statement was adopted by the conference, though only the AAUP and the AAC endorsed it.[54] A great bridge had been crossed.

The colleges and universities did not incorporate the 1925 statement into their by-laws except in very rare instances. Cast in the form of

---

[51] *Ibid.*, p. 103.   [52] *Ibid.*, pp. 102–3.
[53] Letter of Frank Thilly to H. W. Tyler, March 21, 1917, in Seligman Papers.
[54] H. W. Tyler, "The Defense of Freedom by Educational Organizations," in *Educational Freedom and Democracy* (Second Yearbook of the John Dewey Society, New York, 1938), pp. 229–39.

mandatory rules, it was rejected by one board after another as a transgression of charter provisions. Giving equal weight to principles and procedures, it was rejected by presidents and trustees who balked at the formal machinery but accepted the spirit behind it. It was estimated in 1939 that only six or seven boards of trustees in the entire United States had adopted the statement formally.[55] The conviction that what was needed was a statement of policy that invited approval, not a set of rules that required adoption, led to a revision of the code by the AAUP and the AAC in 1938. The new conference at which this was done provided an opportunity to correct the long-standing discriminatory provisions against the lower-ranking members of the profession. A probationary period of six years was specified, after which the teacher, if he was retained, was to be entitled to permanent tenure. Notice of dismissal was to be given one year in advance for all teachers, even those on probation. Finally, the 1938 report declared that "during the probationary period a teacher should have the academic freedom that all other members of the faculty have." Another rift in the academic profession was closed.

The AAC endorsed the 1938 report with several amendments, which necessitated further consideration by the two associations. The new agreement, reached in 1940, changed the probationary period from six to seven years and eliminated the statement that the judgment of what constitutes fulfillment of the obligations of decorum should rest with the teacher.

As the fruit of a quarter-century of thought and labor, the 1940 statement deserves to be quoted in full:

The purpose of this statement is to promote public understanding and support of academic freedom and tenure and agreement upon procedures to assure them in colleges and universities. Institutions of higher education are conducted for the common good and not to further the interest of either the individual teacher or the institution as a whole. The common good depends upon the free search for truth and its free exposition.

Academic freedom is essential to these purposes and applies to both teaching and research. Freedom in research is fundamental to the advancement of truth. Academic freedom in its teaching aspect is fundamental for the protection of the rights of the teacher in teaching and of the student to freedom in learning. It carries with it duties correlative with rights.

Tenure is a means to certain ends; specifically: (1) Freedom of teaching and research and of extra-mural activities, and (2) A sufficient degree of

---

[55] See Henry M. Wriston, "Academic Freedom and Tenure," *Bulletin,* AAUP, XXV (June, 1939), 329.

economic security to make the profession attractive to men and women of ability. Freedom and economic security, hence tenure, are indispensable to the success of an institution in fulfilling its obligations to its students and to society.

ACADEMIC FREEDOM

(a) The teacher is entitled to full freedom in research and in the publication of the results, subject to the adequate performance of his other academic duties; but research for pecuniary return should be based upon an understanding with the authorities of the institution.

(b) The teacher is entitled to freedom in the classroom in discussing his subject, but he should be careful not to introduce into his teaching controversial matter which has no relation to his subject. Limitations of academic freedom because of religious or other aims of the institution should be clearly stated in writing at the time of the appointment.

(c) The college or university teacher is a citizen, a member of a learned profession, and an officer of an educational institution. When he speaks or writes as a citizen, he should be free from institutional censorship or discipline, but his special position in the community imposes special obligations. As a man of learning and an educational officer, he should remember that the public may judge his profession and his institution by his utterances. Hence he should at all times be accurate, should exercise appropriate restraint, should show respect for the opinions of others, and should make every effort to indicate that he is not an institutional spokesman.

ACADEMIC TENURE

(a) After the expiration of a probationary period teachers or investigators should have permanent or continuous tenure, and their services should be terminated only for adequate cause, except in the case of retirement for age, or under extraordinary circumstances because of financial exigencies.

In the interpretation of this principle it is understood that the following represents acceptable academic practice:

(1) The precise terms and conditions of every appointment should be stated in writing and be in the possession of both institution and teacher before the appointment is consummated.

(2) Beginning with appointment to the rank of full-time instructor or a higher rank, the probationary period should not exceed seven years, including within this period full-time service in all institutions of higher education; but subject to the proviso that when, after a term of probationary service of more than three years in one or more institutions, a teacher is called to another institution it may be agreed in writing that his new appointment is for a probationary period of not more than four years, even though thereby the person's total probationary period in the academic profession is extended beyond the normal maximum of seven years. Notice should be given at least one year prior to the

expiration of the probationary period if the teacher is not to be continued in service after the expiration of that period.

(3) During the probationary period a teacher should have the academic freedom that all other members of the faculty have.

(4) Termination for cause of a continuous appointment, or the dismissal for cause of a teacher previous to the expiration of a term appointment, should, if possible, be considered by both a faculty committee and the governing board of the institution. In all cases where the facts are in dispute, the accused teacher should be informed before the hearing in writing of the charges against him and should have the opportunity to be heard in his own defense by all bodies that pass judgment upon his case. He should be permitted to have with him an adviser of his own choosing who may act as counsel. There should be a full stenographic record of the hearing available to the parties concerned. In the hearing of charges of incompetence the testimony should include that of teachers and other scholars, either from his own or from other institutions. Teachers on continuous appointment who are dismissed for reasons not involving moral turpitude should receive their salaries for at least a year from the date of notification of dismissal whether or not they are continued in their duties at the institution.

(5) Termination of a continuous appointment because of financial exigency should be demonstrably bona fide.

The salutary influence of these written ordinances is unmistakable, though not precisely measurable.[56] Generally, they can be said to have conferred three benefits. First of all, they cut through the intellectual tangles in which thinking on the subject of academic freedom had become ensnarled. They indicated, for example, how professors could fight for academic freedom and yet accept the presence of denominational colleges in their midst. They demonstrated how greater faculty participation in choosing and retaining personnel could be reconciled with the unlimited prerogatives granted trustees by the charters. They showed how the need for a competent faculty could be adjusted to the equally strong need for a secure one. Though margins of vagueness remain, and new crises have demanded new formulations, the unending discussion over academic freedom has taken on a cogency and clarity that had been missing before 1915. For all this the AAUP deserves great credit. It was the pioneer, and its achievement inspired other agencies—the National Educational Association, the Progressive Education Association, the

[56] Evaluation of the work of the AAUP is difficult because the central files of the Association are inaccessible and in a very disorganized state. The inner story of the AAUP cannot be written until these files are opened to the historian.

American Civil Liberties Union, the American Federation of Teachers, and, as we have seen, the Association of American Colleges—to take part in the task of codification.[57]

Secondly, the *lex scripta* provided a standard for measuring publicized reforms. Thus, when in 1915 the University of Pennsylvania yielded to public criticism of its handling of the Scott Nearing case and undertook to revise its procedures, the AAUP had a yardstick with which to evaluate this reform. The provision for faculty-trustee cooperation in all dismissals won its approval, but the AAUP committee noted that there was no provision for a trial of scholars based on explicit charges, that there was no provision for judicial proceedings, and that no arrangement was made for eliciting the judgment of fellow specialists.[58] It was now possible to detect and indict the provisions for forms without substance, the variety of gestures without motion.

Finally, the AAUP was effective in getting academic administrators to accept its rules. Not all of its rules, not every administrator. The 1925 statement to the effect that doubtful extramural utterances of a teacher should be referred to a committee of the faculty was so little observed that it was dropped in the 1940 statement. Official recognition of the rules by statutory inclusion was, as we have seen, very rare. Nevertheless, the rules were useful as guides to administrative practice. To take one striking illustration: When the University of Minnesota rescinded in 1938 its action dismissing Professor Schaper during the First World War, it entered a statement upon its records that was a paraphrase of the words of the AAUP.[59] When an institution was ready to be enlightened, it had a formula and a text to draw upon.

ACHIEVEMENTS: THE AAUP AS AN AGENCY OF INVESTIGATION

In the second category of its activities, the AAUP was much less successful. Plunged into investigations from the very beginning, it excited ex-

[57] H. W. Tyler, "Defense of Freedom by Educational Organizations," pp. 243–48. It is interesting to note that the Association of American Universities has not established a committee on academic freedom, and that, aside from cooperating in the 1925 Washington Conference, it has not attempted to legislate on this question.

[58] "Report," Committee of Inquiry on the Case of Scott Nearing, *Bulletin, AAUP*, II (May, 1916), 42–57.

[59] See F. S. Deibler, "The Principles of Academic Freedom and Tenure of the American Association of University Professors," *The Annals of the American Academy of Political and Social Science*, CI (May, 1922), 136–37.

pectations among professors that it was unable and unwilling to fulfill. It neither would be nor could be a police department for ferreting out, a grand jury for sifting, or a trial court for testing all reports of academic injustice. That it *would not* be these things in all cases was assured by its temper and ideology. It did not wish to stiffen resistance by making frontal attacks upon administrators; it preferred to change underlying conditions rather than avenge the crimes which arose from them.[60] But even if it had wished to, it *could not* have served the academic world as policeman, judge, and jury. Finances and personnel had unavoidable limitations. Without an endowment or a subsidy from an outside source, entirely dependent upon a dues-paying membership which before 1940 was fewer than 15,000, the AAUP could not hope to support the battery of lawyers and field workers required for extensive operations. Except for the paid assistance it received from an executive secretary and a legal adviser, the latter appointed in 1926, the AAUP was dependent upon the voluntary help of its members. And there was the rub. To track down a case on a strange campus, the investigator needed the talents of a psychologist, a lawyer, and a philosopher—and an abundance of common sense. Those who were professional crusaders and those who could be easily cajoled were poor material for the job. Thus there were two groups of professors who could at once be eliminated—those who thought all administrators malevolent and those who were too susceptible to their charms. After these discriminations were made, the Association had to take regional factors into account. Since repeated visits to the campus might be necessary, the investigator could not be stationed far away; but since detachment and independence were required, a too close proximity might be undesirable. Finally, some of the most likely prospects for this difficult business eliminated themselves: it was not easy to dislodge a scholar from the peace and quiet of his study and prevail upon him to probe some remote external unpleasantness.

The AAUP had no alternative but to apportion its resources among the cases it received. Whenever possible, and not only out of necessity but out of policy, it tried to use its good offices to mediate between conflicting parties in a way agreeable to both sides. In 1934, it was estimated that for every case written up in the *Bulletin* of the Association, three were settled informally and quietly through mediation.[61] When this approach

---

[60] "Higher Learning in Time of Crisis," *Bulletin*, AAUP, XXVI (October, 1940), 542–46.

[61] Committee A, "Report for 1934," *Bulletin*, AAUP, XX (February, 1934), 99.

failed, the AAUP launched a full investigation into those cases that involved some fundamental question of general principle, or that involved more than one dismissal, or that exemplified a new abuse. In 1934, it was estimated that only half of the non-mediated cases received a full-dress investigation.[62] As a consequence, the AAUP investigations have served a limited purpose—to warn and to illustrate, rather than to avenge and redress.[63] As a consequence, too, the accounts of cases published in the *Bulletin* do not give an accurate picture of the state of academic affairs. On the one hand, they soften the outlines by presenting only a fraction of the abuses that come to the attention of the Association (mediated and non-pressed cases are presented only in statistical form). On the other hand, they make the picture too harsh by detailing only those cases that are not amenable to compromise or conciliation.[64]

Nevertheless, the cases reported in the *Bulletin*—there were 124 of them through 1953—can be categorized in such a way as to yield several interesting conclusions. It is significant that comparatively few of these cases involved a clear violation of the right to free expression. In only 20 of the 94 cases in which the AAUP held the administration to have been in the wrong was the existence of ideological pressure substantiated. In only 17 out of 94 cases was the extramural activity of the teacher one of the grounds for dismissal. On the other hand, in 57 cases, or in almost two thirds, the issues were intramural and largely personal, hinging on the jealousy between a president and a professor, or the conflict between strong personalities, or the petty vindictiveness of someone in high office, or—this was particularly true during the Depression—the decision to cut down the staff in an effort to economize. In 52 cases, the subcommittees found the president to have been autocratic and arbitrary. At one place, a professor and four colleagues were dismissed for having submitted a proposal recommending greater faculty participation in the governing of the college; the subcommittee found the president guilty of "serious ad-

---

[62] *Ibid.*

[63] A. M. Withers, "Professors and Their Association," *Journal of Higher Education,* XI (March, 1940), 126–28, 129; Walter W. Cook, "Address of the Retiring President," *Bulletin,* AAUP, XX (January, 1934), 85–87; Report of Committee A, "Academic Freedom and Tenure," *Bulletin,* AAUP, XX (February, 1934), 98–102; Ralph E. Himstead, "The Association: Its Place in Higher Education," pp. 463–65.

[64] Any teacher in a junior college, a four-year college or a university, of any rank, and regardless of whether he is a member of the Association, has the right to appeal to the AAUP to investigate his case.

ministrative incapacity." [65] At another place, a professor was dismissed for supporting a colleague who had been fired; the subcommittee found grave fault with the president and the trustees.[66] Elsewhere, a professor was dismissed because he refused to endorse a financial drive to build a business college, and because he charged that a disproportionate share of the funds was going to the managers of the campaign.[67] In certain places, presidential highhandedness and stupidity decimated faculty ranks. At DePauw University, during the five-year tenure of G. Bromley Oxnam as president, 60 persons on the faculty resigned, failed of reappointment, or were dismissed.[68] In investigating the Turner case at the University of Pittsburgh in 1934–35, the subcommittee found that 84 teachers of professorial rank had left the university during the last five years, and that administrative practices had "brought into the lives of the men and women of the faculty, and into the lives of those dependent upon them, acute anxiety, worry, and fear." [69] Were these cases not part of the police docket, one would assume that academic relations were utterly bereft of the ordinary decencies. This would not be true, any more than that reports of crime depict average patterns of behavior. But these cases do give color to the belief that administrative, not professorial, incompetence is the great unsolved problem of academic life.

The reported cases also justify the assumption that academic freedom is dependent upon academic tenure and due process. In fully 63 of the 94 cases in which the administration was held to blame, guarantees of tenure were absent and dismissal on short notice was permitted by the institution. Indeed, the absence of law and fixed procedure was the one element that these remiss institutions had in common. They were heterogeneous with respect to size, geographical location, and form of control. They even varied with respect to scholarly importance, though it is true that, with the exception of Pennsylvania, Yale, and Smith, none of the major private or state universities incurred the disgrace of appearing on

[65] "Report of the Committee of Inquiry on Conditions in Washburn College," *Bulletin,* AAUP, VII (January–February, 1921), 126.

[66] "Report on the University of Louisville," *Bulletin,* AAUP, XIII (October, 1927), 443–57.

[67] Report of Committee A, "Academic Freedom and Tenure," *Bulletin,* AAUP, XV (April, 1929), 270–76. The institution was Boston University.

[68] Report of Committee A, "Academic Freedom and Tenure," *Bulletin,* AAUP, XX (May, 1934), 295–302.

[69] Report of Committee A, "Academic Freedom and Tenure," *Bulletin,* AAUP, XXI (March, 1935), 248–56.

the Association's censure list. Clearly, there was a problem antecedent to and inclusive of the problem of protecting freedom, and that was the problem of establishing a government of law, not of whim.[70]

The question of how to penalize offending administrations was a nettling one. Methods of retaliation useful in other situations—the strike, the boycott, the picket line—were not available to the professors. It was therefore proposed that the publication of reports in the *Bulletin*—which had an uncertain punitive effect at best—should be supplemented by an AAUP "blacklist" of disapproved institutions. There was a long debate over this proposal. One side argued that the Association was incompetent to rate institutions, that there could not be just and complete classification, that the penalty would be visited on the innocent—the students and teachers—rather than on the guilty—the administrators—who were often prepared to brazen it out.[71] On the other side, the arguments were that the Association needed sharper weapons than those of moral suasion and publicity, and that the profession needed some device to warn academic candidates to keep away from contaminated places.[72] The tactic finally devised was a compromise between the two extremes. In 1931 the AAUP set up a list of "non-recommended" institutions (not a "blacklist," which carried trade union connotations, nor a list of institutions rated for degree of purity),[73] and it appended to that list the statement that no "censure is visited by the Association upon the whole institution or upon the faculty, but only upon its present administration." [74]

Only its most admiring devotees would claim that the AAUP has carried out its investigative function with a maximum of efficiency. The long time that elapses between the receipt of a complaint and the publication of a final report makes redress difficult and restitution all but impossible. The reports vary in fullness and relevance, and sometimes show the amateur's touch. The fact that institutions remain on the censured list

[70] Frank Thilly, "Presidential Address," *Bulletin, AAUP*, III (February, 1917), 8–9.

[71] See S. P. Capen, "Privileges and Immunities," in *The Management of Universities* (Buffalo, 1953), pp. 46–49.

[72] See L. L. Thurstone, "Academic Freedom," *Journal of Higher Education,* I (March, 1930), 136–38.

[73] In 1935, the word was changed to "ineligible." But since this made members of the faculty of listed institutions ineligible for membership in the Association at a time when they were most likely to join, in 1938 the heading was changed to "censured administrations" and members of those faculties were permitted to join.

[74] See H. W. Tyler, "Defense of Freedom of Educational Organizations," pp. 254–55.

for long periods of time is some indication that this is not as effective a device as it was hoped it would be (though it must also be remembered that the institutions placed on the list are among the more hardened offenders).[75] Frequently, the investigations stirred up so much resentment in administrative quarters that they evoked obstinacy, not remorse.[76] Still, in the balance sheet of forty years of continuous effort, positive contributions must also be entered. The AAUP introduced an apparatus for finding facts in a field that had been ruled heretofore by unevaluated testimony. It threw the light of publicity upon certain institutions wherein for years malpractices had gone undetected. The threat of an investigation was often all that was needed to give administrators second thoughts when they contemplated questionable actions. And in a sense, the very weakness of the AAUP was a healthy reminder that there was no substitute for courage on the part of each professor. Inadvertently, the AAUP gave strength to the maxim: If this shall be the land of the free, it must also be the home of the brave.

THE FIRST WORLD WAR, LOYALTY, AND THE AAUP

The crisis of 1917 plunged the academic profession into vast and unheralded new difficulties. A mob fanaticism arose that put every freedom in jeopardy. The American university, always vulnerable to the opinions of the community, could not escape its coercive spirit. Indeed, professors, being by trade and usually by disposition somewhat more detached from mass obsessions, became the particular targets of the country's enthusiasm and anxiety. All over the nation, patriotic zealots on boards of trustees, in the community, and on the faculties themselves, harassed those college teachers whose passion for fighting the war was somewhat less flaming

[75] Seven institutions were carried on the list for five years or fewer, five for from five to ten years, eight for from ten to fifteen years.

[76] As one example, there is the letter of J. T. Kingsbury, President of the University of Utah, to Nicholas Murray Butler, November 5, 1917: "The professors' committee headed by Professor Seligman of C. U. took for granted that it was treating me and the University of Utah very justly by publishing a blue book against the University of Utah and myself and so prejudicing the professors and institutions through the country as to prevent, if possible, the filling of the places made vacant. . . . Looking back now upon our disturbance I sometimes think that both the regents and myself probably made a mistake in showing Mr. Lovejoy the courtesy we did or in having anything whatever to do with him when he came to Utah to make an investigation." In Cattell Papers, Columbia University Library.

than their own. Suddenly, the gains for academic freedom that had painfully and gradually been won—the greater acceptance of the principle, the beginnings of a regime of academic law—were swept aside. With frightening quickness, the hard-to-learn manners of tolerance yielded to crude tribal instincts of taboo. The academic profession and its young Association confronted the almost total collapse of the moral and institutional safeguards that had been wrought in the slowness of time.

Nothing in the experience of the professors prepared them to deal with the problem of loyalty in a time of national emergency. No other orthodoxy commanded such allegiance; against no other orthodoxy was resistance so difficult to sustain. Unlike other heretics known to the republic, "the slacker," "the pro-German," "the pacifist" were liable to prosecution by the state. Unlike other hunts for heretics, the search for disloyal citizens was not confined to certain well-defined breeding grounds, but extended throughout the community. The new orthodoxy thus transcended every other in its power and its totality. It exceeded religious orthodoxy, for it was not limited by unchanging doctrine; it exceeded economic conventionalism, for it permitted no havens of dissent. Its pharisaical division of the saved and the damned was not only the concern of sectarians, but of every group in society.

In 1917, the cult of loyalty had a particular morbidness. It was widely feared that new Americans, whose loyalties were complicated by immigration, were not sufficiently patriotic. It was widely feared that many Americans, attracted to pacifistic ideals, were not sufficiently bellicose. Though deep and genuine loyalty does not seek or require advertisement, this country, in its insecurity, demanded public display. It encouraged oaths of loyalty—hollow rituals of affirmation; rallies for the sale of war bonds—unity via the spirit of the crowd; patriotic societies—censors of other people's public virtue. For all this, America was pathetically ill-equipped to define the loyalty it demanded. The country was not content to look for the overt forms of disloyalty in treasonable conduct; it sought subtler traces in ideas and ideologies. This was a dangerous course, rendered more so by our disparate traditions. What creed could define Americanism? What social or political stance was manifestly loyal or disloyal? The tendency was for loyalty to become that belief which the inquirer took for granted, disloyalty that belief which raised doubts in some beholder.

To survey only a few of the First World War academic-freedom cases is to reveal the vagueness of the new orthodoxy and the fervor with which it was enforced. In 1918, the Nebraska State Council of Defense submitted to the University of Nebraska Board of Regents a list of twelve professors who had, for one reason and another, "assumed an attitude calculated to encourage among those who come under their influence, within and without the university, a spirit of inactivity, indifference, and opposition towards this war and an undesirable view with respect to the several fundamental questions inseparable from the war." [77] After investigation, it was disclosed that three professors did variously believe in internationalism, impede the sale of liberty bonds, and criticize their more patriotic colleagues. For these transgressions, and after a trial by the board, the three professors were dismissed.[78] At the University of Virginia, Leon R. Whipple, director of the School of Journalism, was charged with disloyalty for a speech in which he declared that "we can win the war only by freeing the spirit of democracy in the Germans by good-will," that "war does not remove the menace of autocracy, [or] make the world safe for democracy," and that Russia will be the spiritual leader of the next generation. The president of the university, paying his respects to Whipple's energy, capacity, and attention to duty as a teacher, considered this speech "a document of disloyalty." After a trial by the Board of Visitors, Whipple was let go.[79] The University of Minnesota's Board of Regents had still another conception of what constituted disloyalty. It dismissed Professor William A. Schaper, chairman of the Department of Political Science, for having said that he did not wish to see "the Hohenzollerns . . . wiped out root and branch." [80] Schaper weighed on Minnesota's conscience: twenty years later the Board of Regents reinstated him, granted him the title of Professor Emeritus, and expunged the earlier verdict from the record. How another generation could regard the same problem and the same evidence is given in the statement written by the Board in 1938:

The Board of Regents sitting in 1938 recognizes with regret and not in a spirit of condemnation of its predecessors that periods of national crisis are characterized by widespread loss in social perspective and a strain upon the values that prevail when conditions are more nearly normal. It would also affirm in these calmer days and against another day of storm and stress that in

[77] *The Nation,* CVI (June 1, 1918), 639.
[78] Charles Angoff, "The Higher Learning Goes to War," *American Mercury,* XI (March, 1927), 188.
[79] Letter of Leon R. Whipple to *The Nation,* CV (December 20, 1917), 690–91.
[80] James Gray, *University of Minnesota* (Minneapolis, 1951), p. 247.

times of crisis the need for adherence to accepted values and traditions and procedures, especially by institutions of higher education, is most necessary.[81]

At Columbia University, an overzealous board of trustees, a dictatorial president, and a distinguished but personally offensive professor were the figures in a loyalty case that shook the academic world. To the Columbia Board of Trustees went the doubtful distinction of being the first private governing board to institute a general program of investigation in order to ascertain, as the minutes have it,

whether doctrines which are subversive of, or *tend to* the violation or disregard of, the Constitution or the laws of the United States or of the State of New York, or which *tend to encourage* a spirit of disloyalty to the government of the United States, or the principles upon which it is founded, are taught and disseminated by officers of the University.[82]

A Committee of Nine, consisting of five deans and four faculty members, was appointed to help the trustees inquire into the state and ultimate tendency of teaching in the university. The Columbia faculty was deeply affronted. The Faculty of Political Science thought the idea of a "general doctrinal inquisition" violated every principle of academic freedom.[83] A number of Columbia's luminaries, including Wesley C. Mitchell, Herbert L. Osgood, James T. Shotwell, and John Erskine, sent an angry rejoinder to the trustees:

The action taken by the Trustees . . . has in fact created . . . a general impression that disloyal doctrines are so extensively propagated by Columbia instructors that the authorities do not deem it sufficient to take action against individual offenders, but contemplate a regulation of instruction that will make such offenses rare if not impossible. Such an impression is both unjust and injurious. It is unjust, because Columbia is not a hot bed of disloyalty. . . . It is injurious because it discredits the loyalty of the University and seems to threaten its liberty.[84]

The Nation saw the absurdity of undertaking a limitless search to find felonious states of mind.

How is the investigating committee to go to work? Will it draw up a formidable questionnaire for all the professors . . . ? Perhaps it will be enough to station the clerk of the trustees near the lecturer's chair. How could there be

---

[81] "Higher Learning in Time of Crisis," *Bulletin,* AAUP, XXVI (October, 1940), 544.

[82] *Minutes of the Trustees of Columbia University,* XXXVII (March 5, 1917), 208. Italics supplied.

[83] Charles A. Beard, "A Statement," *New Republic,* XIII (December 29, 1917), 250.

[84] Petition to the trustees, undated, in Seligman Papers.

"disloyalty" in the awful presence of the clerk? . . . Should the trustees persist in their unexampled inquisition, however, they may expect the turn about which is fair play. The faculty might appoint a committee to investigate *them*. The instructions would be to "inquire and ascertain" whether the trustees were not suffering from a bad state of nerves.[85]

President Nicholas Murray Butler earned another dubious distinction for Columbia: he was one of the few university presidents who formally withdrew the privilege of academic freedom for the entire duration of the war. On June 6, 1917, at a Commencement Day gathering of the alumni, Butler declared that

so long as national policies were in debate, we gave complete freedom, as is our wont, and as becomes a university—freedom of assembly, freedom of speech, and freedom of publication to all members of the University who in lawful and decent ways might wish to inform and to guide public policy. Wrongheadedness and folly we might deplore, but we are bound to tolerate. So soon, however, as the nation spoke by the Congress and by the President, declaring that it would volunteer as one man for the protection and defense of civil liberty and self-government, conditions sharply changed. What had been tolerated before becomes intolerable now. What had been wrongheadedness was now sedition. What had been folly was now treason.

The president had an interesting conception of what was tolerable, and not seditious or treasonable:

This is the University's last and only warning to any among us, if such there be, who are not with whole heart and mind and strength committed to fight with us to make the world safe for democracy.[86]

Loyalty was defined in effect as the particular degree of indignation and bellicosity displayed by President Butler.[87]

Professor J. McKeen Cattell was one of the leading psychologists of his generation; but the psychology at which he was proficient was experimental, not applied. By all accounts he was brash, tactless, and offensive—

[85] "Trustees and College Teaching," *The Nation*, CIV (March 15, 1917), 305.

[86] Commencement Day Address, June 6, 1917, in Columbia University Archives.

[87] That Butler was suffering from war shock and not from any permanent disability is attested by his much-quoted statement on proprietary gifts which he made just after the war in one of his annual reports. An intimate of wealthy men and a political conservative, he was unequivocal in his condemnation of conditional gifts. "Under no circumstances should, or can, any self-respecting university accept a gift upon conditions which fix or hamper its complete freedom in the control of its own educational policies. . . . No university is so poor that it can afford to accept a gift which restricts its independence, and no university is so rich that it would not be impoverished by an addition to its resources which tied the hands of its governing boards." Nicholas Murray Butler, *Annual Report* (1919), pp. 7–8.

not only to the president, with whom he conducted a running battle for years, but to such kind and patient colleagues as E. R. A. Seligman and John Dewey. As early as 1910, President Butler, stung by Cattell's charge that he regularly acted as an autocrat, substantiated the charge by proposing to the trustees that Cattell be removed or that steps be taken to silence him.[88] The trustees did not then take action. In 1913 they moved to retire Cattell without his consent, but certain members of the faculty interceded and helped forestall final action.[89] Cattell was not made prudent by the precariousness of his position. In 1917, he wrote a letter to the faculty in which he referred to the president as "many talented and much climbing" and in which he suggested that the president's house should be expropriated and used for the benefit of the teachers.[90] Once more, the trustees, this time with much faculty assent, were ready to dismiss Cattell, but were headed off by his note of apology. Cattell remained unreconstructed, however: in a letter to Seligman, he criticized his colleagues for taking offense at his *lèse majesté,* and attributed their attitude to "the traditionalism and the conventionalism, the lack of perspective and the lack of humor, which deaden university life." [91] He evidently preferred exhibitionism and acrimony to enliven it.

The ineptness of the president and the trustees matched that of the professor. When they finally discharged him, it was not over the issue of his personality, but over the issue of his loyalty. One supposes that, in the shallow perspective of wartime, this seemed to be the stronger ground, the one most likely to appeal to a public excited by war and Wilsonian rhetoric. But if this was the motive, it was grievously at fault, for it converted a possibly valid case of dismissal for personal unfitness into an indefensible attack upon academic freedom. What Cattell did to precipitate his dismissal was to send a petition (on a Columbia University letterhead) to three Congressmen, urging them not to approve a bill then pending which would have sanctioned the use of American conscripts on European battlefields.[92] With appalling disrespect for the constitutional privi-

[88] Extract from the *Minutes of the Committee on Education* (trustees) (December 22, 1910), in Cattell Papers.

[89] Letter of Edmund B. Wilson to Butler, May 20, 1913; M. I. Pupin to Butler, May 19, 1913, in Cattell Papers.

[90] J. McKeen Cattell, "Confidential Memorandum to Resident Members of the Faculty Club," January 10, 1917, in Cattell Papers.

[91] Letter of Cattell to Seligman, March 8, 1917, in Cattell Papers.

[92] Letters of Cattell to Julius Kahn of California, S. Wallace Dempsey of New York, and E. R. Bathrick of Ohio, August 23, 1917, in Cattell Papers.

lege of petition, the three Congressmen told Butler about it, one of them complaining that Cattell was "sowing the seeds of sedition and treason with the sanction of the institution." [93] That was the final straw. "We have got the rascal this time!" the clerk of the trustees exulted.[94] So eager was the board to make disloyalty the gravamen of their charge against Cattell that they overrode the faculty recommendation that he be retired without any mention of the grounds. They publicly bracketed his dismissal with that of Henry Wadsworth Longfellow Dana, an assistant professor of comparative literature, who was condemned for having encouraged student agitation against the Conscription Act while it too was pending.[95] To cap it all, the trustees issued a statement to the press which erroneously declared that the university's faculties had seconded their action.[96] Incompetence was often a miry ground on which to justify dismissal, but compared to the charge of disloyalty, it was as a high plateau to a swamp.

The swamp was soon to ensnare less offensive Columbia professors. In 1916, Dr. Leon Fraser, instructor in politics at Columbia College, made some critical remarks about the military camp in Plattsburg. For this he was haled before a committee of the trustees, and, in the following year, was discharged. Ironically, Fraser had been engaged to work for the Association for International Conciliation, a pacifist organization, by none other than President Butler—but this had been before pacifism became unacceptable, and the young instructor was not sufficiently resilient to change his mind with the times.[97] Soon afterwards, the eminent historian Charles A. Beard was summoned before the trustees' star chamber. A sensationalistic newspaper had accused Beard of condoning a speaker

[93] Letter of Julius Kahn to Butler, August 27, 1917, in Cattell Papers.

[94] Letter of John B. Pine, Clerk of the Trustees, to Butler, September 21, 1917, in Cattell Papers.

[95] The Committee of Nine asked the trustees to give no publicity to Dana's dismissal, and to grant him a leave of absence without salary for the remainder of the year. In this, as well as in the Cattell case, the trustees overruled the committee of faculty members and deans. *Report of the Committee of Nine* (October 9, 1917), p. 5.

[96] New York *Times,* October 2, 1917. The only support that the trustees received officially from the faculty was a statement from eight members of the Committee on Instruction of the Schools of Mines, Engineering, and Chemistry. Letter to Butler, September 19, 1917, in Cattell Papers. The Committee of Nine, though it recommended the retirement of Cattell, did so without referring to his patriotism. Letter of Seligman to George L. Ingraham, Chairman of the joint committee of the trustees, September 24, 1917, in Seligman Papers.

[97] *Minutes of the Trustees of Columbia University,* XXXVI (May 1, 1916), 292–93; Beard, "A Statement," p. 250.

who was alleged to have said "To Hell with the Flag." Despite his public denial, Beard had to convince the board that he had never condoned that statement. Evidently he did so convince it. But the board did not let him go without casting further aspersions upon his colleagues. Demanding its ounce of prevention, it ordered Beard to warn the other Columbia historians that teachings "likely to inculcate disrespect for American institutions" would not be tolerated. "I repeated my order to my colleagues," wrote Beard, "who received it with a shout of derision, one of them asking me whether Tammany Hall and the pork barrel were not American institutions!" [98] A week after Dana and Cattell fell, Beard handed his resignation to President Butler:

Having observed closely the inner life of Columbia for many years, I have been driven to the conclusion that the University is really under the control of a small and active group of trustees who have no standing in the world of education, who are reactionary and visionless in politics, narrow and medieval in religion. . . . I have, from the beginning, believed that a victory for the German Imperial Government would plunge all of us into the black night of military barbarism. . . . But thousands of my countrymen do not share this view. Their opinions cannot be changed by curses or bludgeons. Arguments addressed to their reason and understanding are our best hope.[99]

Before the loyalty craze had run its course at Columbia, two other professors, Henry R. Mussey, assistant professor of economics, and Ellery C. Stowell, associate professor of international law, also resigned.[100]

The grim story of academic freedom during the First World War is relieved by at least one president's moral courage and one board's emotional calm. In 1916, a story was circulated in the press that a Harvard alumnus was threatening to annul a bequest of $10,000,000 to Harvard unless the openly pro-German professor, Hugo Münsterberg, was deprived of his chair. The Harvard Corporation stated officially that the "University cannot tolerate any suggestion that it would be willing to accept money to abridge free speech, to remove a professor or to accept his resignation." [101] And President Lowell, in the next year's annual report, stood four-square for academic freedom in wartime:

[98] Beard, "A Statement," p. 249.
[99] Letter of Beard to Butler, Minutes of the Trustees, XXXVIII (October 8, 1917), 89–90.
[100] Letter of Mussey to Seligman, November 6, 1917, in Cattell Papers; Minutes of the Trustees, XXXVIII, 145–46, 299.
[101] Henry Aaron Yeomans, Abbott Lawrence Lowell, 1856–1943 (Cambridge, Mass., 1948), p. 316.

If a university or college censors what its professors may say, if it restrains them from uttering something it does not approve, it thereby assumes responsibility for that which it permits them to say. This is logical and inevitable, but it is a responsibility which an institution of learning would be very unwise in assuming. It is sometimes suggested that the principles are different in time of war; that the governing boards are then justified in restraining unpatriotic expression injurious to the country. But the same problem is presented in war time as in time of peace. If the university is right in restraining its professors, it has a duty to do so, and it is responsible for whatever it permits. There is no middle ground. Either the university assumes full responsibility for permitting its professors to express certain opinions in public, or it assumes no responsibility whatever, and leaves them to be dealt with like other citizens by the public authorities according to the laws of the land.[102]

It had taken centuries for Henry Dunster's college to achieve such a high degree of balance and sanity.

For the AAUP, the potion of war produced intense internal conflicts. The Association could not, lest it betray all that it stood for, consider freedom a peacetime luxury. Its docket of academic-freedom cases was filling up with sordid evidences of the censorship that called itself patriotism and the malice expressed in the name of loyalty. At the same time, it had given itself without compunction to those martial symbols and apocalyptic hopes with which America goes to battle. Its historians had given up research to write propaganda tracts for the Committee on Public Information; its scientists were devoting their skills to the multifarious problems of war.[103] Most of its leaders—Arthur Lovejoy, John Dewey, Franklin Giddings, to name only a few—had gladly enrolled in the campaign to sell the war to Americans. In 1918, the AAUP sent an official message to the President of the United States, expressing its "hearty and grateful approval of the course you have pursued in calling the nation to arms against a foe who has ruthlessly violated the rights of law-abiding and peaceful peoples." [104] For this group, loyalty had not one focus but two, and the problem that had to be decided was which would be given precedence.

The report of the AAUP Committee on Academic Freedom in Wartime presented the Association's decision. "There are two sides," it said, "to the duty of the citizen in time of war." The more urgent duty was to help

[102] *Ibid.,* pp. 311–12.
[103] Merle Curti, "The American Scholar in Three Wars," *Journal of the History of Ideas,* III (June, 1942), 241; Guy Stanton Ford, *On and Off the Campus* (Minneapolis, 1938), pp. 73–100; F. P. Keppel, "American Scholarship in the War," *Columbia University Quarterly,* XXI (July, 1919), 171.
[104] *Bulletin,* AAUP, IV (January, 1918), 8.

win it. The other—less obvious and perhaps less appealing—was to preserve democratic institutions. But, it declared, and with this declaration it took its stand on the problem of loyalty, all the processes of democracy cannot go on in time of war.

> When . . . a democracy finds itself forced into war in defense of its rights, of the integrity of the law of nations, and of the safety of democracy throughout the world, it will, if it has any practical wisdom, temporarily adapt its methods of political action and of governmental procedure to the necessities of the grave and perilous business immediately in hand.

What this gospel of expediency portended for academic freedom was soon made apparent. The Committee cited four grounds on which academic authorities might legitimately dismiss professors, and only one of them presupposed prior punitive action by the government. These were: (1) "conviction of disobedience to any statute or lawful executive order relating to the war"; (2) "propaganda designed, or unmistakably tending, to cause others to resist or evade the compulsory service law or the regulations of the military authorities"; (3) action designated "to dissuade others from rendering voluntary assistance to the efforts of the Government"; (4) in the case of professors of Teutonic extraction and sympathy, violating the obligation "to refrain from public discussion of the war; and in their private intercourse with neighbors, colleagues and students, to avoid all hostile or offensive expressions concerning the United States or its government." [105] The various qualifications that the Committee introduced—that trustees should exercise magnanimity in dealing with pacifists, that teachers should be spared the extreme penalty of dismissal on their first offense, that the proceedings should be strictly judicial in character—were of comparatively small importance. The Committee, as the *Nation* put it, "hands over the keys of the castle to the enemy." [106] It assumed that the war had fundamentally changed the conditions of academic freedom. It assumed what Lowell denied, that the university should be responsible for its professors' outside utterances. It accepted the premise that the university might impose greater restrictions of speech upon its members than the state imposed upon its citizens. The unnerved professors of the Committee bear witness that not all the casualties of war are to be found upon the battlefield.

[105] "Report," Committee on Academic Freedom in Wartime, *Bulletin*, AAUP, IV (February–March, 1918), 30. The Committee was composed of A. O. Lovejoy, Edward Capps, and A. A. Young.

[106] "The Professors in Battle Array," *The Nation*, CVI (March 7, 1918), 255.

Though civil liberties were under attack for years after the war, academic freedom suffered most during the period of the war itself. In this respect, the pattern of inquisition in that day differs from the one existing today: academic freedom, relatively little affected during the Second World War, has been severely tried in the post-war, cold-war atmosphere. There are other differences and some similarities between that day and this, which we set down by way of linking the present work to its companion volume.[107] After the First World War, as at the time of writing, disloyalty in a time of national danger was the central problem. At both times "loyalty" was defined with a woolly vagueness. At both times, as suspicion began to fray the social fabric, certain pathological types rose to national prominence: the informer, whose repeated purgations of guilt acquired the public's sanction; the defamer, whose aggressions against his fellows took socially acceptable forms; the investigator, who was allowed to pry and accuse without the customary judicial restraints. Finally, at both times, the public, called upon to judge difficult problems of individual guilt or innocence, took refuge in the passive and naive assumption that where there is smoke there must be fire, neglecting to inform itself as to whether there might not in fact be a smokescreen. These are some of the constants, some of the similarities in tone.

But the differences are more important. Academic freedom faces in some ways a more ponderable threat today. For one thing, the present generation has inherited the burden of the infatuation with Communism in the 1930s, an involvement wider and more compromising than, say, the involvement of the professors of an earlier day in Wobblyism, or Socialism, or pan-Germanism. There are now just enough skeletons in professorial closets—not many, to be sure—to give investigators into "disloyalty" some return for their labors. Moreover, the greater danger in the present situation stems from the nature of the Communists' operations. When Cattell was fired from Columbia in 1917, there was no question about what he had done—he had petitioned Congress not to send our troops abroad; everyone knew where he stood, and the issue for the faculty and for professional opinion was whether this behavior merited that punishment. But the secretive character of Communist activities—in part the result of their repression, in part the result of their masked language and tactics of infiltration—argues for an apparatus of investigation, not to discover the propriety of a professor's act, but to discover

[107] Robert M. MacIver, *Academic Freedom in Our Time* (New York, 1955).

whether the act was ever committed. The alleged act in addition, is rarely as overt as indiscreet speech, rarely as apparent as open indoctrination, but is usually a pattern of association from which subversive intentions are inferred. This makes, or threatens to make, investigation—by trustees, by state legislative committees, by filiopietistic groups—a built-in characteristic of academic life, an organ of administration, interminable because it is nonspecific, incalculable in effect because it rarely relates to professional behavior. And, of course, most important in any comparison is the fact that peace has not yet come after the Second World War to give the tension of superpatriotism a chance to relax, to permit the usual libertarian reaction.

But if these are the ways in which the present crisis seems worse than the previous one, there are other ways in which it seems decidedly better. A more sympathetic and profound understanding of academic freedom is more widespread among teachers, administrators, and trustees today than in 1917. The institutional mechanisms for the defense of academic freedom are far better developed. The prevalence of rules of tenure, the technique developed by the AAUP for investigating cases, are important modern protections. The AAUP, today an organization of 42,000, is a power of some significance in the academic world. In the present climate of opinion, these factors are not sufficient to give courage to the circumspect or timid, but they provide a considerable measure of security for professors who have the hardihood to assert themselves.

No one can follow the history of academic freedom in this country without wondering at the fact that any society, interested in the immediate goals of solidarity and self-preservation, should possess the vision to subsidize free criticism and inquiry, and without feeling that the academic freedom we still possess is one of the remarkable achievements of man. At the same time, one cannot but be appalled at the slender thread by which it hangs, at the wide discrepancies that exist among institutions with respect to its honoring and preservation; and one cannot but be disheartened by the cowardice and self-deception that frail men use who want to be both safe and free. With such conflicting evidence, perhaps individual temperament alone tips the balance toward confidence or despair.

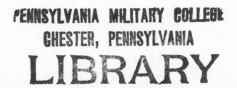

INDEX

INDEX

AAC, *see* Association of American Colleges

AAUP, *see* American Association of University Professors

Abbot, Francis, 335; on scientific competence, 348 f.; on scientific criticism, 354

Abelard: on authority, 14; on faith and reason, 28 f.; *Sic et non,* 29

Aberdeen, University of, 131*n*

Abolitionism, and the colleges, 253-61

Academic freedom, 317; Mather on tutors at Harvard College, 104; contribution to by lay government, 120 ff.; role of college president, 125 f., 305-6; origin in changes in curriculum, 192 f.; and liberalized science teaching, 196-201, 283-93; civil liberties and, 205 ff., 262 f., 382, 403-5; limitations on, in colonial colleges, 210; and Jefferson's plans for the University of Virginia, 238-42; idea of, 261-74; and denominational colleges, 293-303; and the teaching of Darwinism, 326 ff.; new rationale of, 363-66; German concept of, 388 ff.; *Lernfreiheit* and *Lehrfreiheit,* 386 ff.; American reaction to German concept of, 391 ff.; discrepancies in practice of, 395; American code, 407-12; character of infringements upon, 412; cases reported by AAUP involving, 420-51, 469; effect of bureaucratization on, 456; movement to standardize theory and practice of, 474 ff.; AAUP statement of 1940, 488; loyalty cases in wartime, 490-95; and Communism, 505 f.

Academies, English, 76

Act of Supremacy, 74

Adams, Charles Kendall, support of Ely, 430 ff.

Adams, Henry Carter, 377, 416; dismissed from Cornell, 419

Adams, Herbert B., 377

Adams, Jasper, on role of faculty in college government, 236

Adams, John Quincy, 315

Adelard of Bath, 28*n*

Adler, Felix, lectureship at Johns Hopkins, 340

Administration and administrators: limitations upon, 365; spokesmen for higher education, 471; AAUP censure of, 494; *see also* Trustees

Adrian VI, pope, 41

Agassiz, Louis, 292; on Darwinism, 321; charged with atheism, 353

Agreement of Religion and Philosophy, The (Averröes), 33 f.

Agricultural college, 382

Alain de Lille, on authority, 14

Albigensians, 19

Aldrich, Morton A., 442

Alexander, Stephen, 286

Alford, John, 183

Alford Professorship of Natural Religion, Moral Philosophy and Civil Polity, 184, 253

Alien and Sedition laws, 207

Almanac, 200

Alison, Francis, 156

Allen, William, 150*n*

Althoff, Friedrich, 384*n*

Alumni organizations, origin and function of, 313-16

American Association of University Professors (AAUP): Committee A, Report on Academic Freedom and Tenure, 396 f., 407-12, 479, 480-90; Committee G, "Extra-collegiate Intellectual Service," 404*n*; report on violations of academic freedom, 429 f.; establishment of, 468-80; academic-freedom cases, 469; *Bulletin,* 471, 490 ff.; eligibility for membership, 472; founders, 476 ff.; membership, 477, 506; code revisions, 487; state-